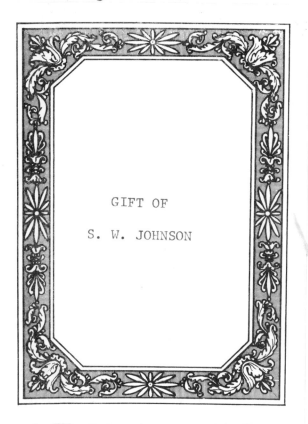

PERSONALITY THEORIES

An Introduction

PERSONALITY THEORIES

An Introduction

Barbara Engler

Union College
Cranford, New Jersey

49-642

HOUGHTON MIFFLIN COMPANY   BOSTON

Dallas   Geneva, Illinois   Hopewell, New Jersey
Palo Alto   London

Printed in the U.S.A.
Library of Congress Catalog Card Number: 78–069596
ISBN: 0–395–26772–2

To my sons,
Ted and Bill

CONTENTS

x   Contents

LIST OF EXERCISES

PREFACE

This book is intended precisely for undergraduates who seek an introduction to the field of personality. It presents the major issues that are involved in personality theorizing within an overall interdisciplinary framework. In one's early years, the quest for self-understanding is largely egocentric, motivated and informed by one's own experiences and understanding. With maturity, one becomes ready to entertain and incorporate the viewpoints of others into one's own understanding. The undergraduate is ready to understand other points of view but is still sufficiently engaged in the earlier phase of self-understanding as to want to see concretely and clearly the impact and relevance of those viewpoints to his or her own life. This book aims to cross that bridge. It is first and foremost a theories text that seeks to present the major theories of personality. Additionally, it attempts to show the relevance of each theory by discussing its personal, therapeutic, and social application.

Further, application is made personally relevant by including self-enlightening exercises informed by the theories under discussion. The exercises are designed to be simple and non-presumptuous. If the student is so motivated, the exercises may be used to arouse his or her interest and enhance personal as well as academic growth.

Most books on personality theory fall into four main categories: comprehensive and sophisticated surveys of existing theories of personality; topical approaches that compare and contrast several theories on certain key issues; behavioral analyses of personality; or adjustment texts that seek to provide experiences that will lead toward effective interpersonal skills and self-actualization. The sophistication of many of them is too difficult for an average undergraduate to grasp. The first three approaches are more useful with advanced students. The fourth, commonly used with undergraduates, frequently promises a great deal but delivers little because a sound theoretical basis is missing.

Personality Theories: An Introduction introduces the major theories that have influenced contemporary psychological thought on the subject of personality. It is suggested that the theories be viewed under seven main headings—Freudian Psychoanalysis, Neo-Psychoanalytic Theories, Behavior and Learning Theories, Trait Theories, Humanist Theories, Cognitive Theories, and Eastern Theories—to provide a coherent, integrated survey of a diverse field. In presenting the theories, four main objectives are sought: to present a clear but concise picture of the major features of each theory; to indicate the basic assumptions and primary methods of research or inquiry that underlie each theory; to show the application of the theory in terms of personal, therapeutic, and social change; and to provide exercises informed by the theories, for use in facilitating self-understanding.

Each theory is presented as concisely as possible for adequate coverage. Further, each theory is developed and presented in the manner that seems most appropriate and clear for that theory. Rather than a standard format of presentation, comparisons within the text itself are used as a more viable way to outline and preserve the distinctive characteristics and contributions of each theory. My aim was to be objective and fair, while providing the reader with frequent bases for comparison.

A significant proportion of space is devoted to Freud's psychoanalytic theory, in recognition of its influence and the fact that many of the other theories have been developed in its stead, as efforts to elaborate on, modify, substitute, or refute. A firm basis in Freudian psychoanalytic theory provides the reader with a distinct focal point from which comparisons and contrasts may be made.

The introductory section poses the question, "What kind of games are these?" This is in recognition of the fact that the subsumption of personality theories under scientific psychology is a relatively new development. Many of the theories that influence contemporary thought did not develop from and do not purport to be strict scientific theory. Rather, they reflect philosophical methods of inquiry and investigation. Thus, an attempt is made to provide the reader with the necessary tools for distinguishing among the different functions of the theories and with appropriate criteria for evaluating them as philosophy, science, and art.

Giving acknowledgments makes one acutely aware that what one is, thinks, and does is due in great measure to having lived in a context of human relationships. I am grateful to my colleagues and students at Union College for their interest, support, and constructive comments concerning this project. I would like to thank the following reviewers for their careful consideration of the manuscript and helpful comments: Larry V. Goff, El Centro College (Texas); Sara H. Hunger, formerly at University of North Carolina, Chapel Hill; and Sam S. McFarland, Western Kentucky University.

I also wish to express my appreciation to a former student and now good friend, Donald Goldsmith, who read every page of the manuscript and offered innumerable constructive suggestions; and to Lois Rioux, one of my teaching assistants, who relieved me with invaluable secretarial services in conjunction with both my instructional duties and the preparation of this manuscript. Finally, I owe an unrepayable debt of gratitude to my sons, Ted and Bill, who shared their mother and permitted the incessant demands and interruptions of her writing to intrude on their lives.

Barbara Engler

CHAPTER 1

Introduction: What Kind of Games Are These?

The question "What is personality?" looks simple enough. A reader about to consider various theories of personality might imagine that a direct answer to that question will be quickly forthcoming. But the answer is not that simple. As a matter of fact, a complete search for that answer would take us back to the early history of the human race. The search for identity, the question of self, was begun when the first person asked, "Who am I?" thereby seeking or reflecting on his or her identity. The diverse answers that people have given to that question have found expression throughout history in various cultural constructs such as philosophy, religion, art, politics, and science. I cannot give a definite, simple answer to the question "What is personality?" because a final answer is yet to be found. Each one of us begins the quest anew; when as children seeking identity, and later as adults reflecting upon our identity, we raise the perennial question "Who am I?" and thus join fellow travelers on the road in search of the self.

While the term *personality* is frequently used, then, it is not easy to define. In common speech, it usually refers to one's public image. Thus, we hear said, "Becky has a terrific personality!" or "If only Jeff had a more dynamic personality." This common usage reflects the origin of the word "personality" in the Latin *persona*, which referred to the masks that actors wore in ancient Greek dramas. Such a concept of social role, however, does not embrace the complexity that is connoted in the long quest for understanding the self.

A psychologist, Gordon Allport, who was trying to arrive at a satisfactory definition of personality for his work, described and classified over fifty different definitions of personality. His effort shows that there is little common agreement among personality theorists on appropriate use of the term. For Gordon Allport, personality is something *real* within the individual that determines his or her characteristic behavior and thought. For Carl Rogers, another personality theorist, the personality or "self" is an organized, consistent pattern of perception of "I" or "me" that lies at the heart of our experiencing. For B. F. Skinner, probably the most well-known psychologist in America, the word "personality" is superfluous. Skinner does not believe that it is necessary or desirable to evoke a concept such as self or personality in order to understand human behavior. For Sigmund Freud, the father of contemporary personality theories, personality was largely hidden and unknown, involved as it is in the dark recesses of the unconscious.

Thus, there is no definition of the word "personality" with which all personality theorists would agree. Each theorist presents us with his or her own understanding of the word informed by his or her theoretical position. While such diversity is confusing, baffling, and even disturbing, it does not imply that the theories are not useful. Each offers insights into the question of the self and, as such, they can be provocative in helping us to formulate our own tentative answers and in guiding our own personal searches.

Since we are referring to theories of personality, the next logical question to raise is, "What is a theory?" Here the reader will be pleased to see that I can give a more definitive answer. However, later I will have to qualify it and point out that there are many different levels of theories. The term "theory" comes from the Greek word *theōria*, which refers to the act of viewing, contemplating, or considering something. A theory is a set of abstract concepts that we make about a group of facts or events in order to explain them. A theory of personality, therefore, is an organized system of beliefs that helps us to understand human nature. Describing a theory as a system of beliefs underscores the fact that a theory is something that we construct in the process of viewing and thinking about our world. Theories are not given or necessitated by nature, rather, they are created by people in their efforts to understand the world. The same data or experiences can be accounted for in many different ways. As we shall see, there have been and are innumerable theories of personality.

As I pointed out earlier, the question "What is personality?" takes us back to early human existence. Early human awareness about the self and the world was prereflective, prephilosophical, and prescientific. It was *before* reflection, philosophy, and science. I am not implying, however, that it was necessarily unreflective, unphilosophical, or unscientific. In time, scholars began to reflect on their insights in terms of specialized fields. Philosophy developed as a mode of understanding and expression. Later, science emerged as a specific methodology for acquiring information.

Classification of personality theories under scientific psychology is a relatively new development. Only in the 1930s did the study of personality become a formal and systematic area of specialization in American academic scientific psychology. Prior to that time, questions about personality were generally included under the broader umbrella of philosophy. While the methods of science and philosophy are distinct, they are not unrelated. Science is an offspring of philosophy. Its methods are the fruit of philosophy's labors. The objective mode of study and investigation characteristic of the modern scientist arises, as we shall see, out of a prior philosophical encounter with the world.

If scientific theories of personality have their origin in philosophy, they also culminate in some form of art or practical application. The art of personality theory is, of course, much older than the science or even the philosophy of it. From earliest times, much has been spoken and written about how to live a good life. As science has developed, however, it has provided us with new knowledge, tools, and methods of self-understanding and improvement. Theories of personality are not mere armchair speculations, but belief systems that find expression in ways that are designed to help us understand and improve ourselves and the world.

Personality theories are a branch of academic scientific psychology, but they also entail philosophy and art. As scientists, personality theorists hope to develop a workable set of hypotheses that will assist us in understanding human behavior. As philosophers, personality theorists seek to explore what it means to be a person. As artists, personality theorists seek to apply what is known about people and behavior to foster a better life. By briefly exploring the areas of interests entailed in the philosophy, science, and art of personality theory, we hope to create a foundation for understanding personality theories and for seeing how they express themselves in these three modes.

THE METAPHOR OF GAMES

The Austrian philosopher Ludwig Wittgenstein (1889–1951) used the phrase "language games" to point out the many different sorts of information that various statements provide. Consider the following two statements: "There is a lion on the lawn" and "The boy came forth a raging lion." Both statements appear to refer to lions. Or do they? The first is an *empirical statement*. The term *empirical* means based on experience; an empirical statement may be tested by observation. To discover whether or not the statement "There is a lion on the lawn" is justified, we would go out and look on the lawn for a species of cat that has a tawny body with a tufted tail and shaggy mane. The second statement, "The boy came forth a raging lion," is a *poetic statement,* a metaphor. Such a statement is not tested by ordinary observation. To test it, we do not go out to see if the boy has a mane and a tail. Hardly! That would be an inappropriate method of testing.

The metaphor of games is useful because games are played according to certain rules. If we want to play a game properly and fairly, we have to understand what its rules are and follow them. Even young schoolchildren know the different rules of baseball and football. To criticize poetry because it does not depict a literal picture of what appears to our senses is to miss the point of what a poetic statement is all about. We have failed to see how it functions as poetry. A similar problem arises in the discussion of personality theories if we fail to perceive the essential and primary function of the statements of a particular theory. That is to say, if we mix our language games.

Each personality theory offers many different statements about human nature. The term *statement* refers to an utterance that makes an assertion or denial. The earliest logician, the Greek philosopher Aristotle (384–322 B.C.), defined the word "statement" as a sentence that can either be true or false. We are going to see that it is a little misleading to call some statements, particularly in science, true, because they cannot be ultimately tested. Thus, for our purposes, it is clearer to define a statement as a sentence that asserts or denies something. It is a sentence to which it makes sense to reply, "I agree" or "I disagree." However, not all statements belong to the same language game or follow the same rules.

Consider the following statements, each of which represents a different language game:

A bachelor is an unmarried man.
All men are mortal,
   Socrates is a man;
   therefore, Socrates is mortal.
Two plus three equals five.
All crows are black.
All people seek what is good.
This sculpture is beautiful.
It is wrong to lie.
Jesus is the Lord.

"A bachelor is an unmarried man" is a definition. It is true by virtue of the way in which we have agreed to use words in our language. "All men are mortal, Socrates is a man; therefore, Socrates is mortal" is a logical syllogism. It follows the rules of deductive logic. "Two plus three equals five" is a mathematical statement whose truth depends on the rules agreed on by mathematicians. We should notice here that while many statements in mathematics correlate with our experiences in the everyday world (two toes plus three toes equals five toes), their truth does not depend on that correspondence. Mathematics also deals with concepts that are not necessarily observable, such as imaginary or negative numbers. The truth of its statements, therefore, depends on the mathematical system we have agreed to play. In base ten, four and seven make eleven; but in base nine, four and seven make twelve. Each of the statements we are considering represents a different specialized field or game. Thus, each must be judged according to a different set of rules.

"All crows are black" is a generalization from empirical observation. I have seen many crows and all of them have been black; therefore, it seems safe to assume that all crows I might meet in the future will also be black. Such statements must always be open to falsification, because the next crow I encounter might be an albino. On the surface, the statement "All people seek what is good" appears to be similar to the empirical observation, but it is not disproved by identifying an exception and pointing to a wicked person. Rather, its evaluation leads us into other kinds of discussion, for that statement is a philosophical assumption. Other statements come from such diverse fields as aesthetics, "This sculpture is beautiful"; ethics, "It is wrong to lie"; and religion, "Jesus is the Lord." No two of these statements are precisely alike even though each one makes an assertion. Students of language spend considerable time and energy distinguishing among different types of statements and indicating the appropriate criteria for each.

The kinds of statements that we are likely to run across in personality theories are statements that reflect a concern with philosophy, science, and art or practical application. Therefore, an examination of these kinds of statements will equip us with the necessary tools for understanding personality theorizing.

PHILOSOPHICAL ASSUMPTIONS

No psychologist or personality theorist can avoid being a philosopher of sorts. As we have seen, the science of personality theorizing has its origins in philosophy. The very act of theorizing, or thinking about what we see, entails making certain assumptions about the world and human nature. Every thinking person, not to speak just of personality theorists, entertains and holds basic philosophical assumptions as he or she reflects on the world and his or her existence. These basic philosophical assumptions deeply and profoundly influence the way in which we perceive the world and theorize about it.

The term *philosophy* comes from the Greek *philein*, "to love," and *sophia*, "wisdom"; it connotes the love or pursuit of wisdom. At root, each one of us is a philosopher insofar as our thinking and reflecting about the world and ourselves entails making basic assumptions and judgments. The search after wisdom, however, involves more than a desire for information to counter our ignorance. Wisdom denotes not merely knowing about something, but knowing what ought to be done and how to do it. The knowledge of wisdom touches our heart as well as our head and enables us to act out of its judgment. Wisdom entails more than appropriating information; it realizes itself in appropriate action. We are all familiar with the fool who may have a great deal of information, but who lacks insight. As philosophers, we make assumptions and judgments about the good life and how to live it.

Traditionally, philosophy has encompassed five types of language and study: logic, aesthetics, ethics, politics, and metaphysics. Logic is the study of correct or normative reasoning; it describes the ideal method of making inferences and drawing conclusions. Aesthetics is the study of ideal forms and beauty; it deals with the nature of the beautiful and with judgments about beauty. Ethics is the study of ideal conduct; it deals with the knowledge of good and evil. Politics is the study of ideal social organization and describes those forms of social and political structures that are most appropriate for human beings. Metaphysics is the study of ultimate reality and attempts to coordinate what is real in the light of what is ideal.

Obviously, very few of us develop complete and articulate stances on each of these issues. Nevertheless, many of our thoughts and statements are concerned with them. Insofar as our thoughts, reflections, and theorizing reflect one or more of these concerns, we can be sure that they are informed by certain basic philosophical assumptions. In the same sense, very few, if any, of the personality theorists that we will consider aim at developing full and complete philosophical pictures of ourselves and the world. They consider themselves psychologists rather than philosophers. Nevertheless, in their psychologizing they raise philosophical issues, and, in doing so, reflect philosophical assumptions.

Recognizing Philosophical Assumptions

It is not my purpose here to introduce you to the nature and character of philosophical statements. Such a topic would take us far afield and belongs more properly to textbooks in philosophy itself. However, it is important to recognize that personality theories entail philosophical assumptions and to identify them when they occur. In what follows, therefore, I shall simply try to give a few criteria that will enable you to recognize philosophical assumptions when they arise so that you will be able to evaluate them accordingly.

The discourses of philosophy frequently posit a distinction between what is and what ought to be. People do not always think logically; nor do they behave in ideal ways. Philosophical statements suggest that things are not necessarily what they appear to be. *What is* is not necessarily *what should be* or *what is really real*. The fact that many people lie or steal does not mean that lying and stealing are right or that lying and stealing constitute the essence of what it means to be human. Whatever appears or happens in our everyday world is not necessarily ultimate.

Since philosophical assumptions do not necessarily represent what happens in the everyday world, the "seeing" of philosophy cannot be the ordinary seeing of our sense organs. Rather, the "seeing" that informs our philosophical assumptions is a special act of cognition, an *extra*-ordinary intuition and visionary mode of apprehension that transcends everyday experience. Philosophical knowledge is ultimately in the form of an *epiphany* (from the Greek *epiphaneia*, which means appearance or manifestation), or a sudden perception of essential meaning.

Philosophical assumptions, therefore, differ from empirical statements, which are based on ordinary observation. Consider again the following statements: "All crows are black" and "All people seek what is good." On the surface, both statements look alike. But to test the first, you would look around to see if there were any nonblack crows, whereas this kind of test would not be appropriate to the second statement. The statement "All people seek what is good" does not refer to something that can be seen in everyday observation, nor does the statement employ empirical observation. Instead, this statement refers to some kind of ultimate reality or its equivalent, which is perceived in a different way.

A common characteristic of philosophical assumptions, therefore, is that they often refer to a reality beyond appearances. They suggest that appearance and reality do not necessarily coincide. "Everything that is real is of the nature of mind" reads a statement of the extreme idealist position in philosophy. This statement contradicts our everyday observation. While it appears to us that many things have a genuine material reality and existence apart from our minds, the statement indicates that, in spite of their appearances, all things are ultimately of the nature of mind.

We want to be careful here because scientific statements often also refer to things that we cannot see in ordinary observation. Many important constructs in science involve imaginary (but not therefore unreal) concepts that cannot be seen with the naked eye or even sophisticated optical equipment. For example, the protons and neutrons of the atom, the basic building blocks of nature, are not visible but are inferred from other observable evidence. The difference lies in the nature of the observation that gives rise to the construct and the way in which it is tested. Statements in science are ultimately, even if indirectly, based on ordinary empirical observation, and their means of test or validation, as we shall see, is different from those of philosophy.

A second characteristic of philosophical assumptions is their tendency to be global. Philosophical assumptions universally embrace the world and all things. A key word to look for is "all" or some equivalent. "Everything that is real is of the nature of mind." "All people seek what is good." These statements transcend the individual and refer to the entire class of which they are speaking. Most important, they allow for no exceptions. This represents a primary distinction between scientific generalizations, which may also be global, and philosophical assumptions.

As we shall see, in science all statements must be open to falsification. In fact, science is required to indicate the conditions under which its statements might be proven incorrect. If an exception is found to a scientific generalization, that generalization must be qualified. When we philosophize, we treat exceptions in an entirely different manner. Suppose a person were to hold the philosophical assumption "All people seek what is good." A critic might counter with an exception: "How can you possibly describe the activities of Richard Nixon as seeking what is good?" As a philosopher, a person might reply, "I agree with you, it would appear that Nixon is a man who did evil, but his evil is only in the world of appearances. In his efforts to do good, Richard Nixon became sidetracked and his actions miscarried. In the process of trying to do what was good, he did something that appears to be evil." The exception is treated in terms of the philosophical assumption itself and explained in light of that view. Philosophical assumptions are not tentative hypotheses to be discarded when evidence contradicts them. There is no way in which an empirical test could be constructed that would enable us to falsify philosophical assumptions. If my philosophy is such that it entails the assumption "All people seek what is good," I will not permit any empirical conditions to dissuade me from my stance. On the contrary, I can account for all exceptions and seeming contradictions in terms of my philosophical assumption itself.

A third characteristic of philosophical assumptions is that they frequently are implicit rather than explicit. An *explicit statement* is one that is clearly stated. Its postulates are clearly delineated, related to one another, and organized into a unified whole. An *implicit statement* is one that is not always clearly stated. Its postulates are not always fully thought through and frequently they are not even recognized by the person who holds them. A person may be unaware that his or her theory is based on certain assumptions about the world. It is often difficult to identify a person's assumptions when they are not stated explicitly. Nevertheless, as we shall see, almost all personality theorists take a stance on certain fundamental philosophical assumptions. For example, a theorist may believe that people are genuinely free to determine their own behavior or that they are primarily controlled by inner or external forces. These explicit or implicit assumptions profoundly and deeply influence a theorist's way of perceiving and understanding the world.

Evaluating Philosophical Assumptions

We have seen that a person's assumptions refer to a reality that is not necessarily apprehended or perceived by ordinary observation. The reality to which philosophical assumptions refer need not be the world of everyday observations, but instead a world of ultimate reality. This means that philosophical assumptions have criteria for evaluation that are different from the criteria for empirical statements or other statements based on ordinary observation. Philosophical assumptions have criteria that are appropriate to the epiphanic vision that underlies them. In empirical science, as we shall see, statements are proven false by the process of perceptual observation. This method is inappropriate for philosophical assumptions. In evaluating a person's assumptions, we cannot set up a crucial test or experiment that will determine whether or not his or her hypothesis is justified. Philosophical assumptions do not function as hypotheses; thus, they have their own criteria or test. As a matter of fact, the best way to spot whether or not a theorist's statements represent philosophical assumptions is to look at the way in which he or she evaluates them.

Philosophical assumptions are based on a special act of epiphanic cognition. They are evaluated by criteria that are appropriate to that mode of knowing. We are going to suggest three criteria for evaluating philosophical assumptions that add up to a fourth and final criterion: compellingness. This addition follows a principle known as gestalt. The term *gestalt* comes from the same German word, meaning "configuration" or "form," and the gestaltist principle implies that the whole is more than the sum of its parts.

The first criterion is that of *coherence*. Are the philosophical assumptions coherent? The verb *cohere* means to hang together. Thus we ask, "Are the philosophical assumptions of a theory presented in a clear, logical, consistent manner, or are they riddled with contradictions and inconsistencies?" A philosophical system may have apparent inconsistencies, perplexing metaphors, or paradoxes and still be coherent, providing that the seeming contradictions are ironed out within the philosophical stance itself so that the final position represents a precise, coherent whole. A person's philosophical assumptions may also be unfinished, that is, open to further growth, but to be coherent they must have a clearly recognizable, consistent thrust.

The second criterion is *relevance*. To be meaningful, a philosophical assumption must have some bearing on our view of reality. If we do not share the same view of reality, as is the case with some earlier philosophies, we will have considerable difficulty judging the assumption. We do not know what its bearing was in earlier times or how it might apply to our contemporary world. This lack of information explains why myths that posit geographical locations for heaven and hell are very difficult for us to appreciate today. Such myths were perfectly appropriate in a Ptolemaic universe where the heavens revolved around the earth, since it seemed perfectly sensible then to think of heaven as up above and hell as down below. However, geographical location is rendered much more difficult in a Copernican universe, which is why contemporary mythic conceptualizations of heaven and hell tend to locate them within the self. Such a concept has more meaning for us today in the light of our contemporary world view. In our modern world, the criterion of relevance further implies the need to be compatible with empirical reality as best we can ascertain it, thus, philosophies are invariably reshaped by scientific discoveries.

The third criterion is *comprehensiveness*. Is the philosophical assumption "deep" enough? In part, this question refers to scope or intended range of coverage. Does it cover what it intends to cover? Further, the criterion of comprehensiveness asks whether or not the treatment of the subject governed by the assumption is profound or merely surface and superficial. A philosophical assumption is surface and superficial if it leaves too many questions unanswered or if it refuses to answer them.

These three criteria add up to the final criterion, which we refer to as *compellingness*. The final and most important question to ask is, "Does the assumption and its underlying philosophy convince you?" A philosophical assumption convinces you if it grabs you where you live in such a way that you find the belief inescapable. It is as if you have to believe in it. Now, it is perfectly possible that a philosophical assumption may strike you as being coherent, relevant, and comprehensive, but in spite of those features it does not compel you to believe it. In such a case, the belief does not move you and you cannot "buy" it. My language here is deliberately passive: "The philosophical assumption grabs you." "You are compelled." This language underscores the fact that philosophical assumptions are not merely subjective opinions that a person has about the world. Rather, philosophical assumptions emerge out of a person's encounter with the world. They entail an active meeting of the person and the world that leads to a position or a stance about reality that the person finds inescapable.

Inevitably, the personality theories that will be described reflect philosophical points of view. Some of the theories are explicitly philosophical. In others, the philosophical assumptions are not clearly stated; they are hidden, but they are nevertheless present. Carl Rogers openly acknowledges that his view of the self is philosophical and that his primary differences with other theorists, such as B. F. Skinner, are philosophical ones. Sigmund Freud initially conceived of his work as devoid of philosophy, but, in the end, he was forced to acknowledge that many of his assumptions functioned philosophically. To the extent to which personality theories entail philosophical assumptions, it is important that we recognize them as such and apply the criteria that are appropriate for them.

EXERCISE:

Examining Philosophical Assumptions

Every thinking person entertains and holds basic philosophical assumptions as he or she reflects on the world and his or her existence. By looking at some common assumptions on philosophical issues held by personality theorists and asking where you stand on these issues, you can become more aware of your own philosophical assumptions and use them as a point of reference as you study the different theories.

Lawrence Wrightsman (1974) has identified six dimensions on which individuals vary in their perception of human nature. Each issue is presented here as a bipolar dimension along which a person's view can be placed according to the degree to which he or she agrees with one or the other extreme. You can rate your own view according to a scale from one to five. If you completely agree with the first statement, rate the issue with a number 1. If you completely agree with the second statement, rate the issue with a number 5. If you only moderately agree with a statement, a number 2 or 4 would best reflect your view. If you are neutral towards the issue or believe that the best position is a synthesis of the two extremes, rate the issue with a number 3.

> 1. *Trustworthiness versus untrustworthiness*
>   a. *People are basically trustworthy, honest, and responsible.*
>   b. *People are basically untrustworthy, immoral, and irresponsible.*
> 2. *Altruism versus selfishness*
>   a. *People are basically unselfish and sincerely interested in others.*
>   b. *People are basically selfish and unconcerned about others.*
> 3. *Independence versus conformity*
>   a. *People basically maintain their convictions in the face of pressures to conform from a group, society, or authority figure.*
>   b. *People basically conform to the views of a group, society, or authority figure.*

4. *Freedom versus determinism*
   a. *People basically have control over their own behaviors and understand the motives behind their behaviors.*
   b. *The behavior of people is basically determined by internal or external forces over which they have little, if any, control.*
5. *Complexity versus simplicity*
   a. *People are basically complicated and hard to understand.*
   b. *People are basically simple and easy to understand.*
6. *Similarity versus variability*
   a. *People are basically very similar in nature.*
   b. *Each individual is unique and cannot be compared with others.*

When you have determined where you stand on each of these major issues, a comparison of your positions can help you assess the importance of these issues to your own understanding of personality. Those assumptions that you feel very strongly about and have marked with a 1 or a 5 probably play a very important role in your personal philosophy. If you are not strongly committed to any particular issue, that issue is probably not as important to you in your thinking about personality.

You should note that there are no correct answers to the questions above. The different personality theorists that I will talk about vary markedly in their position on each of these issues. Each adopts the position that appears most commendable or compelling. A comparison of your own position with that of each theorist will help you to understand why a particular theory does or does not appeal to you.

SCIENTIFIC CONSTRUCTS

As scientists, personality theorists seek to validate or confirm their ideas about personality by generally agreed-upon methods of test. The term *science* comes from the Latin *scire*, "to know." Science is a system of methods of acquiring knowledge based, or purporting to be based, on specific principles. The keystone of science is observation. While science may build elaborate theories, many of which refer to constructs that we cannot directly observe, the ultimate test of its theories rests on empirical observation.

Thus science is empirical. As we have seen, the term *empirical* means based on experience, and the simplest kind of statements in science are empirical ones, such as "There is a lion on the lawn." To know whether or not an empirical statement is justified, a person has to be shown evidence based on sensory data regarding what has been seen, heard, felt, smelled, or tasted. If someone reports, "I see a lion," we can consider the statement in two ways. The person may be saying, "I see a *lion*" or "I *see* a lion." In the first case, we are referring to the object of experience or *objective data*. In the second case, we are referring to an experience of seeing or *subjective data*. Both objective and subjective knowledge refer to empirical data. The difference between them lies in the stance of the observer. In objective knowledge, the stance is I-it, or *extrospective*. The self is looking outward on the world as object. In subjective knowledge, the stance is I-me, or *introspective*. The self is looking inward on its own experience as the object.

Reports that are concerned with the object of experience or extrospective data are relatively simple to verify. We merely indicate the conditions under which the observation may be repeated. If a second observer does not see the reported phenomena, we suggest that the conditions were not clearly specified; for example, the observer looked for the lion on the wrong lawn. Or, we may surmise that the original observer has a distorted sense of perception or experienced a hallucination. Repeated observations of the same phenomena under specified conditions lead to *consensual validation* or agreement among observers. Reports that are concerned with introspective or subjective phenomena are much more difficult to validate consensually. A certain piece of artwork may give me much joy but fail to move someone else. This is because experiential phenomena occur under much more complex conditions than extrospective objects, and they are more difficult to describe. Repeating such introspective observations may require the second observer to undergo extensive training or other experiences in order to duplicate all of the conditions. Undoubtedly, my joy on seeing a particular piece of art depends not simply on the art itself, but also on my mood, personal history, and so forth. Considerable effort is needed to duplicate these observations, but it is not impossible (Tart, 1975).

Since reports that are concerned with introspection or subjective phenomena are much more difficult to validate, some psychologists have tended to ignore them and invest their efforts in extrospective or objective findings. In fact, John Watson (1878–1958), the father of the behaviorist movement, recommended that inasmuch as our thoughts, feelings, and wishes cannot be directly observed by another person, the psychologist should ignore them and simply concentrate on overt behaviors. Few psychologists today, however, would agree with this extreme position. Most personality theorists emphasize that we need to be concerned with both subjective and objective data in order to understand behavior.

Recognizing Scientific Constructs

The simplest kinds of statements in science are empirical ones, based directly on the observation of our senses. When a number of different instances of observation coincide, however, the scientist may make a generalization. A scientific *generalization* is an inductive conclusion that states that something is true about many or all of the members of a certain class. "All rats are colorblind." The evidence for this statement is a number of facts about individual members of the class. I have observed this rat, that rat, and other rats—all of them have been unable to distinguish colors. Therefore, I conclude that all rats are colorblind, even though I have not examined each and every rat.

Because it is impossible for me to examine each and every rat that has existed in the past or might exist in the present or future, my empirical generalization can never be called ultimately true. It must remain open to possible falsification. Still, many of the statements on which we base our lives are empirical generalizations of this sort. They refer to experiences that have happened with such frequency and reliability that it may even strike us as absurd to think that they might be false. Why do we believe that the sun is going to rise tomorrow morning? Because it has risen every other day. While it is true that this conclusion is also based on a systematic understanding of astronomical law, the existential commitment that most of us have to it is based on our own experience. We have no guarantee that the sun will rise tomorrow, but we would probably feel foolish if we acted as if it were not going to.

The scientist also uses definitions. *Definitions*, as we have seen, are statements that are true because of the way in which we have agreed to use words. Some words, such as "bachelor," are easy to define clearly and precisely. Other words, such as "personality," are harder to define and subject to disagreement. To resolve that problem, the social scientist frequently tries to develop operational definitions. An *operational definition* specifies those behaviors that are encompassed in the concept. "Stress" might be operationally defined in terms of the rate of one's heartbeat and extent of one's perspiration as measured by polygraph apparatuses, which translate bodily changes into a printed record. It frequently is difficult to reach agreement on appropriate operational definitions, and at times an operational definition distorts or even misses the concept it is trying to describe. For example, "stress" can also be defined as a subjective feeling of intense anxiety. The virtue of operational definitions, for whatever it is worth, lies in giving us a common ground of reference.

For our purposes, the most important statement to consider in science is that of the scientific construct. A *scientific construct* is a statement that invokes an imaginary or hypothetical concept, which cannot be seen or observed, in order to explain what we can observe. The fact that our construct is imaginary or hypothesized does not mean that it is nonexistent or unreal. It simply means that we cannot directly observe it and have to infer it from the evidence. A familiar imaginary construct is that of IQ or Intelligence Quotient. The concept IQ is an imaginary construct that is used to explain certain behaviors, namely, one's likelihood for academic success. IQ is not an entity that we can see or directly observe. Indeed, it is an error to think of IQ as something substantive in the sense that if one were to cut open a person's brain, one could see the number 110 stamped on it. IQ does not represent something in the ordinary sense. It is properly used as an imaginary concept that may be more or less useful in explaining and predicting behavior. It helps to explain why John, who has a high academic record, performs in a certain way, while Mark, who studies just as hard, has difficulties pulling average grades. Many of our concepts in science, in fact almost all of the important ones, such as the atom with its electrons, protons, and neutrons, cannot be directly seen. They are inferred from other evidence.

Essentially, the scientist, in trying to deal with the everyday world, constructs a para-world. The *para-world* is a world of quantified, logical, and mathematical imaginary constructs that is placed beside the everyday world. By applying particular rules of reference, the scientist can correlate the two worlds and apply conclusions drawn from the para-world to life in the everyday world. Suppose that tomorrow I have to make a trip to a town sixty miles distant. I would like to know how much time I should allot to get there. I know that I can travel an average of forty miles per hour on the road. I transport this situation into imaginary constructs that will fit the mathematical formula: time equals speed times distance. Computation tells me that it will take one and a half hours. But the formula does not guarantee that my trip in the everyday world will actually be completed in that amount of time. Other variables could interfere: traffic might be slow or I could have a flat tire. The para-world that the scientist creates is fruitfully related to the everyday world even though the two worlds are not the same.

Evaluating Scientific Constructs

Although scientific constructs invoke imaginary concepts, they still have their roots in observation. However, they have to be tested indirectly. I cannot test the statement "John has an IQ of 110" in the same way that I can test the statement "There is a lion on the front lawn." I cannot simply look. The statement must be tested indirectly, but the test is still ultimately based on empirical observation.

There is no *one* method of validating constructs in science, rather, science consists of a variety of techniques for evaluating information. Nevertheless, there is one method of testing that has come to be so recognized and identified as characteristic of the scientific enterprise that it is commonly termed the *scientific method*. You should be familiar with it as an example of scientific work. This method is not unique to psychology, but is shared and used by all of the sciences. Essentially, it consists of five steps: recognizing a problem; developing a hypothesis; making a prediction; testing the hypothesis; and drawing a conclusion.

Scientific inquiry, like all inquiry, begins with a "problem" situation. The problem does not arise in the scientific laboratory, but in the everyday world. When there is an outbreak of a new virus, the scientist is called on to develop a vaccine or antidote that could decrease its intensity. We refer to the problem as *extra-* or *pro-*scientific to underscore the fact that the problem arises out of the everyday world and is not created by the method. Instead, the scientific method has been developed to deal with problems such as these.

In order to deal with a problem, the scientist puts it into a question. This elementary step helps to focus attention on what the problem is and what the solution might be. By asking questions, the scientist zeroes in on the problem, specifies it, and makes it more manageable. At the same time, the questions raised structure the search and limit the possible answers. By focusing on one or two aspects thought to be pertinent to a problem, a scientist may temporarily divert attention from other relevant matters. Some critics have argued that in the social sciences we neglect significant problems in our effort to be specific. Their criticism has merit, but it is also necessary to narrow down our problems in order to deal with them effectively.

The second step is to formulate a *hypothesis*, a preliminary assumption that directs further inquiry. Many commentaries emphasize the importance of a preliminary investigation or review of the literature to inform the development of a hypothesis. Such a review entails studying available data about the problem, comparing it to similar problems, and so on. This type of preliminary investigation is helpful and necessary, but we would be misled if we thought of it as distinct from the formation of the hypothesis itself. If a scientist did not have some idea (or preliminary hypothesis) to begin with about the kinds of information that would be useful, he or she would not know what to look for in the first place. Without some tentative hunches about what information is important, one would not know whether to consult baseball scores or car manuals to learn what the problem with a malfunctioning car might be. Thus, a review of the literature does not in itself produce a hypothesis. The hypothesis is created by the scientist as he or she brings creative mental powers to bear on the problem. Some scientists refer to the hypothesis as an "idea" or "hunch"; others go so far as to call it "inspiration" or "divination." The important point is that while the scientific method is a procedure for testing hypotheses, in and of itself it does not generate them. It presupposes them.

There are several conditions for an appropriate hypothesis in science. First, the hypothesis must answer the question posed by the problem. If the problem is an outbreak of a new virus, the hypothesis that my car is malfunctioning probably is not relevant. These two events in all likelihood do not have any relation to each other. But we need to be careful here. Sometimes what initially appears far-fetched may have more relevance than is immediately apparent. This is why "brainstorming" is often suggested when a group of scientists are trying to solve a formerly insurmountable problem. In brainstorming, each scientist tosses out any idea that comes to mind regardless of how irrelevant or foolish it may appear. Later the ideas are considered, and, at times, an idea that initially appeared unrelated proves to have considerable merit.

Second, the hypothesis must be possible. By this we mean that it must not violate any known causal laws. *Causal laws* are established laws of cause and effect. In science, we are not permitted to have any demons or devils jumping into a car during the night and gummying up the works, nor can we have persons able to leap tall buildings in a single bound. These activities violate known causal laws, and such hypotheses are simply not permitted.

Third, the hypothesis must be testable. By "testable" we mean that the scientist must be able to deduce other consequences from the hypothesis beyond the fact that the problem situation exists. To argue that Johnny is lazy because he has a lazy disposition is to argue in a circle and not provide any new or further information. To suggest that Johnny behaves in a lazy fashion because he has a low rate of metabolism is to suggest a hypothesis that provokes further consequences. A blood test might reveal a low level of blood sugar. A poor rate of metabolism might reveal itself in other behavioral symptoms as well.

In discussing the formulation of hypotheses, I have already mentioned the third step of the scientific method, which is to make a prediction from the hypothesis. From our hypothesis that Johnny has a low rate of metabolism, we can predict that a blood test might reveal a low blood sugar level. By placing the word "if" before the hypothesis and inserting the word "then" before the prediction, we can form a complete hypothetical statement: *"If* Johnny has a low rate of metabolism, *then* a blood test will reveal a low blood sugar level." This prediction refers to an experience that we could have if the hypothesis were useful.

The fourth step is to test the hypothesis. By the time the scientist arrives at this point, he or she has a pretty good idea of what the test is going to be because the prediction itself stipulates what sort of test. Some hypotheses are tested very simply by looking somewhere. Others require an elaborate experiment in which variables are carefully manipulated and controlled. In some cases, we may not be able immediately to test the hypothesis. This often happens in the field of astronomy when certain phenomena suggest a new comet or planet. We may be unable to test the hypothesis at the present time because it refers to a future event or we lack sufficient technological equipment. The farthest planets in our solar system were hypothesized long before telescopes were powerful enough to spot them. In other instances, we may not be able to find the evidence that the hypothesis requires. In history, clear-cut evidence, such as relics and written documents, is not always available. But as long as we can stipulate what sort of evidence could test the hypothesis, our hypothesis is considered to be legitimate.

The final step is to draw a conclusion. Many people like to think of scientific constructs as *verified*, that is to say, proven true, once they have passed the test; but logically this is incorrect. A simple illustration clarifies this point. Suppose one were to argue:

If X is a fish, then X can swim.
X can swim.
Therefore, X is a fish.

Obviously, the argument is unsound because something is wrong with the conclusion. I can swim too and I am not a fish. In logic, this is called the *fallacy of affirming the consequent*. It is precisely the same kind of reasoning that we would be following if we were to assume that a construct that held up under testing was thereby true. It is always possible that there are other factors or variables that could account for the test results. Therefore, the scientist never claims that the information yielded by his or her methods is ultimately true. Science progresses by disconfirmations.

Science, because it is ultimately based on observation, always has to be open to falsification. Indeed, the scientist is required to state under what conditions his or her hypothesis could be disproven. The very nature of scientific methods limits the kind of information that they can yield. As we have seen, the scientist in trying to deal with the everyday world constructs a para-world. The truth of the scientist's methods is limited to that para-world. This is why the validating activity of the scientist is never as convincing or compelling as the cognitive act that underlies our philosophical assumptions. While scientific methods cannot be said to yield ultimate truth, they do provide a wealth of useful information that can assist us in living in the everyday world. It is to our advantage, therefore, to act as if the conclusions from our scientific methods are true. The criterion for judging scientific constructs is that of *usefulness* rather than truth.

EXERCISE:

How We Behave as Scientists

The personality theorist George Kelly (1955) has suggested that each one of us behaves like a scientist in one's efforts to cope with the world. You can gain a deeper understanding of your own activities as a scientist by analyzing a recent problem and your efforts to solve it in terms of the steps of the scientific method, which we have just outlined. Suppose one night, when you arrive home, you turn the light switch and nothing happens. "Perhaps the bulb has burned out," you think. You struggle across the room to turn on another light, but it too fails to light. "Maybe the fuse has blown out," you think. With the aid of a flashlight you arrive at the fuse box and replace the fuse. The lights go on and you discard the original fuse.

Analyze the problem, or another one, in terms of the scientific method. How did you identify the problem? What hypotheses did you develop? What predictions did you make about possible experiences that you could have if the hypothesis were useful? How did you test your hypothesis and what conclusions did you draw?

In the process of scientific inquiry, frequently the scientist entertains more than one hypothesis. Each one is checked out in turn in order to rule out those that do not stand up under test conditions. Occasionally, the scientist is left with rival hypotheses. Sometimes, the same phenomena may be accounted for by two or more different hypotheses, both of which stand up under test. At other times, a sufficiently sensitive or crucial test has not been developed to eliminate all of the hypotheses but one.

Given that both are sound hypotheses, how does the scientist decide between them? In general, three criteria have been applied: compatibility, predictive power, and simplicity. Each of these criteria has its advantages and limitations. *Compatibility* refers to the agreement of the hypothesis with other previously well established information. This criterion is a sensible one since it is a lot easier for us to accept a new hypothesis if it is consistent with findings in other areas. However, this criterion should not be too rigidly applied. Science does not necessarily grow in an orderly, straightforward manner, accumulating new facts without ever going back and changing them. There are times in science when a new construct completely shatters earlier theories, forcing us to revise and reconsider them. This is what happened with Einstein's theory of relativity. While the criterion of compatibility is a good rule of thumb, sometimes an incompatible theory proves to be more useful.

Predictive power refers to the range or scope of the construct. Scientists not only seek to explain the phenomena that we observe but also to predict and anticipate them. We have seen that by being testable, a hypothesis is able to generate predictions about experiences that we could have if the hypothesis should turn out to be useful. The more predictions or consequences that we can infer from a hypothesis, the greater its range and usefulness in generating new ideas. It was on this basis that Newton's hypothesis concerning gravitation and his three laws of

FIGURE 1.1 Ptolemaic and Copernican Theories

The Ptolemaic theory (above) held that the sun, moon, and planets revolved in epicycles around the sun. Cumbersome mathematical formulas were required for prediction from the theory. The Copernican theory (below) in which the planets revolve around the sun is a much simpler one.

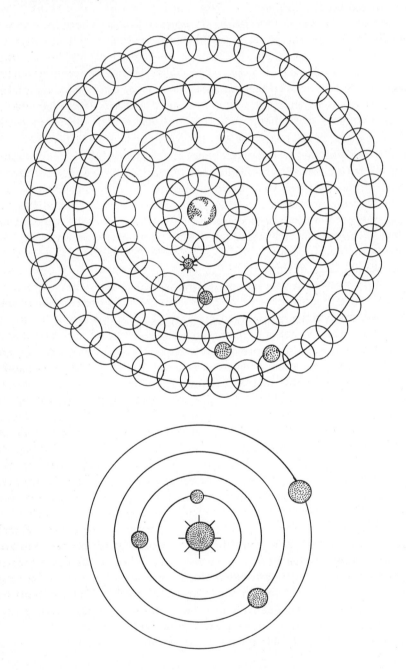

motion were adapted over Kepler and Galileo's theories. On the other hand, too narrow a reliance on this criterion may lead to the notion that the primary value of a construct lies in the amount of research and predictions it generates. Some theories express their scope by integrating and encompassing ideas rather than by generating specific predictions and research projects.

Some refer to the criterion of *simplicity* as "Occam's razor." William of Occam was a medieval philosopher who suggested that explanations ought to be as simple as possible. It was on this basis that the Copernican theory of the universe was accepted over the earlier Ptolemaic theory, which held that the sun, moon, and planets revolve in epicycles around the earth. The Ptolemaic theory has a wide predictive power and could accurately account for the movement of heavenly bodies, but predictions from it entailed cumbersome mathematical procedures. Copernicus's suggestion that the planets revolve elliptically around the sun (Figure 1.1) called for comparatively simpler formulas. This is why today we believe that the earth revolves around the sun, a fact that runs counter to the perception of our senses and that has not been directly observed. Too rigid an emphasis on the criterion of simplicity, however, can be at the expense of accounting for all of the complexity of human behavior. While it is true that our explanations should not be multiplied beyond necessity, the goal is simplicity rather than simplism.

Science and philosophy are complementary methods of investigation. Each has its own rules and procedures for establishing information, and each has its own criteria for judging the validity or soundness of its findings. Both are necessary for the personality theorist. Scientific studies rely on assumptions that can only be established philosophically. The desire to be scientific, however, reflects itself in an effort to test constructs by validating evidence rather than by simply relying on the compelling character of a philosophical assumption (Rychlak, 1968). At the same time, the evidence of scientific methods can never be as strong as the convincingness of an epiphanic insight. Some psychologists have erred in that they have narrowed the scientist's activity to an objective experimental methodology and ignored the philosophical assumptions on which all scientific work is based. Others have assumed that the compelling character of philosophical assumptions is sufficient to establish their credibility as scientific constructs (Rychlak, 1968). Either position is misguided. It is important that we distinguish between science and philosophy so that we can recognize each kind of discourse when it occurs and evaluate it according to the appropriate criteria. At the same time, we also need to evaluate our philosophical assumptions in the light of contemporary scientific information and to judge our scientific findings in terms of their adequacy as philosophy.

If theories of personality have their origin in philosophy and seek to validate their constructs through scientific methods, they also culminate in some form of art or practical application. While personality theories have found application in many areas, such as assessment, research, and social concerns, they are probably best known for their contribution to psychotherapy.

The art of psychotherapy is the effort to apply the findings of personality theory in ways that will assist individuals and meet human goals. The word "therapy" comes from the Greek word *therapeia*, which means to heal; however, psychotherapists are not interested only in healing sick people. They are also interested in understanding "normal" people, learning how they function, and helping them to function more creatively. While in many respects psychotherapy is the flowering of personality theory, it is also the seed of it, as the desire to help people has fostered and nourished the development of personality theories. The two go hand in hand. Many theories of personality cannot be adequately understood without understanding the theory of psychotherapy that accompanies them.

The reader does not need any special introduction to the statements that are used in psychotherapy, because the language of psychotherapy is no different from ordinary language; it consists of a conversation between human beings. As Freud acknowledged, in analysis, "nothing takes place" between the patient and the physician "except that they talk to each other" (1926b). What we need to become aware of, however, are the different goals of psychotherapy and ways of evaluating it.

Goals of Psychotherapy

Joseph Rychlak (1968) has suggested that psychotherapy has three major motives: the scholarly, the ethical, and the curative.

The "scholarly motive" conceives of therapy as a means of understanding the self and human nature. Psychoanalysis, for example, was considered by Freud as a tool for discovering truths about human nature. Freud was only a reluctant therapist, and he did not conceive of the curative side effects of psychoanalysis as its primary function or virtue. His goal was to help the individual acquire self-understanding and to develop a comprehensive theory of human nature, and he developed psychoanalysis as a method of research aimed at that end.

The "ethical motive" conceives of therapy as a means of helping the individual to change, improve, grow, and better the quality of his or her life. The effort here is not to study or understand people as much as it is to create an atmosphere within which people can change if they wish to. Carl Rogers's work represents an example of the ethical motive. His emphasis is on an attitude created by the therapist that permits change to occur within the client, rather than on cognitive understanding or the manipulation of behavior.

The "curative motive" aims directly at eliminating troublesome symptoms and substituting more appropriate behavior. There is an analogy here to the work of medical practitioners who seek to cure people of illnesses. Most behavior therapists, for example, consider that they have been hired to do a job and seek to do it as effectively and quickly as possible. From this point of view, the therapist is conceived of as responsible for creating changes, removing symptoms, and controlling behavior.

Most people enter therapy with the expectation that they will be cured or helped to improve. In this respect, the curative motive is most consistent with the popular view of psychotherapy. Because of this expectation, many people have difficulty, particularly at the beginning, undergoing psychoanalysis or other forms of "insight" therapy. If they stay with it, however, their reasons for being in therapy change, and they begin to appreciate the value of the other motives. Obviously, the reasons for entering, continuing in, and practicing psychotherapy are diverse and mixed. This is why the evaluation of therapy is a difficult issue.

Evaluating Psychotherapy

How does one go about evaluating psychotherapy? What are the criteria that are appropriate to use? In 1952, a British psychologist, Hans Eysenck, stunned the therapeutic community when he issued a report on treatment outcomes that indicated that the improvement rate for patients in intensive and prolonged psychotherapy was only about 64 percent. This rate was less than that of 72 percent for patients who received treatment only from a general practitioner or were in simple custodial care. A second report (1961) did not change the general outlook. However, Eysenck's reports have subsequently been severely criticized, and it is now clear that his results are not the final word on the issue (Smith & Glass, 1977). It appears likely that Eysenck prejudiced his results. Moreover, Eysenck's criterion for improvement was that of "symptom remission." This criterion, while perhaps appropriate for therapies governed by the curative motive, is not necessarily appropriate for those that are conducted for other purposes.

If the proportion of cures were the only criterion by which psychotherapies were to be judged, psychoanalysis and other insight therapies would have long since disappeared from the scene with the advent of more efficient and less costly curative techniques. This, however, has not been the case. If one's criterion, on the other hand, rests on scholarly grounds, psychoanalysis emerges the clear winner. No other method of therapy has provided us with such a wealth of information about the complexity and depth of the human personality.

In brief, each method of psychotherapy must be evaluated in terms of its own goals and purposes. Behavior therapists, who aim at cure, are particularly interested in discovering the proportion of cures associated with various techniques. Ethical theorists, who aim at creating an appropriate climate for therapeutic change and life improvement, have stimulated considerable research and empirical study of those conditions that foster personality change and their effects. They have also raised ethical questions as to the desirability of certain behaviors. Freudian psychoanalysis asks to be evaluated in terms of its effectiveness as a method of research aimed at understanding human nature.

A few words might be appropriate here as to the type of evidence that is used in psychoanalysis to arrive at knowledge, because there is a clear tie-in to the discussion of scientific and philosophical knowledge. From the viewpoint of the analyst the evidence is empirical, although the analyst's techniques are clearly informed by the philosophical assumptions of psychoanalysis. The analyst carefully observes the patient, listens to his or her statements, makes interpretations based on perceived relationships among the elements, and views the subsequent behavior of the patient as confirmation or disconfirmation of his or her hypotheses. Unfortunately, this research is not particularly public or open to widespread consensual validation because of the private and confidential nature of the analytic relationship. From the viewpoint of the patient, however, the evidence is cognitive. The patient's acceptance or rejection of an interpretation is based on its compellingness, which may or may not emerge as a result of its coherence, relevance, and comprehensiveness. In this sense, a patient may reject a perfectly valid interpretation. This possibility explains why psychologists who take a rigorous scientific point of view are frequently suspicious of clinical insight. They recognize that its acceptance or rejection by a patient is not based on scientific grounds.

Nevertheless, it is hard to see how insight could result from the scientific method alone, inasmuch as self-understanding and the understanding of others ultimately rests on philosophical grounds. As Will Durant, the American educator and writer, reminds us, "Science gives us knowledge, but only philosophy can give us wisdom;" and "Every science begins as philosophy and ends as art" (1954).

SUGGESTIONS FOR FURTHER READING

The student who is interested in pursuing Allport's effort to define the word "personality" should see his survey in Chapter Two of *Personality: A Psychological Interpretation* (Holt, 1937). It provides a compact survey of the origin of the word and various ways in which it has been defined.

The Story of Philosophy by Will Durant (Pocket Books, 1954) is a lay introduction to philosophy that tells its story by focusing on the lives and ideas of significant philosophers. The introduction, "On the Uses of Philosophy," helps to place the work of these thinkers in perspective. J. B. Conant's *On Understanding Science* (Yale University Press, 1947) gives a concise introduction to the scientific enterprise. A comprehensive history of psychology is provided in the classic work of E. G. Boring, *A History of Experimental Psychology* (Appleton-Century-Crofts, 1929), a long, detailed book but invaluable to the serious student of psychology.

Books that try to place the study of psychology and personality theory in perspective within the general framework of science and philosophy are more difficult reading, but worth the effort of the interested individual. The following are especially recommended: M. Turner, *Philosophy and the Science of Behavior* (Appleton-Century-Crofts, 1967); D. Bakan, *On Method: Towards a Reconstruction of Psychological Investigation* (Jossey-Bass, 1967); J. Rychlak, *A Philosophy of Science for Personality Theory* (Houghton Mifflin, 1968); and I. Chein, *The Science of Behavior and The Image of Man* (Basic Books, 1972). These books stress the need to develop adequate conceptual structures of science and philosophy within which personality theorizing can flourish and grow as efforts to understand the human being.

PART I

Freudian Psychoanalysis

Of all of the giants of intellectual history, Sigmund Freud emerges with unquestionable stature as a leader in helping us to understand human nature. Freud's contributions towards understanding personality are such that some people believe he did more to enhance our self-understanding than anyone else since Socrates, Plato, and Aristotle, the great philosophers of ancient Greece. Some critics, following a comment of Freud's own, have compared his activities to the Copernican revolution. Even if the comparison is not justified, Freud's achievement is highly significant. Many of the other theories that we will study were developed as efforts to elaborate on, modify, substitute for, or refute the concepts of Freud. Contemporary personality theorizing is, in all likelihood, incomprehensible without a prior understanding of Freud's contribution.

How did Freud come to develop psychoanalysis and its attendant theory of personality? Significant discoveries such as his, of unconscious forces, repression, and pervasive sexual motivation, do not come out of the sky or emerge fully developed without prior preparation. Freud's theory of personality and his contributions to our self-understanding are both a culmination of and a departure from a long history of intellectual thought, which included the particular developments in academic and clinical psychology of the nineteenth century.

The sixteenth- and early seventeenth-century renaissance of science had raised new problems for philosophical speculation about human nature. Copernicus, Kepler, and Galileo had investigated the world by careful observations on the basis of which they made hypotheses. They tested their theories by determining their consequences and carrying out experiments that would show whether or not the predictions from their hypotheses would come about. In short, science emerged with its methodologies of investigation. The empirical methods of the new science gradually overthrew the long-dominant Aristotelian philosophy of nature and gradually led to the conclusion that the physical world operated as a vast machine, a machine whose motion could be measured and described in mathematical laws. After Isaac Newton (1642–1727) formulated and popularized the mechanical laws of motion and the principle of gravity, it was thought possible, at least in theory, to explain the entire physical world in qualitative and mechanical terms. The world that emerged was one that operated as a material system according to fixed laws of nature, and Newton's model of the universe was to dominate all scientific thought to the end of the nineteenth century.

The application of scientific findings was first limited to the inanimate physical world, but inevitably, in the seventeenth century, a movement arose to relate them in a more encompassing fashion. This movement culminated in the mechanistic materialism of an English philosopher, Thomas Hobbes (1588–1679), whose philosophy suggested that nothing existed except matter in motion, which was measurable by fixed qualitative laws. As everything was explainable on the basis of matter and its mechanical laws of motion, Hobbes believed that there was no such entity as spirit, soul, mind, or reason as an immaterial substance. Human thought or behavior was simply the product of the movement of matter. Hobbes extended the thoroughgoing mechanistic concept of the physical world to include human beings and mental life.

The response of the French philosopher René Descartes (1596–1650), "I think, therefore, I am," which reasserted the primacy of thought over matter, was meant to do justice to the conviction that a person is more than a machine without belying or hampering the accomplishments of the new science. In his philosophy, Descartes divided all reality into two separate kinds of substances: *res extensa*, "matter," and *res cogitans*, "mind." Matter included all extended substances: inorganic and animate matter, including human bodies. This realm, Descartes suggested, could be legitimately understood under the scientific categories of mechanistic materialism and its laws of motion. Mind included all conscious states: thinking, willing, feeling, and so forth. Mind was a second kind of substance, immaterial and unextended, which Descartes believed was free of any explanation by mechanical laws. For the first time in history, a sharp distinction between mind and matter was made the basis of a systematic philosophy.

Descartes's well-known response, "I think, therefore, I am," was to have far-ranging consequences. It led people in the West to posit the center of the person in the mind rather than the entire organism. From ancient times, it was well known that both mental and bodily components were involved in personality, but not until after Descartes did the dualism of mind versus matter become a problem. The popular view, following Descartes, was that bodily activities might occur according to the laws of mechanical causality, but mental life was not governed by the same laws of cause and effect.

Descartes's view was too far removed from the emerging science to permit it to remain unchallenged. The life of the mind and human life could hardly remain outside the realm of growing scientific investigation. This development had, by Freud's time, expressed itself in two ways: the doctrine of evolution and the concept of psychology as a science. Thus, during Freud's early childhood, two notable events in the history of science occurred. When Freud was three, Charles Darwin published *The Origin of Species* (1859), a work that revolutionized the concept of humanity by making human beings a part of nature and thus, subjects who could be studied by the scientific method. The next year, Gustav Fechner founded psychology as a natural science by demonstrating that the mind could be studied scientifically and measured qualitatively. He proved it by noting the relation of the intensity of a stimulus to the intensity of a sensation.

Freud's early training and study were in the field of neurology at the physiological laboratory of Ernst Brücke. Brücke's book *Lectures in Physiology* (1874) viewed living organisms as dynamic systems of development that could be understood under the laws of chemistry and physics. Freud initially hoped to extend the work of Brücke and his predecessors into the understanding of the life of the mind. However, subsequent developments, which will be traced in Chapter 2, led Freud to an understanding of personality that was psychological rather than physiological, as he gradually recognized that the dynamics of the psyche could not be comprehended in simply materialistic or physiological terms.

Freud was eventually led to disagree with both the popular view based on Descartes and Brücke's view, which tried to reduce mental processes to physical or chemical causes. To exempt mental life from the determinism characteristic of all other natural phenomena was, in Freud's opinion, to overthrow the entire scientific outlook on the world. It was simply "unscientific" to call slips of the tongue or dreams accidental. According to the laws of determinism, mental life, as well as physical life, must be seen as coherent and connected. But it was also an error to attribute a dream or slip of the tongue to gastric indigestion, fatigue, or other physiological causes as Brücke tended to do. Freud believed that dreams and slips must be meaningful within a comprehensive understanding of psychic life itself.

Freud was heir to many of the problems created in the aftermath of Cartesian philosophy. Lancelot Law Whyte (1960) has suggested that "Descartes by his definition of mind as awareness, may be said to have provoked, as reaction, the European discovery of the unconscious mind." The Cartesian definition of the person as "awareness" rendered a coherent, intelligible continuity of conscious data impossible without the assumption of unconscious processes, because conscious states appear in isolation and are apparently unconnected with one another. The interpolation of unconscious mental acts served to fill the gaps between individual conscious states. At the same time, Freud's work represents an effort to resolve some of the problems created by Cartesian philosophy. For example, in the end, Freud's unconscious forces entail both bodily and mental processes, thus somewhat repairing the Cartesian dualism of mind versus body.

As well as being a giant of intellectual history, therefore, Freud stands out also as something of a mystery. There is no question but that he was a man of his time and culture, but he also sought to overcome the limitations of his own day and age. It would be difficult to find another thinker who was so completely bound to outmoded, inadequate, and traditional forms of thought, yet who so succeeded in breaking those confines and opening the door to new points of view. Freud stood within a tradition of empirical objectivism and claimed to have extended scientific knowledge by placing human psychic life under scientific observation and theory. As such, his hypotheses were rooted and cast in the framework of nineteenth-century biological determinism. Freud was also one of the last of the enlightenment rationalists and showed an almost unqualified faith in human reason. Few contemporary thinkers can agree with these presuppositions today. Yet it was Freud who, in his theory, shattered the optimism of the nineteenth century and destroyed the image of human nature portrayed by a mechanical matrix.

A dynamic figure, such as Sigmund Freud, invariably attracts and repels. A heavy fire of criticism has been directed against almost every Freudian hypothesis, and many of his concepts have been rejected as either reductionistic or projectionistic. Nevertheless, Freud encouraged and made possible a new way of looking at human beings. Freud inspired a group of loyal disciples, who today continue the psychoanalytic tradition.

CHAPTER 2

The Development of Psychoanalysis

The distinguished stature and contributions of Sigmund Freud place him at the forefront of contemporary personality theorists. For over forty years, Freud meticulously studied dimensions of human nature that were previously unknown and unexplored. Developing the technique of free association, he reached far into the depths of his own unconscious life and that of others. In the process, he created a unique method of research, psychoanalysis, for comprehending the human individual. He discovered psychological processes such as repression, resistance, transference, and infantile sexuality. He developed the first comprehensive method of studying and treating neurotic problems. Not only did he revolutionize psychology, but his influence has been felt in all the social sciences, as well as in literature, art, and religion. His position in the history of intellectual thought clearly justifies a concentrated study of his ideas.

SIGMUND FREUD: BIOGRAPHICAL BACKGROUND

Sigmund Freud was born in 1856 in Freiburg, Moravia (a small town in what is now Czechoslovakia), to a Jewish merchant and his young wife. Sigmund was born in a caul, which is to say that a small portion of the fetal sac enveloped his head at birth. His mother took this event, according to folklore, as a sign that ensured the child's future fame. While

Freud did not practice religion as an adult, he remained extremely conscious of his Jewish extraction and identity. His mother, twenty-one at the time of her favored, first son's birth, was loving and protective, and the young boy was passionately devoted to her. Freud's father, Jacob, not a very prosperous wool merchant, was forty-one, almost twice as old as his wife. Jacob was stern and authoritarian, but his son revered him. Only later, through his heroic self-analysis, did Freud realize that his feelings toward his parents were in fact ambivalent, tinged with fear and hate as well as respect and love.

When Sigmund was eleven months old, a brother, Julius, was born, but he died eights month later. A sister, Anna, arrived when Freud was two and a half. Later, four other sisters and a brother joined the family. In the household of Freud's earliest youth, there was also an old Nannie, described by Freud as "ugly," but he was very fond of her and impressed by her religious teachings of Catholicism. Nevertheless, shortly after Anna was born, the nanny was abruptly dismissed for having stolen from the household. Sigmund's large and diverse family was further complicated by the fact that he was born an uncle. Sigmund's father, a widower, had two grown sons by his former marriage, and Freud's elder half-brother was himself a father. Freud and his nephew John, who was one year older than he, were close early childhood companions. Freud was to view their early relationship as very significant to his later development. Many have speculated that Freud's unusual family constellation set the stage for and provoked his later discovery of the Oedipus complex and its parameters.

At the age of four, Sigmund and his family moved to Vienna, where he was to live for almost eighty years. Although he was critical of Vienna, he was influenced by it and would not leave the city until it was overwhelmed by Nazis in 1938, the year before he died. In his youth, Freud was a conscientious student. His parents encouraged his studies by giving him special privileges and expecting the other children to make sacrifices in behalf of their elder brother. He was the only member of the family allotted a tiny room in their modest home. He studied by oil lamp while the others had to make do with candles. A natural student, Freud entered high school a year earlier than normal and stood at the head of the class for most of his days at the Sperl Gymnasium. He demonstrated a considerable flair for languages and was an avid reader, being particularly fond of Shakespeare.

As a child, Freud had dreams of becoming a great general or minister of state, but in reality professional choice was severely restricted for a Viennese Jew. He toyed with the idea of becoming a lawyer but entered medical studies at the University of Vienna in 1873 and graduated eight years later. His studies there took longer than usual as he took his time with those areas that were of particular interest to him. He never intended to practice medicine, being more interested in physiological research. Working in Ernst Brücke's laboratory, he made substantial and noteworthy contributions as a researcher, publishing his findings on the nervous system of fish and the testes of the eel. He developed a method of staining cells for microscopic study and explored the anesthetic properties of the drug cocaine. Practical considerations, including occupational barriers to Jewish people and the desire to marry, however, led him to establish a practice as a clinical neurologist in 1881.

Since the private practice on which Freud depended for a living brought patients suffering from primarily neurotic disorders, Freud's attention became focused on the problem and study of neurosis. *Neurosis* refers to an emotional disturbance, but the disturbance is usually not so severe as to prevent the individual who has it from functioning in normal society. As Freud's goal was a comprehensive theory of humanity, he consistently considered that his study of neurosis would eventually provide a key to the study of psychological processes in general. He studied for a year in Paris with the French psychiatrist Jean Charcot, who employed hypnosis in the treatment of hysteria. He was impressed by Charcot's demonstrations but later rejected hypnosis as a therapeutic technique. Returning from Paris, Freud became deeply influenced by a procedure developed by Joseph Breuer, a Viennese physician and friend, who encouraged his patients to talk freely about their symptoms. Breuer and Freud collaborated in writing up some of their cases in the work *Studies in Hysteria* (1895). Freud's further investigations with Breuer's "talking cure" led to his own development of free association and subsequent psychoanalytic techniques. Eventually, however, Freud and Breuer parted company, as Breuer could not reconcile himself to Freud's emphasis on the role of sexuality in neurosis.

In 1900 *The Interpretation of Dreams*, a book that many consider to be Freud's most important work, was published. Initially, however, the book was ignored by all but a few. Nevertheless, Freud's reputation and prestige grew, and he began to attract a following. He also began to encounter a barrage of criticism and reproaches; some critics accused his work of being pornographic. A psychoanalytic society was founded by Freud and his colleagues and many of Freud's disciples later became noted psychoanalysts: Ernest Jones (his biographer), A. A. Brill, Sandor Ferenczi, and Karl Abraham. Originally, Carl Jung and Alfred Adler were also close associates, but later they left Freud's psychoanalytic movement, to develop and stress other ideas.

In 1909, G. Stanley Hall, noted psychologist and president of Clark University in Worcester, Massachusetts, invited Freud to present a series of lectures. It was his first and only visit to the United States. These lectures contained the basic elements of Freud's theory of personality, and their delivery marked the transformation of psychoanalysis from a small Viennese movement to one of international scope and recognition.

Freud's work, however, was by no means over. He continued to develop and extensively revise his psychoanalytic theory until his death. By the end of his life, psychoanalytic concepts had been applied to and were influencing virtually every cultural construct of humanity. Freud's published works fill twenty-four volumes in the *Standard English Edition*. He died in London in 1939 at age eighty-three, after many years of suffering from cancer of the jaw.

THE ORIGINS OF PSYCHOANALYSIS

Sigmund Freud's concepts must be appreciated historically if they are to be understood. What he completed was not a perfected system. *An Outline of Psychoanalysis*, which he began in 1938, the year before he died, had as its aim: "to bring together the doctrines of psychoanalysis and to state them . . . in the most concise form." But this book was never finished; in fact much of his work has an unfinished character about it. Ideas appear and are dismissed, only to reappear in a new context. His thought moves in phases, forever annulling and synthesizing what has gone before. The only works that Freud systematically tried to keep up to date were *The Interpretation of Dreams* (first published in 1900) and *Three Essays on Sexuality* (1905). In describing Freud's theories, therefore, it is important to recognize that psychoanalysis does not represent a finished, static theory, but rather an ongoing process of discovery about the self.

A logical place to begin discussion of the origins of psychoanalysis is Freud's early collaboration with Joseph Breuer. This, in fact, is how Freud began his discussion of the story of psychoanalysis when he presented it to the American public in his lectures at Clark University. As we have already seen, Freud was deeply influenced by a procedure developed by Breuer, and frequently he credited Breuer with the discovery of the psychoanalytic method. Thus, the beginnings of psychoanalysis may be marked by the case history of one of Joseph Breuer's patients, who is known in the literature as Anna O. (Freud, 1910).

Anna O. was a twenty-one-year old, highly intelligent woman. In the course of a two-year illness beginning in 1880, she had developed a number of physical and mental disturbances. Among her symptoms were a paralysis of the right extremities, difficulty in vision, nausea, the inability to drink any liquids, and the inability to speak or understand her mother tongue. Further, she was prone to states of absence. *Absence* refers to an altered state of consciousness in which there may be considerable personality change and later amnesia or forgetting of events that occurred during that period.

The medical profession of 1880 was quite mystified by illnesses such as these and diagnosed them as cases of hysteria. *Hysteria* referred to an illness in which there were physical symptoms, such as a paralysis, but there was no organic or physiological basis for the problem. Today such disorders are known as *conversion reactions,* in which psychological difficulties are converted into physical ones. The cause of hysteria was a mystery. Because they could not understand or effectively treat the problem, many doctors tended to view patients suffering from hysteria with suspicion and to be punitive in their attitudes toward them. At times, some even went so far as to accuse their patients of feigning or faking an illness.

This reproach did not apply for Joseph Breuer, who treated his patient sympathetically. Breuer noticed that during her states of absence, Anna frequently mumbled several words. Once he was able to get at these words, Dr. Breuer put her under a sort of hypnosis, repeated the words to her, and asked her to verbalize for him any associations that she had to the words. The patient cooperated. What she repeated can best be described as fantasies or daydreams, stories about herself that seemed to center on one particular event of her life: her father's illness and death.

Before he died, Anna's father had had a protracted illness. She had taken care of him until her own illness prevented her from doing so. After she had related a number of these stories, Anna's symptoms were relieved and eventually disappeared. The patient gratefully called the cure the "talking cure," or referred to it jokingly as "chimney sweeping."

The patient at one time was unable to drink any liquids even though it was summer and she had a terrible thirst. In order to relieve herself, she ate fruits, but these did not begin to quench her thirst. One day, while under hypnosis, she began to talk about her English governess, whom she had disliked. She finally told how one time she had entered her governess's room and seen the woman's little dog, whom she hated intensely, drinking water from a glass. Under the circumstances, she had kept her feelings silent, but after she had expressed her restrained anger in the session with Breuer, she asked for a glass of water and had no difficulty drinking it or drinking thereafter.

Her visual difficulties traced back in her memory to a time when she was sitting by her father's bed during his illness and was very worried about him. She was trying to hide her tears so that her father would not see them, when her father asked her what time it was. Since she did not want her father to see that she was crying, it was only with difficulty that she could look at her watch and make out the position of the arms on the dial through the tears that clouded her vision. Recollecting that event restored her to clarity of vision.

Later she recalled another memory that also stemmed from the period when she sat by her father's bed caring for him. A black snake (common in the area in which she lived) appeared in the room and seemed to go toward her father. She tried to drive the reptile away, but it was as if she could not move her arm. She wanted to call for help, but she could not speak. Recalling these events and the emotions they entailed relieved her paralysis and restored her knowledge of her native tongue.

Breuer concluded that the patient's symptoms were somehow determined by traumatic or stressful events of the past and that the recollection of these events had a cathartic effect on the patient. *Catharsis* refers to emotional release. When the patient recalled the events, she did so with a great deal of emotional intensity. This evidently freed her of the symptom to which the emotion had become attached.

By mid-1882, it appeared that Anna was completely and dramatically cured. In any event, Dr. Breuer was anxious to terminate the treatment, because it had become obvious that his young patient was extraordinarily fond of him. Her open proclamations of love and strong demands for his services embarrassed the prudent and reserved Dr. Breuer and also created domestic problems with his wife. When Dr. Breuer announced his intentions to end the case, Anna offered a phantom pregnancy as a final symptom. Dr. Breuer was exceedingly shaken by this turn of events, abruptly dropped the case, and took his wife to Vienna for a second honeymoon. On his return, he avoided the cathartic method in treating future patients. Fortunately, Anna eventually recovered. In time, she became well known as one of the first social workers, striving to improve the rights and status of children and women. The entire case would probably have gone unnoticed in the annals of medical history had Breuer not mentioned it to some of his colleagues, including the young doctor, Sigmund Freud, who was deeply interested.

Sometime later, Freud recalled the Anna O. episode and began to use the "talking method" with his own patients. He had some measure of success, and after observing his own explorations with the technique, came to the following conclusions. At the time of the original traumatic event, the patient had to hold back a strong emotion. He or she was unable, perhaps because of the circumstances that surrounded the event, to express the emotion it evoked in a normal way through thought, word, or deed. The emotion, prevented from escaping normally, had found another outlet and was expressing itself through a neurotic symptom. Further, the patient had forgotten the particulars of these past events. Until they were recalled under hypnosis, the details of the events and the emotions they entailed were not a part of the patient's awareness. Thus, the patient was *unconscious*, or unaware, of these memories; but the unconscious memories were influencing present behavior.

Shortly thereafter, Freud decided to give up hypnosis. In part, it was a practical necessity, since not all of his patients could be hypnotized. He assured his patients that eventually they would be able to remember the traumatic events in a normal waking state. Abandoning hypnosis also proved to be an important step in Freud's discovery of resistances. Freud's efforts in assisting his patients in remembering was a protracted and tedious process. This led Freud to conjecture that although the patient consciously wanted to remember those events, some force within prevented the patient from becoming aware of them and keeping the memories unconscious. Freud labeled this force "resistance." *Resistance* refers to the various obstacles that interfere with the analytic process and that must be overcome if the process is to be successful. Freud assumed that the same forces that originally caused the events to be forgotten were now opposing their emergence into consciousness. These earlier forces he termed "repression." *Repression* is a process that excludes undesirable thoughts or feelings from consciousness. Thus, a twofold concept emerged: repression, a force that renders ideas unconscious; and resistance, one that keeps them unconscious.

Recognizing repression and resistance leads to a very dynamic understanding of *unconscious processes*, or forces of which a person is unaware. When an idea becomes unconscious, it is not simply a matter of its having been filed in a drawer from which it can be easily retrieved, as is the case with ordinary memories of which we are not always conscious. Such memories Freud included in his concept of preconscious. *Preconscious* refers to memories that have temporarily slipped from consciousness but are accessible to consciousness without too much difficulty. You may not immediately be able to recall what you did on your last birthday, but with a little bit of effort you probably could remember. *Unconscious* memories are of a rather different sort. You may recall having been punished as a child but be unable, no matter how hard you try, to remember why you were punished. Such a memory has been repressed and rendered unconscious. It can only be recalled, if at all, with considerable difficulty. When one tries to retrieve such a memory, one discovers that the file drawer is stuck. There is a force, another aspect of the person, that prevents one from opening the drawer and retrieving the memory. This force, the resistance, must be overcome in order for the memory to be recovered.

What were those ideas or thoughts that would be rendered unconscious? Freud discovered that they were *wishes*. He learned that, during the traumatic event, a wish had been aroused that was incompatible with the personal pretensions of the patient. The wish ran counter to the person's ego-ideal or self-concept. Because it is hard for a person to accept the fact that he or she is not what he or she would like to be, such incompatibility causes pain. If it causes too much pain, the incompatible wish is repressed. One of Freud's patients provides an example. This patient's older sister had married a man of whom the patient was very fond. Shortly thereafter, the sister died, and as the girl stood at her sister's bedside for a fleeting moment an idea occurred expressing a wish. It was a wish that her personal pretensions could not permit to enter consciousness. "Now he is free," she thought, "and he can marry me." Shortly thereafter the girl became ill, displaying severe hysterical symptoms. Upon recollecting that scene, the symptoms went away.

Underlying Freud's theory is the concept that events and happenings in our lives evoke strong feelings. These emotions help us to evaluate our world and surroundings in terms of being pleasurable or unpleasurable, loving or hostile, good or bad, and so forth. There may be particular instances in which the immediate expression of one's emotion may be inappropriate, ill advised, or even disastrous. In a civilized world, we cannot express our emotions unchecked. Nevertheless, emotions must ultimately be expressed and find an outlet; they cannot be withheld indefinitely. Ideally, their expression is nondestructive. One acknowledges, accepts the emotion, and then guides it into constructive, or at least harmless, channels of expression. If an emotion is not expressed directly, it will seek expression indirectly. Repressed and unrecognized emotions go underground and begin to emerge in other ways, as in neurotic symptoms.

We repress emotions in order to avoid pain, because the wish the emotion represents conflicts with the self-concept. A certain amount of repression is inevitable and necessary in order for a civilized society to exist. But the repression is not always successful or constructive. Another example, one which Freud gave during his lectures at Clark

University, illustrates the havoc that repressed ideas can render. Suppose, he suggested, that during the course of his lecture, a young man in the back of the room decided to interrupt rudely by laughing, talking, and stamping his feet. Other members of the audience, disturbed by his behavior, forcibly eject the young man from the room so that the lecture may continue. Recognizing that our young man is a rowdy sort who might try to re-enter the hall, they station themselves at the door and hold it shut to ensure that he will not push it open. This unpleasant young fellow, however, refuses to be dealt with in that manner. He bangs on the outside of the door, kicks, screams, and, in short, creates a worse ruckus than he made in the first place. A new solution is required. Some compromise may be necessary. Perhaps the audience will agree to permit the young man back into the lecture hall if he will agree to behave a little bit better.

Freud admitted that his spatial metaphor was somewhat misleading, but it served to illustrate his primary concepts. We eject painful wishes, not permitting them to enter consciousness, but the repressed wishes refuse to behave agreeably. Instead, they create all manner of havoc, produce neurotic symptoms, and so forth. The need, then, is to restore the wishes to consciousness so that we can deal with them realistically.

Freud thought that there are several ways in which we could deal with the wishes once they were brought back into consciousness. First, we may recognize that we were wrong in repressing the wish in the first place. The wish that loomed so reprehensible at the time of the repression may be seen to represent no more than a normal desire of humanity. Therefore we can accept the wish either in whole or in part. Second, we may direct the wish into a higher goal through sublimation. *Sublimation* refers to translating a wish, the direct expression of which is socially unacceptable, into socially acceptable behavior. Third, we might recognize that the rejection of the wish was rightly motivated but also recognize that there is a distinction between thoughts and actions. Therefore, we can control ourselves and do not act on the wish by conscious realistic thought.

Evolving a Psychoanalytic Method

The initial discussion of the origin of psychoanalysis presented it as being simple only for the purpose of abbreviation. In fact, the process proved to be much more complicated than the original simple illustrations of Breuer's and Freud's patients suggest. Essentially, several opposing forces are at work. First, there is the patient who is consciously trying to remember the forgotten events. Second, there is resistance, which persists in keeping the memories unconscious. Finally, there are the repressed emotions that perpetually seek expression. If a wish cannot get out on its own recognizance in its intent to escape, it will seek an outlet in a disguised form. By putting on a mask, it will manage to sneak out and find expression in the person's behavior. Therefore, although the trauma cannot be immediately recollected, it may express itself in a veiled and hidden manner through the memories and thoughts that are recalled. In order to delve behind these surrogates and discover the repressed ideas, Freud developed two primary procedures: free association and the interpretation of dreams and slips.

Free Association This refers to a technique in which the patient is permitted to say whatever comes to mind. Free association was first suggested by Carl Jung, an early colleague of Freud. The patient is told to verbalize whatever comes to mind, no matter how insignificant, trivial, or even unpleasant the idea, thought, or picture might seem. Free association is based on the premise that no idea that occurs to the patient is arbitrary and insignificant. Eventually, these ideas will lead back to the original problem being sought. For example, Breuer's patient did not immediately recollect the scene of her father's death, but her arm was paralyzed, her vision clouded, and she was unable to use her native tongue. In other words, what she did talk about alluded to the hidden event. The instructions for free association are deceptively simple, because, in fact, they are very hard to follow. What happens when we try to verbalize everything that comes to mind? We may be flooded with thoughts and find it impossible to put them all into words. At other times, we may go blank and discover that nothing comes to mind. Also, the thoughts that do come may be very painful to discuss. These intruding ideas are like ore, however, for the analysis eventually reduces them from their crude state to a valuable metal. In the process of free association, the resistance is analyzed, understood, and weakened so that the wish is able to express itself more directly.

EXERCISE:

Free Association

A simple demonstration suggested by Theodore Reik (1956), one of Freud's followers, can convince the reader how difficult yet potentially valuable the task of free association is. The exercise is hardly equivalent to the genuine psychoanalytic situation, but it shares some of its elements and has the advantage of being able to be conducted by anyone. Further, it shows that the value of free association goes beyond its use as a technique in psychoanalysis. It may be employed by the lay person to more fully understand experiences in his or her everyday life. By following the chain of seemingly irrelevant thoughts that we produce, we may come to new insights and original concepts about ourselves.

Modern technology simplifies the demonstration. Availing yourself of a tape recorder, choose a time and place where you can be alone and in relative quiet. *Assume a relaxing position and then try to speak into the recorder whatever thoughts come to mind for a period of one half-hour or more. In general, we try to follow a certain direction in speaking. We try to speak logically and develop points in an orderly sequence. Free association requires that we verbalize whatever occurs to us without such order and restriction. Do not try to control your thoughts, or censor or analyze them. Moral, logical, and aesthetic considerations should be laid aside, and you should concentrate simply on recording whatever comes to mind. Many obstacles block the way. You may be surprised, ashamed, and even afraid of the thoughts that emerge. Social conventions have taught us to be silent on a great many matters. It is difficult to acknowledge hostile and aggressive tendencies, particularly toward those we love. Some of us even have difficulties expressing tender thoughts. Moreover, a petty or trivial thought is often the hardest of all to express. You will be successful if you succeed in verbalizing and recording all of your thoughts, regardless of their significance, importance, pleasantness, or logical order.*

When you are finished, put the tape aside and resume your normal business. After a reasonable amount of time, perhaps the next day, play the tape back. You will be listening to a person who reminds you of yourself in many ways, but in other respects, he or she will be unknown. You will discover that you had thoughts and impulses that you did not realize before. They may seem minor, but they will surprise you. While such a demonstration does not even begin to approach self-analysis, it may make clear the difficulties involved, the potential for self-discovery, and the moral courage required for self-understanding.

The Interpretation of Dreams and Slips In the process of free association, particular attention is paid to slips and dreams. *Slips* refer to bungled acts: a slip of the tongue, a slip of the pen, or a lapse of memory. In these cases, we consciously intend to say, write, or do one thing but something else inadvertently slips out. A word or a name may be on the tip of the tongue, but we have momentarily forgotten it. Many of us dismiss such events as trivial and meaningless, but, to Freud, slips like these are not without meaning. The Freudian theory assumes that in our psychic life nothing is trifling or lawless, rather, there is a motive for everything.

Here, we are making an important distinction between cause and motive. *Cause* implies the action of a material, impersonal force that brings something about. *Motive* refers to personal agency and implies an emotion or desire operating on the will of a person and leading him or her to act. For Freud, all events are *overdetermined*, that is, they have more than one meaning or explanation. To illustrate: a ball is thrown into the air; after traveling a certain distance, it falls to the ground. A causal explanation of this event would invoke laws of gravity to account for the ball's fall. An explanation in terms of motive would emphasize that the ball was thrown by someone. This particular ball would not have fallen at this time if someone had not volitionally thrown it. Both explanations are correct, and they serve to complement each other. Thus, it is not sufficient to argue that we make slips of the tongue because we are tired, although it is true that fatigue may provide the physiological conditions under which a slip may occur. Nevertheless, the slip expresses a personal motive as well. Nor, as we shall see later, is it enough to account for dreams on the basis of indigestion from last night's supper or the presence of β (beta) waves during REM sleep. The dream also expresses a personal intention that merits attention. Freudian theory is particularly concerned with the explanation in terms of motive.

Here is an example of a slip and its analysis, which Freud reported in *The Psychopathology of Everyday Life* (1904). He recalls how a friend was talking excitedly about the difficulties of his generation. The friend tried to end his comment with a well-known Latin quote from Virgil, but he could not finish the line. Freud recognized the quote and cited it correctly: "*Exoriar(e) aliquis nostris ex ossibus ultor*," which literally means "Let someone arise from my bones as an avenger." The forgotten word was *aliquis* ("someone"). Freud's friend was embarrassed, but, remembering the significance that Freud attached to such slips, indicated that he was curious to learn why he had forgotten the word in this instance. Freud took up the challenge and asked his friend to tell him candidly and without any censorship whatever came to mind when he directed his attention to the word *aliquis*. The first thought that sprang to his mind was the notion of dividing the word as follows: *a* and *liquis*. Next came the words: "relics," "liquify," "fluid." These associations had little meaning to him, but he continued and thought of Simon of Trent and the accusations of ritual blood sacrifices that had often been brought against the Jewish people. Next he thought of an article that he had read recently entitled "What Saint Augustine Said Concerning Women." The next thought appeared to be totally unconnected, but following the cardinal rule he repeated it anyway. He was thinking of a fine old gentleman whose name was Benedict. At this point, Freud interjected that he had referred to a group of saints and church fathers: St. Simon, St. Augustine, and St. Benedict. That observation made his friend think of St. Januarius and the miracle of blood. Here, Freud observed that both St. Januarius and St. Augustine had something to do with the calendar and asked his friend to refresh his memory about the miracle of blood. The blood of St. Januarius is held in a vial in a church in Naples. On a particular holy day it miraculously liquifies. The people attach a great deal of importance to this miracle and become very upset if it is delayed. Once it was delayed and the general in command took the priest aside and made it clear to him that the miracle had better take place very soon. At this point in his discourse, Freud's friend hesitated. The next thought was surely too intimate to pass on, and besides, it had little connection. He had suddenly thought of a lady from whom he might get an awkward piece of news. "Could it be," Freud conjectured, "that she missed her period?"

The resolution of the slip was not that difficult. The associations had led the way. Freud's friend had referred to the calendar, the blood that starts to flow on a certain day, the disturbance should that event fail to occur, and the feeling that the miracle must take place. The word *aliquis* and its subsequent allusions to the miracle of Saint Januarius revealed a clear concern with a woman's period. That concern was what was unconsciously occupying the young friend when he made the slip. Often a slip is not so obvious and is revealed only after a long chain of associations. The meaning of the slip, you will note, is not imposed on it from outside, but comes to view only in the course of the person's associations.

A second area explored by free association is that of dreams (1900). For Freud, the dream is the *via regia* or the royal road to the unconscious. Young children's dreams are often very simple to understand. Young children, who wear their personalities on their sleeves as their defenses have not yet masked their motives, dream very simply of the fulfillment of unsatisfied wishes from the day before. The child who has not received what in his or her opinion is a sufficient amount of candy during the day may dream of an abundance of it at night. Folk proverbs reinforce the concept that the dream is the fulfillment of a wish: "The pig dreams of acorns, the goose of maize." "Of what does the hen dream? Of millet."

Adult dreams also express unsatisfied wishes, but, because in the adult many of these wishes have become unacceptable to the self-concept, the dream undergoes a disguise. Therefore, Freud distinguishes between the manifest dream and the latent dream. The *manifest dream* is the dream as it is remembered the next morning. Such a dream appears frequently incoherent and nonsensical. It seems to be the fantasy of a mad person. Nevertheless, it constitutes some kind of story that can be told. The *latent dream* refers to the real meaning or motive underlying the creation of the manifest dream. Analysis seeks to discover the latent meaning that is expressed within the manifest dream. The dream wish, however, has undergone distortion, and its mask must be removed before it will reveal its true meaning.

Dreams provide a particular wealth of information because in dreams a person is more relaxed than during the waking state, and his or her resistance, so to speak, may be caught off guard. The wishes and desires that are forbidden access in normal conscious states have a chance to slip out. Thus, the manifest dream may be described as a disguised fulfillment of repressed wishes.

It is possible, Freud held, to gain some insight into the process that disguises the unconscious dream wishes and converts them into the manifest dream. This process is called *dream work*, and it has many elements. One important element is its use of symbols. A *symbol* is a sign that stands for something else. Some symbols employed in dreams are unique to the individual dreamer and can only be understood in terms of his or her particular history and associations. Other symbols are typical and shared by many dreamers. In some instances, symbols have acquired universal meanings; such universal symbols often find expression in our myths, legends, and fairy tales, as well as in our dreams.

The occurrence of anxiety dreams or nightmares does not contradict Freud's concept that the dream is a wish fulfillment. The meaning of a dream does not reside in its manifest context; thus, a dream that on the surface appears to provoke anxiety may serve to fulfill an unconscious wish on another level. Further, the expression of a forbidden wish, as we have seen, causes anxiety or pain to the conscious self, so an anxiety dream may indicate that the disguise was unsuccessful and permitted the forbidden wish too overt an expression.

EXERCISE:

The Interpretation of Dreams and Slips

You can also use Freud's technique of free association to gain greater insight into your own slips and dreams. Verbalizing into a tape recorder whatever comes to mind in connection with a slip or dream can lead to new understandings about ourselves. It is a fact that all of us dream, even though some of us remember our dreams infrequently. Telling yourself that you want to remember a dream may help you to recollect more of them. Asking yourself immediately upon awakening, "What did I dream?" and then rehearsing the dream over in your mind also helps fix it in memory. Some people who are interested in their dreams keep a special notebook beside their bed so that they can record the dream immediately upon awakening.

In dream interpretation, every element of the dream is important, therefore, you should try to remember small details that arise in dreams, particularly if they are strange or bizarre. Basically, the method of interpreting a dream consists of free associating to each element in the dream. Taking each element one by one, you simply verbalize whatever associations come to mind as you ponder it. Later you can replay the tape and review your associations to see whether you can discover aspects of yourself that were revealed in the dream.

Some examples of dreams that Freud analyzed in the course of his self-analysis and reported in *The Interpretation of Dreams* may help to illustrate the procedure of dream analysis. During the spring of 1897, Freud learned that he had been nominated for the position of professor extraordinarius (assistant professor) at the university. He was pleased even though he did not expect much to come of the nomination. In the past, such proposals had been ignored by the authorities and several other equally qualified colleagues had been waiting in vain for similar appointments. One evening a colleague visited Freud and told him of a confrontation that he had with an authority, in which he asked him whether or not the fact that he was Jewish delayed the promotion. He had received an evasive and noncommittal answer, and as he stated to Freud, "Now, at least I know where I stand." The conversation reinforced Freud's own notion that he would probably not get the promotion because of his own Jewish background.

The next morning, Freud had a dream: My friend R. is my uncle; I have a great affection for him. His face in the dream is somewhat altered, it is elongated and has a distinct yellow beard.

An analysis of the dream (for condensation, I have omitted some of the associations) revealed that Freud had only one uncle, Joseph, who had committed a criminal offense, was arrested, found guilty, and paid the penalty. Freud's father would say that Joseph was not a bad man, simply a simpleton, and in the dream R. appeared to be a simpleton. The composite face seen in the dream illustrates condensation in the dream work. But why would Freud wish to render his friend, for whom he had a great deal of respect, a simpleton? At this point, Freud recalled a conversation with another colleague, N., who had also been nominated for the professorship and who had congratulated Freud on his nomination. Freud shrugged off the compliment, suggesting that the nominations were probably worthless, but N. told him not to be too certain as there was a special problem that had been delaying his. Once a woman had brought criminal charges against N. He had been acquitted, but such matters are known to show their ugly heads in considerations such as these. With these associations, the meaning of the dream was clear. Uncle Joseph represented both of Freud's colleagues: one was presented as a simpleton, the other as a criminal. If religious prejudice was really a determining factor in the delay of his friends' promotions, chances were that Freud's own promotion stood in jeopardy. If, however, in his dream he could account for their rejection by other factors, then his own chances for the appointment would be elevated.

Dreams fulfill our wishes; they do not necessarily represent reality. Freud reported that it was hard for him to analyze his dream. It was embarrassing for him to acknowledge that he had adverse thoughts about his colleagues. Of course, the analysis did not imply that Freud actually felt his colleagues were stupid or criminal; rather, it represented them in that light in order to achieve the wish fulfillment.

Another dream, which Freud traced back to his seventh or eighth year and analyzed some thirty years later, was a particularly vivid one in which Freud's mother, who was sleeping with a particularly calm expression on her face, was carried into the room and laid on the bed by two or three persons with bird's beaks. This dream was particularly important, as it led to a discovery in Freud's theory and also illustrated the fact that dreams are frequently overdetermined. Not only do dreams refer to the unsatisfied wishes of the day before, but also to wishes that stem back to early childhood.

Freud indicated that as a child he awoke crying from the dream, but he became calm when he saw his mother. In his subsequent analysis of the dream, the tall figures with beaks reminded Freud of illustrations in Philippson's version of the Bible. The birds appeared to be Egyptian deities such as are carved on tombs. Freud's grandfather had died shortly before the dream. Before his death, he had gone into a coma and worn a calm expression on his face identical to the expression in the dream. At this level of interpretation, the dream appeared to express a young boy's anxiety over the possible death of his mother. Further analysis led deeper. The name "Philippson" reminded Freud of a neighborhood boy named Philip with whom he used to play as a child. Philip introduced Freud to the slang expression *völgern*, a rather vulgar German phrase referring to sexual intercourse. The term originates from the German word *Vogel*, which means "bird." Thus, on a deeper level, Freud had to conclude that the wish expressed in the dream was that of sexual (and therefore forbidden) desires toward his mother. This dream led Freud to the discovery of the Oedipus complex, which I will discuss shortly, and assisted him in clarifying the nature of repressed wishes and desires.

THE DYNAMICS AND DEVELOPMENT OF PERSONALITY

According to Freud, the nature of our repressed wishes and desires is erotic (from the Greek word *eros*, "to love") and sexual. This reference to sexuality is an aspect of Freud's work that many people find problematic. In part, Freud's emphasis on sexuality is hard to appreciate because it requires understanding how Freud redefined the term "sexuality" and used it in his work. Moreover, the implications of Freud's discovery, quite frankly, offend many of us. Freud's insistent reference to our sexual nature tells us something about ourselves that many of us would prefer not to acknowledge.

The Importance of Sexuality

In his early work, Freud viewed sexuality as a bodily process that could be totally understood under a scheme of tension reduction. The goal of human behavior was simply to reduce the tension created by the accumulation of too much energy and to restore a state of equilibrium or balance. Sexual desires could be compared to a wish to remove an itch. However, as his work developed, Freud began to emphasize the psychological character of mental processes and sexuality. His use of the word *libido* to refer to the emotional and psychic energy derived from the biological drive of sexuality testifies to this shift in his thought.

Freud's desire to emphasize the psychological character of mental processes is also evident in the development of his concept of *drive*. The German word he used was *Trieb*, which has been variously translated as "instinct" or "drive." Since the word "instinct" generally connotes an inborn automatic pattern of activity characteristic of animals rather than humans, translation of the word as "drive" seems more appropriate to Freud's intent. Freud used *Trieb* to refer to a psychological or mental representation of an inner bodily source of excitation. Drives are a form of energy, a driving force that cannot be reduced to either a bodily component or a mental one because they combine elements of both. In his concept of drive, Freud abandoned the earlier attempt to reduce psychological processes to physiological or bodily ones and began to repair the Cartesian rift by recognizing that a comprehensive view of personality must envision body and mind as a unity.

A drive is characterized by four features: source, impetus, aim, and object. *Source* refers to the bodily stimulus or need. *Impetus* means the amount of energy or intensity of the need. *Aim* implies goal and purpose: to reduce the excitation. *Object* refers to that person or object in the environment through which the aim may be satisfied. If Freud had characterized drives simply by source and impetus, he could have continued to think of the sexual drive as simply a bodily process. He also chose to characterize drives by aim and object, which forced him to view sexuality differently and to emphasize its psychological and volitional character. Freud used the verb *cathect* to refer to investing libidinal energy in an object that will satisfy a desire; a person cathects an object that he or she wants. The importance of one's sexual life as a bodily process begins to diminish in favor of one's response to it. For this reason, Freud employs the term *psychosexuality* to indicate the totality of elements included in the sexual drive.

Freud viewed human beings as predominantly hedonists or pleasure seekers. We seek to avoid painful tension and obtain pleasure. In the course of avoiding tension, psychic energy may be displaced. In other words, if the original object intended to satisfy the drive is unavailable, another object may be substituted. The substitution is known as *displacement*. Thus, the sexual drive may be satisfied in many different ways. The displacement of energy from one object to another is a very important aspect of personality development, since it assists in accounting for the incredible variety of human behavior.

Freud suggested that there are two basic groups of instinctual drives. *Life instincts* or drives refer to those forces that maintain life processes and insure propagation of the species. The key to these forces is the sexual drive whose energy force is "libido." *Death instincts* or drives are the source of aggressiveness and reflect the ultimate resolution of all of life's tension in death. While Freud emphasized the importance of the death drive, his discussion of the development of personality centers around the sexual drive.

What is the purpose of sexuality? Traditionally, the answer has been reproduction; propagation of the species was thought to be the primary purpose of sexuality. The medieval theologian Thomas Aquinas (1225–1274) gave classic expression to this position when he argued in *Summa Theologica* that according to natural law the primary purpose of sexuality was propagation of the species. Other goals or purposes of sexual activity were seen to be subordinate and secondary. The pleasure that attended sexual activity was permissible, and even encouraged by Saint Thomas, but he recommended that it should be submissive to and never thwart the primary purpose of reproduction.

If the primary purpose of sexuality is reproduction, certain consequences about sexuality are logically going to follow in our thoughts. Activities of bodily manipulation that do not entail or lead to the involvement of the genitals and thus cannot culminate in reproduction are going to be depreciated or regarded as perverse. It is difficult to concede that young children, prior to the age of adolescence, have a sexual life because their immaturity inhibits reproduction.

The Victorian culture in Vienna, from which Freud's theories emerged, reflected such an attitude. Nevertheless, at the same time Vienna was undergoing a cultural renaissance in philosophy, music, and literature and was seeking the realities that lay behind the façade of the decaying Austrian empire. One such reality was sex, which had been denied by the Victorian ethos. The sexual act was generally viewed as bestial, unrefined, and undignified, but it was tolerated for procreation. There was considerable concern and anxiety over what were thought to be inappropriate sexual activities and perversions. Women and children were thought incapable of sexual feelings. To suggest that a woman or child was capable of such feelings was to cast an evil aspersion on them. Rigid taboos were put on infantile autoeroticism (self-love) and limitations were established on the expression of sexuality in adult life. The body's excretory functions were attended to with embarrassment and prudery was practiced to fanatical extremes. To a large extent, Freud shared his culture's attitude, yet he distinguished himself by relentlessly searching for the reality behind the façade.

Freud suggested that the primary purpose of sexual behavior is pleasure. To be specific, sexual activities aim at producing pleasure in the body. If the primary purpose of sex is pleasure, the door is open to a host of new conclusions. Activities that may not focus on the genitals are included as key ramifications of sexuality to the extent to which they provide pleasure. The young child, who invariably seeks pleasure in the body, may be seen as having a rich sexual life. Activities such as sucking the thumb, previously seen as utterly distinct from sexuality, may come under the purview of sexual activities.

Freud, in effect, turned the traditional concept upside down. This reversion permitted him to account for phenomena that were hitherto inexplicable, such as sexual deviations and infantile sexuality. Such activities may be more clearly understood if pleasure is seen as the primary purpose of sex, and reproduction as secondary. In effect, Freud's redefinition of sexuality is twofold. First, he divorces sex from its previous close restriction to the genitals and reproductive activity. Second, he enlarges the concept of sexuality so that it may include activities, such as thumb sucking and sublimation, that previously were not thought of as sexual.

In Freudian terms, the child, who actively seeks pleasure from many areas of the body, is *polymorphous perverse;* that is, children deviate in many respects from what is thought to be normal reproductive sexual activity. The sexual activity of children is essentially *autoerotic;* children seek pleasure from their own bodies rather than from the body of another person. They find pleasure in sucking their thumbs, exploring their genitals, and so forth. Only in the course of a long history of development do children progress toward normal, mature, heterosexual, reproductive activities.

The Psychosexual Stages of Development

Freud (1905) outlined a path that children travel as they progress from autoerotic sexual activity to normal, mature, reproductive activity. In this journey, the libido or sexual drive cathects itself on various *erogenous zones* or areas of the body that provide pleasure. By passing through a series of stages in which different erogenous zones are important, children move from autoeroticism to heterosexuality.

Oral Stage The first stage is the *oral stage,* which lasts from birth to age one. During this time, the major source of pleasure and potential conflict is the mouth, the primary organ for young infants. From it they receive nourishment, have their closest contact with the mother (in breast feeding), and discover information about the world. The fact that each new object infants encounter is immediately placed in the mouth indicates the importance of this zone. The two main types of oral activity, ingestion and biting, are the prototypes for character types and traits that may develop later on. Because the oral stage occurs at a time when infants are totally dependent on others for sustenance, feelings of dependency arise. Oral activities are also a source of potential conflict because restraints may be placed on them. A mother may seek to discourage thumb sucking or restrain her child from biting the breast. Thus, the focus of greatest pleasure and conflict is located for infants in the mouth.

Anal Stage Freud's second psychosexual stage is the *anal stage*, which is experienced in the second year of life. At this time, the major source of pleasure and potential conflict is the anus. Generally, toilet training occurs during this period. Toilet training involves converting an involuntary activity, the elimination of bodily wastes, into a voluntary one. It frequently represents the child's first experience with an attempt to regulate instinctual impulses. A clash of will may develop. Children may obtain pain or pleasure in either retaining or expelling their waste products. These two primary modes of anal expression, retention and expulsion, are further prototypes for possible future character traits. In their efforts to train their children, parents may forget that control over the sphincter muscles and eliminatory activity is an activity that only the child can perform. As early efforts to discipline children begin, the buttocks are frequently selected as a site on which to inflict pain. Since stimulation in that area causes both pleasure and pain, sadistic (pain inflicting) and/or masochistic (pain receiving) patterns of behavior may emerge. Subsequent forms of self-control and mastery have their origins in the anal stage.

Phallic Stage The *phallic stage* of development occurs between the ages of three and six. The characteristics of this stage are pleasurable and conflicting feelings associated with the genital organs. The child's interest in the genitals does not concern itself with their reproductive function, but with their ability to give pleasure in autoerotic activity and their significance as a means of distinguishing between the sexes. At this time, children discover that not all individuals are similarly endowed. They expend considerable energy in examining their genitalia, masturbating, and expressing interest in sexual matters. They are extremely curious, even though their curiosity outstrips their ability to comprehend sexual matters intellectually. They spin unconscious fantasies about the sexual act itself and the birth process. Their notions are frequently inaccurate and misleading. They may believe that a pregnant woman has eaten her baby and that a baby is expelled through the mouth or the anus. Sexual intercourse is frequently viewed as an aggressive act by the father against the mother.

The pleasures of masturbation and the fantasy life of children set the stage for the *Oedipus complex*, which Freud considered to be one of his greatest discoveries. Freud's concept of the Oedipus complex was suggested by the Greek tragedy of Sophocles in which King Oedipus unwittingly murdered his father and married his mother. The key point is that Oedipus was unaware, or unconscious, of what he was doing. He did not realize that the man whom he met on the road was his own father, nor did he know that the queen whom he married was his mother. At the same time, he played an active role in bringing about his fate. On discovering the truth, he punished himself by blinding himself. Within that Greek myth, Freud perceived a symbolic description of the unconscious psychological conflict that each one of us endures. In brief, the myth symbolizes each child's unconscious desire to possess the opposite-sexed parent and do away with the same-sexed parent.

If the Oedipus complex were simply to be taken literally, many people would have abruptly dismissed Freud's concept as absurd and nonsensical. Incredible as it may seem, Freud suggested that children have incestuous wishes toward the opposite-sexed parent and murderous impulses toward the same-sexed parent. Do children actually desire to perform sexual intercourse and commit murder? Most preschool-age children have no clearly articulated concept of what coitus is all about. Furthermore, even if they had the will, they would lack the means to perform the act. Finally, for the preschool-age-child, the permanence and reality of death is incomprehensible. As a literal depiction, Freud's concept of the Oedipus complex is clearly absurd.

Nevertheless, at this stage in development, the young boy (to tell his side of the story first) has become very fond of his mother, his primary caretaker. He loves her very much, and he wants to love her as fully as possible. He senses that Mommy and Daddy have a special kind of relationship, which he wants to emulate. He becomes frustrated since he cannot envision what the relationship is all about nor perform it in a similar manner. At the same time, he wants his mother's love in return, but he views love quantitatively as a fixed amount. It is as if his mother's love constitutes an apple. Each kiss or sign of attention that his father receives indicates that a big, juicy chunk has been bitten out of that apple, so that less remains for him. He cannot conceive of love as qualitative or as able to increase to fill a void. Viewing love as a quantity, the child perceives his father as a rival who prevents him from obtaining the full love that he desires from his mother. This perception creates wishes and impulses of disposing of the father, an activity the child is powerless to carry out.

The child's feelings are very intense, strong, and conflicting, besides being too difficult for the child to cope with directly on a conscious level. Futhermore, the feelings create guilt because the child's sentiments toward his father are not solely hostile but affectionate as well. The child finds it difficult to cope with ambivalent feelings of love and hostility directed toward the same person. His rivalry culminates in *castration anxiety*, which means that he fears physical retaliation from his father, in particular, that he will lose his penis.

The Oedipus complex is resolved by a twofold process. First, the son gives up his abortive attempts to possess the mother and begins to identify with his father in terms of sexual gender. In *identifying with the same-sexed parent*, he adopts the moral codes and injunctions of his father. This introjection of the parent's standards of good conduct leads to the development of a *superego* or social conscience, which assists him in dealing with his forbidden impulses. By identifying with his father, the boy can through his imagination vicariously retain his mother as his love object, because he has incorporated those characteristics of his father that his mother loves. While he may not have his mother in fact, he can wait until he grows up and then look for "a girl, just like the girl, that married dear old Dad." *

The little girl undergoes a similar complex. Freud deliberately did not dignify it with a separate name, because he wished to underscore the universality of the Oedipal situation. Others have referred to the feminine version as the *Electra complex*. The primary love object for girls is also the mother. Yet girls, on discovering the genitals of the opposite sex, abandon the mother and turn to the father instead, making possible the Oedipal situation in reverse. The disappointment and shame that they feel upon viewing the superior penis leads to jealousy of the male, *penis envy*, a sense of inferiority, and a feeling of resentment and hatred toward the mother, who is held responsible for the effected castration. Reluctantly, the girl identifies with her mother, incorporates her values, and optimally makes the transition from her inadequate penis, the clitoris, as her chief erogenous zone, to the vagina. Because the female Oedipus complex is secondary, Freud suggested that it is never as strong or as effectively resolved as that of the male; thus, the woman's ego-ideal is weaker and she has less capacity for sublimation. Freud's concepts on the development of women have been the subject of considerable criticism and debate. We shall return to this controversy in the next chapter.

Latency Period After the phallic stage, Freud believed that the libido or sexual drive goes underground, leading to a period of *latency*, comparative sexual quiescence, during the early school years. Psychic forces develop that inhibit the sexual drive and narrow its direction. The libido is sublimated and channeled into nonsexual activities. Freud borrowed the term *sublimation* from the field of chemistry where the verb "to sublime" means to pass directly from a solid to a vapor state. Sublimation connotes passing from a lower state to a higher one. Thus, the sexual impulses, which are unacceptable in their direct expression, are channeled and elevated into more culturally accepted levels of activity, such as sports, intellectual interests, and peer relations. Freud was relatively silent about the latency period. He did not consider it a genuine psychosexual stage because nothing dramatically new emerges. Today, the latency period, as such, is questioned by most critics, who suggest it is more correct to observe that children learn to hide their sexuality from disapproving adults.

Genital Stage With the onset of puberty, changes set in which transform the infantile sexual life into its adult form. Freud's final stage is termed *genital* and emerges at adolescence when the genital organs mature. There is a resurgence of sexual and aggressive desires, and the sexual drive, which was formerly *narcissistic* (aimed at obtaining gratification from one's own body), is redirected to seeking gratification from genuine interaction with others. Young adolescents prefer the company of same-sexed peers; however, in time, the object of the sexual drive shifts to members of the opposite sex. The genital stage is the culmination of a long journey from autoerotic sexual activity to heterosexual activity. Mature individuals seek to satisfy their sexual drives primarily through genital, reproductive activity with members of the opposite sex. The *normal* or *mature individual* is defined as one who has realized conventional genital sexuality and all its constituent ramifications as defined by his or her culture. Mature people satisfy their needs in socially approved ways. They accommodate themselves to, function within, and seek to uphold the laws, taboos, and standards of their culture. These ramifications are clearly spelled out for both male and female. The hallmarks of maturity can be summed up in the German expression *Lieben und arbeiten*, "to love and to work." The mature person is able to love in a sexually approved way and also to work productively in his or her community and society.

The lingering effects of the psychosexual stages can be seen in various adult character types or traits. Freud believed deeply that things that happened in the past can influence the present. If the libido, the sexual drive, is prevented from obtaining optimal satisfaction during one or more of the stages, because it has either been unduly frustrated or overindulged, the libido may become fixated on a particular stage. *Fixation* refers to an arrestment of growth in which excessive needs, characteristic of an earlier stage, are created due to overindulgence or undue frustration of desire. Since all of us have fixated libido at some point or another during our psychosexual stages, this dammed-up libido expresses itself in our adult life according to character types or traits that reflect the earlier level of development. Hence, an orally fixated person is likely to be dependent on and easily influenced by others. At the same time, oral personalities are optimistic and trusting to the point of being gullible. Anal personalities tend to be orderly, parsimonious, and obstinate. Most of us, of course, do not reflect a pure type, but these personality traits and their opposites have their origin in the various psychosexual stages.

EXERCISE:

Identifying Psychosexual Character Traits

Salvadore Maddi (1972) has summarized the traits of the various charac-
ter types described by Freud and his followers as bipolar dimensions.
Consider each of the traits in Table 2.1. See if you recognize them as
characteristic of yourself or someone you know. It would be nice if we
could simply state that one polar trait indicates fixation due to frustra-
tion, while the other is due to overindulgence, but in reality such a view

TABLE 2.1 Psychosexual Traits

Oral Traits	
optimism	pessimism
gullibility	suspiciousness
manipulativeness	passivity
admiration	envy
cockiness	self-belittlement

Anal Traits	
stinginess	overgenerosity
constrictedness	expansiveness
stubbornness	acquiescence
orderliness	messiness
rigid punctuality	tardiness
meticulousness	dirtiness
precision	vagueness

Phallic Traits	
vanity	self-hatred
pride	humility
blind courage	timidity
brashness	bashfulness
gregariousness	isolation
stylishness	plainness
flirtatiousness	avoidance of heterosexuality
chastity	promiscuity
gaiety	sadness

SOURCE: Based on information in S. R. Maddi, *Personality Theories: A Comparative Analysis,*
Homewood, Ill.: Dorsey Press, 1972, pp. 271–276.

is too simplistic because many of us swing from one pole to its opposite. Nevertheless, the traits may be seen as attitudes that develop initially during these various psychosexual stages. From a Freudian viewpoint, the existence of any of these traits to a marked degree presents an invitation to explore that stage in our personal history. These basic attitudes emerge from our interactions with significant persons during these phases of development. It is important to point out that although I have described the psychosexual stages chronologically from infancy to adulthood, in psychoanalytic research the understanding of a person's history moves backwards from the present to the past. From a present attitude or trait, we can conjecture that an individual experienced certain difficulties at certain levels of his or her psychosexual development. On the other hand, we cannot suggest with any significant degree of reliability that certain present parental practices will lead to specific character traits in the future.

If the development of personality is seriously inhibited or delayed, it can lead to problems later in life. We have seen how the libido, due to frustration or overindulgence, may become fixated at an earlier stage. A child who persists in thumb sucking well into the preschool years is showing evidence of an inability to satisfy oral needs in a manner appropriate for his or her age. In other instances, under times of stress, the libido may regress to an earlier level of development. *Regression* refers to a temporary reverting to earlier forms of behavior. A child who was completely toilet trained may in a period of stress begin to wet the bed. Extreme instances of fixation and regression are seen to be entailed in neurotic behavior and sexual perversions.

All of the sexual activities that we consider divergent are at some time normal sexual activities for children. Prototypes of sadistic and masochistic forms of behavior, sexual disorders in which a person obtains pleasure by inflicting (sadism) or receiving (masochism) pain, are apparent during the toddler years. Voyeurism, obtaining pleasure from seeing sexual organs or sexual acts, is present in the curiosity of the preschool child. Homosexuality, primary attraction to the same sex, is apparent during the latency period and early adolescence when one's primary association is with same-sexed peers. Thus, sexual diversions may be accounted for in terms of arrested development.

Neurosis is likewise viewed as the product of an inadequate sexual development. In cases of neurosis, the individual continues to mature physically, passing from stage to subsequent stage, but with heavy residues of negative attitudes and emotions that prevent the person from functioning optimally and dealing adequately with stress and anxiety. Such people are bound to their unhappy past and respond emotionally in immature ways. Being unrealistic, these ways are not helpful to them in the everyday world.

Freud's presentation of the stages of human psychosexual development is clumsy, because the gradual transition from one stage to another is not meant to be as distinct as the outline implies. The stages are not disjunct, they merge and meld into one another. Therefore, the age references should not be seen as beginning and end points, but rather as focal points during which the stage is at its height. One stage begins as another concludes. A diagrammatic illustration of them (Figure 2.1) would show each as gradually beginning, swelling to a climax, and then waning as the following stage begins to emerge. The emergence of the genital stage does not signify a complete cessation of the earlier ones, rather, it transforms them in the service of genital aims. Thus, adult behavior is shaped by a complex of earlier conflicts.

Freud's discussion of the psychosexual stages of personality was presented in the framework of nineteenth-century biological determinism and has been soundly criticized for its failure to appreciate deeply enough the influence of social and cultural factors. Nevertheless, it brought forth a conclusion that Freud was never to abandon and that served to overturn almost the entire Western tradition of thought concerning humanity. In Freud's theory, human life is subsumed under a sexual paradigm or model. The way in which people invest their libido determines their future and destiny. Freud employed sexuality as a paradigm for a person's style of life: character is built up by responding to one's sexuality; the way in which a person resolves the Oedipus complex is crucial to his or her adult personality; neurosis represents a fixation at an earlier stage of sexual development. The normal or mature individual is one who has behaved conventionally, having attained the genital level of sexuality and all its constituent ramifications. Furthermore, the development of culture and civilization is made possible by sublimated sexuality. Sexuality becomes the paradigm for human understanding since the totality of all actual and possible human doings may be understood under its rubric. The effect was to rephrase Descartes's dictum "I think, therefore, I am," and render it "I love, therefore, I am."

Ever since the days of the Greek philosopher Aristotle (384–322 B.C.), people had been defined as rational animals because it was thought that reason separated the human being from other forms of life. Freud did not depreciate reason, he sought to cultivate it through analysis; however, he emphatically pointed out that we are essentially emotional beings or creatures of will and desire. In Freud's theory, our reason, which is sublimated sexuality, is no longer the master, it is a servant serving the libido that brought it into being. By making sexuality, instead of reason, the prime mover or motivation of human beings, Freud radically and ineradicably transformed the self-consciousness of Western personality.

FIGURE 2.1 Freud's Psychosexual Stages

Each stage begins gradually, swells to a climax, and then wanes as the following stage begins to emerge.

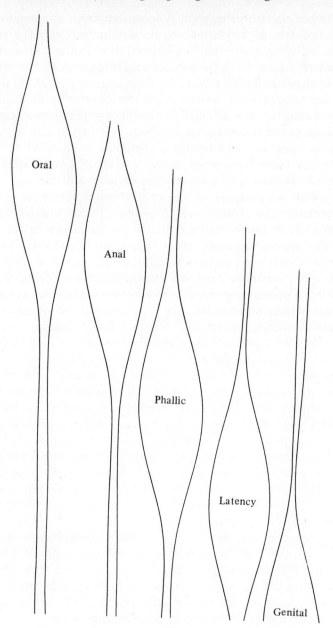

Oral

Anal

Phallic

Latency

Genital

Freud's published works fill twenty-four volumes in the *Standard English Edition of the Complete Psychological Works of Sigmund Freud*, published by Hogarth Press of London, beginning in 1953. The lay reader will find the following most useful as a further introduction to the development of Freud's thought and theory: The *Five Lectures on Psychoanalysis*, which were delivered at Clark University in Worcester, Massachusetts (1909), represent a concise introduction by Freud to his own work. They are included in Vol. XI (1957) of the Complete Works. More extensive presentations by Freud on his general theory are provided in *Introductory Lectures on Psychoanalysis* (1917), Vols. 15–16, 1963; and *New Introductory Lectures on Psychoanalysis* (1933), Vol. 22, 1964. Freud's classic writings on dreams, slips, and sexuality is *The Interpretation of Dreams* (1900), Vols. 4–5, 1953; *The Psychopathology of Everyday Life* (1901), Vol. 6, 1960; and *Three Essays on Sexuality* (1905), Vol. 7, 1953.

The serious student of Freud will also be interested in the three-volume biography, *The Life and Work of Sigmund Freud* (Basic Books, 1953–1957), written by a close friend and follower, Ernest Jones. Briefer, more popular introductions to Freud's life and work are Irving Stone, *Passions of the Mind* (Doubleday, 1971); and P. Roazen, *Freud and His Followers* (Knopf, 1975).

CHAPTER 3

Freudian Theory and Psychoanalysis

Sigmund Freud did not present a completely finished model. His thought moves in phases, forever reviving, amending, discarding, and synthesizing what has gone before. He did not hesitate to set forth tentative formulations. Many of his lectures and writings read as though the author was thinking out loud. Ideas appear, disappear, and then reappear in a new context. Alasdair MacIntyre (1958) suggests that Freud's work is characterized by a "creative untidyness"; "he never presents us with a finished structure but with the far more exciting prospect of working through a number of possible ways of talking and thinking" (p. 79). As Freud's thought reached maturity, certain concepts about the structure of personality and the technique of psychoanalysis acquired a greater degree of sophistication and articulation. His thought moves from the physical, through the psychological, to the *metapsychological*, a term he used to refer to his effort to give the fullest possible description of psychic processes.

THE STRUCTURE OF PERSONALITY

The familiar Freudian concept of the structure of personality as entailing an id, ego, and superego was a rather late product of his thought. Not until 1923 with the publication of *The Ego and the Id* did Freud's final theory of a threefold structure of personality emerge. In discussing this mature tridimensional understanding of the psyche, we must keep in mind that the id, ego, and superego are not three separate entities or mental regions with sharply defined boundaries, rather, they represent a variety of different processes, functions, and dynamics within the person. They originate out of the same organism, blend with one another, and conflict with one another. Freud's description of their interactions and blendings aims to provide a comprehensive picture of the person as a whole.

The Id, Ego, and Superego

The *id* is the "core of our being." Freud borrowed the Latin term *id*, which literally means "it," from the title of a work, *The Book of the Id*, written by Georg Groddeck (1923), who suggested that we are "lived" by unknown and uncontrollable forces. Groddeck, in turn, attributed his use of the word to the German philosopher Friedrich Nietzsche (1844–1900). The id is the oldest and original function of the personality and the basis of the other two. We know little of the id, because it does not present itself to our consciousness in naked form. Therefore, we can only describe it by analogies and by comparing it to the ego. Freud then referred to it as a "chaos, a cauldron full of seething excitations." The id includes all of our genetic inheritance, our reflexes and capacities to respond, and, above all, the instincts and drives that motivate us. It represents our basic drives, needs, and wishes. Further, it is the reservoir of psychic energy that provides the power for all subsequent psychological functioning.

The id operates according to the pleasure principle and employs primary processes. The *pleasure principle* refers to seeking immediate tension reduction. When libido, psychic energy, builds up, it reaches an uncomfortable level of tension. The id seeks to discharge the tension and return to a more comfortable level of energy. In seeking to avoid painful tension and obtain pleasure, the id takes no precautions but acts immediately in an impulsive, irrational way. It pays no heed to the consequences of its actions and therefore, frequently behaves in a manner that may be harmful to the self or others.

The id seeks to satisfy its needs through reflex action and the primary process. *Reflexes* are inborn automatic responses. Such responses are spontaneous, unlearned, and operate without any conscious thought or effort. Sneezing, yawning, and blinking are reflexes. Many of our reflexes are protective in that they help us to ward off dangers in our environment. Others are adaptive and enable us to adjust to the conditions of our environment. Newborn infants have several reflexes that help to ensure their survival. They turn their heads toward the source of tactile stimulation. This "rooting reflex" assists them in locating the nipple. Sucking is also an automatic reflex to enable infants to take in nourishment.

The *primary process* is a psychological activity in which the id seeks to reduce tension by hallucinating or forming an image of the object that would satisfy its needs. Visualizing a forthcoming hamburger or sirloin steak momentarily assuages our hunger pangs; such activity is also called *wish fulfillment*. It is present in the mental functioning of newborns, in our dreams, and in the hallucinations of psychotics. Visualizing a bottle or the breast partly pacifies the infant, but it does not satisfy his or her need. Since the primary process does not distinguish between its wish-fulfilling images and real objects in the external world that would satisfy its needs, the primary process is not very effective in reducing tension. A second structure must develop if the organism is to survive.

The *ego* ("I") emerges in order to realistically meet the wishes and demands of the id in accordance with the outside world. People who are hungry have to be effective in securing food for themselves from the environment in order to meet their needs and survive. The ego evolves out of the id and acts as an intermediary between the id and the external world. It draws on the id's energy, acquires its structures and functions from the id, and endeavors to serve the id by realistically meeting its demands. Thus, the ego is the executor of the personality, curbing the id and maintaining transactions with the external world in the interests of the fuller personality.

While the id obeys the pleasure principle, the ego follows the reality principle and operates according to the secondary process and reality testing. The *reality principle* refers to satisfying the id's impulses in an appropriate manner in the external world. The ego postpones the discharge of tension until the appropriate object that will satisfy the need has been found. While the ego does not prevent the satisfaction of the id, it may suspend or redirect the id's wishes in accordance with the demands of reality. Its task is to satisfy optimally the demands of the organism for pleasure. While the id employs the fantasies and wishes of the primary process, the ego uses realistic thinking characteristic of secondary processes. *Secondary processes* refer to cognitive and perceptual skills that enable an individual to distinguish between fact and fantasy. They encompass the higher intellectual functions of problem solving, which enable the ego to establish suitable courses of action and test them for their effectiveness. Actually, there is no natural enmity between the ego and the id. The ego is a "faithful servant" of the id, which tries to fulfill its needs realistically.

Harbored within the ego as "its innermost core" is the *superego* ("above I"). Heir to the Oedipus complex, it represents introjected and internalized values, ideals, and moral standards of society. The superego is the last function of the personality to develop and may be seen as a precipitate or outcome of the interactions with one's parents during the protracted period of childhood dependency. Rewards and punishments originally imposed on us from without become self-administered as we internalize the teachings and precepts of our parents and society. As a result of the activity of the superego we experience guilt when we disobey acceptable moral standards.

The superego consists of two subsystems: the conscience and the ego-ideal. The *conscience* refers to the capacity for self-evaluation, criticism, and reproach. It admonishes the ego when moral codes are violated and creates feelings of guilt. The *ego-ideal* is an ideal self-image consisting of approved and rewarded behaviors. It is the source of pride and a concept of who we think we should be.

The superego strives for perfection. It seeks moralistic rather than realistic solutions. Practically speaking, the development of the superego is a necessity. The id's demands are too strong, and young children's egos are too weak to prevent them from acting on their impulses. For a period of time, strong introjected moral injunctions—"Thou shalt nots"—are required to curb behavior. But the superego may also be relentless and cruel in its insistence on perfection. Its moralistic demands may resemble those of the id in their intensity, blindness, and irrationality. In its uncompromising manner, the superego may inhibit the needs of the id, rather than permit their ultimate necessary and appropriate satisfaction.

In the mature and well-adjusted personality, the ego is the primary executor. It controls and governs both id and superego, mediating between their demands and the external world. In ideal functioning, the ego maintains a balanced, harmonious relationship among the various elements with which it has to deal. Development, though, does not always proceed optimally. If the id or superego gains control and predominates, imbalance and maladjustment follow. The ego frequently ends up harassed by two harsh masters. One demands instant satisfaction and release. The other places rigid prescriptions on that release. Drawing on an analogy of Plato, Freud described the ego as a charioteer trying to control two strong horses, each of which is trying to run in the opposite direction from the other. Thus, the ego is frequently beset and harassed.

Freud's final picture of personality is that of a self divided against itself. The specific roles played by the id, ego, and superego are not always clear; they mingle at too many levels. The self is seen as created of many diverse forces in inevitable conflict. Freud's picture of the person is not optimistic, but it is an attempt to account for the fact that as human beings we are not always able to cope with our situation. The locus of the problem is to be found in the complex inner dialogue of the self, for "the ego is not master in its own house."

Although the tripartite division of personality appears to be a finished structure, essentially the person is understood as a product of development. The ego and superego are viewed as evolving historically in response to specific historical situations. In the case of the superego, that situation is also interpersonal since it involves other people. It would be wrong to freeze the id, ego, and superego into systems; instead, the personality is created by a dynamic of forces that can be divided against themselves at many levels. Thus, in his mature formulation, Freud holds in tension the biological ground of the self and its development.

EXERCISE:

Recognizing the Id, Ego, and Superego

The reader can gain a more concrete picture of the various functions of the id, ego, and superego by trying to imagine a variety of problematic situations and considering the role of the id, ego, and superego in each conflict. The id asserts our raw untempered desires and wishes; the superego places authoritarian and moralistic strictures on our behavior; and the ego seeks a realistic compromise. Thus, in the case of a young man or woman out on a date with an attractive member of the opposite sex with whom he or she might wish to engage in a sexual relationship, the id would unreservedly exclaim, "I want, I want!" while the superego might legalistically proclaim, "Thou shalt not!" Meanwhile, the ego seeks a realistic solution that fulfills the id's demands within the limitations and customs of that society. In the above instance, such a solution might require waiting until one is more familiar with one's date or until certain social prerequisites have been met. Can you consider what the roles of the id, ego, and superego might be in other situations, such as that of a young child in a department store desiring a piece of sports equipment for which he or she does not have sufficient funds in his or her piggybank?

The Relationship of the Id, Ego, and Superego to Consciousness

There is no easy correlation between the words "id," "ego," and "superego" and the qualities of "conscious," "preconscious," and "unconscious." We have seen that *conscious* refers to processes of which we are aware; *preconscious* refers to psychological material that can easily become conscious when the need for it arises; and *unconscious* refers to material that has been repressed or never permitted to become conscious. At times, Freud tended to make the easy equation of ego with consciousness and id with unconsciousness; he also referred to the unconscious and conscious as systems or topographical locations. His discoveries, reflected in *The Ego and the Id*, that aspects of the ego and the superego are unconscious, as is the id, forced him to revise his theory. He could no longer use "conscious" and "unconscious" in the sense of mental provinces or systems, but simply as qualities that psychological processes have. Thus, in the end, "unconscious," "preconscious," and "conscious" do not imply systems. A spatial metaphor is ultimately misleading. They are properly seen as adjectives describing qualities that psychological processes may or may not have. The attributes of awareness and its opposite may potentially apply to any and all of the psychic structures: id, ego, and superego. The characteristic of being conscious or unconscious is not the vital factor in the conflict among them.

If one were to diagram Freud's picture of the psyche, perhaps the best image would be Freud's own: that of an iceberg nine-tenths of which is submerged under water. The surface of the water represents the boundary between conscious and unconscious. Its line intersects, or potentially intersects, all three functions of id, ego, and superego. But any spatial metaphor is misleading. A topographical image does not reflect Freud's mature understanding of the person as historical. "Id," "ego," and "superego" are best understood as dynamic functions of personality, while "conscious" and "unconscious" are adjectives that describe qualities that these functions may have.

Simple correlations or comparisons are inappropriate, for the dynamic forces within the self are many. The self is not simply divided against itself by id, ego, and superego but divided against itself and the

FIGURE 3.1 The Psyche as an Iceberg
Freud described the psyche as an iceberg, nine-tenths of which is submerged under water.

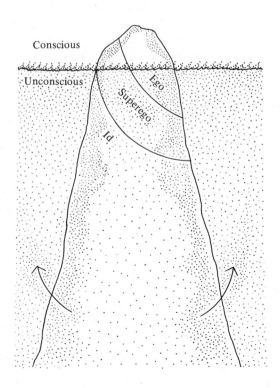

world at many levels. Conflict is the keynote of Freud's final understanding of the self. The self is essentially in conflict, which is inevitable because of the very nature of things. The world, Freud once
wrote, is *anake* (literally: "a lack"), too poor to meet all of our needs.
As the id's demands increase, tension mounts, and the ego becomes
overwhelmed with excessive stimulation that it cannot control. Thus,
the ego becomes flooded with anxiety.

ANXIETY AND THE EGO

Anxiety is an inevitable aspect of the human condition, and a situation
into which we all are thrust by virtue of being born. Birth represents a
situation of privation in which there is a realistic danger that the needs
of the infant will not be gratified. The "birth trauma" may be seen as
the prototype of all later anxiety, insofar as the infant is bombarded
by stimuli of an unpleasurable magnitude and intensity without the
ability to cope with them adequately and provide for their discharge.
This means that anxiety is the key problem with which the developmental and adjustment process has to deal. An inability to cope with
anxiety underlies most forms of neurosis.

Freud made an important distinction among reality anxiety, neurotic anxiety, and moral anxiety. *Reality anxiety* refers to the fear of a
real danger in the external world. *Neurotic anxiety* refers to the fear
that one's inner impulses cannot be controlled. *Moral anxiety* is a fear
of the retributions of one's own conscience. All have their basis in
reality anxiety. A child who is frightened because he was almost hit
by a truck is experiencing reality anxiety. However, a subsequent fear
of crossing wide streets is neurotic in the adult who doubts his or her
own ability to cross safely. The child who refrains from snitching
cookies for fear that he or she might be beaten is experiencing reality
anxiety, but most adults refrain from stealing out of moral anxiety or
the fear of retribution from their own conscience.

The Defense Mechanisms

In order for an individual to cope with anxiety, the ego develops
defense mechanisms, procedures that ward off anxiety and prevent its
conscious perception. Defense mechanisms share two common features. They occur on an unconscious level so that we are not aware of
what we are doing, and they deny or distort reality so as to make it
less threatening. Defense mechanisms are not necessarily maladaptive,
indeed, we cannot survive without them. The stimuli that confront us
as children from our outer and inner worlds are too intense to be borne
in their naked reality. Without some means of warding off the intensity
of our feelings, anxiety would overwhelm and paralyze us. Defense
mechanisms must be created to assist the developing ego in carrying

out its functions. However, should their distortion of reality become too extreme or should they be employed to the exclusion of other more effective means of dealing with reality, defense mechanisms may become maladaptive and destructive. A discussion of the more common defense mechanisms follows.

Repression The key defense mechanism is repression, which is the first means of defense arising before and encompassing all of the others. *Repression* entails blocking a wish or desire from expression so that it cannot be experienced consciously or expressed directly in behavior. The act of repression is involuntary. As a result of repression we are not aware of many of our own anxiety-producing conflicts nor can we remember certain traumatic emotional events from our past. As we have seen, the relief that repression provides is not without cost. Freud's theory has emphasized that emotions demand expression. The repressed emotion continually seeks an alternative outlet, and a continuous drain of psychic energy in the form of resistance is required to prevent its emergence into consciousness. Nevertheless, once formed, repressions are difficult to eliminate.

Projection This term refers to the unconscious attribution of an impulse, attitude, or behavior onto someone else or some element in the environment. An individual who is unconsciously hostile to someone may project the hostility onto the other person. Such a defense reduces anxiety by attributing its source to the external world, which makes it seem easier to handle. Further, it permits us to defend ourselves aggressively against our opponent and thereby indirectly express our impulses. Freud would suggest that those who vigorously wage campaigns against pornography or other sexual practices may be projecting their own sexual impulses onto other people.

Reaction formation This defense mechanism expresses an impulse by its opposite. Hostility, for example, may be replaced by friendship. Frequently, however, the benign substitute is exaggerated, thereby calling into question the genuineness of the feeling. The well-known quote from *Hamlet*, "The lady doth protest too much, methinks," refers to a situation in which reaction formation may have been present.

Fixation This term refers to the lodging of psychic energy at an early stage of psychosexual development, preventing the individual from moving on to the next stage. The overly dependent school-age child may be fixated, thereby prevented from becoming independent.

Regression In *regression* the person moves backward in time to a stage that was less fraught with anxiety and entailed fewer responsibilities. Regression frequently occurs following a traumatic experience.

The child who resumes bedwetting because he is frightened by the prospect of going to school may be showing signs of regression.

Rationalization This defense mechanism entails dealing with an emotion or impulse analytically and intellectually in order to avoid feeling it. As the term implies, it involves fallacious reasoning, since the problem remains unresolved on the emotional level. Aesop's fable about the fox who could not reach the grapes and concluded that they were probably sour is a classic example of rationalization.

Identification In *identification* we reduce anxiety by modeling our behavior after that of someone else. By assuming the characteristics of a model who appears more successful in gratifying needs, we can believe that we also possess those attributes. We may also identify with an authority figure who is resented and feared. Such identification may assist us in avoiding punishment. As we have already seen, identification with the same-sexed parent plays an important role in development of the superego and subsequent personality.

Displacement If an object that would satisfy an impulse of the id is unavailable, we may shift our impulse on to another object. Such substitution is called *displacement*. A child who has been scolded may hit a younger sibling or kick the dog. The substitute object, however, is rarely as satisfying as the original object. Thus, displacement does not bring complete satisfaction but leads to a build-up of undischarged tension.

Sublimation This mechanism entails rechanneling an unacceptable impulse into a more socially desirable outlet. It is a particular form of displacement that displaces the impulse itself rather than the object. Freud suggested that Leonardo da Vinci's interest in painting madonnas may have been a sublimation of his desire for intimacy with his own mother, from whom he had been separated at an early age. Freud also suggested that sublimation was crucial to the development of culture and civilization. However, as sublimation, like displacement, does not result in complete satisfaction, our civilization and culture are purchased at a very high price.

Defense mechanisms, in and of themselves, are not harmful. No one is free of defenses; we need them in order to survive. Defenses protect us from excessive anxiety and frequently represent creative solutions to our problems. At times, however, our defenses become predominant, self-perpetuating, and block further personal growth. At such times, it is helpful for us to try to identify the defense mechanism that acts as a barrier so we may work on it.

Identifying Defense Mechanisms

Defense mechanisms are most easily recognized in preschool-age children who, to borrow Stone and Church's apt description (1973), wear their personalities on their sleeve. Because they have not yet learned to deceive other people, young children's instant translation of their impulses into actions often clearly and colorfully illustrate some of the defenses that we have described. Who has not been present when a young child who has spilled milk or broken an object immediately exclaims, "I didn't do it!"? The child is trying to deny or undo the act through denial and repression. At this age, projection frequently takes the form of blaming a "crime" on a younger sibling or even the family pet.

You can help to familiarize yourself with the various defenses by trying to identify each of the mechanisms in Table 3.1 as you have seen them occur in someone else, and then trying to recognize instances in which you may have used them yourself. It is much easier, of course,

TABLE 3.1   Defense Mechanisms

Repression
characteristics: blocking a wish or desire from conscious expression *example:* being unaware of deep-seated hostilities toward one's parents

Projection
characteristics: attributing an unconscious impulse, attitude, or behavior to someone else *example:* blaming somebody else for what you did or thinking that another person is out to get you

Reaction formation
characteristics: expressing an impulse by its opposite *example:* treating someone whom you intensely dislike in an overly friendly manner

Fixation
characteristics: satisfying an impulse in an immature manner for one's age *example:* protracted thumb sucking

TABLE 3.1 (continued)

Regression

characteristics: returning to an earlier form of expressing an impulse
example: resuming bed wetting after one has long since stopped

Rationalization

characteristics: dealing with an emotion intellectually to avoid emotional involvement
example: arguing that "Everybody else does it, so I don't have to feel guilty."

Identification

characteristics: modeling behavior after someone else
example: imitating one's mother or father

Displacement

characteristics: satisfying an impulse with a substitute object
example: scapegoating

Sublimation

characteristics: rechanneling an impulse into a more socially desirable outlet
example: satisfying sexual curiosity by conducting sophisticated research into sexual behaviors

---

to observe defense processes at work in someone else than to recognize them within ourselves; however, some of the following hints may help you to spot them. Have you ever "forgotten" an important event, such as an assigned test or a dentist appointment? You may also recall momentarily forgetting the name of someone you know quite well. Such activities indicate the tendency we all have to repress. Memory gaps on childhood events, in which you can recall only part of an event but not what preceded or followed, may indicate that the event entailed certain traumatic elements that make it hard for you to remember it completely. Have your parents ever told you about an experience that you had as a child but cannot remember? Do you have any phobias that you know are unrealistic, such as a fear of dogs or of flying? In such instances, you may really be afraid of some of your own inner impulses and have projected your fear onto an external object that makes it easier to handle. Have you ever found yourself behaving in an overly polite fashion in a situation in which you have wanted to be rude? You may have compensated for your impulse by reaction formation. Do you have any persistent immature habits, such as pouting and sulking when things do not go your way? Such behaviors may be signs of fixation. Have you ever provided an alibi for something you did or did not do? Could it have been an attempt to rationalize your behavior? Can you recall ever taking out your anger on someone who was helpless, such as a child or pet? Use of scapegoats is a common form of displacement. What kinds of leisure activities, sports, or creative and artistic activities do you enjoy? Through sublimation you may have been able to redirect certain antisocial impulses into socially approved and constructive behaviors. Sublimation is one of the more productive defense mechanisms available to us. In short, we all have and need defenses. Recognizing the use of a defense mechanism is not an occasion for finding fault with ourselves, rather, it is an opportunity for further exploration of our use of defense mechanisms so that they can be employed to foster instead of hinder growth.

The Synthesizing Functions of the Ego

Freud (1933) wrote, "Where id is, there shall ego be." He might also have written, "Where superego is, there shall ego be." The ego, we recall, seeks to realistically meet the needs and wishes of the organism, in contrast with the id's impulsive efforts to reduce tension and the superego's moralistic and perfectionistic solutions. By strengthening the ego, an individual reduces the power of the id and superego and makes them more easily manageable. Freud believed that becoming aware of our impulses and our reasons for behaving as we do is our greatest tool for strengthening the ego and assisting its synthesizing functions. Becoming aware of one's impulses does not eliminate them or reduce their strength. However, knowledge of one's wishes and desires gives one greater opportunity for satisfying them realistically according to the acceptable outlets of one's culture. All societies provide some means of expressing our sexual and aggressive impulses. Some, to be sure, are more restrictive than others and not all of the measures lead to health. However, without recognizing and understanding our impulses we cannot explore the available options. Further, an understanding of the reasons for our behavior permits us to act out of a conscience that is informed by our ego, rather than blindly obey the precepts of a moralistic and irrational superego.

We have seen that for Freud neurosis basically emerges from an unsatisfactory or arrested libidinal development. An individual falls ill when the satisfaction of his or her erotic needs is denied in the sphere of reality. The person turns to an illness as a surrogate satisfaction and creates a partially satisfying world of fantasy. Neurotics have no peculiar psychic content or functioning of their own that is not also found in healthy people. The mechanisms of id, ego, and superego describe normal and neurotic alike. Each one of us must travel the psychosexual stages. The neurotic is simply one who falls ill from the same conflicts and complexes with which normal people struggle. There are no clearly defined boundaries between illness and health. The primary question is not "Am I normal or neurotic?" but rather "To what degree is my neurosis debilitating?" The concept of neuroses is subsumed under a general image of humanity.

We have briefly traced the story of the development of Freud's therapeutic method, and the discovery of those techniques—free association and dream interpretation—that were to prove so fruitful to psychoanalysis. But the story of psychoanalysis was incomplete until Freud began to come to terms with the phenomenon of the transference.

Early in his work, Freud realized that the relationship between patient and physician was important in determining the outcome of the therapy. Nevertheless, it was with considerable embarrassment that he discovered one of his patients had fallen in love with him. We recall that a similar episode with his patient Anna O. had led Dr. Breuer to abandon the cathartic technique. For a man of such upright moral Victorian character as Freud, such a happening also appeared to pose a threat to and interference with his work. Only after considerable reservations and initial attempts to discourage similar phenomena from occurring did Freud begin to appreciate the dynamics of what was happening. He discovered that the feelings that were expressed toward him as a doctor were not directed at him as a person but rather were repetitions of earlier feelings of love and affection that the patient had for significant persons in his or her life. Thus, Freud was forced to recognize the value of the *transference*, a process whereby the patient transfers to the analyst emotional attitudes felt as a child toward important persons. By deliberately cultivating and analyzing the transference, Freud and his patients were able to learn a great deal.

Freud distinguished between *positive transference*, friendly, affectionate feelings expended on the physician, and *negative transference*, characterized by the expression of hostile, angry feelings. By studying the transference, Freud learned that his patients were relating to him in the same unsatisfactory and inefficient ways in which they had related to other important people in their lives. The transference was simply a new segment of an old affair, repeating infantile and ineffective interpersonal relationships. However, in the safe security of the analytic experience, the patient could rework these earlier unsatisfactory relationships through the current relationship to a satisfactory resolution.

It is difficult to know if Freud himself ever fully recognized the implications of the transference, but its cultivation and interpretation have become crucial to the psychoanalytic technique he fathered. Transference offers the patient an opportunity to relive the emotional conflicts that led to repressions and provides the analyst with a deep understanding of the patient's characteristic ways of perceiving and reacting. The major point here is that in analysis the patient experiences his or her conflicts under a different set of circumstances. The analyst does not respond to the patient with disapproval or rejection as earlier individuals did. Rather, the analyst reacts with insight and understanding, which permits the patient to gain insight into his or her experiences and feelings, and allows for change.

Freud's solution is one of insight, but the insight that psychoanalysis provides is a special kind of knowing that is not intellectual but existential. It touches the heart as well as the head. The solution does not lie in the realm of knowing but in the realm of doing: working through earlier conflicts. Discovering one's self is not only an intellectual act, but also an emotional experience. To use the Socratic expression: "To know is to do." Thus, therapy provides a more effective working through of the situation that provoked the neurosis. As the problem inevitably involves an ineffectiveness in one's psychosexual interpersonal relations, the solution must take place within the happening of a psychosexual interpersonal relationship—the transference. Freud's answer is *insight:* a deeply erotic insightful experience.

In classical analysis, the patient lies on a couch and the analyst sits behind, out of view. The patient is instructed to verbalize whatever comes to mind regardless of how irrelevant, absurd, or unpleasant it may seem. According to the deterministic stance, the patient's free associations are not really free at all, rather, they are determined by unconscious forces and gradually will permit these processes to be more clearly understood. During free association the patient may make a slip of the tongue or refer to a dream, both of which may be interpreted and utilized to assist the patient in acquiring a deeper understanding of the problem.

In the initial phase of analysis, the patient obtains considerable relief just by being able to unburden him- or herself to a sympathetic listener. A positive transference is developed, and the patient frequently believes that the analysis has reached a successful conclusion, even though the work of analysis has barely begun. There are as yet undisclosed and conflicting feelings that the patient has not yet explored. During the next phase, the analyst gently assists the patient in exploring these emotion-laden areas by pointing out and interpreting the resistance in an effort to weaken the patient's defenses and bring his or her repressed conflicts into the open. The analyst's efforts leave the patient angry, anxious, and depressed; therefore the analyst is now perceived as rejecting and unhelpful. Thoughts of prematurely concluding the analysis may again arise. Eventually the negative transference begins to cohere around specific areas. The patient re-experiences crucial episodes from childhood. The unremediated situation of the past includes not simply insufficiently resolved traumatic events but, more important, inadequately resolved interpersonal relationships. The analyst maintains a neutral stance, interpreting the transference and encouraging the patient to re-examine those circumstances in the light of increased maturity. The analyst's stance enables the patient to work through these situations to a more satisfactory conclusion. Lastly, the analyst assists the patient in converting newly won insights into everyday existence and behavior. This emotional re-education enables the new insights to become a permanent part of the patient's personality.

In its traditional form, analysis is a very protracted and expensive procedure. The patient meets with the analyst an average of five times a week for fifty-minute sessions over a period of several years. The procedure requires a considerable commitment in terms of time, effort, and money. However, the goal of psychoanalysis is an ambitious one since its aim is a full understanding, reorganization of, and basic change within the personality structure. Such goals cannot be accomplished quickly or easily. And, as Freud (1917) once wrote, "A neurotic who has been cured has really become a different person . . . he has become his best self, what he would have been under the most favorable conditions."

THERAPY EXCERPTS   **Psychoanalytic Therapy**

In the excerpt below, Lewis Wolberg, a psychoanalytically oriented therapist, assists a relatively new patient in understanding the kind of communication that occurs in psychoanalytic therapy.*

PT (Patient): I just don't know what's causing these feelings. I get so frightened and upset, and I don't know why.
TH (Therapist): That's why you are coming here, to find out the reasons, so you can do something about your trouble.
PT: But why is it that I can't sleep and concentrate?
TH: That's what we'll begin to explore.
PT: But why?
TH: What comes to your mind? What do you think?

* L. R. Wolberg, *The Technique of Psychotherapy*, Grune & Stratton, New York, 1977, Vol. 1, p. 507. Used by permission.

PT: I don't know.

TH: You know, there are reasons for troubles like yours, and one must patiently explore them. It may take a little time. I know you'd like to get rid of this trouble right away, but the only way we can do this is by careful exploring.

PT: Yes.

TH: And to take your anxiety feelings, for example, you may not be aware of the reasons for them now, but as we talk about you, your ideas, your troubles, and your feelings, you should be able to find out what they are.

PT: How do I do this?

TH: When I ask you to talk about your feelings and thrash things around in your mind, you won't be able to put your finger on what bothers you immediately, but at least you will have started thinking about the sources of the problem. Right now, the only thing you're concerned with is escaping from the emotion. That's why you're just going around in a circle. While you're operating to seal off anxiety, you're doing nothing about finding out what's producing this anxiety.

PT: It sounds sort of clear when you say it. (laughs)

TH: Well, do you think you understand what I mean?

PT: What you're explaining now?

TH: Yes.

PT: Yes. (pause) The point is that I keep thinking about myself too much. It's that I feel inferior to everyone. I must win at rummy. When I play golf, I practically beat myself red if I don't get the low score. And this is silly.

TH: What happens when someone beats you at golf?

PT: I get upset and these feelings come.

TH: Now there seems to be some connection here; let's talk some more about that.

As psychoanalytic therapy continues there are frequent long periods of silence on the analyst's part as the patient verbalizes what comes to mind. The patient is encouraged to fantasize about the analyst and these fantasies facilitate the transference. The imagined excerpt below is extremely condensed, but illustrative of what happens.

PT: You don't have anything to say about that? You should say something. (silence) You know it's very frustrating for me to come in here hour after hour and not hear you say anything. I feel as if you can't be bothered, that you don't really care.

TH: That must be very frustrating.

PT: Damn right it's frustrating. There you sit with the answer to my problem, and you don't even care. You won't help me.

TH: My silence bothers you a great deal. What do you imagine that I am thinking when I'm silent?

PT: I told you—that you don't care. Either that or that you're judging me. You've decided I'm not worth it.

TH: You used the word "judge." It seems as if you feel like you're in a court room.

PT: That's right, I'm on trial and you're the judge.

TH: And the verdict is guilty.

PT: Yes, no wonder, I can't talk to you.

TH: Do your feelings seem familiar? Do I remind you of anyone?

PT: Well, hell, yes. Sure. You remind me of my father. Whenever I wanted to do anything, he'd be all over my back.

EVALUATION AND IMPLICATIONS

Educated in the precise methods of nineteenth-century science, Freud established a significant reputation as a medical researcher before he developed the theory of psychoanalysis. At many points in his writings, Freud clearly defined and described the scientific enterprise. He asserted that knowledge is based on empirical observation and dogmatically maintained that his own theories were so based. His concepts, he claimed, were merely tentative constructs to be discarded if later observation failed to confirm them. He frequently revised his theories because new data had emerged that could not be accounted for in terms of his earlier theories.

While his research was not based on controlled laboratory experimentation, much of it was concerned with empirical data. The basic setting for his inquiry was clinical. He made careful observations of his patients in the therapeutic setting. He garnered considerable information from the techniques of free association and dream analysis. Finally, he conducted his own self-analysis, beginning in 1897 and continuing throughout his life. Such data may properly be called empirical as it is based on observation. The fact that the looking is looking in ("introspection") rather than out ("extrospection") does not mean that it is any less empirical, although it might make our test more difficult.

Nevertheless, in determining how Freud's statements function, we have to look not only at the data on which they were initially based, but also at the method of test finally employed. In the spirit of many fellow positivists of his day, Freud, while claiming that he was merely extending scientific knowledge by placing the psychic life of human beings under scientific observation and theory, permitted many of his concepts to function philosophically. He did not permit them to have any exceptions. We have seen that an important criterion of scientific constructs is the requirement that they be open to falsification. The desire to be scientific reflects itself in an effort to test constructs by validating evidence rather than by simply relying on the compelling character of a philosophical assumption. Freud defined many of his concepts as all-controlling factors in everything we do, think, and are. For example, Freud suggested that it is impossible to conceive of any activity that does not reflect unconscious motives as well as conscious ones. The doctrine of unconscious processes was thus lifted out of an immediate empirical construct and made applicable to all actual and possible human behavior. Even the objections to it could be explained in terms of resistance or further unconscious processes. How can one dream a dream or make a slip that would contradict Freud's understanding of the unconscious? Anxiety dreams, seeming exceptions to the statement that all dreams fulfill wishes, can be reconciled to the theory by distinguishing between the manifest dream and the latent one. The distinction between latent and manifest makes it clear that things are not necessarily what they appear to be.

The theory of the life and death instinctual drives, lightly called "our mythology," (Freud, 1933) actually functions as a mythology. Sexuality became a philosophical concept insofar as Freud asserted that all human behavior could be considered in its light. Freud drew conclusions from careful self-observation and observation of his patients in a clinical setting and projected them into philosophical statements. Although Freud invested his theories with an aura of science, in evaluating them he made primary use of philosophical criteria, relying on their compelling power rather than validating evidence.

Nevertheless, Freud's theory has generated a great deal of empirical research and attempts to test the concepts experimentally. Such efforts are all very appropriate as it is certainly permissible and desirable to scrutinize philosophical concepts with modern scientific information. A large body of literature (for example, Sears, 1943, Klime, 1972, and Fisher and Greenberg, 1977) concern attempts to test hypotheses derived from Freud's ideas to see if they function usefully as science. In such efforts, hypotheses informed by Freud's concepts are tested in the laboratory or other settings where variables can be manipulated and controlled. The concepts are translated into operational procedures that allow for unequivocal tests.

Under such scrutiny, some Freudian theories have not been validated. For example, it has become untenable in the light of modern research in biology and embryology to conceive of the female as an inferior and castrated male. Other Freudian concepts, however, appear to stand up nicely under experimental conditions. The concept of repression has been operationally translated to suggest that there is a stronger tendency to forget events identified with unpleasant associations than with neutral or pleasant events. Experimental test of this hypothesis indicates its usefulness.

There appear, however, to be definite limits on the viability and value of treating Freud's concepts simply as scientific constructs. First,

Freud's theory contains many concepts that are by their nature difficult to define operationally. There is no direct evidence that will substantiate concepts such as unconscious processes or repression. Thus, the operational translation of many of Freud's concepts frequently misinterprets and oversimplifies his ideas. The Freudian theory of repression does not simply imply experiences associated with unpleasant thoughts; thus, laboratory studies on repression generally deal with phenomena that are essentially different from the kind of phenomena that concerned Freud. Since the concepts are distorted and minimized, they do not truly represent the constructs in Freud's thought. Further, a simpler rival hypothesis that has greater appeal to common sense can frequently be offered to account for the same phenomena that arise in the laboratory test. According to the rule of Occam's razor, the simpler, less offensive hypothesis is often preferred in science. Finally, Freud's own investigations and those of other psychoanalysts hardly allow for replication due to the conditions of privacy and confidentiality under which they arise.

Such apparent failures do not seriously trouble the psychoanalyst, who tends to view efforts to evaluate Freud's work solely on experimental scientific grounds as ultimately trivial. The analyst points out that it is virtually impossible to test seriously any really important psychoanalytic concept because the experimental method itself necessarily requires us to oversimplify or distort. Such methods are ultimately inappropriate if they are considered to constitute the final test of Freud's theory. The kind of knowing on which psychoanalysis, as well as other scientific work, is ultimately based is epiphanic, a form of knowing that is extra-ordinary because it does not rely on everyday experiences, it transcends them.

Freud acknowledged that philosophy was a goal that had beckoned him all along, for in later years he suggested that his dalliance with science was a detour on the road to a more ultimate quest: a comprehensive philosophy of humanity. In the final analysis, the criteria that compelled Freud and compels many of his followers are largely philosophical. At the same time, the ongoing effort to validate his theories represents the need to evaluate our philosophical assumptions in light of contemporary scientific information.

While Freud changed and revised his theory, in the end he presented a clear, logical, and coherent pattern. To be sure, his theory is not a finished whole. Not only did he continually modify it, but it has been revised, modified, and updated by those within the Freudian tradition as well. Some psychoanalysts, as we shall see, have elaborated on the role of the ego, giving it greater autonomy in its functions in comparison to Freud's emphasis on the id. Others have instituted changes in psychoanalytic therapy. While Freud was frequently unsympathetic to efforts to modify his theory and claimed the ultimate right to declare what properly should and should not be called psychoanalysis,

he was not unreceptive to change that reflected the spirit of psychoanalysis as an evolving movement of a particular form of thought and
investigation. Certain pillars, however, he believed were unassailable
and could not be weakened lest the entire structure of psychoanalysis
tumble. One such pillar was the concept of repression and the recognition that in large measure we are governed by forces of which we are
unaware. Interpretation of transference and resistance remained the
mainstays of psychoanalytic technique. Nevertheless, within this framework, Freud forever presented new points of reference for understanding personality and juxtaposing them against his earlier ones. It is
only fitting that many of his followers do likewise. Thus, his theory
does not constitute a finished structure and system; it is an open one
capable of continued growth. Psychoanalytic theory not only fulfills
the criterion of coherency, it additionally provides a consistent pattern
on which one can build.

The relevance of Freud's theory is evidenced by its remarkable
impact on the Western world. Freud changed, perhaps irrevocably, humanity's image of itself. Since Aristotle, the essence of humanity had
been located in our rational powers and ability to think. This image
found ultimate expression in Descartes's phrase "I think, therefore, I
am." In a post-Freudian world, our self-image is changed. We can no
longer conceive of ourselves as primarily rational animals; rather, we
are pleasure-seeking, sexual creatures driven by our emotions. We have
seen that Freud rephrased Descartes's statement to render it, "I love,
therefore, I am." For many, the gospel of psychoanalysis is not "good
news," because it forces consideration of aspects of ourselves that we
woud prefer to ignore, yet it is virtually impossible to deny Freud his
influence. Freud's accomplishments have been favorably compared with
those of Copernicus, Darwin, and Einstein. Not only did he revolutionize psychology, but his influence has been felt in the social sciences,
literature, art, philosophy, and religion. Freud's name is a household
word. Errors of the pen or tongue are commonly known as "Freudian
slips," and innumerable people cannot make one without wondering
what the unconscious reason is. Freud's theory, then, has relevance for
our time. He grappled with ideas that were, are, and continue to be of
primary concern to us. Because of that his theories interest, allure, and
excite people everywhere.

Freud's theory of personality is comprehensive, challenging, and
profound. His aim was to develop a comprehensive theory of humanity.
He consistently maintained that his study of neurosis would eventually
provide a key to the study of psychological processes in general. Freud's
quest for the truth was unrelenting; no question was too small for him
to consider; no probe was too trivial for him; no psychological process
was too insignificant for his attention. To look for meaning on the
surface was to settle for appearances and superficiality. Only by risking
a plunge into the depths of the unconscious could one discover the truth

about oneself and others. Any contradiction or opposition to his theory was to be met by analysis of the resistance, for only through such thorough analysis could true insight emerge.

Finally, Freud's theory has compelled many individuals. Some critics (see, for example, Ellenberger, 1970) have suggested that Freud founded a school comparable to the philosophical schools of ancient Greece and Rome. With the creation of psychoanalysis, Freud developed a movement, characterized by its own rules, rituals, and doctrine of membership. Training in analysis entails a specific and protracted initiation into the rites of the psychoanalytic society. The didactic (or training) analysis requires sacrifices in terms of time, money, privacy, and the self. This process serves to integrate firmly the initiates into the rituals, tenets, and wisdom of the movement. Some suggest that Freud's major contribution will be seen as the development of the psychoanalytic philosophic cult.

Be that as it may, it is possible that after reading and studying Freud, one may concur that his concepts are coherent, relevant, and comprehensive, yet nevertheless one remains uncompelled. Freud would counter that the insight required for full appreciation of his theory is of a particular kind, perhaps one which can be acquired only through undergoing the kind of analytic self-investigation that he and many of his followers have undertaken. Freud's theory is by no means universally accepted. Indeed, few other positions in the history of philosophical thought have been subject to as much attack, ridicule, and criticism as that of Sigmund Freud. In modern science, only the theory of Charles Darwin has been met with equal scorn and resistance. It is not for the author to indicate to readers an appropriate judgment on their reading of Freud. Such a judgment can only arise from the reader's own encounter with the thought of Sigmund Freud. Nevertheless, Freud's picture of personality is one that for many people compels. His picture of the personality as beset by anxieties, governed by forces of which we are largely unaware, living in a world marked by external and internal conflicts, resolving problems by solutions informed by fantasy or reality, is a concept of personality that many people find inescapable.

CURRENT TRENDS IN PSYCHOANALYSIS

In recent years, psychoanalysts, following Freud's own example of revising and reformulating his concepts, have expanded and enlarged the application of psychoanalytic findings. The theoretical focus of many psychoanalysts has turned from the study of the adult to the study of the child and from investigation of the unconscious to investigation of the ego. There has been an expansion of psychoanalysis as a therapeutic technique. Several psychoanalysts have placed an increased emphasis on social and cultural influences on personality. Efforts have been made to explore the implications of psychoanalysis for understanding women as well as men. Lastly, Freud's concepts have been translated into terms that are easier for the lay person to comprehend. I will briefly mention the first three trends and examine the last three in more detail.

Anna Freud, Sigmund Freud's daughter, has been a pioneer in extending the interests of psychoanalysis to the exploration of the ego and the study of the child. The concepts presented in her classic work *The Ego and the Mechanisms of Defense* (1936) have become an integral part of psychoanalysis. Her observations of children, which extend beyond that of normal or disturbed children growing up in average homes and include children who have met with extraordinary circumstances, such as war, physical handicaps, and parentless homes, have opened the way to a new era of research in psychoanalytic child psychology and application of its findings to a wide area of concerns associated with child rearing.

Margaret Mahler (1976) has explored the processes of separation and individuation by which the child emerges from a symbiotic, or intimate, fusion with the mother and assumes individual characteristics. Her findings have confirmed that the biological birth of an infant and the psychological birth of an individual are not the same. The former is a distinct event, whereas the latter is a gradually unfolding process.

Another group of psychoanalysts, led by Heinz Hartmann, has earned the label of ego psychoanalysts because of their extensive study of the role of the ego in personality development. We recall that Freud believed that in the healthy personality the ego was the primary executor, harnessing and channeling the demands of the id and the superego in order to meet realistically their needs in the everyday world. Freud, however, stressed the influences of the id's unconscious and irrational processes. The ego was never the master of personality but was continually beset by the demands of the impulsive id and moralistic superego. The best Freud could hope for was that, through analysis, one might strengthen the id, but he never granted it autonomous status.

Hartmann (1958, 1964), Rapaport (1959, 1960), and others have suggested that the ego is an important, autonomous force in its own right. Its energy is not necessarily derived from the id, but both ego and id originate in inherited predispositions that follow independent courses of development. Thus, the ego's functions are not limited to the avoidance of pain and the service of instinctual gratification. These theorists have paid considerable attention to the synthesizing and integrative functions of the ego. They have explored its processes of perception, attention, memory, rational thought and action and have shown increased interest in accounting for normal behavior. Hartmann has also suggested that certain spheres of ego activity may be "conflict free," that is to say, that the ego is not perpetually in conflict with the id, external world, and superego. Through experience and adaptation, many of the ego's functions may become increasingly distinct from original instinctive and defensive maneuvers and lead to higher order objectives and goals.

Whereas Freud believed that only psychoneuroses were amenable to treatment by psychoanalysis, other analysts, such as Giovacchini (1975, 1977) and Spotnitz (1976), have expanded the psychoanalytic technique to encompass treatment of more serious psychological problems and character disorders. Recognizing that Freud barely began to explore the wide spectrum of narcissistic and pre-oedipal conditions, they have expanded research into these areas and developed techniques designed to work through transferences and resistances stemming from these phases of psychosexual development.

Other psychoanalysts have turned their attention to cultural and social influences on personality. These were largely neglected by Freud because of the key importance he placed on the biologically determined drives of the id. Alfred Adler (1870–1937), Erich Fromm (1900–   ), Karen Horney (1885–1952), and Harry Stack Sullivan (1892–1949), whom we will consider in subsequent chapters, have all emphasized social determinants of personality. Their theories have gained independent stature and recognition. Within the psychoanalytic movement itself, Erik Erikson (1902–   ) stands out for his recognition of the importance of cultural, social, and historical influences on personality. In his writings, Erikson has also elaborated on Freud's stages of development, trying to make explicit the social dimensions in Freud's work.

Erikson's Psychosocial Stages of Development

In his discussion of the psychosexual stages of development, Freud concentrated specifically on the biological character of the stages; thus, he tended to neglect their social dimension and import. Nevertheless, Freud's stages reflect more than simply a psychosexual development in which the child comes to terms with his or her sexuality. Erikson demonstrates how they also represent a *psychosocial* development, in which the child is trying to understand and relate to the world and others. In effect, Erikson makes explicit the social dimension implied in Freud's work.

Each of Erikson's stages is established around an emotional polarity or conflict that children encounter at certain critical periods. New environmental demands introject positive and negative emotional components into the development of personality. Both emotional components are to some extent incorporated into the emerging person, but if the conflict is resolved satisfactorily, the positive component is reflected

TABLE 3.2 Freud's Psychosexual and Erikson's Psychosocial Stages

	Freud	Erikson
0– 1	oral	trust versus mistrust
1– 3	anal	autonomy versus doubt; shame
3– 5	phallic	initiative versus guilt
6–11	latency	industry versus inferiority
	genital	
12–18	(adolescence)	identity versus role confusion
18–24	(young adulthood)	intimacy versus isolation
25–50	(adulthood)	generativity versus stagnation
50–	(maturity)	ego integrity versus despair

to a higher degree. If the conflict persists, or is not adequately resolved, the negative component predominates. Erikson's first four stages correspond to Freud's psychosexual stages (oral through latency). Erikson subdivides the genital stage into four phases (Table 3.2) that represent growth and development throughout maturity.

Corresponding to Freud's oral stage is Erikson's psychosocial stage of *trust versus mistrust*. At birth, infants are deprived of the constant attention they received in the womb and for a protracted period of time they are highly dependent on others for their care. Certain frustrations are inevitable and socially meaningful, but too much frustration or indulgence may have deleterious effects. The primary dilemma that infants face is whether or not the world and its people are safe, nurturing, and reliable so that they can be trusted to meet the infants' needs. If infants receive unreliable, inadequate, or rejecting care, their world will be perceived as indifferent or hostile. While this crisis is not permanently resolved during the first year or two of life, a foundation is laid that influences the subsequent course of development.

Erikson's second psychosocial stage is that of *autonomy versus shame and doubt*, which arises during the second and third years of life. The primary emotional duality here is that of developing control over the body and bodily activities as opposed to developing a tendency for doubt and shame. The struggle for autonomy is not limited to sessions on the toilet, but extends to many other areas of life as well. Toddlers, who are making rapid gains in neuromuscular maturation, verbalization, and social discrimination, are beginning to explore independently and interact with their environment. These initial tentative explorations may be reinforced or rejected. The negativism of the two-year-old, whose favorite word is "no," is further evidence of children's struggling attempt at developing autonomy. After all, a temper tantrum is simply a momentary loss of self-control. If children develop doubts about their ability for self-control, their doubts may lead to feelings of inadequacy and shame.

The emotional duality that Erikson envisions for the phallic stage (three to five) is that of *initiative versus guilt*. At this period, children are active within their environment, mastering new skills and tasks. Having gained relative independence and autonomy during the toddler years, they are directing their activities toward specific goals and achievements. Their curiosity extends not only to sexual matters but to many other concerns of life as well. If the characteristic word of toddlers is "no," the characteristic word of preschoolers is "why." Their incessant questions are a hallmark of their curiosity. Parental responses to children's self-initiated activities determine the successful or unsuccessful outcome of this stage. If initiative is reinforced, a child's behavior will become increasingly goal oriented. Excessive punishment or discouragement of a child's general stance of initiation may lead to feelings of guilt, resignation, and the belief that it is wrong to be curious about the world and ill advised to be active in it.

During the school years (six to eleven), the primary emotional duality is that of *industry versus inferiority*. The term "industry" refers to work and children's work is at school, where certain new demands are placed on them. No longer are children loved simply for whom they are; they are expected to perform and master the technology of their culture in order to earn the respect of their teachers and peers. Their ability to conform and master the tasks of this level depends in large measure on how successfully they have traveled the preceding stages. A certain residue of each side of the emotional polarities is created as one develops. The question is, which predominates? If children emerge from the preceding stages with a basic sense of trust, autonomy, and initiative, they are ready for the industrious labor that school presupposes. But if their development has left heavy residues of mistrust, doubt, and guilt, they may have difficulty performing at an optimal level. From a psychoanalytic point of view, the child who has not adequately resolved his or her Oedipus complex may not be ready to read. Erikson warns, however, that industry should not be limited to educational achievements, since it also entails a sense of being interpersonally competent in the social world.

The danger during this period is that feelings of inadequacy and inferiority will develop. Children begin to make comparisons between themselves and others and to perceive themselves in a more or less favorable light. The use of inoffensive labels, such as "wolves," "foxes," and "raccoons," to differentiate among children's school performance may slightly minimize but in no way erases a child's consciousness of his or her work as superior or inferior. Children know, or think they know, where they stand.

For Freud, the hallmarks of the genital stage were *Lieben und Arbeiten*, "to love and to work." Erikson divides this period of mature development into four substages. The primary duality during adolescence (twelve to eighteen) is that of *ego identity versus role confusion*.

Ego identity involves developing a self-image that entails "inner sameness and continuity" both in one's own and others' perception of the self. Failure to develop such identity leads to an *identity crisis* and role confusion, in which an individual finds it difficult to be effective in the various roles that society assigns.

Young adulthood (eighteen to twenty-four) is marked by the emotional duality of *intimacy versus isolation*. Intimacy refers to the ability to develop a close, deep, and meaningful genital relationship with other persons. Erikson here applies Freud's dictum "to love and to work" as the model orientation. Isolation entails self-absorption and the inability to develop deep committed relations.

The middle years (twenty-five to fifty) are characterized by the conflict between *generativity versus stagnation*. Generativity entails more than parenthood; it is the ability to be productive and creative in many areas of life, particularly those that show a concern for the welfare of ensuing generations. One actively participates in those elements of the culture that will ensure its maintenance and enhancement. Failure to do so leads to feelings of stagnation, boredom, and interpersonal impoverishment.

Maturity, the final stage of life (fifty to death), is marked by *ego integrity versus despair*. Ego integrity entails the ability to reflect on one's life with satisfaction. Death is not feared, it is accepted, as one among many of the facets of one's existence. Despair refers to regret over missed and unfulfilled opportunities at a time when it is too late to begin again.

Clearly, Erikson builds on Freud's psychosexual stages, but he emphasizes the social determinants of personality. The conflicts that arise are not caused simply by frustration of the sexual drives, but by the clash between the child's needs and wishes and society's expectations and strictures.

Erikson has also extended psychoanalytic inquiry into the area of psychohistorical analysis. He has written biographical studies of historical figures, such as Martin Luther, George Bernard Shaw, and Adolf Hitler, in which he has clarified their lives by means of his theory of the human life cycle and its respective crises.

Psychoanalysis and Femininity

Contemporary psychoanalysts are also re-examining Freud's impact on our understanding of femininity. For many in the feminist movement, Freud's writings have represented oppression rather than liberation. Freud is said to have viewed women as incomplete, inferior human beings whose development is dictated primarily by the absence of a penis. For these women, Freud's theories led to a setback in their self-understanding rather than an advance.

Critical examination of Freud's ideas about women began in the

1920s, long before the current feminist and biological debates. Figures such as Alfred Adler, Helene Deutsch, and Karen Horney questioned Freud's picture of women as inferior and suggested amendments to the psychoanalytic theory of femininity. They suggested cultural, economic, and social factors that could account for the phenomena of penis envy, narcissism, and passiveness that Freud observed. Drawing on their own clinical experience, as well as on cultural, anthropological, and literary evidence, they showed how Freud's concepts were frequently a product of his social and cultural milieu. More recently, the penetrating critiques of feminists Betty Friedan (1963), Kate Millett (1970), and Phyllis Chesler (1972) directed attention to Freudian concepts that were prejudicial to women and also suggested that psychoanalysis itself was guilty of perpetuating a model of normalcy for women that maintained the status quo.

New research on sexuality has also forced us to re-evaluate Freud's work. Masters and Johnson's (1966) findings on the female orgasm and the role of the clitoris have called into question Freud's distinction between clitoral and vaginal orgasms. Recent discoveries in the areas of endocrinology and embryology suggest that women are not "castrated men," but rather, men are "masculinized females." The original libido appears to be feminine rather than masculine as Freud suggested. We now know that mammals begin fetal life as females and that masculinization is a subsequent result of the action of fetal androgens according to genetic prescription. The clitoris is not a miniature penis, rather, the penis is an "exaggerated clitoris" (Sherfey, 1972). Studies in gender identity suggest that sex assignment and rearing, rather than genitals per se, play a major factor in sexual identification (Stoller, 1973).

While Freud was sexist and chauvanistic, his writings are equally sexist and confining for both men and women. His discussion of the psychosexual stages and development of the male, no less than the female, are permeated with the notion of biological determinism and shares the same characteristics of inevitability. Still, it was Freud's analysis that permitted us to begin to recognize the kinds of psychological development produced within a patriarchal society.

In assessing Freud's statements on men and women, we need to distinguish between his astute empirical observations of the attitudes and feelings of the people of his day and subsequent conclusions he drew about the essential characteristics of masculinity and femininity. In many respects, the picture that he painted of women represents accurate empirical descriptions of the prevailing feelings, mood, and self-understanding of the women of his era. At a time in which virtually everyone believed implicitly in the traditional sex roles, it is no surprise that women perceived themselves as inferior and secondary. That childhood feelings should be verbalized in terms of penis envy or castration anxiety is understandable when it is clear that those who possessed a penis were afforded more prestige and worth.

In spite of his predilection for biological determinism, Freud assisted us in recognizing that culture and society shape and direct our sexual expression and do so in a way that is not necessarily optimal. Freud helped us to realize that if we wish to understand a person's development we must do so in terms of that person's particular history. A woman's devaluation of her femininity is a developmental effect of her history, not an inevitable consequence. With this in mind, contemporary psychoanalysts like Juliet Mitchell (1975) are re-examining Freud's theories and showing how they provide essential and inescapable insights for women's psychological and political liberation.

Transactional Analysis and Gestalt Therapy

Finally, Freud's concepts have been translated into terms that are easier for the lay person to understand. Eric Berne, the founder of transactional analysis (TA), had been associated with psychoanalysis for fifteen years when he introduced a new vocabulary (1961) that simplified the conceptualization of human relationships. Berne suggests that in our relations with the self and others, we alternate playing the roles of Child, Parent, or Adult. In many respects, Berne's ego states parallel Freud's tripartite division of the personality: Child = id, Parent = superego, and Adult = ego. However, it is easier to comprehend how we frequently play the role of a Child or a Parent rather than an Adult in our interpersonal relations than it is to understand the sophisticated Freudian concepts.

The *Child* consists of a recording of those feelings and experiences we had when we were children. It encompasses our hurts, angers, and affections. The Child is not childish but childlike. In our Child ego state, we tend to respond spontaneously, to strike back, or to defend ourselves, reflecting the natural, adapted, and rebellious aspects of our childhood. As we grow up, we also incorporate into our personality the admonitions, looks, gestures, and moral injunctions of significant adults. Our *Parent* is both nurturing and controlling. In our Parent ego state, we tend to scold, punish, or impose value judgments on other people. As Adults, we seek to evaluate and make realistic choices among the alternatives that confront us. Thus, in our *Adult* ego state, we seek information, weigh alternatives, and are not threatened by angry or punitive statements from others.

The point is not to eliminate the Child or the Parent, both of which have positive aspects, but to examine their data in the light of the data accumulated by the Adult. Thus, we need to ask whether or not the wisdom of the Parent is true and applicable today and whether or not the feelings of the Child are appropriate to the present (Harris, 1969).

In any given situation, an individual generally acts out of one or more of these ego states. Where the other individual plays a parallel or complementary role, a reciprocal relationship exists. But if the other person does not go along, there is a crossed relationship that is mutually unsatisfying. Berne's classic example is that of a husband and wife where the husband, operating in an Adult state, asks, "Where are my cufflinks?" A complementary Adult response might be: "I haven't seen them," or "On top of your bureau." However, if the wife responds defensively as a Child: "How am I supposed to know where they are?" or judgmentally as a Parent: "You should take better care of your things," a crossed relationship exists that stops communication or causes trouble.

In other respects, Berne's system draws heavily on the thought of Alfred Adler, whose position I will discuss in the next chapter. Each individual develops a life script that expresses his or her attitude to him- or herself and others. The four positions (Harris, 1969) are:

I'm OK, you're OK
I'm OK, you're not OK
I'm not OK, you're OK
I'm not OK, you're not OK

These attitudes influence the *games* people play or the transactions that they have with one another.

Each child begins life in the position of I'm not OK, you're OK because of the inferiority the infant feels. Ideally, however, with sufficient strokes, an individual assumes the stance of I'm OK, you're OK. *Strokes* are activities that fulfill physiological and psychological needs, and they are essential for human survival and self-fulfillment. Initially, we are dependent on others for our strokes; later, we learn to give them to ourselves from our nurturing Parent. Too often, however, we receive or give *cold pricklies*, negative strokes, which lead to a less optimal position.

Transactional analysis seeks to help an individual understand how he or she views him- or herself and others and to analyze the kinds of interpersonal transactions or games that he or she plays. Particularly suitable for groups, TA assists people to develop a more objective view of themselves and others.

Frequently, transactional analysis is used in conjunction with gestalt therapy. Frederick (Fritz) Perls, the founder of gestalt therapy, was also trained in Freud's psychoanalytic method. *Gestalt therapy* emphasizes awareness and seeks to discover the how and now of behavior. When we are unaware, or unconscious of our behavior, it is unavailable to us for constructive use. By directly experiencing our present feelings, we can begin to utilize more of our potentiality.

Fritz Perls suggests that many people are *phonies*; they put on an act, play games, live false roles. In doing so, they disown part of themselves. Our *Topdog* (superego or Parent) harasses our *Underdog* (our inner, frightened, weaker self). As we become aware of our phony behavior, we become frightened of behaving in a genuine way. However, we also begin to realize how we have limited and constricted ourselves.

The gestalt therapist seeks to structure the therapeutic situation in such a way that the patient is able to confront him- or herself and experience his or her actual present feelings. An emphasis is placed on nonverbal behaviors to show the frequent inconsistency between our verbal and nonverbal statements. If a patient states that she is frightened but has a smile on her face, Perls would point out that a frightened person does not smile and seek to explore the meaning of her smile. The gestalt therapist approaches a dream by asking the person to play all of the persons or objects in his or her dream. Fantasizing is encouraged. The therapist does not play a doctor role but seeks to express him- or herself authentically. These techniques seek to tap our hidden potential and permit previously unused energies to surge forward in a process of integration.

The current lively debate that Freud's psychoanalysis is engendering in these and other areas is testimony to its continued impact and importance.

SUGGESTIONS FOR FURTHER READING

Freud's final theory of a threefold dynamic of personality was presented in *The Ego and the Id* (1923), published in Vol. 19 of *The Standard English Edition of the Complete Psychological Works of Sigmund Freud* (Hogarth Press, 1961). Freud's re-evaluation of the problem of anxiety and the defense mechanisms is included in *Inhibitions, Symptoms and Anxiety* (1926), Vol. 20, 1959. The various introductory lectures cited in the previous chapter provide useful information on the development of psychoanalysis as a therapeutic technique. However, the reader may also enjoy two later essays on the subject: "Analysis Terminable and Interminable" and "Constructions in Analysis" (both written in 1937), included in Vol. 23, 1964, in which Freud tries to realistically assess the benefits and limitations of psychoanalysis.

Secondary sources that provide a comprehensive picture of Freudian theory are C. Brenner, *An Elementary Textbook on Psychoanalysis* (Doubleday, 1955) and C. S. Hall, *A Primer of Freudian Psychology* (World, 1954). The classic review of empirical studies seeking to validate Freudian concepts is R. Sears, *Survey of Objective Studies of Psychoanalytic Concepts* (Social Science Research Council, 1943). For an update on more recent efforts, see P. Klime, *Fact and Fantasy in Freudian Theory* (Metheun, 1972) and S. Fisher and R. R. Greenberg, *The Scientific Credibility of Freud's Theory and Therapy* (Basic Books, 1977).

Erik Erikson's eight stages of man are included in *Childhood and*

Society (2nd ed.) (Norton, 1963). Readers who are interested in contemporary re-evaluations of psychoanalytic views on femininity are referred to Juliet Mitchell, *Psychoanalysis and Feminism* (Vintage, 1975), and my own "Freud's Sexual Politics: Heresy or Heroism," *Anima* 1976, 2(2), 62–71. Eric Berne's *Games People Play* (Grove, 1964) and Thomas Harris's *I'm OK—You're OK* (Harper & Row, 1969) are useful introductions to transactional analysis. Fritz Perls's best-known book, *Gestalt Therapy* (Julian Press, 1958), was written in collaboration with R. F. Hefferline and P. Goodman. Richard G. Abell's *Own Your Own Life* (Bantam, 1977) describes a psychoanalyst's tardy discovery of the value of these approaches, both in his own life and in his therapeutic approach.

PART II

Neo-psychoanalytic Theories

It was no doubt inevitable that a dynamic figure like Sigmund Freud would both attract and repel. Freud developed a group of loyal followers. However, some of his followers became dissatisfied with orthodox psychoanalysis, defected from the movement, and founded their own schools of thought. Carl Jung, Alfred Adler, Karen Horney, and Erich Fromm were all deeply indebted to Freud and psychoanalysis. Freud's psychoanalytic theory provided a major impetus for their work. At the same time, each reacted in varying ways against Freud's theory and developed his or her own position. In many instances, certain developments in these theories have been identified as valuable elaborations or adjuncts to classical psychoanalysis. Nevertheless, each theorist presented his or her theory as one that could stand by itself.

Most of the neo-psychoanalytic theorists, in particular Adler, Horney, and Fromm, react against Freud's instinctualism or the view that the primary motivational forces of personality lie in instinctual drives. They criticize Freud for overemphasizing the importance of sexuality in personality. They recognize that many of Freud's patients expressed conflicts that centered around sexual desires, but this may have been largely due to the strict Victorian ethic under which Freud's patients were raised. Their own patients did not necessarily share these conflicts. Instead, they displayed a more global set of problems. Although Jung does not reject an instinctual basis of personality, he also criticizes Freud's emphasis on sexuality, suggesting that it is ultimately reductionistic as it reduces any and all activities to sexual ones. Jung's point is that sexuality itself must be seen as symbolic, having a mysterious quality of otherness that cannot be fully circumscribed and described.

In place of instinctual forces, Adler, Horney, and Fromm stress the social forces that shape personality. Horney emphasizes factors within the family that affect personality. Adler and Fromm also examine forces within the society at large. While they object to Freud's emphasis on instinctual drives and intrapsychic structures of personality, they do not adopt a radical environmentalist position and suggest that personality is entirely shaped by society. They continue to recognize that there are forces within the self that assist in shaping personality. Thus, both human nature and the role of society are considered by these theorists.

Several neo-psychoanalytic theorists emphasize anxiety as a central problem of the self. For example, Horney suggests that anxiety is the basic human condition with which a person has to deal. Here she is reminiscent of Freud's later view that anxiety is the basic human condition into which we are thrust. But she differs from Freud in that she does not see anxiety as an inevitable part of the human condition. She suggests that anxiety is created by social forces rather than by the human predicament itself.

Each of the neo-psychoanalytic theorists is more optimistic than Freud about human potentialities and the potentiality of society. They see human nature and the individual personality as flexible and changeable. Each posits forward-moving tendencies within the self leading toward growth and health. Jung posits the drive toward self-actualization, a concept that has been picked up by many subsequent theorists. Adler, Horney, and Fromm suggest that obstacles to growth are imposed by the society rather than by human nature itself. Both Adler and Fromm envision the creation of a utopian society that will more adequately meet and fulfill human potentialities. In short, the neo-psychoanalytic theorists replace Freud's pessimism with a much more hopeful note.

Many neo-psychoanalytic concepts may be seen as elaborations on the original Freudian theory. Jung expands on unconscious forces. Fromm elaborates on the personality types. Horney clarifies the ego-ideal. Adler's compensatory dynamics and Horney's adjustment mechanisms may be seen as elaborations of the Freudian defense mechanisms. Perhaps they could see farther because they were standing on the shoulders of a giant.

We have seen how in many respects Freud's theory was a product of nineteenth-century thought, rooted and cast in the framework of a now outdated biological determinism. While many of his concepts helped to shatter the nineteenth-century understanding of human nature, they require revision to meet the demands of the twentieth century and remain abreast of intellectual thought. In the early twentieth century, the disciplines of psychology, sociology, and anthropology developed as distinct methods of investigation. The neo-psychoanalytic theorists were able to take advantage of these emerging fields in revising Freud's theory and developing their own points of view.

Neo-psychoanalytic theories tend to be philosophical in their approach rather than scientific. These theories developed out of a clinical setting. The authors were physicians who developed their theoretical structures in the context of the therapeutic setting of treating patients. While their methods and results are frequently empirical, being based on observation, they could not be described as rigorous or precise scientific techniques. Moreover, neo-psychoanalytic theorists are critical of a narrow scientific experimental approach because it tends to be reductionistic and does not permit the finer nuances of the doctor-patient relationship and concepts based on it to emerge. They tend to consider proof a matter of the internal coherency or consistency of a theory and its ability to illumine the human condition. This "coherence theory of truth" is characteristic of the philosopher. The scientist, on the other hand, employs a "correspondence theory of truth," which asks whether or not a theory corresponds to what we can observe—the empirical evidence (Rychlak, 1973).

There are clear ethical themes in the writings of neo-psychoanalytic theorists. Illness is viewed as the failure to develop one's better side and to live by an appropriate ethic. Jung once suggested to a patient that his primary problem was a moral one. Adler believed that a faulty lifestyle developed out of the failure to cultivate one's social interest. Fromm spoke of a humanitarian conscience as inherent to a productive orientation. Horney considered the pursuit of self-knowledge a privilege and a responsibility. Thus, we could suggest that a commitment to or sympathy with one or more of these theories represents a commitment to or sympathy with the way of life espoused by the theory. To the degree to which one agrees with parts or all of a theorist's position, one tends to accept his or her philosophy. His or her view compels.

CHAPTER 4

Two Early Defectors: Jung and Adler

As we have seen, Freud developed a group of loyal disciples. Some of his followers eventually became dissatisfied with orthodox Freudian psychoanalysis, defected from the movement, and founded their own schools of thought. In this chapter, we shall consider two early defectors: Carl Jung and Alfred Adler. Actually, it would be unfair to consider Jung and Adler only as defectors from the psychoanalytic movement. Both men were mature scholars in their own right, with their own developing ideas, before they encountered Freud. While each was closely associated with Freud for a period of time, each went on to develop an independent theory of thought; and, as we shall see, each developed divergent patterns that contrast markedly with orthodox psychoanalysis and with each other. While each is indebted to Freud, Carl Jung and Alfred Adler have earned independent stature and recognition as personality theorists in their own right.

CARL JUNG: ANALYTICAL PSYCHOLOGY

Carl Gustav Jung was born in 1875 in Switzerland, where he lived all his life. He was the only surviving son of a poor country pastor and scholar of the Reformed church. Jung described his father as conventional and kind, but weak. He respected his father even though he had difficulty communicating with him, especially in matters of religion, which were of deep interest and concern to Jung throughout his life.

CARL JUNG

Skeptical of the orthodox faith in which he was reared, he searched relentlessly for adequate answers. This search is reflected in his psychology with its interest in religion, mythology, and the occult.

His mother was a more powerful person. Jung felt that she was a good mother, but she suffered from emotional disturbances. He was later to describe her as possessing two personalities. She alternated between being kind and loving and harsh and aloof. Jung's family constellation and ambivalent attitude toward his mother is echoed in his psychology, which emphasizes maternal images of woman as protector and destroyer rather than the paternal images of Freudian psychoanalysis.

Jung described his childhood as lonely and his personality as introverted. Two brothers had died in infancy before Jung was born and his sister did not arrive until he was nine. The young boy frequently played by himself, inventing games and carving a small companion out of wood to console himself. These long periods of solitude were later to find expression in his self-analysis. His psychology was also to reflect his predilection for being alone. Maturity for Jung is not defined in terms of interpersonal relations, as it is for Freud, but in terms of integration or balance within the self.

As a child, he not only had several close contacts and brushes with death, but he was also familiar with illness. When he was a young child his mother had to be hospitalized for several months, leaving him in the care of an elderly aunt and family maid. During his youth a series of fainting spells caused him to miss over six months of school. The boy enjoyed the consequent freedom from formal studies that his illness afforded him and the opportunity to explore other areas that interested him but were not in the traditional academic curriculum. However, shortly after he overheard his father's anguished comment to a friend, "What will become of the boy?" his health was restored and he resumed formal schooling. Later, he suggested that this experience taught him the meaning of a neurosis.

Jung originally wanted to be an archeologist, but due to financial circumstances he could only afford to attend the University of Basel, which did not offer courses in that area. Therefore, he chose to study medicine. He was planning to specialize in surgery when he came across a textbook by Krafft-Ebing, a German neurologist (1840–1902), that described psychiatry as invariably subjective. The description provoked Jung's interest. Here was a field that might provide the key to some of the dreams, mysteries, and obscure happenings that he had been trying to fathom.

His first professional appointment was as an assistant in a mental hospital in Zurich. Here he studied and worked with Eugen Bleuler, a well-known psychiatrist. Later, he became a lecturer at the University of Zurich. He established a private practice and developed a word-association test in order to study emotional reactions.

Carl Jung first met Sigmund Freud in 1907 after having corresponded with him about their mutual interest for a short period. The two men were highly impressed with each other and with each other's work. That meeting began an intense personal and professional relationship. For some time Freud regarded Jung as his heir apparent, and he looked on him with all of the affection that a father has for his son. When the International Psychoanalytic Society was founded, Jung, with Freud's endorsement, became its first president. The men traveled together to Clark University where both had been invited to lecture. Nevertheless, in 1913, Carl Jung broke away from Freud and his school. The break was "a great loss" for Freud and shattering for Jung, who entered a period of extensive inner disorientation in which he could not read or write, and which eventually led to his self-analysis. Many reasons underlaid the break with Freud. The most pronounced point of disagreement was Jung's rejection of Freud's emphasis on sexuality. Whereas for Freud all higher intellectual processes and emotionally significant experiences are ultimately substitutions for sexuality and can be understood thereby, for Jung sexuality itself must be seen as symbolic. Sexuality and the reality it represents has a mysterious quality and cannot be fully analyzed or completely depicted.

Thereafter, Jung developed his own school of thought, which eventually came to be known as *analytical psychology*. He wrote extensively and his highly original theories were informed by a vast array of concerns including Eastern religions, mythology, and alchemy. Although such subjects are frequently considered to be scientifically suspect, Jung felt that they were essential to the psychologist and indispensable in understanding the mysterious forces of the unconscious. He died in 1961 at the age of eighty-five after a long and fruitful life.

The Nature and Structure of Personality

Whereas Freud described the structure of personality in terms of three forces that are in perpetual conflict—the id, the ego, and the superego—Carl Jung conceived of the structure of personality as a complex network of interacting systems that strive toward eventual harmony. The primary ones are: the *ego*, the *personal unconscious* with its *complexes*; and the *collective unconscious* and its *archetypes*. Jung also talked about two primary attitudes and four basic functions, which together constitute separate but related aspects of the *psyche* or total personality.

The *psyche*, or total personality, refers to all psychological processes: thoughts, feelings, sensations, wishes, and so forth. Jung used the terms *psyche* and *psychic*, rather than "mind" and "mental," to avoid the connotation of the latter with consciousness and to emphasize that the psyche embraces both conscious and unconscious processes.

Jung and Freud differed in their approaches to the unconscious. Freud tended to emphasize a view of the unconscious as essentially materials that have been repressed, whereas Jung emphasized a concept of the unconscious as the source of consciousness and the matrix of new possibilities of life.

The Ego Jung's concept of the ego likewise differed from Freud's. For Freud, the ego was ideally the executor of the personality. While Freud initially thought that the ego was primarily conscious, he belatedly realized that a large portion of the ego was unconscious and beyond conscious control or awareness. Still, for the mature, healthy adult, the ego is the center of the personality.

Jung's concept of the ego is quite different. For Jung, the ego is equivalent to one's conscious perception of self. Thus, Jung suggests that the ego is responsible for our feelings of identity and continuity. It is through our conscious awareness of our feelings that we establish a sense of self. The ego, however, is not the true center of personality for Jung. This runs counter to our everyday point of view in which the ego is generally taken to be the center of personality. Most of us identify ourselves or our center as that awareness or consciousness that we have of ourselves. For Jung, as we shall shortly see, the true center of personality is located elsewhere. Jung compares the conscious aspect of the psyche to an island that rises from the sea. We notice only the part above water, even though a much greater land mass lies below, which can be compared to the unconscious (Fordham, 1953).

FIGURE 4.1 Jung's Concept of the Unconscious

The Jungian notion is that each individual ego is an island, joined to others by the collective unconscious.

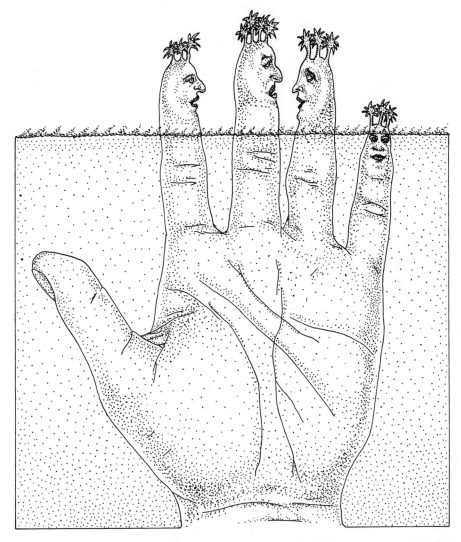

Redrawn from *Psychology Today* Magazine. Copyright © 1976 Ziff-Davis Publishing Company.

The Personal Unconscious The region immediately adjacent to the ego is termed the *personal unconscious*. It is a land that is not always covered by sea and, thus, can be reclaimed. Here those contents that have been put aside (for our consciousness can only hold a few items at a time) reside and may be easily retrieved. The personal unconscious also includes those experiences of an individual's life history that have been repressed or forgotten. This is an aspect of the unconscious that, as we have seen, Freud also emphasized. These forgotten experiences are accessible to consciousness even though becoming aware of some of them may be an arduous process.

Experiences are grouped in the personal unconscious into clusters containing a certain theme. These clusters Jung refers to as complexes. A *complex* is an organized group of thoughts, feelings, and memories about a particular concept (1934). A complex may be organized around a particular person or object. One of Jung's examples is a complex concerning motherhood (1954a). One's mother complex refers to the cluster of ideas, feelings, and memories that have arisen from our own particular experience of having been mothered. It also draws into it other experiences of mothering to which we have been exposed. Each new instance of mothering that we encounter is drawn into our mother complex, and understood and interpreted by it. For example, my associations to motherhood pertained first and foremost to my own mother; later, they included other instances of mothering that I may have seen or read. This concept of mothering deeply and individually affects my understanding of what it means to be mothered and to mother. As you can see, Jung's concept is very far removed from the everyday definition of a "mother complex" as the inability to disengage oneself from one's mother's apron strings.

Jung described a man who believed that he was suffering from a real cancer, even though he knew that his cancer was imaginary. The complex, Jung wrote, is "a spontaneous growth, originating in that part of the psyche which is not identical with consciousness. It appears to be an autonomous development intruding upon consciousness" (1938). A complex may act like an independent person, behaving autonomously of our conscious self and intentions.

A complex is said to have a constellating power, which means that the complex has the ability to draw new ideas into it and interpret them accordingly. It can be compared to a magnet that attracts related experiences. The more drawing power a complex has, the more powerful it may become. A complex may be conscious, partly conscious, or unconscious. Certain elements of it may extend into the collective unconscious. Some complexes appear to dominate an entire personality. Hitler is frequently described as being driven by inner forces to obtain power.

The Collective Unconscious Whereas the personal unconscious is unique for each individual, the *collective unconscious* is shared. Jung referred to the collective unconscious as "transpersonal"; that is to say, it extends across persons. It consists of certain potentialities, potential ways of being, that we all share because we are human beings (1936). Jung sometimes referred to the collective unconscious as the psychic residue of human evolutionary development. Essentially, he said that all people, because they are human beings, share common characteristics.

All human cultures, regardless of their distinctness and diversity, share certain things in common: all human beings live in groups and develop some form of family life or society in which roles are assigned for various members. These roles may vary from society to society, but all human groups assign them. All human beings share certain emotions such as joy, grief, or anger. The conventions for feeling or expressing these emotions may vary, but the emotions themselves are shared. All human beings develop some form of language and symbolization. While the particular words may vary, the concepts and symbols are commonly shared. Thus, certain symbols reappear again and again from society to society, and they may be seen to have a common meaning. One such symbol, Jung suggested, is the *mandala* (1955a), a concentrically arranged figure, such as the circle, the wheel, or the cross, which Jung saw appearing again and again in his patients' dreams and in the artwork of all peoples in all cultures. He suggested that the mandala represents the self striving toward wholeness. The collective unconscious, then, consists of predispositions or possibilities of behaving in certain ways because we are human.

Within the collective unconscious, lie the archetypes. An *archetype* is a universal thought form or predisposition to perceive the world in certain ways (1936). The word "predisposition" is crucial to Jung's concept of the collective unconscious and its archetypes. It emphasizes potentialities, for the archetypes represent different potential ways in which we may express our humanness. The archetypes can never be fully known or described. They appear to us in personified or symbolized pictorial form. The archetypes may penetrate into consciousness by means of myths, dreams, art, ritual, and symptoms. Insofar as they represent the total latent potentiality of the psyche, it is helpful for us to get in touch with them. In doing so, we go beyond developing our individual potentialities and become incorporated in the eternal cosmic process. Jung described several archetypes. The list below is by no means exhaustive, but it will serve to introduce some of Jung's most widely recognized and discussed archetypes.

The Persona The *persona* refers to the social role that one is assigned by society and one's understanding of it. The term comes from the Latin word *persona*, which we have seen refers to the masks that actors wore in ancient Greek dramas. Thus, one's persona is the mask that one wears in order to fulfill the demands of society. Each one of us, as we have seen, is assigned particular roles by our society. I am assigned roles as wife, mother, and professor. The persona represents a compromise between one's true self and the society as to what one should appear to be. To neglect the development of a persona is to run the risk of becoming asocial and gauche. On the other hand, if one identifies too completely with one's persona, one may play the role at the expense of his or her true self.

The Shadow The *shadow* encompasses those unsocial thoughts, feelings, and behaviors that we potentially possess. It is the opposite side of the persona, in that it refers to those desires and emotions that are incompatible with our social standards and ideal personality. It could be described as the devil within. Jung's choice of the word "shadow" is deliberate and designed to emphasize its necessity. There can be no sun that does not leave a shadow. The shadow cannot be avoided and one is incomplete without it. Jung agreed with Freud that such base and unsocial impulses may be sublimated and channeled to good ends. To neglect or try to deny the shadow involves us in hypocrisy and deceit. Angels are not suited for existence on earth. Jung suggested a need to come to know our baser side and recognize our animalistic impulses. To do so adds dimension and credibility to personality as well as increased zest and vitality for life.

The Anima and Animus Each one of us has assigned to us a sex gender, male or female, based on our overt sexual characteristics. Yet none of us is purely male or purely female. Each of us has qualities of the opposite sex in terms of biology and also in terms of psychological attitudes and feelings. Thus, the *anima* archetype is the feminine side of the male psyche and the *animus* archetype is the masculine side of the female psyche. The anima and the animus are precipitates of collective and individual human experience throughout the ages pertaining to the opposite sex. They assist in enabling us to relate to and understand the complementary sex. For Jung, there was a distinct difference between the psychology of men and women. Jung believed that it was important that one express these opposite-sex characteristics in order to avoid an unbalanced or one-sided personality. If one exhibits only the traits of his or her assigned sex, the other traits remain unconscious, undeveloped, and primitive. Those of us who have difficulty in understanding the opposite sex probably are not in tune with our anima and animus.

The Self The central archetype in Jung's understanding is that of the self. The *self* represents the striving for unity of all parts of the personality. It is the organizing principle of the psyche, which draws unto itself and harmonizes all the archetypes and their expressions in complexes and consciousness. The self, rather than the ego, is the true midpoint of personality. Thus, the true center of one's personality is not to be found in rational ego consciousness. Freud had already begun to discover this truth, but he wanted to rescue human beings from irrationality and so he made ego consciousness central. For Jung, the true self lay on the boundary between conscious and unconscious, reason and unreason. The development of the self is life's goal, but the self archetype cannot begin to emerge until the other personality systems have been fully developed. Thus, it usually does not become evident until one has reached middle age. Jung spoke of the realization of the self as a goal that lies in the future. It is something to be striven for but rarely achieved.

Other Archetypes Jung described numerous other archetypes of the collective unconscious. Some of these are birth, death, rebirth, power, magic, the child, the hero, God, the demon, the earth mother, and the wise old man. The point is that one cannot deny or destroy these archetypes. If one tries to, for example, if one says that God is dead, the archetype will reappear in an unlikely place, because the archetypes cannot be destroyed. God will simply change into something else that will evoke human worship. Therefore, it is helpful for us to get in touch with the archetypes, as they represent our latent and inevitable personality.

EXERCISE:

Active Imagination

Jung developed methods for getting in touch with the archetypes. One of these methods is active imagination. *You are invited to imagine your shadow, anima, animus, or one of the situations reflected in the archetypes, such as birth or death. Place yourself in a comfortable position, relax, and close your eyes. Then, begin to fantasize a scene involving the relevant archetype. You might imagine what the fantasized archetype would say to you and enter into a dialogue with it. If a scene becomes too difficult or produces anxiety, you should discontinue it. Such archetypal fantasies may assist in providing insight and intuitions about the relevance of Jung's concepts for the self.*

Because the archetypes also appear in dreams in the form of people, animals, or symbols, you may try to understand them by placing yourself in the role of one of the figures in your dreams. Here you speak as if you were that dream individual or object. You describe yourself, indicate what you wanted to express in the dream, and relate to other figures in the dream. Remember that every person, object, or event in a dream is a product of your own creation and thus has to do with you. Therefore, by acting out the part of a dream image, you may come to understand it more fully. In your imagination, you can relive a dream or complete one that was unfinished. You can even go back and change the ending of a dream. Such creative fantasy can be a powerful force, Jung pointed out, just as slaying dragons in one's imagination may be preparatory to slaying them in real life. Such fantasies may assist you in learning to cope with threatening situations.

Many of us today are concerned with liberating ourselves from the traditional male and female sex roles. In this connection, exploration of

*our opposite-sex archetypes, the anima and animus, through the tech-
nique of active imagination, can be particularly valuable for us. Historically, the male has been associated with aggressiveness, analytic and
instrumental thought, emotional control, and self-concern; while the
female has been identified with passivity, intuitive and expressive
thought, emotionality, and concern for others. According to Jung, each
of us shares the components of our sexual opposite. If we do not get in
touch with the other side of our personality, we run the risk of being
lopsided and missing a valuable dimension of our experience. Failure
to comprehend the anima or animus makes it difficult for us to understand and communicate with our opposite-sex counterparts. Furthermore, the opposite-sex characteristics, if unconscious, may unexpectedly
seize and possess us. An anima-possessed male is nagging, stubborn,
or moody; an animus-possessed female is overdominant and demanding.
Getting in touch with the anima or animus entails permitting oneself to
feel and experience the opposite-sex characteristics. For a man, this
means permitting himself to feel vulnerable and hurt and to cry. For
a woman, it entails feeling and expressing her aggression. Taking note
of the anima and animus as they appear in our dreams and letting them
speak to us helps to foster the opposite sex role. In dreams, the anima
variously appears as a virgin, a mother, or a witch. The animus often
takes the appearance of a Prince Charming, a savior, or a sorcerer.
These polarities reveal how we often tend to think of the opposite sex
as either good or evil. Realistically, it is neither, though, also, it is
both. Our perception of the anima and the animus changes as we begin
to notice them and feel their influence in our lives.*

The Attitudes Jung referred to two basic attitudes or psychotypes
(1933a). The *introverted* attitude is one of withdrawal, in which the
psyche is oriented inward toward the subjective world. The *extroverted*
stance is one of expansion, in which the psyche is oriented outward
toward the external, objective world. These words have become so commonplace in today's vocabulary that most of us readily identify ourselves as introverted or extroverted. Jung labeled himself an introvert
and Freud an extrovert. Yet this labeling refers simply to the dominant
or more developed attitude. The conscious extrovert is an introvert in
his or her unconscious and vice versa.

The Functions Equally important to Jung's typology are the four
functions (1933b). *Functions* are ways of perceiving the environment
and orienting experiences. The function of *sensation* refers to sense
perception of the world. *Thinking* entails giving meaning and understanding to the world. The function of *feeling* involves weighing, valuing, and judging the world. Lastly, *intuition*, perception via the unconscious, informs us of the atmosphere surrounding experience and future
possibilities. These functions group themselves into opposite pairs.

Thinking and feeling are said to be rational functions because they both require acts of judgment. Sensation and intuition involve immediate experiences. Jung suggested that one of these functions tends to be dominant or superior in each individual and its opposite weaker and inferior. A professor, for example, may have so cultivated his intellectual and cognitive powers that the feeling and intuitive aspects of his personality are submerged. While primitive and undeveloped, they may nevertheless invade his life in the form of strange moods, symptoms, or projections. A synthesis of the four functions is required for an actualized self.

In developing his concept of the collective unconscious, Carl Jung believed that he was making a unique, unprecedented contribution to depth psychology. He pointed out that Freud's concept of unconscious forces was limited to the concept of the personal unconscious—experiences that have been repressed or forgotten. Yet Freud disclaimed Jung's plea for originality, stating that he had known all along that the unconscious is collective. And, of course, there are certain archetypal patterns in Freud's understanding of the unconscious. The psychosexual stages involve predispositions toward acting out the human drama in certain ways. The Oedipal situation that we all experience is a collective archetypal myth. Symbols in dreams may be unique to the individual, but also shared. Thus, a concept of collected unconscious forces is implied in Freud's theory although certainly not clearly articulated. And whereas Freud emphasized the unique unfolding of unconscious forces in the individual's life history and personal unconscious (thus, it is not enough to know that one has gone through the Oedipal situation, one must fully experience its particular unfolding within one's distinct family constellation), Jung emphasized the shared and collective aspects.

Psychic Energy

For Freud, the dynamics of personality consists of libido, the sexual drive. People are motivated by eros. Jung also uses "libido" to refer to psychic energy, but his use is not to be confused with Freud's definition of libido. Jung uses the term in a more generalized fashion as an undifferentiated life energy (1948b). *Libido* refers to an appetite that may refer to sexuality and to other hungers as well. It reflects itself as striving, desiring, and willing. Psychic energy operates according to the principles of equivalence and entropy, which is to say that it seeks a balance and moves the person forward in a process of self-actualization.

Although Jung does not reject an instinctual basis of personality, he criticizes Freud's emphasis on sexuality, suggesting that it is ultimately reductionistic, or simplistic, as it reduces any and all activities to sexual ones. Jung's point is that sexuality itself must be seen as symbolic, having a mysterious quality of otherness that cannot be fully circumscribed and described.

Self-actualization

Jung did not clearly outline stages in the development of personality as Freud did in his concept of psychosexual stages. He suggested that the self is in the process of self-actualization.

Although the concept of *self-actualization* was fully expounded by Jung, it cannot be said to be new with his thought. The origin of the principle takes us back to the Greek philosopher Aristotle (384–322 B.C.). Aristotle held that everything has a *telos*, a purpose or goal, that constitutes its essence and indicates its potentiality. Thus, every acorn has the essence of treeness and the potential to become a mighty oak. In the same way, each one of us has the potential to develop into a self, that is, to actualize, fulfill, and enhance our maximum potentialities. This viewpoint is essentially *teleological*, or purposeful. It explains the present in terms of the future with reference to a goal that guides and directs our destiny. Whereas Freud's view was primarily a causal one, comprehending personality in terms of antecedent conditions of the past, Jung maintained that both causality and teleology are necessary for a full understanding of personality.

While development is largely forward moving, regression may occur under conditions of frustration. Such regression is not viewed negatively by Jung. Rather, it may, in the end, facilitate the forward movement of progression. By exploring the unconscious, both personal and collective, the ego may learn from past experiences and resolve the problem that led to the regression. Whereas for Freud a neurosis represents the return of the repressed, for Jung it is the insistence of the undeveloped part of the personality on being heard and realized.

Self-actualization entails individuation and transcendence (1916, 1939). In *individuation*, the systems of the individual psyche achieve their fullest degree of differentiation, expression, and development. *Transcendence* refers to integration of the diverse systems of the self toward the goal of wholeness and identity with all of humanity. Jung's concepts of individuation and transcendence are difficult for the average Westerner to understand. In Western psychology, we generally think of personality as referring to an individual's uniqueness. We suggest that personality is what makes one individual different from all other people. People who do not appear to be unique are often said to "lack personality." Jung suggests that this aspect, individuation, is a lower level of total personality development. He believes that, following individuation, we need to experience transcendence. In the process of transcendence, a deeper self or essence emerges that unites a person with all of humanity and the universe at large.

Thus, as the self actualizes, a process that begins to occur only late in life and that is never fully completed, it perpetually rises above itself to a greater enhancement, fulfillment, and realization of itself and humanity. If we view the psyche as a wheel, the hub of which is the archetype of the self, we can suggest that the true self emerges when

FIGURE 4.2 The Coincidence of Opposites

If we were to view the psyche as a wheel, the hub of which is the archetype of the self, the true self emerges when the opposites coincide. The resulting image is, of course, a mandala.

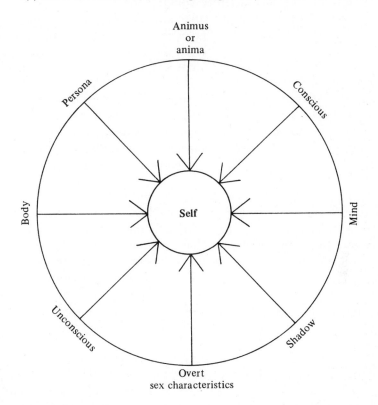

the opposites coincide. The true person does not consist of the conscious or unconscious, mind or body, persona or shadow, overt sexual characteristics or complements, but of all of these. This coincidence of opposites is the ultimate goal of personality development in the Jungian view. Whereas for Freud, the person is inescapably in conflict, for Jung, the person ultimately seeks harmony.

Jungian Psychotherapy

Neurosis is viewed by Jung as a person's attempt to reconcile the contradictory aspects of his or her personality. One side of the psyche, such as the conscious, adaptive, social self, may be exaggerated at the expense of the darker, unconscious aspects of the personality of the individual.

It is difficult to describe Jung's method of psychotherapy specifically as he did not clearly outline his procedures as Freud did. Further, Jung maintained that no one approach is suitable for everyone. The individual who has had difficulty in accepting the sexual and aggressive aspects of his or her life may well require a Freudian interpretation. But for others, or at different stages in development, the Freudian understanding may be insufficiently comprehensive.

In classical Freudian psychoanalysis, the analyst remains detached and reveals little of his or her personal feelings and reactions in order to facilitate the transference, whereas the Jungian analyst enters into a personal relationship with the patient and is ready to throw his or her entire personality into the work. Therapy is a "dialectical procedure," a dialogue between doctor and patient, conscious and unconscious. While the couch may be used to facilitate procedures such as active imagination, for the most part analyst and patient sit facing each other. The Jungian also sees patients far less frequently than the Freudian analyst. The frequency of visits depends on the stage that the patient has reached.

During the early stages of treatment, there is a need for *confession*. Such confession is generally accompanied by emotional release and is viewed by Jung as the aim of the cathartic method originated by Breuer and Freud. But Jung points out that emotional release, in itself, is not therapeutic any more than temper tantrums or other emotional outbursts are curative in and of themselves. For Freud, conscious intellectual understanding and insight renders the catharsis effective. Jung emphasizes that the presence of the other, the therapist, who supports the patient morally and spiritually as well as intellectually, makes the confession curative.

Projection and transference play an important role in Jungian analysis, though Jung added to Freud's concept of transference the recognition that not only significant persons from the patient's past are projected onto the analyst but also archetypal figures. Jung also viewed the sexual components of the transference as symbolic efforts on the patient's part to reach a higher integration of personality. In contrast to Freud, Jung did not think that transference was a necessary precondition for therapy to occur.

Jung's attitude toward dreams differs from that of Freud. Whereas Freud treated dreams as the expression of unconscious wishes, Jung understood dreams as having a prospective function as well as a retrospective one. By *prospective* function Jung meant that the dream represents an effort by the person to prepare for future events. Dreams also have a *compensatory* function; they are efforts to complement the patient's conscious side and speak for the unconscious. Thus, dreams speak to us of the future, revealing those aspects of our personality that we have tended to ignore and need to stress further in our movement toward wholeness.

In interpreting dreams, Jung uses the *method of amplification* (1951) rather than the method of free association. In free association, each dream element is the starting place for a chain of association that may lead far afield from the original element. In amplification, one focuses repeatedly on the element and gives multiple associations to it. The dream is taken exactly as it is with no precise effort to distinguish between manifest and latent contents. The therapist joins the patient in efforts to unfold the dream's meaning, adding personal associations and frequently referring to mythology, fairy tales, and the like in order to extend the dream's meaning. Whereas Freud tended to deal with dreams singly, Jung uses a series of dreams that the patient might report. By analyzing a series of dreams the inner life of the patient unfolds, which is taken as a guide to true-life meanings for the patient.

As a therapist, Jung also values the use of active imagination as a means of facilitating self-understanding and the use of artistic production by the patient. He encourages his patients to draw, sculpt, paint, or develop some other art form as a means of listening to their inner depths. In all of this, obedience to the unfolding inner life is emphasized and encouraged as the appropriate, ethical fulfillment of one's humanity.

EXERCISE:

The Mandalas in Your Life

Mandala *is a Sanskrit word that means "magic circle." The mandala is one of the oldest religious symbols and is found throughout the world. A mandala is usually circular in appearance, but at times it appears in the form of a square or a squared circle and contains other geometric forms. The earliest known form of mandala was the sun wheel. Throughout the East, the mandala is a common symbol that stands for wholeness and unity and is used as an aid in meditation. The yin and yang symbol of Chinese Taoism is clearly a mandala because of its circular form. In the West, mandalas appear in the four-sided cross, symbols of the Trinity, and in stained glass patterns of Gothic cathedral rose windows. Nature itself has provided us with many mandalas, such as the atom and the snowflake.*

It is interesting that Jung found the mandala symbol occurring spontaneously in the dreams and images of his patients. He believed that the mandala is an archetypal symbol of wholeness than can aid us in integrating our personality. Practically all of us doodle. Take a few minutes to look at your doodles to see if you can identify any mandala in them. If you can, you have confirmed Jung's position that the mandala is a spontaneous symbol of expression shared by all humankind. Jung also believed that it is useful for a person to try to create his or her own mandalas. Simply draw a circle, a square, or a combined figure, and complete it in a manner that expresses your feelings and interests at the moment. Studying the mandalas that we draw and noticing subsequent changes that we make over a period of time can give us insight into our personality.

FIGURE 4.3 Mandalas

Mandalas appear in the symbolism of the East and West, in nature, and in our doodles.

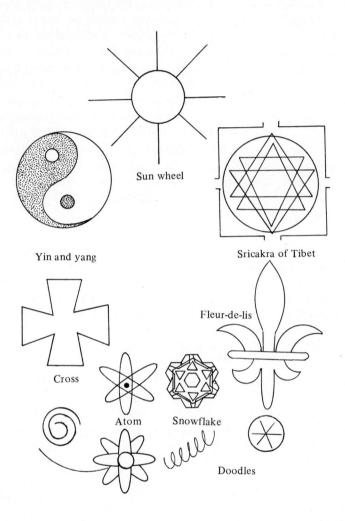

Sun wheel

Yin and yang

Sricakra of Tibet

Fleur-de-lis

Cross

Atom

Snowflake

Doodles

Jung believed that our art forms are important ways by which we synthesize conscious and unconscious forces. Our drawings, paintings, and other creative activities reflect aspects of our unconscious selves. Such art forms are not to be judged in terms of aesthetics, but understood as attempts at self-expression. If you are interested in exploring yourself through the medium of art, first draw, paint, or make some other effort at creative expression. Then try to explain what your creation means to you intellectually and emotionally. Take note of your self-discoveries. Develop a series of creative works and reflect on them in order to notice the changes that occur.

Jung's emphasis on wholeness and integration was not always easy for his patients to appreciate. Those who came seeking comfort found something else: Jung's insistence that they integrate the suffering into their lives. One patient reported that she dreamed she was commanded to descend into "a pot filled with hot stuff." She immersed herself to the shoulders, but Jung came and pushed her deep into it, commenting, "Not out but through!" (Hull, 1971).

Just as Jung recognizes that no one method of therapy is appropriate for everyone, he also realizes that the goals of therapy differ for different individuals at different points in their lives. Self-actualization is a goal that is fully realized by very few. Most of us settle for some lesser sort of balance. Perhaps this is rightly so, as trying to come to terms with the darkest side of our psyches may place us in severe jeopardy and risk that can be genuinely overwhelming. Thus, the quest into the collective unconscious is not always wise or timely. The therapist must carefully consider the situation and the patient. Usually the first half of life is devoted to development of one's adaptive self, the ego and the persona. Only in the second half of life, when outward adjustment is no longer a problem, does it become possible to conduct the kind of inward quest about which Jung finally speaks. Thus, the specifically Jungian mode of interpretation is particularly relevant to those patients who are in the second half of life. A majority of Jung's patients, particularly in his later years, fell into that category.

Evaluation and Implications

Psychology, as we have seen, may be conducted as science or as philosophy. Throughout much of its recent history, particularly in America, psychology has tried to be a laboratory science like physics or physiology. Psychologists try to understand psychological phenomena and human behavior by conducting experiments under controlled laboratory conditions. They try to develop theories, general laws of behavior that can function usefully as science.

Jung's concepts are particularly difficult to study in the laboratory. As with Freud, it is virtually impossible to define operationally many of his terms or to develop a crucial test that would serve to disprove them. Further, Jung's interest in the occult has led many critics to dismiss him as a mystic.

Many of Jung's discoveries were, as were those of Freud, made in the clinical setting. These were empirical observations of his patients in the course of treatment and research. He also obtained information from sources outside the treatment room. Observations of other cultures, studies of comparative religion and mythology, symbolism, alchemy, and the occult afforded him a wealth of information. Jung considered these sources secondary but legitimate. His stance was not that of a believer but that of a psychologist seeking to illumine the mysteries of the human psyche. He considered the comparative method of study, such as that used in history and anthropology, a valuable approach for science.

Although Jung spoke frequently of God, he bracketed the question of God's factitiousness. Whether or not God exists is not a question that Jung tried to answer. That which has no effect on us might as well not exist. Analytical psychology posits the existence of the archetypal God image—not God. Insofar as the archetype of God has a demonstrably clear effect on us, God is a psychic fact and a useful concept in our psychology.

Jung did not believe that the psychologist should be bound to an experimental scientific approach. In introducing his concept of teleology, he criticized the current scientific atmosphere for limiting its concepts to those of causality. After all, he pointed out, the concepts of cause and goal are not themselves found in nature, they are imaginary constructs imposed by the scientist. Jung urged a broader scope and conceptual design for the scientist. However, his suggestions have generally been rebuffed, and scientific psychology has until recently ignored Jung's analytical psychology. Nevertheless, Jung has indirectly influenced developments in psychology. The concept of self-actualization, which is clearly teleological, is echoed in the theories of Rogers, Allport, and Maslow.

Jung indicated that he was more interested in discovering facts than in developing a system of personality. He held that the theories he did develop were based on empirical data. At the same time, Jung also raised philosophical questions and suggested philosophical answers. To suggest that questions about human nature should be answered empirically is itself a philosophical position. Fundamentally, the Jungian quest may be viewed as a philosophical or religious one. For Jung, the fundamental power of self-understanding and cure stem from an appropriate Weltanschauung or philosophy of life. Even more, attuning oneself to one's unconscious forces is a religious experience entailing acceptance of God. To be sure, the God that is accepted may not be the traditional deity of theism; rather, it is an indwelling god, a natural spirit within the universal psyche of man. While Jung has been largely ignored by experimentally oriented psychologists, theologians have found his work very fruitful. His concept of God as revealing himself through the collective unconscious is particularly attractive to theologians who seek a more relevant articulation of traditional theistic concepts.

In recent years, the *Annual Review of Psychology* has reported a resurgence of interest in Jung's thought. Jung's emphases on inborn qualities, the duality of human nature, symbolism, and the importance of inner experiences, factors that at one time led psychologists to neglect his work, are now seen as important, if not indispensable, for understanding personality.

Jung's comments about the anima and the animus lead quite naturally to the concept of an androgynous ideal. *Androgyny* refers to the presence of both masculine and feminine qualities in an individual and the ability to realize both potentialities. At present, increased research is being done in the area of androgyny as a possible mode of viewing human nature and of offering increased liberation for both men and women (see Kaplan and Bean, 1976).

Jung's ideas have also appealed to those who are discontent with Western society and its modes of exploration and who seek to expand their self-understanding by studying Eastern thought with its emphasis on introspection and experience. Jung's thinking complements the recent interest in the East.

ALFRED ADLER: INDIVIDUAL PSYCHOLOGY

Alfred Adler, second of six children born to a successful merchant, was born in 1870 and raised in a suburb of Vienna. He described his childhood as difficult and unhappy. He suffered from rickets, a deficiency disease of childhood that affects the bones and made him clumsy and awkward. Initially, his parents pampered him, but when his younger brother was born he sensed that his mother transferred her attention

ALFRED ADLER

to him. He felt dethroned and turned to his father who favored and expected great things from him.

When he was three, he saw his younger brother die in the next bed. Twice during his early childhood Adler was run over in the streets. His fear of death was further increased by a bout with pneumonia that he experienced at the age of four. Later, he traced his interest in becoming a doctor to that near-fatal illness.

At school he was only an average student. Indeed, at one point his teacher suggested that his father take him out of school and apprentice him to a shoemaker. Nevertheless, he rose to a superior position in school, especially in mathematics, which he originally had had the greatest difficulty in mastering. In spite of his physical handicaps, he developed courage, social interest, and a feeling of being accepted in his play with other children. He was to carry an interest in and joy in being in the company of others throughout his life.

His weak physique and inferior feelings during childhood were later to find expression in his concepts of organic inferiority and the striving for superiority. His sensitivity toward being the second son was reflected in his interest in the family constellation and ordinal position of birth. His efforts to get along with others found expression in his later conviction that the human being is a social animal and in the Adlerian concept of social interest.

Adler studied medicine at the University of Vienna, where Freud had received his medical training. Although he trained as an eye specialist, he became a general practitioner and later established himself as a practicing neurologist and psychiatrist. In 1902 he was invited by Freud to join a group of weekly discussions on psychoanalysis. This group eventually grew into the Vienna Psychoanalytic Society, of which Adler was the first president, and later, the International Psychoanalytic Association.

There are many stories concerning Adler's association with Freud and their subsequent split. Adler was never a student of Freud's nor was he ever psychoanalyzed. He joined the discussions because he was interested in psychoanalysis, but from the beginning, he discovered points of disagreement. By 1911 these differences appeared crucial. Adler was invited to state his position to the society, which he did, but since his views were denounced, he resigned and about one-third of the members left with him.

Adler founded his own group and attracted many followers. He served in the Austrian army during World War I. Afterwards he assisted the government in establishing child guidance clinics in Vienna. Although he and Freud both practiced in Vienna during the 1920s and early 1930s, they did not associate with each other.

Adler visited the United States frequently and came here to live in 1935 to escape the Nazi regime. He continued his private practice, accepted a position of professor of medical psychology at the Long Island

College of Medicine, and lectured widely. He died suddenly in 1937 of a heart attack while on a lecture tour in Scotland; he was sixty-seven.

From the beginning, Adler's theory of personality was open to growth and evolution. While he never contradicted his earlier ideas, his theory became more comprehensive and inclusive as his work matured. Adler chose the term *individual psychology* for his conception of personality because he was interested in investigating the uniqueness of personality. Nevertheless, he realized early in his theorizing that the individual could not be considered in isolation or apart from the whole situation. His emphasis shifted from a stress on *intrapsychic* ("within the psyche") phenomena such as were found in Freud to an appreciation of *interpsychic* ("interpersonal") relations. Adler's theory culminated and found its ultimate expression in his insistence that understanding a particular individual entails comprehending his or her attitude in relation to the world. Thus, for Adler, the human person emerged as primarily a social creature rather than a sexual creature. According to Adler, we are motivated by social interests and our primary life problems are social ones.

Social Interest

A leading concept of Adler's individual psychology is his emphasis on the importance of human society. Human society is crucial not simply for the development of an individual personality, but also for the orientation of each and every behavior and emotion in a person's life.

Human beings, as all living creatures, are driven by certain innate instincts, drives, or needs. All living organisms feel an impulse to maintain life, which causes them to seek food and sustenance. They have a compulsion to propagate the species, which finds its expression in sex. While much of the behavior of lower animals appears to be regulated by instincts, this is not true of human behavior. Human beings have tamed their instincts and subordinated them to their attitudes toward the environment. At times, human beings deny or disobey their natural instincts because of their social relations. A prisoner may die rather than betray his country. A young child may refuse food if she believes that such a tactic puts her at the best advantage in a power struggle with her parents. A young woman may renounce her sexual desires if she believes it is in her best social interest to do so.

This shaping of instinctual expression in terms of one's attitude toward the environment suggests that underlying all other instincts and needs is the innate characteristic of social interest (1939). *Social interest* refers to that urge in human nature to adapt oneself to the conditions of the environment. Social interest expresses itself subjectively in one's consciousness of having something in common with other people and of being one of them. It expresses itself objectively in cooperation with others toward the betterment of human society. This innate social characteristic, while common to all, is not automatic, nor does it invariably find constructive expression. It must be nurtured and cultivated if the individual is to achieve adequate fulfillment of the complex demands of his or her society and work toward its perfection.

Finalism

The personality and characteristics of an individual are developed by the attitudes that he or she adopts toward his or her social environment in early childhood. This occurs and is made possible through the goal-oriented activity of the human psyche. Adler stresses the fact that the movement of all living things is governed by goals. We cannot think, feel, will, or act, except with the perception of some goal (1927). To try to understand human behavior in terms of external causes is to fail to understand psychic phenomena, because psychic phenomena can only be comprehended when regarded in terms of a goal. If I know a person's goal, I begin to understand in a general way what is happening. It is this focus on ultimate goals that permits us to understand and recognize the unity of the human personality. Once a person's goal has been recognized, it is possible to see how the movements and behavior of that individual fall into line with both the goal and the plans that he or she has evolved for achieving the goal.

When an individual behaves in a certain way we naturally ask why. Past efforts to answer that question emphasized material and mechanical explanations. Sigmund Freud showed us that in answering this question it is not enough to look for physiological causes, we must also try to understand the psychological motives underlying behavioral events. However, Freud was misled by the principle of causality into regarding these motives as past and looking to the past for the explanation of all human behavior. Adler emphasized the purposefulness of human behavior by recognizing that the motivational force of every human action is the goal or future orientation of that action. This means that for Adler the human psyche is teleologically oriented. We will recall from our discussion of Jung that the term *telos* means a purpose or goal. Adler agreed with Jung that teleology is necessary for a full understanding of personality. For Adler, the goal that the individual pursues was the decisive factor. Adler referred to this concept of goal orientation as the principle of *finalism* (1930).

Adler suggested that many of our guiding goals are fictions. His use of the term "fiction" is puzzling, because the point is not that a fiction is false. Adler indicates that we cannot know whether or not our goals are true or false because there is no way in which we can scientifically test them. The term *fiction* comes from the Latin root *fictio*, which means "to invent," "fashion," or "construct." We are unable to have a complete understanding of things as they really are, so we structure our own idea of reality. "Fictions" are the individual's or group's cognitive construct or subjective interpretations of the events of the world. They are philosophical assumptions. We assume that it is best to tell the truth, that all people are basically good, or that hard work will eventually pay off. In Adlerian vocabulary, such basic concepts or philosophical ideas are *fictional finalisms*. Adler was indebted to an earlier philosopher, Hans Vaihinger, for his concept of fictional finalisms. Vaihinger wrote a book, *The Philosophy of "As-if,"* in which he suggested that people create ideas that guide their behavior. Fictional finalisms cannot be tested against reality, because they are not scientific hypotheses that can be put to a crucial experiment. They are constructs or inventions of the human psyche that arise out of its encounter with the world. Under the influence of a fiction, people behave "as if" their goals were true. If people believe that it is to their best advantage to be honest, they will strive to be so, even though there is no way in which they can ultimately test that belief as a hypothesis. It is important to note that psychologists also often pose fictional finalisms in their discussion of the good life. Concepts such as the "healthy personality" and "self-actualization" function as fictional finalisms and cannot be empirically tested.

A fiction may be healthy or unhealthy. Adler's point here is that it is inappropriate to judge a fiction as true or false, right or wrong; rather, the goal should be judged according to its usefulness. Adler's concept of the *usefulness* of fictional finalisms should not be confused with the concept of usefulness as it is employed in reference to scientific hypotheses, which was discussed in the introductory chapter. For Adler, a goal is useful if it fosters productive living and enhances our lives. The scientific hypothesis is useful if it can generate predictions about experiences that we might observe. Adler's point is that while fictions do not have any counterpart in reality, they do vary in terms of their usefulness: some goals foster productive living while others are harmful and hinder adjustment. Belief in a deity and the desire to serve him has shown itself to be a valuable fiction for many individuals. For others, however, belief in God and the desire to please him has had deleterious effects. Whether or not God really exists is beside the point; the point is that belief in God has a demonstrable effect, positive or negative, on the behavior and life of an individual. Healthy individuals (and psychologists, we might add) continually examine the effectiveness of their fictions and alter their goals when they are no longer useful. They maintain their fictions in a state of flux in order to meet the demands of reality.

Striving for Superiority

Adler suggested that the psyche has as its primary objective the goal of superiority. This is the ultimate fictional finalism for which all human beings strive and that gives unity and coherence to the personality. Initially, Adler conceived of the primary motivating force as aggression. Later, he identified the primary drive as a "will to power." Finally, he refined the concept of a drive toward power and suggested that the essential dynamic of human nature lies in its striving for superiority (1930).

Adler's concept of the striving for superiority does not entail the everyday meaning of the word "superiority." He did not mean that each of us innately seeks to surpass one another in rank or position, nor did he mean that we seek to maintain an attitude of exaggerated importance over our peers. Rather, the drive for superiority entails the desire to be competent and effective in whatever one is striving to do. The concept is similar to Jung's idea of self-actualization. Each one of us seeks to actualize, fulfill, and enhance our human potentialities. We strive for completion and unity—to be our best possible self. Thus, we seek to be superior within our own selves, not necessarily in competition with others. Adler frequently used the term *perfection* as a synonym for the word "superiority." This term can also be misleading unless we recognize its origin in the Latin *perfectus*, which means "to complete" or "make whole."

The striving for superiority may take on the form of an exaggerated lust for power. An individual may seek to exercise control over objects and people and to play god. The goal may introduce a hostile and fighting tendency into our lives in which we play games of dog eat dog. But such expressions of the goal for superiority are abortive and do not reflect its constructive nature.

The striving for superiority is innate and part of the struggle for survival that human beings share with other species in the process of evolution. Life is not motivated by the need to reduce tension or restore equilibrium as tended to be the case for Freud, instead, life is encouraged by the desire to move from below to above, from minus to plus, from inferior to superior. This movement entails adapting oneself to and mastering the environment. The particular ways in which individuals undertake this quest are determined by their own unique history and style of life.

Inferiority Feelings

To be human, Adler suggests, is to feel inferior. The sense of inferiority is a part of the human condition that all persons share. Feelings of inferiority have their origin in our encounter as infants with the environment. Throughout the whole period of childhood we feel inferior in our relations with parents and the world. As human infants, unlike other animals, we are born immature, incomplete, and incompetent to satisfy even our basic needs. There is a protracted period during which we are almost totally dependent on other people for our survival. Feelings of inferiority thus reflect a fact of existence. Children, in comparison to adults, are weak and inferior. Such feelings are inescapable, but also invaluable, as they provide the major motivating force that leads to growth. From our inferior position as children, we develop our goals of superiority. Our efforts and success at growth and development may be seen as attempts to compensate for and overcome our imagined or real inferiorities and weaknesses. Thus, feelings of inferiority are not deviant but are the basis for all forms of human accomplishment and improvement in life (1927).

The concept of human nature as driven by feelings of inferiority first came to Adler during his practice of general medicine. He observed that many of his patients localized their complaints in specific body organs. He hypothesized that in many cases an individual is born with a potentially weak organ that may not respond adequately to external demands (1917). This "organ inferiority" can have profound effects on both the body and the psyche. While it can have a harmful effect and lead to neurotic disorders, it can also be compensated for and lead to optimal achievements. A classic historical example of compensation is found in the story of the ancient Greek, Demosthenes, who suffered as a child from a speech impediment. Nevertheless, he learned to overcome his stuttering and became a great orator by forcing himself to shout in front of the ocean with pebbles in his mouth. Later, Adler broadened the concept of organ inferiority to include any feelings of inferiority, whether actual or imagined.

In his early writings, Adler termed the compensation for one's inferiorities the *masculine protest.* At the time, he associated inferiority with femininity. This concept finds common expression in our references to "the weaker" or "the stronger" sex. Adler himself was soon to become dissatisfied with this shortsighted view. Women may well be biologically different from men, but they are not on that account inferior. Later, he was to emphasize that inferiority has nothing to do with femininity; rather, it is a condition of existence that affects males and females alike. In that sense, Adler became an early proponent of women's liberation. He felt that none of the biological differences favored the male or justified a theory of inferiority of women. Basically, he recognized that the assignment of inferiority to women was a social assignment rather than a biological one.

Style of Life

Each individual seeks to cope with his or her environment and develop superiority in a unique way. This principle is embodied in Adler's concept of the *style of life,* which was a primary theme in his later writings (1929a, 1931). Each of us shares the common goal of striving for superiority, even though there are many different ways by which we may achieve this goal. One individual may try to develop competence and superiority by developing intellectual skills. Another may seek self-perfection by capitalizing on physical strengths and powers. These different lifestyles develop early in childhood. Adler suggests that the lifestyle is pretty clearly established by the time a child is five years old. Thereafter it remains relatively constant. It can be changed, but only through hard work and self-examination.

The style of life results from a combination of two factors: the inner goal orientation of the individual with its particular fictional finalisms, and the forces of the environment that assist, impede, or alter the direction of the individual. Each individual's style of life is unique because of the different influences of our inner self and its constructs. Adler imagines that no two individuals ever had or could have the very same style of life. Even identical twins respond to their environment in different ways.

Among the factors that lead to different lifestyles are the ordinal position of birth and different experiences in childhood. Adler does not postulate any stages of development, but he emphasizes the importance of the atmosphere of the family and the family constellation. *Family constellation* refers to one's position within the family in terms of birth order among siblings and the presence or absence of parents and other caretakers. Adler hypothesizes that the personalities of oldest, middle, and youngest child in a family are apt to be quite dissimilar simply by virtue of the different experiences that the child has as that particular member of the family group (1931). Older children tend to be more intelligent, achievement oriented, conforming, and affiliative, whereas younger children are more aggressive, ambitious, sociable, and dependent. The only child tends to be more like an older child, whereas middle children show a combination of the above characteristics. The family constellation becomes further complicated when one considers additional possibilities such as the only brother among sisters, twins, the only child, and so forth.

Family atmosphere refers to the quality of emotional relationships among members of the family. This atmosphere assists in determining whether or not the child will react actively or passively, constructively or destructively in the quest toward superiority. Children who are spoiled or neglected were thought by Adler to be particularly predisposed to a faulty style of life. The spoiled child is one who is excessively pampered and protected from life's inevitable frustrations. Such a child is actually being deprived of the right to become independent and learn the requirements of living within a social order. Parents who spoil a child make it difficult for the child to develop social feelings and become a useful member of society. The child grows to dislike order and develops a hostile attitude toward it. The neglected child is one who is unwanted and rejected. Such a child is virtually denied the right to a place in the social order. Such rejection arouses resistance in the child, feelings of inferiority, and a tendency to withdraw from the implications of social life. Adler points out that child-rearing practices frequently consist of a continuing alternation between indulgence and rejection. The spoiled child demands undue attention and regard, which eventually leads to parental anger and punishment that are often interpreted by the child as rejection. While few parents actually reject their children, many children feel humiliated and defeated.

Although parental "rejection" is overcome when parents learn better ways to handle their children, Adler stresses that the individual is fully responsible for the meaning attached to parental behavior and action. Many of us harbor deep feelings of having been rejected by our parents when in actuality they gave us their best efforts. Thus, in the end, only the person can assume responsibility for the style of life that he or she has adopted.

The Creative Self

A concept that Adler considered to be the capstone or climax of his theory is that of the *creative self* (1964). In a sense, I have been referring to the creative self all along. It is the self in its creative aspects that interprets and makes meaningful the experiences of the organism and that searches for experiences that will aid in fulfilling the person's unique style of life. In other words, the creative self establishes, maintains, and pursues the goals of the individual. Adler's concept of the creative self underscored his belief that human nature is essentially active, creative, and purposeful in shaping its response to the environment.

The concept of the creative self also offers further testimony to Adler's affirmation that individuals make or create their own personalities. We construct our personalities from the raw materials of our heredity and environment. In his concept of the creative self, Adler restored consciousness to the center of personality. Adler believed that we are aware of everything we do, and, that through self-examination, we can understand why we behaved in a certain way. The forces of which we are unaware are simply unnoticed; they are not buried in a sea of repression.

Adler's position here was in such direct contrast to that of Freud that it is no wonder the two could not collaborate. While Adler was not unaware of unconscious forces, he minimized them by reducing unconsciousness to simple temporary unawareness. He opposed Freud's determinism by emphasizing the vast extent to which a person can achieve conscious control over his or her behavior. People, Adler argued, may become largely aware of their deepest impulses and fictional finalisms, and, with conscious intent, create their own personalities and lifestyles that will achieve their deepest goals. In the end, Adler's position was almost the complete antithesis of Freud's, which emphasized that our behavior is largely determined by forces of which we are unaware. Freud offered his followers the hope of being able to endure and live without crippling fear of one's unconscious conflicts, but he never offered freedom from them. By restoring consciousness to the center of personality, by again coronating the king Freud had struggled so valiantly to dethrone, Adler aroused Freud's ire. To Freud, Adler was re-espousing the very illusion that Freud had sought to destroy.

Nevertheless, for many people, Adler's optimistic view provides a welcome contrast to the pessimistic and conflict-ridden picture of human nature shown in psychoanalysis. It is comforting to believe that we make and create our personalities. Once again, we may be masters of our fate. In his optimism, Adler foreshadowed the humanistic school of personality, which I shall discuss later.

Adlerian Psychotherapy

Neuroses, according to Adler, entail unrealistic life goals or fictional finalisms (1968). Goals are not realistic unless they take into account our capacities, limitations, and social environment. A person who felt extremely inferior or rejected as a child may set goals that are too high and unattainable. A person of average intelligence cannot expect to perform at a consistently outstanding level in academic work. Some individuals adopt goals that are unrealistically low. Having felt defeated and unable to cope with certain situations, such as marriage, people may seek to avoid situations in which they could develop and perfect those skills that would enable them to perform effectively.

Neurotics also choose inappropriate lifestyles as a means of attaining their goals. In their efforts to compensate for feelings of weakness, neurotics tend to overcompensate. *Compensation* entails making up for or overcoming a weakness. *Overcompensation* refers to an exaggerated effort to cover up a weakness that entails a denial rather than an acceptance of the real situation (1954). The bully who persists in attempting to force others to play his way may be overcompensating for a difficulty in working cooperatively with others.

Adler's terms "inferiority complex" and "superiority complex," phrases that have become commonplace in our vocabulary, also describe neurotic patterns. If an individual feels highly inadequate, we suggest that he or she is suffering from an *inferiority complex*. In Adlerian terms, there is a gulf between the real person and his or her excessively high life goals. If an individual exaggerates his or her importance, we use the label *superiority complex*. In Adlerian terms, such an individual has overcompensated for feelings of weakness. Both complexes have their origin in a person's responses to real or imagined feelings of inferiority.

Adler suggests that neurotics actually live a *life lie*. Their style of life belies their actual capacities and strengths. They act "as if" they were weak, "as if" they were doomed to be losers, when in fact, they could create a constructive existence for themselves. They capitalize on imagined or real weaknesses and use them as an excuse rather than a challenge to deal constructively with life. They employ *safeguarding tendencies*, compensatory devices, that ward off feelings of inferiority in a maladaptive rather than adaptive fashion. To be sure, we all use such protective defense mechanisms at times, but neurotics employ them in an exaggerated manner and degree.

Adlerian therapy aims at restoring the patient's sense of reality, examining and disclosing the errors in his or her goals and lifestyle, and in cultivating social interest. Adler did not establish strict rules or methods for treatment; he believed that the patient's lifestyle should determine the procedure. On the whole, Adler's approach was more informal than Freud's. He abandoned the use of the couch, suggested that the patient sit facing the therapist, and reduced the frequency of contact between patient and doctor.

The first goal of the Adlerian therapist is to establish contact with the patient and win his or her confidence (1929b). Such confidence is won by approaching the patient as a comrade, rather than an authority, and thereby eliciting cooperation. Whereas Freud viewed the transference, in which a patient works through earlier unsatisfactory relations by projecting them onto the doctor, as essential to the effectiveness of treatment, Adler suggested that therapy is effective because healthy features of the physician-patient relationship are *transferred*, or carried over, into the patient's life. Such transference need not have regressive features and is simply another name for the cultivation of social feeling.

Second, the therapist seeks to disclose the errors in the patient's lifestyle and provide insight into his or her present condition. The therapist tries to lead the patient gently and gradually to the point where the patient is able to recognize the errors in his or her goals, lifestyle, and attitude toward life. Early memories of childhood and dreams were seen by Adler to be excellent sources of information about a person. Together, early memories and dreams enable us to trace an individual's "life line" or lifestyle. Early memories frequently summarize the essential characteristics of our stance toward life, because the lifestyle is generally chosen by the time we are four or five and our selective memory thereafter tends to reflect experiences that are in line with our basic attitudes. For example, Adler observed that the first memories of doctors often entail the recollection of an illness or death. Dreams, rather than reflecting the past, are goal oriented. They reveal the mood that we want to feel and suggest how we intend to deal with a problem or task of the immediate future. Taking note of the options that we choose to follow in our dream life gives us further insight into our style of life.

EXERCISE:

Tracing the Life Line

Adler's method of "tracing the life line" may be used as an interesting preliminary technique for understanding your own primary goals and lifestyle. Your early memories probably refer to experiences that are in line with your basic attitude, and they may be used by you to justify your present stance. It is unimportant whether or not the memories are factual and really happened. Even imagined memories may be revelatory. Jot down or record your earliest memories. When you have finished, pretend that you are an observer studying someone else's actions and behavior. Ask yourself, "What goal might another person be trying to accomplish by acting in this manner?" Then compare the attitude expressed in your early memories to those that are currently present in your dreams. In our dreams, we are not bound by realistic or common-sense solutions to our problems. Our fantasies reveal the way in which we would like to cope with issues in our lives. Running away from a dream monster may be indicative of the desire to run away from a current problem. Being paralyzed in a dream may suggest a style of playing helpless in the face of pressing demands. Look for consistencies and similar postures in your early memories and current dreams. If the goals therein appear unattainable, or the lifestyle ineffective, you may wish to examine further their usefulness.

Do not be discouraged, however, if your investigation leaves you with questions rather than answers. It may be that you will be unable to discover a consistent or comprehensible pattern. Adler emphasized that it is difficult for a person to recognize his or her own lifestyle. It is sufficient that we begin to become aware of our early memories and dreams and of their potential for assisting our self-understanding. Adler pointed out that changes in our goals and lifestyles also find reflection in our dreams. Significant changes in attitude and our approach to living express themselves in our dreams. In the course of successful therapy, Adler also discovered that patients frequently recall new, previously overlooked memories that are more consistent with their newly won lifestyle.

Adlerian therapy seeks to encourage the patient to face present problems and to develop constructive means of dealing with them. While the therapist does not make decisions or assume responsibilities for the patient, he or she may structure or suggest situations that will assist in cultivating the patient's own skills. Such deliberate attempts to encourage enable the patient to accept new tasks and responsibilities. In this sense, the therapist plays the role of an educator who re-educates the neurotic in the art of constructive living. Additionally, Adler sought to minimize latent feelings of rejection and resentment and to cultivate feelings of social interest and good will. Adler believed that only by subordinating our private gain to public welfare can we attain true superiority. The true and inevitable compensation for all the natural weaknesses of individual human beings is that of social justice for all.

Evaluation and Implications

Adler's commitment to a philosophical viewpoint emerges clearly in his discussion of fictional finalisms. Human beings, he asserts, are goal-oriented organisms. All of human behavior may be comprehended in terms of its contribution and adherence to a goal. Difficulties in living are the result of an inappropriate philosophy and its accompanying faulty lifestyle. Reality, the ultimate fact of existence, is embodied in the concept of social interest. It is by recognizing and cultivating the need for social justice that a person can fulfill his or her ultimate potentiality.

Adler adds to the criteria for judging philosophical assumptions the criterion of usefulness. A philosophy is useful if it fosters productive living and enhances our lives. As such, he follows the pragmatic philosophy of William James (1842–1910), who argued that the meaning of a statement lies in the particular enriching consequences it has for our future experiences and quality of life. Not all philosophers would agree with this position; some would argue that it is important to acknowledge honestly the truth even if it increases one's difficulty in living. Nevertheless, James' and Adler's emphasis on the importance of the usefulness of our goals and constructs has attracted a large following of psychologists and personality theorists.

Adler's theory stemmed from his clinical observations. While he occasionally indulged in an empirical study to validate his findings, such efforts played a minor role in his work. Some attempts have been made to test Adler's birth-order theory and look for common characteristics in firstborns, and so on, but the results are inconclusive (Vockell, Felker, and Miley, 1973). One needs to remember that Adler simply suggested that there is a tendency for birth order to have different effects. He did not make firm predictions. To have done so would have been to run counter to the primary postulate of his psychology, which emphasized that each individual develops his or her own style of life and no two individuals may be presumed to be identical.

Adler reacts against Freud's instinctualism or the view that the primary motivational forces of personality lie in instinctual drives. In place of instinctual forces, he emphasizes the factors in society that shape personality. On the other hand, he does not adopt a radical environmentalist position and suggest that personality is entirely shaped by society. There are forces within the self, such as the drive for superiority and the creative self, that assist in shaping personality. Nevertheless, Adler is more optimistic than Freud about human potentialities and the potentiality of society. Human nature is flexible and changeable. There is a forward-moving tendency within the self, the drive for superiority, which implies that obstacles to growth are imposed by the society rather than by human nature itself. At the same time, through the creative self, human beings basically create their own personalities. In the end, Adler envisions the possibility of creating a better society through cultivating our social interest.

Adler's emphasis on the social forces that shape personality influenced subsequent neo-psychoanalytic and other theorists. We have already noted his influence on transactional analysis. Albert Ellis's system of rational-emotive therapy (1973), which emphasizes that behaviors are a function of beliefs, draws on Adler's individual psychology, as does William Glasser's reality therapy (1965) with its emphasis on pragmatic common sense. Adler's optimistic conceptions also influenced the humanist school of thought, which we will consider subsequently. Thus, Adler's ideas have become widespread even though several of them are not recognized as Adlerian.

Many of Adler's concepts have been particularly useful in helping the lay person develop more effective methods of child rearing and education (Dreifurs, 1952–1953). Adler emphasized again and again the value of education. As creative selves, we construct the primary forces that shape our existence: our goals and lifestyles. We can change these, should they become maladaptive, through insight into our errors. Thus, education and training are of the utmost importance. Through education, Adler believed that our innate and shared concept of social interest and justice could be made to flower and to provide the final and most appropriate form of compensation for our individual weaknesses. Adler was active in child guidance clinics and involved in penal reform. He was attracted to the political movement of socialism and many hours of his later years were devoted to specifying ways of educating for social justice.

SUGGESTIONS FOR FURTHER READING

Carl Jung was a voluminous writer. His *Collected Works* have been published in this country by Princeton University Press, beginning in 1953. While statements about his theory are scattered throughout these works, Volumes 7, 8, and 9 present the major features. Because Jung is a difficult writer to follow, the lay person would be best advised to begin his or her study with books that are more directed to the general public. *Man and His Symbols* (Doubleday, 1964) is probably the best introduction to Jungian psychology. It was written by Jung and several of his disciples. Jung's autobiography, describing the spiritual journey that led to his position, is found in *Memories, Dreams, and Reflections* (Random House, 1961). A statement of the major principles of analytic psychology as well as the theory of types and functions is included in

Psychological Types (Harcourt, Brace, 1933). Several of Jung's lectures were also collected in a basic introduction entitled *Modern Man in Search of a Soul* (Harcourt, Brace, 1933).

Also recommended are the *Freud/Jung Letters* (Princeton University Press, 1974). The best secondary sources introducing Jung's ideas are F. Fordham, *An Introduction to Jung's Psychology* (Penguin, 1953), and C. S. Hall and V. J. Nordby, *A Primer of Jungian Psychology* (Mentor, 1973).

Alfred Adler also wrote a great many books and articles. The classic introduction to Adlerian thought is *The Practice and Theory of Individual Psychology* (Harcourt, Brace, 1927). A shorter summary, "Individual Psychology," appears in C. Murchison, (Ed.), *Psychologies of 1930* (Clark University Press, 1930). Selections of Adler's writings have also been edited and presented by H. L. and Rowena R. Ansbacher (Basic Books, 1956, 1964).

For biographical data and an assessment of Adler's contemporary influence, the reader is referred to H. Orgler, *Alfred Adler: The Man and His Work* (New American Library, 1972); H. Musak (Ed.), *Alfred Adler, His Influence on Psychology Today* (Noyes Press, 1973); and M. Sperber, *Masks of Loneliness: Alfred Adler in Perspective* (Macmillan, 1974).

CHAPTER 5

Social Psychoanalytic Theories

As we have seen, many of the theorists who followed Freud reacted against his instinctualism or the view that the primary motivational forces of personality lie in instinctual drives. In particular, they criticized Freud for having overemphasized the importance of sexuality in personality. They acknowledged that in nineteenth- and early twentieth-century Vienna, where a strict Victorian ethos prevailed, it may well have been that many of Freud's patients expressed conflicts that clustered around guilt feelings toward their sexual desires. Such conflicts, however, appear to be less frequent in other societies where social and economic factors often seem to play a primary role. We have already seen a shift away from intrapsychic factors and toward interpsychic and social forces in Alfred Adler's theory.

Karen Horney and Erich Fromm emphasize the forces in society that shape personality. Horney stresses the forces within the family that influence personality. Fromm points beyond toward factors within the society at large. Drawing on their own clinical experience, as well as on cultural, anthropological, and literary evidence, they show how Freud's concepts are frequently a product of his social and cultural milieu. In the process, they develop their own theories of personality informed by the emerging social sciences of sociology and anthropology, which stress that personality is primarily a social product. At the same time, however, they remain within the psychoanalytic framework, conceiving of themselves as rejuvenators of psychoanalytic theory in line with the newer sciences, rather than pioneers embarking on new theories.

KAREN HORNEY

KAREN HORNEY: PSYCHOSOCIAL ANALYSIS

Karen Danielson Horney was born in 1885 near Hamburg, Germany, into an upper-middle class family that was economically and socially secure. Her father was of Norwegian descent and her mother was Dutch. As a child, Horney sometimes traveled with her father, a sea captain. While Horney admired her father, he was frequently stern and morose. His intense gazes frightened her and he was often critical of her intelligence, interests, and appearance. Because of her father's long absences from home, Karen Horney spent considerably more time with her mother, a dynamic, attractive, freethinking woman, who had the greater influence on her daughter. Karen was a devoted daughter to her even though at times she felt her mother may have favored her older brother. Mrs. Danielson encouraged her daughter to become a physician at a time in which it was unusual for women to enter that profession and in spite of rigid opposition from her husband. It was not the first time that the differences of temperament in Horney's parents led to discord. Eventually they separated and Horney's mother moved near Freiburg, where her daughter was pursuing her studies at the university. Later, Horney was to stress in her writings the role that a stressful environment plays in nurturing basic anxiety. Lack of love and encouragement, quarrelsome parents, and other factors in a stressful environment lead to feelings of rejection, worthlessness, and hostility. She acknowledged these feelings in herself as a result of her own childhood and strove hard to overcome them.

Horney received her degree in medicine from the University of Berlin. Thereafter she associated with the Berlin Psychoanalytic Institute. She was analyzed by Karl Abraham and Hans Sachs, loyal disciples of Freud, who were two of the foremost training analysts of the day.

In 1909 she married Oscar Horney, a Berlin lawyer. They had three daughters. As a result of different concerns, and her increased involvement in the psychoanalytic movement, they were divorced in 1937. The challenges of being a career woman, a mother, and of dissolving a marriage that was no longer viable gave her considerable insight into the problems of women. She was one of the first to speak directly to the issue of feminine psychology.

Horney spent most of her life in Berlin, but in 1932 she was invited to come to the United States and assume the position of associate director of the Chicago Psychoanalytic Institute. Two years later, she moved to New York City, opened a private practice, and taught at the New York Psychoanalytic Institute.

Coming to America during the great depression, she began to appreciate more and more the role of environmental factors in neurosis. Her patients were not troubled primarily by sexual problems, but with keeping a job and paying bills. Economic, educational, occupational, and social pressures seemed to be foremost in inducing neurotic behavior. While earlier she had had disagreements with the Freudian point of view, orthodox psychoanalysis with its stress on genetic and instinctual causes of behavior appeared increasingly one-sided. Eventually her dissatisfaction led her to leave the orthodox movement and found the Association for the Advancement of Psychoanalysis and the American Institute of Psychoanalysis. She assumed the position of dean of the Institute until her death, of cancer, in 1952.

Karen Horney did not develop a personality theory per se. She felt that her ideas lay primarily within the framework of Freudian psychoanalysis, and she subscribed to a great deal of Freud's work and theory. She sought to overcome the limitations in Freud's thought by emphasizing social and cultural factors and minimizing biological ones with their characteristic stress on sexuality. Her writings and teachings centered primarily on the neurotic aspects of behavior. However, in doing so, they help us to account for and understand why we behave as we do. By looking at Horney's conception of neurosis, we can infer how she would define normal behavior and also how she would construct a theory of personality.

Basic Anxiety

A primary concept underlying Horney's thought is that of basic anxiety (1945). As human beings our essential goal and challenge is to be able to relate effectively to other people. *Basic anxiety* results from

feelings of insecurity in these relations. In basic anxiety, the environment as a whole is dreaded, because it is seen as unrealistic, dangerous,
unappreciative, and unfair. Children are not simply afraid of their own
inner impulses or of punishment because of them, as in Freud's concepts
of neurotic and moral anxiety, they also feel at times that the environment itself is a threat to their development and innermost wishes. A
variety of negative conditions in the environment can produce the lack of
security entailed in basic anxiety: domination, isolation, overprotection,
hostility, indifference, inconsistent behavior, disparagement, parental
discord, lack of respect and guidance, or the lack of encouragement and
warmth. Children's fears are not unrealistic, but real. In a hostile environment, the ability of children to use their energies and develop self-
esteem and reliance is, in fact, thwarted. Children may be rendered
powerless in the face of these encroachments on their environment.
Their biological dependency and the lack of parental fostering of adaptive self-assertive behavior may leave them helpless. While children may
endure a certain amount of frustration and trauma, it is essential,
Horney believes, that they feel safe and secure.

Neurotic Trends

In the face of adverse circumstances, people develop certain defense attitudes or strategies that permit them to cope with the world and
afford a certain measure of gratification (1937). Specifically, we use
these strategies to deal with or minimize feelings of anxiety and to assist
us in effectively relating to others. Where they become exaggerated or
inappropriate these strivings may be referred to as *neurotic trends*. The
trends are not instinctual in nature but highly dependent on the situation in which a person lives. Horney criticizes Freud for his image of
neurotic needs as instinctual or derivative of the instincts. She places
environmental factors at the center of personality development.

Each of these neurotic trends leads to a certain type of behavior in
interacting with other people. Horney distinguishes three primary directions or modes of relating to others (1945).

Moving Toward In moving toward people, we accept our own
helplessness and become compliant in order to win the affection of
others, depend on them, feel safe, and thus minimize feelings of anxiety.

Moving Against In moving against people, we assume and accept
the surrounding hostile environment and rebel and resist other people.
In this way, we seek to protect ourselves, control others, attain revenge,
and reduce feelings of anxiety.

Moving Away In moving away from people, we feel that we have
little in common with others. We isolate ourselves and keep apart,

creating a world of our own. By relying solely on ourselves, we seek to eliminate the anxiety that arises out of involvement with others.

Later in her writings, Horney (1950) expanded these social orientations or directions toward other people so that they encompassed a general basic orientation that people may have toward life itself. The three primary movements became:

The self-effacing solution or an appeal to be loved.
The self-expansive solution or a striving for mastery.
Resignation or the desire to be free of others.

These patterns are reflected in the ten basic neurotic needs Horney described in her text on self-analysis (1942). Although the ten neurotic needs were articulated earlier, they may be seen as specific manifestations of an individual's general basic orientation.

Needs that reflect the solution of self-effacement:
1. The exaggerated need for affection and approval.
2. The need for a dominant partner in life.

Needs that reflect the solution of self-expansion:
3. The exaggerated need for power.
4. The neurotic need to exploit others.
5. The exaggerated need for social recognition or prestige.
6. The neurotic need for personal admiration.
7. The exaggerated ambition for personal achievement.

Needs that reflect the solution of resignation:
8. The neurotic need to restrict one's life within narrow borders.
9. The exaggerated need for self-sufficiency and independence.
10. The neurotic need for perfection and unassailability.

Normal or mature individuals resolve their conflicts by integrating and balancing the three orientations that are present in all human relations. They are able to express each mode at the appropriate time. Neurotics express one mode at the expense of the other aspects of their personality. They fail to recognize that tendencies to react according to the other orientations exist, and they actively, although unconsciously, repress them. Their repression, of course, is not successful, as the repressed tendencies continue to seek expression and increase their anxiety. Thus, they transform normal strivings and trends into pathological and neurotic ones.

The Idealized Self

Karen Horney (1950) distinguishes between the real self and the idealized self. The *real self* represents that which a person actually is. The *idealized self* represents that which a person thinks he or she should

FIGURE 5.1 The Normal and Neurotic Self
Circles can be used to represent the real and idealized self in Horney's theory of personality.

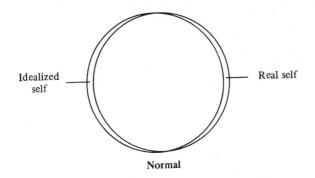

Idealized self —— —— Real self

Normal

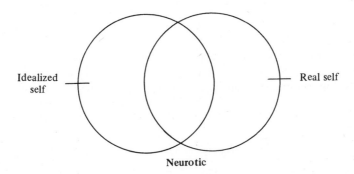

Idealized self —— —— Real self

Neurotic

be. This idealized self is used as a model in assisting us to develop our potential and achieve self-actualization. The dynamic of creating an idealized self in order to facilitate self-realization is universal and characteristic of each of us. In my attempt to be a competent teacher I posit an ideal of what an effective teacher is like. In the normal individual, the idealized self and the real self largely coincide. There is not much discrepancy between them and the idealized self is based on a realistic assessment of one's abilities and potentials. But in the neurotic, the real self and the idealized self are distinct or separated. This situation can be represented diagrammatically by circles as is shown in Figure 5.1, above. In the normal individual, the circles coincide. In the neurotic, they are increasingly distinct.

A person is only able to recognize and develop those aspects of the real self that coincide with the idealized self. Thus, as neurosis becomes more severe, an increasing amount of the powers and potentialities of the real self may be rendered unavailable for cultivation. In an extreme neurosis, the individual may completely abandon the real self for the

FIGURE 5.2 The State of Alienation

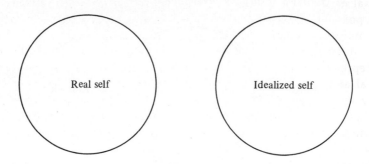

sake of the idealized self. Horney refers to this situation as one of *alienation*. The person abandons his or her real self for the sake of the idealized self and renders the two completely distinct (see Figure 5.2). In doing so, the person loses his or her true source of strength, as our only source of strength comes from whom we really are. Horney sometimes referred to this extreme form of alienation as *the devil's pact*.

For example, should an individual have the concept that in order to be a good person, he must never feel jealous, he might posit an idealized self that does not permit feelings of jealousy. Because his idealized self does not include jealous feelings, he may be unable to acknowledge feelings of jealousy that arise. Therefore, the part of his real self that does experience feelings of jealousy is denied. The individual becomes estranged from a part of himself.

A classic illustration clarifies Horney's point: normal individuals, by and large, are happy with and function within the everyday world. Neurotics are unhappy with the everyday world. Therefore, they build castles in the sky. They function in the everyday world, but to the extent that they are dreaming about their castles at the expense of the everyday world, they do not function as effectively as they might. Extreme neurotics abandon the everyday world and attempt to go and live in their castles in the air. Such total identification with the idealized self renders such individuals virtually unable to cope with the everyday world.

Horney's concept of the idealized self may be seen as a constructive revision or correction of Freud's concept of the ego-ideal. We recall that Freud's concept of the superego included two components: an introjected social conscience and an ego-ideal that was an idealized image consisting of approved and rewarded behaviors. The ego-ideal was the source of pride and provided a concept of who we think we should be. In her elaboration of the ego ideal, Karen Horney rejects the instinctual basis of Freud's concept of the superego that was derived from the self-destructive instinct. Instead, Horney emphasizes social factors that influence the development of an idealized self. Furthermore, Horney does not view the idealized self as a special agency within the ego, but as a special need of the individual to keep up appearances of perfection. She also points out that the need to maintain an unrealistic idealized self does not entail simply repression of "bad" feelings and forces within the self. It also entails repression of valuable and legitimate feelings that are repressed because they might endanger the façade. The repression of sexual and aggressive feelings and emotions that are thought to be socially undesirable frequently carries with it repression of spontaneous feelings, wishes, and judgments that are legitimate and constructive to individual growth. A woman, for example, may through the repression of her sexual desires attain an appearance of being socially and morally uncorrupt, but this façade is achieved at the expense of her not fulfilling her sexual desires and it may lead to her losing touch with other important messages from her body.

Feminine Psychology

Karen Horney's interest in feminine psychology was stimulated by two factors. First, psychoanalysis was created by a male who spoke almost entirely of men and boys. Second, certain clinical observations appeared to Horney to contradict Freud's theory of the libido. Freud had considered the psychology of women only from a male point of view. In his concept of libidinal development he had reduced sexual attitudes and activities to instinctual and inevitable processes that ignored the role of culture and society.

Freud had suggested that penis envy was largely responsible for a woman's development. Women, he suggested, viewed themselves, as he himself viewed them, as castrated males. Karen Horney suggested that Freud's hypothesis of penis envy as the primary determining factor in the psychology of women was not very useful. She pointed out that both men and women may develop fantasies about castration in their efforts to cope with the Oedipal situation. She further observed that many men and boys express jealousy over the woman's ability to bear and nurse children. She termed this phenomena *womb envy* and suggested that womb envy and penis envy are complements (1967). The appearance of these attitudes does not necessarily reflect unsatisfactory development or harmful emotions, but rather the mutual attraction and envy that the sexes have for each other.

Horney believed that the essence of sexual life lies in its biological creative powers. It follows that a greater role in sexual life belongs to the female because she is the one who is able to bear and nurse children. The woman's capacity for motherhood demonstrates her "indisputable superiority." This superiority is recognized by the male and is the source of intense envy.

Womb envy, rather than being openly acknowledged by the male, has often taken subtle and indirect forms, such as the need to disparage women, belittle their achievements, and deny them equal rights. Similar attempts to deal with these feelings have led men to equate the term "feminine" with passiveness and to conceive of activity as the prerogative of the male.

Both men and women have an impulse to be creative and productive. Women can satisfy this need naturally through procreation. Men can satisfy their need only indirectly, through accomplishments in the external world. Thus, Horney suggests that the impressive achievements of men in work or other creative fields may be seen as compensations for their inability to bear children.

The woman's sense of inferiority is not constitutional but acquired. In a patriarchal society, the attitude of the male has predominated and succeeded in convincing women of their supposed inadequacies. But these are cultural and social factors that shape development, not biological ones. If a "flight from womanhood" can be observed in our society, it is due not to instinctual developments but to the experience of real, social, and cultural disadvantages that women have suffered under. Sexual unresponsiveness, Horney points out, is not the normal attitude of women. It is due to cultural factors rather than the problem itself of being a woman. Our society, as has been well acknowledged, is a male society, and therefore for the most part it is not amenable to the unfolding of women and their individuality.

While Karen Horney's psychology of women, which is almost a direct inversion of Freud's theory, has met with criticism from several feminists who do not concur that the essence of being a woman lies in motherhood, her interest and contributions to feminine psychology have been very valuable. In her own life she struggled valiantly to resolve some of the problems that face women in contemporary culture. She successfully combined motherhood with an active career.

Self-Analysis

Psychoanalysis was first developed as a medical method of treatment for neurotic disorders. Karen Horney suggested and demonstrated that it can also be an assistance to normal personality development (1942). Through the process of self-analysis, significant gains may be made in self-understanding and in freeing human beings from inner bondages that hinder them in developing their best potentialities.

While Karen Horney acknowledged that self-analysis is difficult and painful, she believed that it is possible. The world in which each one of us lives is familiar to us because it is our world. Because it is ours, in certain respects we can understand it better than any outside observer can. While it is true that many of us have become estranged from parts of our world and desire not to see them, the fact remains that knowledge about our world is available to us. By observing and then using our observations, we can gain access to those aspects of our world that we have neglected.

To those critics who were concerned that self-analysis might be dangerous, Karen Horney pointed out that the advantages that might accrue from self-analysis outweigh any possible dangers. The likelihood of danger is minimized in self-analysis because of the fact that an individual who is attempting to analyze him- or herself will simply fail to make observations that might be intolerable and lead to further personality disorientation. While self-analysis can never be considered as an adequate substitute for professional analysis in situations of neurosis, its possible benefits for enhancing individual development merit its attention, consideration, and use.

Occasional self-analysis, Horney pointed out, is engaged in by each one of us when we try to account for the motives behind our behaviors. A man who falls in love with a wealthy widow might ask whether the desire to share her money plays a primary part in his feelings. A student who fails a test that she thought was unfair might ask whether she had properly prepared for it. An individual who yields to another in a disagreement might ask if he gave in because he was convinced that the other's point of view was superior or whether he was afraid of a possible argument. Such analyses are a common phenomenon in normal living.

Systematic self-analysis differs in degree rather than kind. It entails a serious and protracted effort for self-understanding undertaken on a regular basis. Karen Horney suggests that people in analysis face three primary tasks: to express themselves as freely, completely, and frankly as possible; to become aware of their unconscious driving forces or neurotic trends and discover their causes, manifestations, and effects; and to develop the capacity for changing those disruptive attitudes, thereby improving their relationship with themselves and other people.

The first task of analysis is achieved by free association. I have already described the major features of the process in conjunction with its development in the work of Sigmund Freud. One attempts to become aware of any thoughts, feelings, or wishes that come to mind. In professional analysis, one verbalizes his or her feelings. In self-analysis, it is sufficient to take note of one's associations. It may be helpful to record them on tape or to jot down key words that may be useful in reviewing them later. While free associating, it helps to remember that one is not presenting material for someone else to listen to or to read. The only audience is oneself and the sole purpose is to further self-understanding.

In free association, we try to express what we really feel, not what we think we are supposed to feel according to past tradition or moral standards. We need to give free range to our feelings, even though they may seem to be ridiculous. Even if we think that we should not have been bothered by a hurtful comment, we should permit and encourage ourselves to feel the full pain and hurt that the comment evoked. While we cannot bring out feelings that are deeply repressed, we can try not to check those that we can feel.

During free association, we abstain from reasoning or critical evaluation. The task of the moment is simply to take note of whatever thoughts or feelings come to mind. As long as the thoughts flow freely, there is no reason to stop them. At some point, they may stop flowing, or we may become curious as to their meaning. Then, we might wish to begin some preliminary exploration into the meaning of our associations by making tentative interpretations. Here we bring reason into play, but it should not be used exclusively. We need to be guided by our hunches and intuitions. Becoming aware is not simply an intellectual process but an emotional experience as well.

As we attempt to explore the meaning of our associations, Horney suggests that we let our attention be guided by our interests. What is the material that attracted your attention, aroused your curiosity, or struck an emotional chord? No observation should be regarded as unimportant. Every detail is potentially meaningful. We might ask, Why does this particular thought or feeling come up just now? What is its meaning in this particular context? It is helpful to pay attention to repetitive themes or sequences. Such repetitions suggest material that is of concern.

It is also useful to look for contradictions and exaggerations in our reactions and emotions. Frequently, we suspect that we are overreacting to a situation. In analysis we do not criticize ourselves for overreacting but try to feel that reaction, acknowledge it fully, and understand why it is so enormous. Dreams and fantasies should be heeded. We will also benefit from paying attention to themes that we have omitted or quickly passed over. If a feeling arises that we would prefer to ignore or pass over lightly, it may possibly be a sign that the feeling is of greater significance than we have been ready to acknowledge before.

Any interpretation that we make as to the meaningfulness of our associations needs to be regarded as tentative. It is not necessary to accept any more than we can believe. Interpretations are tentative hypotheses that await further confirmation; they are not definite conclusions. As we begin to feel that we are recognizing personal difficulties, we may begin to try to understand those factors that are responsible for our problems. We may try to investigate what elements in the past, such as our rearing, could have contributed to the problem. At the same time, we might try to think of weak spots in our own personality that continue to contribute to the difficulty. Understanding the influences of the past is important in comprehending how we got where we are, but the past is over and done with. Unless we can recognize how we continue to perpetuate the problem into the present, we will be unable to cope with it more effectively.

A key problem in any analysis is that of dealing with resistances.

Resistances are defenses or maneuvers that aim at maintaining the status quo. We all seek to maintain certain aspects of our personality that have come to be of value to us and that appear to hold the promise of gratification and security even though they may have long ceased to be really useful.

It is difficult but not impossible to become aware of these resistances. Resistance is anything that interferes with the analytic progress. We can suspect resistance if we are depressed, tired, or apprehensive, but do little to try to clarify or understand the problem. If, in a period of personal difficulty, we discover that we are shunning analysis of the problem, resistance is a likely factor at work. Resistance also manifests itself in blind spots, factors that we have ignored or whose meaning and importance we failed to understand.

A major step in dealing with resistances is the recognition that they do occur. One of our biggest problems is our tendency to minimize our feelings. We believe that we should not feel that way and therefore we concentrate on trying to feel differently, rather than recognizing the feeling for what it is and trying to understand it. Resistance is not an evil, it is a normal part of human development and an invitation to further investigation.

We deal with resistance, also, by free association. Before associating, however, it is helpful to try to review our associations of what preceded the blockage. In associating to a resistance, we consider the blockage itself and let our thoughts freely wander from there. Afterwards, we again try to understand the meaning of our associations.

An example adapted from one of Horney's cases may help to suggest how the associations that we make in analysis may reveal forces and processes of which we were previously unaware. A young man begins his free association by considering that he had a bad night and that he feels very depressed. His secretary is ill with the flu. This disturbs him because her illness interferes with his business and he is also afraid that he might catch it. He is also reminded of a physician who upset and confused him by not clearly indicating the contents of a drug that was prescribed. Next, the young man entertains thoughts of a tailor who did not deliver a coat when it was promised. He also thinks about the injustices that are done to small countries in Europe.

A main theme in these associations is annoyance at external events in the outside world. The young man is annoyed by those aspects of the environment that do not fulfill his needs and desires. His secretary's illness threatens to infect him; his physician's lack of specificity threatens to confuse him; his tailor's tardiness inconveniences him. He wishes that that world were such as not to frustrate him. The fact that the world does frustrate him strikes him as unfair. He feels defenseless—like a small country in Europe. In his associations he makes others responsible for his difficulties. Conspicuously absent from his thoughts are those aspects of his own personality that might be contributing to the problem or ways in which he might more constructively deal with his environment. If the young man were able to recognize in his associations his tendency to blame others for his problems and thereby avoid his own responsibility, he would be better prepared to work out his own solution for them.

Karen Horney points out that a major problem in analysis is that of being overly self-critical. Frequently, we are so eager to engage in self-blame and reproach that we indulge in recriminations against ourselves rather than make attempts to understand ourselves. It may help to remember that an individual is not to blame for the development of his or her neurotic tendencies. They were developed as a means of protection when all other means had failed, at an age when few other options were available. One's neurotic trends should simply be regarded as given factors of the situation at hand. When we find ourselves indulging in self-criticism, we would do well to try to understand why it is so important to us to be so critical.

The third step in analysis, developing the capacity to change our attitudes, follows automatically in a successful analysis. Genuine insights into one's personality free energies that were previously engaged in perpetuating neurotic trends for use in constructive changes. Horney believes that the organism has a forward-moving tendency, which is similar to the concept of self-actualization. This natural forward movement permits us to grow and to change. The alterations that occur in analysis are not necessarily changes in our overt or noticeable behavior, rather, they are changes in the attitudes that underlie our behavior. Change in underlying attitudes alters the effect and impact of our actions even though the differences in our overt behavior may be imperceptible to the casual observer.

Horney acknowledges that there are limitations to self-analysis. Complete self-understanding is an unattainable goal. The severe neurotic is not open to changes through self-analysis, because without outside help he or she will be unable to penetrate the defenses that mask and protect neurotic trends. We need to remain open to the possibility and desirability of professional help. Self-analysis is no substitute in those cases where professional analysis is mandated. Nevertheless, within limitations, self-analysis can be a valuable tool toward self-understanding.

EXERCISE:

Self-Analysis

While there is no prescribed recipe, Karen Horney's general suggestions may be used by the reader who is interested in pursuing self-analysis. Horney considered the pursuit of self-knowledge a privilege and a responsibility that all of us can use to advantage.

In developing your own self-analysis, beginning by investigating one problem area that you can clearly identify will facilitate matters. Each analysis produces its own sequence or order of events. Problems of which you are unsure need not be tackled immediately. They will emerge in the course of analysis if they are genuine problems. Nor is it necessary to feel that you should explore every depth of your inner life. It is enough to begin with problems that are obvious to you.

Suppose you are concerned about your interrelationship with your parents. Following the steps outlined above, you would begin your analysis by making free associations about your parents. When thoughts stop flowing or a particular item provokes your curiosity, you might stop and begin tentatively to interpret your findings. This in essence is the heart of the analytic process: free association followed by reflection on one's thoughts. In the process, you may discover certain resistances that impede your analytic work. Further free association is helpful in dealing with such resistances.

In working through a problem, sometimes it helps to raise specific questions. You might ask, "Is my relationship a realistic matter of concern?" "Are the interpersonal standards that I have set commensurate with my abilities and willingness to change things?" "Can I identify specific problem areas?" "In my own opinion, what am I doing that might account for a poorer relationship than I desire?" "What is the simplest thing that I might do about it?" These questions can be rephrased to take account of other problems. Raising questions like these and attempting to answer them can set forth positive tendencies toward growth.

Evaluation and Implications

A number of critics (see Hall and Lindzey, 1978) have asked whether or not Karen Horney and other neo-psychoanalysts do much more than simply elaborate on concepts that were implied in Freud's writings but not clearly expressed. Is anything added that is really unique? We have seen how social forces were implied in Freud's theory of the psychosexual stages of development even though they were not clearly articulated. Freud's aim in therapy ("Where id is, there shall ego be") represented his effort to give the individual, through psychoanalysis, more creative control in shaping his or her personality. Thus, much of the work of the neo-psychoanalysts can be seen as elaborations, albeit frequently constructive ones, on the original Freudian theories. Horney clarifies the ego-ideal; her adjustment mechanisms may be seen as an elaboration of the Freudian defense mechanisms; she expands upon the psychology of women by looking at the other side of the Freudian coin. To repeat, the question is, in any or all of these concepts are we really given anything new that cannot be comprehended under Freud's original concepts? The heart of this critique is that in developing their own theories, the neo-psychoanalysts have discarded a number of the Freudian concepts that were considered crucial to psychoanalysis. The biological grounding of human existence is minimized; gone is the stress on sexuality. Gone also is Freud's hardheaded realism, or, if you prefer, pessimism. Freud could not be as optimistic as Karen Horney.

Karen Horney was not interested in abstract thinking and she did not do a great deal of reading in the area of philosophy. Nevertheless, her ideas are in tune with many philosophical concepts that have been introduced by other therapists. Her goals in therapy are growth oriented, optimistic, and life affirmative. She set goals of assisting people in becoming more aware of a larger world and participating in a fuller cosmos. Toward the end of her life, she became interested in Zen Buddhist writings and practices.

At the same time, Horney was an astute observer and talented clinician. She frequently tested, revised, and discarded her theories in the light of new observations. Horney asserted that certain therapeutic approaches will bring forth desired and predictable changes in behavior. These changes can be observed in the course of therapy if not in a rigorous laboratory experiment. Horney believed that her method and theory must be open to scientific investigation and research. While her theories have not generated much specific laboratory experimentation, as they do not lend themselves easily to objective test, her theory and technique have been found useful by many clinicians. Several aspects of her technique are discussed in current Freudian literature as useful adjuncts, or additions, to psychoanalysis (see Wolman, 1954).

ERICH FROMM: HUMANISTIC SOCIAL ANALYSIS

Erich Fromm was born in Frankfurt, Germany, in 1900, the only child of a deeply orthodox Jewish family. At the age of thirteen, Fromm began to study the Talmud, beginning an interest in religious literature and an admiration of the German mystic Meister Eckhart (1260?–1327?) that has remained throughout his life. In his later years, Fromm has not formally practiced religion, but he has referred to himself as an "atheistic mystic," and it is clear, as it is with Freud, that Fromm's early religious experiences left a distinct mark on his personality and work. The moral and committed tone of his writings has a quality that has been described as reminiscent of the Old Testament prophets. He has been deeply interested in religion and both his early and recent writings reflect his concern.

Fromm never wrote a great deal about his early childhood. In his few comments, he described his early family life as tense and acknowledged that his parents were probably neurotics. His mother was "depression-prone," and his father, an independent businessman, "moody" and "overanxious." Young Erich was fourteen years old when

ERICH FROMM

World War I broke out. He was impressed, almost to the point of being overwhelmed, by the irrationality of human behavior as it showed itself in the brutalities of war. By 1919 he had identified his political attitude as socialist but he hesitated to join the party and actively engage in politics at that time. Instead, he pursued formal studies in sociology and psychology at Heidelberg and received the Ph.D. in 1922.

The early 1920s was a time of vibrant excitement in the academic community. Nineteenth-century scholars such as Comte, Spencer, and Marx had opened the door to the analytical study of human behavior and social institutions. Fromm was influenced by all of these men, but Marx in particular impressed him, and later Fromm attempted a synthesis between the concepts of Marx and those of Freud.

The new disciplines of psychology, sociology, and anthropology were emerging as distinct fields of investigation within the academic community. At the same time, efforts to bridge these fields and build common interdisciplinary foundations for understanding social institutions and human behavior were arising. Sigmund Freud himself had observed that all psychology must ultimately be social psychology because it involves the interaction of the individual and his culture. Although Erich Fromm never personally met or worked with Freud, he took an active role in the growing movements of psychoanalysis and social psychology. Fromm's approach has been described, therefore, as humanistic social psychoanalysis.

Erich Fromm was trained in analysis in Munich and at the Institute of Berlin. He was one of the early *lay analysts*, which is to say that he had no formal medical training. The desirability of a medical background for the practice of psychoanalysis is a matter that is still currently debated. Most psychoanalysts in America view psychoanalysis as primarily a medical method of treatment for neurotic disorders and therefore consider a medical background indispensable. Freud, however, had argued against medical training as the optimal background for an analyst and had advocated the training of lay people. He felt that analysis should be viewed as more than simply a method for the treatment of neurosis and suggested that it should also be seen as a broad cultural force that could lend insight into such areas as sociology, philosophy, art, and literature. Erich Fromm's rich and broad understanding of the social sciences and philosophy were to enrich his understanding of psychoanalytic theory and its applications. At the same time, these interests eventually led to his severance with orthodox psychoanalysis and his criticism of Freud for his unwillingness to acknowledge the importance of social and economic forces in shaping personality.

In 1933, during the depression, Fromm came to the United States. He has been a popular instructor at several institutes and universities in this country, and has also conducted a private practice. Since 1951, he has been living and teaching in Mexico.

The Basic Human Condition: Loneliness

A major theme of Erich Fromm's writings is the concept of loneliness (1941). To be human is to be isolated and lonely, because one is distinct from nature and others. Loneliness represents the basic human condition, according to Fromm, and it is this characteristic that radically separates human nature from animal nature. As the human race has gained more freedom by its transcendence over nature and other animals, its people have become increasingly characterized by feelings of being apart and isolated. The condition of loneliness finds its ultimate expression in the problem of death. Unlike other animals, we know that we are going to die. This knowledge leads to a note of despair. While we have vast potential, we know that our life span is too short to realize it. Most of us, therefore, find death incomprehensible and unjust—the ultimate expression of our loneliness.

In response to the basic condition of loneliness, human beings can resolve their problems by working with one another in a spirit of love to create a society that will optimally fulfill their needs, or they can use the freedom that they gain by being human to submit to other people or forces in a form of bondage. Such an escape mechanism will alleviate feelings of isolation but it does not creatively meet the needs of humanity or lead to optimum personality development.

Existential and Historical Dichotomies

Fromm posits a number of conditions that arise simply from the fact of one's existence—the fact that one exists. Loneliness is one of these. Fromm refers to these conditions as dichotomies (1947). A *dichotomy* is a two-horned dilemma or problem that has no solution because none of the alternatives it presents are entirely satisfactory. We desire immortality, but we face imminent death; we would like to be at one with nature, but we transcend it; we desire to know the truth, but there are limits to our knowledge. In short, we desire a certain kind of world, but we find the world into which we were born unsatisfactory. Dichotomies such as these are termed *existential dichotomies* because they arise from the very fact of our existence.

Finding the given world unsuitable and unsatisfactory, we create and try to make for ourselves a more satisfactory environment. In doing so, we may further create *historical dichotomies,* which are dilemmas or problems that arise out of our history because of the various societies and cultures that we have formed. The inequitable distribution of wealth among persons is a historical dichotomy, as is our long history of war. It is important that we not confuse or interlabel the two. Historical dichotomies are created by people and thus they are not inescapable, as existential dichotomies are. Instead, they are products of history and, therefore, open to change.

Together existential and historical dichotomies structure our limitations and potentialities. They serve as the basis for our aspirations and hopes, but, at the same time, they also generate our frustrations.

Basic Human Needs

The existential dichotomies that characterize the human condition give rise to five basic needs (1955). These needs stem from our existence and they must be met in order for a person to develop fully. Our primary drive is toward the affirmation of life, but unless we can structure our existence in such a way that it fulfills our basic needs, we either die or become insane.

The five basic needs are:

Relatedness Erich Fromm believes that the ability to relate to other people and love productively is not innate or instinctive in human beings. As people, we have to create our own relationships. We may seek to relate to others by submission or dominance, but these ultimately prove defeating. Only productive love, which retains the distinct character and integrity of the self, prevents narcissism, or self-isolation, which results from the failure to develop effective relationships.

Transcendence Human beings need to rise above the accidental and passive creatureliness of their animal existence by becoming active creators. If we cannot solve the problem of transcendence by creativeness, we turn to destructiveness, which is an abortive method of fulfilling this drive.

Rootedness Rootedness refers to the need to feel that one belongs. Initially we find such belonging in our natural tie to our mother, but only insofar as we find new human roots in a feeling of universal comradeship with all human beings can we feel at home in the world as a responsible adult.

Sense of Identity Human beings need to become aware of themselves as separate selves and individuals. This sense of "I" requires experiencing oneself as distinct from others and as the center and active subject of one's powers. Failure to develop a sense of identity as a unique individual leads us to develop a sense of identification by unquestioning conformity to a group or whole.

The Need for a Frame of Orientation and Devotion Each one of us needs a stable and consistent frame of reference by which we can organize our perceptions and make sense out of our environment. Such a thought system may be rational or irrational, true or false, but it is mandated by the very character of being human and leads to our devotion to a particular world view.

Human beings create society in order to fulfill these basic needs that arise independently of the development of any particular culture. The five needs are given with the fact of our being human. But the type of society that humans create structures and limits the way in which the basic needs may be fulfilled. In other words, human personalities develop in accordance with the opportunities that their particular society allows. For example, in a capitalistic society, acquiring money is a means of establishing a sense of identity. A person who is unable to acquire money in a capitalistic society may have a difficult time establishing a sense of identity unless he or she is able to identify with some major corporation or find some other means of distinction. Thus, one's final personality represents a compromise between his or her inner needs and the demands of the society.

Personality and Character Orientations

Fromm (1947) defines *personality* as the totality of an individual's psychic qualities, which includes *temperament*, one's mode of reaction, and *character*, the object of one's reaction. Whereas temperament is largely given with one's heredity and is therefore fixed, character is largely developed through experience. A person may by temperament react quickly or slowly, strongly or weakly, but what he or she is quick or strong about depends on character. Character refers to a system of strivings or objectives that underlies one's behavior. It is those forces that motivate a particular person to act, feel, and think in a certain way.

Fromm identified five character types that are common in Western society (1947). The traits that emanate from each type have both positive and negative qualities, but on the whole, Fromm saw the first four types as largely unproductive. The first three types are reminiscent of Freud's oral and anal character types, and parallels can be drawn between Freud's and Fromm's typologies. However, in his discussion of the marketing orientation, Fromm is generally thought of as having gone further and developed a character type that is not inherent in Freud's thought, but new and innovative.

The primary difference between Erich Fromm's theory of character types and orientations and that of Sigmund Freud is that Freud envisions the fixation of libido in certain body zones as the basis for future character types, while Fromm emphasizes the fundamental basis of character in the different ways in which a person may relate or orient him- or herself to the world. Because a person's character is determined in large measure by his or her culture and its objectives, it is possible, Fromm suggests, to speak of social character, qualities that frequently are found among the people of a particular culture.

The Receptive Orientation Receptive people feel that the source of all good things is outside of themselves, therefore, they believe that the only way to obtain something they want is to receive it from an outside source. They react passively, waiting to be loved.

The Exploitative Orientation Exploitative people, like receptive ones, feel that the source of all good things is outside, but they do not expect to receive anything good from others. Therefore, they take the things they want by force or cunning. They exploit others for their own ends.

The Hoarding Orientation Whereas receptive and exploitative types both expect to get things from the outside world, hoarding personalities are convinced that nothing significantly new is available from others. Therefore, they seek to hoard and save what they already have. They surround themselves by a wall and are miserly in their relations to others.

The Marketing Orientation The modern marketplace is the model for Fromm's fourth character orientation, in which the concept of supply and demand, which values an article of commerce in terms of its exchange worth rather than its use, is the underlying value. Marketing personalities experience themselves as commodities on the market. They see their personality as a package that is to be sold, and they develop those character traits that they believe will assist them best at any particular moment in terms of being bought at the market. They are as they believe others desire them to be. Their basic character is empty. They may be described as opportunistic chameleons, changing their colors and values as they perceive the forces of the market to change.

The Productive Orientation Fromm's description of the productive orientation tries to go beyond Freud's definition of the genital character, which simply suggested that the mature individual is capable of functioning adequately sexually and socially. Fromm seeks to describe an ideal of humanistic development and moral stance that characterizes the normal, mature, healthy personality. Freud's dictum "to love and to work," taken symbolically, denotes the meaning of productiveness. But the productive orientation refers fundamentally to an underlying attitude, a mode of relatedness, that governs the productive person's relationship to the world. These individuals value themselves and others for whom they are. They find themselves as the center of their powers and they are able to realize their potentialities constructively. In using their powers productively, they relate to the world by accurate perception of it and by enlivening and enriching it through their own creative powers.

In particular, the productive character comprehends the world through love and thinking. Love enables a person to break down the walls that separate one person from another. Productive love, as we shall see, entails four basic elements: care, responsibility, respect, and knowledge. Productive thinking is controlled by the nature of the object as well as the nature of the subject. It denotes being affected by and responding to an object that is seen for what it is and not for what one wishes it to be. It also entails being aware of one's own position as an observer and being able to relate to what is observed.

In reality, no individual represents exclusively one of the character orientations Erich Fromm described. We always deal with blends. There is no individual whose total orientation is productive, and no one is completely lacking in productivity. Further, each of the character structures has positive and negative aspects. Indeed, the productive type might be described as a culmination of the positive attributes of the other forms.

Humanistic versus Authoritarian Ethics

A further characteristic of the productive orientation is the use of humanistic rather than authoritarian ethics (1947). Whereas *authoritarian ethics* have their source in a conscience that is rooted outside the individual, *humanistic ethics* represent true virtue in the sense of the unfolding of a person's powers in accordance with the law of his or her human nature and the assumption of full responsibility for his or her own existence.

Fromm's concept of the authoritarian conscience is influenced by Freud's concept of the superego, which referred to the dictates and moral values of the parents and other significant authority figures internalized and introjected into the self. The prescriptions of the authoritarian conscience are not determined by one's own values but by those of others. Fromm points out that the source of authority is not limited to parents or other significant persons from childhood, it may also be anonymous or impersonal institutions, such as cultural traditions, the scientific and philosophical ethos of one's time, or current public opinion.

Simply because an ethic is authoritarian and external does not mean that it is arbitrary and contrary to human nature. Fromm acknowledges that many of the precepts that underlie great religions may reflect humanistic ideals. All too frequently, however, the authoritarian conscience and its ethics are not based on the nature of human beings and their genuine needs. In contrast, a humanistic ethic is grounded on the true requirements of human nature. Furthermore, its source is in the individual's true self and response to his or her total proper functioning as a human being rather than in external authority. Whereas a comparison could be drawn between Fromm's concept of the humanistic conscience and Freud's idea that the conscience of the mature person is primarily informed by the ego rather than the superego, Fromm does not believe, as Freud did, that an authoritarian conscience is a necessary precondition of a humanistic one.

EXERCISE:

Our Convictions

Fromm notes that it is very difficult for us to appreciate how often we escape our essential loneliness by yielding to authoritarianism rather than realizing productively our freedom and being guided by our inner consciences. We rationalize the fact that we are controlled by others in such a way as to conceive of ourselves as free individuals. In that way, we foster the illusion that we are living by our own free decisions. Fromm has described a favorite experiment that he often uses with patients. He asks them to spend an afternoon writing down all of the things of which they are really convinced. They might begin with the statement that the earth revolves around the sun. Their statements must be convictions of which they are absolutely certain, not simply opinions or probabilities. A statement does not count unless one would be willing to stake his or her life on it. You are encouraged to try Fromm's experiment before reading further.

Fromm notes that most people initially see the task as a simple one.

When they attempt to do it, however, it becomes increasingly more diffi-cult, and many discover that their only conviction is that they are not really convinced of anything! The difficulty relates not only to matters of intellectual conviction, but also to questions of inter- and intrapersonal relations. How many people do you feel you can really count on? How many people can you trust with a secret that, if revealed, could destroy your life? Is there any matter on which you would unflinchingly stand in the face of any and all opposition? Or do you, and perhaps other people as well, have a price?

Basic Interpersonal Relationships

The various character orientations come into being, in part, because of the particular love relationship that a child has experienced with his parents. Fromm does not outline any particular stages in personality development, but he describes three basic kinds of relationships that may exist between a parent and a child (1956).

Symbiotic Relatedness In symbiotic relationships, two persons are related in such a way that one or the other of the parties loses or never attains his or her own independence. One person is swallowed by the other person, a method that is indicative of the *masochistic* form of the symbiotic relationship. Or, one person may swallow the other person, a means that occurs in the *sadistic* form.

Withdrawal-Destructiveness The withdrawal-destructive relation-ship is characterized by distance rather than closeness. The relationship is one of apathy and withdrawal or direct expressions of hostility and aggression.

Love Love is the productive relationship to others and the self. It is marked by mutual respect and the fostering of independence for each party.

The various character types may be seen as products of the early forms of parent-child relationships. The receptive character originates in a masochistic response to a symbiotic relationship. The exploitative type emanates from a sadistic pattern developed by the child who reacts destructively to parental withdrawal. The marketing orientation is the behavior pattern of a child who reacts to parental destructiveness by withdrawal. The productive orientation has its roots in the relationship of love.

The Art of Loving

Love, Erich Fromm asserts, is an art. Its theory and practice can be mastered, but only if we make mastery of the art of love a matter of ultimate concern. Much of Fromm's theory of love is indicated in earlier aspects of his personality theory. We have seen how productive love is the true creative answer to human loneliness. Symbiotic relationships are immature or pseudo forms of love.

Genuine productive love entails the four elements of care, responsibility, respect, and knowledge (1956). *Care* implies active concern for the life and growth of the loved person. *Responsibility* denotes an ability and readiness to respond to the needs, expressed or unexpressed, of the person who is loved. *Respect* refers to the ability to see the other person as he or she is and to be aware of his or her unique individuality. *Knowledge* entails the experience of union with another person in which there is no room, and no need, for knowledge in the sense of grasping his or her innermost secret. One realizes that the other person remains an enigma, or mystery, but he or she can be known, nevertheless, in the act of love.

Love is an attitude or orientation of character that refers to the relationship of a person to the world, not simply to one object. Nevertheless, the kind of object that is loved permits us to distinguish among various types of love (1956).

Brotherly love is the sense of responsibility, care, respect, and knowledge of another human being. It is the fundamental kind of love that underlies all types.

Motherly love is the unconditional affirmation of a child's life and needs. It entails care and responsibility that enable the child to grow and an attitude that instills in the child a love of life. Whereas brotherly love occurs between equals, the nature of motherly love is one of inequality, since the child needs the love that the mother gives. The child must grow, however, and the essence of motherly love is to permit the child to become a completely separate human being.

Erotic love is the craving for union and fusion with one other person. It is exclusive, but in its union and fusion with one individual it expresses its love for all mankind and life. It entails attraction to a particular individual, but it is also an act of will as it involves a decision and a promise to commit one's life totally to another person.

Self-love expresses the fact that love is an attitude that is the same toward all objects, including the self. Fromm acknowledges that there is a widespread belief that it is selfish and wrong to love oneself. Love for the self and love of others are frequently seen to be opposite, and it is assumed that to the extent one loves oneself, one has less love to give to others. The idea that love for others and love for oneself are mutually exclusive is false. In fact, love of others is rooted in the ability to love oneself, to affirm one's own life, happiness, growth, and freedom. Love of self entails the same four elements of care, responsibility, respect, and knowledge directed at oneself. Nevertheless, Fromm believes that most people find it very difficult to genuinely love themselves. Selfishness and self-love are not identical but opposite. The selfish person loves him- or herself too little and thus is not capable of loving others. Love, according to Fromm, is not a fixed quantity like an apple that must be divided, but like wine in a cup that, when full, overflows.

Love of God springs from the need to overcome separateness and achieve union. The term "God," here, refers to the highest value and indicates the most desired good of a person. In its mature form, love of God becomes love of truth, love, and justice, and the realization of that which "God" stands for in the self. Fromm's concept of God is not the traditional theistic concept, rather, it is an ultimate concern with reality that creatively answers the dilemmas of existence. There is a similarity between Fromm's notion of realizing the God within and Jung's archetypal God image. Both refer to an innate tendency to grow and realize our potential, which if fostered brings out the divine in humanity.

There can be no prescriptions for the practice of love. It, like any other art, requires discipline, concentration, patience, and a supreme concern with its mastery. In particular, the ability to love requires the overcoming of narcissism. In *narcissism* we experience as real only that which exists within our selves. Love entails recognizing our subjective elements and being able to see other people and things objectively. Thus, emerging from narcissism or self-encapsulation requires development of humility, objectivity, and reason. We must strive for objectivity in each situation and to recognize those times when we are bound by our subjective feelings. We need to try to recognize the difference between our picture of another person, as it is narcissistically determined by our feelings about and interests in the person, and the person's reality as it exists apart from our own needs and emotions.

In addition, the art of loving requires the practice of faith. Fromm understands faith as a character trait that pervades the entire personality. It is not a specific belief but a stance rooted in productive intellectual and emotional activity. Faith entails a conviction in the truth of one's vision and experience of the world and in the reliability of oneself and others. An example of such faith is the confidence of a parent in a child's ability to grow, to love, to be happy, and to develop his or her potential. Without such faith, parents feel compelled to manipulate their children, to put into them what is desirable and suppress what appears to be undesirable. Parents can have this faith only to the extent to which they have realized their own potential and are confident in their own ability to love and act productively.

EXERCISE:

Cultivating Faith and Concentration

We have seen that there can be no prescription for the practice of love. Its mastery requires discipline, patience, and concentration. In The Art of Loving, *Fromm does not provide any recipes, but he does* point out a few initial steps that might be helpful. Love entails faith. Elsewhere, Fromm has pointed out that it is very difficult for many of us to have faith in a highly "technetronic" society (1968) where meaningful interpersonal relationships are scarce. The assembly line worker who does the same chore hour after hour, day after day, year after year, usually does not interact relevantly with the people around him or her and therefore feels dehumanized. Many of us feel as if we have been reduced to identification numbers in a computerized society.

The first step in developing faith is to notice when and where we lose faith. In what particular situations are you most apt to feel that it is difficult to communicate meaningfully with others around you? Second, it helps to try to recognize the instances in which we behave like cowards, such as when we fear losing our jobs. Look through closely and try to examine the rationalizations that you employ to alleviate technological stress and to cover up for loss of courage. Society may function in the above fashion because while we stress that we are afraid of not being loved, our real fear is that of loving, for love requires courage, openness, and the willingness to commit oneself without guarantee.

In a rapidly changing society, many of us have difficulty concentrating, which is also essential for love. Fromm suggests the following as an aid in developing concentration. Sit in a relaxed position and close your eyes. Try to visualize a white screen and to remove any thoughts or pictures that interfere. Then try to follow your breathing. Do not try to think about it or force it, but simply follow and sense it. While doing this, try to develop a sense of "I," or yourself, as the center of your powers and the creator of your world. Repeating this exercise once or twice a day for a period of twenty minutes or longer can help us to focus our attention. The reader may notice a similarity between this exercise and certain meditational practices of the East. Fromm was considerably interested in Eastern religion and philosophy and believed that they are particularly relevant to self-understanding.

Necrophilous and Biophilous Orientations

More recently, Fromm (1964, 1973) has suggested a further pair of character orientations. The first, the *necrophilous character*, is attracted to that which is dead and decaying and seeks to take that which is living and destroy it. The second, the *biophilous character*, is synonymous with the productive orientation where one is a passionate lover of life who seeks to further the growth of living things. Fromm acknowledges that this pair is informed by Freud's life and death instincts, but he points out that for Freud both instincts are givens of our biology, whereas for Fromm life is the normal biological impulse. The desire to destroy emerges only when life forces are frustrated. Thus, necrophilia is not parallel to but an alternative to biophilia.

Fromm argues that human beings are not genetically aggressive. The destructiveness and cruelty that we display toward one another cannot be explained in terms of our animal heredity but must be comprehended in terms of the way in which we differ from animals. As living organisms, we all are programmed to respond with biologically adaptive benign aggression, which acts as a vital defense against threat. Malignant aggression, however, develops when life forces are frustrated. It is a potential rooted in the condition of being human that is realized when certain negative political and social factors are present. Destructive aggression, therefore, is a propensity of character rather than an innate or learned behavior.

A classic example of the necrophilous character is Adolf Hitler, who was fascinated and obsessed with death and destruction. In Fromm's careful description and analysis (1973), Hitler emerges as a narcissistic and withdrawn personality who, because he could not change reality, falsified, denied it, and engaged in fantasy. Hitler's coldness, apathy, and self-indulgence led to failures early in life and humiliations that resulted in a wish to destroy. This wish could not be recognized; instead, it was denied and rationalized as defensive maneuvers and actions undertaken on behalf of the glorious emerging German nation. What is unique is not the personality of Adolf Hitler, but the sociopolitical and historical situation that permitted a Hitler to rise to a position of great power. Fromm believes that malignant forms of aggression can be substantially reduced when socioeconomic conditions that favor the fulfillment of human needs and potential are developed in a particular society.

Society

We have seen that a dominant emphasis in Fromm's discussion of personality is the role that society has in structuring, shaping, and limiting personality. In his writings Fromm has analyzed and carefully studied different social and cultural situations and their effects on human nature (1947, 1955).

Society is necessary in order for human beings to fulfill their needs. We are social animals and cannot live without developing some form of social organization. We create society in order to fulfill our needs, but the type of society that we create, in turn, structures and limits the way in which our needs may be filled. Furthermore, for a particular society to function adequately, it is absolutely necessary that the people within that society be shaped to satisfy its demands. Otherwise, that particular system of society cannot be maintained. In a capitalistic society, for example, individuals must produce and consume goods. If they do not, a capitalistic society cannot be sustained. Nevertheless, if a particular society makes demands on its members that are contrary to their nature, that society warps and frustrates their human potential. In fact, to date,

Erich Fromm believes that no society has yet been developed that has been able to meet all of the basic human needs constructively. He has outlined specifically how both capitalism and communism have failed in their efforts to satisfy basic human needs productively. He has pointed out that while a great deal of lip service is given to the ideal of love in a capitalistic society, most of its relations are, in fact, governed by a principle of fairness in which we give unto others only as much as they give unto us.

Taking Erich Fromm's discussion of love seriously, and attempting to implement it in our society, would require rather drastic changes in our social relations. Fromm is optimistic about the possibility of a society being designed and created that would be able to meet human needs constructively. In such a society, he suggests that individuals would relate to one another lovingly, transcend nature creatively, and respond productively. Each individual would experience him- or herself as the source of power and would relate realistically to the world. Erich Fromm has spelled out specific reforms, and at one point labeled his ideal society *Humanistic Communitarian Socialism*. He suggests that such a society would realize the goals posited by Marxist philosophy and the choice of life offered by psychoanalysis.

While Fromm does not imply that personality is entirely shaped by society, he suggests that obstacles to growth are imposed by the society rather than by human nature itself. Since human beings create the societies in which they live, Fromm can envision the creation of a utopian society that would more adequately meet and fulfill human potentialities. Fromm replaces Freud's pessimism and discontents with optimism and hope. Freud could not be so optimistic as to envision human creativity sufficiently powerful to eliminate the problems that are inherent in human nature and civilization itself. Some critics (see Hall and Lindzey, 1978) have criticized Fromm's utopian dreams as unrealistic. If we have the potential to develop a perfect society, why have we repeatedly failed to do so? In his later writings, Fromm is sobered by our failures to achieve some of our goals, but he remains optimistic, believing that as long as life exists there is hope (1970).

Most recently (1976), Erich Fromm has distinguished between two modes of existence that are competing for the spirit of humanity. The *having mode*, which relies on the possessions that a person *has*, is the source of the lust for power and leads to isolation and fear. The *being mode*, which depends solely on the fact of existence, is the source of productive love and activity and leads to solidarity and joy. A person whose being depends solely on the fact that he or she *is* responds spontaneously and productively and has the courage to let go in order to give birth to new ideas. It is not necessary to remain trapped in a cruel and hostile world. However, radical spiritual and social changes are required. Central to these changes is the basic choice that we must make between the modes of having and being.

Fromm has written little about his technique of therapy. While he has deviated to some extent from the orthodox psychoanalytic approach, he employs a form of free association, places considerable value on the interpretation of dreams, and recognizes the importance of analyzing the transferences that arise in therapy. He has indicated that he is more active than Freud in his role of therapist and employs the term *activating* to describe the therapist's interventions to facilitate progress. Fromm also emphasizes that the therapist must feel within him- or herself what the patient is talking about and recognize the common humanity that both of them share. The therapist must existentially acknowledge within his or her own self the many feelings and impulses that the patient describes. In short, nothing human may be alien. Fromm suggests that it is this element of *empathy* that permits competent therapists to give back what their patients are really saying as compared to what they think they are saying, and that enables their patients to recognize that their inner feelings are shared by others.

Erich Fromm describes the psychoanalytic method of investigation as genuinely scientific. Its essence is the observation of facts. Over the protracted period of an analysis, the analyst observes many facts about his or her patient. He or she draws inferences from these observations, forms hypotheses, considers these hypotheses in the light of further facts that emerge, and eventually arrives at a conclusion on their possible validity. While the theoretical models of the psychoanalyst do not lend themselves to scientific falsification by means of experiment, nevertheless, they are based on many hours of careful empirical observation within the clinical setting. Thus, while the method of verification is different from that of the natural sciences, Fromm believes that it is a reliable method.

Fromm rejects *scientism* or the exclusive reliance on a narrow conception of science, deeming it inadequate for the full comprehension of human nature. He realizes, more clearly than many, that the process of scientific activity begins with an epiphanic vision that is informed by the scientist's philosophy. Fromm's own analysis is a speculative and transcendental one, incorporating several vantage points that initially may appear contradictory. He has drawn insights from such fields as religion, philosophy, psychology, sociology, and economics, permitting them to illumine his theory.

An example of the type of scientific research that Erich Fromm encourages was published in 1970. Psychologists, anthropologists, historians, and other experts joined together in an interdisciplinary field study of a Mexican village, which was published under the title *Social Character in a Mexican Village*. Their findings about the village's history, economic and social structure, belief systems, and fantasies appear to confirm Fromm's theory of social character.

Fromm's psychobiography of Adolf Hitler is reminiscent of Erik Erikson's psychohistorical analyses of the lives of famous people. Erikson studied individuals such as George Bernard Shaw, Mahatma Gandhi, and Martin Luther. Such studies provide fascinating reading and provoke considerable speculation about the reasons why certain significant historical figures behaved as they did. However, their validity is difficult to ascertain, because it is virtually impossible to test empirically their hypotheses.

In his writings, Fromm has tried to develop a norm or ethic that presents the best answers to the problem of being human. Fromm considers as ethical those behaviors that are most appropriate in unifying, harmonizing, and strengthening the individual. Observation can assist us in determining which behaviors facilitate those goals. Fromm's efforts to study human behavior empirically and responsibly within a particular philosophical point of view have led to his rich ethical convictions and transcendental approach.

SUGGESTIONS FOR FURTHER READING

Karen Horney's writings have attracted a large lay audience. They are clear and easy to read. *New Ways in Psychoanalysis* (Norton, 1939) describes Horney's disagreements with Freudian theory: her belief that its stress on instinctual determinants is one-sided and needs to be rounded out by the consideration of cultural and social elements. *The Neurotic Personality of Our Time* (Norton, 1937), *Our Inner Conflicts* (Norton, 1945), and *Neurosis and Human Growth* (Norton, 1950) outline Horney's theory of neurosis. Identifying ten neurotic needs in the earliest book, Horney's thought develops through the concept of three social orientations and, later, three general orientations to life. In the last book, Horney introduces the concept of the idealized self. *Self-analysis* (Norton, 1942) familiarizes the lay person with the methods and techniques of psychoanalysis. It is an invaluable work for any individual who is interested in pursuing his or her own self-understanding through analysis. Karen Horney's writings on the psychology of women have been brought together in *Feminine Psychology,* edited and with an introduction by Harold Kelman (Norton, 1967).

Erich Fromm's writings have had a vast appeal. He is one of the theorists most likely to be read by the lay person as he wrote expressly for them. Fromm's first, and in the eyes of many most important, book is *Escape From Freedom* (Holt, Rinehart and Winston, 1941). In it he explores the problem of human freedom and our tendency to submit to tyranny or authority. *Man For Himself* (Holt, Rinehart and Winston, 1947) discusses the problem of authoritarian versus humanistic ethics and outlines his five character orientations. *The Sane Society* (Holt, Rinehart and Winston, 1955) describes the five basic human needs and considers the effects of capitalism and other social forms on character development. Fromm's most popular work is *The Art of Loving* (Harper & Row, 1956), which outlines his theory of love. The distinction between the necrophilous and biophilous orientation and Fromm's case study of Adolf Hitler are included in *The Anatomy of Human Destructiveness* (Holt, Rinehart & Winston, 1973). Fromm's latest work, *To Have or To Be* (Harper & Row, 1976), offers us a choice of two primary modes, one of which offers the potential of growth.

PART III

Behavior and Learning Theories

A dominant trend in American psychology has been the behaviorist movement with its emphasis on learning and the influences of the environment in shaping personality. The development of modern physics, astronomy, biology, and chemistry, beginning in the early seventeenth century, ushered in new modes of understanding the world and the self. Natural science, which dealt with phenomena by objectively measuring them, became a model for the psychologist to emulate or follow. Informed by the philosophy of John Locke and the British empiricists, behavior and learning theorists have sought to perfect the methodology and techniques of psychology, thereby raising it toward the sophistication of the natural sciences.

John Locke (1632–1704), an English philosopher, sought to apply to psychology the inductive tests and scientific methods of Francis Bacon, an earlier British philosopher (1561–1626), who was the forerunner of the empirical tradition. Locke believed that all our knowledge comes from our senses and through experience. At birth, he suggested, the mind is a "tabula rasa," or blank slate, on which sense experience writes in a myriad of ways. While Locke did not deny that the mind might be active in selecting and molding the data of sensation, his phrase "tabula rasa" expressed empiricism in its classic form, just as Descartes's "I think, therefore, I am" had expressed the essence of rationalism.

Rationalism refers to the philosophical view that the mind, in and of its own accord, can formulate ideas and determine their truth. *Empiricism*, however, suggests that human knowledge arises slowly in the course of experience through observation and experiment. To be empirical means to be based on experience, be it sensory or introspective. Descartes and Locke agreed that sense experience was an inadequate basis for a full understanding of the outside world. Descartes, however, believed in the power of the human mind to overcome the limitations of sense data and arrive at truth, whereas Locke was skeptical about the understanding of any truth outside of the data of our senses. Modern behavior and learning theory have been heir to Locke's agnosticism and belief that valid knowledge arises out of experience and needs to be continually checked by its accordance with it.

Behaviorists emphasize learning and experience as the primary determinants of behavior. Rather than postulating complex personality structures and dynamics within the individual, they focus on those factors in the environment that shape an individual's behavior. While internal structures are not necessarily denied, they are minimized or eliminated in favor of external forces. Behavior theories have also become increasingly committed to a rigorous methodology that studies behavior experimentally. Whereas Freudian and neo-psychoanalytic theories had their origin in a clinical setting, most behavior and learning theories have originated in the psychological laboratory. Several of the constructs of personality pertinent to the behaviorist point of view have come out of findings that have emerged from laboratory studies and experiments dealing with *infrahuman* (lower than human) species. Theoretical speculation is shunned in favor of careful observation and experimentation. The rigorous methodology of the behaviorist approach has permitted precision and economy in theory construction as well as clear empirical foundations for the major concepts of the theories.

Although modern behavioral theory is singularly American, the historical background of the approach can also be traced to the Russian psychologist Ivan Pavlov (1849–1936), who demonstrated and articulated a form of learning known as *classical conditioning*. In a classic laboratory experiment, Pavlov took a hungry dog and presented it with food, an *unconditioned stimulus* that normally elicits salivation, an *unconditioned*, or *automatic, response*. Then he simultaneously paired the food with the sound of a bell, a neutral stimulus that does not normally elicit salivation. The dog salivated to the paired food and sound of the bell. After several presentations of both food and bell, Pavlov was able simply to present the sound of the bell, and the dog would salivate. The sound of the bell had become a *conditioned stimulus* that elicited a *conditioned response* of salivation. In other words, Pavlov showed that by pairing an unconditioned stimulus with a conditioned stimulus, he could elicit a response that previously would have been elicited only by the original stimulus. We can represent this diagrammatically in the following way:

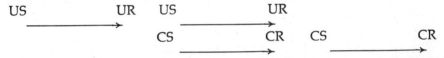

In the process of his experimental work with dogs, Pavlov discovered and demonstrated a number of additional principles that have become basic to the understanding of learning. He noted that the food acted as a reinforcer. A *reinforcer* is an event that increases the likelihood of a particular response. It was the food that had originally underlaid the connection between the bell and the salivation. To sustain the conditioned response it was necessary to present the food again from time to time along with the bell. Pavlov discovered that if he did not occasionally do this, the conditioned response of salivating to the sound of the bell would disappear. Technically speaking, the response would undergo extinction. *Extinction* refers to the tendency of a response to disappear if it is not reinforced. Pavlov also observed the phenomena of *generalization* and *discrimination*. He noticed that once a dog had been conditioned to salivate to the ringing of the bell, the dog would also tend to salivate to other similar stimuli, such as the ringing of a buzzer. This phenomena constitutes *generalization*. On the other hand, the dog could be taught to *discriminate* among different stimuli so that it would salivate only to a particular tone of a bell.

Another major figure in the history of behaviorist theory is John Watson (1878–1958), who is commonly known as the father of behaviorism. John Watson expanded classical conditioning into a theory of behaviorism in which he recommended that psychology emphasize the study of overt rather than covert behavior. *Overt* behaviors are those that we can observe directly, such as motor movements, speaking, and crying. *Covert* behaviors are those that only the individual who actually experiences them can directly observe, such as thoughts, feelings, and wishes. Watson believed that for psychology to be an empirical science, it should base itself on phenomena that can be seen by an outside observer. Much of what psychologists had traditionally talked about were phenomena that could not be directly observed by an outsider. Thoughts, feelings, and wishes can be subjectively observed by the person who is having them through the process of introspection. However, they cannot be observed directly by another individual. Because such processes cannot be objectively observed through extrospection, Watson suggested that psychology should ignore them and limit itself to discussing only the overt behaviors of an individual.

This recommendation created a curious situation. The term "psychology" refers to the study of the psyche. In common parlance, "psychology" is often thought to refer to the study of the mind. However, Watson pointed out that it is virtually impossible to observe mental processes directly. He suggested that the psychologist should act as if the mind did not exist and simply concentrate on overt behavior. In a sense, what Watson proposed was a "psychology without the *psyche*." Nevertheless, Watson's point of view was quickly adopted by many American psychologists. The behaviorist movement became the dominant movement in psychology in America. Even today, the distinctive characteristics of American psychology reflect closely Watson's emphasis on objectivity and extrospection.

Another figure in the history of learning theory is Edwin Thorndike (1874–1949). Thorndike conducted several experiments with animals in order to gain further understanding of the learning process. He formulated many important laws of learning. The law that is particularly important for our purposes is Thorndike's *law of effect*, which states that when a behavior or a performance is attended by satisfaction, it tends to be stamped in or increase. If the performance is attended by frustration, it tends to decrease. We now recognize that the law of effect is not necessarily universal. Sometimes frustration leads to increased efforts to perform. Still, most psychologists believe that the law of effect is generally true.

A final figure to consider here is Clark Hull (1884–1952). Hull developed a systematic theory of learning that was based on the concept of *drive reduction*. Hull's point was that learning occurs only if a response of the organism is followed by the reduction of some need or drive. For example, the infant learns to suck a bottle of milk in order to relieve its hunger. If sucking the bottle did not result in some drive or need reduction, the infant would not learn to perform that activity. Hull's theory of learning greatly influenced the personality theory of John Dollard and Neal Miller, whom I will discuss in Chapter 6.

Part III presents several major contributors of the behavior and learning approach to personality theory and shows their outstanding influence on psychology today.

CHAPTER 6

Psychoanalytic Behavior and Learning Theories

The interpersonal theory of psychiatry of Harry Stack Sullivan and the learning theory of John Dollard and Neal Miller are informed by the insights of Freud and his followers. They borrow and utilize many Freudian concepts, but in doing so, they integrate them with the ideas and methodology of behaviorist psychological research on learning and behavior.

Strictly speaking, Sullivan is not a behaviorist. Nevertheless, his theory veers in the direction of behaviorism because of his emphasis on the study of personality characteristics that can be directly observed in the framework of interpersonal relationships. In Sullivan's theory, he stopped trying to reckon with unseen and private mental processes within the individual (intrapsychic) and began to concentrate on interpersonal processes that can be verified by observation of the individual within his or her social context. In his emphasis on operational definitions and extrospective stance Sullivan resembles the behaviorists, and so may be seen as a transitional theorist in the American movement of behaviorism (Rychlak, 1973). John Dollard and Neal Miller's orientation has been called *psychodynamic behavior theory* since "it is a major effort to integrate some of the fundamental ideas of Freudian psychodynamic theory with the concepts, language, and methods of experimental laboratory research on behavior and learning" (Mischel, 1971). Chapter 6 provides an overview of the ideas of these men.

HARRY STACK SULLIVAN: INTERPERSONAL PSYCHIATRY

Harry Stack Sullivan was born in 1892 in Norwich, New York. He was the only surviving child of poor Irish Catholic farmers, who had to struggle to provide the basic necessities for their son. A shy, awkward boy, he had difficulty getting along with the other children in the predominantly Protestant Yankee community in which he lived.

While Sullivan suggested that ethnic and religious differences were the primary contributors to his feelings of isolation as a child, personality difficulties created by his home life and own personality were probably equally contributory. Sullivan did not have a close relationship with his father, whom he described as "remarkably taciturn." His mother, a complaining semi-invalid, was the more ascendant figure in his life. Mrs. Sullivan resented the fact that through marriage, she, a Stack, from a professional middle-class family had sunk in social, educational, and economic status. Her son bore the brunt of her laments, tales of earlier family prominence, and unrealistic dreams.

When Sullivan was eight and a half, he developed a close friendship with a thirteen-year-old sexually mature adolescent boy. It appears that this relationship had overt and expressed homosexual characteristics (Chapman, 1976). Sullivan later wrote that close relationships between a same-sexed young child and an early blossoming adolescent invariably leads to homosexuality (1972). As an adult, he admitted with regret that he never achieved a heterosexual genital relationship. Although he was discreet in his personal life, Sullivan was frequently thought of as being homosexual.

In school Sullivan was a superior student. He was valedictorian of his high school class and won a state scholarship to Cornell. Encouraged by one of his teachers, he decided to become a physicist in order to rise above his poverty. At Cornell, however, his grades fell and in his second year, he was suspended for academic failure. During the next six years, Sullivan earned enough money to enter the Chicago College of Medicine and Surgery, an inferior school that he later described as a "diploma mill," suggesting that it granted degrees for payment of tuition rather than academic performance. The school closed in 1917, the same year in which Sullivan received his degree.

The shabby education that Sullivan received had detrimental effects in his later life. He never learned to write well, and he did not have a solid formal training in scientific methodology and research. At no time did Sullivan receive any formal training in psychiatry, and, therefore, there were gaps in his medical knowledge. He was also relatively ignorant of many cultural subjects. Nevertheless, Sullivan worked hard at self-instruction, and his lack of formal education may have freed him from some of the set attitudes and prejudices that a standard education can foster.

Sullivan entered psychiatry at the age of thirty when he was appointed to the staff of Saint Elizabeth Hospital in Washington, D.C. Many psychiatrically disturbed veterans were housed at Saint Elizabeth. Here Sullivan developed a working knowledge of psychiatry through his work with patients and his attendance at lectures, seminars, and case history presentations. He later suggested that his patients, most of whom were young male schizophrenics, were his primary teachers. In 1923, Sullivan moved to the Sheppard and Enoch Pratt Hospital. His devotion and energy in working with patients and his descriptions of his therapeutic techniques brought him to the forefront of American psychiatry. In 1924, he added to his duties at the hospital the responsibility of being an adjunct faculty member at the University of Maryland Medical School.

In 1930, Sullivan moved to New York and established a private outpatient practice. While he was in New York he had some three hundred hours of personal psychoanalysis under Clara Thompson. It is possible that his analysis was not conducted according to classical Freudian lines, as Clara Thompson was heavily influenced by Sandor Ferenczi, a defector from the Freudian viewpoint.

In 1933, Sullivan assisted in founding the William Alanson White Psychiatric Foundation, named after a neuropsychiatrist who had greatly influenced Sullivan's work. He founded the journal *Psychiatry* to make public his own views. In his later years Sullivan served as a consultant to the Selective Service Board and to UNESCO.

In 1939, he returned to the Baltimore-Washington area. He maintained a busy professional life and continued to have close contact with professional activities in New York. But his later years were spoiled by poor health. He was nursed and cared for through several serious illnesses by an adopted son and close students. He died suddenly in Paris in 1949, while returning from an executive board meeting of the World Federation for Mental Health.

Harry Stack Sullivan suffered from emotional problems all of his life. He had difficulties in maintaining relationships with other people. These problems and his acknowledged frequent isolation no doubt contributed to his sensitivity and insight in dealing with other people. He could not stand apart but recognized his own human weaknesses in the patients whom he was treating (Chapman, 1976).

Personality: Its Interpersonal Basis

Sullivan defines *personality* as the characteristic ways in which an individual deals with other people in his or her interpersonal relationships (1953). He believed that it was meaningless to think of an individual as an object of psychological study, as an individual develops and exists only in the context of relations with other people. Interpersonal relations constitute the basis of personality.

Whereas Sigmund Freud's psychoanalysis is largely *intrapsychic*, emphasizing the structures and dynamics of the individual person, Sullivan's theory is *interpersonal*, emphasizing relationship with others. Sullivan did not believe that it was necessary to invoke complex imaginary psychic constructs, such as an id, ego, and superego, in order to explain how a person behaves. He suggested that it is more useful to observe and describe how a person relates to other individuals in his or her environment.

Indeed, the very term *personality*, itself, is only a hypothesis for Sullivan (1964). It is merely an imaginary construct that is used to explain and predict certain behaviors. It would be a mistake, Sullivan suggests, to try to reify the concept of personality and to consider personality as a separate entity apart from the interpersonal situations in which it emerges. Thus Sullivan's definition of personality as the characteristic ways in which an individual relates to others stresses the empirical components that we can directly observe. We can see, hear, and feel that an individual is relating to other people in certain ways, such as in a passive or dominant fashion. One's interpersonal relationships can be empirically observed by others.

While he conceives of personality as only a hypothesis, nevertheless, as we shall see, Sullivan identifies and describes some of the patterns and processes that may be included within that concept.

Anxiety is a central concept of interpersonal psychiatry. Sullivan uses the term in a very broad sense. *Anxiety* refers to any painful feeling or emotion. Thus, anxiety includes doubt, shame, guilt, feelings of inferiority, loathing, as well as anxiousness and other undefinable feelings that cause pain. Anxiety is the result of tension that may arise from organic needs or social insecurity. Sullivan's primary concern was with the anxiety that arises from social insecurity.

Sullivan points out that anxiety can be observed and described. The anxious person can give an account of how he or she feels. Many times, anxiety can be observed by looking at the individual's physical appearance and reaction. Physiological changes within the body that are indicative of anxiety, such as heart rate, can also be measured.

Anxiety is interpersonal in origin. Human beings, Sullivan held, are surrounded with anxious feelings from birth. The first feelings of anxiety are transmitted by the mother because her concern for the adequate care and welfare of the child implies the need for caution against dangers like illness or accidents. These anxious feelings are empathetically perceived by the child.

Anxiety threatens a person's self-esteem. Sullivan employs the term *self-esteem* broadly to mean all of those feelings of competence and personal worth that hold a person together. Feelings of anxiety may result from either real or imagined threats or dangers to the child's sense of security. Anxiety may have both productive and destructive effects. In mild or moderate amounts, it may serve as a warning system and motivate an individual to seek effective measures of tension reduction. In large amounts, it confuses and leaves an individual incapable of effective solutions. Deep anxiety may bind a person to ineffective interpersonal relationships and patterns. It limits the ability to observe what is happening and thereby avoid repeating mistakes.

In our relationships with others, we are aware to some extent of what we are doing and why we are doing it, and we are to some extent unaware of these things. Sullivan rejects the notion of substantive unconscious forces whose existence cannot be demonstrated. Nevertheless, he appreciates the fact that an individual may be unconscious or unaware of certain of his or her motives and behaviors. A person's awareness or lack of awareness of his or her own behavior can be objectively demonstrated by talking with the person and observing his or her actions. The ease with which a person can become aware of his or her interpersonal relations varies from individual to individual and with the person as well. Some facets of our behavior can be much more easily brought to our attention than others. Thus the relationship between conscious and unconscious is very flexible.

If we are unaware of our interpersonal relationships, we cannot learn anything from them. It is as if certain events had not occurred because we do not experience them. Thus, when we are unaware, we cannot profit from our experiences and learn new patterns of relating to others. On the other hand, when we are aware of the pattern of our interpersonal relationships, we can modify and change them.

Awareness and unawareness occur in the present; but they may influence a person's perception of the past and future. An individual who believes that he or she is inept may only be aware of the way in which he or she bungles things. This lack of awareness of one's true abilities and accomplishments distorts the person's view of his or her past performances and cripples future activities.

Unawareness is caused by anxiety. We are unaware of those factors in our interpersonal relationships that might cause us pain or anxiety. The ease with which we may become aware of these things depends on the anxiety we would experience in becoming aware. Yet, by experiencing that anxiety and becoming aware, we are able to change in healthier directions.

Security is the opposite of anxiety. It is not simply the absence of anxiety but a state of emotional well-being, self-confidence, and optimism in which there are no painful feelings or emotions. Complete security, or *euphoria,* is an unattainable goal. Nevertheless, each of us seeks to develop those interpersonal relationships that will decrease our anxiety and increase our security.

In our efforts to reduce anxiety and increase security, each of us employs many different security operations of which we are usually unaware (1963). A *security operation* is an interpersonal device that a person uses to minimize anxiety and enhance security. These security operations may have positive or negative effects and be healthy or unhealthy. They are healthy if they increase our security without jeopardizing our competence in interpersonal relations. They are unhealthy if the security that they provide is obtained at the expense of the development of more effective interpersonal skills. Unhealthy security operations merely blunt our anxiety; further, they may lead to other painful emotions and psychiatric illness.

There are many parallels between Sullivan's notion of security operations and Freud's concept of defense mechanisms. Both are processes of which we are unaware and means by which we reduce anxiety. The primary difference lies in Sullivan's stress on what is observable. Sullivan's emphasis is not on an intrapsychic activity, such as repression, but on the way in which a person may become disassociated and disconnected with certain aspects of his or her experience of the world. Sullivan points out that security operations are not unobservable processes going on inside an individual. They are processes that we can observe as they arise in the matrix of interpersonal relationships. In simple situations, security operations can be clearly perceived; in complex situations, we may conjecture or imagine them.

Some of the security operations that Sullivan describes are:

Sublimation   This is the expression and discharge of uncomfortable feelings in ways that are interpersonally acceptable. A child demonstrates sublimation in learning to release anger verbally rather than by hitting or kicking the object of his or her anger. We recall that sublimation is also one of Freud's defense mechanisms, but we should note how Sullivan reconceives it to include an emphasis on learning in an interpersonal situation.

Selective Inattention   This security operation is the failure to observe some factor in an interpersonal relationship that might cause anxiety. A husband may not notice his wife's flirtations with other men because those activities threaten his own self-esteem. Sullivan considers selective inattention a very powerful and potentially dangerous security operation. Extensive selective inattention may blind us to what is going on in our world and make it difficult for us to cope with events effectively.

"As if"   This involves an individual behaving as if he or she were someone else in interpersonal relations. In "as if" we act out a false but practical role. One may act "as if" he or she were stupid, to fulfill the expectations of others, when in actuality he or she is not. For the mentally disturbed person "as if" may mean acting as normally as possible. Again, we can see both positive and negative consequences of the security operations. Through the mechanism of "as if," a person may discover that his or her capacities are greater than he or she thought. Through the security operation of "as if," we may convince ourselves that we are competent by behaving consistently in a competent fashion.

The Development of Personality and Its Processes

Sullivan stresses that personality arises developmentally as the result of a person's interaction with the environment. He is quick to point out that the concept of personal individuality, or the belief that each individual is unique, is an illusion. Our tendency to think of ourselves as distinct individuals fails to take account of the fact that in order to communicate and relate to other people, we have had to adjust our potentialities to the necessities of getting along with others. One's personality is shaped by these interactions. The "self" is a system that arises out of innumerable social situations by which we become aware of ourselves in terms of our relationships to other people. It is futile, according to Sullivan, to try to study an individual's personality as if it existed as a discrete entity. Rather, we should concentrate on the ways in which an individual relates to other people. We can observe certain processes in an individual's interpersonal relations and the processes can be used to describe his or her personality. Two such processes that we can perceive in interpersonal relations are dynamisms and personifications.

Dynamisms A *dynamism* is a pattern of energy transformation that characterizes an individual's interpersonal relations (1953). Dynamisms result from experiences with other people. Many, but not all, of the dynamisms that Sullivan describes employ a particular body zone by which to relate to the environment. Here his work is reminiscent of Freud's emphasis on the importance of bodily zones.

The description of a dynamism that occurs in infancy may help to clarify Sullivan's concept. Bodily processes within the infant cause the child to feel hungry. These physiological processes provide the source for a dynamism's energy. The infant cries, and by doing so, summons his or her mother. Thus, the flow of energy initiates an interpersonal contact between mother and child. The mother nurses the child and her activities lead the infant to respond in certain ways, such as feeling satisfied and behaving contentedly. A dynamism or pattern of energy characteristic of an individual's interpersonal relationship has emerged.

In later childhood and adolescence, of course, the dynamisms become much more complex. For example, a person who characteristically relates to others in a hostile manner is expressing a *dynamism of malevolence*. The child who is afraid of strangers illustrates the *dynamism of fear*. The young male who during adolescence seeks sexual relations with young women is expressing the normal *dynamism of lust*.

One of the more significant dynamisms is that of the self or *self-system*. This dynamism develops as a result of anxiety. The self-system is made up of all of the security operations by which an individual defends him- or herself against anxiety and ensures self-esteem. Basically, it is an individual's self-image, which has been constructed on the basis of his or her interpersonal experiences. Sullivan suggests that the concept of self is no more than a response to the interpersonal relationships in which one has been involved. The course of development of the self dynamism is charted by the child's recognition of situations of potential anxiety, that is, parental disapproval and rejection, and his or her attempts to avoid them.

Out of the child's experiences with rewards and anxiety, three phases of what will eventually be "me" or the self-system emerge. The *good-me self* refers to the content of awareness when one is thoroughly satisfied with oneself. It is built up out of an organization of experiences that were rewarding and characterized by a lack of anxiety.

The *bad-me self* is based on anxiety and refers to the content of awareness that is organized around experiences that one tries to avoid because they are anxiety producing. The *not-me self* is a gradually evolving image of aspects of the self that are regarded as dreadful and that cannot be permitted conscious awareness and acknowledgment. These dynamisms are processes rather than structures. They are behavior patterns that have come to characterize one's interpersonal relationships. But they can result in a dissociation of the self in which certain experiences literally become cut off from identification with the self.

EXERCISE:

Good-Me, Bad-Me, Not-Me

You can begin to appreciate Sullivan's distinction of three phases of the self in regard to your own personality by trying to recognize certain experiences that might fit into each phase of your own self-system. Take a sheet of paper and divide it into three columns. Label them "good-me," "bad-me" and "not-me." In the column headed "good-me" make a list of those feelings and experiences you have that make you feel thoroughly content with yourself. For example, someone compliments you for a job you agree was well done, or a significant event enhances the relationship of yourself and a friend, the intense satisfaction you feel when you are relaxed and simply enjoying the pleasure of being you. In the column headed "bad-me" make a list of those experiences and feelings that you have when you are anxious and dissatisfied with yourself. For example, you have just been taken advantage of, been caught in telling a lie, or have done something that met with the disapproval of someone very close to you. In the column headed "not-me" list those experiences and feelings that you believe are totally alien to yourself. These would include activities or feelings that you find very difficult, if not impossible, to recognize or express. For example, committing murder, engaging in certain forms of sexual behavior, or defying particular moral and ethical norms.

These three phases of the self-system emerge out of experiences that make us feel anxious because they threaten our security. We have seen that complete security, or euphoria, is an unattainable goal. Still, each of us seeks to cultivate situations and relationships that will decrease our anxiety and increase our security. Listed below are some areas that many people are concerned about with regard to security: academic security, job security, financial security, intrapsychic and interpersonal security, and health security. Which of these concerns are most important to you? What steps do you find yourself taking to ensure that you will be secure? Do any of these measures resemble Sullivan's security operations?

Personifications A *personification* is a group of feelings, attitudes, and thoughts that have arisen out of one's interpersonal experiences (1953). Personifications can relate to the self or to other persons. The child, for example, develops the personification of the *good-mother* and the *bad-mother* out of his satisfying and anxiety-producing experiences with his or her own mother. In fairy tales, these personifications find expression as the good fairy and wicked stepmother or witch.

An individual's personifications may not be accurate. Indeed, they rarely are. In extreme cases, they may lead to extensive parataxic distortions, which I will describe later on. Nevertheless, personifications persist and are influential in shaping our attitudes and actions toward other people.

Personifications that are shared by a majority of people in any given culture are called stereotypes. *Stereotypes* are prejudgments that we make about people on the basis of their membership in certain groups. Many stereotypes, such as "all Irish are politicians," "all blacks are lazy," or "all professors are absent-minded," are based on inadequate observation. Rather than facilitating our interpersonal relations with members of those groups, they frequently serve to hinder them.

Stages of Development Sullivan outlined six stages in personality development prior to adulthood (1953). In his discussion of the stages and their primary dynamisms and cognitive processes, Sullivan frequently emphasized bodily zones, such as the oral and genital zones. In that sense, his stages are reminiscent of Freud's. However, the stages themselves were thought by Sullivan to be determined socially rather than biologically. That the period of adolescence is seen to be crucial is evidenced by the fact that three of the stages refer to it.

Infancy Infancy refers to the period from birth to the emergence of meaningful speech. During this period, there is an emphasis on the significance of oral experiences. The child's perception of the nipple and his or her mother as good or bad, perceptions that crystallize around the feeding situation, will have a major impact on his or her later view of objects and persons within the environment.

Childhood Childhood extends from the emergence of meaningful speech to the development of the need for playmates. During this period, the child's primary emotional tasks consist of developing healthy relationships with his or her parents.

The Juvenile Era The juvenile era begins with a strong need for playmates and ends with a need for intimacy with peers of the same sex. The juvenile era provides a broader social environment that may be useful in fostering new and more effective patterns of interpersonal relations.

Preadolescence Preadolescence is marked by the need for intimacy with a same-sexed peer and ends when sexual maturation ushers in adolescence. This "chum" relationship, as Sullivan describes it, is important because it is the beginning of genuine human relationships. One develops a close intimate *reciprocal* relationship with another person. In healthy preadolescence, the relationship is not scarred by overt homosexual genital activity.

Early Adolescence Early adolescence begins with physical sexual maturation and leads to the eventual development of a stable heterosexual pattern for the satisfaction of genital sexual feelings. Prior to adolescence, Sullivan believed that sexual impulses play an insignificant role in personality development. During adolescence, the lust dynamism emerges and impells an individual to seek intimate relations with persons of the opposite sex. Genital sexual activity in these relationships is an implied but not necessarily realized goal.

Late Adolescence Late adolescence begins when the individual has established a stable pattern for expressing his or her feelings of lust through heterosexual genital activities. It is a period of integration and stabilization during which the individual achieves the kinds of social, vocational, and economic adjustments that his or her society considers characteristic of the adult. Adulthood is characterized by full stabilization. However, personality is never considered by Sullivan to be fixed and rigid. Blind chance, or the unpredictable and uncontrollable interpersonal situations into which a person is thrown, continues to be important in shaping an individual's interpersonal relations and in determining his or her health or illness.

Although Sullivan does not specify ages for his stages, they can be seen as corresponding roughly to certain common school ages. Infancy refers to the first year of life. Childhood embraces the preschool years. The juvenile era encompasses the elementary school years. Preadolescence is characteristic of the junior high school period. Early adolescence generally occurs during the high school years, and late adolescence occurs during the normal college years.

Cognitive Processes Sullivan describes three *cognitive processes* or modes by which we experience the world and relate to others during the course of personality development. The three cognitive modes, prototaxic, parataxic, and syntaxic, occur developmentally and show that we experience the world differently at different levels of development.

The first and lowest level is the *prototaxic experience*, which is characteristic of the infant. In this experience there is no distinction between the self and the external world. Awareness is diffused and undifferentiated. The child directly perceives certain sensations, thoughts, and feelings, but he or she does not think about them or draw any conclusions. The child is simply involved in what William James (1842–1910), a popular American psychologist and philosopher at the turn of the century, referred to as a "stream of consciousness." The prototaxic mode is a necessary precondition for the other two. From the masses of undifferentiated sensations, the child gradually distinguishes among three different things: material objects, people, and him- or herself. This distinction moves the child into the next level of experience.

The *parataxic experience* sees causal relations between events that happen together. However, the causal relations that it perceives are not those of reality or logic. It involves making generalizations about experience, usually on the basis of proximity. The infant whose cry has brought the mother to nurse assumes that with his or her crying he or she has produced the milk. Superstitions are examples of parataxic thinking. The person who has had a bad experience after seeing a black cat assumes that the black cat is the cause of his or her misfortune. Random movements or patterns that are reinforced at an inopportune time may be repeated or avoided because they are thought to be the cause of the satisfying or anxiety-producing situation. Parataxic thinking is characteristic of the young child whose mind is too immature to understand the causal laws of nature. Yet Sullivan suggested that much of our thinking does not advance beyond the parataxic level. Parataxic distortion may lead us to react to another person as if he or she were someone else. Thus, a man may assume that his boss will be domineering because his father was. When he treats his boss as if he were his father, he illustrates a parataxic distortion.

The highest level of cognitive activity is that of *syntaxic experience,* which entails the use of symbols and relies on *consensual validation,* or agreement among persons. Syntaxic experience relies upon symbols that have an agreed-upon meaning that is shared by other people in one's culture. The use of language is a primary example of such symbols. Young children originally associate their utterances with a general feeling of power and magic. When they cry "Mama" all sorts of exciting things happen. Later, they learn, with some disappointment, that the word "Mama" is not a personal magical pronouncement that carries within itself a certain response like the "open sesame" of ancient fairy tales that opened cavernous doors, but rather a socially agreed-upon name for one's mother. The acquisition of language provides an excellent example of Sullivan's understanding of the developmental process. When a word has been consensually validated, that is, been given an agreed-on meaning by members of a society, it loses its personal meaning and power, but the validation enables individuals to communicate with one another and provides a common ground for understanding experiences. Syntaxic thought begins to develop in childhood and increases during development so that ideally as adults our experience is almost completely symbolic and dependent on syntaxic modes of cognition.

Sullivan's method of psychotherapy is one of the most carefully worked out and fully described non-Freudian systems. It has been adopted by a large number of psychiatric practitioners. Essentially, Sullivan views and describes psychotherapy as an interpersonal process in which one person assists another in resolving problems of living (1954).

During an interview patient and therapist sit across from each other in comfortable chairs. However, to avoid the nervousness that might arise from staring at each other continually, Sullivan suggests that the therapist turn his or her body at a 45- or 90-degree angle away from the patient. The therapist is still in full view of the patient, but this position frees them both from the need to look continually at each other, while permitting them to look if they so desire.

Sullivan uses the concept of participant observation to define the nature of psychiatric inquiry and treatment (1954). The concept of *participant observation* refers to the fact that the psychiatrist is engaged in observing one or more interpersonal relationship in which he or she is an active participant. While observing what is going on, the psychiatrist is also affecting that relationship by participating in it. By his or her attitude, posture, comments, or questions, the psychiatrist alters the other person's behavior. Sullivan suggests that it is absurd to imagine that a psychiatrist could obtain from his or her patient data and/or behaviors that are uninfluenced by the therapist's own behavior in the relationship.

Sullivan, who spent his youth doing manual labor on his father's farm, suggests that psychotherapy is the hardest work he knows. It requires continual alertness, honesty, and flexibility on the therapist's part. The therapist is invariably emotionally involved in the therapeutic process. He or she may be interested, bored, frustrated, or angry. The therapist must continually try to be alert to his or her reactions, understand them, and keep them at a minimum in order to continue to be an alert observer. Not only is psychotherapy hard work, it also must not be expected to provide the usual satisfactions of ordinary interpersonal relationships. The therapist does not look for friendship, gratitude, or admiration from the patient. He or she aims simply to have the patient understand him- or herself better. The therapist's rewards come from knowing that he or she is doing a job well and is being reasonably paid for it.

The work of psychotherapy primarily involves dealing with the patient's anxiety, lack of awareness, and security operations. These processes reduce a person's awareness and make it difficult for the person to assimilate and understand his or her experiences so that he or she might profit by them. Exploring these areas is painful to the patient because it increases anxiety. Nevertheless, it is necessary in order to broaden his or her awareness. Part of the psychiatrist's task is to keep anxiety at an optimal level for furthering the therapeutic process. A certain amount of anxiety is necessary to motivate the patient to continue to work on his or her problems. Too much anxiety, however, can overwhelm and paralyze. Sullivan does not hesitate to ask directed and probing questions in order to focus attention on a problem. He also makes statements designed to reduce the patient's anxiety so that he or she can talk more fully about a pain-laden area. For example, he might say, "Why do you think that is so horrible?" The fact that the therapist does not express alarm over the patient's behavior is, in itself, reassuring.

A major portion of the therapy is spent in examining the two-person interpersonal relationship that exists between the therapist and the patient. This is one sample of the patient's interpersonal life that is made available for direct study through therapy. During therapy, the patient frequently begins to treat the physician as if he or she were someone else. Freud labeled this phenomenon transference. In Sullivan's terms, the patient develops a *parataxic distortion*. A patient who had a harsh authoritarian father may react to the therapist as if he or she were also harsh and authoritarian. Such parataxic distortion is not unique to therapy. It occurs in everyday life as well. Normally, however, it simply invites puzzled or angry responses from other people and interferes with effective interpersonal relationships. In therapy, it is an invitation for further exploration and study that can be used to increase the patient's self-awareness of what is happening in his or her interpersonal relationships. Eventually the parataxic distortion must be destroyed so that the patient can work cooperatively with the therapist.

In addition to examining the patient-therapist relationship and dealing with anxiety and security operations, psychotherapy involves exploring the patient's past and current relationships with others. These can be explored to see how they reiterate the processes that have been observed in the present patient-therapist relationship. Sullivan also pays attention to immediate interpersonal crises. These provide a wealth of information, especially if they can be tied to similar crises in the past. Lastly, Sullivan discusses future interpersonal relationships by asking what the patient thinks his or her relationships with certain people will be like in the future. Sullivan refers to such an exploration of the future as *constructive reverie*. Through constructive reverie the therapeutic process can take into account and deal with the patient's expectations and apprehensions about the future.

EXERCISE:

Constructive Reverie

Constructive reverie provides another opportunity for the reader to further his or her own self-understanding. You can engage in constructive reverie by asking yourself what you think your relationship will be like with regard to your mother, your father, each sibling, peer group, lover, or spouse, and others in a month, a year, five years from now, and ten years from now. When you have finished outlining your expectations, ask yourself whether or not they are realistically based. Then check to see whether or not you feel comfortable with these projections of the future. If you are uncomfortable, what are some of the things that you might do in order to change these projections?

In his discussion of therapy, Sullivan paid considerable attention to the interview, which was his term for the interpersonal process that occurs between the patient and therapist. The *interview* refers to a single session or series of sessions that are held between a patient and therapist. The length of each individual session and of the series varies depending on the needs of each patient and other realistic factors. Sullivan suggests that each interview and the course of psychotherapy itself be composed of four parts: the inception, the reconnaissance, the detailed inquiry, and the termination (1954).

During the *inception,* the patient describes the problems that have brought the patient into therapy or that concern him or her during a particular session. At this time, the interviewer is a quiet observer who is attempting to determine the reasons why the patient has entered into therapy and the nature of his or her problem.

The therapist initiates the *reconnaissance* by his or her own comments and questions. Through his or her questions the therapist develops a case history and tentative hypotheses about the patient. Should a patient have difficulty in answering a question, Sullivan might invite the person to free associate by simply asking, "Well, what does come to mind when I ask you that question?" However, Sullivan is critical of free association as a primary therapeutic technique. He also distrusts protracted introspection when it is not carried out in the context of a dialogue between two persons. He suggests that free association and introspection need to be continually questioned and further verified in a dialogue.

During the *detailed inquiry,* the interviewer tests his or her hypotheses by asking detailed questions that zero in on specific instances in the patient's past and present interpersonal relationships that would confirm or disprove the therapist's hunches. He or she listens, probes, and observes. The therapist will also interpret the patient's behavior in order to facilitate understanding. Such interpretations must be carefully made and timed if they are not to fall on deaf ears. By identifying the patient's selective inattention and inadequate self-system, the therapist assists the patient in dealing with them.

In his discussion of dreams, Sullivan shows that he believes that any distinction between a manifest and a latent dream is presumptuous. The dream should be taken at face value as an indication of what we are not like in our everyday conscious life. Sullivan suggests that the key to understanding dreams lies in recognizing their interpersonal nature. In our dreams, we project onto other people or objects our own dynamisms, which we may be unaware of. The dream actually serves the purpose of relieving tension and securing those satisfactions that are not present in everyday relations.

During the *termination*, the interviewer summarizes what has been learned, prescribes some kind of action that the patient might take in regard to his or her problem, and assesses the probable effect of these actions. Sullivan believes that each interview should have a structured conclusion. This is true of each particular session as well as of the therapy as a whole. The patient should gain some benefit from each and every session even if it is only clarification of a minor point. Some form of insight, limited though it may be, should be provided at the conclusion of each interview.

Sullivan views therapy as an uncovering process that provides insight into an individual's interpersonal relations. Such insight removes obstacles to growth and permits the patient to channel his or her own self-healing powers toward constructive progress. It is inaccurate to suggest that the therapist "cures" the patient. He or she merely acts as a catalyst, permitting the patient's own curative powers to come forth.

Evaluation and Implications

There is little question but that Sullivan was aware of the need for validating evidence in personality theory. He emphasized that his theory was grounded on empirical data and observation. He did not invoke imaginary concepts that could not be tested. If a hypothesis was not open to empirical scrutiny, it was rejected. Although he was primarily a clinician, Sullivan encouraged both clinical and experimental study in the development of a theory of personality.

In his concept of dynamism as energy transformations, Sullivan is in tune with twentieth-century physics, which since Einstein (1879–1955) and Planck (1858–1947), physicists who ushered in the modern era, has viewed the universe in terms of the flow and transformation of energy. The nineteenth century had understood the universe in terms of material objects and forces, according to a Newtonian mechanical analogy. Thus, Freudian psychoanalysis described personality processes as forces of varying strengths that collide with one another. In comparison, Sullivan's increased use of energy constructs is more consistent with the predominant twentieth-century scientific approach to nature.

Sullivan's vocabulary is also consistent with modern information and communication theory, which stresses interpersonal relations. At the same time, Sullivan's concepts closely follow Freud's and many of his ideas have been incorporated into the mainstream of psychoanalysis. The primary difference may be one of vocabulary (Corsini, 1977).

Sullivan's work has generated research related to his interpersonal theory. His interest in the therapeutic process has spurred considerable research in techniques of interviewing. Some of these projects are described in *Psychiatry*, the journal Sullivan developed to announce his ideas. The effort to test Sullivan's concepts has been hampered, however, by the fact that they remain difficult to define operationally and to test empirically. Although his concepts have a clear empirical reference, they are frequently stated in a vague or ambiguous manner that is difficult to translate for experimental testing purposes. It is hard, for instance, to distinguish between dynamisms and personifications, two key concepts of his thought.

Although he was an empiricist, Sullivan was not naive in his reliance on empirical data. His concept of participant observation shows us that he was all too aware that the scientific method cannot be purely objective because it is always influenced by the participation of the observer. He was, therefore, an empiricist, who was both naive yet sophisticated, and who led the way to a behaviorist approach to the study of personality.

JOHN DOLLARD AND NEAL MILLER: PSYCHOANALYTIC LEARNING THEORY

John Dollard and Neal Miller were both born in Wisconsin. They taught and worked together at the Institute of Human Relations at Yale University. This institute was founded in 1933 in an effort to explore the interdisciplinary relationships among psychology, psychiatry, sociology, and anthropology. Dollard and Miller's joint efforts resulted in a personality theory based on Hull's reinforcement theory, but that combines those findings with psychoanalytic theory. This integration has resulted in a behaviorist theory that has become truly representative of the mainstream of American psychology. Students of psychology will find this theory familiar as many introductory texts present the subject in a manner that conforms closely to Dollard and Miller's position.

Both Dollard and Miller brought their own distinctive interests and concerns to their collaborated efforts as well as their joint interest in the principles of learning and the concepts of psychoanalysis. John Dollard was born in 1900. He was granted the A.B. from the University of Wisconsin and the M.A. and Ph.D. from the University of Chicago. His primary interests were in sociology and anthropology. He was a strong advocate of interdisciplinary studies. Neal Miller was born in 1909. He was granted the B.S. from the University of Washington, the M.A. from Stanford, and the Ph.D. from Yale. His primary interests

JOHN DOLLARD

NEAL MILLER

　Behavior and Learning Theories

lay in experimental psychology. Both men undertook psychoanalytic training, each has held a number of significant positions, and each has authored several books or articles, in addition to their affiliation with and collaboration at the Institute of Human Relations.

Habits: The Structure of Personality

Dollard and Miller emphasize the key role of learning in the development of personality. Therefore, they place less stress on the aspect of personality structure. They suggest that the structure of personality can be defined very simply as habits (1950). *Habits* refer to some kind of learned link or association between a stimulus and response that make them occur together frequently. Habits represent a very fluid and temporary structure in personality theorizing because habits can appear and disappear. Because they are learned, they may also be unlearned. This is a much simpler concept of the structure of personality than we have encountered heretofore and represents an even stronger emphasis on environmental forces. The primary concern of Dollard and Miller's theory is not to develop an elaborate structure of personality, but to specify those conditions in the environment under which habits are acquired or unlearned.

Drives: The Motivation of Personality

Dollard and Miller suggest that the primary motivation or dynamic underlying personality development is that of *drive reduction* (1950). Drawing heavily upon Hull's theory of learning, they point out that drive reduction is at the heart of behavioral theory. Reducing a drive is reinforcing to an individual, and thus an individual will behave in such a manner as to relieve the tension that is created by strong drives.

Dollard and Miller distinguish between primary and secondary drives. *Primary drives* are those drives that are associated with the physiological processes that are necessary for the organism's survival. Examples would be the drives of hunger, thirst, and need for sleep. We rarely observe primary drives in a direct form because society has developed some means of satisfying the drive before it becomes overwhelming. Most of us begin to feel hungry and to eat around about the time that other people in our society eat meals. Thus, primary drives, by and large, are satisfied through secondary drives. *Secondary drives* are drives that are learned and acquired on the basis of primary drives. Dollard and Miller consider them to be elaborations of the primary drives. A person is motivated to eat at a particular time, to earn money in order to buy food, and to satisfy other drives of physical comfort in the normal mode of his culture.

Dollard and Miller also distinguish between primary and secondary reinforcers. *Primary reinforcers* are those that satisfy primary drives, such as food, water, or need for sleep. *Secondary reinforcers* are originally neutral, but they acquire reward value on the basis of their having been associated with primary reinforcers. Money is a secondary reinforcer, as is wine or an exotic dish. A mother's smile or a word of praise are also secondary reinforcers as they are associated with a state of physical well-being.

The Learning Process: Key to the Development of Personality

The key to understanding personality is the learning process, a process whereby we acquire habits and develop specific behavioral responses. The infant begins life with certain basic genetic and biological equipment, but his or her personality is shaped primarily by learning. As infants, we appear on the scene with a specific organic makeup, the primary drives, a few specific reflex responses, and an innate hierarchy of response. We begin life with the basic equipment needed to satisfy our drives, but the specific behaviors that we will use to satisfy them are learned or acquired. An infant quickly learns to suck deliberately in order to obtain food. Acquisition of the specific behaviors that characterize adult life occurs through the learning process.

Reflex responses are automatic responses to specific stimuli. All of us blink automatically to avoid an irritant to the eye or sneeze to eliminate an irritant to the nose. We pull our hand away reflexively should it touch something hot. An infant will turn its head in the direction of something that touches its cheek and begin to suck. Such reflexes are important for our survival. By *hierarchy of response*, Dollard and Miller mean that there is a tendency for certain responses to occur before others. For example, an infant might innately seek to escape from certain unpleasant stimuli before it would cry. An animal innately runs to avoid a shock rather than cringe and bear it in pain. If a response is unsuccessful, however, an organism will try the next response on the hierarchy. If that does not work, the next will be tried, and so forth. Learning, in part, involves reinforcing and/or rearranging the response hierarchy.

Dollard and Miller suggest that the learning process can be broken down into four main conceptual parts (1950):

Drive A *drive*, as we have already seen, is a stimulus impelling a person to act, but in no way does the drive direct or specify his or her behavior. It simply impels.

Cue A *cue* refers to a specific stimulus that tells the organism when, where, and how to respond. The sight of a bottle acts as a cue directing the infant to suck. The ringing of a bell or the time on a clock is a cue to students to enter or leave the classroom.

Response A *response* is one's reaction to the cue. These responses occur in a hierarchy. Thus, we can rank a response according to its probability of occurring. We can tell in a given situation that one response is more or less likely to occur than another response. But this innate hierarchy is not rigidly fixed or permanent; it can be changed through learning.

Reinforcement Reinforcement refers to the effect of the response. Effective reinforcement consists of drive reduction. If a response is not reinforced by satisfying a drive, it will undergo extinction. Extinction does not eliminate a response, it merely inhibits it, enabling another response to grow stronger and supersede it in the response hierarchy. If present responses are not reinforcing, the individual is placed in a *learning dilemma*. He or she will try different responses until one is developed that satisfies the drive.

EXERCISE:

The Learning Process

The four steps in the learning process as outlined by Dollard and Miller can be fruitfully used to help us understand some of our own habits and frequent responses. Choose a habit that you engage in frequently. Remember that "habit" simply means a learned association between a stimulus and a response. The habit may be positive, such as locking your car when it is parked in a questionable neighborhood, or negative, such as overeating. What are the basic underlying primary and subsequent secondary drives that your behavior seeks to fulfill? What are the specific cues that trigger your response? What are the consequences of your behavior that reinforce the habit? Such an analysis may assist you in discriminating between cues that trigger specific behaviors and reinforcements that strengthen them. Later in the chapter I will suggest ways to develop more appropriate responses where you are dissatisfied with your present behavior.

Research Concerning the Learning Process

Dollard and Miller have conducted extensive studies on reinforcement (1950). Their experiments have shown that *immediate reinforcements,* those that immediately follow a response, are much more effective than *delayed reinforcements,* those that are delayed. Dollard and Miller also distinguish between *positive reinforcements,* or rewards, and *negative reinforcements,* or punishments. They acknowledge that negative reinforcement is effective in extinguishing responses, but they point out that negative reinforcements frequently have unpleasant side effects. A

FIGURE 6.1 Plotting a Gradient

The gradient of reinforcement may be plotted on a graph, which shows that immediate reinforcement is more effective than delayed reinforcement.

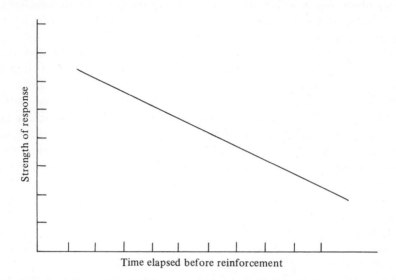

Time elapsed before reinforcement

person may obey but develop a feeling of resentment or hatred toward the parent or authority who punishes.

In order to study further the learning process, Dollard and Miller have used the concept of gradient. A *gradient* refers to the changing strength of a force. Essentially it means that the strength of a force may be plotted on a graph in order to show the changes in strength that occur in different circumstances. Thus, a gradient of reinforcement may be plotted on a graph to illustrate clearly the changes in behavior that occur when reinforcement is given immediately, when it is withheld for a short period, or when it is delayed for a long period of time.

Gradients may also be employed to measure the phenomenon of *generalizations*, that is, the tendency for learning to transfer to another situation depending on the degree of similarity. We can also employ gradients of discrimination to measure the tendency to make fine distinctions in a behavior response depending on the differences in cues.

Dollard and Miller suggest that essentially all human behavior can be comprehended in terms of the learning process. It is through the learning process that one acquires secondary drives. These drives may form a very complex system, but the underlying process by which they are developed is essentially the same: drive, cue, response, reinforcement. Even our higher mental processes can be understood in terms of the learning process. A chain of thought simply involves an internalized process of drive, cue, response, reinforcement, in which one thought serves as a cue for the next thought and so forth.

As psychologists, Dollard and Miller are concerned not only with the principles of learning, but also with the conditions of learning. Dollard and Miller state emphatically that human behavior can be comprehended only within the social context in which it occurs (1941). Just as one could not predict a rat's behavior without knowing where in a T-maze its food is placed, one cannot understand the behavior of a human being without knowing his or her "maze" or social environment.

Studies in Frustration and Conflict

Dollard and Miller have conducted a great number of studies in the area of frustration and conflict (Miller, 1944, 1951b, 1959). *Frustration* occurs when one is unable to satisfy a drive because the response that would satisfy it has been blocked. If the frustration arises from a situation in which incompatible responses are occurring at the same time, the situation is described as one of *conflict*. In conflict, a response is blocked by a competing response.

Conflicts, in brief, entail some sort of opposition between tendencies we have to approach or avoid certain objects and goals. Dollard and Miller distinguish among several different types of conflict. In an *approach-approach conflict*, the individual is simultaneously attracted to two goals that have positive value but that are incompatible. I wish to see a particular TV special tonight, but a book just arrived that I am anxious to read. In an *avoidance-avoidance conflict*, a person faces two undesirable alternatives. He or she cannot escape in either direction without meeting one of these negative goals. A student does not wish to study for a test but does not want to fail the exam. In avoidance-avoidance conflicts, should the conflict be intense and the two alternatives too painful, the individual may, if possible, leave the field. In our example, the student might withdraw from the course. A third kind of conflict is *approach-avoidance*. In an approach-avoidance conflict, one and the same goal both attracts and repels the individual. A classic example of an approach-avoidance conflict is the blind date. One anticipates a blind date with mixed feelings. One may meet the boy or girl of one's dreams; on the other hand, one may face a boring evening. These conflicts may be simply diagrammed, as is shown in Figure 6.2. The diagrams are simplified representations of complex situations. In everyday life, of course, the situation is seldom so simple. Therefore, it is often necessary to talk about and plot compounded situations of conflict, such as a *double approach-avoidance conflict* in which at one and the same time an individual may be dealing with multiple goals that both attract and repel.

The value of these graphic presentations lies in the fact that if we could assign specific numbers to the intensity of the forces involved, we could also predict a person's actions in reference to a particular goal.

FIGURE 6.2 Diagramming Conflicts

The conflicts that Dollard and Miller describe may be diagrammed simply as shown here.

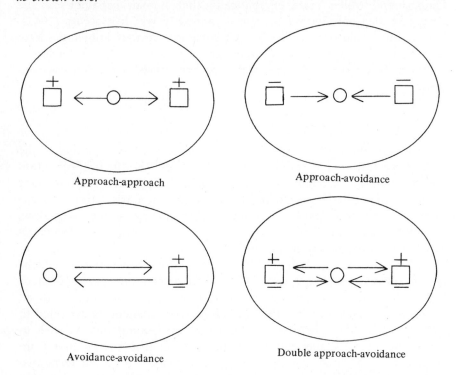

Approach-approach

Approach-avoidance

Avoidance-avoidance

Double approach-avoidance

Human situations are so complex that such prediction is not possible at the present time. But Dollard and Miller have conducted experiments with infrahuman species that have permitted some degree of prediction.

In a classic experiment, rats were placed in a harness attached to a leash so that measurements could be made as to how hard they pulled on the leash in order to arrive at or avoid a particular goal (Brown, 1948). In one case, the goal was food. Here the experimenter noted that the pull on the leash became greater the nearer the animal came to the food. This enabled the experimenter to plot the gradient of approach. In another situation, rats were placed in a similar device where they had learned to expect an electric shock at the goal. In this experiment, they were placed near the goal and permitted to run away. The experimenter noted that they pulled harder at the harness when they were near the goal than after they had gotten some distance away from it. This enabled him to plot the gradient of avoidance. It was discovered that both the tendency to avoid and the tendency to approach reach their highest point near the goal. However, the gradient of avoidance is steeper than the gradient of approach. The rats pulled harder at the harness to avoid the shock than they did to obtain the food.

Knowing these facts, and having obtained these measurements, the

FIGURE 6.3 Gradients of Avoidance and Approach

The gradient of avoidance is steeper than the gradient of approach. Therefore, if a rat were placed in position A, it would be likely to run away from the goal, but if it were placed at position B it would go toward the goal until the gradient of avoidance becomes strongest.

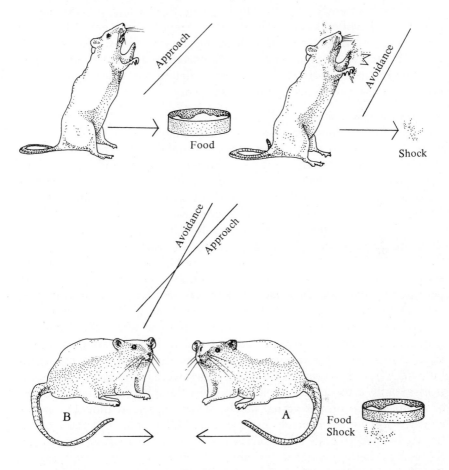

experimenter was able to predict what a rat would do if it were placed in any particular position within a box from which it had learned that it would receive both food and a shock at the goal, as Figure 6.3 shows. If an animal were placed in the box at position A, it would be likely to run away from the goal because the gradient of avoidance is stronger. But if it were placed in position B, it would be likely to begin to approach the goal until it reached the point where the gradient of avoidance became stronger.

Ideally, if we could measure the complex forces that impel human behavior, and if we could develop sophisticated formulas that would encompass all of the variables involved, we could predict the behavior of lower species, and we could also predict complex human behavior. Dollard and Miller's theory has been quite successful in predicting the behavior of simple laboratory animals under controlled conditions. They have not been as successful in predicting complex human behavior.

The Integration of Learning Theory and Psychoanalysis

In their attempt to integrate learning theory and psychoanalysis, Dollard and Miller have adapted many Freudian concepts. However, they have redefined them into learning theory terms. For example, Dollard and Miller appreciate the importance of unconscious forces underlying human behavior, but they redefine the concept of unconscious processes in terms of their own theory.

Unconscious Processes Dollard and Miller refer to two main determinants of unconscious processes. First, they suggest that we are unaware of certain drives or cues because they are unlabeled. These drives and cues may have occurred before we learned to speak and therefore we were unable to label them. In any given society, certain cues may be unconscious, because the society has not given them adequate labels. In our society, we have essentially one word for snow, although we might further describe it as dry or slushy. In certain Eskimo cultures, there are thirty or more different words for the various textures of snow. Such a society is certainly much more aware of the different variations in snow than we are. Distortions in labeling may also effect one's conscious perception. Through distorted labeling, an emotion, such as fear, may become confused with another emotion, such as guilt. Thus, an individual may react in frightening situations as if he were guilty due to a distortion in labeling. Second, Dollard and Miller suggest that unconscious processes refer to cues or responses that once were conscious, but which have been repressed because they were ineffective. *Repression* is essentially a process of avoiding certain thoughts. It entails the loss of ability to use proper verbal labels. Thus, repressed thoughts are no longer under verbal control. Dollard and Miller point out that repression is learned like all other behaviors. When we repress, we do not think about certain thoughts or label them because they are unpleasant. Avoiding these thoughts reduces the drive by reducing the unpleasant experience.

Dollard and Miller make a clear distinction among suppression, repression, and inhibition. *Suppression* refers to the conscious, deliberate stopping of a thought or an action. A mother may wish to make a verbal attack on her child, recognize the wish, and consciously suppress the impulse to belittle him or her. Thus, suppression entails stopping a thought or action by conscious design and intent. *Repression* is the unconscious counterpart of suppression. It is an unconscious learned response of not thinking. *Inhibition* refers to prevention of a response from occurring, because that response conflicts with other strong responses that are unconscious and not under verbal control. Even though an appropriate stimulus may be present, the response is prevented from occurring due to unconscious competing responses. Inhibition frequently lies behind the problem of impotence or frigidity. The problem is not that the individual lacks a sexual drive, but that he or she is prevented from carrying it out or responding to sexual cues because of unconscious conflicts.

In the same way, Dollard and Miller articulate many of the other defense mechanisms that Freud outlined: projection, identification, reaction formation, rationalization, and displacement. In each case, however, they are seen as learned responses or behaviors and they are articulated in terms of learning. For example, identification entails imitating the behavior that one has learned from another. Displacement is explained in terms of generalization and the inability to make proper discriminations.

EXERCISE:

Suppression

Suppression can be an important adaptive device that enables us to curb inappropriate responses, since suppression entails the conscious, deliberate stopping of a thought or action. Any learned or secondary drive can be suppressed. First, identify certain behaviors or desires that you would like to stop because they lead to unproductive results, such as a quick temper, obsession with being popular, or a tendency always to blame yourself. Recognizing these impulses and taking steps to avoid their expression can help us to achieve other goals that are more important to us. When the cues that normally trigger the unproductive response occur, try to engage in other activities that will divert your attention away from the problematic impulse. The old adage that one should count to ten before expressing his or her anger is a simple device that permits suppression. If you find yourself beginning to engage in certain behaviors like self-incrimination, you might try to stop and recognize those factors in the situation that you could not realistically control before further blaming yourself. Obviously, we cannot suppress all of our desires and impulses, but practice in suppression can help us acquire greater self-control.

Unlike suppression, repression and inhibition are not under conscious control. Thus, their effect is often negative rather than positive. Professional intervention is often mandated to assist in lifting repressions and inhibitions, because we are not aware of the source.

Critical Stages of Development Dollard and Miller's restatement of the concepts of Freudian psychoanalysis into learning terms can also be seen in their discussion of critical stages of development. They posit four critical training stages in child development. These are the feeling situation in infancy, cleanliness training, early sex training, and the training for control of anger and aggression. These are critical periods in the child's development in which social conditions of learning imposed by the parents may have enormous consequences for future development. The parallel to Freud's stages is obvious. The conflict situation of feeding in infancy is reminiscent of Freud's oral stage, cleanliness training is reminiscent of Freud's anal stage, and early sex training as well as the effort to control anger and aggression are elements of Freud's phallic stage. Dollard and Miller agree with Freud that events in early childhood are vitally important in shaping later behavior. Further, they suggest that the logic of these events may be comprehended within the learning process as they have outlined it. Whereas Freud's stages unfold biologically, the outcomes of Dollard and Miller's stages are controlled by the learning process. Thus, the infant whose cry when hungry brings immediate relief in the sense of being fed learns that self-generated activity is effective in reducing drives. If the infant, however, is left to "cry it out," he or she may learn that there is nothing self-generated that can be done to reduce the drive and begin to develop a passive attitude toward drive reduction.

Freudian concepts like fixation and repression are also reinterpreted in the light of learning theory principles. *Repression* is understood as returning to an earlier pattern of response because a present behavior pattern has been frustrated. *Fixation* is described as being arrested at an earlier pattern of response because new, more appropriate behaviors have not been learned. Thus, in their incorporation of Freud's theories, Dollard and Miller have reconsidered his ideas in the light of learning theory principles and elaborated them in those terms.

Dollard and Miller's translation of Freudian concepts into learning theory terms has stimulated a great deal of scientific research and experimental testing of Freud's concepts (1941, Miller, 1944, 1951a, 1959). However, in incorporating Freudian concepts into learning theory, Dollard and Miller do not give a precise translation of Freud. Whereas for Freud, anxiety, conflict, and repression were inevitable aspects of the human condition, for Dollard and Miller they are learned responses. Thus, there are significant differences between Freud's concepts and Dollard and Miller's articulation of them. However, by incorporating and transforming many of Freud's concepts into the terms of learning theory and experimental psychology, they have rendered Freud more palatable to a large number of people. It is less threatening to us to believe that unconscious processes and defense mechanisms are learned and may therefore be unlearned. In Freud's theory, such processes were universal and inescapable. One could merely try to recognize them in order to cope with them more effectively.

Psychotherapy

We have seen that for Dollard and Miller behavior is learned in the process of seeking to reduce drives. Abnormal behavior is similarly learned, but in the neurotic, the behaviors that have been learned are frequently self-defeating and unproductive. Dollard and Miller refer to neurosis as a "stupidity-misery-symptom" (1950). The word "stupidity" does not mean that the neurotic is unintelligent or dumb. Rather, it means that the patient has strong, unconscious, and unlabeled emotional conflicts, usually of the approach-avoidance type. His or her stupidity lies in the fact that the problem has not been labeled. Because the neurotic has not labeled the problem, he or she does not discriminate effectively. The neurotic generalizes and applies old, ineffective solutions to current problems and situations. A young man whose father was a tyrant may have learned in early childhood that he had to react to his father meekly in order to avoid his father's wrath. Unable to discriminate between his father's attitude and the attitude of other authority figures in his life, the young man may generalize his response to his father to later authority figures who in fact are not tyrants. In such situations, his meek response may not be the most appropriate one. Dollard and Miller suggest that "neurotic conflicts are taught by parents and learned by children" (1950). Because they are learned habits and patterns of response, however, they can be unlearned and new habits may be established in their place.

Therapy involves unlearning old, ineffective, unproductive habits and substituting new, more adaptive, and productive responses for them. Dollard and Miller refer to two phases in therapy (1950). In the *talking phase*, neurotic habits are studied, examined, and identified so the patient may unlearn them. Essentially, this procedure entails providing appropriate labels for the patient's responses. When we label a repression appropriately, the repression is lifted because we have erased the distortion. The reader may recall the fairy tale of Rumpelstiltskin, who loses his demonic powers once he is confronted with his name. When the repressions are correctly identified and labeled for what they are, their power to harm the individual disappears.

Accurate labels assist one in discriminating between stimuli and appropriate responses to them. Accurate labels also serve to rectify those situations in which cues have been mislabeled. The young boy who accidentally breaks an expensive vase may fear his mother's anger. If his mother not only responds in anger but also with accusations of deliberate intent on the boy's part, the young boy may begin to feel guilt as well. In the future, fear-provoking situations may be compounded with feelings of guilt. Labeling helps to clarify and discriminate in these situations.

Dollard and Miller employ free association and interpretation in their therapy, particularly during the talking phase. They refer to the therapist's interpretations as *successive approximations* in which the therapist tries to provide increasingly more accurate labels for the patient's response.

The second phase of therapy is the *performance phase*. During this phase, the patient acquires new, more adaptive and productive responses and habits and he or she is encouraged to apply them. Deliberate training in suppression can be helpful. The patient can be trained to suppress, that is, to consciously stop or limit those thoughts and actions that reinforce old habits. At the same time, he or she deliberately exposes him- or herself to new cues that will evoke different responses.

Dollard and Miller's theory of therapy represents a bridge to the more directive and active therapies of other learning theories. It is pragmatic and action oriented. While Freud thought it necessary to work through past problems for an analysis to be successful, Dollard and Miller believe that historical recollection and the abreaction of past events is effective only if it is instrumental in creating change. If historical recollection is unnecessary for change to occur, it is only a short step to exclude that emphasis on the past and concentrate on the behaviors of the present as subsequent learning theorists do.

Dollard and Miller also suggest that in order for the patient to sustain the new habits and responses that he or she has learned in therapy, a habit of self-study needs to be developed. *Self-study* refers to self-observation and analysis. We have already encountered this idea in conjunction with Karen Horney. Such self-study should be taken whenever we sense that a problem is emerging. We need to examine our responses and determine their appropriateness. The habit of self-study assists the patient after therapy in continuing to reinforce what he or she has learned.

Reciprocal Inhibition: A Related Form of Therapy

Joseph Wolpe (1915–   ) is a psychiatrist whose method of treatment is also based largely on the application of learning principles established in the laboratory. He was born in 1915 to an orthodox Jewish family who had immigrated from Lithuania to the Union of South Africa. He received his medical training at the University of Witwatersrand in South Africa. Originally attracted to psychoanalysis, he rejected Freud's theory because he believed that scientific research did not give it empirical support. On the other hand, he found in the work of Clark Hull a systematic theory of learning that he could expand.

Wolpe developed his methods of treatment after conducting a series of experiments with animals in which he created experimental neuroses in the animals and then attempted to cure them. In one study, he gave electrical shocks to cats who were in a restricted environment and could not escape. The cats showed a high level of anxiety and other neurotic symptoms and were unable to eat when placed in the experimental apparatus. Wolpe was able to cure his cats by feeding them in a series of laboratory apparatus with graduated similarity to the one in which they had received the shocks. Eventually the cats were able to eat in the original training apparatus without any overt signs of anxiety.

On the basis of his findings, Wolpe developed the principle of reciprocal inhibition (1958). *Reciprocal inhibition* entails the introduction of a competitive response that will interfere with the original maladaptive or nonproductive response. Wolpe suggests that anxiety is an automatic response that an organism exhibits in the presence of painful or harmful stimuli. If anxiety becomes too intense during the process of conditioning, it may lead to neurosis, in which one becomes anxious about subsequent stimuli that are not really harmful. However, if a response that competes with anxiety can be made to occur at the same time the anxiety-evoking stimulus is presented, it can weaken the relationship between the stimulus and the anxiety. By developing a competitive response, the anxiety may be inhibited.

Wolpe suggests that neurotic anxiety can be counterconditioned by creating other behaviors that are antagonistic to the anxiety. He has developed a number of different therapy techniques, but the common denominator of them all is reciprocal inhibition, which entails introduction of a competitive response that will inhibit the original nonadaptive or nonproductive response. The particular technique employed with any given patient is determined after an extensive interview process that helps to clarify what stimuli are causing the problem and what would be the best tactics to employ in eliminating the symptoms.

Systematic Desensitization In systematic *desensitization* the patient is conditioned to stop responding with anxiety to the stimulus and to substitute a new response. Wolpe has discovered that relaxation is often a very successful competing response. It is very difficult for a person to feel anxious in a situation in which he or she is deeply relaxed. Thus, the first step in systematic desensitization is to train the patient in deep muscle relaxation. In the course of a series of six or seven sessions, the patient is taught how to relax various parts of the body so that eventually he or she is able to relax practically at will.

EXERCISE:

Learning to Relax

We are all aware of the calm ease in our bodies when we are lying or sitting in a position of rest. Joseph Wolpe, however, has developed a method of relaxation that permits individuals to relax even beyond that point by helping them become aware of the activities involved in tensing various muscle groups and then letting go. The following exercise* may be useful in assisting you to increase your normal level of relaxation.

* Adapted from Joseph Wolpe, *The Practice of Behavior Therapy*, 2nd ed., New York: Pergamon Press, 1973.

To begin the exercise, seat yourself comfortably in a desk chair and grip the arm of the chair with one hand. Notice the different sensations produced in your forearm and hand. The sensations in your hand are primarily due to touch and pressure, whereas the sensation in your forearm is due to muscle tension. Carefully study the tension of the muscles in your forearm, as these are the muscle contractions that you will seek to relax. Relax and observe the contrast in feeling. It is important to note that this letting go is also an activity, but it is of a negative kind. It is the negative activity of letting go or relaxing the muscles that you wish to learn.

By progressively concentrating on different muscle groups, tensing and relaxing each in turn, you can, through practice, increase your ability to let go and enter progressively deeper states of relaxation. As your body becomes more relaxed, you will begin to notice further sensations. The usual ones are tingling, numbness, or warmth. These sensations indicate a degree of deep muscle relaxation that goes beyond the usual state of rest. Each of the following techniques is useful in locating particular muscle groups that you may want to relax.

The Arms   Ask a friend to grip your wrist while you bend your arm against that resistance. This activity will make you aware of tension in your biceps. Straighten your bent elbow against your friend's resistance in order to feel the tension in muscles along the back of your upper arm. Once you have located these muscles, practice relaxing your arms by gradually increasing the negative activity of letting go. Place your hands comfortably in your lap and allow the muscles of both arms to relax.

The Facial Region   Raise your eyebrows and wrinkle your forehead to create an anxious expression. Slowly and gradually relax them. Close your eyes tightly, then let them relax. In turn, wrinkle your nose, purse your lips and press them together, clench your jaw and bite your teeth together. As you relax your jaw, your lips will part slightly. Press your tongue hard against the backs of your lower teeth, and then let it fall back into your mouth. These activities assist in locating the muscles of the forehead, eyes, lips, jaw, and tongue.

The Neck and Shoulders   Concentrate on the sensations present at the back of your neck as you maintain your head in an erect posture. As you relax these muscles, the head will fall forward. Hold your arm in a horizontal position and then move it backward, forward, and up to the ear to become aware of the muscles in your shoulders.

The Back, Abdomen, and Thorax   Contract your back muscles by arching your spine. Tighten your abdominal muscles and make your abdomen hard, as if you were expecting a punch in the belly. Breathe in deeply, fill your lungs, and notice the tension created as you hold your breath. As you exhale, you will automatically relax.

The Lower Limbs   Bend your toes in order to locate muscles within *your foot. Press your toes on the floor to tense your calf muscles. Move your foot backward and forward. Straighten your knee and try to bend it against resistance. Place your hand on the inner side of the knee and move your leg against that resistance. These activities assist in locating various muscles of the lower limbs.*

Perfect relaxation will not be achieved the first time, but with practice you can become increasingly aware of various muscle groups and the sensations involved as you relax them. Your body will become heavy and you will feel increasingly tranquil as you arrive at deeper and deeper levels of relaxation.

The second step in systematic desensitization is to construct anxiety hierarchies. Wolpe will ask the patient to identify all of the sources of his or her anxiety. These sources are grouped into common themes. Each theme is itemized and the patient is asked to rank each item, placing the item that is most disturbing at the top of the list and the item that is least disturbing at the bottom. The following is an example of part of a hierarchy of fears developed by one of Wolpe's patients, a twenty-four-year-old art student whose severe anxiety over examinations had led to several failing grades.

Hierarchy of Examination Fears
1. On the way to the university on the day of an examination
2. In the process of answering an examination paper
3. Standing before the unopened doors of the examination room
4. Awaiting the distribution of examination papers
5. The examination paper lies face down before her
6. The night before an examination
7. One day before an examination
8. Two days before an examination
9. Three days before an examination
10. Four days before an examination (1958)

Once the patient is trained in deep muscle relaxation and anxiety hierarchies have been constructed, the desensitization process itself begins. First weak and later progressively stronger anxiety-arousing stimuli are presented to the patient to imagine as he or she reclines in a deeply relaxed state. The patient is asked to imagine him- or herself four days before an examination. At the sign of any anxiety the patient is asked to inform the therapist and the scene is discontinued until the patient is able to relax again. Eventually the patient is able to imagine scenes of greater intensity and duration with less and less anxiety and increasing relaxation. In short, a competitive response has been established.

The following description of systematic desensitization is taken from Joseph Wolpe's account of his procedures.* The patient is the twenty-four-year-old art student whose hierarchy of examination fears was presented earlier. After having trained the patient in deep muscle relaxation and agreed on a scale for reporting anxieties, the therapist proceeds to bring about a deep state of relaxation in the patient and introduces the first desensitization session:

TH (Therapist): I am now going to ask you to imagine a number of scenes. You will imagine them clearly and they will generally interfere little, if at all, with your state of relaxation. If, however, at any time you feel disturbed or worried and want to draw my attention, you can tell me so. As soon as a scene is clear in your mind, indicate it by raising your left index finger about one inch. First, I want you to imagine that you are standing at a familiar street corner on a pleasant morning watching the traffic go by. You see cars, motorcycles, trucks, bicycles, people, and traffic lights; and you hear the sounds associated with all these things.
After a few seconds the patient raises her left index finger. The therapist pauses for five seconds.

TH: Stop imagining that scene. By how much did it raise your anxiety level while you imagined it?

PT (patient): Not at all.

TH: Now give your attention once again to relaxing.
There is again a pause of twenty to thirty seconds.

TH: Now imagine that you are home studying in the evening. It is the twentieth of May, exactly a month before your examination.
After about fifteen seconds Miss C. raises her finger. Again she is left with the scene for five seconds.

TH: Stop that scene. By how much did it raise your anxiety?

PT: About fifteen units.

TH: Now imagine the same scene again—a month before your examination.

At this second presentation the rise in anxiety was five SUDs [Subjective Units of Disturbance] and at the third it was zero. . . . Having disposed of the first scene of the examination hierarchy, I [the therapist] could move on to the second. . . . Freedom from anxiety . . . was achieved in seventeen desensitization sessions, with complete transfer to the corresponding situations in actuality.

---

* J. Wolpe, *The Practice of Behavior Therapy*, 2d ed., Pergamon Press, New York, 1973.

Assertive Training In *assertive training* the patient is taught to express his or her feelings in various everyday situations. Training in assertion is not limited to training in aggression. The patient is taught to express friendly and affectionate feelings as well as angry and hostile ones. Wolpe points out that many of us have been trained to inhibit expression of our feelings in social situations in order to be considered polite and socially graceful. Because of this we may let others take advantage of us without objecting to their behaviors, or we may feel inhibited in expressing the positive feelings we have toward other people. Assertive training entails being taught to stand up for what one feels. If an individual butts in front of somebody in a line saying, "I'm sure you won't mind," that person should be able to say, "I'm sorry, but I do mind, please go back to the end of the line."

Wolpe has found behavioral rehearsal a useful adjunct in assertive training. *Behavioral rehearsing* is a form of role playing. Wolpe will play the role of someone who is giving the patient difficulty, such as a boss who frequently asks the patient to work overtime when it is inconvenient. Through behavioral rehearsal the patient may be able to assert him- or herself and point out that it would be an imposition, rather than timidly and continually give in. Behavioral rehearsal may also help one envision a compromise in which both parties are satisfied.

Aversion therapy Although Wolpe rarely considers aversion therapy the first choice of treatment, he has explored its use. The technique of *aversion therapy*, also known as *avoidance counterconditioning*, entails coupling an unpleasant stimulus of strong avoidance response, such as an electric shock, with an undesired response. This technique has been used in the treatment of alcoholism and drug addiction. Alcoholics have been given an emetic, a drug that induces vomiting, and then given an alcoholic beverage. The patient vomits violently as a result of the emetic, which is given in close proximity to the alcohol. After several such sessions the patient may begin to feel queasy or nauseous at the sight or smell of alcohol and lose the desire to drink it. Aversion therapy has been used to eliminate such undesired behaviors as drinking, gambling, nail biting, overeating, and homosexuality. It was graphically described in the book and film *Clockwork Orange*. Such aversive techniques will not usually be effective, however, unless the patient is also exposed to other stimuli that will reinforce the expression of the desired response. Otherwise, when the inappropriate response is no longer negatively reinforced, it may demonstrate spontaneous recovery. To those critics who point out that aversive therapy entails sadistic control, Wolpe points out that it should not be used unless the patient voluntarily agrees that this particular treatment technique is in his or her best interest.

Evaluation and Implications

Behavior and learning theories of personality have developed from laboratory studies and experimentation rather than from clinical work with patients or theoretical speculation. Behavior and learning theorists claim to base their statements on empirical evidence and have shown a definite willingness to submit theoretical differences to observational tests. They recognize, perhaps more than many other theorists, that a theory is useful or not useful in terms of its effectiveness in leading to predictions that can be tested. As scientific theories, therefore, behavior and learning theories have been very attractive to many psychologists because of their appeal to validating evidence.

It is not always clear, however, whether or not statements such as "learning takes place via drive reduction" or "personality is composed of habits" function simply as scientific generalizations in Dollard and Miller's theory or have taken on the aura of philosophical commitments. Repeated animal studies may suggest the usefulness of these concepts, but they cannot convince us of their ultimate truth.

Nor is the empirical evidence always as supportive as Dollard and Miller imply. What an organism can learn is limited by *species specific behavior*, complex, rather than reflex, behaviors that occur in all members of a species. Some stimuli are more relevant to a particular species than others. Possible responses also differ. Pigeons peck, chickens scratch, and pigs root. It is difficult, if not impossible, to alter these behaviors. One cannot easily generalize from a rat to a human being.

As we have seen, Dollard and Miller have taken many of the concepts of Freudian psychoanalysis and rendered them into the imaginary constructs of a scientific theory. They have provided his concepts with operational definitions and shown that they can be tested experimentally. Many consider this a substantial contribution to the viability of Freud's concepts. Whether psychoanalysis has gained or lost in the process, however, is a matter of considerable debate (Rapaport, 1953). Some would point out that in the process of translation, Freudian concepts have lost considerable dynamism and been emptied of their original intent. Others suggest that Freud's in-depth clinical study of humans is far more illuminating for understanding the dynamics of human personality than Dollard and Miller's research with rats.

Nevertheless, the viewpoint of Dollard and Miller has been central to the field of personality since they first published their major work, *Personality and Psychotherapy*, in 1950. Dollard and Miller's system of personality seeks to emulate a pure scientific model and places a great deal of emphasis on empirical research. As such it has generated a large group of supporters.

Sullivan did not care to write much about his ideas; he published only a few articles for technical journals. He did not express his thoughts for lay people and avoided writing for his colleagues save to inform them of certain concepts and treatment techniques that he had found useful in working with patients. Only one book, *Conceptions of Modern Psychiatry*, was published during his lifetime. It was privately printed by friends through the William Alanson White Psychiatric Foundation in 1947, against Sullivan's better judgment. After his death, however, Sullivan's followers collaborated in publishing seven volumes of his ideas. These works consist of transcripts of his lectures and seminars. They are difficult reading because of uneven quality and organization, but they provide a written expression of his ideas.

The Psychiatric Interview (Norton, 1954) is probably of most interest to the lay person. It deals with the evaluation of patients and is the clearest of Sullivan's works. *The Interpersonal Theory of Psychiatry* (Norton, 1953) contains his last full series of lectures and emphasizes his concepts of personality development. *The Fusion of Psychiatry and Social Sciences* (Norton, 1964) consists of seventeen articles, two of which are valuable in portraying the transitional character of his work as a bridge from psychoanalysis to behaviorism: "The Data of Psychiatry" and "The Illusion of Personal Individuality."

Three good secondary sources about Sullivan and his thought are Patrick Mullahy, *The Contribution of Harry Stack Sullivan* (Hermitage House, 1952); Dorothy Blitsten, *The Social Theories of Harry Stack Sullivan* (William Frederick Press, 1953); and A. H. Chapman, *Harry Stack Sullivan: His Life and His Work* (Putnam, 1976).

Dollard and Miller have jointly written two books that describe their effort to develop a theory of personality. Of primary interest is *Personality and Psychotherapy: An Analysis in Terms of Learning, Thinking, and Culture* (McGraw-Hill, 1950). In this work, the authors outline how they have applied the concepts of learning theory to reconsider many of the insights and observations of Freudian psychoanalysis. In it, Freud's theory of personality, therapeutic concepts, and procedures are translated into learning theory terms. The book is an outstanding introduction to the learning and behavior approach to personality.

Social Learning and Imitation (Yale University Press, 1941) represents an early attempt to apply Hull's principles of learning to the study of personality. It is a good introduction to an effort to use learning theory to understand personality.

Individually, and in collaboration with each other and others, Dollard and Miller have written several articles. Some of these are cited in the Bibliography. Joseph Wolpe's therapy techniques for clinical practice are included in *The Practice of Behavior Therapy* (Pergamon, 1973).

CHAPTER 7

Social Behavior and Learning Theories

Social behavior theories analyze personality development in terms of principles derived from learning theory and seek to apply their findings to social situations. The group of theorists that we will consider in this chapter share with John Dollard and Neal Miller, as well as the earlier behaviorists, the belief in the importance of learning for shaping personality. They differ from them, however, in that they reject the psychoanalytic concepts of Sigmund Freud and are pragmatic rather than theoretical in their work. Social behavior and learning theories have come to represent a predominant position in American psychology today.

The most well known is the controversial, yet highly influential, B. F. Skinner, who espouses a point of view known as *radical behaviorism*. Skinner explicitly states that he is not concerned with positing any internal underlying motivations or structures that may be said to constitute personality. His sole concern is to study, predict, and control behavior. Thus, he provides us with a rigorous application of the methods, data, and concepts that emerge out of the scientific study of learning.

Albert Bandura and Richard Walters have emphasized the significance of social factors in learning. They criticize learning approaches to personality that emphasize animal studies and individual learning situations for their limited conceptions. By viewing the person within his or her social context, Bandura and Walters believe that a fuller picture of the learning process will emerge. Julian Rotter has contributed to the study of learning an appreciation of the subjective expectations that a

person brings to a situation, and he has suggested a preliminary formula that will enable us to predict a person's behavior in any given situation. Lastly, Walter Mischel has made major contributions to the understanding and treatment of abnormal behaviors and social problems.

BURRHUS FREDERIC SKINNER: RADICAL LEARNING THEORY

Burrhus Frederic Skinner is without doubt the most well-known and influential psychologist in America today. Skinner was born in 1904 in Susquehanna, Pennsylvania. His father, a conservative Republican, was an ambitious lawyer who eventually earned a substantial income but was unable to recognize his own success. His mother was bright, beautiful, and of high moral standards. A younger brother, of whom he was fond, died suddenly at the age of sixteen. Skinner was reared in a warm, comfortable, and stable home, imbued with the virtues and ethics of small-town, middle-class Americans at the turn of the century. His parents did not employ physical punishments, but their admonitions and warnings succeeded in teaching their son "to fear God, the police, and what people would think." His parents and grandparents, to whom he was close, taught him to be faithful to the puritan work imperative, to try to please God, and look for evidence of God's favor through "success."

As a child, Skinner was fascinated with machines and interested in knowing how things work. He spent many hours building things. He constructed the usual childhood wagons, slingshots, and model airplanes, and he also tried his hand at inventing things. He developed a mechanical device to remind himself to hang up his pajamas, a gadget that enabled him to blow smoke rings without violating his parents' prohibition against smoking, and a flotation system to separate ripe from green elderberries. For many years he tried to design a perpetual motion machine, but it did not work.

Skinner was also interested in animal behavior. He caught and brought home a number of the small wildlife of the woodlands in western Pennsylvania, such as snakes, lizards, and chipmunks. At a county fair, he was highly impressed by a troupe of performing pigeons. Skinner later was to train pigeons and other animals to play Ping-Pong, guide a missile to its target, and perform other remarkable feats.

At school Skinner was an excellent student. He majored in English at Hamilton College, a small liberal arts school in upstate New York, and he seriously thought of becoming a writer. He sent a few short stories to the well-known poet, Robert Frost, who encouraged him in his writing aspirations. He decided to take a year or two off to write, but he quickly became discouraged and decided he could not write as he "had nothing important to say." During this interlude, he read books by Ivan Pavlov and John Watson. These men impressed him, and he decided to begin graduate studies in psychology at Harvard. He received the Ph.D. in 1931.

He taught at the University of Minnesota for nine years and was chairman of the department of psychology at Indiana University, before he returned to Harvard in 1948, having established a reputation as a major experimental psychologist and having written his influential book *Walden II*, which describes a utopian society based on psychological principles. To this day he continues to work at Harvard, following a rigorously disciplined schedule.

A Theory of Personality without Personality

Skinner is the leading heir and advocate of the behaviorist position. It could be said that, in many respects, Skinner has taken the beliefs and concepts of John Watson's behaviorist theory to their logical extreme. He concurs with Watson that it is unproductive and foolish to refer to concepts or structures of the personality that cannot be directly observed. Since we cannot directly observe personality constructs such as an id, ego, or superego, it is virtually useless for us to invoke them. We have seen that Dollard and Miller developed a psychoanalytically oriented behavioral theory in which they combined the insights of Freud's psychoanalytic position with the principles and concepts of learning theory. Skinner takes the logical step that follows from Dollard and Miller's approach. If a stimulus-response theory of psychology can account for all of the overt behaviors that psychologists seek to explain, why not omit the psychoanalytic underpinnings and concepts and simply rely on behaviorist principles (Rychlak, 1973)? Skinner, therefore, has developed a psychology that concentrates not on the person but solely on those variables and forces in the environment that influence a person and that may be directly observed. Thus, Skinner presents behaviorism and learning theory in its purest and most extreme form.

In many ways, Skinner appears to be out of place in a book that concentrates on theories of personality. Skinner has not provided any theory of personality, rather, he has described those variables and forces in the environment that shape an individual's overt behavior. Indeed, Skinner suggests that it is ultimately futile to invoke any concept of personality whatsoever. The effort to understand or explain personality in terms of internal structures such as an id, ego, or superego is to speak in terms of "fictions," because the terms are not very helpful. First, they are presented in such a way that they cannot be directly observed. Second, it is very difficult to deduce from them operational definitions; and, lastly, it is virtually impossible to develop systematic and empirical means of testing them (1953).

Because such concepts are not easily dealt with or managed by the scientist, Skinner simply proposes that we ignore them and any other type of internal structure of personality. Instead, he suggests that we concentrate on the environmental consequences that determine and maintain an individual's behavior. Thus, Skinner suggests that in order to understand a person, it is unnecessary to posit any internal structure of personality. One can simply consider the person as if he or she were empty and observe how changes in the environment affect his or her behavior. For Skinner, the term "personality" is ultimately superfluous, as behavior can be completely comprehended in terms of responses to different forces or factors in the environment.

At the same time, Skinner believes that it is also unnecessary and misleading to posit internal forces or motivational states within a person because their intensity cannot be measured. Skinner does not deny that such states occur; he simply sees no point in talking about them because they cannot be operationally defined. Rather than try to determine how hungry an organism is, Skinner tries to determine what variables or forces in the environment affect the individual's eating behavior. What is the effect of the time period that has elapsed since the last meal was eaten? What are the consequences of the amount of food consumed? Such factors in the environment can be specifically defined, measured, and dealt with empirically.

Skinner, therefore, does not posit any structures or dynamics of personality whatsoever. Some of his critics suggest that Skinner begins with the doctrine of the "empty organism" or the "unopened box" (e.g., Boring, 1946). These terms were not coined by Skinner, and he objects to them as well as to the label "stimulus-response theorist." Skinner fully acknowledges that at birth the infant is not a tabula rasa or blank slate. The newborn is an organism with a certain genetic inheritance, certain reflex capacities, and other abilities to respond, as well as certain drives and motivational states that set it in motion. These factors are given and cannot be changed. Thus, Skinner suggests that their study is of little value. It is more important and useful to show how behavior can be modified or changed by the environment than to show how it occurs from internal structures or forces.

The Development of Behavior Through Learning

At birth, the human infant is simply a given bundle of capacities but his or her consequent behaviors can be comprehended in terms of learning. Thorndike's law of effect stated that when a behavior or performance is attended by satisfaction it tends to be stamped in or increased. If the performance is attended by frustration, it tends to decrease. Omitting Thorndike's reference to internal states, Skinner comes up with a very simple definition of reinforcement. A *reinforcement* is anything that increases or decreases the likelihood of a response. It is the effect of one's behavior that determines the likelihood of its occurring again. If a young child cries or whines, perhaps he or she will get parental attention and be reinforced. If the behavior results in reinforcement, chances are the child will repeat that behavior pattern. If the behavior does not result in reinforcement, that is, if the child is ignored and does not receive attention, then it is likely that the behavioral response will cease and the child will behave in alternate ways to find patterns of behavior that are reinforced.

Operant Conditioning Skinner distinguishes between two types of behavior: respondent and operant (1938). *Respondent* behaviors refer to reflexes or automatic responses that are elicited by a stimulus. A beam of light causes the pupils of one's eye to contract. If the knee is tapped on the right spot, the leg jerks forward. When our fingers touch hot metal, we reflexively pull our hand away. Such behaviors are unlearned. We are not taught to perform them, they occur involuntarily and automatically.

Respondent behaviors may, however, be conditioned or changed through learning. Respondent behaviors were involved in Pavlov's demonstration of classical conditioning. Pavlov's dog learned to salivate to the tone of a bell. An infant learns to suck at a nipple. These are reflexes or automatic responses that have come to be performed in the presence of the previously neutral stimulus through the process of association.

Operant responses are responses that are emitted without a stimuli necessarily being present. They occur spontaneously. Not all of a newborn's movements are reflex responses. Some of them are operant behaviors in which the infant acts on his or her environment. An infant swings an arm or moves a leg and certain consequences follow. These consequences determine whether or not the response will be repeated. Skinner believes that the process of *operant conditioning* is of far greater significance than simple classical conditioning. While classical conditioning most assuredly occurs and governs much of our behavior, many of our behaviors cannot be accounted for in those terms. Rather, they are originally spontaneous behaviors whose consequences determine their subsequent frequency.

There is a clear distinction between the nature of a respondent behavior and an operant behavior. A respondent behavior is evoked or elicited by a stimulus. Operant behavior is emitted or freely made by the organism. The nature of reinforcement also differs in classical conditioning and operant conditioning. In classical conditioning, the stimulus is the reinforcement and it precedes the behavior. In operant conditioning, the effect of the behavior is the reinforcement. Thus, in operant conditioning the reinforcement follows the behavior.

Operant conditioning can be systematically described by depicting the behavior of a rat in an operant conditioning apparatus, a piece of laboratory equipment that Skinner designed in order to train animals and conduct research. Commonly known as a "Skinner box," the apparatus makes possible controlled and precise study of animal behavior.

When a food-deprived rat is first placed within the box, it may behave in a variety of random ways. The rat may first walk around the box and explore it. Later, the rat may scratch itself or urinate. In the course of its activity the rat may at some point press a bar on the wall of the box. The bar pressing causes a food pellet to drop into a trough under the bar. The rat's behavior has had an effect on the environment. The food acts as a reinforcement, increasing the likelihood of that behavior occurring again. When it occurs again it is reinforced. Eventually, the rat begins to press the bar in rapid succession, pausing only long enough to eat the food.

Operant conditioning can be schematically diagrammed as follows:

$$S \; \text{-----} \rightarrow \quad R \quad (\text{response})_1$$

$$(\text{situation}) \qquad R_2$$

$$R_3$$

$$R_4$$

.

.

.

$$R_n \quad (\text{operant response desired})\text{----Reinforcement}$$

When a food-deprived rat is conditioned in a Skinner box to press a bar and is reinforced for that behavior with food, we can predict pretty accurately what the rat is going to do in subsequent sessions in the Skinner box. Furthermore, we can control the rat's behavior by changing the reinforcement. As Skinner observes, the person who controls reinforcement has the power to control behavior. The person who is reinforcing determines the desired behavior. The organism emits a variety of behaviors. When the desired behavior occurs, it is reinforced. Appropriate reinforcement increases the likelihood of that behavior occurring again.

Shaping Frequently the behavior that one wishes to train an organism to do is a complex, sophisticated one that the organism would not naturally be expected to do shortly after entering the box. Suppose one wished to train a pigeon to peck at a small black dot inside a white circle. If one were to wait until that behavior spontaneously occurred, one might wait a very long time. Therefore, Skinner developed and employs a procedure termed *shaping*, in which he deliberately shapes or molds the organism's behavior in order to achieve the desired behavior. In shaping, undifferentiated behavior of the organism is gradually molded according to an ordered series of steps until it increasingly approximates the desired behavior.

Initially, the pigeon moves randomly about the box. When it moves in the direction of the circle, it is reinforced by a pellet of food in the trough below the circle. The next time it approaches the circle, it is again reinforced. Later, it is required to approach the circle more closely before it is reinforced. Later still, it is not reinforced until it pecks the white circle. Finally, the pigeon is reinforced only for pecking at the small black dot within the circle. Through shaping, an organism may be led to develop a behavior that it might never have emitted spontaneously.

Through shaping, Skinner has been able to induce behaviors in animals that they would not normally do. Some of these are unique and remarkable feats. Skinner himself taught pigeons how to play Ping-Pong. During World War II, he trained pigeons for use in air-to-ground missiles. He trained them to peck at objects that were projected onto a screen in such a way that they could guide a missile. His pigeons never actually were put to work guiding missiles, but Skinner showed that it was possible for them to do so. Through behavioral-shaping methods, other animal trainers have been able to produce unusual tricks and feats. A rabbit may be trained to jump into the seat of a toy fire truck and ring the bell. Animals have been taught to play musical instruments and baseball, jump through fiery hoops, dance complex steps, and to perform other tricks. If you have a pet dog, chances are you have trained it to perform a few simple tricks and you have done so by shaping its behavior through reinforcement.

Skinner believes that most animal and human behavior is learned through operant conditioning. Certainly the process of learning to speak one's native tongue involves reinforcing and shaping of operant behavior. The young infant emits certain spontaneous sounds. These sounds are not limited to the sounds of the parents' native tongue but represent all possible languages. Initially, the infant is reinforced by parents for simply babbling. Later, the child is reinforced for making the sounds that approximate meaningful words in his or her native language. Eventually the child is reinforced only for meaningful speech. Thus, the process of shaping is entailed in the process of learning to speak, as well as many other human behaviors.

EXERCISE:

Classical and Operant Conditioning

The reader can easily demonstrate the processes of classical and operant conditioning. Eye blinking is a normal reflex response that we commonly make when an irritant enters our eyes. We do not, however, normally blink simply because we hear certain words, such as "personality." But one can condition a subject to blink to the sound of the neutral word "personality," by means of the following simple process of classical conditioning. Standing close to your subject, focus a soda straw near one of his or her eyes and gently puff to elicit blinking. A few trials should help you determine the distance and strength of puff that is most effective. Then, in a rhythmic pattern say the word "personality" before you puff into your subject's eye. Repeat the process several times in rapid succession. State the word "personality." Pause for less than a second. Puff into your subject's eyes and wait for the blink. Eventually your subject will begin to blink just to the sound of the word "personality," before you have a chance to puff on the straw. Classical conditioning has occurred. Of course, you do not need to fear that your subject will be fated to blink at the sound of the word "personality" for the rest of his or her life. When the response is no longer reinforced by the original stimulus, it will undergo extinction.

You can easily demonstrate the process of operant conditioning by having a friend agree to behave as if he or she were reinforced by the sound of your clapping. Choose a simple uncomplicated behavior that you would like your subject to perform. Appropriate tasks might be to pick up a book lying on a table, to turn a light switch on or off, or to write (anything) with a piece of paper and pencil. Initially, you reinforce your subject by clapping whenever he or she moves in the direction of the vicinity in which the desired behavior is to be performed. Next, you require your subject to be very close to the area. Later, you only reinforce when he or she appears to be attending to the object of the desired behavior: the book, the light switch, or the paper and pencil. Eventually, you will reinforce your subject only for performing the desired task.

After the demonstration, you might ask your subject how he or she felt during the process of conditioning. Some subjects report that they feel quite frustrated when put in the position of a rat in a Skinner box. You might recognize the demonstration as a version of the game "Hot or Cold" that many children play. This is Skinner's point. He suggests that learning has always occurred through reinforcement, but that we now have the opportunity to study it scientifically and employ it systematically.

Schedules and Types of Reinforcement A practical necessity led Skinner to explore the effect of different schedules of reinforcement. In the 1930s, commercially made food pellets were not available. Skinner and his students found that it was a laborious, time-consuming process to make the eight hundred or more food pellets a day that were necessary to sustain his research. Skinner wondered what the effect would be if the animal was not reinforced every time it performed the desired behavior. This question led to the investigation of various schedules of reinforcement.

Skinner has described three schedules of reinforcement and indicated their effectiveness (1967). In *continuous reinforcement*, the desired behavior is reinforced each time that it occurs. The pigeon or rat is given a food pellet every time that it pecks the small black dot or presses the bar. A continuous schedule of reinforcement is extremely effective in initially developing and strengthening a behavior. However, if the reinforcement is stopped, the response quickly disappears or undergoes extinction.

In *interval reinforcement*, the organism is reinforced after a certain time period has elapsed, regardless of whether or not the desired response has occurred. Interval reinforcement may be given on a fixed or variable basis. If it is *fixed*, the same time period elapses each time (such as five minutes). If it is *variable*, the time periods may differ in length.

Chances are that at some time or another during the interval, the desired behavior has occurred. Thus, the reinforcement continues to produce a level of response that is more difficult to extinguish than responses that have been continuously reinforced. However, the level of response tends to be lower than the level produced by other kinds of schedules. Further, if the organism can anticipate the interval, the response may increase just before the anticipated reinforcement and drop significantly afterwards.

This type of reinforcement schedule occurs frequently in the everyday world. A teacher of young children permits them all to go out for recess at the end of the period allotted for arithmetic. An employee may be paid at the end of each week. A student is given exams at certain intervals within the semester. In each of these cases, the reinforcement is essentially independent of the individual organism's performance. Inefficient as it may be, we continue to employ this kind of reinforcement when other schedules might be more effective.

In *ratio reinforcement*, reinforcement is determined by the number of appropriate responses that the organism emits. A pigeon may be reinforced after it pecks the small black dot five times. A factory worker may be paid according to the number of pieces that he or she completes. Ratio schedules of reinforcement may also be fixed or variable. If they are *fixed*, the number of responses required prior to reinforcement is stable and the same each time. If they are *variable*, the number of appropriate operant behaviors that must occur prior to reinforcement changes from time to time. While a continuous schedule of reinforcement is most effective for initially developing and strengthening a behavior, a variable ratio schedule is most effective thereafter in maintaining it. Responses maintained under the conditions of variable ratio reinforcement are highly resistant to extinction and less likely to disappear. Gambling casinos have learned this lesson well. Their use of the principle of variable ratio schedules keeps many an addicted gambler at the table long after money allotted for gambling has disappeared.

Skinner suggests that further research in this area and the systematic application of effective schedules of reinforcement will give greater efficiency in shaping desired behavior. Skinner points out that under the condition of free reinforcement, where reinforcement is haphazard or independent of the organism's behavior as in interval reinforcement, the behavior that immediately preceded any given reinforcement may be increased even if it is not the desired behavior. Take the situation of a pigeon who is on an interval schedule of reinforcement for pecking a black dot. Perhaps, by chance, just prior to the arrival of the food pellet, the pigeon began to groom itself, smoothing its feathers with its beak. The pigeon may go through a protracted period of grooming as if it were that behavior that was being reinforced. Skinner refers to such behaviors as "superstitions," and he suggests that many ineffective habits and common superstitions have their origin in such chance reinforcement.

Skinner has also explored the effectiveness of different types of reinforcement. He concurs with Dollard and Miller in distinguishing between *primary reinforcers*, which are unlearned and by their very nature reinforcing, and *secondary reinforcers*, which in and of themselves are meaningless but that can acquire a learned reinforcing value by their association with primary reinforcers. Skinner also refers to *generalized conditioned reinforcers* (1953), which are learned reinforcers that have the power to reinforce a great number of different behaviors. These reinforcers, such as praise and affection, can be given by anyone. Furthermore, an individual can bestow them upon him- or herself. Ideally, as we grow older, we move from primary reinforcers to more generalized types of reinforcers. Young children initially respond appropriately for food or other things that meet their basic needs. Later, they respond appropriately for pennies, an allowance, or gold stars. Ideally, they associate these reinforcers with the simultaneous praise and affection that accompany them. Eventually, it is hoped that children will work primarily for the reinforcement of praise, which can be self-given.

Skinner distinguishes among positive reinforcement, punishment, and negative reinforcement (1972). *Positive reinforcement* is anything that serves to increase the frequency of a behavior. *Punishment* is an undesirable consequence that follows a behavior and that is designed to stop or change it. *Negative reinforcement* refers to unpleasant stimuli that can be changed or avoided by certain behavior. Skinner's distinction between punishment and negative reinforcement merits special attention. The difference lies in whether or not the unpleasant consequence can be avoided. If it can be avoided, it is a negative reinforcement. Speeding tickets are negative reinforcers, because one can avoid getting a speeding ticket by driving within the speed limit. If the unpleasant consequence cannot be avoided, it is punishment. Placing an animal in a compartment in which it is going to receive an electric shock regardless of how it behaves is punishment because the shock cannot be avoided. The father, who is angry and determined to spank his son is going to do so regardless of how the son pleads or cries.

Punishment may stop or block a behavior, but it does not necessarily eliminate it. The organism may simply seek other means toward acquiring the same ends. Punishment creates fear, but if the fear is diminished, the behavior will recur. Punishment can also lead to undesired side effects. The punished person may respond with anger, hatred, and helplessness. In short, other undesirable behaviors may be induced by punishment.

The effects of negative reinforcements are unpredictable. At times they are effective, at other times they are not. All too frequently they appear to be simply the threat of punishment, and thus, they are easily confused with punishment and can lead to similar undesired consequences. In order to avoid speeding tickets, a driver may install a CB radio in his or her car in order to know when it is "safe" to speed.

Skinner suggests the use of methods different from either punishment or negative reinforcement in order to eliminate behaviors that are not desired (1953). One may ignore the behavior until it undergoes extinction or one may permit satiation to occur. *Satiation* entails permitting the person to indulge in the behavior until he or she tires of it. A child may be allowed to turn a light switch on and off until he or she becomes bored. One may also change the environment that provokes the behavior. Fragile objects may be placed out of a young child's reach. Finally, one can promote behaviors that counteract and inhibit the undesirable behaviors through positive reinforcement.

Skinner emphasizes that positive reinforcement is most effective in initiating and maintaining desired behaviors. However, he points out that the area of positive reinforcement merits careful further study. All too often we do not recognize how we inadvertently give positive reinforcement to a behavior that is not deemed desirable. The child who is seeking attention may actually be positively reinforced by a parental scolding, rather than negatively, because the scolding affords the child attention. By identifying our reinforcement patterns, we can strengthen those that are most effective and develop more efficient means of controlling behavior.

Behavioral Change

Skinner explains maladaptive or neurotic behavior in terms of the learning principles that sustain and maintain it. The neurotic or psychotic is one who has been conditioned by his or her environment to behave in inappropriate ways. If we wish to change an individual's behavior, we can restructure his or her environment in such a way that it will no longer sustain his or her maladaptive behavior and it will reinforce desirable behavior. Thus, in describing neurosis, Skinner does not find it necessary to refer to concepts like repression or conflict. These explanatory fictions are not necessary because maladaptive behavior can simply be reduced to the variables in the environment that reinforce and sustain it.

The role of therapy is to identify the behaviors that are maladaptive, remove them, and substitute more adaptive and appropriate behaviors through the process of operant conditioning. There is no need to review the individual's past or encourage reliving it. Therapy is not dependent on self-understanding or insight. Some insight may occur, but such self-understanding is not necessary for behavioral change. Therapy consists simply of restructuring the environment in such a way that undesired behaviors are eliminated and more desired behaviors are substituted.

The contrast between Freud and Skinner emerges clearly in their attitudes toward therapy. As we have seen, Freud's intent was primarily scholarly. He sought to increase an individual's self-understanding, and psychoanalysis is relatively uninterested in specific behavioral change. Skinner's interest, on the other hand, is totally pragmatic and curative. Behavior modification seeks to eliminate undesired behaviors by changing the environment within which they occur.

Skinner's approach toward behavior modification has been notably successful in areas where traditional insight therapy has failed or is inappropriate. One of its more spectacular successes has been in the area of dealing with mute individuals who, for obvious reasons, are not amenable to traditional therapies, which are largely based on talking. A pioneer in employing many of Skinner's techniques in the attempt to teach autistic and mute children to speak is Dr. O. I. Lovass. Lovass (1967) has employed a systematic program of shaping consistent with Skinner's description of operant conditioning. First, Lovass identifies something that is reinforcing to the child. Since food is generally reinforcing for children, it is commonly employed. Initially, Lovass reinforces the child with a small piece of food every time he or she makes a sound. Gradually he shapes these sounds until they approximate words. Eventually, he reinforces the child only when he or she communicates in full sentences, and so forth. The reinforcement of food is coupled with praise and affection so that the type of reinforcement grows from primary and secondary reinforcers to generalized conditioned reinforcers that can be self-applied. These methods are also generalized to include training in other desired behaviors.

Since sustaining the newly learned behavior depends on maintaining a supportive environment, Lovass includes parents and other significant figures in his program of behavior modification. Parents and other influential figures such as teachers are taught to apply systematically the same reinforcers to similar situations in the home or school. In this way the circle of the environment is widened to permit greater control.

The several techniques employed by behavior and learning therapists may be considered *directive* rather than *nondirective*. In psychoanalysis, the course of the therapy is determined primarily by the patient's free associations, which bring to light materials for interpretation and understanding. In that sense, the patient rather than the analyst directs the course of the therapy. With behavior modification techniques, the therapist constructs a specific situation and confronts the patient with specific stimuli that are designed to facilitate unlearning of the undesired response and substitution of more appropriate behaviors. In doing so, the therapist firmly directs the course of the treatment. The patient is given specific directions to follow and may even be given homework assignments to carry out between sessions. A frequent assumption of directive techniques is that the therapist is in a better position than the patient to determine what are and what are not appropriate behaviors and what techniques are most effective in creating behavioral change.

Skinner's influence has also extended into the area of therapeutic communities. His methods and techniques have been employed in schools for the mentally retarded, mental institutions, and rehabilitation centers. In many of these institutions, a *token economy* has been established. The patient is reinforced for appropriate behaviors by being given tokens of some kind that may subsequently be exchanged for special privileges or things that the patient would like to have. Making one's bed, getting dressed, talking to other patients, and other desirable behaviors are reinforced by tokens that can be exchanged for candy, cigarettes, TV watching, and other amenities that would not normally be provided.

The influence of Skinner's programs may also be seen in the area of education. With Sidney Presley, Skinner developed the teaching machine, an electronic device whereby students may be taught without the need for an ever-present human instructor. Skinnerian principles also underlie numerous systems of individualized and programmed instruction. In such programs, the work is broken down into small units that must be mastered before a student is permitted to proceed to the following unit. The student is virtually being shaped as he or she masters the material. There is immediate reinforcement in the sense of immediate feedback to the student on correct and incorrect answers. There are many who suggest the need for a more systematic application of Skinnerian learning principles in our schools.

Lastly, Skinner's concepts and principles have been applied systematically in industrial and business settings to encourage greater productivity. One executive estimates that his company saved two million dollars over a three-year period through a performance-improvement system based on accurate feedback and positive reinforcement (Feeney, 1972).

Social Utopias

Skinner's interest in and concern with the environment that molds and shapes the individual has led quite naturally to his interest in the design of an ideal environment or a utopian society. We have seen, through behavior modification, how Skinner has been able to induce behaviors in animals that have never been seen before. Some of his techniques offer the possibility of training infrahuman species, such as the pigeon, to handle routine work that is currently being done by human beings. Suppose one could train a pigeon to spot defective parts on an assembly line? Properly trained and reinforced, the pigeon would not be as inclined to be distracted from work by boredom as is often the case with human beings who are assigned routine tasks. The pigeon might even prove more accurate. Skinner suggests that human behavior could also reach new heights and potentialities by appropriate optimal environments.

In order to facilitate the rearing of his second daughter, Skinner developed an *air crib*. The air crib was enclosed in glass and provided an optimal germ-free environment for the child during her sleeping hours. Temperature and humidity were kept at an optimal level, eliminating the need for clothing and blankets. Toys and interesting playthings were close at hand. The crib afforded the child greater freedom of movement, and it relieved the mother of many of the tedious chores normally connected with the routine of child rearing, enabling her to concentrate on other activities and positive ways of relating to the child. Skinner's eldest daughter was sufficiently impressed with the air crib to raise her own child in one. While the air crib has by no means acquired mass popularity, many parents have chosen to use one.

In 1948 Skinner wrote *Walden II*, a book in which he describes his concept of a utopia. Walden II is the name of a behaviorally engineered society designed and run by benevolent psychologists who employ a program of positive reinforcements. The main characters in the book are Frazier and Burrhus. Frazier is the psychologist who founded Walden II. Burrhus is a professor of psychology who is initially quite critical of the community, but who at the end of the novel decides to live in Walden II. Because positive reinforcement rather than aversive means are used to shape behavior in Walden II, the residents seek those reinforcers and willingly behave in socially responsible and productive ways.

In 1971 Skinner wrote *Beyond Freedom and Dignity*, in which he again cogently argues for the creation of a behaviorally engineered society. Skinner points out that most of the major problems that confront society today are problems that involve human behaviors. War, overpopulation, ghettos, unemployment, inflation, and so forth are all problems that are caused by human activity or lack of it. What we need is a behavior technology that will enable us to cope with these problems.

Skinner further argues in *Beyond Freedom and Dignity* that an adequate behavioral technology cannot be established unless we are willing to give up many "fictions" or falsehoods that we have long cherished. We must give up the notion that people are in any way, shape, or form, responsible for their own behavior. We must also give up the notions of dignity or worth. We must recognize that human behavior is controlled by forces in the environment. Only by acknowledging those forces of control and systematically applying them will we be able to develop a society that can cope with the problems that confront us today.

Skinner asserts that there is no such thing as an ego, personality, soul, or mind in any individual that can somehow be called free. We must give up the conceit that human beings are autonomous; people are not free. The concept of free will is a fiction, superstition, or myth. One cannot legitimately think of another person as being responsible for his or her actions. Individuals should neither be punished for inappropriate behavior nor given credit for appropriate behaviors. The clue to our behaviors lies within the environment, not within the individual.

A human being is nothing more than an organism, a bundle of behavior, shaped by his or her environment. Through evolution, the environment shaped the behavior that survives in our genes. After birth, environmental conditioning shapes each of us in this life. If one wishes to control or change human behavior, it may be done by controlling the environment.

In his utopian speculations, Skinner shifts gears from the scientist to the social philosopher. Presenting us with a form of social Darwinism, Skinner suggests that progress may be defined as the survival of a culture. A culture that assists its members in adapting to their environment in order to obtain what they need and avoid what is dangerous is a culture that will help them to survive. In short, cultural practices persist because they have an adaptive value. The survival of a culture depends on evolving those practices that will enable the members of that society to cope with their physical environment and the other cultures that surround them. "Survival is the only value according to which a culture is eventually to be judged" (1971).

For a culture to survive, the individuals within that culture must be encouraged to work for its survival. The individual exists not for him- or herself but for the good of his or her society. Positive reinforcers must be developed that will shape human behavior and induce individuals to work for the survival of the culture. Illusions of individual freedom must be surrendered in favor of the survival of the culture at large.

We need more, not less control, Skinner argues. To his critics, Skinner points out that human beings are already controlling and being controlled. The processes of controlling should not be denied; they should be studied and understood so that we can learn to implement them effectively in developing the society that we want. We have the power to develop a behavioral technology that will assist us in achieving these ends. To ignore this is to run the risk not of no control but rather of continued ineffective or deleterious control.

EXERCISE:

Developing Self-Control

On the individual level, Skinner points out that his techniques can be used by the individual to develop ways to manipulate his or her own behavior. Each one of us can eliminate those behaviors that we deem inappropriate or undesirable and substitute more desirable behaviors by a simple process of modifying our own personal environment.

The student who has difficulty studying may set up a schedule of systematic rewards for him- or herself after he or she has studied for a predetermined period of time. He or she can develop positive reinforcers that may be enjoyed after passing a test with a certain grade. An overweight woman may deliberately avoid purchasing those foods that tempt her and so make them unavailable in her immediate environment. She might purchase a new outfit in a smaller size and work toward the day when it can be worn. *An individual who wants to stop smoking can deliberately avoid lighting up a cigarette in those situations that automatically seem to call for one. He or she could wait fifteen minutes after each meal, before allowing him- or herself to smoke. An individual could switch to a less enjoyable brand or limit the number of cigarettes that he or she carries around. Several current organizations, such as Smokeenders and Weight-watchers, use techniques informed by Skinnerian principles to assist their members.*

In developing a program of self-control, first, decide on a particular behavior pattern that you would like to modify. Make a list of graduated objectives that would shape you in developing a more appropriate behavior. Do not be overambitious. Select only one problem area and break it down into small, manageable steps. Consider the techniques that would help you achieve your objectives. Are there any factors in your environment that you could change in order to facilitate the development of more appropriate behaviors? A student who has difficulty studying might consider the time and place that he or she normally studies. Is it an area and time that is free from distractions and interruptions? Perhaps you would study more effectively in the library. Leaving the phone off the hook during study hours can eliminate intruding phone calls. Finally, you should develop a systematic schedule of reinforcements for appropriate behaviors that lead toward your objectives. Make sure that the reward is something that you value and are willing to work for. And then be sure that you employ it as a means of reinforcement.

Evaluation and Implications

Skinner has provided a great deal of experimental data and research to support his ideas. Further, more than any other contemporary theorist, he has stimulated research to validate the concepts of behaviorism. His own work has been characterized by the intensive study of individual subjects, primarily of infrahuman species, and the careful control of laboratory conditions through automated apparatus, as well as an emphasis on variables easily modified by manipulating the environment.

Skinner's concepts clearly evolved from experimental laboratory investigations and he has shown considerable respect for well-controlled data. His constructs have received considerable empirical test and the concepts of his stimulus-response theory have held up very well indeed under the scrutiny of the scientific method. His theory is elegant in its simplicity. It has admirable qualities in terms of its ability to predict and control behavior, particularly in infrahuman species. Although he set out to avoid theorizing, he presents a theory of human behavior, if not personality, and even plays the role of a social philosopher.

But Skinner is not completely clear in recognizing the kinds of evidence on which his various statements are based. He frequently presents his social philosophy as if it were an empirical science with all the appropriate validating evidence. For example, Skinner has made the empirical observation that an individual may be controlled by manipulation of his or her environment. This is an empirical statement that has held up under observational test. However, from that empirical observation, one cannot jump to the conclusion that human beings are *nothing but* organisms controlled by their environment and claim that the conclusion is based on simple validating evidence. The conclusion entails a philosophical commitment as well. For a scientist to make that jump and refer to the conclusion as "science" is to commit the logical blunder of the "fallacy of affirming the consequent," which was described in Chapter 1.

As an empirical scientist, Skinner protects himself when he argues that concepts of the self, an ego, or freedom are useless fictions in a science. He does not find them useful in developing a scientific theory. However, Skinner goes beyond developing a scientific theory. When he begins to design his utopia, he invokes values and ethical commitments. He suggests that the value of a society lies in its survival and that human beings should give up the conceits of freedom and dignity. These are ethical conclusions, not empirical ones. As such, they need to be evaluated in terms of their adequacy as philosophy.

Skinner's theory represents a strong position in American psychology today. It is an influential theory. We have seen that Skinner's behavioral modification techniques are being used for rehabilitation, among other practical applications. There are those who strongly recommend that Skinner's techniques and practices be introduced into the schools and eventually into the home so that every child will be exposed to them. Skinner is by no means isolated in his thoughts and recommendations. He has a large number of followers who are willing and ready to implement his behavioral modification practices on a large scale.

Some personality theorists have criticized Skinner on the basis that he has not really developed a theory of personality at all. They allege that Skinner has no place for the person in his theory, rather, that he talks about the environment. Skinner would agree with this critique. He is not, strictly speaking, a personality theorist. Indeed, he argues that a theory of personality is not necessary. He suggests that most theories of personality falsely reassure us and delude us into thinking that we can understand or explain our behavior. Skinner is not interested in understanding or explaining behavior, rather, he is interested in predicting what behaviors will occur under certain conditions and in manipulating those conditions so that behavior can be controlled. He has devoted his attention to spelling out laws that govern behavior rather than to developing a theory of personality.

We have seen that Skinner's theory has been effective in making predictions and in effecting control. His theory is particularly effective in dealing with the behavior of infrahuman species; it is also effective in dealing with human behavior when that behavior occurs under situations of positive or negative reinforcement. In everyday terms, we would say that it is effective in dealing with human situations that are surrounded by reward or punishment.

Skinner's theory is less successful, however, in accounting for other areas of human behavior. While there can be no question that operant conditioning, reinforcement, and shaping play a large role in the child's acquisition of language, these concepts alone do not provide for a full explanation of how the child learns to speak. Skinner's theory cannot account for certain phenomena in language development. He cannot account for the child's creative use of language. He does not tell us how it is possible for the child to come up with a new sentence that he or she has never heard before. Nor do Skinner's concepts account for the meaningful errors that the child makes in learning to speak. When a child says, "I branged it home," chances are he or she never heard the verb "branged," but the error is illuminating because it shows us that the child understands the use of the suffix -ed in expressing the past tense without the assistance of formal lessons in grammar.

Skinner talks about self-control, and he suggests that his theories may be used by the individual to develop techniques of self-control. Although Skinner refers to these phenomena, his concepts cannot account for or explain the ability of individuals to create such programs of self-control. Nor do his theories accommodate the fact that at times an individual, even if he or she is motivated to change, cannot apply these programs effectively. Skinner would suggest that in such cases, an individual may be using ineffective controls or even inadvertently reinforcing the very behaviors that he or she wishes to eliminate. But these arguments do not fully convince us that Skinner's stimulus-response theory can accommodate the issues that are involved in a person's ability or inability to develop and effectively utilize the techniques of behavior modification. Saint Paul reminds us, "For the good that I would I do not: but the evil which I would not, that I do" (Romans 7:19). It seems paradoxical that, on the one hand, Skinner avows that human behavior is wholly determined, but on the other hand, he enjoins the possibility of self-control.

Nor can Skinner's own behavior and theory be comprehended solely in stimulus-response terms. Skinner has asserted that all behavior is determined by the environment. If that statement is true, then it must logically follow that Skinner's own statements are determined by his environment. Thus, his own behavior as a theorist would be equally open to change by manipulation of the environment.

Of all of the theorists discussed in this book, B. F. Skinner and Sigmund Freud have generated the most controversy and criticism. Both

FIGURE 7.1 One Critique of Skinner

Some critics have suggested that Skinner's estimate of human behavior can be summed up by looking at the laboratory animal with which he conducted a great deal of his early research.

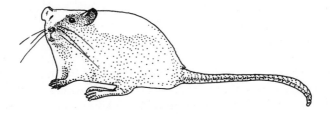

of their theories are in some way offensive. They offend us because they attack our illusions of being in full control of our behaviors. For Freud, the individual is motivated by forces of which he or she is unaware. For Skinner, the individual is totally shaped by forces within his environment. Earlier, Freud described three blows to human self-esteem: the *cosmological* blow afforded by Copernicus's discovery that the earth was not the center of the universe; the *biological* blow dealt by Darwin when he demonstrated that humans are not different or superior to animals, but have their origin in animals and are related to them; and the *psychological* blow afforded by Freud himself when he asserted that the ego is not the master in its own home. Skinner extends yet another blow to human self-esteem: there is no ego and we are completely determined by forces in the environment.

Both Sigmund Freud and B. F. Skinner suggest that we, as human beings, are not in control of ourselves. Yet their response to the discovery of our lack of self-control differs widely. Freud, who is a pessimist, offers us some hope, through the painful process of self-understanding, of gaining a small margin of control over the unconscious forces of which we have been unaware. Skinner, who is an optimist, believes that the answer lies in recognizing our lack of control, renouncing our ambitions of control, and committing ourselves to being more effectively controlled by a behaviorally designed technology.

RECENT TRENDS IN SOCIAL LEARNING AND BEHAVIOR THEORIES

In recent years, some personality theorists have taken the concepts of learning and behavior theories out of the animal laboratory where they concentrated on infrahuman species, such as the rat and the pigeon, and applied and tested these concepts more directly with people and interpersonal situations. Their studies have tried to introduce into the laboratory setting conditions that are more similar to the everyday life of people. These applications and tests have broadened many of the original learning theory concepts and also integrated them with other movements in modern psychology. Social learning and behaviorist theories have added new constructs that have reintroduced the organism (O) into the stimulus response formula (S–R), rendering it once again S–O–R.

Albert Bandura and Richard Walters: Observational Learning

Albert Bandura (1925–   ) and Richard Walters (1918–1967) have emphasized the area of observational learning. *Observational learning* entails learning that occurs without any direct reinforcement (1963). Skinner's studies had suggested that reinforcement is a necessary condition for learning and for the acquisition, maintenance, and change of behavior. Bandura and Walters point out that people not only learn from the consequences of their own behavior, but also by observing other people and events. They suggest that almost any behavior can be learned by an individual without the direct experience of reinforcement.

This kind of learning is frequently called *vicarious* learning or *passive* learning. A food-deprived rat who is learning to run a maze for food may in its initial trials ignore a dish of water that has been placed along the path of the maze. Later, having been deprived of water, it runs directly toward the water dish, which demonstrates that it had learned where the water was even though it was not directly reinforced for doing so.

The most famous study of observational learning in human beings was conducted by Bandura and involved a large inflated plastic Bobo doll (1963). Different groups of children were shown movies of adults playing with the doll in a number of different ways. In one instance, the adult vigorously attacked the doll. The adult hit and kicked the doll while angrily shouting. Other children saw an adult model who was nonaggressive and paid little attention to the doll. Later, when the children were given the opportunity to play with the Bobo doll themselves, their behavior was very similar to that of the particular model they had seen. This demonstrates that children can learn new responses simply by observing other people's behavior.

Whether or not an individual actually performs the behaviors that he or she has learned may be facilitated by reinforcements, but it is not dependent on them. Children who saw the model rewarded for his or her behavior were more likely to imitate the model than those who saw the adult's behavior punished. However, this does not mean that their learning of the behavior depended on reinforcement. We need to draw a distinction between *acquisition,* what a person has learned and can do, and *performance,* what a person actually does. Most of us have the theoretical know-how to rob a store. We are acquainted with the behaviors that are entailed in committing that crime. However, this does not mean that we will go out and do it.

Bandura and Walters point out that there is a great discrepancy between our acquired and performed behaviors; the fact that a person does not actively perform certain behaviors does not necessarily mean that he or she has not learned them. One reason why our performance is not equivalent to our acquisition is that we have learned from observing the consequences of others' behavior. We have observed what happens to individuals who violate the law, and that prevents most of us from doing so.

Many of our human behaviors can be accounted for by observational learning. We learn to speak by imitating our parents' words. We learn sex-appropriate behavior by modeling ourselves after the same-sexed parent. Modeling can influence not only what we do, but also what we perceive. Socialization itself entails observing and imitating the models of a particular culture.

Learning through observation suggests that the link between stimulus and response cannot be as simple or direct as Skinner suggested. Some mediation involving the individual's cognitive processes must be interposed between the stimulus and the response. Bandura and Walters have suggested four interrelated mediational processes (1963): *attentional processes*, in which we learn from a model by paying attention to the model's behavior; *retention processes*, in which imitation of a model entails remembering how the model behaved; *motor reproductive processes*, in which imitation of a model also entails practicing and translating the observed behavior into action; and *incentive and motivational processes*, in which performance entails motivation because no behavior will occur without sufficient incentive.

A primary difference between Skinner's position and that of Bandura and Walters is this introduction of mediational processes that serve as intermediaries between the environment and behavior. We have seen that Skinner did not believe it was desirable to invoke any internal forces in order to account for behavior. He felt that it was sufficient simply to stipulate the variables in the environment that produce certain behaviors. Bandura and Walters retort that a stimulus does not automatically elicit a response, rather, it sets into activity certain mediational processes that then produce behavior. Without hypothesizing certain mediational processes within the individual, we cannot account for more complex forms of learning that are clearly observable, such as learning through imitation. Bandura and Walter's position makes necessary the reintroduction of internal processes into a theory of personality. Thus, an understanding of personality entails more than the comprehension of overt behaviors in relation to external stimuli; it needs to bring into play as well internal factors within the organism, such as cognitive elements, images, and words, that also shape behavior.

It is difficult to study social modeling in a natural setting because of the many variables that cannot be controlled. Therefore, most of Bandura and Walters's experiments have been performed under controlled laboratory conditions. These experiments have shown that both children and adults can develop complex patterns of behavior, emotional responses, and attitudes through exposure to live or filmed models (Bandura, 1969). Some of these experiments were designed to investigate the acquisition of aggressive responses. As we have seen, children imitated the aggressive behavior of adults toward a large inflated doll. Bandura suggests that many of the aggressive behaviors prevalent in our society are acquired by our wide exposure to aggressive behavior. Children practice what their parents do, not what they preach, as a classic cartoon illustrates. The cartoon depicts a father spanking his small son, and the caption reads, "This will teach you not to hit kids who are littler than you."

Bandura has been very concerned with the aggressive models that our culture provides. In particular, he suggested that frequent exposure to aggression and violence through television encourages children to behave aggressively. Experimental studies suggest that what children see on television affects their behavior; thus, frequent exposure to aggressive behavior on television may increase the likelihood of violent behavior in our society (Murray, 1973). On the other hand, violence played a major role in the world of children long before the advent of television. Ancient myths and classic fairy tales, which stimulate a child's fantasy, are replete with violence. Other studies show that a child who is stimulated to engage in aggressive fantasies shows a marked decrease in aggressive behavior (Singer, 1973). In short, scientific evidence has not yet conclusively linked increased violence in the United States to the materials presented on television. Further, the problem may not be simply a question of frequency but also may involve the quality and character of the aggressors and victims of violence, the situation that provokes it, and the consequences.

Since observation is central in the learning of behaviors, it also has a useful place in modifying undesirable behaviors. Bandura and Walters have added the systematic use of modeling as an aid in changing behaviors to the techniques of behavior modification. Phobias, or irrational fears, and other emotional reactions have been effectively altered by having the patient watch a model respond in the same situation in more appropriate ways. Through modeling Bandura was able to eliminate a strong snake phobia in adults (1976). The subjects watched filmed and live models progressively interact with snakes and were later encouraged to touch the snake with the model.

Bandura has responded strongly to charges that behavior modification entails manipulation of human beings and denial of their freedom (1969). He points out that while behavior is influenced by the environment, the individual is not a helpless robot. Responses are self-activated by the individual who chooses to emulate a response. The reintroduction of cognitive processes means that we are not shaped solely by outside forces in the environment. The client comes to the therapist with a request for help in changing his or her behavior. The relationship is not that between a controller (however benevolent) and an unwitting subject, it is a contractual relationship between two consenting individuals. Furthermore, Bandura suggests that behavior modification increases rather than limits an individual's freedom. The individual with a strong phobia is not really free but crippled by his or her behavioral responses. By altering these responses, we can increase individual freedom.

Julian Rotter

Julian Rotter (1916–   ) has contributed to the study of learning an analysis of the subjective expectations that a person brings to a situation and that informs his or her response in that situation. Concurring with Bandura and Walters on the need to reintroduce cognitive processes between a stimulus and a response, Rotter points out that a social learning theory must be much more complex than the simplified theories of animal behavior heretofore presented. In particular, social learning theory needs to analyze and understand four different variables in order to predict a person's behavior in any given situation (1975).

The first variable is the behavior potential (BP). *Behavior potential* refers to the likelihood that a particular behavior will occur. In testing situations, a student may depend on a number of different behaviors, such as hard studying, cheating, feigning illness, and so on. Each of these responses may be seen to have a given potential for any given individual. One behavior may be said to be more or less likely to occur than the others. A second variable is the expectancy construct (E). The *expectancy construct* refers to the individual's subjective expectation about the outcome of his or her behavior. It is his or her estimation of the probability that a particular reinforcement will occur if he or she behaves in a certain way in a given situation. What does Johnny expect will be the outcome of his temper tantrum? The third variable is the reinforcement value (RV). The *reinforcement value* indicates the importance or preference of a particular reinforcement for an individual. In a given situation, Johnny may refuse to wash Dad's car if he thinks that the only reward he will receive for it is a verbal thank you. On the other hand, he might well be anxious to wash the car if he believes that he might receive a couple of dollars for the chore. The fourth main variable is that of the situation (s). *Situation* refers to the psychological context in which the individual responds. Any given situation has different meanings for different individuals, and they will affect the response.

Given these four variables, Rotter suggests that we can relate them in a specific formula that will enable us to predict a person's behavior in any given situation.

$$BP\ x,s_1\ Ra = f\ (Ex,\ Ras_1 + RVa,\ s_1)$$

The formula may be read as follows: "The potential for behavior x to occur in situation 1 in relation to reinforcement a is a function of the expectancy of the occurrence of reinforcement a following behavior x in situation 1 and the value of reinforcement a in situation 1" (1975).

If we could substitute the appropriate numbers for the above variables, we could predict the behaviors that would occur in any given situation. Of course, to date, social learning theorists have not been able to develop the precise techniques of observation and measurement that would enable them to discover the appropriate numbers.

Rotter also points out that expectancies vary in terms of their generality. Prior to taking a particular mathematics test, an individual student may have a rather specific expectancy about his or her ability to pass it. On the other hand, because of past experiences, a student may expect to do well or poorly in all of his or her courses due to generalized expectancy.

Rotter suggests that people form generalized expectancies that lead them to conceive of reinforcing events as either being beyond their control or dependent on their own behavior (1966). In order to measure the degree to which people adhere to one or the other of these poles, Rotter developed the *Internal-External Scale* (I-E Scale), a forced-choice questionnaire. Internally oriented individuals assume that their own behaviors and actions are responsible for the consequences that happen to them. Externally oriented individuals believe that the locus of control is out of their hands and that they are subect to the whims of fate, luck, or others. Subsequent studies have shown that internals usually perform more effectively than externals and that they are more resistant to influence from others. While an extreme reliance on either pole might be unhealthy, it appears that an internal orientation is more conducive to mental health. Nevertheless, internally oriented individuals also have their limitations. They tend to experience more shame and guilt and often assume more responsibility for themselves and others than is appropriate. Further research with the I-E Scale may be useful, as an individual's belief as to the locus of control clearly appears to influence his or her behaviors.

Walter Mischel

Walter Mischel (1930–   ) has emphasized behavioral specificity in his discussion of human behavior (1968). *Behavioral specificity* means that an individual's behavior is determined by the specific situation in which he or she finds him- or herself. A person will behave consistently or in the same manner in different situations only to the extent that these situations lead toward similar consequences. Such behaviors that are uniformly reinforced become generalized. Frequently, however, the consequences of our behavior vary considerably in different situations. When the consequences are different we learn to discriminate among different situations and behave accordingly. We learn through prior conditioning to distinguish among the kinds of responses that are appropriate in different situations.

Mischel has observed that it is not abnormal for an individual to react aggressively in certain situations, but meekly in other situations. Which reaction a person shows at any particular moment depends on discriminative stimuli: where he or she is, who he or she is with, and so forth. It is unnecessary and even undesirable to posit generalized traits or underlying motivations to account for an individual's behavior. Rather, Mischel suggests it is preferable to view behaviors as relatively discrete and governed by comparatively independent causes and sustaining conditions.

Mischel's emphasis on behavioral specificity leads to quite a different understanding of the cause of personality difficulties than that of psychoanalytic theory. This difference may be illustrated by the case of Pearson Brack (1968).

Pearson Brack was an American aviator who served as a bombardier in Tunisia during World War II. During his ninth mission, Brack's airplane was heavily damaged by flak. The airplane jolted, rolled, and began to dive. The pilot was able to avoid crashing, but during the fall Brack was cruelly tossed about in the craft and suffered severe injuries that required a month's hospitalization. When he appeared recovered, he was returned to flight duty. However, on his subsequent two missions he began to experience fainting spells as the plane began to rise to an altitude of about ten thousand feet. It was obvious that he could no longer continue his work.

A psychoanalytic therapist might conclude that Brack's fainting was connected to deep underlying anxieties that stemmed from early childhood and that had been tapped by the near-fatal plane accident. The trauma of the accident was not in itself causative, rather, it was a symbol that precipitated the expression of earlier childhood anxiety. Thus, an understanding and change of Brack's responses in subsequent flights would entail probing into his childhood to uncover the anxieties that the flight had tapped and working them through to a more adequate resolution.

The social behavior therapist would note that Brack's injury occurred when the plane was at an altitude of about ten thousand feet, and that his fainting spells began as subsequent planes neared such an altitude. He or she would suggest that during the accident Brack had become conditioned to certain situational or altitudinal cues. Subsequently, similar cues evoked the reaction of fainting. In this point of view, Brack's behavior can be explained in terms of current conditions that appear to control it. Recommended treatment would entail a program of desensitization to those particular situational or altitudinal cues.

Underlying these theoretical differences is the distinction between the concept of *displacement,* which is central to psychoanalytic thought, and the concept of *discrimination,* which is essential to social learning theory. Psychoanalytic theory suggests that basic underlying motivations and emotions seek expression. If they cannot be expressed directly, they will seek another outlet. In lay terms, we often refer to this phenomena as *scapegoating.* A male worker who becomes annoyed with his boss on the job may not openly show his feelings of anger and frustration in the office. When he goes home, he takes it out on his wife and children. The anger that he expresses toward them is not really directed at them at all, rather to an earlier situation. According to psychoanalytic theory, a person's responses in the present frequently are responses that are inappropriate for the current situation because they are displaced from earlier unresolved conflicts.

The concept of *discrimination* assumes that there are no deep underlying motives that seek expression. Rather, we respond specifically in certain situations according to prior learning, which entails our ability to discriminate among appropriate kinds of responses in different situations. Given the example above, the social learning theorist would suggest that the man recognizes that it is not safe to express openly his angry feelings with his boss. Therefore, on the job, he suppresses the expression of such feelings. At home, however, he recognizes that should he become annoyed, it is safe to express his anger openly. There is no connection between his anger on the job and his anger at home. His response is different at home simply because he has discriminated between different situations.

Which theory is correct? At this point, we cannot definitively answer that question. From the viewpoint of science, we have two rival hypotheses. However, each of these theories is also informed by very different philosophical assumptions.

Evaluation and Implications

The learning and behavior theory approach represents a relatively recent alternative to the study of personality. In 1913, John Watson published his famous article "Behaviorism," and in 1919, he spelled out the details of his approach in *Psychology from the Standpoint of a Behaviorist.* The application of learning principles to behaviors in the everyday world is even more recent, spanning only the last three or four decades. Indigenous to America, the behavioral approach has come to represent the dominant approach in the American academy with its emphasis on experimental research. It has attracted a large number of followers who are enthusiastically applying the findings of empirical studies in the laboratory to the study of human behavior.

Many psychologists are attracted to learning and behavior theories of personality because they appear to be "more scientific" alternatives to the less explicit and less empirically validated constructs of other personality theories. Behavior and learning theories tend to be elegant in their simplicity. Moreover, their constructs claim to have a wide predictive range. As such, learning and behavior theories have been praised as excellent examples of scientific theory construction and function.

Other critics would point out, however, that the concept of science emulated by learning and behavior theorists is often tied to an outdated nineteenth-century positivistic philosophy that is not consciously recognized. *Positivism* was an intellectual movement that claimed that philosophy was an imperfect mode of knowledge to be superseded by the empirical sciences. It narrowed the scientist's activity to an objective experimental methodology and failed to recognize that all scientific work is based on philosophical assumptions. As scientists, we cannot eliminate the philosophical assumptions that undergird our work. It is important, however, that we become aware of them so that we can examine them. In their efforts to be scientific, learning and behavior theorists frequently neglect to look at the philosophical commitments that inform their work.

Learning and behavior theory constitutes a shift from introspection to extrospection as the primary methodology of the psychologist. As we have seen, *introspection* refers to looking inside; it is the examination of one's thought processes and sensory experiences. *Extrospection* refers to looking out; it is the examination of what is outside the self. Prior to Watson, psychology emphasized introspection. Psychoanalysis, for example, examines the individual's own thoughts, feelings, and wishes. Watson's emphasis on overt behavior turned the gaze of the psychologist outward, to the observable behavior of others. It is important to note that both introspection and extrospection refer to empirical data that are observable. However, the growth and popularity of behaviorism was accompanied by a tendency to view introspection as somehow "less scientific," even though it, too, is empirical. In their emphasis on extrospection, learning and behavior theorists may have unduly limited the psychologist's activity.

Critics also point out that the efforts of learning and behavior theorists to translate concepts into operations frequently distort personality constructs. Their selection of appropriate investigations to test these constructs has also been questioned. Critics further point out that learning and behaviorist theorists have tended to ignore data that is inconsistent with their findings and at times have made untenable generalizations.

In their discussion of personality, behavior theorists have emphasized the process of learning. They have been less concerned with describing personality structure or explaining and identifying causes of behavior other than situational or environmental ones. With their emphasis on environmental factors, they have tended to ignore or minimize organic, genetic, social, and personal determinants of behavior. These variables are probably more important than learning theory allows. We have seen that several animal responses appear to be biologically controlled and cannot be conditioned at all. We do not hear of a pigeon being taught to press a bar with its toes or of a rat taught to peck at a dot with its nose. Many complex social responses, such as facial expressions, imprinting, and stranger anxiety, appear to be innate. To assume that any response can be associated with any stimulus through conditioning is to be naive.

Further, human behavior is much more diverse and flexible than learning theory permits. While learning theory appears to be able to account for the learned behaviors of lower animal species and for the learned habits and simple behaviors of human beings, it is less able to account for complex human behaviors like decision making, errors, and perversity. The mechanistic view of human nature as a machine whose output depends on the input provided does not account for the creativity of many human behaviors. The social behaviorists who emphasize the development of expectancy and other internal variables, while reintroducing covert factors, are nevertheless better able to account for the complexity of human behavior.

It has been suggested that the behaviorist preoccupation with the learning process renders these theories partial and incomplete. A more holistic approach is needed rather than the simple analysis of component parts. Finally, it is difficult to determine what is a normal and healthy personality within the confines of learning theory or any science based on validating evidence alone. How can we empirically determine what is good? We have seen that such value judgments rely on ethical commitments. In spite of the claims that they are simply empirical scientists, learning theorists raise ethical questions in their attempts to manipulate and change behavior. However, their science does not give us the means to account for and evaluate their ethical stance. Nevertheless, the learning and behavior approach has had a profound impact on psychology in America, and, undoubtedly its influence will continue to be felt.

SUGGESTIONS FOR FURTHER READING

A classic statement of John Watson's behaviorism may be found in his book *Behaviorism* (Norton, 1925). For students who are interested in a historical introduction to the experimental movement in psychology, E. G. Boring, *A History of Experimental Psychology* (Appleton-Century, 1929) is an encyclopedic survey.

B. F. Skinner's most influential work is *The Behavior of Organisms* (Appleton-Century-Crofts, 1938), in which he formulates a theory of behavior in terms of the principles of conditioning. However, the lay person will probably be more interested in *Walden II* (Macmillan, 1948), Skinner's visionary fantasy of a utopia based on principles of behavioral engineering, and *Beyond Freedom and Dignity* (Alfred A. Knopf, 1971), a continuation of his utopian speculations raising questions about traditional concepts of freedom and responsibility.

Students may also be interested in *The Technology of Teaching* (Appleton-Century-Crofts, 1968), in which Skinner applies his principles to the problem of learning in our schools. Those who are interested in the more technical presentation of his work are urged to turn to *Science and Human Behavior* (Macmillan, 1953); *Contingencies of Reinforcement: A Theoretical Analysis* (Appleton-Century-Crofts, 1968); and *Cumulative Record* (Appleton-Century-Crofts, 1968), a collection of his research papers and detailed analyses of his experiments.

Summaries of research by Skinner and his followers may be found in W. K. Honig's *Operant Behavior: Areas of Research and Application* (Prentice-Hall, 1966); R. W. Lundin, *Personality: A Behavioral Analysis* (Macmillan, 1969); J. L. Williams, *Operant Learning: Procedure for Changing Behavior* (Brooks-Cole, 1972); and D. Rimm and J. Masters, *Behavior Therapy: Techniques and Empirical Findings* (Academic Press, 1974). In addition, *The Journal of Applied Behavior Analysis*, *Behavior Research and Therapy*, and *The Journal of the Experimental Analysis of Behavior* publish findings relevant to Skinner's theory.

Albert Bandura and Richard Walters's most important work is *Social Learning and Personality Development* (Holt, Rinehart, and Winston, 1963), in which they describe modeling and observational learning in social contexts and compare it with reinforcement learning. Bandura's *Principles of Behavior Modification* (Holt, Rinehart, and Winston, 1969) gives implications of observational learning for therapy.

The social learning theory of Julian Rotter is presented in *Social Learning and Clinical Psychology* (Prentice-Hall, 1954), which is an excellent introduction to the cognitive approach to learning. Walter Mischel's distinction between displacement and discrimination is found in *Personality and Assessment* (Wiley, 1968).

PART IV

Trait Theories

From time immemorial, people have attempted to describe one another by sorting their many differences into general categories. Thus, one of the most persistent approaches to personality theorizing is the type and trait approach. People can be described as tall or short, fat or slender, blond, brunette, or redheaded. Differences in behavior may then be thought to be attributable to the different general characteristics. Such typologies have endured and are reflected in common stereotypes such as, "Fat people are jolly," or "Redheads are hot tempered."

Classifications frequently appear in science. Biologists classify living things into genera and species. Appropriate classification of living things increases our knowledge of them. When we classify, we describe an organism as having a certain property that is shared by other members of the same class. Classifying a particular animal as a carnivore and another as a herbivore tells us that the one eats meat and the other plants. Considerable sophistication and knowledge are required, however, to develop a scientific classification system that is genuinely useful. At first glance, one might be tempted to classify a bat as a bird, because it flies, and a whale as a fish, because it lives in the sea. Both bats and whales, however, are more usefully classified as mammals because they are warm-blooded, bear their young alive, and nurse them. The latter characteristics are more fruitful as the base for a classification system.

Classifications are hypotheses that assist us in understanding general laws of cause and effect. For the scientist, one classification system is better than another if it is more useful in generating predictions, scientific laws, and further explanatory hypotheses. A classification is most important when it acts as a clue suggesting that other characteristics are also present. Thus, the most useful characteristic in science would be one that is causally joined with many other properties. Such a characteristic is more useful because it helps us to formulate a minimum number of causal laws that have greater predictive power and that lead to the simplest general explanatory concepts. Because we do not know ahead of time what the laws of cause and effect generated by our classification system will be, and because causal laws are themselves hypotheses, any classification system that we develop is itself an hypothesis. The taxonomy, or classification, of the biologist reflects his or her hypothesis as to which characteristics of living things are most important for formulating a minimum number of causal laws. If further study suggests that other characteristics are more important, the earlier classification system is abandoned in favor of a better one. Thus, in the course of the history of biology, the classification system of the Swiss botanist Linnaeus was adopted, used, and later rejected in favor of a newer one.

One of the earliest efforts to describe personality in terms of categories was made by an early Greek physician, Hippocrates (460?–377? B.C.), and later adapted, refined, and popularized by Galen (ca. 120–

200). Their work has earned them the respective titles of "Father of Medicine" and "Father of Modern Physiology." (Hippocrates' name continues to be associated with the oath embodying a code of medical ethics that is taken by physicians today.) Hippocrates suggested that personalities could be classified according to the predominance of certain body *humors*, or fluids. The four humors—blood, phlegm, black bile, and yellow bile—corresponded to the four basic elements of the world articulated by a fifth-century B.C. Greek philosopher, Empedocles: air, water, earth, and fire. Hippocrates, and later Galen, thought that each of these fluids entered into the constitution of a body and together determined, by their relative proportions, a person's health and temperament. A predominance of blood led to a *sanguine* character, which was marked by sturdiness, high color, and cheerfulness. Phlegm, or the white mucus we cough up, was a cold, moist fluid that in excess caused sluggishness. Thus, the *phlegmatic* personality was slow, solid, and apathetic. Black bile was a humor secreted by the kidneys or spleen. Its predominance led to the *melancholic* temperament, which was characterized by depression. Yellow bile was secreted by the liver and infused the *choleric* personality, which tended to be irascible, hot-tempered, and violent.

While the humoric theory on which Hippocrates' and Galen's concepts were based may strike us as quaint and outdated, their theory presages many concepts in modern psychology and continues to influence some theorists (for example, Hans Eysenck, whose theory is referred to in Chapter 8). Galen was interested in glandular secretions; contemporary investigations suggest a relationship between *hormones* (chemicals released into the bloodstream by the endocrine glands), emotions, and behavior. Further, the ancient vocabulary has permeated our language. We suggest that someone is in a "good humor" or a "bad humor." The terms "sanguine," "melancholic," and "phlegmatic" are common in Western literature. We meet them frequently in William Shakespeare's plays and still encounter them in colloquial use.

An early modern typology was developed by Ernest Kretschmer, a German psychiatrist (1888–1964). He suggested that people could be placed into categories on the basis of their *morphology*, or body measurement. Different clusters of personality traits were linked to different body types because hormonal secretions created both the shape of the body and personality characteristics. *Asthenics* were thin, long-limbed, and narrow-chested. They tended to be aloof, withdrawn, shy, and sensitive. *Pyknics* were short, fat, and barrel-chested. They were inclined to fluctuations in mood—either jovial, lively, and outgoing; or deeply melancholic and depressed. *Athletics* were balanced in physique and muscular development, and they tended to be energetic, aggressive, and sanguine. Kretschmer's theory had the advantage of further suggesting that there is a typical body structure for each of the two main forms of mental illness: schizophrenia and manic-depression. The

FIGURE 8.1 The Four Temperaments

The four temperaments depicted in a fifteenth-century Zurich manuscript. Photographs from the Bettman Archive.

asthenic type was associated with schizophrenia and the pyknic type with manic-depression.

Kretschmer's theory was criticized because it was difficult to fit everyone into a proper category and many people did not behave according to their assigned body type. The difficulty was that Kretschmer could not envision mixtures; he believed that everyone was a pure type. Still, Kretschmer's theory provided a springboard for further psychological research and study.

In order to avoid the problems that Kretschmer's theory encountered, recent theories tend to describe individuals in terms of traits rather than types. Whereas *typologies* imply distinct, discrete, and separate categories into which an individual can be placed, *traits* refer to continuous dimensions that individuals possess to varying degrees. Modern trait theories recognize that individuals vary considerably with regard to the same characteristic. We can speak of two types of stature—tall or short. Within any given population, however, we find a continuous gradation of statures from tall to short. Most of the population, moreover, tends to fall in the middle, being neither extremely tall nor extremely short. Height is an example of a continuous dimension that varies among individuals. Such continuous dimensions are referred to as traits.

Traits, like typologies, are hypothetical constructs that are used to explain behavior. Trait theories vary as to whether or not traits imply any real existence within the person. Some suggest that a trait should simply be regarded as an imaginary construct, an inference from overt behavior, that helps us to explain behavior (Cattell, 1950). Others maintain that traits are not just imaginary constructs but have a real existence within the subject (Allport, 1961). While the traits may not at present be subject to direct empirical observation and test, in the future it may be possible to establish their existence empirically.

Part IV examines a number of different trait theories and describes their influence today.

CHAPTER 8

Psychometric Trait Theories

Trait theories employ traits to account for the consistency in people's behavior and to explain why different individuals respond differently to the same stimuli. Broadly defined, *traits* are dispositions that determine behavior. Traits are inferences from overt behavior. Like any imaginary construct that cannot be directly observed, they must be inferred from behavioral signs. In developing their theories, some trait theorists make frequent use of *psychometrics*, the quantitative measurement of psychological characteristics through statistical techniques. Chapter Eight concentrates on the contributions of two major trait theorists who use psychometrics extensively: William Sheldon and Raymond Cattell.

If a trait theory is to be useful, the traits postulated need to go beyond the overt behaviors that an individual shows. Just as any successful hypothesis in science refers to future experiences that we might have if the hypothesis turns out to be useful, a successful trait construct goes beyond simply asserting that a particular behavior pattern exists. To argue that John is lazy because he has a lazy disposition is to argue in a circle and not provide genuinely useful information. To argue that John is honest, thoughtful, and disciplined because of an underlying source variable or trait of ego strength is a much more useful way to proceed. The underlying trait of ego strength accounts for the surface manifestation and also permits us to speculate about other related characteristics, such as assertiveness or confidence, that John will also display. Both Sheldon and Cattell have made a concerted effort to insure that the traits they hypothesize are genuinely useful constructs. After discussing their theories, the practical application of trait theories and their pervasive influence in our lives will be discussed.

WILLIAM H. SHELDON: CONSTITUTIONAL PSYCHOLOGY

William Sheldon was born in 1899 in Warwick, Rhode Island. He grew up on a farm. His concern with animals was fostered by his father, a naturalist and animal breeder. A close understanding of different breeds and various animal behaviors underlies many of his concepts about the causes of human behavior, and his love of animals is reflected in his writings.

He earned an A.B. degree from Brown University in 1919. Later, he was granted the M.A. from the University of Colorado. He received both the Ph.D. in psychology and the M.D. from the University of Chicago in 1926 and 1933, respectively. During his graduate work he taught at the University of Chicago, Northwestern University, and the University of Wisconsin. On receiving his medical degree, he served on the staff of the Children's Hospital in Chicago and he was awarded a fellowship that permitted him to study abroad. He was primarily interested in studying with Carl Jung, but he also was able to visit Freud and Kretschmer.

On his return, Sheldon secured a professorship of psychology at the University of Chicago. From there he moved to Harvard where he taught and conducted research for several years. During World War II, he served as a flight surgeon in the Army Air Force. In 1947, he accepted an appointment as Director of the Constitution Laboratory, College of Physicians and Surgeons, Columbia University, and remained in that post until 1959. From 1959 to 1970 he was a clinical professor of medicine at the University of Oregon Medical School. At the time of his death in 1977, Dr. Sheldon was associated with the Biological Humanics Center in Cambridge, Massachusetts.

Sheldon's primary concern was to establish a relationship between physique and temperament and to apply these findings. He strongly believed that physical structure is a primary determinant of behavior. Further, he identified a set of objective variables or characteristics that can be measured to use in describing physique and temperament. Finally, in order to test his hypothesis that a given physique and a given temperament are related, he conducted extensive correlational studies and statistical analyses.

Primary Components of Physique

In his classic study, Sheldon (1940) identified three primary aspects of bodily constitution. In order to facilitate and standardize the technique of identifying physical components, Sheldon photographed four

WILLIAM SHELDON

thousand men of college age. The subjects were photographed from three angles: front, back, and side. Three extreme variations in physique stood out as departing most widely from the "average" male physique. Study of several examples of each extreme enabled Sheldon to identify those aspects that determined each extreme.

The first component Sheldon termed endomorphy. *Endomorphs* have a predominance of soft roundness throughout the body. Their digestive tract appears to dominate their bodily appearance. The second component Sheldon termed mesomorphy. *Mesomorphs* have a predominance of muscle, bone, and connective tissue. Their physique is generally hard, heavy, and rectangular. The third component was termed ectomorphy. *Ectomorphs* have a predominance of linearity and fragility. Relative to their mass, they have the greatest surface area and sensory exposure to the outside world. Their brain and central nervous system are also more predominant. A lay person might wish to define the three basic types as a tendency to be fat, muscular, or thin, but as we shall see, this is somewhat misleading. Sheldon viewed the three types as extreme extensions of early layers of the embryo. Shortly after conception, the inner cell mass of the fertilized ovum, or egg, differentiates into three distinct layers. The *endoderm*, or inner skin, develops into the internal organs and digestive tract. The *mesoderm*, or middle skin, becomes bones and muscles, while the *ectoderm*, or outer skin, develops into the central nervous system and outer covering of skin. In each of his three physiques, Sheldon suggested that one of these embryonic layers predominates and influences personality.

These three basic components were viewed as first-order variables. A *variable* is a characteristic that can be measured or controlled. For simplicity, each component has been described as a pure type. But such cases, Sheldon believed, are extremely rare or nonexistent. Rather, each component is best viewed as a continuous variable of which different individual physiques can exhibit different amounts that we can measure. Most people are a combination of all three physiques.

In order to objectify the procedure of determining the degree of each component exhibited by a particular individual physique, Sheldon established several measurements of the human body based on different bodily regions. These indexes served to distinguish among the extreme variants as well as to identify those physiques that lay midway along the scale. Careful study of the photographs, using these criteria of measurement, enabled Sheldon to assign numbers to the scales for the three components.

In order to express a given individual's body type, Sheldon employed a *somatotype*. Each individual in Sheldon's sample of college men was ranked according to the degree to which he exhibited a particular component. Sheldon ranked his subjects on a scale of 1 to 7. The number 1 was assigned when the component was exhibited to the least degree. The number 7 indicated the maximum manifestation of the component. This procedure made it possible to express each individual's physique in terms of three numbers, one for his position relative to the scale for each of the three components. These three separate numbers constituted an individual's somatotype. Thus, the somatotype 7–1–1 indicates that an individual's physique is extreme in endomorphy and expresses a minimum of the other two components. The somatotype 4–4–4 characterizes the individual who is at the midpoint of all three components.

The somatotype is seen as an enduring physical component that is not subject to change by weight gain or loss, or nutritional factors. This is why the definition of fat, muscular, or thin ultimately misleads. A better comparison is to the concept of bone structure. Each one of us can be described as having a light, medium, or heavy bone structure that does not vary as we grow taller or gain weight. Starve an endomorph and you do not end up with an ectomorph; you simply end up with an emaciated endomorph.

Primary Components of Temperament

In order to discover whether or not basic components could also be found in reference to temperament, Sheldon examined the literature on personality for different behavioral traits. He added other variables that he had observed from his own clinical and general observation. A final list of fifty traits was developed.

Sheldon's next step was to study a group of thirty-three young men for a period of one year. He observed them in their everyday life and during weekly clinical interviews. At the end of that period, he rated each man on each of the fifty experimental traits, again using a seven-point scale. The interrelationship of these traits was then studied by a correlational analysis to discover whether or not there were any nuclear clusters of traits that appeared to go together and that might represent the same underlying variable.

Three main clusters or groups of traits appeared. Sheldon (1942) labeled them as follows: *viscerotonia* referred to a general love of comfort, relaxation, sociability, people, food, and affection; *somatotonia* referred to a predominance of muscular activity and vigorous bodily assertiveness, and thus a tendency to seek action and power; and *cerebrotonia* referred to a predominance of restraint, inhibition, and the desire for concealment.

Sheldon formulated the hypothesis that certain physiques and temperaments were different expressions of the same genetic factor. These extremes were governed by the *viscera* (or digestive tract), the *soma* (or body), and the *cerebrum* (or head). To be precise, Sheldon predicted that endomorphy would go along with viscerotonia, mesomorphy with somatotonia, and ectomorphy with cerebrotonia.

In order to test his hypothesis, Sheldon somatotyped two hundred college men, and after extensive observations also rated each of them on the three temperamental characteristics. He then made a correlational study between their physiques and temperaments.

Correlations: A Statistical Tool

Correlations are a statistical tool for making comparisons. Simply stated, they are numbers that express a positive or negative relationship. While there are several different formulas for determining correlations, the final number is one that ranges from +1 to −1. Correlations indicate the extent to which two events are covariants, or occur together. A correlation does not in and of itself imply a causal relationship; it simply indicates to what extent two events or variables occur together. For example, there is a high correlation between blond hair and blue eyes. This is not to say that blond hair causes blue eyes, but rather to point out that a great many people who have blond hair also have blue eyes. Nevertheless, where two variables have a high positive correlation it is reasonable to hypothesize further that there may be a common causal factor.

A correlation of + or −0 to + or −.20 is considered indifferent or negligible. There is no implied relationship between the two events. A correlation of + or −.20 to + or −.40 is a low correlation. It is present but it is slight. A correlation of + or −.40 to + or −.70 is considered a substantial or marked correlation. There appears to be a clear relationship. A correlation of + or −.70 to + or −1.00 is considered high or perfect. The relationship appears definite. Positive numbers indicate that the events are covariants, or occur together. Negative numbers indicate an inverse relationship or the degree to which the events do not happen together.

The Relation of Physique to Behavior

The correlations that Sheldon discovered among his physiques and temperaments suggested a surprisingly high relationship between certain given physiques and temperaments. The specific positive correlations (1944) were as follows:

endomorphy and viscerotonia	+.79
mesomorphy and somatotonia	+.82
ectomorphy and cerebrotonia	+.83

These correlations were even higher than Sheldon himself had expected. They appear to support the hypothesis that physical constitution plays a large part in motivation and temperament. Sheldon believed that body build and temperament, therefore, are primarily the result of heredity. We should note, however, that Sheldon depended on correlational procedures, which yield noncausal data, to assess the relationship between these variables.

We should also note that Sheldon's original research in somatotyping involved only males. He subsequently conducted some work in female somatotyping, but an *Atlas of Women* comparable to the *Atlas of Men* (1954) has yet to appear. Sheldon suggested that women tend to be more endomorphic and to display a smaller range of body types. Nevertheless, he believed that a correlation between physical constitution and temperament can be found in women as well as men.

EXERCISE:

Estimating Your Somatotype

You can estimate your own somatotype by the following crude mea-surement.* Read the following three scales. Study each statement and ask yourself whether that item is generally characteristic of you. Place an X next to those sentences that are characteristic of you. Do not worry about items that appear contradictory. If you are uncertain about an item, do not mark it.

* Adapted from the short scales for temperament in W. H. Sheldon, *The Varieties Of Temperament*, New York: Harper, 1942, p. 26. Used with permission of Dr. Sheldon.

SCALE A

_____ 1. I am relaxed in posture and movement.

_____ 2. I love physical comfort.

_____ 3. I am slow to react.

_____ 4. I love to eat.

_____ 5. I dislike eating alone.

_____ 6. I feel pleasant after a meal.

_____ 7. I like ceremony and ritual.

_____ 8. I love people.

_____ 9. I am friendly to everyone.

_____ 10. I am miserable if someone doesn't like me.

_____ 11. I am oriented to people rather than to things.

_____ 12. I am easygoing.

_____ 13. I am tolerant.

_____ 14. I am complacent.

_____ 15. I am a deep sleeper.

_____ 16. I am malleable, finding good points to both sides of an argument.

_____ 17. I enjoy talking about my feelings.

_____ 18. I am relaxed, happy, and talkative under alcohol.

_____ 19. I need people when I am troubled.

_____ 20. I am oriented toward childhood and family relations.

Total _____

SCALE B

_____ 1. I am assertive in posture and movement.

_____ 2. I love physical adventure.

_____ 3. I am energetic.

_____ 4. I need and enjoy exercise.

_____ 5. I like to dominate and have power.

_____ 6. I love risks and chances.

_____ 7. I am bold and direct in manner.

_____ 8. I have physical courage in combat.

_____ 9. I am competitively aggressive.

_____ 10. I am unsentimental.

_____ 11. I dislike small closed-in places.

_____ 12. I am ruthless and unsqueamish.

_____ 13. I have an unrestrained voice.

_____ 14. I have a high tolerance for pain.

_____ 15. I am generally noisy.

_____ 16. I was an early maturer.

_____ 17. I am quick to make decisions.

_____ 18. I am assertive and aggressive under alcohol.

_____ 19. I need to act when I am troubled.

_____ 20. I am oriented toward goals and activities of youth.

Total _____

SCALE C

_____ 1. I am restrained in posture and movement.

_____ 2. I am overly quick to respond physically to an event such as a possible accident.

_____ 3. My reactions are immediate and precise.

_____ 4. I love privacy.

_____ 5. I am hyperattentive and mentally alert.

_____ 6. I am emotionally restrained and keep my feelings secret.

_____ 7. I avoid looking directly at others.

_____ 8. I prefer small intimate groups rather than large ones.

_____ 9. I avoid talking to other people.

_____ 10. I resist habits and routines.

_____ 11. I dislike wide open places.

_____ 12. My attitudes are hard for others to predict.

_____ 13. I am generally quiet.

_____ 14. I am hypersensitive to pain.

_____ 15. I have poor sleep habits and am often tired.

_____ 16. I look younger than my age.

_____ 17. I am introverted and a deep thinker.

_____ 18. I abstain or avoid getting intoxicated with alcohol.

_____ 19. I need to be alone when I am troubled.

_____ 20. I am oriented toward things that older people enjoy.

Total _____

When you have marked the sentences that describe you, add the number of items that you checked on each scale and divide each total by three, rounding off to the nearest whole number. The resulting three-digit number will provide you with a rough somatotype, showing the degree to which you possess each of the core components. A yields a rough measurement of Endomorph-Viscerotonia. B describes Meso-morph-Somatotonia. C depicts the Ectomorph-Cerebrotonia. While you probably checked some items on each scale, you probably showed a predominance in one.

It is only fair to caution you, however, that the above exercise is not presented as a valid measuring device nor does it even come close to approximating the careful scrutiny Sheldon gave his subjects. But it does permit you to begin to assess the value of Sheldon's work as a means of self-exploration.

Since Sheldon asserted that his temperament characteristics hold true over time, you might wish to assess further the accuracy of your somatotype by asking your parents or a friend who has known you for a long time to rate you both as you were several years ago and as you are now. These findings can be compared with your self-rating and own historical recollection.

Sheldon's interest in biological determinants or causes of behavior led him to be less interested in how personality develops than most other theorists. While he agreed that certain childhood events may be important in determining adult behavior, he believed that biological factors are more important. Specific physiques may provoke certain childhood or infantile experiences and lead to distinct adult forms of behavior. Thus, the biological factors rather than the childhood experiences are the key causal factors. Sheldon recommended that parents, teachers, and others who are interested in the developmental process seriously consider the child's somatotype. They then can assist the child in developing aspirations and expectations that are consistent with his or her physique and temperament and avoiding those that are incompatible.

Evaluation and Implications

Sheldon's conclusions have not been uncontested. One criticism is that Sheldon did not insure that the measurements of physique and temperament were made independently of one another. Since he himself rated both the physique and temperament of his subjects, it is possible that he unwittingly influenced his various ratings by his prior knowledge of the subjects. Second, environmental responses to a particular type of physique may be more important than Sheldon realized. Commonly accepted stereotypes lead us to expect certain behaviors from certain types of physiques. An identical aggressive act from a strong muscular person and a small frail one usually draws different responses. Many people expect a strong muscular person to behave aggressively and they accept his or her aggressive behaviors as natural. The frail individual, on the other hand, has more difficulty in establishing a pattern of recognized aggressive responses. Thus, individuals with particular physiques may find certain responses ignored or punished in their environment and other kinds rewarded. The consequent similarities in temperament may, therefore, be due to environmental responses as well as to constitutional factors. Components of physique and temperament establish limits and potentialities for adult behavior. Nevertheless, environmental effects may determine to what extent a person is able to fulfill those potentialities.

Sheldon's firm conviction was that given knowledge of an individual's somatotype, one could make certain accurate predictions about his or her temperament. Several efforts have been made to replicate his studies. The results have been mixed. While some research supports his findings, other studies either do not support it or contradict it (see Rees, 1961, and Lindzey, 1967, for summaries of relevant research). Nevertheless, Sheldon laid the groundwork for and helped to create a current movement in personality theory—psychometric trait theory—that has had a vast effect.

Sheldon's research is firmly grounded in empirical studies and validating evidence. His introduction of continuous variables rather than discrete categories represents a distinct advance over the earlier typologies. His conscientious research provides an excellent example of the use of psychometrics in personality theory. Nevertheless, even if we agree that there is a correlation between physique and temperament, we have no proof of a causal relationship between the two events. A correlation is a measure of covariance; it does not inform us about causes and effects. Further, while Sheldon looked toward constitutional factors to account for human behavior, he did not explain how body type influences temperament and disposition. This is why his theory has not been widely adopted. His primary contribution was to provide us with a means of measuring and describing physique and temperament. Psychologists who value quantitative methods have used his work as a springboard for the development of even more sophisticated psychometric techniques (such as factor analysis, which will be described in the section on Cattell). Recent developments in psychophysiology, the study of the effects of physical processes on mental ones, emphasize the need for a constitutional psychology that explores how biochemistry, as well as body structure, influences personality and behavior. There is little doubt but that Sheldon was correct in asserting a correlation between physique and personality. The relationship, however, may not be as significant as Sheldon believed, and the explanation for that relationship is yet to be found.

RAYMOND CATTELL: FACTOR THEORY

Raymond Cattell was born in Staffordshire, England, in 1905. He describes his childhood as a happy one. His parents set high standards of behavior but gave their children considerable freedom in choosing their activities. Considerable outdoor activity and competition with his brothers characterized his youth. England became involved in World War I when Cattell was nine. He later acknowledged that the war had a significant impact on him. He saw trainloads of injured men being transported to a converted hospital near his home. The sight impressed upon him the "brevity of life." He became more serious and inclined to work.

Raymond Cattell received his B.S. from the University of London in 1924 at the age of nineteen. He majored in chemistry and physics, but his interest in social concerns led him to pursue psychology, in which he earned a Ph.D. in 1929. His graduate work was also taken at the University of London where he studied under Spearman, a distinguished psychologist who developed the procedure of factor analysis that Cattell would later employ.

The following years were difficult. Employment was difficult to come by for a psychologist, so Cattell worked at several part-time jobs. He was a lecturer at Exeter University and he established a clinic in Leicester. Meanwhile, he also continued his individual research. The depressed economy and his own poor health led to several lean years, during which he was haunted by poverty and his marriage broke up. Nevertheless, he remained steadfast in his dedication to his work. He was anxious to apply Spearman's technique of factor analysis to the study of personality.

In 1937, the University of London awarded Cattell an honorary doctor of science for his contributions to research in personality. That same year he received an invitation to serve as a research associate to E. L. Thorndike at Columbia University in New York. Subsequently, he

became a professor of psychology at Clark University and later at Harvard. In 1945, he was offered a research professorship at the University of Illinois, which enabled him to devote his full time and energy to his research. Cattell is presently a resident professor at the University of Hawaii at Manoa.

Cattell has received several honors and made significant contributions to the study of personality. He has published a phenomenal number of books and articles on a number of different topics. Although his primary emphasis has been on the study of personality through the techniques of factor analysis, he does not lack interest in or concern with other areas of psychology. His interest in clinical psychology led him to attempt to develop a more scientific foundation for analyzing personality structure. More recently, in 1973, he established a nonprofit Institute for Research on Morality and Self-Realization in Boulder, Colorado. Here he hopes to bring together his scientific concerns with social and religious ones.

Cattell's Trait Approach to Personality

Raymond Cattell's theory of personality is highly complex. Because it is complex and relies on the sophisticated technique of factor analysis the theory is neither widely read or understood by the general public. This is unfortunate, as Cattell's theory has and is generating a great deal of research that will probably have a considerable impact in applied areas of psychology and education. Some familiarity with his work is important for the lay person who wishes to have some understanding of modern personality theory.

Cattell begins with a general and preliminary definition of personality: "Personality is that which permits a prediction of what a person will do in a given situation" (1950). He believes that a full definition of personality must await further investigation into the types of concepts that are included in the study of behavior. His general statement may be expressed in the formula $R = f(P, S)$, which reads: A response (R) is a function (f) of the person (P) and the stimuli (S). Cattell observes that the response and the stimuli can be precisely determined in an experiment in which the experimenter carefully structures the situation. However, the person is a less well-known factor that needs further exploration. Cattell believes that the investigation of traits will assist us in understanding the structure and function of the person.

Cattell's preliminary definition of personality as "that which permits a prediction of what a person will do in a given situation" immediately provides a striking and important comparison between his interest and method of personality research and that of other theorists, such as the Freudians. Freud developed psychoanalysis as a means of understanding one's self and developing a comprehensive theory of human nature. He was not particularly concerned with the efficacy of psychoanalysis as a predictive tool, but with the compelling character of the vision of one's self or humanity that it provided. Cattell, on the other hand, is concerned with the *heuristic value* of constructs about personality, or the power of a construct to predict future events. His stance is that of the empirical scientist who derives from his or her theory propositions that are subject to empirical test. In a sense, prediction is more difficult than explanation, as it is easier to account for events that have happened than it is to predict them. Prediction is also useful in that it enables us to anticipate what will happen in certain situations. On the other hand, a theory may have considerable predictive power and garner an impressive array of validating evidence, but still fail to provide a comprehensive or compelling explanation. In his theorizing, Cattell provides an exemplary example of a scientist who is concerned with validating evidence.

Cattell believes that the exploration of traits will assist us in understanding the structure and function of personality. Knowledge of underlying traits will allow us to make predictions about our own behavior and that of others. Cattell defines *traits* as mental or imaginary constructs that are inferences from overt behavior that we make in order to account for its regularity and consistency. Traits are hypothetical constructs that permit us to generate conclusions about subsequent behavioral events. While Cattell is interested in the physical and neurological components that influence behavior, he does not maintain that the traits that he is exploring necessarily have any real physical or neural status.

Cattell distinguishes between surface traits and source traits (1950). *Surface traits* are clusters of overt behavior responses that appear to go together, such as integrity, honesty, self-discipline, and thoughtfulness. *Source traits* refer to the underlying variables that seem to determine the surface manifestation, in this case, perhaps, ego strength.

Cattell believes that the distinction between surface and source traits is important in order to avoid the futility of circular arguments such as John is lazy because he has a lazy disposition. The study of source traits is valuable for several reasons. Because they are probably few in number, source traits permit economy in describing an individual. Second, source traits presumably have a genuine structural influence on personality and thus determine the way we behave. Thus, knowledge of a particular source trait may permit us to go beyond mere description and make predictions about additional behaviors that we might observe further.

Source traits may be divided in terms of their origin into constitutional traits and environmental-mold traits. *Constitutional traits* have their origin in heredity or the physiological condition of the organism, whereas *environmental-mold traits* originate from influences of our physical and social surroundings.

Both source and surface traits may also be labeled according to the way in which they express themselves. *Dynamic traits* refer to traits that motivate an individual toward some goal. *Temperament traits* refer to traits that describe how a person behaves in order to obtain his or her goal. *Ability traits* refer to traits that determine how effectively a person is able to achieve his or her goal.

From extensive research, utilizing factor analysis techniques, Cattell has identified sixteen basic temperament and ability source traits that he suggests represent the "building-blocks" of personality (1966). Initially, Cattell did not name the traits, he identified them with an alphabetical letter. Later, he gave them technical names. However, they may best be understood by the lay person by the popular labels that they have received. These labels are presented as bipolar, or opposite, dimensions, which means that a high score on one end of the dimension indicates a low score on the other and vice versa.

Sixteen Basic Source Traits

outgoing	—	reserved
more intelligent	—	less intelligent
emotionally stable	—	emotionally unstable
assertive	—	humble
happy-go-lucky	—	sober
strong conscience	—	lack of internal standards
adventuresome	—	shy

tough-minded	—	tender-minded
trusting	—	suspicious
imaginative	—	practical
shrewd	—	forthright
apprehensive	—	self-assured
experimental	—	conservative
group-dependent	—	self-sufficient
casual	—	controlled
relaxed	—	tense

EXERCISE:

Measuring a Source Trait

You can roughly measure yourself on one of Cattell's sixteen basic source traits by taking the following self-report questionnaire.* For each of the items below select the answer (a or b) that best applies to you.

1. *I would rather be*
   a. *an engineer*
   b. *a social science teacher*
2. *I could stand being a hermit*
   a. *true*
   b. *false*
3. *I am careful to turn up when someone expects me*
   a. *true*
   b. *false*
4. *I would prefer to marry someone who is*
   a. *a thoughtful companion*
   b. *effective in a social group*
5. *I would prefer to read a book on*
   a. *national social service*
   b. *new scientific weapons*
6. *I trust strangers*
   a. *sometimes*
   b. *practically always*

The following answers are indicating of an outgoing temperament: 1. b, 2. b, 3. a, 4. b, 5. a, 6. b. If you answered all the questions this way, you probably have a very outgoing personality. If you answered

* Questionnaire is based on information from Raymond Cattell, *The Scientific Analysis of Personality*, Aldine, Chicago, 1965, Table A, p. 70.

most of them the other way, you probably are reserved. Most people fall somewhere in the middle.

Cattell describes two kinds of dynamic source traits that underlie surface dynamic traits or attitudes. The *erg* is a constitutional dynamic trait. Cattell prefers the neutral term "erg" over words like "instinct" or "drive" because it avoids loose connotations or associations. The term "erg" comes from the Greek word *ergon*, which means "work" or "energy." Ergs refer to motivational factors that are innate or constitutional. Cattell has identified seven ergs through factor analysis (1958):

Seven Ergs

sex

gregariousness

parental protectiveness

curiosity

escape (fear)

self-assertion

self-indulgence

A *sentiment* is an environmental-mold dynamic source trait. It is acquired or learned through our associations with the physical or social environment. It is a deep, early established feeling toward important cultural objects, such as persons or social institutions. An erg is permanent, because it is constitutional. Its intensity may increase or decrease, but the erg itself will not disappear. A sentiment, on the other hand, is less permanent because it is learned through our associations with our environment. Thus, a sentiment may be unlearned and disappear. Some of the sentiments that Cattell has identified are:

Sentiments

career or profession

sports and games

mechanical interests

religion

parents

spouse or sweetheart

self

The dynamic traits may be thought of as related to each other in a *dynamic lattice* or network (1950). The lattice shows that the traits are related according to the principle of subsidiation. *Subsidiation*

FIGURE 8.2 The Dynamic Lattice

Cattell suggests that the dynamic traits may be thought of as related to one another in a dynamic lattice. Adapted from Raymond Cattell, Personality: A Systematic, Theoretical, and Factual Study, McGraw-Hill, New York, 1950, p. 158, and used with permission of Dr. Cattell.

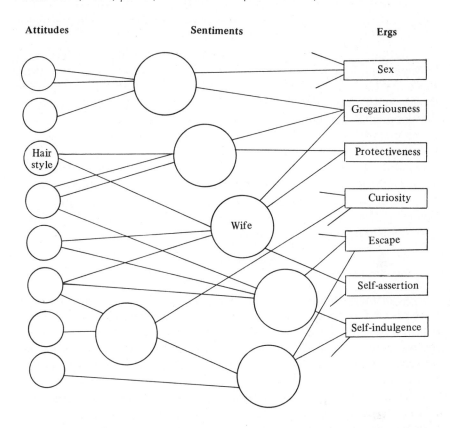

means that certain traits are subsidiary or secondary to other traits. In general, attitudes are secondary to sentiments, which, in turn, are secondary to ergs. In other words, ergs are the basic motivating forces. Thus, each sentiment may be seen as subsidiary to and expressive of one or more ergs. A man's sentiment about his wife may be related to the ergs of sex, gregariousness, protection, and self-assertion. One's surface attitude and behavior, that is, one's attitude toward his wife's hairstyle, is influenced by that sentiment as well as other sentiments. Surface attitudes reflect sentiments that, in turn, express ergs.

In Figure 8.2 the ergs are represented by the rectangles at the right. The large circles in the middle represent sentiments. Each sentiment is subsidiary to one or more ergs. The small circles at the left reflect attitudes toward particular behaviors. Each attitude is secondary to one or more sentiments, therefore it expresses those sentiments and also the ergs that inform the sentiments.

A particularly important sentiment is that of the self. The *self-sentiment* refers to a person's self-image. It is reflected in almost all of the attitudes that a person holds. Cattell suggests that the self-sentiment plays a crucial role in integrating the expressions of all the various ergs and other sentiments. Although it is one of the latest sentiments to develop, it plays a major role in controlling the structure of personality.

Cattell acknowledges the importance of learning in personality development and has described stages in personality growth. While these are not major emphases in his theory, they serve to correlate his theory with other theoretical positions, such as learning theory and developmental psychology, and indicate the connection among learning, development, and personality traits. Many of Cattell's studies have tried to analyze the changes that may occur in different personality traits during different age ranges. For example, in adolescence there appears to be an increase in adventurousness and ego stability and a decrease in apprehensiveness and suspiciousness. Cattell believes that further studies offer the promise of someday developing a full outline of developmental trends in personality traits.

The Identification of Traits

A primary impact of Cattell's personality theory has been his methods and techniques of researching and identifying traits. Cattell's primary tool has been factor analysis, which will be described shortly. However, before Cattell could apply this tool, it was necessary for him to gather large masses of data from a great many individuals in a variety of different ways.

Cattell garnered his data from three primary sources (1965). The first is *life records* and is called *L-data*. L-data refers to observations of a person's behavior in society or everyday life. Examples of L-data would be an individual's school record, number of automobile accidents, job performance reports, and so forth. L-data, therefore involves ratings made by other people on the individual concerned. The second source involves questionnaires or self-reports and is known as *Q-data*. You were engaged in self-reports when you answered the inventories on your somatotype and tendency to be outgoing or reserved. Questionnaires permit self-ratings by the person involved. Thus, they may or may not be truthful. Cattell uses a variety of questionnaires or scales. While he acknowledges that there are difficulties in assessing the accuracy of self-reports, he believes that they are an important mode of gathering data. Finally, Cattell uses objective tests or *T-data*. Cattell employs the term *objective* in an unusual way. By "objective" Cattell means that a test is constructed in such a way that the subject taking it cannot know what a particular test or test item is designed to measure. Thus, it is difficult for a subject to fake the test or distort his or her responses. This definition of objectivity differs considerably from the definition of most other psychologists, as we shall see.

All of the data garnered from these sources is then subjected to the complex, sophisticated statistical technique of factor analysis. *Factor analysis* is essentially a correlational procedure, but it involves more than just one or two correlations. It is a procedure that interrelates many, many correlations at one time. In this way a number of intercorrelations among many different variables may be determined. It is not unusual for a factor analysis study to involve as many as one hundred or more different variables. Obviously, such a study involves a great deal of mathematical computation, and only the advent of the modern computer has made factor analysis a feasible technique for personality description.

Basically, factor analysis aims at describing larger amounts of data by smaller, more manageable units. Using complex mathematical formulas, it reduces the data to the smallest number of relatively similar dimensions or clusters, which are referred to as factors, that can be used to account for the wider variety.

For example, beginning with as many as one hundred surface personality traits, through factor analysis one can discover which of the traits cluster and occur together with the greatest frequency. These traits may then be umbrellaed under a common source trait. One can thereby reduce the number of traits to be dealt with and make them more manageable and easier to handle.

In the end Cattell hopes that he can use the information garnered to facilitate the prediction of behavior. Given the ability to describe an individual in terms of various traits, and the understanding of how these traits enter into certain behavior response patterns, we would be able to apply this information to a particular instance. Eventually, we will be able to predict how a particular individual might respond in a given situation. Cattell (1965) suggests that this may eventually be done by means of a *specification equation*:

$$R = s_1T_1 + s_2T_2 + s_3T_3 + \ldots + s_nT_n$$

This forbidding equation simply means the following: The response (R) equals the sum of the characteristics of the person ($T_1, T_2, T_3 \ldots T_n$). Each trait is weighted according to its relevance to the particular situation. That rating constitutes the situational index ($s_1, s_2, s_3 \ldots$). If a particular trait is highly relevant to the response, its corresponding situational index would be high. If a particular trait is irrelevant to a response, the situation index would be zero. If the trait inhibits or detracts from the response, the situational index would be negative. The model is basically a very simple one.

For example, suppose R were to stand for classroom performance of a professor. The factor of intelligence would be very important because an instructor needs to understand the subject and know how to communicate it to others. Thus, the characteristic of intelligence would be assigned a high situational index. The characteristic of assertiveness might also be important, but less so than intelligence. Therefore, it would be assigned a lower number. Each trait that is relevant to classroom performance would be included until all the elements in the equation are filled in. We would then be able to predict how a candidate might behave in the classroom.

Cattell's formula is based on addition and thus it has been criticized for not providing for possible interrelations or interactions among traits. Cattell acknowledges that we may eventually need more sophisticated formulas, but suggests that his specification equation is a useful starting point.

The Influence of Heredity and Environment on Personality

In comparison to other theorists, Cattell has been particularly interested in assessing the relative importance of heredity and environment in shaping traits and personality. He has studied this problem by a technique known as *Multiple Abstract Variance Analysis* (1960). It will be easier for you to simply remember the abbreviated name of MAVA. MAVA studies twins and siblings who have been reared together or apart. As you may know, identical twins develop from a single fertilized ovum or egg. Thus, they possess an identical genetic makeup, but singletons are unique in their genetic composition. Comparisons of identical twins with other individuals under various environmental conditions can give us an estimate of the degree to which differences in traits are due to differences in genetics or in environment.

Cattell's studies have indicated the importance of heredity in a number of traits, such as intelligence. Studies have shown that identical twins, even if reared apart, are similar with respect to IQ. This is not to say, however, that heredity is the sole determinant of intelligence. Heredity probably places limits on an individual's potential intelligence, but environment determines where within that range his or her actual IQ score will fall. Current research suggests the ratio of influence is heredity sixty percent and environment forty percent. Other twin studies have suggested the possibility of a strong genetic influence on certain mental disorders such as schizophrenia. Findings like these have led Cattell to suggest in *A New Morality from Science: Beyondism* (1972) the importance of selective breeding as a means of cultivating desired traits.

In his research into the effect of the environment on personality, Cattell has also directed his attention to the social context within which a person develops. He has suggested that objective measures may be employed to describe groups just as traits are used to describe individuals. These measures indicate the group *syntality*, which refers to the behavior of the group as a whole or its "group personality" (1948). Cattell's point is that we need to understand the interaction between an individual personality and the syntality of the groups that influence him or her, such as school, peers, and religious associations. Cattell has conducted considerable research into the syntality of small groups and has also suggested a set of factors for describing the syntality of nations and larger groups.

Evaluation and Implications

It should be obvious that Cattell's theory is based on highly objective and precise scientific techniques. Further, he has generated an enormous amount of research data. A perusal of the sections on personality in the *Annual Review of Psychology* over the last decade and a half attests to the significance of his contributions and also provides a concise introduction to the research that Cattell's theory has generated. Critics have pointed out that his method is not as objective as it initially appears to be (Hall and Lindzey, 1978). While it is true that subjectivity may enter into several different steps of Cattell's research process, it is impossible for any scientific methodology to eliminate completely the factor of subjectivity. Cattell's methodology and his goal of predicting behavior are an outstanding example of the use of validating evidence in the empirical scientific tradition.

Cattell's theory also reflects the current emphasis in psychology on quantitative methods and empirical data. Few other theorists have been as precise or operational in their definitions. Furthermore, few other theorists have been as rigorous in subjecting their concepts of underlying personality variables to empirical test. In terms of strict methodology and vast quantity of research, Cattell's theory deserves respect and consideration.

In a later book, *A New Morality from Science: Beyondism* (1972), Cattell advocates that a system of ethical values be developed on the foundation of science. He suggests that by adhering to scientific experiment and empirical observation, valid moral rules may be constructed. Recognizing that traditional revealed religion has faltered badly in the face of science, Cattell urges scientists to reconstruct what they have torn down and to develop out of their scientific discoveries a new and more valid moral imperative. Beyondism rests its case on the scientific theory that humanity is in the process of evolutionary advance in a physically and biologically evolving universe. Moral laws need to be developed that will foster and insure this evolutionary process. Such ethics will enable us to adapt to a wider range of circumstances and thus produce a better chance of survival.

As we have seen, science is the daughter of philosophy. Her methods and objective mode of study and investigation rely on assumptions that can only be established philosophically. Cattell fully recognizes that the initial steps of the scientific method are the product of intuition. In and of itself, the scientific method does not generate hypotheses, it presupposes them and provides a procedure for testing them. Strictly speaking, Cattell's new morality cannot be said to arise from science. Science may have discovered the process of evolution, but the judgment that such evolution is good and should be fostered is a value judgment and, as a value judgment, it takes us outside the realm of validating evidence itself into the realm of philosophy. Still, Cattell raises moral issues, such as the desirability of selective breeding, that deserve serious consideration by all who are interested in the future development of the human race. Herein lies the value of science for Cattell and others who cherish the importance of validating evidence: in science, intuition is subsequently checked by explicit logic and experiment.

A Related Trait Theorist: H. J. Eysenck

An English psychologist, Hans J. Eysenck (1916–   ), has extended the search for personality dimensions and traits into the area of abnormal behavior. He has suggested that there are two fundamental trait dimensions of personality:

emotional stability — neuroticism
introversion — extroversion

The *emotional stability versus neuroticism dimension* refers to an individual's basic adjustment to his or her environment and the stability of behavior over time. The *introversion versus extroversion dimension* reflects the degree to which a person is usually outgoing and participative in his or her relations with other individuals.

Eysenck has been influenced by Jung's typology of introversion and extroversion as well as by the constitutional psychology of Kretschmer and Sheldon. Indeed, Eysenck even includes the earlier classification of Hippocrates and Galen in his overall discussion of personality traits. Eysenck suggests that the traits that have been discovered by factor analysis may be summarized as shown in the diagram in Figure 8.3. The inner circle shows Hippocrates' and Galen's four temperaments. The outer ring shows the results of factor analysis studies of the intercorrelations among traits. The traits may be seen to reflect the two fundamental dimensions of emotional stability versus neuroticism and introversion versus extroversion. Eysenck believes that there is a clear biological basis to personality (1967). Certain constitutional structures render individuals more or less susceptible to certain personality traits and characteristics.

FIGURE 8.3   The Intercorrelation of Traits

The inner circle shows Hippocrates' four temperaments. The outer ring shows the results of factor analysis studies of the intercorrelations between traits done by Eysenck and others. Adapted from H. J. Eysenck and S. Rachman, The Causes and Cures of Neurosis; An Introduction to Modern Behavior Therapy Based on Learning Theory and the Principles of Conditioning, *Edits/Knapp, San Diego, 1965.*

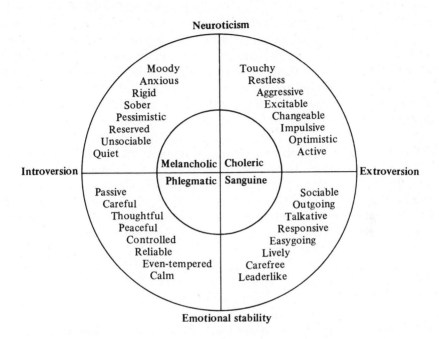

More recently, Eysenck has conducted investigations into the dimension of psychoticism versus nonpsychoticism. A *psychosis* is an abnormal personality disturbance commonly known as insanity. It is usually characterized by loss of or distortion of reality testing and inability to distinguish between reality and fantasy. Disturbances are found in thought, emotion, and motor behavior, and the person may have hallucinations or delusions. Eysenck's investigations reflect his interest in extending the search for personality dimensions and constitutional factors into the area of abnormal behavior.

In his studies, Eysenck has employed a method, called criterion analysis, that is related to factor analysis but is more deductive. In factor analysis, conclusions are drawn as a result of the clusters that appear in the process of factoring. *Criterion analysis* begins with a clear hypothesis about possible underlying variables; then statistical analyses are conducted in order to test the hypothesis.

Eysenck is interested in the influences of heredity on personality and also the influence of learning and conditioning. Eysenck's theory as a whole bridges the gap between trait and learning approaches to personality.

APPLICATION OF TRAIT THEORIES

The average individual has undoubtedly been directly influenced by the trait approach to personality to a greater degree than any other approach. Rare is the individual who has not at some time or other been assessed by some device based on the trait approach. Possibly the major contribution of the trait approach has been its provision of concepts and measures by which we can assess individual differences and test hypotheses concerning personality. This procedure has been made possible by development of psychometric tests that measure psychological characteristics through carefully designed questionnaires and statistical techniques. Such techniques have been fostered by the trait approach. Of course, a primary concern of any individual taking a psychological test is the soundness of the psychometric assessment instrument. Here validating evidence has served to check the intuitions and hunches that played a primary role in earlier personality assessment. Contemporary psychometric tests seek to fulfill four primary criteria: standardization, objectivity, reliability, and validity.

A test is *standardized* if it has been pretested on a large and representative sample in order to provide test norms. Standardization informs us of the average score and the range of score variability for a particular test. The process of standardization makes it possible for us to know whether or not any given individual's score is high, low, or average.

A test is considered to be *objective* if it can be given and scored in such a way that subjective bias of the scorer is avoided. Note that this definition of objectivity differs considerably from Cattell's use of the term to refer to a test constructed in such a way that the subject cannot know what the test item measures. The common definition of the criterion of objectivity refers to the process of scoring. If a test is objective, any qualified examiner can present it in the same way to any particular subject and obtain the same score as other qualified examiners. Obviously, objectivity is easier to obtain if the test responses are clearly delineated, as in a multiple-choice or true-false test where each response clearly indicates a certain factor. It is more difficult, but nevertheless possible, to develop objective criteria for scoring protracted written or verbal responses. Such criteria provide for objectivity in evaluating interviews, written essays, projective techniques, and so forth.

A test is *reliable* if it consistently gives similar scores over time. An analogy may be drawn to an oven thermometer that must register the same degree each time for the same amount of heat in order to be a consistent and useful measuring device. If it were not reliable we could not depend on it when we bake cakes and roast meats to the desired degree of doneness. Similarly, a reliable test is one that consistently gives similar scores over time. If an individual were to be given an alternative form of the same test, his or her score should be similar.

Lastly, a test needs to be valid. A test is *valid* if it measures what it is supposed to measure. Validity is the most difficult criterion of all to meet. Virtually all psychologists agree that certain recognized intelligence tests are valid measures for predicting school performance. They are not at all so certain, however, that these tests are valid measures of that elusive quality "intelligence." Problems encountered in defining and measuring intelligence will be discussed in the next section. A test may be reliable without its being valid. Thus, my thermometer may consistently give the same readings to the same amount of heat but be off by twenty-five degrees. If a test meets the criteria of validity, however, it is reliable.

Psychometric testing had its origins in the psychological laboratories established at the end of the nineteenth century. An early pioneer was an English scientist, Sir Francis Galton (1822–1911), who tried to develop an inventory of human abilities. Of course, the first efforts in psychometric testing appear clumsy and naive in comparison with today's sophisticated techniques. Since Galton's time, there has been a continuous and systematic attempt to study personality traits qualitatively with the use of better tests.

Intelligence Testing

The story of intelligence testing is probably the most impressive example in the history of psychology of an effort to develop a sound assessment technique. In the late nineteenth century, there was no real agreement on the nature of intelligence or on the kinds of tests that might be used to measure it. An operational definition specifying behavioral signs of intelligence was needed to determine whether intelligence could be predicted from different types of tests such as sensorimotor, verbal, and so forth. It was decided that school grades would be an acceptable criterion.

At the beginning of this century, two French psychologists, Binet and Simon, agreed at the request of the educational ministry to try to predict the school performance of Parisian children in order to identify those children who would be unable to benefit from the already overcrowded schools. The test they devised consisted primarily of items that were concerned with complex thinking (imagery, memory, comprehension, judgment, reasoning) rather than sensorimotor skills. Subsequent research on the scores that they obtained showed: performance increasing with age; a positive correlation with independent teacher estimates of the children's brightness; and a positive correlation with school grades. This set of measures, thought to reflect a factor of general intelligence, became the basis for the classic Stanford-Binet Intelligence

Test, which has been a standard for all subsequent research on mental ability testing.

The Stanford-Binet Test, now many times revised, is actually a series of subtests, one or more for each year of age. For each age, the child of normal intelligence is expected to be able to perform certain tasks. For example, a child of five according to the 1960 version of the test is asked, among other things, to complete a drawing of a man with no legs; to fold a paper square twice into a triangle after a demonstration; to define two of the three words "ball," "hat," and "stove"; to copy a square; to assemble two triangles into a rectangle; and to recognize similarities and differences in selected pictures. A child of twelve is expected to define words such as "haste," "lecture," "skill," "pity," and "curiosity"; to repeat five digits backwards; to recognize the absurdity in statements such as "It was so hot outdoors that Bill Jones had to wear a heavy overcoat, gloves, and scarf"; and to explain situations depicted in complex pictures.

Binet introduced a scoring method based on the concept of mental age (MA). For each given age level, the average child is expected to pass a certain number of items appropriate to that age. In the child of normal intelligence, mental age and chronological age (CA) are the same and the child succeeds in most of the tasks appropriate to his or her age as well as a few above it. Children who complete a significant number of additional or fewer items have a higher or lower MA than their CA. The relationship between CA and MA is the basis for computing the numerical IQ or intelligence quotient.

Binet's formula for IQ is

$$IQ = \frac{MA}{CA} \times 100$$

Thus, a child with an MA of 120 months and a CA of 100 months (for ease in computation, both ages are converted into months) would have an IQ of 120. MA was determined by the number of items successfully passed, CA by the number of months since the child's birth. Today, however, the final numerical IQ is assigned by referring to tables that indicate the IQ applicable to the score of an individual of a certain age.

Other widely used individual tests of intelligence have been developed by David Wechsler: the Wechsler Adult Intelligence Scale (WAIS); the Wechsler Intelligence Scale for Children (WISC); and the Wechsler Preschool and Primary Scale of Intelligence (WPPSI). The WISC and WAIS are now used much more often than the Stanford-Binet. Since individual tests like the Binet and Wechsler scales are time-consuming and expensive to administer, group tests are even more commonly used. Chances are at one time or another you have taken a group intelligence test. It may have been the Otis-Lennon Mental Ability Test, which is one of the best known.

Empirical studies show a high positive correlation between scores on present respected intelligence tests and certain kinds of behaviors: academic grades and related kinds of performances. Thus, the story of intelligence testing is a good example of the psychologist's successful attempt to predict behavior. Nevertheless, as an operational definition, academic success is probably an inadequate indicator of what most of us consider intelligence to entail: the ability to think intelligently. Most of us can readily think of examples of very bright people, such as Einstein, who did poorly in school. Thus, there have been many criticisms of the adequacy of our present intelligence tests as a basic indicator of potential.

One of the most stringent criticisms of intelligence tests is that they are culturally biased. Most of the items presuppose information that is familiar to children from a typical white middle-class culture. Other children, who have not been exposed to the specific knowledge required in the test, may do poorly, not because of a lack of reasoning ability, but because of unfamiliarity with the terms and concepts presupposed in the items. Adrian Dove, a black sociologist, has pointed out that black ghetto children, for example, have their own culture and language, which is frequently overlooked in regular intelligence tests. In order to illustrate the problem, he developed his own exam, the Dove Counterbalance General Intelligence Test, also known as the "Chitling Test."

EXERCISE:

The "Chitling Test"

Just for fun, you might enjoy testing yourself on some of the items of Dove's "Chitling Test." * *The test was primarily circulated underground, but it also appeared in some newspapers.*

1. *A "hankerchief head" is: a. a cool cat, b. a porter, c. an Uncle Tom, d. a hoddi, e. a preacher.*
2. *Which word is most out of place here? a. splib, b. blood, c. gray, d. spook, e. black.*
3. *A "gas head" is a person who has a: a. fast-moving car, b. stable of "lace," c. "process," d. habit of stealing cars, e. long jail record for arson.*
4. *"Down-home" (the South) today, for the average "soul brother" who is picking cotton from sunup until sundown, what is the average earning (take home) for one full day? a. $.75, b. $1.65, c. $3.50, d. $5, e. $12.*

* Adrian Dove, "Taking the Chitling Test," © 1968 by the New York Times Company. Reprinted by permission.

5. "Bo Diddley" is a: a. game for children, b. down-home cheap wine, c. down-home singer, d. new dance, e. Moejoe call.

6. If a pimp is up tight with a woman who gets state aid, what does he mean when he talks about "Mother's Day"? a. second Sunday in May, b. third Sunday in June, c. first of every month, d. none of these, e. first and fifteenth of every month.

7. "Hully Gully" came from: a. East Oakland, b. Fillmore, c. Watts, d. Harlem, e. Motor City.

8. If a man is called a "blood," then he is a: a. fighter, b. Mexican-American, c. Negro, d. hungry hemophile, e. Redman or Indian.

9. Cheap chitlings (not the kind you purchase at a frozen food counter) will taste rubbery unless they are cooked long enough. How soon can you quit cooking them to eat and enjoy them? a. 45 minutes, b. two hours, c. 24 hours, d. one week (on a low flame), e. one hour.

10. What are the "Dixie Hummingbirds"? a. part of the KKK, b. a swamp disease, c. a modern gospel group, d. a Mississippi Negro paramilitary group, e. Deacons.

Those who are not "culturally deprived" will recognize that the correct answers are: 1. c, 2. c, 3. c, 4. d, 5. c, 6. e, 7. c, 8. c, 9. c, 10. c.

We do not have an adequate definition of intelligence. Theorists are presently working on developing a more appropriate definition. L. L. Thurstone (1941) has suggested that intelligence is composed of seven primary mental abilities: verbal comprehension, word fluency, number, space, associative memory, perceptual speed, and general reasoning, plus some "general factor" common to all of them. J. P. Guilford (1967) rejects the concept of a general intelligence factor and suggests that there are at least 120 different factors of intelligence. Each factor represents the ability to carry out one of five different types of mental *operations* or activities on one of four different *contents* or materials and to come up with one of six different *products* or end results. Thus, intelligence may best be understood as the interaction among three basic processes: 5 operations times 4 contents times 6 products equals 120 factors. Also, Guilford points out that most standard IQ tests ignore many of these factors. He and his followers have tried to develop tests that will help to differentiate among them. Guilford has observed that there are wide individual differences in people's ability to deal with different kinds of materials. Some individuals excel at working with numbers or other symbols; others work best with concrete objects. Most standard IQ tests ignore many of these differences.

Personality Assessment

Practical circumstances also stimulated the first efforts at personality assessment. During World War I, Woodworth developed a Personal

FIGURE 8.4 Factors of Intelligence

Guilford suggests that intelligence may best be understood as the inter-
action among three basic processes: 5 operations times 4 contents times
6 products equals 120 factors. From information based on J. P. Guilford,
The Nature of Human Intelligence, McGraw-Hill, New York, 1967.

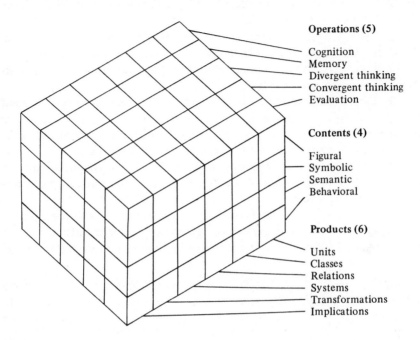

Operations (5)

Cognition
Memory
Divergent thinking
Convergent thinking
Evaluation

Contents (4)

Figural
Symbolic
Semantic
Behavioral

Products (6)

Units
Classes
Relations
Systems
Transformations
Implications

Data Sheet as a means of screening out those men who were not psychologically fit for military service. It was a simple questionnaire that
asked the men to respond affirmatively or negatively to over one hundred
items that were thought to reflect problematic symptoms if too many
answers were in the affirmative. According to modern standards, the
test was grossly oversimplified. Too many of its questions were obvious, such as "Do you ever wet the bed?" and "Do you worry a great
deal?" Nevertheless, the Woodworth Personal Data Sheet was a forerunner of many subsequent self-report questionnaires that were developed, some of which are used today.

One of the most carefully researched questionnaires is the Minnesota Multiphasic Personality Inventory (MMPI). The MMPI is made up
of 550 self-report items or printed statements to which one may answer
"true," "false," or "cannot say." The items cover a wide range of topics
and differ in style. Typical items might be

I am bashful.
Sometimes I think I might commit suicide.
I cry easily.
It is wise to trust others.

The test items, presentation, and scoring are objective and standardized. The test has also been checked for reliability and validity by comparing its results with other indexes or measures. Items on the MMPI have been sorted into ten basic clinical subscales that are designed to measure different tendencies of pathology or abnormal behaviors:

1. *Hs*   *hypochondriasis:* concern about health
2. *D*   *depression:* tendency to feel despondent or depressed
3. *Hy*   *hysteria:* tendency to use physical illness to solve or avoid problems
4. *Pd*   *psychopathic deviance:* tendency toward unsocial impulsive behavior
5. *Mf*   *masculinity-femininity:* the degree to which one's interests follow traditional sex preferences
6. *Pa*   *paranoia:* feelings of persecution and suspiciousness
7. *Pt*   *psychasthenia:* tendency toward obsessions or compulsions
8. *Sc*   *schizophrenia:* tendency to lose contact with the environment and experience personality disintegration
9. *Ma*   *hypomania:* tendency to be mentally or physically overactive
10. *Si*   *social introversion:* tendency toward introversion or extroversion

Recent research has made clear that the scales do not really measure the disorders for which they were originally named. Thus, it would be misleading to suggest that the scales actually tap the entities whose labels they bear. Their meaning emerges only through correlations and associations with other tests and measures.

In order to counter the problems of possible falsification of test items by a subject who is taking the test, the MMPI also includes four validity scales. A *cannot say scale* indicates the number of items left blank. A high score in this scale indicates evasiveness. The *L (lie) scale* measures the tendency an individual might have to falsify items in order to present him- or herself in a good light. It includes items that any honest person would have to answer in the indicated manner: "I get angry sometimes" (true) or "I have never told a lie" (false). The *F (frequency) scale* measures the tendency to answer questions in an unusual way. The *K (correction) scale* indicates a tendency to become defensive while taking tests.

The results of an individual's answers on the MMPI may be presented in the form of a *profile* or graph that facilitates comparison of any given individual's score with the norm. Figure 8.5 shows a profile. In interpreting the results of the MMPI, an individual's scores are compared with average scores and the distribution of scores around the norm. Abnormally high scores, above a t-score of 70, are given attention,

FIGURE 8.5 A MMPI Profile

The results of an individual's answers on the MMPI may be presented in the form of a profile.

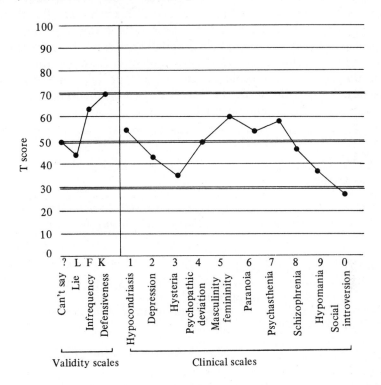

but the pattern of subscale scores is most important. Specific types of profiles are more common among persons with certain pathological symptoms. Although it is not a perfect device, the MMPI represents one of the most widely used and influential techniques today. It was originally designed and is still employed as an aid in the diagnosis of psychiatric patients, where it has shown itself to be a better diagnostic tool than independent psychiatrists' judgments. The MMPI is also widely used in personality research. Several hundred additional scales have been developed using the basic 550 items of the MMPI and other similar items.

An example of a psychometric assessment device influenced by the MMPI is the California Psychological Inventory (CPI). Unlike the MMPI, which concentrates on pathological patterns, the CPI is designed to measure a wide range of normal behaviors. The CPI contains eighteen subscales: dominance, capacity for status, sociability, social presence, self-acceptance, sense of well-being, responsibility, socialization, self-control, tolerance, good impression, communality, achievement via conformance, achievement via independence, intellectual efficiency, psychological-mindedness, flexibility, and femininity. Three of these subscales also function as validity scales.

In order to cope with the problem of falsification in personality inventories and to measure deeper lying aspects of personality, some psychologists also employ projective techniques. *Projective techniques* refer to the kinds of tests that Cattell described in his reference to "objective tests" or T-data. The theory behind these tests is that the subject cannot anticipate what a "correct" or "wrong" answer to the item might be because the stimulus is deliberately ambiguous. In answering the test items, the subject will project some of his or her own personality characteristics into the response and thus reveal something about his or her attitudes, feelings, and so forth.

EXERCISE:

Projective Techniques

What is it like to take a projective-type test? Look at the inkblot in Figure 8.6 and write a full description of everything you see in the blot.

FIGURE 8.6 Rorschach Inkblot
This is a sample of the inkblots used in the Rorschach Test. What do you see in it? Reprinted with permission from Bruno Klopfer and Helen H. Davidson, The Rorschach Technique: An Introductory Manual, Harcourt Brace & Jovanovich, New York, 1962.

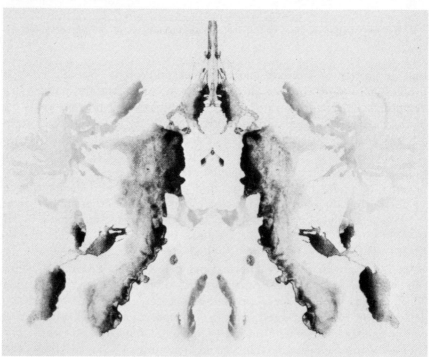

When you have finished, look at the picture in Figure 8.7 and describe in your own words what that picture means to you by making up a story for it. Tell what led up to the events shown in the picture, what is happening, what the characters in the picture are thinking and feeling, and how the event will turn out. When you have finished working with both figures, read the material below about the Rorschach Test and the Thematic Apperception Test, which will give you a general idea of how these assessment devices are evaluated.

FIGURE 8.7 Thematic Apperception Test Picture
This is a sample of the pictures in the Thematic Apperception Test. What story does the picture tell? What led up to the events in the picture? What is happening? How are things going to work out? Reprinted by permission of the publishers from THEMATIC APPERCEPTION TEST by Henry A. Murray, Cambridge, Mass.: Harvard University Press. Copyright © 1943 by the President and Fellows of Harvard College; © 1971 by Henry A. Murray.

Two of the best known projective devices are the Rorschach Test and the Thematic Apperception Test. The Rorschach Test was developed by a Swiss psychiatrist, Herman Rorschach, in 1921. It consists of a series of ten separate inkblots similar to the one in Figure 8.6. The subject is requested to look at each inkblot and tell what he or she sees. Responses are noted in terms of location, physical aspects of the blot, content, and originality. These responses are then compared to standardized norms. A subject who tends to respond to the blots as a whole might be considered generally to think in terms of abstractions, whereas one who concentrates on every minor aspect of the blots may show an absorption in detail.

The Thematic Apperception Test (TAT) was developed by C. D. Morgan and H. A. Murray in 1935 as part of a Harvard Psychological Clinic research program. It consists of a series of ambiguous pictures such as Figure 8.7. The subject is asked to make up stories for the pictures telling what led up to the event, what is happening, what the characters in the picture are thinking and feeling, and how the event will turn out. The person's responses to the TAT suggest how he or she thinks of him- or herself in relation to the physical and social environment. Through the data, the examiner can infer how the subject relates to other people and molds the environment to meet his or her needs. Again, special scoring guides permit the examiner to determine what the test responses indicate.

The main advantage of projective techniques is that they disguise the purpose of the test. Because the stimuli are ambiguous and the subject is free to respond in any way that he or she chooses, it is difficult for the subject to know what would be an appropriate answer. Thus, it is difficult to fake a "correct" response as there are no "correct" answers. Projective techniques are often derived from the psychoanalytic concepts of Sigmund Freud, who suggested that we project our unconscious attitudes and feelings onto other people and stimuli. In psychoanalysis itself the anonymous figure of the analyst invites the analysand to fantasize about the analyst. These fantasies are then carefully studied to determine the unconscious feelings and attitudes that have been projected onto the analyst. In that sense, analysis itself makes considerable use of a projective technique. The difficulty with projective tests is that they are very hard to score in an objective manner that avoids subjective bias and the projection of the scorer. Both the Rorschach and the TAT have manuals with explicit directions for scoring, and personnel who administer these tests are extensively trained. These measures have helped to some degree to insure consistency among scorers.

Other psychometric tests based on the trait approach are aptitude tests, achievement tests, and interest tests. *Aptitude tests* measure an individual's ability to learn a new skill or task. An example is the Scholastic Aptitude Test, taken by many prospective college students, that indicates a person's ability to learn college material. Aptitude tests have been widely used in industry to determine the likelihood of an individual's performing well in a new job. *Achievement tests* measure how much an individual has already learned. Examples are the Iowa and Stanford achievement tests, which show one's level of achievement in different academic skills and compare these levels with national norms. *Interest tests*, such as the Strong Campbell Interest Inventory, tell something about the pattern of a person's interests and how that pattern compares with those of persons in various vocations. Such tests do not measure aptitude or ability, only the similarity of a person's interests to those of others successful in a particular area or field.

Evaluation and Implications

Psychometric measuring devices and techniques have not been used without controversy. Many individuals view such tests as an invasion of personal privacy and are wary of the use to which the test results may be put. Most of the constructs supposedly indicated by these tests cannot be measured directly. Often the validity of the tests is assumed rather than demonstrated. We can account for the usefulness of a test only in terms of its predictive power. But suppose its predictive power is incorrect? On the basis of a "carefully designed" test, we might imagine a situation in which an individual might be imprisoned for the rest of his or her life simply because of the high probability that he or she might commit murder. Such a situation may seem far-fetched, yet individuals are turned down for jobs or denied educational and other opportunities on the basis of such tests.

On the other hand, the wise and judicious use of appropriate assessment techniques can be invaluable in developing individual and group potential. As early as the fourth century B.C., the Greek philosopher Plato advocated careful use of assessment techniques in the shaping of his ideal society, the Republic. He urged teachers to note the dominant traits of their students in order to select and prepare them for the appropriate class in society: workers, guardians, or philosopher-kings. An accurate understanding of one's limitations and potentialities is important for self-actualization. The point to remember, however, is that there is a distinction between a person's inclination to behave in a certain way and the fact of behaving in such a way. Many personality tests have shown themselves to be accurate predictors, but they are not guarantees of certain behaviors. Furthermore, as scientific tools, they must remain open to falsification, and our use of them needs to reflect that fact.

Simplicity and explicitness are key attributes of the trait and type theory approach. Trait theories promise an economy in their description of personality. Moreover, they are also operational. Behaviors are clearly and specifically defined. While many other personality theorists have tried to understand personality through intuitive and speculative methods, modern trait theorists are eminently scientific in their approach. Their search is for objective and replicable procedures for understanding personality. Although the subjective bias or intuitions that lie at the root of any scientific theorizing cannot be denied, trait theorists, more than many others have been rigorous in submitting their hypothetical constructs to empirical test. Such an emphasis on clarity and rigorous standards of measurement is surely commendable. Contemporary trait theorists are excellent and praiseworthy models for applying the use of validating evidence to the study of personality.

SUGGESTIONS FOR FURTHER READING

A concise statement of Sheldon's research up to 1944 is found in his article "Constitutional Factors in Personality," in J. McV. Hunt (ed.) *Personality and the Behavior Disorders* (Ronald Press, 1944). The initial historical orientation is somewhat tedious, but it is followed by an apt summary and description of his research that is interesting reading. A more comprehensive work is W. H. Sheldon, C. W. Dupertuis, and E. McDermott, *Atlas of Men: A Guide for Somatotyping the Adult Male of All Ages* (Harper & Row, 1954), in which Sheldon revises and modifies some of his earlier positions. Sheldon's techniques for measuring physique and temperament are outlined in W. H. Sheldon, S. S. Stevens, and W. B. Tucker, *The Varieties of Human Physique: An Introduction to Constitutional Psychology* (Harper & Row, 1942), and W. H. Sheldon and S. S. Stevens, *The Varieties of Temperament: A Psychology of Constitutional Differences*, both published by Harper & Row, 1942. For summaries of relevant research attempting to replicate Sheldon's studies, see Rees, 1961, and Lindzey, 1967 (full references are given in the Bibliography).

Cattell has been a prolific writer, authoring over 30 books and 300 articles. His work is technical and difficult to digest. However, an introductory primer to his theory, which is not too technical, is provided in *The Scientific Analysis of Personality* (Penguin, 1965), aimed at a lay public. Also readable and exciting because of the ethical issues that it raises is *A New Morality From Science: Beyondism* (Pergamon, 1972). Beyond that the interested reader has a vast array of primary sources to choose from. Cattell's most recent findings are included in Raymond B. Cattell and Ralph M. Dreger, *Handbook of Modern Personality Theory* (Hemisphere Publishing Corporation, 1977). A broad critical review of Cattell's work is found in an article by S. B. Sells, "Structured measurement of personality and motivation: A review of contributions of Raymond B. Cattell," *Journal of Clinical Psychology*, 1959, *15*, 3–21. For summaries of research that Cattell's work has generated, the reader is advised to consult the selections on personality in recent issues of the *Annual Review of Psychology*. Volumes 15, 16, 18, 19, and 20 are especially recommended.

The following books are recommended for students who are interested in psychometric assessment: A. Anastasi, *Psychological Testing*, 3rd. ed. (Macmillan, 1968); J. M. Sattler, *The Assessment of Children's Intelligence* (W. B. Saunders, 1974); and P. E. Vernon, *Personality Assessment: A Critical Survey* (London: Tavistock, 1969).

CHAPTER 9

Gordon Allport: A Humanistic Trait Theory

When a group of clinicians were asked which personality theorist was most influential for them in their everyday work, the name of Gordon Allport ranked second only to that of Sigmund Freud. Gordon Allport is a theorist of monumental influence; he has received almost every professional honor offered by his colleagues in psychology. With the possible exception of Raymond Cattell, Gordon Allport has explored the concept of "trait" more fully than any other personality theorist. At the same time, however, Allport's concern to do justice to the complexity of personality led to a particularly fertile theory that paved the way for the humanistic approach. Allport describes his theory as eclectic. The term *eclectic* refers to selecting the best from a variety of different concepts and methods. Allport is critical of narrow conceptions of personality and research. He believes new methods of study are required to capture the richness and fullness of an individual's personality. His emphases on the uniqueness of the individual, the contemporaneity of motives, and a holistic view of the person point in the direction of the humanist theories, which we will consider in Part V.

BIOGRAPHICAL BACKGROUND

Gordon Allport was born in 1897 in Indiana and grew up near Cleveland, Ohio. He was the son of a country doctor, and he described his practical but humanitarian home life as one characterized by "plain

Protestant piety and hard work." Allport has written little about his childhood, but he has indicated that he spent much of it alone. He was adept at language, but poor at sports and games.

After he graduated from high school, his brother Floyd, who also became a distinguished psychologist, encouraged him to apply to Harvard, where he had gone. Thus began Gordon Allport's close long-time association and devotion to that university. As an undergraduate, he concentrated in both psychology and social ethics, and in his spare time engaged in social service activities. He led a boy's club in Boston's West End, served as a volunteer probation officer for the Family Society, and assisted other groups.

Upon graduation, he accepted an opportunity to teach English and sociology at Robert College in Istanbul, Turkey, in an effort that can be seen as an early forerunner of the Peace Corps. Enjoying teaching, he accepted a fellowship from Harvard for graduate study in psychology. He received his Ph.D. only two years later, in 1922. His dissertation, "An Experimental Study of the Traits of Personality," showed an interest in the area of traits that was to endure. It was also the first American study on personality traits.

Another fellowship for travel abroad followed. Allport spent the first year studying the gestalt school in Germany, a branch of psychology that emphasizes the study of perception. The second year was spent at Cambridge. On his return he became an instructor in social ethics at Harvard, where he developed and taught what was probably the first course offered in personality in this country. In 1926 he left Harvard to accept an assistant professorship in psychology at Dartmouth, but in 1930 he returned to Harvard, this time to stay. His contributions to Harvard were many. Most notably, he was an early advocate of interdisciplinary studies and a leader in the creation of the department of social relations, which combined degree programs in psychology, sociology, and anthropology. His professional honors were manifold. He was a popular and respected teacher. He died in 1967, one month before his seventieth birthday.

THE NATURE OF PERSONALITY

Allport described and classified over fifty different definitions of personality before he developed his own definition in 1937. After working with this definition for many years, he revised it in 1961. His final definition is: "Personality is the dynamic organization within the individual of those psychophysical systems that determine his characteristic behavior and thought."

Key Concepts in Allport's Definition

Zeroing in on some of the key concepts that Allport employs can help us to understand his definition of personality more fully. The term *dynamic* implies that personality is moving and changing. It is not static or fixed, it is a process in forward movement. The term *organized* implies that while personality is moving it is also organized and composed of systems that are not chaotic but structured. The term *psychophysical* implies that personality entails components of both the mind and the body. The term *system* implies that personality is a complex of elements that interact in a meaningful way. The term *determine* has a twofold implication. Not only is one's personality structured by the past, but in turn one's personality also directs and determines the future. The *determining tendencies* of one's personality predispose one to certain behaviors. Personality not only "is something," it "does something." The term *characteristic* implies that each individual is unique. Even the behaviors that we share with others are essentially individual and peculiar to oneself. Although we can compare and contrast persons, no one is exactly like anybody else. Even identical twins are different because each develops in his or her own unique environment. Each person can be understood only in terms of who he or she is.

Allport's definition makes it clear that to him the concept of personality is not a mere fiction or imaginary concept but a real entity. He wants to suggest that one's personality is somehow really there. He refers to the concept of personality as a hypothetical construct, because it is currently unobservable since it cannot be measured empirically. However, Allport suggests that it is an inescapable inference that may someday be demonstrated directly as a real existence within the person, involving neural or physiological components. Allport reminds us that at one time the planet Pluto was a hypothetical construct, postulated long before any telescope could observe it. In time, science was able to point directly to it. In time, Allport also hopes that neurophysiological and psychological research will show us the way to locate directly our present hypothetical construct of personality.

In defining personality, Allport distinguishes among the terms: *personality, character*, and *temperament* (1937). The terms "character" and "temperament" are frequently employed synonymously with "personality." Allport believes that these usages are misleading, and that it is of value to distinguish between these concepts. *Personality* is a neutral concept that attempts to describe without placing any value judgment on its description. The term *character* has a connotation that suggests a certain moral standard or code of behavior against which a person's actions or behaviors may be evaluated or judged. Thus, we speak of a person as having a "good character." Character, therefore, is an ethical term that may be applied to personality: character is "personality evaluated." The term *temperament* refers to a class of raw materials from which personality is fashioned. It refers to biological or psychological dispositions. These phenomena are dependent on one's constitutional make-up and are primarily genetic in origin. Thus, temperament embraces an individual's heredity, disposition, or emotional structure. Temperament is not a finished, unchanging product, but a raw potential that is shaped by the emerging personality.

Personality as Open and Discontinuous

Allport argues for an open system in personality theory (1960). We have seen that the word "system" is included in his definition of personality in order to indicate that personality is composed of a group of elements that interact in a meaningful way. Allport observes that systems or concepts of personality may be considered closed or open. A *closed system* is a concept of personality that admits little or nothing new from outside of the organism to influence or change it in any significant way. In a closed system, one's personality is seen as complete within itself or as simply responding automatically to stimuli within the environment. An *open system* is one that conceives of personality as having a dynamic potential for growth, reconstitution, and change through extensive transactions within itself and also with its environment.

Allport suggests that Skinner's stimulus-response theory and

Freud's theory of psychoanalysis tend to be closed or semiclosed systems, as they do not fully envision personality as a dynamic growth system that has extensive transactions with its environment. Stimulus-response theory concentrates on a view of the organism as limited to responses to stimuli in the environment. Its emphasis is on the intake and output of matter and energy. There is little consideration of the creative response of the person who interacts with the environment. Indeed, personality, as we have seen, is minimized or considered insignificant in stimulus-response theory. Psychoanalysis describes the ego as seeking to maintain a balance among the id, superego, and the outside world. This emphasis on *homeostasis*, or balance and equilibrium, leads to a stress on stability and permanence rather than on growth and change in the concept of personality. The emphasis of psychoanalysis is on the past rather than the future.

Allport describes a fully open theory as one that allows for a dynamic growth process within the organism and extensive interactions with the environment. Completely open theories of personality suggest that as the organism develops, it increases in complexity and becomes something more than it was. Such systems also conceive of personality as the patterning of different experiences that characterize the interaction of the individual with his or her environment. The individual is seen as participating in extensive transactions with various elements and situations that call on him or her to assume different roles. An open theory does not lose sight of either the individual or the environment but encompasses both. By their extreme emphasis on either the environment or the individual, Allport believes that stimulus-response theory and psychoanalysis lose sight of the whole.

Another way to state the distinction between open and closed systems of personality is to refer to continuity theories versus discontinuity theories. A *continuity* theory is one that suggests that the development of personality is essentially the accumulation of skills, habits, and discriminations, without anything really new appearing in the person's make-up. Growth basically is envisioned as an increasing accumulation of more and more skills, habits, and so forth. No significant changes occur except in the number of items assembled. The clearest example of a continuity theory, again, is Skinner's stimulus-response theory. According to Skinner, a stimulus enters the organism and a response is emitted. While the organism may have the capacity to store, summarize, and delay responding to those stimuli, its output is understood largely in terms of its input. Changes are merely quantitative relative to the amount of inputs. Continuity theories, therefore, posit closed systems of personality.

A *discontinuity* theory is one that suggests that in the course of development, an organism experiences genuine transformations or changes so that it reaches successively higher levels of organization.

Here growth is conceived as qualitatively different and the system is open. Walking is considered very different from crawling, talking is viewed as discontinuous with babbling and so forth, even though these behaviors emerge out of the earlier ones. If we picture personality as an organism into which inputs are given, a continuity theory merely sees the inputs accumulating, whereas a discontinuity theory suggests that at times during the development of the organism, the organism reorganizes, regroups, and reshapes these inputs so that the structure of personality changes radically. Such theories view the person as active in consolidating and integrating his or her experience. Change is qualitative rather than merely quantitative. Theories that posit stages of development of personality have the potential to imply discontinuity, because each stage entails a different organization of personality than the stage before it. Freud's psychoanalytic theory, while outlining stages of development, did not fully realize this potential because of its primary emphasis on the individual and intrapsychic factors. Elements within Freud's theory point toward discontinuity, but it remains semiclosed.

The view of personality as open and discontinuous does not lend itself very well to the study of personality by the methods traditionally practiced in academic psychology and that seek to discover general laws that apply to all individual cases. Allport wished to explore the uniqueness and openness of personality, but some of these aspects of personality can only be studied by procedures that have not been considered strictly scientific. Allport pointed out that the methods and techniques of animal experimentation and study within the psychological laboratory are not necessarily suitable for a full understanding of human nature. In his own research, he recognized the value of other methodologies and incorporated influences from other fields, such as literature, philosophy, art, and religion, as well as science. He suggested that an open system of personality paves the way for the invention of new methods of research that aim at rigor, but do not forfeit the study of certain aspects of personality because present scientific methodologies cannot embrace them.

TRAITS

Allport is generally considered a trait psychologist. According to Allport, an individual's traits have a real and vital existence. In order to emphasize his belief in the reality of traits, Allport proposed a biophysical conception of them as neuropsychic structures (1937). This is to say that traits are genuine, bona fide structures within a person that influence behavior. They are not simply labels that we use to describe or classify behaviors.

We can compare Allport's view with that of Cattell, who does not assert that the traits hypothesized through the process of factor analysis necessarily have any real physical or neural status. Allport, on the other hand, defines a *trait* as a determining tendency or predisposition to respond, and he suggests that traits may be considered the ultimate reality of psychological organization. The trait, just as personality, is not in principle unobservable. While it is true that we cannot now directly observe them, in time, trait theorists may be able to measure traits empirically, just as astronomers were later able to observe hypothesized planets.

Allport distinguished between individual traits and common traits (1937). In his later writings, to clarify his position, he used the terms *common traits* and *personal dispositions*. The difference between them is that personal dispositions are unique and peculiar to each individual. Because no two people are exactly alike, no two persons can be said to possess identical personal dispositions. On the other hand, there are times when we wish to make comparisons among individuals. To do so, it is necessary to posit the imaginary construction of common traits that are shared. In a sense, common traits are more nominal (existing primarily in name as convenient fictions for making comparisons) than veridical (really there). Nevertheless, Allport would not wish to concede that they are nonexistent.

The primary importance of the distinction between common traits and personal dispositions is the way in which each is studied. The concept of common traits lends itself to traditional psychometric research, whereas the concept of personal dispositions requires new methodologies that permit the unique individuality of the person to emerge.

In order to clarify his concepts of traits, Allport distinguishes between traits and other determining tendencies. A *habit* refers to a determining tendency that is narrow and limited. Several habits, integrated together, make up a trait that is more generalized. Regularly brushing one's teeth is a habit that, together with others, may compose the trait of cleanliness. Traits are also more general than attitudes. An *attitude* has an object of reference; one has an attitude toward some object—one's country or exploration in space. An attitude is also either positively or negatively disposed toward the object. One is for or against Women's Liberation. The definition of a trait is broader; a trait is a more generalized disposition.

Establishing Common Traits

We have seen that in order to discover roughly comparable traits among individuals, it is necessary to posit the existence of common traits. While no two persons can be said to possess identical traits, we can discover roughly comparable traits, or hypothetical traits that allow us to compare the predispositions that are held in common or shared with other persons. Normal people in any given culture tend to develop along roughly comparable modes or lines of adjustment. In a competitive society, most individuals develop a level of assertiveness or ascendance that can be compared with the level of assertiveness in others. There are several aspects of personality in respect to which all people in a given culture may be compared. A *common trait*, therefore, is a hypothetical construct that refers to those aspects of personality in respect to which individuals within a given culture may be compared.

In order to establish common traits, Allport employs traditional scientific methodology and psychometric techniques. In order to determine whether or not a person is aggressive, we would want to establish the frequency, range, and intensity of his or her aggressive behaviors. We would ask how often the aggressive behavior occurs, how broadly it is applied in different situations, and how strong the reaction of aggression is. These criteria of frequency, range, and intensity are quantifiable; that is to say, they can be measured.

The statistical proof for the existence of a trait is found in different measures of reliability. As we have seen, *reliability* refers to the consistency of or the degree to which a person's score on a variable does not change on repeated testings. The reliability of a trait can be determined in many ways. Observer reliability is determined by noting whether or not judgments about an individual's behavior are confirmed by several different observers. Repeat reliability is established by re-administering the same test or an alternate version to a subject and noting whether or not approximately the same score reappears. Internal reliability refers to the fact that if an individual behaves in a certain way in one situation, he or she will also behave in other situations in a manner that is similar to others who share the same trait. Internal reliability is established by finding out whether or not test items correlate with one another and with the total score for a large population of people. If, for all the people who take the test, high scorers on one item have a clear tendency to be high scorers on other specified items, the test is thought to have internal reliability and be a consistent measurement of a common trait.

In brief, the hypothesizing of common traits suggests that if one kind of behavior is usually associated statistically with other kinds of behavior, there is evidence that a trait underlies the behaviors. If that evidence is derived from a large population of people, it may be assumed to be a common trait. Many common traits—preferred patterns shared by many individuals—have been established in this manner. Allport cites ascendance-submission, neuroticism, extroversion-introversion, authoritarianism, manifest anxiety, the need for achievement, masculinity-femininity, and conformity.

A usual characteristic of common traits is their normal distribution among the population. The bulk of people have average scores, and the rest gradually taper toward the high and low extreme scores. If these

FIGURE 9.1 The Normal Curve

Allport suggests the most common traits show a normal distribution among the population.

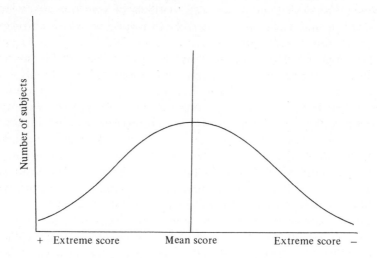

scores were plotted they would form a bell-shaped curve, which is called the *normal curve of distribution*. Such a curve is shown above. Most scores cluster around the *mean* or average. The normal curve permits us to compare individuals with respect to a common trait. High or low scores can be considered to be deviations from the group norm.

Recognizing Personal Dispositions

We have seen that while comparisons may be made among individuals, in the last analysis, no two individuals are exactly alike. Each one of us is a unique historical event with a complex singular personality. In order to distinguish among common traits, which are primarily nominal and enable us to make comparisons between an individual and a group, and individual traits, which are unique to each person, Allport employs the term *personal disposition*. A personal disposition is, like a trait, a general determining characteristic, but it is unique to the individual who has it. Although comparisons cannot be made among personal dispositions, personal dispositions are necessary if one is to reflect accurately the personality structure of a particular individual. While common traits place individuals into comparable categories, personal dispositions, if correctly diagnosed, more accurately describe the individual in his or her uniqueness.

Each one of us has personal dispositions that are of greater and lesser importance. If a personal disposition is so pervasive that almost every behavior of the individual appears to be influenced by it, it is referred to as a *cardinal disposition.* An example would be an extreme lust for power that is so intensive that virtually every act of the individual can be seen to be governed by that desire. Allport believes that cardinal dispositions are quite rare. Nevertheless, some historical figures, such as Napoleon, have been described as possessed of a cardinal disposition like the lust for power.

Central dispositions refer to highly characteristic tendencies of an individual. They provide the adjectives or phrases a person might use in describing the essential characteristics of another individual in a letter of recommendation. Allport suggests that the number of central dispositions that are necessary to describe the essential characteristics of an individual normally varies between five and ten. *Secondary dispositions* are more specific, focused tendencies that tend to be situational in character and less crucial to the personality structure. A person might have a large number of these. A man might be domineering and aggressive at home in his role as father but behave submissively when confronted by a police officer who is giving him a ticket.

While rating scales or testing instruments are useful for determining common traits, they are less useful in determining personal dispositions. Still, they can be helpful, as significantly high or low scores on common traits may suggest areas where personal dispositions may be found. Analysis of an individual's behaviors may also be a useful method of locating personal dispositions. If the investigator has data on a large number of behaviors of an individual available, he or she can look for recurring patterns. This method was used in a classic study known as *Letters from Jenny,* which will be discussed in more detail. Over three hundred letters written by a woman throughout middle and old age were analyzed; they revealed a number of unmistakable central dispositions. We can also test hypothesized personal dispositions. Having hypothesized that an individual possesses a certain central disposition, we can make a prediction about his or her subsequent behaviors. We could then count his or her behaviors to see how many of them manifested the characteristic. Finally, studies of individuals in the clinical setting afford an excellent opportunity for investigating personal dispositions.

Allport suggests that some personal dispositions are highly *motivational* while others are merely *stylistic.* A person's interests, ambitions, and values clearly initiate his or her behavior. Other dispositions tend to direct or steer behavior rather than initiate it. Behaving politely tends to be a stylistic disposition rather than a motivational one. One is not usually polite for the sake of just being polite, but for the sake of a deeper motive.

Finally, Allport points out that dispositions are not entirely consistent nor are they autonomous. A disposition is identified by its focal quality, not by its independent status. The behavior it leads to is also influenced by other dispositions. One situation may evoke one personality disposition, while another situation evokes a different one. Effective adjustment requires flexibility. Thus, a given individual may display contradiction and conflict in spite of his or her other consistencies.

EXERCISE:

Central Dispositions

Think of a close friend or someone who you know well. On a blank sheet of paper, try to describe his or her personality by jotting down those words or phrases that express his or her essential characteristics. Include those qualities that you consider of major importance in an accurate description. Then do the same thing for yourself. Count the number of words or phrases necessary to describe your friend or yourself. Chances are the number varies between five and ten. Allport suggests that the number of highly characteristic central dispositions along which a personality is organized generally falls within that range. In his own research the average was seven. Does your own evidence support this hypothesis?

THE PROPRIUM

It is in his concept of the proprium that Allport's humanistic orientation can most clearly be seen. Allport coined the term "proprium" in order to avoid a number of meanings that have been associated with the terms "ego" or "self." Frequently these names simply beg the question. They are catchall phrases for those elements of personality that cannot be accounted for in any other way. Allport's *proprium* refers to the central experiences of self-awareness that a person has as he or she grows and moves forward.

The prefix *pro-* is important. Allport conducted a study to learn how frequently words containing the prefixes *re-* and *pro-* appear in psychological literature and language (1960). The prefix *re-* means "back" and connotes backward movement, whereas the prefix *pro-* means "forth" and connotes forward movement. Allport discovered that words with the prefix *re-* outnumbered words with the prefix *pro-* nearly five to one. From psychoanalysis, we have terms like "repression" and "regression." Stimulus-response theory abounds with terms like "reflex," "reaction," "response." All these terms suggest a backward direction and preoccupation with the past rather than the future. They suggest that personality can be accounted for in terms of past events. In order to avoid these connotations and to emphasize that personality moves forward toward the future, Allport coined the term "proprium."

EXERCISE:

Re- and Pro- Prefixes in Psychology

You might find it illuminating to duplicate Allport's study of the frequency of the prefixes re- *and* pro- *in psychological literature. Look at the glossary and index of an introductory psychology text or personality text. Compare the number and frequency of use of* re- *compounds with that of* pro- *compounds. Then examine your own language and that of other people in describing human behavior. How much richer is our vocabulary in terms such as "react," "respond," "reinforce," "repress," and "regress" than in terms like "proceed," "program," and "propriate"? Of course, not all* re- *and* pro- *compounds are relevant to the point Allport is trying to make. To be precise, we should include only those* re- *compounds that connote happening again, passivity, or being acted on and only those* pro- *compounds that connote forward movement and intentionality. Even so, the disproportion will probably surprise you. Allport notes that in psychological literature the terms "reflex," "reaction," "response," and "retention," taken together, appear one hundred times more frequently than any single* pro- *compound, with the exception of the terms "problem solving" and "projection." Yet the term "projection" is most commonly used in a reactive sense.*

Propriate Functions

The proprium is defined in terms of its functions or the things that it does. Allport refers to these as *propriate functions*. None of them are innate, rather, they develop gradually over time as an individual grows from infancy to adulthood. Allport describes seven propriate functions (1961): sense of bodily self, identity, self-esteem, extension of self, self-image, self as rational coper, and propriate striving. Together, these activities of the proprium constitute an evolving sense of self as known and felt.

Infants are not aware of themselves as individuals. They cannot distinguish between themselves and other objects. Experiences simply happen to them. They have no "self" that mediates between a stimulus and a response. Thus, their reception and reaction to the world is unreflective. Most infants, like the author's own son, upon discovering the foot, put it into the mouth like any other object. The first time my son did this, he bit it and began to cry. He did not realize that his foot was a part of his body nor did he realize that it was he that had hurt him. Gradually, out of an undifferentiated whole, the infant comes to distinguish between inner and outer. The external world is discovered first. Later the child discovers a "reciprocal sense of I."

The first propriate function to emerge is that of the sense of *bodily self*. It consists of sensations in the body and entails coming to know one's body limits. Certain parts of the body are emphasized as more important than others. Thus, young children, when instructed to wash the face and hands, wash the palms and front of the face but invariably overlook the back of their hands and behind their ears. Most of us, even as adults, tend to locate the self in the head region. This bodily sense, which is learned, remains the foundation of our self-awareness.

The second propriate function is the sense of *self-identity*. It refers to the awareness of inner sameness and continuity. The young child learns his or her name and who it refers to. He or she knows that "Johnny" or "Mary" is "I." Even though we change over time, shedding our body cells and developing new personality characteristics, each of us is sure that he or she is the same self, the same "I" in spite of the changes. The sense of self-identity does not emerge full-blown; it grows slowly through trial and error, confusion and uncertainty. Further, the sense of the distinction between "I" and "not-I" varies from culture to culture. In the Western world, there is a sharp delineation between self and not-self. In other cultures, the distinction is less sharp.

Allport suggests that the first two propriate functions begin to emerge from eighteen months onward. Between the ages of two and three the third propriate function *self-esteem* develops. Self-esteem refers to the feelings of pride that develop as the child develops his or her ability to do things. It is comparable to Erikson's stage of autonomy, which reflects the child's need to feel that he or she can control him- or herself and other objects. Two-year-olds are eager to do things for themselves and do not want others to help them. One mark of the child's emerging sense of self-esteem is negativism. The child employs the word "no" to assert his or her freedom from adult control. A certain amount of negativism is necessary for the development of self-esteem.

Between the ages of four and six, two other propriate functions emerge: self-extension and self-image. *Self-extension* refers to a sense of possession. Children recognize that certain toys and certain people belong to them and identify them as, "my ball," "my daddy." The sense of bodily self strengthens and bodily parts, particularly the genitals, become very important. Self-extension leads into a valuing of others because of their relationship to oneself. In the adult years one's children are perceived as extensions of the self. Young children's self-extension is highly egoistic. They consider that the world exists for their benefit. In the adult, egocentric self-extension is replaced by reciprocity, in which one recognizes the legitimacy of the other.

Self-image refers to a sense of the expectation of others and its comparison with one's own behavior. The child comes to understand parental expectations and to see him- or herself as fulfilling or not fulfilling those desired roles. This early self-image lays the foundation for development of conscience and, later, intentions and goals.

Between the ages of six and twelve, the propriate function of *self as rational coper* develops. Children discover that they can use their own rational capacities to solve problems. They begin to perceive of themselves as active, problem-solving agents, who can develop a sense of competence in what they do. Allport compares the self as coper with Freud's concept of the ego as the executor of the personality.

Lastly, during adolescence, the propriate function of propriate striving emerges. *Propriate striving* refers to the projection of long-term purposes and goals and the development of a plan to attain them. Such propriate striving is essential for the development of self-identity, which Erikson had pinpointed earlier as the primary feature of adolescence.

Together, these seven aspects of selfhood constitute the self as known and felt: the proprium.

Personality Development

Allport's discussion of the development of the proprium (1961) is eclectic. He borrows from many different theorists the principles and concepts that he believes are most valuable in describing the changes that occur. He does not speak of specific stages in personality development other than the seven aspects of the proprium. Nevertheless, it is clear that there is a marked difference between the infant and the adult. The infant is described as a dependent, impatient, pleasure-seeking, "unsocialized horror." The infant, largely governed by unlearned biological drives, can tolerate little delay in the fulfillment of those drives and reflexes. The infant has the potentialities for personality, but "can scarcely be said to have personality" (1961). Given the appropriate security and affection, the child will grow in the direction of developing a proprium. The child will be transformed from a biologically dominated organism to a psychologically mature adult. Motives will become autonomous. The adult person, therefore, is discontinuous from the child. The adult emerges from the child but is no longer governed by the child's needs.

Not only is there a radical discontinuity between the child and the mature adult, but Allport also suggests that there is a radical discontinuity between healthy adults and neurotics. The life of neurotics is marked by cognitive crippling. In their efforts to find security, neurotics react in rigid, inflexible ways. Such individuals continue to behave as children, dominated by infantile drives and conflicts. Their propriums are undeveloped and their motives remain tied to original needs.

Functional Autonomy

Allport suggests that major changes in motivation occur as the individual develops out of the total dependency of infancy and assumes the social responsibility characteristic of the adult. He suggests that an adequate theory of human motivation must meet four requirements.

First, *the theory should acknowledge the contemporaneity of motives.* Motives exist in the present. The past does not necessarily determine present motives. It should not be invoked unless past motives can be shown to be dynamically active at the present time.

Second, *the theory should be pluralistic* and allow for many different motives. Reducing all motives to one basic type of motivation, such as sexual desires or drives, usually results in an oversimplification. Motives are too diverse to be encompassed under one common denominator.

Third, *the theory should emphasize the importance of cognitive processes.* An individual's intentions, desires, and reasons for doing something are important keys for understanding his or her behavior. Allport's use of the word "intentions" is deliberate. Intentions point forward in time rather than backwards, as they connote purpose, conscious planning, organization, and foresight.

Fourth, *the theory should permit the concrete uniqueness of motives.* Many theories describe motives in the abstract, referring to allegedly common motives that all humans share. John's desire to become a sculptor may be seen as a sublimation of his sexual desires. Mary's concern to earn money may be seen as a secondary drive. While general theories of motivation may help us to understand how particular motives have come about, they do not help to clarify the variety of present motives and their unique concreteness.

Allport's concept of *functional autonomy* (1937, 1961) represents his effort to avoid the limitations of backward-looking theories and to fulfill the criteria for a successful theory of motivation outlined above. Allport is well known for his concept of functional autonomy, but the concept itself has been very controversial. The concept of functional autonomy implies simply that adult motivation is not necessarily tied to the past. A given behavior may become a goal in itself regardless of its original intention. Thus, adult motives are not necessarily related to the earlier experiences in which the motive or activity initially appeared.

For example, let us imagine that young Johnny's father was a baseball fan. During his spare time and on Saturdays he played baseball with his son. Originally, Johnny played baseball with his Dad to gain his attention and to please him. During his school years, Johnny also played baseball with the other children in his neighborhood and was an active member of Little League. He discovered that he was competent in the game, and what is more, he enjoyed it. During high school and college, he played in the school's intramural sports program. Later, he was recruited to play with a major league. Today, as he is standing at bat for the Yankees or Dodgers, does it make sense to insist that his motive for playing baseball continues to be that of pleasing his father? Does it not seem more reasonable to suggest that he plays because he enjoys the game and the financial rewards that it brings? His present motives are entirely different and free from his original motives. There may be a historical tie, but there is no functional tie. His motive is functionally autonomous.

Allport refers to two levels of functional autonomy: perseverative functional autonomy and propriate functional autonomy.

Perseverative functional autonomy refers to acts or behaviors that are repeated even though they may have lost their original function; however, they are not controlled by the proprium and have no genuine connection with it. A teen-age girl may, in a spirit of rebellion against her parents, begin to smoke cigarettes, which she knows will annoy them. As an adult, she may continue to smoke cigarettes, long after her period of teen-age rebellion. Perseverative functional autonomy refers to repetitive activities, such as compulsions, addictions to drugs or alcohol, ritualistic or routine behaviors. Such actions are free of the original motives that spurred them into being, but they cannot be said to be governed by the proprium.

Propriate functional autonomy refers to those acquired interests, values, attitudes, intentions, and lifestyle that are directed from the proprium and are genuinely free of earlier motivations. Abilities frequently convert into interests. The person selects those values that are important. He or she then organizes these motives in a fashion that is consistent with his or her self-image and lifestyle. In short, there is a radical discontinuity between the motivation of the infant and the healthy adult.

Allport acknowledges that not all behaviors are functionally autonomous. Some processes that are not are: drives, reflexes, constitutionally determined capacities such as physique and intellect, habits, primary reinforcements, infantilisms and fixations, some neuroses, and sublimations. At times it is difficult to determine whether or not a motive is functionally autonomous. Further, certain motives may only be autonomous to a certain degree. Nevertheless, Allport believes that many of the motives of the healthy, mature adult may be considered to be governed by propriate functional autonomy. Allport's rationale for developing the concept of propriate functional autonomy is the desire to underscore the concept that we live in the present, not in the past. Allport does not say that there is no continuity between the present and the past, rather, the healthy adult individual is not bound to the past. He or she is free to live in the present and the future unencumbered by the past.

Allport's concept of functional autonomy has been the subject of a great deal of controversy and criticism. In presenting his theories to the public, Allport's concern has been to teach and provoke interest rather than make statements that are above reproach. Thus, it is often very difficult to differentiate between what he assumes and what he has established through empirical procedures. The concept of functional autonomy is not a construct that lends itself to operational definition, predictions, or empirical tests. The phenomena that Allport explains as functionally autonomous can also be explained by rival constructs. Further, Allport does not clearly describe the developmental processes that underlie functional autonomy. He fails to explain how or why it occurs (Hall and Lindzey, 1978).

Still, Allport's concepts are highly congruent with recent developments in personality theory. His emphasis on discontinuity is picked up by the phenomenological and cognitive theorists, whom I will discuss in Part VI. His concept of functional autonomy and propriate functions harmonize with certain recent expansions in psychoanalysis. The goal of psychoanalysis is to strengthen the functioning of the ego. The intent of the reconstruction of the past in psychoanalysis is to permit the patient to work through the past so that it loses its grip on the individual. By becoming aware of one's unconscious motivations, one is free to behave differently in the future if one so wishes. Thus, the intent of psychoanalysis is congruent, if not synonymous, with the development of propriate functional autonomy.

A Definition of Maturity

Allport is one of the earliest modern personality theorists to devote his attention to the mature, healthy personality rather than to the immature, neurotic one. As we have seen, Allport believes that there is a radical discontinuity between the neurotic and healthy personality. Allport concurs with Carl Jung that too many personality theorists center their discussion of personality on the characteristics of the neurotic and view health simply as the absence of neurotic symptoms. He suggests that we need a positive definition of health that will enable us to point to an ideal in adult life. In his discussion (1961), Allport posits six criteria of maturity.

Extension of the Sense of Self The mature adult is one who has radically extended the boundaries of self. Mature adults genuinely participate in important realms of human achievement. They are not simply active, their egos are totally involved in many spheres of human activity. They are interested in others and consider the welfare of others as important as their own. Their sense of self is not limited to their own selves but embraces many interests.

Warm Relating of Self to Others The mature person is able to relate intimately to other persons in appropriate situations. Mature people respect others and appreciate the common humanity that all of us share. Thus, they are compassionate and able to tolerate many differences in human beings. In their relationship to others, they neither impose themselves on others nor hinder their own freedom of self-identity.

Emotional Security (Self-Acceptance) The mature person is able to tolerate the frustrations of daily living. Mature people are able to accept themselves and their emotional states. Thus, their emotions, even though they are not always pleasant, do not lead them into impulsive acts or actions that hurt others. They are sufficiently secure in who they are to accept themselves and not wish to be somebody else. They have control over themselves without the need for overcontrol.

Realistic Perception, Skills, and Assignments The mature adult has an efficient and accurate perception of him- or herself and the world. Mature adults do not need to create a fantasy world but live in "the real world." They are problem solvers and have developed the appropriate skills to complete their assigned tasks and work. Moreover, their work is not a burden to them, it is a responsibility whose challenge can be accepted without self-pity.

Self-objectification (Insight and Humor) Self-insight is difficult to acquire. The mature person possesses knowledge of him- or herself to a high degree. Mature people know what they can do, they know what they cannot do, and they know what they ought to do. They have no need to deceive either themselves or other people. An important corollary of insight is a sense of humor. Mature individuals are able to laugh at themselves rather than feel threatened by their human weaknesses. Such humor is to be distinguished from the ordinary sense of the comic. All too often our sense of humor simply releases sexual or aggressive impulses by degrading other people and in turn trying to elevate ourselves. The sense of humor to which Allport refers entails recognizing the ludicrous behaviors we share with others because of our common humanity.

Unifying Philosophy of Life Maturity entails a clear understanding of life's goals and purposes. In the mature person, this philosophy is clearly marked and outwardly focused. It is strongly informed by a set of values that may but does not necessarily include religious sentiments. In the mature individual, religion has acquired an intrinsic value rather than an extrinsic one. In distinguishing between intrinsic and extrinsic religion, Allport conceives of religion as *intrinsic* when the religious quest is perceived as an end in itself. Religion is *extrinsic* when it serves other purposes, such as to enhance one's social standing or self-esteem. Further, a unifying philosophy of life is governed by a generic conscience. The *must* conscience of childhood is replaced by the *ought* conscience of the adult. Whereas the child's values are introjected from others, the adult's values arise from his or her own chosen style of being and are based on propriate judgments. Allport's distinction is reminiscent of Fromm's distinction between the authoritarian conscience and the humanistic conscience.

Essentially, maturity for Allport is summed up by expression of the propriate functions to a high degree and freedom from one's past. Allport has indicated that human beings are always in the process of *becoming* (1955). The urge to grow and fulfill oneself is present from birth. We have the ability to develop and follow a creative lifestyle. Further, with maturity we can consciously design and effect our plans without being hindered by unconscious forces of the past. His theory holds echoes of Jung's concept of self-actualization and Adler's construct of the creative self.

METHODS OF RESEARCH

Although Allport's theory has generated little empirical research itself, Allport has written extensively on methods of inquiry and investigation that are useful for the study of personality, and some of his own research in the area is considered classic.

Allport points out that personality is so complex that every legitimate method of study should be included in its pursuit. As we have seen, an open system of personality does not lend itself to analysis through narrowly defined scientific procedures or methods. Allport is critical of those who limit their research to traditional scientific methods and do not encourage or permit the study of personality concepts that are not easily submitted to empirical test. At the same time, he is also critical of applying methods appropriate to the study of neurotic individuals to the normal individual. He suggests that the information gained through projective techniques (such as the Rorschach inkblot test and the Thematic Apperception Test) is not really different from what we can obtain by asking an individual to describe him- or herself, and it runs the danger of presenting a distorted portrait overemphasizing unconscious and irrational elements (1953).

Allport observes that there have been two main approaches to the study of personality. The *dimensional* (or nomothetic) approach studies large groups of individuals in order to infer general variables or universal principles. The *morphogenic* (or idiographic) approach centers on the individual, employing techniques and variables that are appropriate to understanding the uniqueness of each person.

The emphasis, particularly in American psychology, has been on the dimensional approach. Much of our research in psychology is conducted along these lines. Large groups of subjects are examined in order to determine the frequency with which certain events occur. Normalcy is often conceived of as that behavior that occurs most regularly. The behavior that is normal for a two-year-old is that behavior that is shared in common by most two-year-olds. Psychologists look for common traits that are shared by a large number of the population.

The individual is studied to see if and where he or she deviates from the norm.

Morphogenic approaches aim at discovering laws that govern the particular individual. While such methods are difficult, time consuming, and often expensive to evolve, their aim is to account for the unique event that is theoretically just as open to lawful explanation as is the frequent event. An example of a morphogenic approach that we are already familiar with is psychoanalysis, which is an extensive investigation into the historical development and psychic structure of one individual.

While most of Allport's own research was of the dimensional type, he urged the development and greater use of morphogenic approaches as an ultimately better technique for understanding and predicting behavior. This is consistent with Allport's emphasis on the uniqueness of each individual. Allport was also a pioneer in developing morphogenic approaches to the study of personality.

With Philip Vernon and Gardner Lindzey, Allport developed a Study of Values Scale, which is a dimensional measurement designed to get at individuality. The scale measures six common traits originally delineated by Spranger (1928): the theoretical, aesthetic, social, political, religious, and economic. Because the test reflects the relative strengths of these six values within one's own personality, one individual's score cannot be compared with anyone else's. A person who scored lowest in aesthetics might be more aesthetic than a person whose highest value was aesthetics, because he or she might have a stronger set of values to begin with. The final profile that emerges on the test is individual, personal, and relevant only to the individual who has taken the test. The test has been widely used in counseling and vocational guidance and has proved to be a significant research tool in studies of selective perception.

Another outgrowth of Allport's personality theory has been his interest in religion as a healthy, productive aspect of human life. In order to introduce religion into the comprehensive study of personality, Allport wrote *The Individual and His Religion* (1950), in which he presented religion as a normal rather than primarily neurotic human phenomenon. Allport's distinction between intrinsic and extrinsic orientations in religion has contributed to research on understanding the relation between religion and prejudice. Churchgoers on the average are more prejudiced than nonchurchgoers, even though most advocates of treating all people equally are religiously motivated. Allport discovered a curvilinear relationship between religion and prejudice. The extrinsic attitude is correlated with prejudice, but the intrinsic is correlated with very low prejudice (1968).

In the 1940s, over three hundred letters written by a woman (Jenny Masterson) between her fifty-ninth and seventieth year to a young married couple came to Allport's attention. He and his students analyzed these letters to determine Jenny's central dispositions. In studying these documents, Allport tried to note the frequency with which certain themes or ideas appeared. He asked other people to read the letters and assess Jenny in terms of her traits. He also discussed Jenny's personality in terms of different personality theories. Allport believed that the study of personal documents, such as diaries, autobiographies, and letters, can be a potentially valuable morphogenic approach. Such study cannot be sloppy or loose but must be conducted under clear scientific guidelines, some of which need further refinement.

Allport and Philip Vernon initiated research into expressive behavior during the early 1930s. *Expressive behavior* refers to the study of an individual's manner of performing. Every behavior has a coping and expressive aspect. The *coping* aspect refers to what the act does to deal with or adapt to the task at hand. The *expressive* aspect refers to how the act is done. When you listen to a lecture you concentrate on what the lecturer is saying (the coping aspect of his or her behavior), but you also take note of how he or she is delivering the lecture. The lecturer may be nervous or relaxed; he or she may talk in a loud or soft voice. These expressive aspects of behavior prompt you to make certain inferences about the lecturer as a person.

Ordinarily we pay more attention to coping behavior than to expressive behavior. But expressive behavior, because it is more spontaneous, can be highly revelatory of basic personality aspects. Allport and others conducted considerable research on several expressive features of personality: the face, voice, posture, gesture, gait, and handwriting. They discovered that there is a marked consistency in a person's expressive behavior. In some instances, Allport was able to deduce certain traits and make accurate judgments about an individual's personality. Allport acknowledges that research is not yet at the point where the study of expressive behaviors can provide a full guide to psychodiagnosis. Nevertheless, he suggests that further research in this area is highly desirable because a person's expressive manner and style may be the most important factor in understanding the personality.

EXERCISE:

Expressive Behavior

Allport suggests the following simple experiment as an illustration of the consistency of our expressive movements (1961). Draw four lines on a sheet of paper. On the first three lines, sign your name as you usually sign it. On the last line, try to make an exact copy of your signature on the third line. Then compare the lines. You will probably discover that the first two signatures are much more alike than the last two. The instructions for the first three lines, "Sign your name as you usually sign it," were the same and permitted maximum freedom for expressive consistency. The last line was a conscious attempt to make an exact copy of the previous signature. Expressive consistency was suppressed and every movement became deliberate.

Allport points out that other areas of investigation employ methodology that can be fruitfully applied to the study of personality. Fields such as literature, philosophy, art, and religion offer techniques that can be valuable adjuncts to the personality theorist. The basic tools of psychological study—observation and interpretation—are shared with all human quests for knowledge. We observe an event and we interpret its significance. Many techniques may assist us in our goals and they need to be appreciated for their potential contribution to scientific knowledge.

EVALUATION AND IMPLICATIONS

Allport was not a practicing psychotherapist. His background was largely that of the university. His theory of personality is eclectic, and he did not develop a specific technique of therapy. Allport suggested that there is a radical discontinuity between the normal mature adult and the neurotic. Whereas the neurotic might well be troubled by unconscious forces, Allport conceived of the normal healthy individual as largely conscious of his or her impulses and desires. Unconscious forces are simply not all that powerful. Allport once indicated that the most important question that a therapist could ask a patient was not "Where have you been?" but "Where do you want to go?" (Evans, 1970).

Allport's personality theory is highly creative. While many of his ideas are reminiscent of other theories, he combined these insights with his own to develop a truly distinctive and unique approach. His own original concepts, such as the proprium and functional autonomy, while highly controversial, are extremely stimulating and provocative.

Allport related the following anecdote about his meeting with Sigmund Freud (Evans, 1970). Shortly after college, he was traveling in Europe and sought an audience with Freud. When he arrived, Freud sat silent, apparently waiting for Allport to state the reason for his visit. Allport was simply curious. Nevertheless, an incident came to mind that he thought might interest Freud, because it concerned a phobia that appeared to be set very early in life. He told him about an event that had happened on the streetcar on the way to Freud's office. A small boy who was obviously afraid of dirt kept saying to his mother that he didn't want to sit on a dirty seat or next to a dirty man. When Allport finished, Freud looked at him and said, "And was that little boy you?"

Allport was surprised, but he regained his composure and changed the subject. Still, he was shaken and he never forgot the incident. He began to feel that Freud's ascription of most behaviors to unconscious motives was incorrect. An alternative theory of motivation was necessary. In his own theory, Allport did not probe into the dark side of personality; he did not concur with Freud's emphasis on sexuality and unconscious motivations.

In his emphasis on the uniqueness of the individual, the contemporaneity of motives, and holistic view of the person, Allport foreshadows theories that we will consider in Part V. Indeed, the emphasis in his theory is not on the past, but on forward movement. Allport has not developed a school of followers, but his theory has had considerable impact, as attested to by the frequent references to Allport in psychological literature. Further, his work offers a bridge between traditional academic psychology, with its emphasis on psychometrics and dimensional studies, and clinical psychology, which concentrates on a more morphogenic approach to the understanding of personality.

Allport insisted that personality is so complex that every legitimate method of study should be included in our efforts to comprehend it. He respected and utilized the methods of rigorous science. At the same time, he suggested that alternative methods need to be discovered that will help us to understand the uniqueness of each individual. In the end, Allport fully realized that in order to understand the human being as a whole, it is necessary to comprehend an individual philosophically as well as psychologically. "The philosophy of the person is inseparable from the psychology of the person," he wrote (1961). Indeed, any psychological stance, Allport pointed out, is implicitly linked to basic philosophical assumptions.

SUGGESTIONS FOR FURTHER READING

Gordon Allport was a prolific author whose many writings have a clear didactic or teaching intent. He sought to describe and illustrate his concepts vividly. His writings are enjoyable to read and of great interest to the student of personality.

Allport's pioneer effort in the field of personality theory was *Personality: A Psychological Interpretation* (Holt, 1937). This work constitutes the initial presentation of his theory: distinguishing between common and individual traits and introducing the concept of functional autonomy. A revised and updated statement of his position is given in *Pattern and Growth in Personality* (Holt, Rinehart, and Winston, 1961). In this work, Allport introduces the concept of personal disposition and emphasizes the uniqueness of each individual. The book is highly readable and strongly recommended as an introduction to Allport's thought. *Becoming: Basic Considerations for a Psychology of Personality* (Yale

University Press, 1955) underscores Allport's humanistic and futuristic approach. In it he discusses the criteria for maturity. Also recommended are *The Person in Psychology: Selected Essays* (Beacon Press, 1968), which contains a group of Allport's important articles; and *The Individual and His Religion* (Macmillan, 1960), which offers a psychological interpretation of religion as a normal phenomenon of human behavior.

PART V

Humanist Theories

In recent years a number of theories have arisen that present themselves as alternatives or complements to the major positions discussed so far. The humanist theories, as we shall refer to them because of their emphasis on human potentiality, are critical of what have been the two major forces in psychology: psychoanalysis and behaviorism. The humanists disagree with the dark, pessimistic, and largely negative picture of personality that emerges in Freudian psychoanalysis. They also disagree with the limited picture of the person as a machine or robot that emerges from the behavioral and learning theory approach. The humanists suggest that the study of neurotics or infrahuman species is not particularly enlightening for the study of personality. Health is more than the absence of neurotic symptoms. There is a radical difference between a rat in a Skinner box and a human being in the everyday world. The humanists also frequently reject the assumption of long-term motivations, dispositions, or traits that is inherent in the psychoanalytic and trait approach. Instead, the humanists emphasize a view of the person as an active, creative, experiencing human being who lives in the present and subjectively responds to current perceptions, relationships, and encounters. The humanist view of personality is a positive, optimistic one that stresses the tendency of the human personality toward growth and self-actualization.

Humanist theories are discontinuity theories rather than continuity theories. We have already seen that a continuity theory suggests that the development of personality is essentially the accumulation of skills, habits, and discriminations, whereas a discontinuity theory suggests that in the course of development there are genuine transformations or changes so that one's personality reaches successively higher levels of organization. To use Allport's terminology, discontinuity theories strive to be open rather than closed.

Humanist theories are generally proactive rather than reactive. *Proactive* theories view the human being as acting on his or her own initiative rather than simply reacting. The sources of behavior are perceived as lying within the individual, who does more than just react to stimuli from the outside world. Furthermore, humanist theories suggest that the human being is motivated toward growth, increased stimuli, and self-actualization. Other theorists, such as Freud and Dollard and Miller, suggested that human nature seeks primarily to maintain an internal state of equilibrium and balance through drive reduction. Such a state of balance is known as *homeostasis*. The humanists see personality as motivated toward new opportunities for growth and fulfillment. Individuals do not merely seek to reduce tension, they also seek new stimuli and challenges that will further their growth. Such a goal is known as *heterostasis*.

Humanist theories have their origin in many sources. Not all of their concepts and ideas are entirely new. Gordon Allport's emphases on the uniqueness of the individual, the contemporaneity of motives, and holistic view of the person are consistent with the humanistic approach. Indeed, it was he who first stressed the value of discontinuity and proactive theories of personality. Alfred Adler conceived of the individual as positing goals, moving forward, and seeking to attain those goals. This concept reappears in humanist thought. Carl Jung referred to the principle of self-actualization, stressing our positive tendencies and strivings for growth. Thus, in a sense, Alfred Adler and Carl Jung may be seen as precursors or forerunners of the humanist stance. Other influences include gestalt psychology, phenomenology, and existentialism.

The term *gestalt* means "configuration." In psychology, it has come to refer to the study of how organisms perceive objects and events. Gestaltist psychologists such as Max Wertheimer (1880–1943), Wolfgang Kohler (1887–1967), and Kurt Koffka (1886–1941) pointed out that the way in which an object or event is perceived depends on its surroundings or context. Each part of a whole is dependent on all of its other parts. Thus, the basic tenet of gestalt psychology may be summed up in the phrase, "The whole is more than the sum of its parts."

Although Kurt Lewin (1890–1947) was not a gestaltist, he was influenced by the gestalt point of view. He was also impressed by Einstein's theory of relativity, which spoke of "fields of force" in physics rather than simply inert matter. Kurt Lewin suggested that Einstein's field theory could be applied to aspects of psychology as well as physics. Behavior may be seen as occurring in an environmental field of psychological forces comparable to the fields of gravity and electromagnetics in physics. This is to suggest that an individual cannot be studied in isolation, but must be studied within the context of the larger environment in which he or she finds him- or herself. The way in which an object or an event is perceived does not depend solely on the object or thing in itself, but rather on the context in which it presents itself. In Lewin's terms, a person can only be comprehended in terms of his or her life space.

The term *phenomenology* refers to the study of phenomenon or appearances. It comes from the Greek *phainomenon*, which means "that which appears or shows itself." Edmund Husserl (1859–1938) was the father of modern phenomenology in philosophy, which seeks to describe the data, or the "given," of immediate experience. In psychology, phenomenology has come to mean the study of human awareness and perception. Phenomenologists stress that what is important is not the object or the event in itself, but how it is perceived and understood by the individual. From phenomenology, the humanist theories have drawn their emphasis on current experiences, the here and now, and their emphasis on subjectivity as the primary mode of awareness. The emphasis is not on the object or event itself, but on how the individual perceives his or her experiences.

A third major force that has influenced the humanist approach is the existentialist movement in philosophy. Existentialists such as Sören

Kierkegaard (1813–1855), Jean Paul Sartre (1905–   ), and Martin Heidegger (1889–1976) have focused on the analysis of what it means to be or to exist. The existentialist movement is a bewildering one that defies simple definition. We can clarify it, however, by comparing two possible postures that a person might have at a football game. The first is that of the spectator up in the stands; the second is that of the player on the field. Both spectator and player are involved in the football game, but there is a considerable difference in their involvement. The spectator may get very agitated and excited as the game proceeds. He or she may urge and cheer on a favorite team. But his or her involvement is very different from that of the player. The outcome of the game does not depend on the activity of the spectator, who remains outside the game as an observer. The outcome depends very much on how the player behaves and performs on the field. What he or she does is not indifferent to the game. The player cannot stand back and observe the game while involved in it.

The posture of existentialism is that of the player, and the game of existentialism is the game of life. In the game of life, existentialists point out, we cannot play the role of a detached or uninvolved spectator because we are already participants in the game.

Existentialists have made clear the limits of objectivity in our understanding. Objectivity is a goal that many of us prize. We believe that unless we are objective, our emotions and prejudices will come between us and the facts and cloud our reasoning processes. At times, however, objectivity prevents understanding. Some truths, such as understanding what it means to be, are not discovered by objectivity, but by intense personal involvement. Objectivity tells us that the study of a rat's behavior in a Skinner box tells us something about ourselves, but we do not really understand ourselves except as we enter into personal relations with others.

In their insistence that ultimately human knowledge is interpersonal, the humanists are indebted to the thought of existentialist philosopher Martin Buber (1878–1965), whose book *I-Thou* made a classic distinction between knowing that is transpersonal (I-Thou) and knowing that is objective or subjective (I-it). In his book, Buber describes an entirely different way in which the world, particularly the world of persons, reveals itself to us. Knowledge is not simply objective (of an external object) or subjective (of the self), but also interpersonal, arising out of the encounter of human beings with one another. Understanding through encounter is just as real as understanding through objectification. Most personality theorists have tended to reduce persons to I-it descriptions. For example, Cattell describes a person with sixteen numbers. Humanist theorists would suggest that real persons— Ted Clifford, Kathy Kapner—are not "known" by this process, rather, they are abstracted.

Existentialism begins with personal existence. It asks, what does it mean to be a self? It questions the purpose and nature of existence. It views each individual as an agent with free choice, who is responsible for his or her actions. Each one of us carves out our own destiny. We are literally what we do. From existentialist thought, the humanists have drawn their emphasis on choice and responsibility and their ethic that a worthwhile life is one that is authentic, honest, and genuine.

Carl Rogers, who is probably best known as the originator of client-centered psychotherapy, emphasizes subjective perception in the development of the self. His method of treatment has been adopted by many counselors. Abraham Maslow is frequently considered the leading spokes person of the humanistic point of view in psychology. In his description of the process of self-actualization, he emphasizes our positive potential for growth and fulfillment.

CHAPTER 10

Carl Rogers's Self Theory

For Carl Rogers, a person's behavior is completely dependent on how he or she perceives and understands the world. We react to events according to our understanding of them. Such a theory of personality emphasizes the self as an important element of experience; and it is largely due to Carl Rogers's efforts that the self has re-emerged as a valuable construct for understanding personality. In modern psychology, the concept of the self had fallen into disrepute. Notions of an immortal soul that was free of material causality or of an "inner manikin," that is to say, a little person within directing our behaviors, appeared to be leftover remnants from earlier religious or philosophical viewpoints that hardly appealed to contemporary scientific mentality. Carl Rogers, however, considers the self to be neither of those. The *self* is simply Rogers's term for those psychological processes that govern our behavior. It is a scientific construct that helps us to account for certain phenomena.

Carl Rogers is best known, however, as the originator of client-centered psychotherapy, a technique that focuses attention on the person or client seeking help. Rogers's technique has been widely adopted for the treatment of minor personality disorders. Moreover, it has greatly influenced education and other areas of social concern.

BIOGRAPHICAL BACKGROUND

Carl Rogers was born in 1902 in Oak Park, Illinois, a suburb of Chicago. He was the fourth born of six children, five boys and one girl. His

family was a close-knit one that valued work and religion. Rogers's parents, educated and conservative middle-class Protestants, instilled in their children high ethical standards of behavior and emphasized the importance of hard work.

Rogers recalls that he had little social life outside of his large family, but this did not bother him. He was an avid reader and early in life developed a certain level of independence. When he was twelve, the family moved to a farm. Farm life spurred his interest in science and increased his ability to work independently. He was fascinated with the literature that his father brought home about scientific agriculture. Rogers worked hard at his chores on the farm; he reared lambs, pigs, and calves. He also collected, studied, and bred moths. A superior student, Rogers entered the University of Wisconsin, a family alma mater, with the full intent of studying agriculture. However, in his second year, he decided to prepare for the ministry. After his graduation in 1924, he married Helen Elliot, a childhood friend, and drove to New York City in a secondhand Model-T coupe to begin preparation for the ministry at Union Theological Seminary.

Rogers's fate, however, was not to become a minister. During his final years at college, Rogers found himself departing from his parents' fundamentalist ways of thinking. The liberal philosophical approach toward religion fostered at Union Theological Seminary and insights gained from participation in several YMCA conferences led him to feel that he could not work in a field that would require him to profess a specific set of beliefs. This was a difficult period for both Rogers and his parents, but it nurtured Rogers's growing conviction that the individual must ultimately rely on his or her own experiences. Rogers's interests were turning toward psychology; therefore, he transferred to Columbia University Teachers College, where he was introduced to the philosophy of John Dewey and began his training in clinical psychology.

In 1931, Rogers received the Ph.D. and joined the staff of the Rochester Guidance Center, where he assisted in developing a highly successful child study department. Here, Rogers first met what was to be many years of opposition from members of the psychiatric profession who felt that psychologists should not be permitted to practice or have any administrative responsibility over psychotherapy. In 1939, when Rogers was made the director of the center, a vigorous campaign was waged to unseat him. No one criticized his work, but the general opinion was that a psychologist simply could not do this kind of work. Fortunately, the board of trustees decided in Rogers's favor.

In 1940, Rogers accepted an appointment as professor of psychology at Ohio State University. He worked with intellectually adept graduate students and began to articulate clearly his views on psychotherapy. In 1945, he moved to the University of Chicago where, as professor of psychology and executive secretary of the counseling center, he again championed his view that psychologists could effectively conduct therapy. Rogers felt strongly that no single discipline or profession had a stronghold in the matter of understanding human nature. Rogers worked hard to demonstrate the responsible character of his work. He clarified the processes that underlie therapeutic change and he supported his findings and methods with impressive research data. It was largely due to his efforts that clinical psychology became a respectable field and that psychiatry and psychology have become somewhat reconciled, conceiving themselves as two professions in search of a common goal. This reconciliation and challenge were reflected in his appointment as professor of psychology and psychiatry at the University of Wisconsin in 1957. Since 1963, Rogers has been a fellow at the Center for Studies of the Person in La Jolla, California.

THEORY OF PERSONALITY

Carl Rogers's theory of personality, which emphasizes the self, developed out of his clinical experience in working with patients. His therapy provided a wealth of observations that were extremely useful to him in formulating a theory of personality. In turn, his theory helped to clarify and elucidate his practice.

The Phenomenal Field

Rogers maintains that each individual exists in a phenomenological field or world of experiences of which he or she is the center (1959). The *phenomenal field* refers to the total sum of experiences. It consists of everything that is potentially available to consciousness at any given moment. This entails both conscious and unconscious experiences. As you read you may not be aware of the pressure of the chair on your buttocks, but when attention is drawn to this fact you can become acutely conscious of it. Conscious experiences are those that have been symbolized. The organism, however, reacts to all of its experiences, symbolized or unsymbolized.

The organism responds to the field as it perceives it. Rogers's emphasis here is on the individual's perception of reality. For social purposes, we agree that the perceptions commonly shared by others in our culture are the correct perceptions. However, from the viewpoint of psychology, reality is essentially a very private matter. Two individuals walking along at night may see an object by the road and respond very differently. One, thinking that it is a large bear, may be afraid; the other, perceiving a tree stump, may be indifferent. We test our "reality" by further perceptions. Small white grains in a bowl may initially be perceived as sugar. But if they taste salty, we perceive them to be salt. The individual's perception rather than the reality in itself is what is most important. Suppose a young boy were to come to Carl Rogers with the complaint that his father was dogmatic, authoritarian, and dictatorial. In fact, an impartial observer might conclude that the father was open and democratic. Rogers would point out, however, that what the father is really like is not important; what is important is how the boy perceives his father (1951).

It follows that the best vantage point for understanding an individual is that of the individual him- or herself. Rogers points out that the individual is the only one who can fully know his or her field of experience. Meaningful understanding of another person's behavior is not imposed by an outside observer interpreting behavior from an external frame of reference, it is acquired by understanding his or her behavior as he or she perceives it. Rogers acknowledges that it is not always easy to understand behavior from the internal frame of reference. We are limited to the individual's conscious perception of his or her experiences. Also, our knowledge depends on communication that is often faulty. Nevertheless, such an empathetic understanding of the experiences of another is probably much more accurate in reflecting the basic laws of personality process and behavior.

Self-Actualization

The organism reacts as a whole to its phenomenal field. Change in any one area creates alterations in other areas. The primary tendency of the organism is to maintain, actualize, and enhance itself. This self-actualizing tendency follows lines laid down by heredity. The particular type of seed that is planted determines whether or not the flower will be a chrysanthemum or a snapdragon, but the environment can greatly influence the resulting bloom. An optimal environment that provides adequate nourishment, sun, and water leads to a healthy bloom. Conditions of drought or excessive heat may stifle the plant. The process of actualization is neither automatic nor effortless; rather, it involves struggle and even pain. Rogers points out that the young child does not take a first step without a struggle. The child falls and may be hurt. Yet the desire to grow moves the child forward.

Behavior is the "goal-directed attempt" of the organism to meet its needs as it perceives them (1951). Rogers's definition is very different from that of the learning theorists, who see behavior largely as a response to stimuli, or that of the psychoanalysts, who stress unconscious determinants of behavior. Behavior is a response to one's perception of his or her needs. Rogers's definition emphasizes the subjective perception of the person and the goal-directed activity of the organism.

The forward movement of self-actualization can occur only when the choices and options that are open are clearly perceived and adequately symbolized by the organism. When choices are unclear, the individual is unable to differentiate between progressive and regressive behavior. Given a clear choice, however, Rogers suggests that we will always choose to grow rather than move backwards.

Rogers points out that emotions accompany and usually facilitate the process of self-actualization. Pleasant emotions accompany the attainment of a goal. Even emotions that we generally think of as unpleasant, such as fear or jealousy, have a positive effect of integrating and concentrating our behavior on a goal. The intensity of the emotion varies according to the perceived significance of the behavior toward achieving the goal. Jumping out of the path of an oncoming truck is accompanied by very strong emotions, particularly if this behavior is seen as crucial to life or death. Unless they are excessive or inappropriate, emotions facilitate goal-oriented behavior.

Carl Rogers's view of the emotions is a very positive one. He does not believe that emotions in and of themselves are worrisome, troublesome, or shameful. Emotions simply are, and they have a positive effect in leading us toward goal-directed activities. Fully experiencing one's emotions facilitates growth. The denial or distortion of emotions may permit them to raise havoc in our lives. Whereas in the psychoanalytic point of view the impulses of the id are savage, ignoble, and in need of civilization, Rogers has a more optimistic view of our basic motivational strivings and urges. He suggests that self-actualization occurs most freely when the person is open and aware of the full totality of his or her experiences, be they sensory, visceral, or emotional. Repression is not necessary in Rogers's viewpoint. The person who utilizes his or her senses and emotions, trusting them fully, is the person who is permitting the process of self-actualization to develop.

The Self

Out of the interaction of the organism and the environment, there emerges the self, or a concept of "who I am" (1951). The self-concept is a portion of the phenomenal field that has gradually become differentiated. Composed of those conscious perceptions and values of "me" or "I," the self-concept may or may not include the totality of the organism's experiences. The self, then, is an object of perception as well as a process. It is the person as he or she perceives him- or herself to be. Thus, we have a distinction between *the organism*, or real self as process, and *the self* as perceived, or object.

As young children interact with their environment, they gradually acquire ideas about themselves, their world, and their relationship to that world. They experience things that they like or dislike, and things that they can or cannot control. Those experiences that appear to enhance one's self are valued and incorporated into one's self-image; those experiences that appear to threaten the self are denied and rendered foreign to the self.

The self-concept frequently includes values that are taken over from other people rather than reflected from the actual experiences of the organism. A young boy quickly learns that his parents withdraw their affection when he hits his baby brother. Even though hitting his brother is a satisfying act, the boy forfeits his acknowledgment of its satisfaction in order to conceive of himself as lovable to his parents. Through introjection, values may become divorced from the organism's actual experiences.

When children deny or distort the symbolization of their experiences, they are no longer aware of them. They begin to experience the attitudes of others, such as their parents, as if these were the direct experiences of their organism. The "self" that one forms, therefore, may be at variance with the real experience of one's organism. An individual may come to experience any expression of anger as bad, through such distortion. He or she can no longer accurately perceive that at times its expression is satisfying. In such cases, the experiences of the self and that of the organism do not coincide.

Rogers does not believe that it is inevitable for the self-structure to be formed on the basis of denial and distortion. The child values the experiences of his or her organism as positive or negative. If a parent is able to accept genuinely the child and his or her feeling of satisfaction and simultaneously accept his or her own feelings that certain actions are inappropriate, the parent can help the child curb such actions without threatening the integrity of the child's self-concept.

The parent can make it clear that he or she disapproves of the action of hitting the baby. Nevertheless, the feelings of satisfaction from the aggression and the child's desire are recognized and accepted. Such recognition provides the child with an accurate symbolization of his or her own experience. The child can weigh the satisfaction obtained from hitting the baby with the satisfaction he or she gained from pleasing the parent and then act accordingly. The child would not need to deny his or her own satisfaction nor to identify his or her own reaction with that of the parent.

The experiences that occur in one's life are either symbolized, ignored, denied, or distorted. If an experience is symbolized, it is perceived and organized into a relationship with the self. Generally, such experiences are related to the needs of the self. Experiences are ignored if one cannot perceive any relationship between the experience and the self-structure. One simply fails to pay attention to irrelevant experiences. Experiences are denied or distorted if they appear to be inconsistent with the self-structure. Young women who are brought up to believe that aggression is unfeminine may deny or distort their natural feelings of anger and find it difficult to be assertive because they seek to behave in ways that are feminine. In short, the individual's awareness is highly dependent on his or her self-concept. It is very difficult for an individual to permit the intrusion of a perception that is at variance with the self-concept. One tends to regard such perceptions as alien or foreign. The experiences occur in reality and the organism reacts to them, but they are not symbolized or recognized by the conscious self. Rogers calls this process subception. *Subception* refers to a discriminating evaluative response of the organism to its experience that precedes conscious perception.

Congruence and Incongruence

There is a need for the self as perceived and the real self, the organism, to coincide or to be congruent. A state of *congruence* exists when a person's symbolized experiences reflect the actual experiences of his or her organism. When one's symbolized experiences do not represent the actual experiences, or if they distort them, there is a lack of correspondence between the self as perceived and the real organism. In such a situation, there is *incongruence* and possible maladjustment. Diagrammatically, we can show this with overlapping circles, much as we described Karen Horney's distinction between the real self and the ideal self. When the circles representing the self-concept and the organism largely coincide, the person is in a state of congruence and harmony. As the circles become separate and distinct, incongruence develops and maladjustment may occur.

When an individual denies or distorts significant sensory and visceral experiences, certain basic tensions arise. The self as perceived,

FIGURE 10.1 The Total Personality

From Client-Centered Therapy *by Carl R. Rogers. Copyright © 1951 by Carl R. Rogers. Reprinted by permission of Houghton Mifflin Company.*

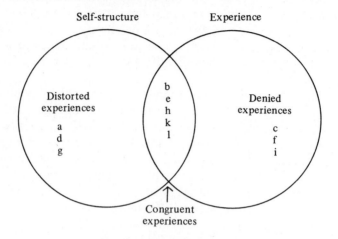

A personality in a state of psychic tension

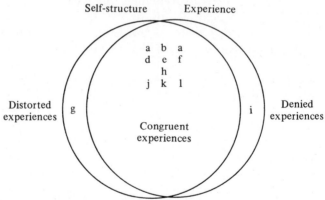

A personality in a state of relative congruence wherein more elements of experience have been integrated into the self

which primarily governs behavior, is not an adequate representative of the true experiences of the organism. It becomes increasingly difficult for the self to satisfy the organism's needs. Tension develops and is felt as anxiety or uncertainty.

Rogers offers the following example of maladjustment (1951). A young mother conceives of herself as a "good and loving mother." She cannot recognize her negative, rejecting attitudes toward her child because they do not coincide with her self-image. Nevertheless, these negative attitudes exist, and her organism seeks aggressive acts that would express these attitudes. She is limited to expressing herself only through channels that are consistent with her self-image of being a good mother. Since it is appropriate for a good mother to behave aggressively toward her child when the child is bad, she perceives a great deal of the child's behavior as bad and punishes the child accordingly. In this manner, she can express her negative attitudes but retain her self-image of being a good mother.

When the self-concept is congruent with the experiences of the organism, one is free from inner tension and psychological adjustment exists. Rogers makes it clear that he does not advocate the free and unrestrained expression of all our impulses and emotions. Part of the reality of the organism's experience is that certain social and cultural values require suppression of certain activities. Nevertheless, one's self-concept can include both the desire to behave one way and the desire to behave in other more socially accepted ways. If parents can accept their feelings of rejection for their children as well as their feelings of affection, they can relate to their children more honestly.

When people become aware of and accept their impulses and perceptions, they increase the possibility of conscious control over their expression. The driver who is adept on icy roads knows the importance of going "with the skid" in order to gain control over the car. In the same manner, when one accepts all of his or her experiences, he or she acquires better self-control.

Development of Personality

Carl Rogers does not posit any specific stages of personality development from infancy to adulthood. He concentrates on the way in which the evaluations of others impede or facilitate self-actualization. Although the tendency to actualize follows genetic determinants, Rogers notes that it is subject to strong environmental influences.

The young child has two basic needs: the need for positive regard by others and the need for positive self-regard. *Positive regard* refers to being loved and accepted for who one is. Young children behave in such a way as to show their strong need for the acceptance and love of those who care for them. They will undergo significant changes in their behavior in order to attain positive regard.

In an ideal situation, positive regard is *unconditional*. It is given freely to children for who they are regardless of what they do. *Unconditional positive regard* is not contingent on any specific behaviors. A parent can limit or curb certain behaviors that he or she finds undesirable by objecting only to the disapproved behaviors and not disapproving of the child and his or her feelings. A parent who sees a child scribble on the wall may say, "Writing on the wall destroys it. Use this blackboard instead." Here, the parent limits his or her remarks to the behavior itself. But the parent says, "You are a bad boy (girl) for writing on the wall," he or she has shifted from disapproval of the behavior to disapproval of the child. Such regard is no longer unconditional.

Frequently, positive regard is merely conditional. *Conditional positive regard* is given only under certain circumstances. Children are led to understand that their parents will not love them unless they think, feel, and act as their parents want them to. Such conditional positive regard tells the child that he or she is acceptable only if he or she behaves in certain ways. The parent who says, "You are a bad boy (or girl) for writing on the wall," is, in effect, saying to the child, "I will not love you if you write on the wall." In such cases, the parent is imposing *conditions of worth*, specifying the provisions under which the child will be accepted. Such conditions of worth may lead the child to introject values of others rather than of the self and lead to a discrepancy between the self-concept and the experiences of the organism.

Positive self-regard follows automatically if one has received unconditional positive regard. Children who are accepted for who they are come to view themselves favorably and with acceptance. It is very difficult, however, to view oneself positively if one is continually the target of criticism and belittlement. An individual who is merely given conditional positive regard may find it very difficult to acquire self-respect. It is clear that for Rogers, how an individual regards him- or herself depends in large measure on the kinds of regard he or she has been given by others. Inadequate self-concepts, feelings of inferiority or stupidity, frequently arise because a person has not received adequate positive regard from others.

Rogers's point is that the valuation of others plays a significant role in development of the self-structure. If conditions of worth are posited, the self-concept may be distorted. For example, suppose a young boy who is jealous of his baby sister begins to hit her with a toy truck. Mother can stop the behavior: she can remove the truck. She can also remind Johnny that it is harmful to hit his sister. But if she also conveys the message that he is a bad boy and she will not love him if he feels jealous of his sister, she posits a condition of worth. Johnny's options are now limited: he can concur that he is a bad boy; he may acknowledge that his mother does not like him; or he can decide that he is not jealous of his sister and does not want to hit her with a truck. Each of these options denies certain aspects of the truth. In order to meet his mother's conditions of worth, he must deny some aspects of the experiences of his organism. In effect, the child has to put on blinders. Suppose he decides that he is not jealous of his sister. His organism remains jealous but he is unable to perceive that jealousy, because to perceive it would make him anxious lest he lose his mother's love. Introjected values take the place of his own, and he becomes divided against himself.

In the course of development, any experience that is at variance with the emerging self-concept is denied entrance into the self because it is threatening and evokes anxiety. If children are taught that it is wrong to feel angry, they may begin to perceive the emotion of anger itself rather than certain unconstructive behavioral expressions of anger as dangerous or incorrect. In order to fulfill the conditions of worth, a child may become unable to perceive the very feelings of anger when they develop. Rogers would point out that there are people who literally cannot perceive when they are angry because they have been taught that the feelings of anger themselves, rather than certain actions that may emanate from those feelings, are wrong and inappropriate.

The primary distinction here is between feelings and actions. Feelings simply are. They have an important value in that they help us to understand our experience. Actions may or may not be appropriate. Some of them have to be curbed or prevented if we are going to live together in society.

When an experience is denied entrance into the self, it is not simply ignored, rather, it is falsified by the pretense that it does not exist or by distortion. In psychoanalytic terms, the experience is repressed. As Rogers explains it, an object or event may be *subceived* or unconsciously perceived as a threat (1951). While it produces visceral reactions in the organism, it is not consciously identified; instead, the mechanisms of denial or distortion prevent the threatening experience from becoming conscious. Rogers points out that some people will adamantly insist on a self-concept that is clearly at odds with reality. A young woman who believes that she is inferior and receives a raise may believe that the boss felt sorry for her, rather than take credit where credit is due. The person who has achieved a significant goal may enter into a deep depression. One's self-concept may be so poor that one cannot realistically permit him- or herself to enjoy what has happened.

It is clear that for Rogers psychological adjustment is a function of the congruence of the self with reality. The individual who has an accurate perception of his or her self and environment is free to be open to new experiences and to fulfill his or her potential.

EXERCISE:

Q-Sort Test

One technique that Rogers has used for studying a person's self-concept is known as the Q-sort technique. The Q-sort test uses a packet of one hundred cards that contain descriptive statements or words that can be used to describe the self. The person is given the cards and asked to sort them into a prearranged distribution, which resembles the normal curve, according to his or her self-perception.

The reader may explore this technique by making and sorting his or her own set of cards. Make a list of different ways in which you might perceive yourself, or copy the list of twenty-five items in Table 10.1 onto individual index cards. First, sort the cards into seven different piles, ranging from "least like me" to "most like me." In order

TABLE 10.1 Suggested Ways of Perceiving the Self

I make strong demands on myself.
I often feel humiliated.
I often kick myself for the things I do.
I doubt my sexual powers.
I have a warm emotional relationship with others.
It is difficult to control my aggression.
I am responsible for my troubles.
I tend to be on my guard with friendly people.
I am a responsible person.
I usually feel driven.
Self-control is no problem for me.
I am disorganized.
I express my emotions freely.
I feel apathetic.
I am optimistic.
I try not to think about my problems.
I am sexually attractive.
I am shy.
I am liked by most people who know me.
I am afraid of a full-fledged disagreement with a person.
I can usually make up my mind and stick to it.
I can't seem to make up my mind one way or another.
I am impulsive.
I am afraid of sex.
I am ambitious.

to have your distribution follow the normal curve, you will need to place most of the cards in the middle piles indicating that the characteristic is somewhat like you, but not the most or least like you. Your final distribution should be like this:

pile #

least like me	1	2	3	4	5	6	7	most like me
no. of cards	1	2	5	9	5	2	1	

After you have sorted the cards to describe your self-concept as you perceive it, you may wish to re-sort the cards to describe your ideal self—the person that you would most like to be. A comparison of these two sortings will give you a rough idea of the discrepancy between your self-concept and your self-ideal. You might also wish to ask some friends to sort the cards as they perceive you, to gain an idea of the image you project to others in comparison with your own self-perception.

Carl Rogers is best known for the method of psychotherapy that he developed: *nondirective* or *client-centered* therapy. Rogers not only originated this type of therapy, but he has also carefully studied it to determine what makes it work. As a scientist, he has tried to define operationally the conditions that underlie successful therapy to generate hypotheses that can be empirically tested.

Conditions for Therapeutic Change

Rogers's studies have suggested that there are six necessary and sufficient conditions for therapeutic change. By *necessary*, Rogers means that the conditions are essential and must be present. By *sufficient*, he means that these six conditions are all that is required. Not only does Rogers maintain that these six conditions underlie his method of therapy, but he also suggests that they underlie any successful therapeutic technique.

First, there must be *a relationship between persons*. A psychological contact between two or more persons must be present. Rogers does not believe that significant personality change occurs outside of a personal relationship. Insight does not come about by reading a book or punching a computer. It entails a relationship between persons.

Psychoanalysis also emphasized the relationship between doctor and patient. However, Freud emphasized the transference relationship in which the patient projects onto the analyst the feelings and emotions that he or she had toward earlier significant persons in life. Rogers is not talking about the transference relationship, rather, he is talking about the *actual and real relationship* that exists between therapist and client. Rogers suggests that it is an error to view the relationship between the doctor and patient as merely a transference relationship. To be sure, the transference is one part of it, perhaps a very important part, but at the same time there is a real and actual relationship between patient and doctor that cannot be reduced to just the elements of a transference. The minute two people are together there is a relationship between them. Psychotherapy entails fostering and cultivating a particular type of relationship that is conducive to personality change.

The second condition is that *the client is in a state of incongruence*. There is a discrepancy between the actual experiences of the organism and his or her self-concept. Because of this, the client is anxious and vulnerable.

The third condition is that *within the confines of the therapeutic relationship, the therapist is congruent*. He or she is genuine, integrated, free, and deeply aware of his or her experiences within the relationship. Rogers points out that the therapist need not be a paragon of mental health in all aspects of his or her own life. He or she may have short-comings and difficulties in other situations. But within the relationship of therapy, the therapist needs to be congruent.

The fourth condition is that *the therapist experiences unconditional positive regard for the client.* The therapist does not posit any conditions of worth. Rather, he or she conveys to the client an attitude and feeling that Rogers terms "acceptance." *Acceptance* essentially means a nonjudgmental recognition of oneself and the other person. It permits each person to be him- or herself and to recognize who he or she is, without placing any restrictions or value judgments on either one's behavior. Through his or her acceptance the therapist lets the other person be.

The fifth condition is that *the therapist experiences an accurate, empathetic understanding of the client's awareness of experiences and communicates it to the client.* Empathy refers to the ability to participate in another person's feelings as if they were one's own, but never lose sight of the "as if." Through empathy, the therapist is able to put him- or herself in the client's shoes without trying to wear those shoes or lose his or her own shoes. The therapist understands the client's internal frame of reference and communicates this understanding, largely through statements that reflect the client's feelings.

The sixth and final condition is that *the client perceives the acceptance and empathy that the therapist has.* The therapist will have created a nonthreatening atmosphere and positive feelings of acceptance that will permit the client to explore his or her feelings and experiences more fully. Because the threat to the self-structure is diminished, the client is able to perceive and examine experiences that are inconsistent with his or her self-concept and to revise the concept so that it becomes more congruent with the actual experiences of the organism.

Given these six conditions, Rogers believes that positive, constructive personality changes will occur. In a climate of unconditional positive regard, the patient will be able to explore those feelings and experiences that were previously denied or distorted. In doing so, the patient's self-concept will gradually become more congruent with the actual experiences of his or her organism. Carl Rogers suggests that all successful therapy, not just his mode of client-centered therapy, shares these six conditions. The factor that essentially makes psychotherapy effective is an underlying attitude of acceptance on the part of the therapist that is perceived by the client.

Responses to Emotional Communications

Rogers does not employ any special techniques, such as free association or dream analysis, in his therapy. The direction of the therapy is determined by the client. Whereas in psychoanalysis the instructions are, "Say whatever comes to mind," in Rogerian therapy, if there were any instructions, they would be, "Talk about whatever you would like to talk about." These two instructions are very different. The client determines what will be discussed, when, and to what extent. This is why Rogers's form of therapy has been labeled "client-centered." If a client does not want to talk about a particular subject, he or she is not pressed to do so. The client does not even have to talk at all if he or she does not want to. Rogers feels strongly that his clients have the ability to understand and to explore their problems, and that given the appropriate therapeutic relationship, that is, an attitude of acceptance, they will work toward further self-actualization.

In Rogerian therapy, the therapist communicates the attitude of acceptance largely through statements that reflect the client's feelings. We can understand this better by distinguishing between different kinds of responses to emotional communications. Rogers developed a number of studies in which he explored how people communicate in face-to-face situations (1952). Consider the following hypothetical communication: "The doctor keeps telling me not to worry, but I'm frightened of this operation." There are many different ways in which one could respond to such a statement. Rogers discovered that most responses fall into one of five categories: probing, evaluative, interpretative, reassuring, and reflective. Each of these responses tends to lead toward a different consequence.

Probing Response A probing response seeks further information. One might ask, "What is it about the operation that frightens you?" Additional information can be very helpful in assisting the listener in understanding the problem. All too frequently, however, a probing response is taken by the speaker to be an infringement upon his or her privacy. He or she may inwardly react, "That's none of your business." In such a case, the speaker might clam up and the listener would lose the opportunity to explore the feelings further. Rogers would recommend that a probing response be avoided or presented in such a way that the speaker is free to drop the subject if he or she chooses. One might simply ask, "Would you like to talk about it?" in which case the speaker is free to say, "No, I'd rather not," if he or she finds the subject too painful.

Evaluative Response An evaluative response places a value judgment on the person's thoughts, feelings, wishes, or behavior. One might say, "You shouldn't be afraid of the operation." Evaluative responses may have their place when the listener is specifically asked to give his or her opinion or wants to disclose his or her own values or attitudes. However, because evaluative responses are judgmental, they tend to detract from an attitude of basic acceptance of the other individual. Our natural tendency to approve, disapprove, judge, or evaluate another person's comments is a primary barrier to understanding in communication. Evaluative responses frequently close the door to further communications rather than open it. Often they lead to a defensive reaction in the speaker and to a situation in which each party simply looks at the problem from his or her own point of view. When one is defensive, he or she is no longer open to further exploration of the anxiety that he or she is trying to defend him- or herself against.

Interpretative Response   An interpretative response is an effort on the listener's part to tell the speaker what his or her problem really is or how he or she really feels about the situation. One might say, "That's because you're afraid of being unconscious during the operation." Interpretation is a technique that is frequently employed in intensive therapy. In the hands of a trained and skilled technician, it can be a valuable adjunct to assist in developing insight. But in the hands of an amateur, interpretation can be a dangerous tool. In the first place, the interpretation may be wrong. Second, if an interpretation is correct, it must be properly timed. If an interpretation is ill timed, it will be rejected, because the speaker was not ready for it. If an interpretation is rejected it may have the further side effect of making the speaker feel misunderstood and less likely to discuss the issue further. For these reasons any interpretation should be presented only tentatively and left open for further confirmation. Further, an interpretation should be timed so that it is not given until just before the speaker is about to make the same discovery about him- or herself. When properly used, and given with skill, empathy, and integrity, interpretations can be potent catalysts for growth.

Reassuring Response   A reassuring response attempts to pacify or soothe the speaker's feelings. It implies that the speaker need not feel the way he or she does. One might reply, "Many others have come through the same operation well." Reassuring responses may be helpful in letting the speaker know that he or she is accepted or in encouraging a person to try out new behaviors that might help to resolve a problem. However, reassurance is frequently perceived by an individual as an attempt to minimize his or her problem. At the moment he or she does not care about other people. The speaker is concerned with his or her own dilemma. Introducing other people's problems or one's own in an effort to pacify may suggest that the listener is not taking the speaker's problem seriously or wants to dismiss it.

Reflective Response   The reflective response seeks to capture the underlying feelings that are expressed in the original communication. One might say, "You're very scared." An effective reflective statement does not simply restate or echo the original words or thoughts of the speaker, it tries to zero in on the underlying emotion that was expressed.

It is most effective if the listener uses his or her own words and responds in a manner that matches the depth of the original communication.

A distinction should be made between a reflective response and mere restatement. A *restatement* repeats the *thought* of the original comment, whereas a reflective comment seeks to express the underlying *emotion*. Reflective responses are useful because they tell the speaker that the listener is interested and understands what he or she is trying to say. A reflective response is most likely to encourage the speaker to elaborate and explore his or her problem further. In addition, it assists the listener in coming to understand the other person's internal frame of reference. For these reasons, it is probably the most fruitful response to employ, particularly for a lay person and even for a skilled therapist in the initial phases of a relationship.

Nevertheless, Rogers found that in everyday life the responses were used in the following order of frequency: (1) evaluative, (2) interpretative, (3) reassuring, (4) probing, and (5) reflective. Apparently, we could use practice in cultivating the reflective response.

EXERCISE:

Responding to Emotional Communications

One of the simplest yet most effective ways to develop skill in cultivating the reflective response is to practice it with another person. The next time you become deeply engrossed in a conversation or an argument, agree to obey the following rule. Each person may speak only for him- or herself after he or she has reflected the thoughts and feelings of the previous speaker accurately and to that person's satisfaction. What initially sounds simple proves difficult, but it leads to a much more constructive discussion as it focuses on understanding one another rather than simply presenting different points of view.

You might also read the following emotional communications, imagine how you might respond, and try to write responses for each one that fit into each of the five categories.*

1. Mr. Jones is such an unfair teacher, I just failed another one of his tests.

2. I got so annoyed when John stood me up last night, I wouldn't come to the phone when he called.

3. I'm so depressed, I don't know what to do! Here I am twenty-nine and still unmarried.

4. I'm really worried about Bill. His grades have fallen and I think he may be into drugs.

* Communications adapted from E. H. Porter, Jr. *Therapeutic Counseling,* Houghton Mifflin, Boston, 1950, pp. 33–40.

5. *What should I do about Bob? I like dating him, but I think he wants to get too serious.*

6. *That new kid in class really tees me off. He's such a braggart.*

7. *I think I'll leave home, my parents don't understand me and they make such unfair restrictions.*

8. *I know I should do something about the problem, but I just can't bring myself to face it.*

It is helpful to compare your responses with those that others make. Discuss where and how your responses might be improved. Finally, analyze the comments that you hear people make in group situations. Note the frequency with which each type of response occurs.

Actually, there is no written exercise or book that can improve your ability to communicate reflectively. It requires continual practice, interaction, and feedback from others. Nevertheless, in everyday communications, one can try to attune oneself to the kinds of responses that are offered. One can ask oneself, "Do my responses reflect what the speaker really means?" One can also ask the speaker if one is reflecting him or her accurately by prefacing or ending a comment with a phrase such as, "Do you mean . . ." or ". . . is that it?"

Supportive versus Reconstructive Psychotherapy

Different methods of psychotherapy vary in their ambitions. Some therapies aim at maintaining or modifying adaptive behaviors, while others seek to reorganize the entire basic personality structure. At one end of the spectrum, psychoanalysis stands as a clear example of reconstructive psychotherapy. Through analysis of the resistances and transference the analyst seeks to remove defenses so that the patient can communicate his or her true feelings and integrate his or her personality. On the other hand, many psychotherapeutic techniques are best characterized as supportive, since they seek to strengthen adaptive instincts and defenses, without necessarily tampering with the underlying personality structure.

In both instances, maladaptive behavior can be viewed as defensive behavior that has gone awry. In order to protect him- or herself against anxiety, the individual develops defense mechanisms or denials and distortions. These defense mechanisms have both constructive and destructive features. They are positive and constructive in that they ward off anxiety that would be too painful to bear in its full impact. Yet the defenses may become destructive in that they prevent us from recognizing and acting on our innermost feelings. Supportive psychotherapy seeks to strengthen and bolster adaptive defense mechanisms to assist the person in more effectively coping with his or her anxieties. Reconstructive psychotherapy entails weakening those defenses that have become maladaptive so that the original emotions and anxieties can be re-experienced and more effectively resolved.

Both modalities of treatment have their place. Some patients require supportive psychotherapy, whereas others benefit more from an intensive reconstructive psychotherapy. Age, the nature of the problem, and the ability to withstand stress are a few of the many factors that need consideration prior to selection of a preferred method of treatment. In some cases, according to some theorists, support of neurotic defenses is necessary to prevent an outbreak of psychosis.

A young woman who was reared in a home in which sexual impulses and behaviors were frowned on and considered dirty might experience anxiety over her own sexual desires. Her parents, who are heirs of a Victorian attitude, taught her that sex was ugly and, at best, simply to be tolerated. She lives, however, in a culture that does not necessarily share these views. An introductory acquaintance with the Kinsey Report and other recent studies on sexual behavior and mores convinces her of the increasing incidence of young and older people who not only engage in sexual activities but openly enjoy them. Her knowledge of the contemporary world undercuts a number of parental myths, such as "Nice girls don't kiss until they become engaged," or "Girls who do it are punished by becoming pregnant." Moreover, she notes that an increasing number of scientific studies suggest that expression of one's sexuality is desirable in terms of mental health. For such a young woman, supportive therapy can be very helpful in assisting her in coming to terms with the acceptability of her sexual desires and urges. In an atmosphere that is free of the earlier parental conditions of worth, she can express her feelings without fear of punishment. At the same time, supportive therapy can assist her judgment and help her to recognize the genuine lack of wisdom in the values that she was taught as a child.

But in other instances, supportive therapy will not be sufficient. Many young women have been fully aware of the ignorance and stupidity of the sexual views that were inculcated in them as children. But, as children, they were taught so well to repress their sexual feelings that it is very difficult for them to know or even experience their own sexual desires and impulses. Even though such an individual may know and be fully convinced on an intellectual level of the possibility of optimally and constructively expressing her sexual feelings, she finds herself inhibited. Her sexual response is prevented from occurring by underlying unconscious conflicts. In such a situation, which is frequently marked by an inability to be orgasmic, supportive therapy might not be enough. Reconstructive therapy may be necessary. Her defenses will need to be analyzed and weakened so that the underlying unconscious conflict can emerge and be worked through.

Whereas supportive therapy takes the existing personality structure and strengthens its desirable features, reconstructive therapy seeks complete rehaul and reconstruction of the personality. One might compare the one to slipcovering a chair with a new fabric to give it a new lease on life, and the other to an upholstery job in which the chair is stripped to the frame and then rebuilt. Clearly, reconstructive psychotherapy is a much more intensive, protracted undertaking, which helps to account for the length and the duration of psychoanalysis. Although he is not adverse to providing insight when the occasion merits it, Rogers's approach tends to be supportive rather than reconstructive.

This is not to say that one technique is better than the other; rather, we need to recognize that for different people, in different circumstances, and, perhaps, even at different times in their lives, one approach may be more suitable than another. Such variation may also help to account for the fact that Rogers's therapeutic technique has been particularly successful with college-age students, many of whom are not seriously impaired but are undergoing a difficult period of identity during which supportive therapy may be very helpful. Carl Rogers points out that we all can benefit from therapy. Although we may not be suffering from overt problems that seriously affect our lives, we may not be functioning as well as we would like. Rogers himself has acknowledged that at one particularly stressful period of his life he was treated by a colleague. He was thankful that he was able to develop a method of therapy and train therapists who were not only independent but also able to offer him the kind of help that he needed. Since the time that he himself received therapy, Rogers has believed that his own work with patients has been increasingly free and more spontaneous.

Changes in Rogers's View of Therapy

Rogers's earlier writings on therapeutic technique stressed the idea that the potential for better health lies in the client. The therapist's role was essentially that of making the kinds of reflective responses that would enable the client's potential to flower. Later, Rogers shifted from his emphasis on technique to the counselor's need to develop an interpersonal relationship in which experiences could come into awareness. In his later writings, Rogers has stressed the need for the therapist to be present as a person in the relationship. While Rogers continues to recognize the importance of nondirection, believing that the client must remain in charge of his or her own life, he maintains that the therapist needs to be aware of his or her own feelings and free to express them without imposing them on the client. Negative as well as positive feelings may be presented, simply posed as data that the client is free to cope with as he or she chooses. The therapist may point out that a client is boring him or her. This is not a mandate for the client to change, but a factor within the interpersonal relationship that the client might wish to deal with.

In recent years, Rogers has also been less interested in individual therapy and more interested in group therapy as well as broader social concerns. He is a leader in the field of encounter groups and has also sponsored some interracial and intercultural groups. He has written about education and other issues in contemporary psychology and society.

THERAPY EXCERPTS   Client-Centered Therapy

In client-centered therapy, the therapist's main objective is to reflect the client's feelings. The therapist, in this case Carl Rogers, may disclose some of his or her own feelings but does so without making value judgments. In the excerpt below, the client, a thirty-year-old divorcée, begins by expressing conflict over whether or not to tell her nine-year-old daughter Pammy that she has had sexual relationships with men since her divorce.*

CL (client): I almost want an answer from you. I want you to tell me if it would affect her wrong if I told her the truth, or what.

TH (therapist): I sure wish I could give you the answer as to what you should say to her.

CL: I was afraid you were going to say that.

TH: Because what you really want *is* an answer.

The client begins to explore her relationship with her daughter and realizes that she is not sure whether or not her daughter would accept her "shady" side, because she is not certain she accepts it herself.

CL: You're going to sit there and let me stew in it and I want more.

TH: No, I don't want to let you just stew in your feelings, but on the other hand, I also feel that this is the kind of very private thing that I couldn't possibly answer for you. But I sure as anything will try to help you work towards your own answer. I don't know whether that makes any sense to you, but I mean it.

CL: I can tell that you really do mean it.

The client focuses further on the conflict she experiences between her actions and her inner standards. Again, she presses for an answer.

TH: I guess, I am sure this will sound evasive to you, but it seems to me that perhaps the person you are not being fully honest with is you, because I was very much struck by the fact that you were saying, "If I feel all right about what I have done, whether it's going to bed with a man or what, if I really feel all right about it, then I do not have any concern about what I would tell Pam or my relationship with her."

CL: Right. All right. Now I hear what you are saying. Then all right,

* Adapted from B. D. Meader and C. R. Rogers, "Client-Centered Therapy," in R. Corsini (ed.), *Current Psychotherapies*. Reproduced by permission of the publishers, F. E. Peacock Publishers, Inc., Itasca, Ill., 1973.

then I want to work on accepting me then. I want to work on feeling all right about it. That makes sense. Then that will come natural and then I won't have to worry about Pammy. I guess I wanted you to tell me what to do, because I can't quite take the risk of being the way I want to be with my children unless an authority tells me that . . .

TH: I guess one thing that I feel very keenly is that it's an awfully risky thing to *live*. You'd be taking a chance on your relationship with her and taking a chance on letting her know who you are, really.

CL: I wish I could take more risks, that I could act on my own feelings of rightness without always needing encouragement from others. I know what I'd like to do is to level with Pammy and tell her the kind of a person that I really am.

TH: You'd like to tell her the truth.

CL: Yes, I would. Now I feel like "now that's solved" and I didn't even solve a thing; but I feel relieved. I feel like you have been saying to me—you are not giving me advice, but I do feel like you are saying, "You know what pattern you want to follow, Gloria, and go ahead and follow it." I sort of feel a backing from you.

TH: I guess the way I sense it, you've been telling me that you know what you want to do, and yes, I do believe in backing up people in what they want to do.

The Empirical Validation of Psychotherapy

Carl Rogers has been exceptionally open to the empirical test of his theories. The private, confidential character of clinical treatment has made it very difficult to study in its natural setting. With the permission of his clients, however, Rogers has introduced the tape recorder and camera into the treatment room. He does not believe that they detract from the therapy. Within a short time, both client and therapist forget about the recording equipment and act naturally and spontaneously.

The recordings Rogers has made have provided a group of actual transcriptions of therapeutic sessions that can be observed and studied. The sessions have been analyzed in various ways. A classification system permits us to note the kinds of statements made by both the client and the therapist. Rating scales monitor the progress and change that occurs during therapy from the viewpoints of both the client and the therapist. The Q-sort technique has been used to measure changes that occur throughout therapy. In short, Rogers has provided and given an impetus to developing means for ongoing empirical research on the processes of therapy and the self.

From his studies, Rogers concluded that there is a clear predictability to the therapeutic process. Given certain conditions, such as the six basic conditions outlined earlier, certain predictable outcomes may be expected. The client will express deep motivational attitudes. He or she will begin to explore and become more aware of his or her attitudes and reactions. The client will begin to accept him- or herself more fully and will discover and choose more satisfying goals. Finally, the client will begin to behave in a manner that indicates greater psychological growth and maturity.

THE FULLY FUNCTIONING PERSON

Carl Rogers, like many other humanist theorists, has suggested certain ideas as to what constitutes the mature person or an ideal model of human living. *Fully functioning person* is the phrase Rogers uses to indicate the individual who is functioning at an optimal level, either as a result of his or her own development or of psychological treatment. Rogers describes five characteristics of the fully functioning person (1959).

Openness to Experience   The fully functioning person is aware of all of his or her experiences: sensory, visceral, and emotional. Fully functioning people are not defensive and do not need to deny or distort their experiences. They can recognize a feeling even if it is inappropriate to act on it. During a lecture, a young man may experience the desire to have sexual relations with the young girl sitting next to him. He refrains from acting at the moment because he recognizes that such action would be imprudent, but the feeling does not threaten him. Fully functioning people can recognize both negative and positive emotions and permit them to enter into their self-system. They are able to listen to their innermost selves and are not afraid of being introspective.

Existential Living   The fully functioning person is able to live fully and richly each moment of his or her existence. Each experience is potentially fresh and new. Fully functioning people do not need rigid preconceived structures to impose on and by which to interpret each happening. Every event can speak for itself. They can deal with new, unpredicted, and unexpected situations. They are not predetermined, but processes that grow with each experience. Thus, they are flexible and spontaneous. They discover the structure of their experiences in the process of experiencing them.

Organismic Trust   The fully functioning person trusts in the feel of his or her own organism. Fully functioning people are independent of the judgment of others. They may take other people's opinions and the consensus of their society into account, but they are not bound by them. The locus of their decision making lies within themselves. They do what they believe is right. They could be described as men and women of conscience. They are principled, but their principles are their own, not introjected from others.

Experiential Freedom   The fully functioning person operates as a free choice agent. Fully functioning people do not feel compelled by others or by some alien aspect of themselves. They assume responsibility for their decisions and behavior. Obviously, they are subject to the laws of causality. One's behavior is largely determined by one's genetic make-up, past experiences, and social forces. Nevertheless, fully functioning people subjectively feel free to be aware of their needs and to respond accordingly.

Creativity   The fully functioning person lives constructively and effectively in his or her environment. The spontaneity and flexibility characteristic of fully functioning people enable them to adjust adequately to changes in their surroundings and to seek new experiences and challenges. Free from constraints, they move confidently forward in the process of self-actualization.

Rogers emphasizes that his is not a "pollyanna," or naively optimistic, point of view. Terms such as "happy," "blissful," or "contented" do not necessarily describe fully functioning people; rather, such people are challenged and find life meaningful. Their experiences are "exciting," "enriching," and "rewarding." Self-actualization requires the "courage to be" and the willingness to launch oneself into the process of life.

Carl Rogers welcomes and encourages empirical and scientific validation and test of his theories. He also openly and refreshingly acknowledges that he is a philosopher and that the primary differences between his theory and other theories lie in the realm of philosophy.

ROGERS'S CRITIQUE OF SKINNER

Carl Rogers fears that the formulation of human life according to the terms of behavioral science has the potential to lead to some dangerous implications. He has been particularly vigorous in his critique (1961) of the social and philosophical implications that arise out of B. F. Skinner's position. Skinner has argued that strategies for behavioral control have become a historical reality. While it is true that at times throughout our history these controls have been used improperly, we now have the ability to design and implement constructive social conditions in which all of the skills of scientific management are utilized.

Carl Rogers is concerned that the kind of society that Skinner has depicted is one that would be used to control the individual and rob each of us of our personhood. The goals of science are those of control and prediction. Science brings with it the power to manipulate. We manipulate, however, in terms of certain predecided goals or purposes. In short, all science depends on the prior subjective choice of purposes and goals. That choice lies outside of the scientific endeavor itself. In and of itself, the scientific method cannot establish the truth, it can only test hypotheses that may or may not be useful. The hypotheses it chooses to test reflect the scientist's value systems.

If we value the ability to control other people, our scientific technology can tell how to achieve this goal. On the other hand, if our value is to increase individual freedom and creativity, our scientific technology can facilitate these ends as well. If we wish to determine whether increased control is "better" than increased freedom and creativity, science can also study these two values, but it can do so only in terms of another value that we have imposed. Thus, if we value an orderly society, we can determine whether increased control or creativity is better for achieving it. If we value subjective human happiness, again, we can determine whether increased control or creativity is most pertinent. In either event, however, the value or goal that directs the scientific enterprise lies outside of it.

Some have suggested that the scientific endeavor gradually can evolve its own goals. Rogers points out, however, that this overlooks the original and continuous subjective choices that underlie our science and are prior to it. To conceive that our values might emerge from science is to misconceive the origins and limits of our science.

Rogers suggests that we need to make explicit the goals that we choose for our science to serve. If we choose as our goal to manipulate others and render them submissive to societal aims, our scientific technology can assist us in meeting these ends. However, if we choose as our goal to increase human freedom, responsibility, and spontaneity, our scientific technology can also serve these ends. Carl Rogers, the scientist, studies the predictability of the therapeutic process, not to predict his clients' behavior, rather, to render his clients less predictable, more free and spontaneous. Such a utopia may be less easily defined, but it is one that Rogers, the philosopher, would prefer.

EVALUATION AND IMPLICATIONS

Carl Rogers has done a great deal to bring the human being back into the primary focus of psychological study. He has attracted a large following of people who prefer his optimistic, nonmanipulative view to the pessimism of psychoanalysis and the reductionism of behaviorism. Psychologists have welcomed his reintroduction of the importance of subjectivity and perception as determinants of behavior. His therapeutic techniques have been widely applauded and adopted. Their usefulness in helping troubled people has been demonstrated, as has their potential application to a broad range of social concerns.

While Rogers's position has enormous appeal, it has also provoked a fair amount of criticism. Rogers's emphasis on subjectivity and the individual's internal frame of reference as a primary perspective for psychological study has made things difficult for a psychology that has traditionally stressed the role of the external observer. As we have seen, introspective reports are much more difficult to validate than extrospective reports. In Rogers's research a great deal of stress is placed on self-reports. Critics point out that self-reports may be deceptive. In the past, such difficulties led scientific psychology to reject firmly the notion of any self or psychic agent. Even though the self in Rogers's theory is no longer a philosophical concept, but a name for a group of processes, these processes are difficult to study objectively.

The major criticism that has been made of Rogers's position is that it is based on a simplistic concept of phenomenology and does not reflect a sophisticated understanding of the complexity of the processes underlying human awareness. To suggest that the person is the most important source of information about him- or herself, because the person is the only one who can be fully aware of his or her experiences, is to minimize how continually and frequently human beings deny or distort the truth about themselves to themselves. Many of us seem bent on self-deception rather than on self-understanding. Although Rogers acknowledges that there are experiences of which a person may be unaware through the processes of denial and distortion, he does not believe that repression is inevitable. Under the proper conditions of unconditional positive regard, he suggests that repression can be avoided. Moreover, Rogers holds that an atmosphere of acceptance is sufficient to lift repression. Critics suggest that this belief is naive and that Rogers fails to recognize the power and intensity of unconscious forces. He does not appreciate the extent to which most people conceal from themselves their innermost thoughts and feelings.

To permit a client to say simply whatever he or she wants to say may be in certain cases to perpetuate the process of self-deception. If one is not required to say whatever comes to mind, one can easily avoid painful topics. However, precisely those topics we do not want to explore may be the locus of our difficulty and their analysis would penetrate our defenses. To be sure, the discussion of painful subjects is threatening, but a certain amount of threat may be necessary in psychotherapy to recreate the original conditions that led to the repression and to permit the unconscious forces to enter consciousness. Perhaps we can only truly know ourselves as we permit ourselves to be known by another.

On the other hand, Rogers's analysis of the therapeutic process has shed considerable light on the phenomenon of therapy itself. In particular, Rogers's discussion of the attitude of acceptance on the part of the therapist toward the client is a helpful correction of Freud's overemphasis on the transference. As Rogers points out, it is the underlying actual and real personal relationship between the therapist and client that fosters personality change. The types of relationships that are conducive to change merit further investigation.

Rogers's theory has given rise to a great deal of further study and research, particularly concerning the concept of the self and the process of psychotherapy. His emphasis on human potentiality and freedom provides an attractive alternative to theories that emphasize the idea that we are largely controlled by external or unconscious forces. We have seen that his therapeutic approach has found wide application and led to constructive techniques in diverse areas, such as education, industry, and social reform. He has tremendous appeal to those who share his humanistic and optimistic philosophy of the human being.

SUGGESTIONS FOR FURTHER READING

Carl Rogers is a lucid writer whose works are relatively easy for the lay person to understand. In *Counseling and Psychotherapy* (Houghton Mifflin, 1942), Rogers first introduced his nondirective therapy technique, gave examples, and compared it with other therapeutic methods. *Client-Centered Therapy* (Houghton Mifflin, 1942) reflects the change in name Rogers gave his technique in order to focus attention on the client as the center of the therapeutic process. This book discusses the practice and implications of client-centered therapy and also describes his theory of personality and behavior. With Rosalind Dymond, Carl Rogers edited *Psychotherapy and Personality Change* (University of Chicago Press, 1954), which presents thirteen empirical studies investigating hypotheses that have arisen out of the client-centered approach. In a group of significant articles organized into the book *On Becoming a Person* (Houghton Mifflin, 1961), Rogers describes his own experiences as a therapist, his view of the fully functioning person, the place of research in psychotherapy and its implications for education, family life, and group functions. Also included is Rogers's critique of B. F. Skinner. Finally, *Freedom to Learn* (Charles E. Merrill, 1969) discusses ways of making classroom learning more relevant and meaningful to students. He explains how the atmosphere that makes learning effective is similar to those attitudes that are conducive to personality change in therapy.

Summaries of his own research may be found in a book edited by Rogers, *The Therapeutic Relationship and Its Impact* (University of Wisconsin Press, 1967) and the Rogers and Dymond book mentioned above. For a discussion of the research generated by self-theory, the reader is referred to R. Wylie's chapter on "The Present Status of Self-Theory" in E. F. Borgotta and W. W. Lambert, *Handbook of Personality and Research* (Rand McNally, 1968).

CHAPTER 11

Abraham Maslow's Theory of Self-Actualization

Abraham Maslow has been described as the spiritual father of American humanism. An articulate, persuasive writer, he has described humanist psychology as a "third force" in American psychology. He criticized both psychoanalysis and behaviorism for their pessimistic, negative, and limited conceptions of human nature. The study of crippled people (neurotics), characteristic of psychoanalysis, he wrote, can only lead to a crippled psychology. The study of human nature as a machine, typical of behaviorism, cannot comprehend the whole person. Maslow offered his view as a complement rather than an alternative to these two other forces. He did not reject the contributions that psychoanalysis and behaviorism have made, but he believed that the picture of human nature needs to be rounded out. In particular, Maslow sought to emphasize the positive rather than the negative side of human nature. The brighter side of humanity is emphasized in his concept of the self-actualized person.

BIOGRAPHICAL BACKGROUND

Abraham Maslow was born in 1908 in a poor Jewish district of Brooklyn, New York. The first of seven children, his parents were Russian immigrants. As his father's business as a cooper (one who makes or repairs wooden casks and tubs) improved, Maslow's family moved out

ABRAHAM MASLOW

of the slums and into lower-middle-class neighborhoods. As a result, the young Abraham found himself the only Jewish boy in the neighborhood and a target of anti-Semitism. Taunted, isolated, friendless, and lonely, he spent a great deal of his early years cloistered in the library in the companionship of books.

His father was an ambitious man who instilled in his children a desire to succeed. At an early age, Abraham delivered newspapers. Later he spent several summers working for the family company. Today, that company, Universal Containers, Inc., is a large, successful barrel-manufacturing corporation, run by his brothers. Maslow was not close to either of his parents. He was fond of his father but afraid of him. He described his mother as schizophrenic and later wondered how he had turned out so well in spite of his unhappy childhood. His mother's brother, however, was a kind and devoted uncle, who spent a great deal of time with his nephew and may have been responsible for Maslow's mental stability.

Maslow attended New York City schools through the eighth grade and then the Brooklyn Borough High School, where he had an excellent record. At the age of eighteen he entered New York City College, where the tuition was free. His father wanted him to study law. Law, however, totally disinterested him, and his grades fell. The next two years were marked by confusion. Undecided about his studies and in love with a girl of whom his parents disapproved, he floundered, spending time at Cornell, returning to New York City, and trying to escape by going to the University of Wisconsin.

Within a few months of his arrival at Wisconsin, he announced his intentions of marrying his sweetheart. She returned with him to Wisconsin. Later, he suggested that life didn't begin for him until he married and began studying at Wisconsin. The supportiveness of his wife encouraged his academic work. Further, he had discovered John Watson and was totally absorbed in behaviorism, which he saw as a very practical way of improving society. During his college and graduate years, Maslow received a solid grounding in empirical laboratory research. He worked as an assistant to William H. Sheldon, although he was not personally enamored of Sheldon's theory of the varieties of temperament. He also studied animal behavior, working with Harry Harlow, a well-known psychologist who conducted extensive research with rhesus monkeys. Maslow's own doctoral research concerned the sexual and dominance characteristics of monkeys.

After receiving the Ph.D. from Wisconsin in 1934, Maslow returned to New York. He worked as a research assistant to Edwin L. Thorndike and then began to teach at Brooklyn College. New York was a vibrant place for a young psychologist during the thirties. Many European psychologists, psychiatrists, and others of the intelligentsia who had come to America to escape the Nazis were in New York. Maslow eagerly met and learned from them. He was influenced by Max Wertheimer, a founder of the gestalt school, Erich Fromm, Karen Horney, and Alfred Adler. He was also impressed by the anthropologist Ruth Benedict, who inspired him with her optimism about the potentialities of society.

Within such an eclectic climate, it was probably inevitable that Maslow's interest in behaviorism would diminish. The birth of his first daughter was the "thunderclap that settled things" once and for all. All of his experimentation with rats and primates did not prepare him for the mystery of the child. S-R theory might explain what was observed in the laboratory, but it could not account for human experiences. The advent of World War II also profoundly affected Maslow. His attention turned more fully to research on the human personality in an effort to improve it, "to show that human beings are capable of something grander than war and prejudice and hatred" (Hall, 1968).

Maslow remained at Brooklyn for fourteen years. In 1951, he moved to Brandeis University where he stayed until one year before his death in 1970. These later years at Brandeis were again marked by a feeling of isolation, in spite of the fact that Maslow had become a very popular figure in the field of psychology. Perhaps it was simply Maslow's nature to be a loner. He clarified and refined his theories, and shortly before his death had embarked on a fellowship that was to have enabled him to undertake a large-scale study developing a philosophy of economics, politics, and ethics informed by humanistic psychology.

Motivational processes lie at the heart of Maslow's theory. The primary motivating force of human nature is the drive to self-actualize. This means that human beings seek more than the simple fulfillment of biological drives or to restore an equilibrium and balance. Human beings are interested in growing rather than simply avoiding frustration. Indeed, as one human desire is satisfied, Maslow suggests another arises to take its place. Maslow describes the human being as a "wanting animal" who is almost always desiring something. In his or her drive to self-actualize, the individual moves forward toward growth, happiness, and satisfaction.

Maslow makes a distinction between two broad groups of motivational tendencies: motivation and metamotivation (1971). *Motivation* itself refers to reducing tension by satisfying deficit states or lacks. It entails *D-needs* or *deficiency needs*, which arise out of the organism's requirements for physiological survival or safety, such as the need for food or rest, and motivate the individual to engage in activities that will reduce these drives. Thus, motivation and the D-needs are powerful determinants of behavior.

Metamotivation refers to growth tendencies. It entails *B-needs* or *being needs*, which arise out of the organism's drive to self-actualize and fulfill its inherent potential. B-needs do not stem from a lack or deficiency; rather, they push forward toward self-fulfillment. Their goal is to enhance life by enriching it. Rather than reducing tension, they frequently increase it in their quest toward ever-increasing stimuli that will facilitate life lived to the fullest.

Motivation and the D-needs take precedence over metamotivation and the B-needs. The deficiency needs must be satisfied first. An individual who is wondering where his or her next mouthful of food is going to come from is hardly able to be concerned with the esteem that he or she receives from other people or with spiritual goals like truth or beauty. Thus, the needs may be conceived as arranged in a hierarchy, in that the needs at the bottom must be satisfied before those at the top can be fulfilled.

In his hierarchy, Maslow (1970) describes five basic needs. In order of their strength they are: physiological needs; safety needs; belonging and love needs; self-esteem needs; and self-actualization needs. Each lower need must be satisfied before an individual can become aware of or develop the capacity to fulfill the needs above it. As each need is satisfied, the next higher order need develops and attains importance. Some individuals, because of their circumstances, find it very difficult to satisfy even the lowest needs. The higher one is able to go, however, the greater psychological health and self-actualization he or she will demonstrate.

FIGURE 11.1   Maslow's Hierarchy of Needs

Maslow suggests that human needs may be conceived of as arranged in a hierarchy in which the needs that stand at the bottom must be satisfied before those at the top can be fulfilled.

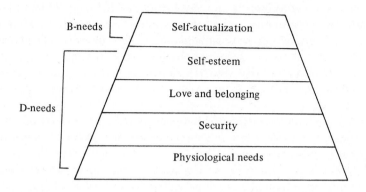

Physiological Needs   The strongest needs of all are the physiological needs. These needs are those that pertain to the physical survival and biological maintenance of the organism. They include the need for food, drink, sleep, oxygen, shelter, and sex. For most of us in America, physiological needs are satisfied almost automatically. However, in those cases where biological needs are not met for a protracted period of time, an individual will not be motivated to fulfill any other needs. The person who is really starving has no other interest than obtaining food. Several experiments and tales from real life have indicated the overwhelming behavioral effects produced by a lack of food, sleep, or other life-sustaining needs (1970). Only when these needs have been met is an individual capable of turning toward the satisfaction of higher needs. Gratification of these needs renders them less important and permits other needs to appear.

Safety Needs Safety needs refer to the organism's requirements for an orderly, stable, consistent, and predictable world within which to feel secure. Most normal, healthy adults have satisfied these needs, but they can be seen clearly in young children and neurotics. The young child, who is helpless and dependent, clearly prefers a certain amount of structured routine and discipline. The absence of these elements makes him or her anxious and insecure. Too much freedom is threatening because a child does not know what to do with it. The neurotic frequently behaves like the insecure child, compulsively ordering his or her world and avoiding strange or different experiences. In general, the mature adult, assured of the basic stability of his or her world, is open to the new and unexpected.

Belonging and Love Needs Once the physiological and safety needs are met, needs for love and belonging arise. The individual seeks affectionate and intimate relationships with other people. He or she needs to feel part of various reference groups, such as the family, neighborhood, gang, or a professional association. Maslow notes that such needs are increasingly more difficult to meet in our fluid and mobile American society in which families are splintered and individuals frequently do not live in the same place for very long. Such problems may account for the recent rise and interest in encounter groups, communes, and new styles of living together.

The need for love entails the ability to receive love and to give it. Clinical studies show that the absence of love withers growth and the fostering of human potential. Love is as necessary as food for a full human life. Those who have not received adequate love as children are unable to love adequately as adults.

Maslow did not identify love with sex, nor did he believe, as did Freud, that love is derived from sex. Sex in and of itself is a purely physiological need. While it is true that sex is one mode of expressing the need for love and to love, sex and love are not identical. Love, rather than being physiological, involves a healthy, mutual relationship of trust, in which each person is deeply understood and accepted.

Self-esteem Needs Maslow described two kinds of esteem needs— the need for respect from others and the need for self-respect. Self-esteem entails competence, confidence, mastery, achievement, independence, and freedom. Respect from others entails recognition, acceptance, status, and appreciation. When these needs are not met an individual feels discouraged, weak, and inferior. Healthy self-esteem is a realistic appraisal of one's capacities and has its roots in deserved respect from others. For most people, the need for regard from others diminishes with age because it has been fulfilled and the need for self-regard becomes more important.

Self-actualization Needs If the foregoing needs have been met, the needs for self-actualization emerge. These needs are difficult to describe because they are unique and vary from person to person. In general, self-actualization refers to the desire to fulfill one's highest potential. If an individual on this level does not fully exploit his or her talents and capacities, he or she is discontent and restless. In Maslow's words, "A musician must make music, an artist must paint, a poet must write, if he is to be at peace with himself" (1970). Each of us has different potentialities and capacities. There is no standard format for self-actualization; thus, specific forms of self-actualization differ from individual to individual.

Self-actualization is possible only if the lower needs have been sufficiently met so that they do not detract from nor engross a person's basic energies. Thus, a number of preconditions are necessary for self-actualization. First, the individual must not be preoccupied with physiological or safety needs. Second, he or she needs to feel secure in his or her relationships with others and in him- or herself. Lastly, self-knowledge is required so that one may recognize and seek to fulfill one's own abilities.

As a person moves higher in the hierarchy, he or she is less and less preoccupied with the deficiency needs (D-needs) and more and more concerned with the being needs (B-needs). For all intents and purposes, the basically satisfied person no longer has the needs for safety, love, or esteem, because these needs have been met. Rather than organizing their behavior toward tension reduction, individuals whose deficiency needs are satisfied continually seek new stimuli and opportunities for self-actualization. They may, in fact, seek states of increased optimal tension in order to enhance their self-fulfillment.

In metamotivation, B-needs take precedence over D-needs. The values or goals that arise out of B-needs are valued as ends in themselves rather than as means to other ends. One seeks truth for truth itself rather than its service to some other purpose. Thus, the B-needs or values connote states of "being" rather than states of "becoming." Some of these growth needs are: wholeness, perfection, completion, justice, aliveness, richness, simplicity, beauty, goodness, uniqueness, effortlessness, playfulness, truth, and self-sufficiency. In short, the motivation of those who are living on a B-level is radically discontinuous with that of those who are still striving to satisfy deficit states.

In addition to the hierarchy of needs just outlined, Maslow posits the needs to know and understand as important (1970). These form a small but powerful hierarchy of their own, in which the need to know is more potent and prior to the need to understand. Children, by nature, are curious; when their cognitive impulses are satisfied, they seek further comprehension and understanding. Maslow also mentions the importance of aesthetic needs. Some people actually become ill when they are confronted with ugliness. These needs are not sharply delineated from the needs of the earlier hierarchy, they overlap with them and are interrelated.

Maslow describes all the needs of the human being as *instinctoid* or inherent to human nature (1970). He recognizes that human beings cannot be said to have instincts in the sense that lower animals do. The term *instinct* generally refers to species-specific behaviors that are automatic and unlearned. Some of these are very complex: the spider builds sophisticated webs; the salmon goes upstream to spawn. These activities are not taught, they are innate. Whatever instincts human beings may possess are so heavily overlaid by learning that some psychologists suggest it is more accurate to say that human beings have no instincts whatsoever. Maslow points out, however, that as humans we have *instinctoid tendencies* or instinct remnants. While it would be incorrect to suggest that every female of the human species has a maternal instinct that immediately directs her in caring for her young, it is correct to observe that most human beings have a strong desire to tend and care for their children. We need to nurture and develop those skills and attitudes that will enable us to fulfill our instinctoid tendencies. In the human species, the instincts of the lower species are replaced or overlaid by drives, needs, and motives. Nevertheless, we need to become more sensitive to and aware of our instinctoid remnants so that we can identify and nourish them.

A number of clinical experiments have demonstrated that the needs that Maslow describes are essential for optimal human life and development. Studies of children in institutions where they do not receive adequate love and attention show that these children do not develop normally, in spite of the fact that all of their physical needs are met (Spitz, 1951). Maslow's own clinical experience showed that individuals who satisfy their basic needs are happier, healthier, and more effective, whereas those whose needs are frustrated display neurotic symptoms (1970). Furthermore, other clinicians, such as Karen Horney and Carl Rogers, have pointed out that given the appropriate conditions, the individual chooses to move forward and grow. From where does such a choice or impulse come, unless it is inherent in the individual? Psychologists speak of *species-specific* behavior, that is, an inborn tendency for members of a biological subgroup to behave in a certain way. Chickens tend to stratch for their food, whereas pigs root for it. Maslow suggests that the species-specific characteristics of human beings include the hierarchical needs and a drive toward self-actualization. Of course, for an adequate test of Maslow's theory that human needs are arranged in a hierarchy in which the satisfaction of lower needs leads to the emergence of higher needs, we would have to conduct extensive longitudinal studies (Maddi and Costa, 1972). Such studies have not yet been conducted.

EXERCISE:

Motivation

You can begin to assess the level of motivation that primarily influences you by carefully analyzing the reasons for your behavior. Over the course of an entire day, take careful note of all of your activities. Ask yourself why you did what you did and try to locate your motivation on Maslow's hierarchy of needs. Do not forget to pay attention to little things that occurred while you were in the middle of another activity. You may have interrupted your study time to prepare a snack, go to the bathroom, or talk with a friend. Try to observe which needs you met in a routine fashion and which demanded your full attention. While you may have found yourself motivated on all levels of Maslow's hierarchy, chances are that you satisfied your physiological and safety needs more or less automatically and concentrated your efforts on meeting other needs that are higher in the hierarchy. In addition, it would be informative to observe the activity of young children of various ages and note the different motivations governing their behavior in order to test Maslow's hypothesis that lower level needs become less pressing and higher level needs assume greater dominance with age.

THE STUDY OF SELF-ACTUALIZED PERSONS

Maslow has been described as preoccupied with healthy persons rather than with neurotics. He conducted an extensive, although informal, study of a group of persons whom he considered to be self-actualizers. His study was initially private and motivated by his own curiosity rather than by the normal demands of scientific laboratory research. Thus, it lacked the rigor and distinct methodology characteristic of strict empirical study. Nevertheless, the study generated such interest among other psychologists that Maslow felt it was wise to publish his findings (1970). He admits that his findings represent only an initial, tentative attempt to study optimum health, but they may serve as a focal point for further empirical research.

Maslow defined a *self-actualizing person* as one who is fulfilling him- or herself and doing the best that he or she is capable of doing. His subjects consisted of friends and personal acquaintances, public figures living and dead, and selected college students. Some of the figures included in his study are well known, such as Abraham Lincoln, Thomas Jefferson, Eleanor Roosevelt, Albert Einstein, and Albert Schweitzer. Others are not as well known and several of them were never identified publicly. In his initial study of three thousand college students, Maslow found only one individual who could be termed self-actualizing. He hypothesized that self-actualizing tendencies probably increase with age. Thereafter, he limited his studies of the college population to the most well adjusted 1 percent of the Brandeis College population. Not all of his subjects were deemed fully actualized. He divided them into categories: cases, partial cases, and potential or possible cases. Studying these individuals, their personalities, characteristics, habits, and abilities, enabled Maslow to develop his definition of optimal mental health.

Techniques of Inquiry and Research

In his study of self-actualized individuals, Maslow used whatever techniques appeared to be most appropriate to the particular situation.

In dealing with historical figures, he analyzed biographical material and written records. With live subjects, he also utilized in-depth interviews and psychological tests, such as the Rorschach inkblot test and the Thematic Apperception Test. He obtained global impressions from friends and acquaintances. In some cases, he found that he had to be rather surreptitious because a number of his subjects were suspicious of the intrusions that his research constituted on their privacy.

By ordinary standards of laboratory research, what Maslow did in his study was not research. He was quick to acknowledge that his investigation was not conducted along strict scientific lines. His descriptions were not based on standardized tests. Moreover, his definition of a self-actualized person tends to be a subjective one: the self-actualized person is he or she whom Maslow deems to be self-actualized. Nor were his conclusions obtained from controlled experimental situations. Nevertheless, Maslow points out that the canons of rigorous scientific procedures would not have encompassed or permitted research into the problems that he was studying. Further, he presented his data as only an initial observation and effort to study health as opposed to neurosis. He hoped that future studies would yield more information as to the nature of self-actualization and confirm or disconfirm his own hunches and expectations.

Characteristics of Self-Actualizers

Maslow lists several characteristics of self-actualized persons that emerged out of his study (1970). For simplicity, these characteristics may be grouped under four key terms or dimensions: awareness, honesty, freedom, and trust (1969).

Awareness Self-actualizers are characterized by awareness. They are aware of the inner rightness of themselves, of nature, and of the peak experiences of life. This awareness emerges in an *efficient perception of reality*. Self-actualizers are accurate in their perception of the world and comfortable in it. They can see through phoniness and assess the real motives of other people. They have a clearer perception of reality and realism in areas such as politics and religion, which permits them to cut through extraneous issues and recognize true ones. They have a higher acuity or sharpness of perception. Colors appear brighter and more vibrant to them than to the average person. They have a more efficient sense of smell. Their hearing is more precise. Studies have suggested that mental illness may entail impaired perceptions. The neurotic does not perceive the world as accurately as the healthy person. To some schizophrenics, the world is flat, merely two-dimensional, and colors are dull. For others, colors are enhanced. The distinction between health and illness appears to be cognitive as well as emotional.

Self-actualizers display a continued *freshness of appreciation*. They can appreciate again and again the basics of life. Each sunrise and sunset refreshes them anew, and each new flower is an event that never loses its miraculous quality. Familiarization does not lessen the miracle. Self-actualizers have no preconceptions of what things ought to be. They are open to experience and let each experience speak for itself.

The self-actualized person frequently experiences what Maslow refers to as a peak experience. A *peak experience* is an intensification of any experience to the degree that there is a loss of self or transcendence of self. These kinds of experiences are often termed mystical or religious, but Maslow emphasizes that they do not necessarily entail religion. A peak experience may be provoked by a secular event as well. Events that may be mundane and ordinary to others, such as viewing a work of art or reaching a sexual climax, may be the sparks that trigger or provoke a peak experience.

During a peak experience, the individual not only experiences an expansion of self, but also experiences a sense of unity and meaningfulness in his or her existence. For that moment, the world appears to be complete, and he or she is at one with it. After the experience is over, and the person has returned to the routine of everyday living, the experience lingers on. It has an illuminating quality that transforms one's understanding so that things do not seem to be quite the same afterwards.

Maslow distinguishes between "peakers" and "non-peakers." Non-peakers tend to be practical and efficient. Peakers tend to be more aesthetic. Maslow believes, however, that all human beings are potential peakers. Some people have peak experiences but they suppress them and therefore do not recognize them when they occur. In other cases, one may inhibit a peak experience, thereby preventing its occurrence.

EXERCISE:

Peak Experiences

The following checklist of characteristics of peak experiences can be useful to you in evaluating events that have happened in your own life.* It can also serve as a focal point for discussion with other people. Think of a meaningful experience that you have had. Does it fulfill any of the criteria listed below?

1. A peak experience is fully attended to with a high degree of concentration. The person is detached, passive, and objective, able to attend to the experience without having to evaluate, compare or judge it.

* Based on information from A. Maslow, *Religions, Values, and Peak Experiences*, Viking, New York, 1964. Used by permission of Kappa Delta Pi, A Honor Society in Education, owners of the copyright, Box A, West Lafayette, Indiana 47906.

2. The universe is perceived as an integrated united whole that is both meaningful and perfect.

3. The person is not conscious of time or space and there is a loss of ego or forgetfulness of self.

4. The person experiences wonder, humility, and reverence in the face of the experience. He or she is ready to listen and to learn. Negative emotions disappear. Some individuals experience a feeling of death and rebirth.

5. The dichotomies or conflicts of life tend to be transcended or resolved.

6. The person moves close to his or her real self, feels more like a person, and becomes more loving, accepting, spontaneous, and open.

7. The person feels responsible, an active creator who has a great deal of free will.

8. The peak experience is felt as self-validating and self-justifying.

9. After a peak experience, people characteristically feel lucky, fortunate, or graced. A common reaction is "I don't deserve this."

10. The peak experience leaves wholesome after effects that linger on.

Self-actualizers show a high degree of *ethical awareness*. They are clear about the distinction between good and evil. Self-actualizers have definite ethical standards, although their standards are not necessarily the conventional ones; rather, they know what for them is right and do it.

Self-actualizers are able to distinguish between the end goal that they are striving for and the means by which they are accomplishing it. For the most part, they are focused on ends rather than means. At the same time, they often consider as ends activities that are simply means for other people. They can enjoy the journey and appreciate it as well as the destination.

Honesty Self-actualizers are characterized by honesty. This honesty permits them to know their feelings and to trust them. They can trust the wide range of feelings—love, anger, and humor—present in interpersonal relations.

Self-actualizers have a *philosophical sense of humor* rather than an ordinary one. Most humor expresses hostility, superiority, or rebellion against authority. Common jokes and wisecracks do not strike the self-actualizer as funny. His or her humor is more closely allied to philosophy. It is essentially an ability to laugh at the ridiculousness of the human situation and to poke fun at our shared human pretensions. Such humor was characteristic of Abraham Lincoln, whose jokes were not at other peoples' expense. Such humor is spontaneous rather than planned. Often it cannot be repeated or retold. Maslow suggests that he once felt this humor in a room full of "kinetic art." It seemed to him to be a "humorous parody of human life, with the noise, movement, turmoil, hurry and bustle, all of it going no place" (1970).

Self-actualizers experience *social interest* or a deep feeling of kinship with humanity. Maslow borrows Adler's term *Gemeinschafts-gefuhl*, which means "brotherly love," to describe the identification with humanity that is expressed. While on occasions they may experience feelings of anger, impatience, or disgust, they have a general sense of identification, sympathy, and affection for the human race and all its members.

Self-actualizers form deep, profound *interpersonal relations*. However, they are highly selective and therefore have a small but close circle of friends. They have no need for admirers or large groups of disciples although at times they may attract such followers, creating a situation that they try to handle with tact. Their love of others may be described as a love-being-love rather than a love-deprived-love. They are involved with the being of the other person rather than with having the love of a person who cares for them. This love stems from a fullness of being rather than a state of deprivation and need.

Their love is not indiscriminate. At times they are quick to anger; they can speak harshly to others and express righteous indignation where a situation calls for it; yet their attitude is one of pity rather than attack. They react to the behavior rather than to the person.

Self-actualizers display a *democratic character structure*. They are free of prejudice, tolerant, and acceptant of all people regardless of their background. They listen and they learn from those who are able to teach them. They react to others on the basis of character rather than on the basis of race, creed, or social status.

Freedom Self-actualizers experience a high degree of freedom. This freedom permits them to be detached and to withdraw from the chaos that surrounds others. They are free to be independent, creative, and spontaneous.

Self-actualizers show a high degree of *detachment* and a *need for privacy*. They enjoy solitude and like to be alone. Many of us avoid being alone and compulsively seek the company of other people. Self-actualizers relish and require times when they can be by themselves. While they are not secretive, they often stand apart from other people. Maslow discovered that many of them did not particularly welcome his questions or think in terms of seeing a therapist, because they considered such activities a violation of their privacy.

This ability to be detached extends to other areas as well. It permits the self-actualizer to concentrate to a greater degree than the average person. While others may become excited and involved in the storm of things around them, self-actualizers remain above the battle, calm and unruffled.

Free to be themselves, self-actualizers are also free to let other people be. They are not afraid of letting other people be who they are. As parents, this means they have the ability to refrain from meddling with a child, because they like the way he or she is growing. They do not feel that they have to interfere when it is not necessary. They do not need to make decisions for or overprotect the child. They can permit the child to experience the consequences of his or her own behavior without overprotecting.

Self-actualizers are *autonomous and independent* of their physical and social environment. Motivated by growth rather than by deficiency, they do not need to depend on the world or others for their real satisfaction. Their basic needs and gratifications have been met, therefore, they are free to depend on their own development.

Autonomy also entails the ability to be a free choice agent and to govern oneself. Maslow suggests that self-actualizers have more free will than other people. Their activity stems from themselves rather than from their physical or social environment.

Maslow found that without exception all of his self-actualizers demonstrated *creativity*, originality, or inventiveness. This is not to say that they possess a special talent akin to that of a Mozart or a Picasso, rather, that they have a drive and a capacity to be creative. They do not necessarily write books, compose music, or produce art; instead, their creativeness is projected onto and touches whatever activity they undertake. The carpenter or clerk is creative in his or her work, adding a personalized touch to whatever he or she does. Self-actualizers even perceive the world creatively, as a child does, envisioning new and different possibilities.

Self-actualizers are *spontaneous,* simple, and natural. They are free to be what they are in any given moment. While their behavior is often conventional, they do not allow conventionality to hamper or prevent them from doing the things that they deem important. They are acutely aware of their feelings, thoughts, and impulses and do not hide them unless their expression would hurt others. Their codes of ethics are autonomous and individual, based on fundamentally accepted principles rather than on social prescriptions.

Trust Self-actualizers demonstrate a high degree of trust. They trust themselves, their mission in life, others, and nature.

Self-actualizers are generally *problem centered* rather than focused on themselves. They have a high sense of mission in life. They are task oriented and commit themselves to important tasks that must be done. They live and work within a wide frame of reference that does not permit them to get bogged down in what is petty or trivial. Problems outside themselves enlist most of their attention.

Self-actualizers demonstrate *acceptance of self, others, and nature.* They accept themselves without disappointment or regret. They recognize but are not particularly bothered by their shortcomings. This is not to say that they are smug or self-satisfied, rather that they accept their weaknesses and frailties as given. They are not embarrassed about the bodily processes that humans share with animals. The needs to eat, defecate, and express their sexuality do not distress them. They feel guilty about characteristics that they could and should improve on, but they are not overrun with neurotic guilt about many things. They can respect their own limitations, thus, their guilt arises from realistic rather than neurotic sources. In the same way, they can accept the necessities of reality and human life. As Maslow points out, they are not disturbed because water is wet, rocks are hard, and grass is green. They can live with these things. Healthy people do not feel bad about what is per se, but about differences between what is and what might realistically be.

Self-actualizers are not well adjusted in the normal sense of the term, which entails conformity with one's culture; they show *resistance to enculturation.* Essentially, they live in harmony with their culture, yet they remain somewhat detached from it. Often they are labeled "odd-ball," as they do not always react in the expected fashion. They generally conform in matters of dress, speech, and food, and other matters that are not of primary concern to them. But where an issue is important they are independent in their thought and behavior. This resistance to enculturation leads to their transcendence of any one particular culture. Thus their identification is with humanity as a whole rather than any one particular group.

Maslow acknowledged that the picture he draws of the self-actualized person is a composite. No one person that he studied possessed all of the above qualities. Each of them demonstrated the characteristics to varying and differing degrees. Furthermore, Maslow emphasized that self-actualizers are not perfect. They show many lesser human failings. They frequently have silly, wasteful, or thoughtless habits. At times they are vain and take too much pride in their achievements. They lose their tempers. Because of their concentration on their work, they often appear absent-minded, humorless, or impolite. At times their kindness toward others leads them to permit others to take undue advantage of them. At other times they may appear to be ruthless and inconsiderate in their relations with other people. Some times they are boring, even irritating. In sort, they are not perfect; yet, Maslow's definition of self-actualization did not imply perfection: it merely suggested that an individual was basically fulfilling him- or herself and doing the best that he or she was capable of doing.

The principles and values of self-actualizers differ from those of the average person. Perceiving the world in an essentially different manner, they are not threatened by it and do not need to adopt a morality of self-protection. Maslow suggests that a great deal of that which passes as moral and ethical standards may simply be "by-products of the pervasive pathology of the average" (1970). The conflicts and anxieties that threaten the average person are simply not present. Self-actualizers can welcome differences and need not be afraid of them. Their value systems are not organized around the values of the deficiency needs. These have been satisfied, so self-actualizers can devote themselves to the values that concur with the B-needs. Thus, at one and the same time, their values are universal and reflect shared humanity, but also distinct, individual, and unique.

Maslow concluded that self-actualization entails the ability to transcend and resolve dichotomies. The usual oppositions between heart and head, reason and emotion, body and mind, work and play that fragment most of us do not exist as antagonists, because they are seen as functioning together simultaneously. For example, the distinction between being selfish and unselfish is no longer bothersome. Self-actualizers can recognize that every act is at one and the same time selfish and unselfish. That which is done for the benefit of others is frequently that which benefits the self. Maslow suggests that in the self-actualized individual the id, ego, and superego work cooperatively together. Thus, healthy individuals are both quantitatively and qualitatively different from the average.

EXERCISE:

Rating of Self-Actualization

The following self-report questionnaire,* may be useful in helping you determine to what extent you perceive yourself as having self-actualizing characteristics. Study each characteristic carefully and then rate yourself on a scale of 1 to 5—1 (always like me) to 5 (never like me)—according to how you feel that you honestly fit into each description.

1. I tend to have a more efficient perception of   1   2   3   4   5
reality than other people, and I am comfortable in
the world.

2. I generally accept myself, others, and nature.   1   2   3   4   5

3. I am spontaneous and can do things on the spur   1   2   3   4   5
of the moment without the need for advance planning.

* Based on pp. 153–174 from *Motivation and Personality*, 2nd edition by Abraham H. Maslow. Copyright © 1970 by Abraham H. Maslow. Reprinted by permission of Harper & Row, Publishers, Inc.

4. I am more concerned with problems that involve society or others than with my own problems. 1 2 3 4 5

5. I enjoy and need to be alone. 1 2 3 4 5

6. Most of the time I believe that I am a free-choice agent, governed by my own free will and undetermined by outside agents. 1 2 3 4 5

7. I am able to appreciate simple things, such as a sunrise, flower, or baby, again and again. 1 2 3 4 5

8. I frequently experience "peak experiences" in which there is a loss of self. 1 2 3 4 5

9. In spite of occasional anger, impatience, or disgust, I experience a deep feeling of kinship with other humans. 1 2 3 4 5

10. I tend to have a few close friends rather than a large number of acquaintances. 1 2 3 4 5

11. I am tolerant, free of prejudice, and relate to people equally no matter what their race, religion or creed may be. 1 2 3 4 5

12. I have a clear and distinct sense of what is right and wrong for me. 1 2 3 4 5

13. My humor is generally nonhostile and philosophic. 1 2 3 4 5

14. I am original and perceive the world in a creative fashion. 1 2 3 4 5

15. While I generally conform to society, it does not frighten me to be independent in my thought and behavior. 1 2 3 4 5

Compute your average total score. Do not take your results too seriously. Remember that this is not a valid test as it has not been standardized nor compared with other measures of self-actualization. It is offered simply as an exploratory device. Also recall that in his initial study of three thousand college students, Maslow found only one whom he could describe as self-actualized. Nevertheless, it might interest you to note those areas where you rated yourself high and others where you felt you were low. Can you think of any reasons for these discrepancies? Also, you might wish to have a close friend or two rate you on the scale and consider the differences that emerge.

In order to develop a rating scale that would adequately measure the qualities inherent to self-actualization, the terms that are used to describe self-actualization would have to be operationally defined. We would need to specify exactly what behaviors constitute efficient perception, acceptance of self and others, spontaneity, and so forth. Maslow has not done this, although he has suggested ways in which his descriptions could be converted into hypotheses that could be empirically tested. It is important to remember that Maslow conceived of his work as merely preliminary. He recognized that considerably more scientific research needs to be done in the area of human potentialities.

For some years research on Maslow's concept of self-actualization was slow, since an adequate assessment device for measuring the variables of self-actualization was lacking. Recent years have seen the development of the Personal Orientation Inventory (POI) by Shostrom (1965). The POI is considered to be a reliable, valid measure of self-actualization and it has led to increased empirical research related to Maslow's constructs.

MASLOW'S COMMENTS ON THERAPY

Abraham Maslow was not a practicing therapist. He did not develop any new theory or method of therapy. However, he made several comments about therapy (1970) that are worth attention. Maslow made a distinction between basic needs therapy and insight therapy. *Basic needs therapy* refers to therapeutic procedures that meet the primary needs of people: safety, belonging, love, and respect. *Insight therapy* refers to the deeper, more protracted effort of self-understanding that leads to profound motivational changes. Maslow suggested that both forms of therapy are best understood by beginning with a study of the effects of those elements that gratify or thwart basic human needs.

Basic human needs can be satisfied only by other human beings. An individual cannot satisfy these needs by him- or herself, nor can they be satisfied by "trees, mountains, or even dogs" (1970). Harry Harlow's experimental research with monkeys demonstrated the importance of mothering or "contact comfort" (1959). When infant monkeys were deprived of this mothering, they failed to develop normally. Additional animal studies have stressed the importance of imprinting (Lorenz, 1952). *Imprinting* refers to the bond of attraction that develops between an offspring and usually its mother. Imprinting appears to be an inborn behavior pattern that develops at a particular time. If the mother is unavailable, an unnatural object of affection may replace the natural object. Thus, goslings have come to prefer a football or tin can over their natural mother if during the critical period only the artificial object was present. There is reason to believe that some form of imprinting may occur in human babies as well. While imprinting is not the same as love or loving, it is a process by which a love object is introduced. Studies have shown that a lack of adequate love during infancy may lead to deleterious effects later on. It is crucially important that during the first year of life a human infant develop a close bond of attachment to a significant other who has cared for the child (Mahler, 1976). Without such an attachment, infants show signs of apathy and later an inability to love. It appears that individuals are unable to express love unless they have first received it.

Thus, the first and primary criterion for therapy is a relationship between human beings. On this point Maslow concurs with Carl Rogers. Yet Maslow goes on to point out that the kind of relationship that satisfies our basic needs is not a unique relationship, but one that shares the fundamental qualities found in all good human relationships. The relationship of therapy is not at its base unique, because it shares the primary characteristics of all good human relationships.

What is needed is a more careful study of all of those relationships that foster and fulfill the satisfaction of our needs of safety, belongingness, love, respect, and ultimately, self-actualization. A constructive marriage, close friendship, or healthy parent-child relationship permit these satisfactions to occur. Thus, every human relationship is potentially a therapeutic one. One task of psychology is to try to identify and foster those qualities that make for good human relations as opposed to poor ones. We can then foster those relationships that enable us to grow.

Maslow criticizes Freud for limiting his discussion of the relationship that emerges in analysis to the elements of transference. By failing to recognize the underlying relationship between analyst and patient and by focusing almost entirely on the elements of transference, Freud failed to perceive the healthy character of the relationship. In effect, Freud suggested that the only feelings a patient could have toward the analyst were those of a positive or negative transference. In return, the only emotions an analyst could have toward the patient were those of countertransference. Thus, in Freud's discussion of analysis, the only feelings that emerge in the relationship are sick or neurotic ones. Freud failed to articulate the fact that it is only because a basic healthy relationship underlies the process of analysis in the first place that elements of transference can arise, be sustained, analyzed, and worked through.

If the qualities of relationship that emerge in psychotherapy are the qualities that are found in any good, healthy relationship, we should look more closely at those everyday therapeutic happenings that occur in good marriages, good friendships, and good jobs. We ought to try to expose ourselves and others to these kinds of situations. It also follows that each human being is potentially a therapist who can function in a therapeutic way insofar as he or she can enter into these kinds of relationships that are based on love and respect. We should approve of, encourage, and teach these fundamentals of sound human relationships and foster the development of lay psychotherapy.

Hand in hand with Maslow's increased respect of the importance of lay psychotherapy goes a clear recognition of the necessity for trained practitioners. There are times when the normal therapeutic processes of life fail, and insight therapy, conducted by a trained psychotherapist, is irreplaceable. A person who is severely ill may not be able to benefit from basic needs therapy. He or she may have given up trying to satisfy his or her basic needs in favor of satisfying neurotic ones. In such a situation, when basic need gratification is offered, the patient may not be able to receive it. If the patient is offered affection, he or she may be afraid of it, misinterpret it, and reject it. In these instances professional insight therapy is mandated.

Insight therapy is not only invaluable for those neurotics for whom basic needs therapy is no longer helpful; it is also a valuable method by which relatively healthy persons can acquire insight and facilitate their own self-actualization. Unfortunately, psychoanalysis and psychotherapy have not become as effective or active forces of individual and cultural self-understanding as they have the potential to be. The emphasis, particularly in America, on therapy as a medical method of treatment has prevented its entrance into other fields. Interestingly, Freud did not originally conceive of analysis as simply a method for treating neurotics. That, he wrote, "is only one of its applications, the future will perhaps show that it is not the most important one" (1927). Freud also recommended that since it would be impossible to analyze each and every parent, teachers might undergo analysis in order to avoid passing on unconscious conflicts to children. Maslow picks up this suggestion, pointing out that if relatively healthy people are deeply touched by therapy, it is all the more important to invest our energies on them, particularly if they happen to be in key therapeutic positions, as teachers, social workers, and physicians. An increased proportion of time spent in didactic or training analyses, such as are presently undertaken by potential psychoanalysts, could have a profound effect on society. Additional considerations ought also to be given to furthering group therapy and personal growth groups.

EVALUATION AND IMPLICATIONS

Maslow's portrait of the self-actualized person is optimistic, generating a great deal of confidence in human potential. Nevertheless, some critics suggest that his picture may be simplistic, neglecting the arduous processes that are actually entailed in growth and development. It is clear from Maslow's description that the number of people who actually achieve self-actualization is relatively small, less than 1 percent of the population. Obviously, the possibility of self-actualization is limited or even closed to large numbers of the human population, whose environment has yet to meet the lesser needs depicted in Maslow's hierarchy. Concepts such as the self-actualized person may be elitist and apply only to a select few. More attention needs to be given to the processes within the individual and society that permit self-actualization to flower. In Maslow's words, "How good a human being does society permit?" (1970).

Maslow's discussion of self-actualization is descriptive rather than functional. He describes the characteristics of the self-actualized individual, but he does not tell us how these characteristics may be concretely acquired. He suggests that in the self-actualized individual dichotomies are transcended. In Freudian terms, the id, ego, and superego work together cooperatively. But is this picture realistic? Perhaps it is simplistic to hope to reduce all conflict, and more justified to assume that we can merely strengthen the ego, enabling it to be more effective in its executive functions. Freud, we recall, was pessimistic about reducing human conflict. Still, the very presence of self-actualizing individuals suggests that we can improve our human condition.

Maslow clearly points in a direction away from that of pure science and into the broader outlines of philosophy. He acknowledges that his portrait of self-actualization is part of a larger evolving philosophy of human nature. He reminds us that all too frequently we conceive of science as an autonomous method that exists in and of itself, governed by its own distinct rules, and totally divorced from human beings or human values. We forget that human beings create science, establish its goals, and use its technology for their own human purposes. Thus, Maslow again reminds us that it is misleading to think science is value free, since its procedures are employed for human purposes. One may use science to create mechanistic robots out of human nature or one may use it to increase human freedom and potential. Maslow suggests that we should conceive of science as a problem-solving activity rather than a specific technology. Only the goals and ends of science can dignify or validate its methods.

SUGGESTIONS FOR FURTHER READING

Maslow's best-known work is *Motivation and Personality* (Harper & Row, 1970), which presents his theory of personality and describes in full his concepts of the hierarchy of needs and self-actualization. Originally published in 1954, it was completely revised shortly before his death. *Religions, Values, and Peak Experiences* (Viking, 1964) presents Maslow's argument that religion be viewed as a normal, potentially healthy phenomenon and studied scientifically. In this work he outlines his concept of peak experiences, although he does not limit them to religious experiences. Nevertheless, Maslow points out the need of human beings for spiritual expression, and he suggests that science can assist us in understanding this need and its expressions. *Towards a Psychology of Being* (D. Van Nostrand, 1968) is a collection of papers in which Maslow discusses his theory of B-values as well as peak experiences and self-actualization; the book also makes clear Maslow's humanistic stance as opposed to those who present a mechanistic or negative picture of human nature. Maslow's last work, *The Farther*

Reaches of Human Nature (Viking, 1971), is a cumulative effort to integrate his theory with the latest developments in science. It covers topics such as biology, creativity, cognition, and synergy.

Two readable secondary sources on Maslow's thought are Frank Goble, *The Third Force: The Psychology of Abraham Maslow* (Grossman, 1970) and Colin Wilson, *New Pathways in Psychology: Maslow and the Post Freudian Revolution* (Taplinger, 1972).

PART VI

Cognitive Theories

The term *cognition* refers to the process of knowing. The most recent theories of personality are cognitive theories, which emphasize the processes by which an individual becomes aware of the world and makes judgments about it. The research and theoretical assumptions of cognitive theories attempt to understand the mental activities involved in perception, learning, remembering, thinking, problem solving, and decision making. Cognitive theories stress that an individual's behavior is not simply determined by the environment, but also, and primarily, by his or her attitudes, expectations, and beliefs.

The recognition of cognitive elements in personality structure and development is not new. Cognitive aspects have played a role in many of the theories we have considered. The early structuralists, under Wundt, used introspection in order to understand the contents of the mind. Sigmund Freud's discussion of how a person often distorts reality in his or her efforts to cope with it reveals an underlying concern with cognitive issues. More recently, in the psychoanalytic movement, ego psychoanalysts have emphasized the processes of cognition and perception in their articulation of ego development. Social learning theories reintroduced cognitive elements that had been dismissed by Watson and Skinner. They pointed out the need to interpose cognitive processes between a stimulus and a response in order to understand behavior. In Bandura and Walters's theory, mediational processes serve as intermediaries between the environment and overt behavior. Julian Rotter emphasized the subjective expectations that inform a person's response to a situation. Humanist theories demonstrated a high degree of concern with cognitive matters. Their phenomenological orientation led them to emphasize that an event in the external world cannot influence an individual and his or her behavior until it becomes a part of his or her conceptual framework.

What distinguishes the cognitive theories from other theories that we have studied is their stress on cognition as the primary factor in personality development. While other theorists have recognized the importance of cognition, they did not make it the mainstay of their theory. Sigmund Freud emphasized emotional processes of the heart rather than intellectual processes of the head. The behaviorists' concern was primarily with the end product or final overt responses to the environment rather than with intermediate subjective processes that led to the behavior. The analysis of environmental stimuli was a more major concern. Cognitive theories, on the other hand, view cognition as the primary factor governing personality and behavior. It is this factor that they seek to clarify.

Cognitive theorists pay little or no attention to many functions of personality that have concerned other theorists. They have little or nothing to say about drives, needs, emotion, motivation, or behavior. Nevertheless, they include these factors by perceiving them as elements or aspects of personality that are controlled by the higher cognitive processes. Obviously, basic biological needs must be met before a person can engage in higher cognitive functions, but it is more fruitful to begin our personality theorizing at the point where lower needs have been satisfied and to concentrate on the higher order functions that distinguish human nature and behavior.

Cognitive theorists share many assumptions with humanist theorists. They too are strongly influenced by the phenomenological approach in psychology and stress the importance of subjective human awareness and perception. For the most part, they are not concerned with objective reality, rather, in the way in which a person perceives, understands, and interprets the world in which he or she lives. Cognitive theorists also view the individual as active rather than passive in transactions with the environment. The person is seen as a creative, experiencing human being who is living in the present and subjectively responding to current perceptions and relationships. The emphasis again is on the present rather than the past. Further, cognitive theories are developmental theories since they emphasize that cognitive processes develop through growth and maturation. They are also discontinuity theories because they view advanced levels of cognitive development as qualitatively different reorganizations and advances over earlier stages.

Two earlier psychologists who helped to foster cognitive theory are Donald Hebb (1904–   ) and Heinz Werner (1890–1964). Neither Hebb nor Werner was a personality theorist, but each was instrumental in bringing to the fore the importance of the study of cognitive processes and development.

Hebb argued that an infant's perception is not immediate, as was previously supposed, but builds up gradually. Initially, the infant does not perceive specific objects, only global unities. With time, perceptual differentiation emerges, and the child can make specific identities. Hebb's classic work, *The Organization of Behavior* (1949), suggested a two-phase process of mental development and encouraged psychologists to stay abreast of and tie in their theories with the latest findings in neurophysiology. His work presages contemporary interest in that area. Hebb also stimulated research into the effects of early deprivation and enrichment on later perceptual development. He viewed early experience as crucial for determining subsequent behavior, suggesting that it shapes the direction of later perception much as early pruning and staking determine the growth of a tree.

Heinz Werner was deeply committed to the study of principles of development as a dimension of primary concern in understanding the individual. Through development, he suggested, an individual moves from syncretic ("global") perceptions of the world to clearly articulated constructs. Initially, the infant's perception of his or her environment is vague and diffuse. With experience, the child learns to differentiate among specific objects and their component parts. These parts are then reintegrated into a new and more meaningful whole. Development, therefore, is a process of increasing differentiation and hierarchical integration. The progression is from whole, to part, to more meaningful whole.

Werner was interested in all types of development. He suggested that development not only entails the movement from global to articulated perceptions, but also the movement from rigidity to flexibility in thought and action, as well as the progression from living in an uncertain, chaotic world of infancy to dwelling in a stable, dependable one. Development, Werner maintained, is multilinear; it occurs on many different lines of functioning at the same time, though not always at the same level. A person may be sophisticated in one area of development yet primitive in another. Thus, at times we see intelligent adults take refuge in rigid or ritualistic behavior because they have not yet made the transition to a stable world in which behavior can be flexible and varied. Werner agreed with Freud that adult personality may be seen as stratified or arranged in layers according to different stages in development. What happens during each stage is influenced by what has preceded it. In his interest in all types of development, Werner's concerns were broader than those of the cognitive theorists who follow and conceive of development primarily in terms of intellectual progression.

Part VI concentrates on the viewpoints of two contemporary cognitive theorists. Jean Piaget, a Swiss psychologist whose work is increasingly finding recognition in the United States, has extensively studied the process of how children come to know and understand the world. George Kelly, an American psychologist whose work is also being given increased attention, introduced the notion of the person as a scientist who develops personal constructs in order to understand, make predictions, and act on the world.

CHAPTER 12

Jean Piaget's Theory of Cognitive Development

Jean Piaget is not generally classified as a personality theorist; he is thought of primarily as a child psychologist or educator. Piaget himself prefers to be identified as a genetic epistemologist. *Genetic epistemology* refers to the study of how knowledge is acquired, with an emphasis on the genetic component, and Piaget is, indeed, best known for his theory of knowledge acquisition. For over four decades, Piaget and his colleagues in Geneva have been pursuing a clinical study of children's thought processes. Nevertheless, Piaget's methods of studying knowledge and his ideas about cognitive processes are attracting increased attention from personality theorists who believe that the study of cognitive elements is important for understanding personality. His comprehensive and extensive theory of the development of intelligence is beginning to be recognized as a valuable source of information for understanding the development and structure of the human personality. For these reasons, the inclusion of Piaget in a text on personality theory appears justified and wise.

BIOGRAPHICAL BACKGROUND

Jean Piaget was born in 1896 in Neufchatêl, Switzerland. He attributes his realistic orientation to life and his ability to work systematically and meticulously to his father, a writer and authority on medieval literature. Piaget describes his mother as basically kind, energetic, and intelligent,

but somewhat neurotic. Her poor mental health made family life difficult, and the young Piaget adjusted to his unfortunate situation at an
early age by imitating his father and taking "refuge in both a private
and a non-fictuous world."

As a youth, Piaget was intellectually precocious. His first paper,
an article describing a rare albino sparrow, was published when he was
ten years old. Afterwards he wrote to the director of the local museum
of natural history and received permission to study that gentleman's extensive collection of birds, fossils, and shells. Piaget was still in high
school when, on account of his noteworthy publications, he was asked to
serve as the curator at the Museum of Natural History in Geneva. Reluctantly, he declined the offer as he still had two more years to study
for his diploma.

Piaget's undergraduate and graduate work were taken at the University of Neufchatêl where he received his Ph.D. in zoology and wrote
his thesis on mollusks. While he was interested in the natural sciences,
Piaget's interests were expanding widely into other areas, such as psychology and philosophy.

After receiving his doctorate, Piaget felt somewhat lost and restless.
Experimental laboratory work seemed irrelevant to the basic problems
that interested him. He was concerned with the issue of epistemology,
the problem of how we know. The psychoanalytic emphasis on solitary
meditation struck him as dangerous. He was not sure what direction he
wanted to follow. In a stroke of good fortune, however, he had an opportunity to go to Paris and work at the laboratory in the grade school

where Albert Binet had developed his famous intelligence test, the forerunner of the well-known Stanford-Binet. While testing children in the laboratory, Piaget found that he was fascinated with the reasoning processes of his young subjects. He was particularly interested in understanding their wrong answers. At Binet's school, Piaget developed his own method of research, a method that he further pursued as director of studies at the J. J. Rousseau Institute in Geneva. Through careful questioning and study of the responses of young children, Piaget was able to discover several principles of mental growth.

Initially, Piaget's findings were not very well received, particularly in America. He was viewed as a peculiar old man, wearing a blue beret and smoking a meerschaum pipe, who tramped along the shores of Swiss lakes and frequently stopped to converse with young children. He was criticized for his methods of talking to children, his results, and his interpretations of them.

It was the efforts of educators, men such as Jerome Bruner and David Rapaport, who were seeking new curricula and curricula materials in the 1950s and 1960s, that first brought Piaget's work to the serious attention of American scholars. Piaget's concept of the child as an active participant in learning was seen by these astute men to have radical potentialities for education. In 1969, Piaget received an award from the American Psychological Association for his substantial contribution to psychology.

Piaget is an indefatigable worker who follows a strict, self-imposed schedule. His research has been continuous, and his writings fill more than eighteen thousand pages in over thirty books and hundreds of articles. He has taught at the University of Geneva and has traveled to address groups on child development and other issues. His contributions have spanned the fields of biology, philosophy, logic, psychology, and education. In America, his impact is only beginning to be felt. His influence on contemporary psychology may eventually be seen to be second only to that of Sigmund Freud.

COGNITIVE DEVELOPMENT

Jean Piaget considers the child an active agent in trying to understand and comprehend the world. The child's mind is not passive, rather, it is active in its efforts to structure and make sense out of experiences. Piaget points out that children have ideas about the world that they have neither inherited nor learned, as these terms are commonly understood. Young children, for example, believe that all moving things, even inanimate objects, are alive. Such notions cannot be inborn, because they are revised as the child gets older. Nor can they have been learned, because adults characteristically do not deliberately teach such false notions to children. Piaget suggests that the child's ideas involve both mental structures and experience. The behaviors of children should not be seen as merely the repetition of reinforced movements, but appreciated for the novel inventions that they are.

As a biologist, Piaget is impressed by the continual adaption that mollusks and other organisms make to their environment. He conceives of human intellectual development in a similar fashion. He considers cognitive acts as ways in which the mind organizes and adapts to its environment. The intellectual activity of an organism is simply one aspect of the fuller process of adaptation, whereby an organism through its functioning adjusts to the world in which it lives.

The organizing mental structures of the mind are neither fixed at birth nor learned, they develop in a sequence of maturational stages or mechanisms. This is to say that in growing from infant thought processes to mature logical thought, the child passes through a series of stages at which times he or she employs different mechanisms. While the stages are not fixed rigidly by age, each level presupposes the preceding one and could not occur without it. Thus, no child can skip any stage, as each mechanism requires the accomplishments of the one before it. Each mechanism is more complex as it reconstructs the earlier one and surpasses it. Thus, according to Piaget, each subsequent stage is more adequate and adaptive than the one that went before it.

Piaget uses the word *schema* to refer to the child's cognitive structure or framework of thought. Just as the stomach is a body structure that enables animals to digest their food, a schema is a mental structure that enables the intellect to adapt to its environment. Simply stated, schemas are categories by which people organize and understand the world. They permit us to make distinctions and to generalize among varying stimuli. Initially, the young child has only a few schemas by which to understand the world. Gradually these are increased. Adults employ a manifold variety of schemas in their efforts to comprehend the world.

As children move from one stage to another, two primary mechanisms assist in the development of schemas. *Assimilation* refers to the ability to incorporate new ideas, objects, and experiences into the existing framework of one's thought. *Accommodation* refers to the ability to change one's schema in order to introduce new ideas, objects, or experiences. The author's young son, trying to identify a squirrel, quizzically asked, "Kitty?" His activity illustrates both assimilation and accommodation. He was groping to find an appropriate label for a new stimuli. Since the squirrel seemed to approximate a cat, that was the best label that he could come up with. At the same time, his query indicated that while he perceived similarities between the squirrel and a cat, he also sensed that there were differences. His query initiated the process of accommodation and the learning of a new label, namely, "squirrel."

When a previous schema is no longer adequate, children change their schema in order to incorporate new experiences. The processes of assimilation and accommodation assist children in adapting to the world by restoring cognitive balance or equilibrium between their framework of thought and their experience. At first, children seek to assimilate new experiences into their existing frame of reference. When they are unsuccessful, they change their frame of reference in order to include the new experience.

Piaget suggests that the earliest schemas of children are reflexive in nature, involving the senses and bodily activity. Young infants actively explore the environment with their mouths. When a new toy or object is given to a baby, it is immediately placed in the mouth. These simple reflexive schemas are the forerunners of later, more sophisticated mental schemas.

Children's intellectual activity during the first eighteen months is described by Piaget as *sensorimotor*. At this time, infants do not use language or symbols; instead, they explore the world through their actions. A study of their behaviors clearly conveys to us a concept of their intelligence. A one-year-old who wants to play with a toy that lies out of reach on a blanket will pull the blanket toward his or her body in order to get the toy. This act, which Piaget terms a *schema of action* to distinguish it from later more complex *schemas of operation*, is, while simple, nevertheless an intelligent act. A schema of action is a general sensorimotor response that is employed to resolve a number of different problems. A schema of operation is a complex function whereby an individual operates on the world by using concepts and symbols. The infant employs many different schemas of action—sucking, biting, hitting, banging, pulling, shaking, and kicking—in an effort to explore the world.

Whereas during the first eighteen months, children's intellectual activity is sensorimotor and preverbal, afterwards their intellect may be described as *conceptual* or operational, because they make use of symbols and language. They operate on the world rather than simply act on it. In their sensorimotor activity, children seek practical solutions to immediate problems. As they progress into conceptual stages, they begin to seek knowledge as such and increasingly use words and symbols to direct their activity and understand their world. Piaget suggests that conceptual intelligence occurs in three basic stages: preoperational (18 months to 7 years), which is marked by the emergence of language; concrete operations (7 to twelve years), which is marked by reliance on specific objects; and formal operations (12 years and older), which entails the ability to employ logic and abstract ideas (1963).

The Sensorimotor Period

Piaget divides the sensorimotor period into six developmental substages (1952). The first four generally arise during the first year and the remaining two usually occur during the first six months of the second year. Each stage is marked by new patterns of behavior that clearly distinguish it from the preceeding stage. In his writings, Piaget discusses the general behavioral characteristics and the child's concept of objects and causality for each stage.

Reflexes (Birth to 1 Month) The earliest behavior of infants is reflexive. Piaget points out, however, that reflexes like sucking, grasping, crying, and other body movements are not simply automatic responses to external stimuli. Frequently an infant initiates reflexive activity. Thus, newborn babies often make sucking movements even though no nipple is present. Within a short period of time, infants learn, through practice, to suck more efficiently. Thus, the first substage is marked by the more effective use of reflexive activity as a means of adapting to the environment.

Piaget describes the young infant as egocentric. The term *egocentrism* means that an individual sees the world only from his or her point of view and is unaware that other points of view exist. Egocentrism in the newborn means that the infant is not aware of him- or herself as a subject in a world of objects. Infants cannot distinguish between themselves and their environment. Nor can newborns differentiate between experiences that arise within their bodies and those that arise outside it. While called egocentric, the newborn, strictly speaking, does not yet have an ego or any awareness of self. The newborn is egocentric—without an ego. Piaget believes that children's awareness of external things as objects and themselves as subjects develops slowly out of sensorimotor experience. Since they lack any concept of objects, infants also lack any awareness of cause-and-effect relationships. In effect, the child must, in time, construct his or her own self, the world of objects, and the concept of causality (1954).

Primary Circular Reactions (1 to 4 Months) During the second substage of sensorimotor development behaviors become more deliberate, and infants begin to re-enact certain activities for the pleasure that they provide. Through close observation of his son Laurent, Piaget was able to notice a steady progression in hand-mouth coordination, in which the child learned to successfully place his hand in his mouth and gradually to suck simply the thumb rather than the whole hand (1952). During this period, infants become more adept at sucking, moving their hands, following objects with their eyes, and discriminating among sounds. Although infants appear to be aware of objects at this time, they do not seem to notice any effect that their own activity has on the external world. In this sense, their behaviors lack intentionality. Actions are performed for their own sake rather than oriented toward external goals.

Secondary Circular Reactions (4 to 8 Months) During the third substage, behaviors increasingly are directed toward objects and events outside of the infant's own body. At this time infants repeat behaviors that have an interesting effect in their environment. Whereas in the second sub-stage, the child re-enacted responses for the intrinsic pleasure that the activities themselves gave, at this time he or she engages in responses in order to see the change that takes place in the environment. The behavior here is clearly more intentional and involves a growing relationship to external objects. The baby who discovers, by accident, that he or she can move a mobile hanging over the crib by pulling a cord will repeatedly pull the cord and watch the swinging mobile.

These behaviors show that the infant is developing a preliminary concept of objects. Infants begin to recognize that objects exist apart from themselves and that their behaviors can have an effect on those objects. They also begin to anticipate the position of moving objects, looking in the direction in which a falling object is going to land. These behaviors reveal a greater sophistication in object consciousness than existed previously.

Coordination of Secondary Reactions (8 to 12 Months) During the fourth substage, children begin to use responses that were developed earlier to achieve specific goals. Babies, at this time, push or kick obstacles to get to the toys behind them, not just to see the object displaced. Their activities become means to an end rather than ends in themselves. They demonstrate originality in their ability to employ behaviors previously mastered in new situations. They coordinate earlier secondary reactions, such as pushing or grasping a toy, to achieve specific goals.

Objects appear to have a greater degree of permanence for infants of this age than they had before. Infants in this phase no longer act as if an object has evaporated when it is hidden; instead, they begin to look for it. A rattle hidden under a blanket is quickly retrieved. Babies also begin to realize that other people and objects in their environment can be sources of activity. A child will grasp the hand of a parent and gesture for the parent to repeat an activity. Younger infants behave as if no actions begin outside of their own bodies.

Tertiary Circular Reactions (12 to 18 Months) At about one year of age, children begin to vary their activities in their efforts to explore the environment. They deliberately change their manipulation of a toy or an object in order to see the different consequences that their various actions will have on the object. They drop toys from varying heights and examine the different ways in which they fall. In this way one-year-olds discover, through trial-and-error experimentation, new ways to solve problems and deal with external objects. If a problem is unresolvable by one activity, the child will experiment with another. Such behaviors represent an important step in intellectual problem solving, providing the basis for later more sophisticated activity.

Also, at about one year of age, children begin to demonstrate clearly that they are aware of the permanence of objects. If an object is hidden in sequence in more than one place, a child is able to find it in the last place where it was hidden. Previously, if a rattle, first hidden under a red pillow, was subsequently hidden under a blue pillow, the child would look for it only under the red pillow. This was true even though the act of hiding the rattle under the blue pillow was done before the child's very eyes. Thus, the one-year-old learns to search for objects in more than one place. Objects are also recognized and employed more clearly as the source of distinctive activities that occur outside of the self.

Mental Combinations (18 to 24 Months) During the sixth substage, children move from sensorimotor intelligence to conceptual intelligence. Children begin to think before they act and to consider the effects of their actions. This is to say that children begin to internally represent objects in their minds and solve problems symbolically before they act. Piaget reports the following observation of his daughter Lucienne after he had hidden a watch chain in a matchbox (1952). Lucienne looked at the narrow slit of the slightly opened box and thoughtfully opened and shut her mouth several times. Then she pulled at the small opening of the box in order to make it bigger and obtain the chain. Lucienne was mentally thinking about possible ways to solve her problem before acting on it. In order to do this, she must have been able to imagine or internally represent an event without actually enacting it. This ability to internalize combinations can result in dramatic insights and sudden comprehension. The child can now solve problems internally.

Representation enables children to locate objects that they have not seen being hidden. Clearly, then, children by this age know that objects have permanence. Children of this level are no longer bound to their own immediate perceptions, they are able to represent objects in their minds. Through representation, children can also begin to predict a cause-and-effect relationship. When Piaget's son Laurent could not open the garden gate because it was blocked by a chair, he quickly went around the wall, moved the chair, and triumphantly opened the gate (1954). Thus, object concept and the awareness of causality are deeply strengthened by the ability to represent objects.

The child at the age of two is cognitively very different from the infant at birth. He or she internalizes activity rather than simply relying on overt actions. From this point onward, intellectual development occurs primarily in the conceptual sphere and is symbolic rather than motor.

EXERCISE:

Sensorimotor Activities

The reader can best appreciate the value of Piaget's work by duplicating some of his observations with young children. The following informal tests of infant behavior can help to illustrate the concepts of objects and object permanence. Observe infants in each of the age levels indicated, carry out the suggested procedure, and observe and compare the baby's response with the anticipated response.

1. One to two months
Procedure: move an object across the infant's line of vision and then let it pass out of his or her line of vision.
Anticipated response: the infant's eyes will follow the stimulus until it goes out of the line of vision. When it is out of sight, the infant will not look for it.

2. Three to six months
Procedure: hold an object within the infant's visual field and then place it outside the visual field.
Anticipated response: the infant will grab at the object which he or she can see but will not reach for the object outside of the visual field.

3. Four to eight months
Procedure: drop an object in front of the infant.
Anticipated response: the infant will follow the object's fall and search for the object on the floor.

4. Nine to twelve months
Procedure: permit the infant to watch you hide an object under a handkerchief. After the infant has found it, hide it again, but then secretly remove the object so that when the handkerchief is taken away the object is not there. After observing the infant's response, hide the object again under the handkerchief, remove it, and hide it under another handkerchief.
Anticipated response: the infant will reach for the object under the handkerchief and will show surprise when it is not present. The infant will continue to look for the object under the first handkerchief but will not look under the second one.

5. Twelve to eighteen months
Procedure: repeat the procedure for nine to twelve months.
Anticipated response: the child will look for the object under the second handkerchief or in the last place that it was hidden.

6. Eighteen to twenty-four months
Procedure: show the child a small toy animal in a box. Place the animal and the box under a handkerchief. Remove the box but do not remove the animal.
Anticipated response: the child will look for the animal under the handkerchief.
Procedure: Show the child a coin in your hand. Close your hand and hide the coin under a handkerchief. After observing the child's response, further complicate the test by placing the coin in your hand and your closed hand under a series of objects. Leave the coin under the last object.

Anticipated response: when the child does not find the coin in your hand, he or she will look under the handkerchief. The child will also be able to follow your sequential movements and search for the coin under the series of objects.

Most children and infants of the above ages will react according to the anticipated responses. If the child you have selected differs from the anticipated response, try the experiment listed for the age level just above or below. The child's behaviors should give you a pretty clear indication of his or her sensorimotor development in terms of object concept and permanence.

Preoperational Thought (2 to 7 Years)

The cognitive activity of a child at two is qualitatively very different from that of an infant at birth. Reflexive activity has been replaced with conscious, deliberate, thought-out problem-solving activity. In the course of the preoperational stage, children increase their ability to represent objects and events within their minds and they become less dependent on sensorimotor activities for solving problems. Piaget does not divide the stage of preoperational thought into further substages; instead, he talks about different kinds of activities and thoughts that the child is or is not able to master.

Symbols and Language The use of symbols marks the beginning of preoperational thought. At first, children's symbols may be abbreviated forms of actions, like Lucienne's opening and closing of her mouth to indicate the opening and closing of the match box. Later, children use objects as symbols of other things in their play. A doll becomes a live baby, a stick is a gun, and a block of wood can be a car. The phenomenon of language emerges side by side with the use of symbols. The development of language is important because it enables children to use words as symbols for objects and ideas.

Initially, children use holophrases, or one-word sentences, to express their thoughts. By age four, however, most children have a marked sophistication in the use of language. They have mastered many of the rules that govern the construction of words and sentences in their native tongue and they can speak in full and complex sentences.

According to Piaget, the most significant accomplishment during the preoperational period is this emergence of language. Language is not a prerequisite of cognitive development, because the basic elements of intelligent behavior have already occurred during the sensorimotor period prior to the child's ability to speak. Indeed, Piaget believes that sensorimotor cognitive development is a necessary prerequisite for language (1967). However, the development of language, once it emerges, greatly facilitates cognitive development and enhances its speed and range.

Egocentrism During the preoperational period, the speech of children displays clear indications of *egocentrism*, concern with the self and its own needs rather than others. Preschool-age children frequently make no real effort to communicate with other people, nor do they show concern over whether or not they are understood. It is as though children of this age speak to themselves in the presence of other people and do not care whether or not other people hear the words. Thus, groups of preschool-age children engage in what Piaget calls *collective monologues*. Each child talks about a different subject: her dog, his birthday, her truck, and so on, at the same time, and none shows any distress that the conversation is not reciprocal.

Egocentric speech never predominates, but as children become older their speech becomes markedly more *sociocentric* or communicative. They begin to consider the listener and the listener's viewpoint, and they attempt to influence or exchange ideas with other people. Egocentric speech demonstrates how young children are prisoners of their own points of view. They are unable to see how things are looked at or understood by someone else. They operate as if their own ways of observing, experiencing, and behaving are the only ways. Their egocentrism is not selfish or intentional because they are unaware that other points of view exist. According to Piaget, the process of cognitive growth entails losing this egocentric stance and becoming able to step outside one's own experiences and thoughts to consider different perspectives. Throughout all of the periods of cognitive development, however, egocentrism continues in different guises. Adolescents, for example, are egocentric in their feelings and unable to comprehend that others feel differently about a situation than they do.

Children's social development can also be observed in the way in which they play games that have rules. Piaget notes that preschool-age children do not understand the rules of classic games, such as marbles. Thus, they make up their own rules for playing the game. Fortunately at this age, usually everybody can win and nobody has to lose. By the age of seven, however, children in most Western cultures begin to understand the rules and to play cooperatively and competitively. They establish rigid rules and identify winners and losers. Their behavior is markedly more social, involving other people.

Children's reasoning during the preoperational period is largely egocentric and personal, influenced by their own needs and wants. As adults, we reason *inductively* from the specific to the general or *deductively* from the general to the specific. Preschool-age children, however, reason *transductively* from the specific to the specific. If two things happen together, they are assumed to have a causal relationship.

Lucienne once reasoned that it could not be afternoon because she had not yet taken her nap.

Personal motives dominate the preschool child's understanding of causality. The *animism* of earlier years, in which everything is conceived of as alive, is replaced with *artificialism*, the schema that all events are to be accounted for in terms of personal motives. When three-year-olds persist in asking questions, they are not looking for explanations in terms of natural law. An explanation in terms of the chemical composition of the leaf in response to the question, "Why do the leaves turn color?" fails to satisfy them. But an answer that involves a humanlike purpose, such as a story about Jack Frost and his paintbrush, makes sense to them.

Reversibility, Centration, Conservation, Class Inclusion A further quality of preoperational thought is the absence of reversibility. *Reversibility* refers to the ability to go back to the beginning of a chain of thought and start over again. If water is poured from a short, wide glass into a tall, thin one, as in Figure 12.1, the four-year-old believes that there is more water in the tall glass because the water level is higher. Part of the problem is that the child cannot imagine reversing the process to

FIGURE 12.1   Reversibility
Preschool-age children cannot realize that the amount of water remains the same when it is poured from a short, wide glass into a tall, thin one.

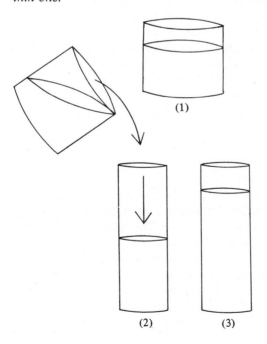

(1)

(2)   (3)

see that the amount of water is unchanged. Irreversibility prevents development of logical thought. The child who cannot reason that if A is less than B, B must be greater than A, is unable to solve problems in logic.

The child's inability to recognize that the amount of water poured from one glass to another remains the same also illustrates the predominating characteristic of *centration*. Preschool-age children tend to center or base their conclusions on the perceptually dominant characteristics of what they see. If a child is asked to compare two rows of pennies in which the first row contains five pennies placed close together and the second row contains four pennies placed farther apart (see Figure 12.2), the child will generally identify the second row as having more pennies because it is longer.

The lack of reversibility and the inability to decentrate are clearly illustrated in the problem of conservation. *Conservation* refers to the ability to recognize that the amount, weight, or volume of matter remains the same regardless of changes in its position or shape. A row of five pennies remains a row of five pennies whether or not the pennies are grouped close together or far apart. The amount of water does not change when it is poured from a tall to a short glass. In the preoperational period, children are generally unable to conserve. They identify the longer row as having "more" pennies and the taller glass as having "more" water. They are unable to hold one dimension constant in the face of other dimensions that have changed.

Preoperational thought is further marked by the inability to classify consistently objects into appropriate groups. Young children, given a variety of objects to sort, may sort them by shape or color. However, they sometimes mix objects of different classes together and they do not always include all of the objects that belong together in the same group. By five years of age, children can sort objects consistently, putting all of the objects of the same shape or color into one group, but they still have

FIGURE 12.2 Centration
The preoperational child will generally identify the second row as having more pennies because it is longer.

not developed *class inclusion*. Piaget (1952) gave a group of five-year-olds a set of eighteen brown and two white wooden beads. The children were able to acknowledge that all of the beads were made out of wood and to indicate those beads that were brown. However, when he asked the children, "Are there more brown beads or wooden beads?" the children replied that there were more brown beads because the brown beads were greater in number. They did not recognize that the class of brown beads was included in the class of wooden beads.

By the end of the preoperational period, the beginnings of reversibility, decentration, conservation, and class inclusion appear. At about age five or six, the child is able to make simple reversals. At age six or seven, the child starts to decenter perceptions. At age five or six, the child demonstrates conservation with number. Later, other conservation skills follow. The ability to conserve volume, because it entails all of the other abilities to conserve (weight, area, substance, and number), comes last and is delayed until about age eleven or twelve. At about age seven, comprehension of class inclusion is demonstrated. These characteristics represent important developments in the child's emerging powers of reason. The child of seven bears little resemblance to the child of two. He or she is beginning to acquire many rules and concepts not possessed earlier. The initial demonstration of mastery of the above concepts indicates that the child is ready to pass into the next stage.

EXERCISE:

Mastering Conservation

Again, duplicating some of Piaget's informal experiments with children will illustrate his concepts. Choose children of ages four, seven, and eleven. Follow the procedures below and ask the child to explain his or her answers.

1. Present the child with two identical short glasses filled with the same amount of water. Have the child understand that the amount of water is the same in each glass. Then, in front of the child's eyes, pour the water from one glass into a taller, thinner one. Ask a question such as, "Suppose you were very thirsty and wanted to drink a lot of water. Which glass has the most water?"

2. Present the child with two identical rows of five small pieces of candy. Have the child identify that the number of candies in each row is the same. Then, in front of the child's eyes, make one row longer by enlarging the spaces between the candies. Ask the child, "Which row has more candies?"

Compare the responses of children of different ages. Frequently the responses are obvious. If a child says, "That one is more because it is bigger (or longer)," it is obvious that the problem of conservation has not been mastered. If the child says, "They are both the same, because the water came from the same glass (or they both have five candies)," it is clear that the problem of conservation has been mastered. Sometimes, however, children's responses surprise and confuse us because our questions were unclear to them. If a child says, "There is more in that glass (row) because I was thirstier (hungrier) when I had it and I'm not thirsty (hungry) now," it's anybody's guess as to where he or she stands on the issue of conservation. In such a case, you may need to rephrase your question several different ways until you get an answer that indicates the level of comprehension.

Concrete Operations (7 to 11 Years)

During the ages of seven to eleven, children are generally in the period of concrete operations and they begin to think logically. Piaget uses the term *concrete operations* to refer to the set of logical skills or complex mental actions that children develop at this time to deal with objects. These skills include addition, subtraction, classification, serialization, conservation, and relational expressions. All of these operations are reversible and can be turned around. Children of this age level recognize that subtraction is the reversal of addition and that if one object is larger than another object the second object must be smaller. At this time, however, the children's operations are tied to specific objects or experiences. They need concrete objects or things in front of them in order to perform mental activities. It is only natural that children first learn to count, add, and subtract with their fingers and toes. Children at this stage have difficulty performing operations internally in their heads with no objects present. In general, they cannot apply their developing logic to purely verbal or hypothetical problems. This is to say that given a purely hypothetical or verbal problem, children of this level usually cannot solve it symbolically. But given the same problem in terms of specific objects, children of this age can deal with it effectively. For this reason concrete implements, such as Cuisinaire rods for arithmetic, facilitate the problem-solving behavior of early-school-age children.

Sociocentric Thought Children at the age of concrete operations are less egocentric in their thinking and their behavior is markedly more social. They know that other points of view exist that are different from their own. They can imagine what an object would look like to someone else who looks at it from a different direction. They also begin to recognize the need to validate their own thoughts through social interactions with others. Thus, children begin to take note of and consider the opinions and ideas of others.

Transformation The ability to engage in reversals permits children in the stage of concrete operations to deal with transformations or changes. In one experiment, Piaget showed young children semicircular shapes of wire that he then straightened. He asked the children to draw the successive stages in the change of the wire's shape. In addition, he asked the children to verbalize what had happened and select sketches of the wire during the various stages. Between the ages of four and seven, children could not draw or otherwise represent the successive stages. In general, they referred only to the initial and final stages. After the age of seven, however, they could describe the changes successively and also anticipate them. These behaviors showed that they understood the relationship between successive steps.

Logical Operations The important feature of the period of concrete operations is that children's mental processes have become logical. Logical operations are essentially reversible mental actions that have become internalized. They presuppose some awareness of conservation, and they are not isolated but exist within a system of other related operations. Reversability is a primary logical operation. Two other logical operations that the child masters during this phase are seriation and classification.

Seriation refers to the ability to arrange objects in a sequential order according to increasing or decreasing size. While preschool-age children may be able to arrange three objects in a series, they cannot arrange larger groups or perform that activity in their heads. Since numbers occur in a serial order, the concept of seriation obviously is crucial to performing arithmetic problems. The ability to seriate generally emerges at about the same time as conservation skills arise and with respect to the same dimensions of quantity or number, weight, and volume.

Coupled with seriation comes the ability to make transitions and equivalences. If A is bigger than B, and B is bigger than C, A must be bigger than C. Likewise, if A equals B, and B equals C, A must equal C. Younger children do not recognize these necessary implications.

During the stage of concrete operations, the children's growing ability to classify begins to encompass the concept of class inclusion. Children of this age have no difficulty recognizing that there are more wooden than brown beads in the earlier experiment, because they can now cope simultaneously with two kinds of classes without focusing on only one dimension. They begin to recognize that cats are animals as well as cats and that the class of animals includes the class of cats. This behavior is indicative of a significant level of abstraction that will make additional logical problem-solving processes possible.

Formal Operations (12 Years to Adulthood)

Another major shift in the child's cognitive ability occurs with the beginning of adolescence. Piaget refers to this stage as the period of formal operations to differentiate it from the preceeding period. The essential difference is that adolescents and adults are no longer tied to concrete and specific objects in their logical thought. They can perform all of the operations entirely in their heads. During this period, children's cognitive structures become mature. They acquire all of the cognitive structures and mental powers of an adult. This does not mean that their thinking is equivalent to that of an adult, rather, it means that they have developed the potential to begin to think as adults do. The content, function, and use to which they may apply their intellectual powers will be enriched throughout adulthood, but all of the structures of intelligence have emerged.

Adolescents, who can think in their heads, are able to apply their logical operations to a much wider range of problem-solving activities than school-age children who are tied to the concrete. Because concrete operational children are still strongly influenced by their perceptions, they have difficulty in solving hypothetical problems, complex verbal problems, or problems dealing with the past and the future. They cope with each problem as an individual, separate unit and cannot see that certain problems belong together or are of a common type. They apply one kind of problem-solving activity to a problem at a time and are unable to coordinate the different kinds of problem-solving skills that can be applied to the same task. Adolescents, on the other hand, are able to integrate and coordinate their skills and apply them simultaneously to the task at hand because their operations have become formalized.

The distinction between concrete and formal operations is nicely illustrated in the manner in which children of different ages tackle a problem such as: "I am thinking of a number between one and one hundred. Can you guess the number within ten questions?" The child at the level of concrete operations simply guesses at different numbers using no particular strategy until by trial and error he or she happens on the correct number. Adolescents at the level of formal operations tackle the problem systematically. They classify the numbers in a logical pattern and ask questions such as: "Is it over fifty?" or "Is it an even number?" thereby narrowing the possible solutions.

In addition, formal operations entail the ability to follow the steps of the scientific method. Individuals at this level systematically understand the problem, develop a hypothesis, deduce the consequences of the hypothesis, test it, and draw a conclusion. They have become fully capable of deductive logic and their thought moves from the general to the specific. During the period of concrete operation, inductive logic, which moves from specific to general, prevailed.

Individuals at the stage of formal operations demonstrate a more adequate and mature understanding of causality. Their understanding of cause and effect has shifted from the predominant egocentrism, which manifested itself in animism and artificialism, to an objective understanding of causality as a coherent system of relationships among events. They are ready to cope with events in terms of natural laws of cause and effect.

Freed from the literal mindedness of earlier periods, the adolescent can deal with the abstract and think about the logic of an argument independently of its particular content. Further, the adolescent is aware of his or her own thought processes and can reflect on them. All of these features give the cognitive structures of formal operations a much greater power and range.

The sophisticated potentialities of formal operations enable adolescents to deal with a number of problems that cannot be solved by concrete operations. When Piaget (1928) asked youngsters: "Edith is fairer than Susan; Edith is darker than Lilly; who is the darkest of the three?" most children under twelve had difficulty answering his question. Also, if a hypothetical statement precedes a logical argument, such as "Suppose water boiled at seventy degrees Fahrenheit . . .," a younger child tends to assert that the statement is false and the problem cannot be solved. The older child accepts the hypothetical assumption and goes ahead with the logic of the argument. Freed from the perceptual and the concrete, the adolescent is ready and easily able to handle sophisticated types of problems such as these.

Nevertheless, Piaget observes that there are still differences between the thought of the adolescent and that of the adult. He suggests that these differences are primarily due to the egocentrism that continues to influence adolescents during this period. As each new structure of thought is first acquired, it is applied in an egocentric fashion. When infants first identify objects as external, they think of them solely in terms of their meaning for them. Children in the preoperational phase cannot distinguish between their own thoughts and those of others. Children in the stage of concrete operations cannot distinguish between thoughts in themselves and their own perceptions. Egocentrism in adolescents refers to their inability to distinguish between what is logical or ideal and what is realistic. Adolescents have acquired the powers of logical thought and they can think logically about the world and its problems. But they believe that the world should conform to logical, rational norms and they are unable to comprehend that this is not always the case (1969). In this sense, adolescents are still trying to adjust the world to their own viewpoints. To the adolescent, dreams of glorious reform in which the world is transformed by correct ideas are a genuine and real possibility. In this sense, adolescents are, to use Wadsworth's phrase, "idealistic social critics" (1971). In adulthood, their idealism recedes as they increasingly come into contact with the real world. By the time children reach adolescence, their cognitive structures become mature. There is a qualitative difference in the way in which they think and the way a younger child thinks.

Piaget's stages are neither rigid nor linear; the age limits are flexible and the stages progress in a cumulative rather than linear fashion. The chronological ages that Piaget suggests as norms merely indicate the period at which most children may typically be expected to display certain behaviors. Piaget reminds us that there is a wide diversity among individual children. Further, the behaviors of one stage do not disappear with the successive stage; instead, the activities of the following stage complement the earlier behaviors. Nor is process through the various stages automatic. Maturation, physical experience, social interaction, and the internal mechanisms of equilibrium are all variables that influence and affect the transition from stage to stage. However, according to Piaget, each child must go through the stages in the same order. Each subsequent stage presupposes the preceding one and cannot occur without it. The stages of cognitive development that Piaget has outlined represent a path that we all trod in the journey from childhood to adulthood.

MORAL DEVELOPMENT

In addition to his study of the intellectual development of the person, Piaget has also explored the area of moral development, which he considers simply another function of overall cognitive growth. By *moral judgment*, Piaget refers to a person's understanding of why certain behaviors are right or wrong. Piaget's studies led him to suggest (1932) that there are two broad phases in the development of moral judgment.

The first phase, *moral realism* (ages three to ten), is marked by the belief that moral laws are as fixed and unchangeable as the physical laws that the child is just discovering. This stage is further marked by the tendency to judge the merit of a behavior on the basis of its consequences rather than its intent, to think of behaviors as either totally right or totally wrong, and to believe in imminent justice: that the appropriate punishment or reward automatically follows wrong and right acts. The second stage, the *morality of cooperation* (ages ten and older), refers to the person's recognition that rules are developed and sustained by social agreements. At this time, children realize that rules can be changed, that there may be more than one side to a moral issue, and that intentions, rather than punishments and rewards, are a preferable basis for judging people's behavior.

Lawrence Kohlberg (1964), an American psychologist, has extended Piaget's study of the moral judgment of the child. Kohlberg presented children with a number of different *moral dilemmas*, such as: "If a man's wife is dying, and he cannot afford the drug that will cure her, should he steal for the drug?" or "If a dying woman begs the doctor to let her die because of her pain, should the doctor continue measures to sustain her life?"

Moral Dilemmas

Before reading further, study the above dilemmas carefully, formulate your own answers to them, and write an explanation of each answer. When you have finished reading the brief discussion of Kohlberg's theory that follows, try to analyze your answers and identify them as representative of a certain level of moral development in terms of the criteria that he suggests.

On the basis of children's answers and reasons for their answers to the dilemmas that he posed, Kohlberg suggested that moral development follows three main levels with six substages.

Level 1: Preconventional During the preconventional period the child judges behavior in terms of its consequences. The first stage is *punishment and obedience oriented.* The child obeys adults or rules in order to avoid being punished. A child at this level might reply to the dilemma concerning the drug, "If he steals the drug, he'll go to jail," or "He'll get in trouble if he lets his wife die." The second stage reflects an *instrumental-relativist orientation.* At this phase, the child is a "naive hedonist," who believes that behaviors are good if they bring pleasant consequences and bad if they yield unpleasant ones. A child at this level might reply, "If he steals the drug, his wife will get better," or "If he gets caught stealing, he might have to go to jail."

Level 2: Conventional During the conventional period, the child judges behavior in terms of the norms and expectations of his society, family, or social group. The third substage is a *"good boy—nice girl"* orientation. Good behavior is conceived as that which pleases, helps, or is approved by other people. At this level a child might reply, "His family would think he was a bad husband if he let his wife die," or "People will say he is a criminal if he steals." The fourth stage is oriented toward *law and order.* Laws and rules are conceived as fixed and absolute and obeyed for their own sake. A child at this level might answer, "It's his duty to save his wife," or "If he steals, he's guilty of breaking the law."

Level 3: Postconventional During the postconventional period, which seldom appears before adolescence, an individual judges behavior in terms of abstract moral values and his or her own conscience. Stage five is a *social contract, legalistic orientation.* Laws and rules are seen as utilitarian social contracts that may vary from group to group or person to person. An individual at this level might answer, "He'd lose other people's respect if he didn't steal the drug and save his wife," or "It's a rule of our society that one should not steal." The sixth stage reflects *universal ethical principles*. At this level, what is right has become a decision of individual conscience based on self-chosen standards of ethical principles of justice and respect that are seen to have universal implication. An individual who is operating at this level might respond, "A human life is more important than any other moral value. Without upholding the inherent worth of an individual over other values, we could have no principles of justice or love."

More recently, Kohlberg (1973) has postulated a seventh stage in moral development that has marked religious overtones. The connotations of this level are reminiscent of Erikson's final stage of integrity versus despair, in which one reflects on his or her life and is able to accept it. Kohlberg points out that moral development does not necessarily end in young adulthood but continues into maturity. The development through moral stages is not automatic, however, nor is it always complete. Not all individuals make the transition to the higher levels of moral development. Some individuals make the transition intellectually but not emotionally or functionally. Thus, it is not unusual to see adults behave or defend their actions in a manner that reflects an earlier stage of development.

METHODS OF RESEARCH AND INVESTIGATION

Piaget's research techniques are quite different from the experimental model that has dominated American psychology. Experimental research entails testing hypotheses under rigorously controlled laboratory conditions, and specified variables, as well as subsequent analysis of the results through sophisticated statistical procedures. Piaget's work has not been experimental in that sense. His method was basically descriptive and clinical. He observed the behavior of children, asked them carefully designed questions, and paid attention to their responses. His work was thorough, systematic, and subjected to meticulous analysis, even though it was not experimental in the limited sense of the term. At times, Piaget followed his intuition; he did not hesitate to change his questions with different children if he felt that it would be helpful to rephrase or reorder them. His work has been criticized because the number of children that he observed was relatively small and the children did not always receive the same treatment. In more recent years, he has increased the number of his subjects and followed a more rigorous experimental model. In light of the criticisms made of his work, however, Piaget points out that typical experimental procedures are not necessarily the most appropriate ones for exploring the area of cognitive development or other matters of concern for personality. In the course of his research, Piaget has amassed a tremendous amount of information about the development of cognitive processes and suggested explanations for that development.

Piaget's theory has generated a considerable amount of research by other psychologists. Each year the *Annual Review of Psychology* has extensive sections on research devoted to Piagetian concepts. For the most part, research appears to confirm that Piaget's basic description of the sequence of cognitive stages is accurate, particularly for children in Western cultures. Critics question, however, the universality of his sequence and the way in which he accounts for the changes in development. Piaget's sequence is meant to be crosscultural, outlining the development from immaturity to maturity without presupposing any specific cultural matrix within which that development must occur. There is little doubt but that Piaget's statements about developmental changes in conservation of mass, class inclusion, and serialization are generally true for Western children. Subsequent research, however, has not clearly established that his stages are universal across cultures. In his explanation of changes in development, Piaget posits internal mental processes and suggests that the child acquires different operations or ways of thinking. Critics point out that alternative, simpler explanations might be possible (see Siegel, Roerper, and Hooper, 1966).

Piaget's studies of moral development have also generated considerable empirical research by Kohlberg (1964) and others. Many of the studies appear to support Piaget's view; however, his hypotheses have not been uncriticized. Kohlberg studied non-Western as well as Western cultures, and his research suggested that the same basic pattern of acquiring moral values is found in every culture and develops in the same order. The answers of children in Malasia, Taiwan, and Mexico, as well as the United States reflect the same stages and progression. A primary difference is that stage five thinking appears to come earlier and be more conspicuous in the moral reasoning of adolescents in the United States. However, since it is present in other countries too, it is not a purely American phenomenon.

Drawing their inspiration from Piaget's work, other researchers have expanded on areas of interest consistent with his theory. Jane Loevinger (1969) has described the ego's development in terms of striving to master, integrate, and make sense out of experience by progressive differentiation and hierarchization through stages. Jerome Bruner (1973) and Jerome Kagan (1972, 1973) have extended Piaget's work in their discussions of children's cognitive development and the implications of Piagetian theory for education. Breger (1974) has developed a model that combines Piaget's cognitive stages and Freud's psychosexual ones.

EVALUATION AND IMPLICATIONS

Piaget's studies and research demonstrate a deep concern and interest in the structure and development of the cognitive aspects of personality.

While Piaget does not minimize or ignore other personality aspects, he has not tried to develop a comprehensive theory of personality.

In American psychology, the deep concern with environmental factors led to an emphasis on learning and studying the processes by which behavior can be modified through experience. For the most part, American psychologists after Watson, particularly in the behavior and learning tradition, have not been concerned with the influence of heredity or maturation in the development of personality characteristics. The impact and significance of the work of Jean Piaget has forced the psychologist, and in turn the personality theorist, to pay attention once again to factors such as heredity and maturation.

We have seen that Piaget conceives of cognitive development in the human personality as a parallel to the biological adaptation of all living organisms to their environment. Just as living organisms adjust biologically to the world in which they live, so human beings adjust intellectually to the world. The basic outline of cognitive development is shared by all humans. At the same time, however, Piaget (1961) recognizes that there are certain variables that influence the course of development. Maturation, equilibrium, experience, and social interaction with others all assist in fostering the unfolding inner process of cognitive activity. Of these variables, maturation and the tendency toward equilibrium clearly depend on the organism itself with its genetic endowment and potentialities. Experience and social interaction, however, depend on external events and forces outside of the individual person. Thus, Piaget does not really take sides in the age-old nature versus nurture controversy. He recognizes that both factors are involved in the development of personality. Neither nature nor nurture, in and of itself, bears the entire burden of personality structure and development.

Piaget has not discussed the question of motivation in any great length or detail. However, his theory implies that motivation is intrinsic, having its source within the organism, rather than due to external forces. Piaget suggests that the need to know the world comes about as a result of the existence of the organism and its functions. For the organism to function, it must know its world. Thus, its needs arise out of its very functioning. Once the processes of assimilation and accommodation begin to occur, motivation may be considered to be self-activating and perpetuating (1952). Thus, Piaget does not concur with the behaviorist and learning theory concept of reinforcement as a sufficient explanation for behavior. His theory points to the need to explore further the area of internal motivation.

Two major implications of Piaget's work are the concepts of critical periods and readiness. During certain phases of growth, known as *critical periods*, the organism is highly responsive to certain influences that may enhance or disrupt its development. This is particularly clear in embryonic development, where timing is of the upmost importance. If certain organs do not develop properly at certain given points, they fail to evolve normally. The same kind of phenomenon also appears to be true of intellectual and emotional development, although perhaps it is not quite as irreversible. There are certain critical periods during which a person is more receptive to certain kinds of intellectual and emotional stimuli and influence. The concept of *readiness* is closely allied to the concept of critical periods. If a person is not prepared or disposed to learn a particular concept, he or she will be unable to do so because the necessary prerequisite schema are not present. Individuals vary as to their readiness to learn and develop because of the variables of maturation, experience, social interaction, and equilibrium. The concepts of critical periods and readiness have crucial implications for both education and psychotherapy. Neither students nor patients are going to be able to learn or change their behavior unless they are prepared and the necessary prerequisites have been met.

Although Piaget's theory does not represent a fully developed theory of personality, it is clear that his findings have a great deal to offer to the personality theorist. Some critics (such as Breger, 1974) have pointed out possible parallels between Piaget's stages of cognitive development and the stages that other theorists, such as Freud and Erikson, have posed. The potential coordination of Piaget's levels with Freud's psychosexual stages or Erikson's psychosocial ones offers the possibility of constructing a more comprehensive theory of development. Thus, Piaget's theory is rich in providing materials on which personality theorists may draw in developing theories of personality that more accurately portray the individual in all of his or her fullness.

SUGGESTIONS FOR FURTHER READING

Piaget's works are not easy for the average lay person to comprehend. Most of his writings were first published in French and later translated into English. He introduces many unfamiliar words and concepts that are difficult for an untrained person to understand. In addition, a full comprehension of what he says often requires some sophistication in mathematics, epistemology, and logic. Thus, the reader who is interested in pursuing Piaget's thought further might be best advised to first look into a good secondary source. Barry Wadsworth's *Piaget's Theory of Cognitive Development* (David McKay, 1971) is a good introduction aimed at students in psychology and education. Also quite readable is David Elkind's *Children and Adolescents: Interpretive Essays on Jean Piaget* (Oxford University Press, 2d ed., 1974). Jean Flavell's *The Developmental Psychology of Jean Piaget* (D. Van Nostrand, 1963) is an excellent introduction to Piaget's theory and subsequent research on it. However, it is a much more difficult book.

Of Piaget's own works, *The Origins of Intelligence in Children* (International Universities Press, 1952) traces the manifestations of sensori-motor intelligence during infancy. *The Construction of Reality in the Child*, translated by Margaret Cook (Basic Books, 1954) describes the child's early perceptions of objects, space, people, and time. Both of these books include Piaget's careful observations of his own children. *The Moral Judgment of the Child* (Harcourt, Brace, and World, 1932) describes Piaget's careful studies of how children distinguish between right and wrong and their basis for these judgments.

CHAPTER 13

George Kelly: Constructive Alternativism

George Kelly's theory of constructive alternativism invites us to look at personality in a new and different light by conceiving of each individual as a scientist. A fundamental property of being human, Kelly suggests, is our ability to create various constructs, or patterns of meaning, that enable us to understand our world. On the basis of these different constructs, we make predictions about events and use these predictions as guides to help us act. As such, our activity parallels that of the scientist. Kelly's theory is a purely cognitive one. He concentrates entirely on how people variously construe, or interpret, events. Everything of importance, one might say, goes on in the head.

Reading Kelly is like entering a new terrain, as he avoids many of the concepts traditionally present in personality theorizing. Kelly is forthright in describing the differences between his approach and that of others. "It is only fair," he wrote, "to warn the reader about what may be in store for him. In the first place, he is likely to find missing most of the familiar landmarks . . . For example, the term *learning*, so honorably embedded in most psychological texts, scarcely appears at all. That is wholly intentional; we are for throwing it overboard all together. There is no *ego*, no *emotion*, no *reinforcement*, no *drive*, no *unconscious*, no *need*" (1955). It is not that these concepts are entirely omitted from Kelly's work; rather, they are given new meanings and incorporated into his philosophy of constructive alternativism.

GEORGE KELLY

BIOGRAPHICAL BACKGROUND

George Kelly was born on a farm in Perth, Kansas, in 1905. His father
was a Presbyterian minister, but ill health prevented him from actively
leading a church congregation. Kelly's parents were devout funda-
mentalists who practiced their faith, prescribed hard work, and rigorously
shunned the evils of dancing, drinking, and card playing. As an only
child, Kelly received extensive attention and love. His mother, in particular, was devoted to him.

Kelly's early education was somewhat sporadic. He attended a one-
room country school and was taught by his parents at home. He was
sent to Wichita, Kansas, for high school, where he attended four different schools. He studied for three years at Friends University and received the B.A. degree one year later (1929) from Park College. Kelly
had majored in physics and mathematics and planned a career in
mechanical engineering. However, his interests were turning to social
problems. While holding a number of different jobs related to engineering and education, he pursued a master's degree in educational sociology
at the University of Kansas.

In 1929, Kelly was awarded a fellowship of study at the University
of Edinburgh in Scotland. He earned a bachelor of education degree

there based on his previous academic experience and his year of residency in Scotland. Kelly wrote his dissertation on the problem of predicting teaching success and discovered that his interests were turning to psychology. On his return to the United States, he enrolled as a doctoral student in psychology at the State University of Iowa. He received the Ph.D. in 1931 with a dissertation on speech and reading disabilities.

Kelly began his career as an academic psychologist in the middle of the depression of the 1930s. Opportunities for work in physiological psychology, his speciality, were scarce, so he turned his attention to clinical psychology, a growing field. During the next twelve years, Kelly taught at Fort Hays Kansas State College and developed a program of traveling psychological clinics that sought to identify and treat emotional and behavioral problems in students in the state's public school system. His experience with the clinics was crucial to his later development and theorizing. Not committed to any one theoretical approach, Kelly experimented with several different methods in his work with students referred for counseling. His position gave him a unique opportunity to try out innovative as well as traditional clinical approaches. His work with the clinics sparked several ideas that later found application in his own theory of personality and therapy.

World War II briefly interrupted Kelly's academic career. He enrolled in the navy as an aviation psychologist, headed a training program of local civilian pilots, and worked for the bureau of medicine and surgery, gaining recognition for his clinical services. After the war, a significant demand for clinical psychologists appeared. Returning servicemen required help with personal problems. Clinical psychology came to be seen as an essential part of health services. Kelly played a leading role in fostering the development and integration of clinical psychology into the mainstream of American psychology. After teaching one year at the University of Maryland, he joined the faculty of Ohio State University as professor and director of clinical psychology. During the next twenty years at Ohio State, Kelly built a distinguished program of clinical psychology and refined and published his theory of personality.

In 1965, Kelly received a prestigious appointment to the Riklis Chair of Behavioral Science at Brandeis University. This appointment would have given him great freedom to pursue his research, but he died one year later at the age of sixty-two.

Kelly did not publish a great deal, but he lectured extensively in the United States and abroad and he exerted considerable influence on psychology through his personal impact on his students and friends. In his later years, he spent considerable time suggesting how personal construct theory could be applied to help resolve social and international problems. He held several important positions, such as president of both the Clinical and Counseling Divisions of the American Psychological

Association. He assisted the development and also served as president of the American Board of Examiners in Professional Psychology.

CONSTRUCTIVE ALTERNATIVISM

George Kelly's theory of personality is unashamedly based on his philosophical position of *constructive alternativism:* the assumption that any one event is open to a variety of interpretations. Kelly observes that while the world is real and happening, in and of itself, it does not automatically make sense to us. We have to create our own ways of understanding the events that happen to us. In effect, there is no reality outside our interpretations of it. Take, for example, the situation of a boy who is late for school. His father may think that it is because the boy is lazy. His mother may suggest that her son is forgetful and daydreams on the way to school. His teacher may view the pupil's tardiness as an expression of his distaste and hostility toward academic work. His best friend might see it as an accident. The boy himself could construe his lateness as an indication of his inferiority. The event itself is merely a given datum, but it gives rise to many different alternative constructions that may lead to different actions. For Kelly, the objective truth of a person's interpretations are unimportant because they are unknowable. What is important is their implications for behavior and life.

In our efforts to understand the world, we develop constructs or patterns that make the world meaningful to us. We look at the world "through transparent patterns or templates" of our own creation. It is as if each person can only view the world through sunglasses of his or her own choosing. The variations of color or tint that each person selects provides for the many different views that we have of the world (Schultz, 1976). Kelly points out that no one construct or pattern is final and a perfect reflection of the world. There is always an alternative construct that might do a better job of accounting for the facts that we perceive. Thus, our position in the world is one of constructive alternativism, as we change or revise our constructs in order to more accurately understand it.

George Kelly suggests that we look at ourselves and other people as scientists, an image that he notes psychologists are quick to ascribe to themselves but perhaps not as readily to other people. In positing an analogy between the human person and the scientist, Kelly suggests that the posture we take as we attempt to predict and control the events in our world is similar to that of the scientist who develops and tests hypotheses. In our efforts to understand the world, we develop constructs that act as hypotheses that make the world meaningful to us. If these patterns appear to fit our subsequent experience, we find them useful and hold onto them. If we construe the world or certain events as hostile, we will act in certain ways to protect ourselves. If our protective behaviors appear to be useful ways to cope with the events, we will continue to hold onto the hostile interpretation. If the pattern or construct is a poor one, that is to say, if it does not lead to behaviors that help us adjust to events in our world, we will seek to alter or change the construct in order to develop a better one. Just as the scientist employs hypotheses to make predictions about certain consequences that might happen if the hypotheses were true, people employ their constructs to predict what is going to happen to them in the future. Subsequent events are then used as indicators that the predictions and underlying constructs were correct or that they were misleading.

For example, at the beginning of a semester, students develop certain constructs or ideas about the subjects that they are studying. Usually, these constructs are based on a very limited sample of the actual course or the professor's behavior. One student may conclude that a particular course will be a snap, requiring a minimum of time and preparation. Another student may conclude that the same course will be a challenge, requiring considerable work and effort. As the semester progresses, each student acts on and gradually tests his or her preliminary hypothesis for its accuracy. The lectures, reading assignments, written papers, and tests are all subsequent events that serve to confirm or disconfirm the initial suspicions. By the middle of the semester, a student has a much clearer idea of the accuracy of his or her original constructs concerning the course. Should the original hypothesis seem valid, chances are the student will continue his or her present mode of handling the course work. However, if subsequent events suggest that the original construct was incorrect, the student will reevaluate and change the construct, developing new patterns of behavior that are more in line with the revised construct.

The example of a student's behavior in a college course is simply an example in miniature of what happens to us all at all times in our lives. As was pointed out earlier, the world is not a fixed given that can be immediately comprehended and understood. In order to understand the world, we have to develop constructs or ways of perceiving it. During the course of our lives, we develop many different constructs. Further, we engage in the process of continually testing, revising, and modifying them. As none of our constructs are ultimate, alternative constructs that we could choose from are always available. Thus, a person is free to change his or her constructs in an effort to make sense out of, predict, and control the world.

Although Kelly encourages us to think of the person as a scientist, his discussion of the way in which we validate personal constructs involves the compelling character of philosophical insights as well as the application of scientific methods. Kelly suggests that a construct is validated if the anticipations based on it occur. Validation refers to the compatibility between one's predictions and one's observation of the outcome, both of which are subjectively construed. This form of every-day validation does not precisely parallel the controlled procedures of the scientist who in testing hypotheses does not look for events that will verify them but rather sets up conditions that might falsify them. In a well-designed experiment, one's anticipations are of little consequence to the outcome of the hypothesis (Rychlak, 1973). It would appear that people are philosophers as well as scientists, or, at least, that the scientific activities in which they engage are predicated on a philosophical stance. Kelly recognizes this fact in his candid acknowledgment that his view of the person as scientist is based on the philosophical position of constructive alternativism.

FUNDAMENTAL POSTULATE AND COROLLARIES

In order to present and explain his theory, Kelly sets forth one basic assumption or fundamental postulate and then elaborates on it with eleven corollaries (1955).

Fundamental Postulate

The *fundamental postulate* reads: "A person's processes are psychologically channelized by the ways in which he anticipates events."

Probably the most important word in Kelly's primary assumption is *anticipates*. Essentially, Kelly suggests that the way in which an individual predicts future happenings is crucial to his or her behavior. As scientists, people seek to forecast what is going to happen. They orient their behaviors and ideas about the world toward the goal of accurate, useful predictions. According to Kelly, the future, rather than the past, is the primary impetus of behavior.

The other words that Kelly includes in his fundamental postulate are also carefully chosen to convey the important elements of his theory. The term *person* indicates Kelly's interest in the individual person as a whole rather than in groups or part of a person. Kelly uses the term *processes* to underscore that he conceives of the person as a behaving organism that is already in motion. He does not find it necessary to postulate internal or external forces that impel or control behavior; the existence of the organism itself implies motivation. The word *psychologically* specifies the range of Kelly's concern and his desire to give a purely psychological description of processes rather than another kind of description. *Channelized* describes Kelly's conception of psychological processes as organized into a structured but flexible network that permits, yet also limits, a person's behavior. Lastly, the word *events* indicates that human constructions refer to the real world and are an effort to predict and to cope with it.

Corollaries

Each of the eleven corollaries that Kelly presents to elaborate his fundamental postulate focuses on a primary word that helps sum up the essence of these supportive statements and his theory.

Construction The term "construe" means to place an interpretation on an event. As we have seen, the universe is not an automatically knowable given. We must create constructs or ways in which to understand it. Kelly suggests that in our construction or interpretation of events, we look for themes that happen over and over again. Even though no two events are exactly identical, we can detect similarities and differences in them that guide our expectations of other events in the future.

Individuality No two people interpret events in the same way. Each of us experiences an event from our own subjective point of view. Our views cannot be identical because each one of us plays a different role even when we are involved in the same event. This corollary underscores Kelly's belief that it is the subjective interpretation of an event, rather than the event itself, that is most important. The individuality corollary does not mean, however, that we cannot share our interpretations of events. Many of our constructs are shared with or similar to those of other people. This is particularly the case among people who have a common background and culture. Thus, it is possible for us to share our interpretations of the world by mutually construing how the other might understand it.

Organization Our interpretation of events in the world is neither haphazard nor arbitrary. Each one of us organizes his or her constructs in a series of ordinal relationships in which some constructs are more important and others are less important. Our constructs may, therefore, be seen as constituting a hierarchy in which some constructs are subordinate to others. The construct "good" may include the concept of "intelligent." Our hierarchy of concepts is not rigid; rather, it changes from time to time in light of subsequent events. Nevertheless, the fact that our constructs fall into an organized pattern means that we develop a system of constructs rather than simply a number of isolated ones.

Dichotomy In making an interpretation about an event, Kelly believes that we not only make an assertion about it, but we also indicate that the opposite quality is not characteristic of it. A dichotomy is an opposite, and Kelly suggests that all of our constructs are of a bipolar form. When we construe that a person is strong, we also imply that the person is not weak. If our constructs did not imply a choice between opposite poles, they would be meaningless. We would not know how to understand them. This dichotomous form of our constructs provides the basis for constructive alternativism.

Kelly suggests that the smallest number of elements in a construct is three things. Our assertion about one thing implies that at least one other thing is like it and at least one other thing is not. Thus, when we say Jane is beautiful, we intimate that at least one other person is also beautiful and at least one other person is not. At its root, therefore, a construct is made up out of a minimum of three elements and two relationships. It asserts how two things are alike and how they differ from a third.

Choice We have seen that each construct is composed of three elements and two opposite poles. Kelly suggests that in developing our constructs, each person tends to choose the pole that seems to be most helpful in expanding his or her anticipation of future events. We can expand our interpretation of future events in two ways. We can narrowly define our constructs and make them more explicit. Such definition leads to greater security and certainty about a few things. On the other hand, we can extend our construct system by making it more inclusive. The latter method of expansion often makes us temporarily uncertain but eventually leads to a wider understanding. Thus, Kelly believes that we do not always choose the tested construct or path of security. If it appears that a new construct will enhance our future anticipations, we may be adventurous and risk uncertainty for the sake of enriching the ultimate predictive power of our construct system. The choice corollary is a very important one. Underlying Kelly's whole position is the belief that a person is free and able to choose from among the various alternatives the construct that will be most useful.

Range Each one of our constructs has a certain range or focus. Few, if any, constructs are appropriate for interpreting all events. Thus, Kelly notes that the construct of *tall versus short* is useful for describing people, trees, or horses, but virtually useless for understanding the weather. Some people apply their constructs broadly, while others limit their constructs to a narrow focus. Kelly suggests, for example, that one person may use the construct of *respect vs. contempt* to include a wide variety of interpersonal relationships, while another individual might use it in a much more limited sense to refer only to aspects in a court proceeding. In order to understand an individual's constructs, we need to take into account both what is and what is not included in their range.

Experience Kelly believes that people change their interpretation of events in the light of later experience. Subsequent experiences serve as a validating process by which the accuracy of our anticipations can be checked out and tested. If a construct does not prove helpful in anticipating future events, it is reformulated and changed. Such reconstruction forms the basis for learning that, Kelly suggests, is taking place at all times. It is hardly necessary to postulate a distinct theory of learning when learning is fully comprehended within the theory of personal constructs.

Modulation The term *modulation* refers to change. Kelly believes that the extent to which changes may occur within our constructs depends on the existing framework and organization of the constructural system. Constructs are more or less *permeable,* that is, they are more or less open to change and alteration. Concrete constructs are rather difficult to change because of their specificity in definition and limited range. The construct *fluorescent versus incandescent* is useful to apply to different kinds of light, but beyond that, it has a very limited range (Bannister and Fransella, 1971). Other constructs may be more or less widely applied. The construct *good versus evil* might be narrowly conceived by one individual so as to contain relatively few experiences. In that case, it would be very difficult for that individual to change his or her construct of *good versus evil.* For another individual, the same construct might be much more permeable and easily penetrated by new experiences.

Kelly suggests that a construct that limits its elements to its range only is a *preemptive concept.* Preemptive concepts are very specific and difficult to penetrate, because they categorize the world in rigid ways and do not permit it to be conceived of differently. "Nothing but" statements or assumptions frequently reflect preemptive thinking. Kelly points out that when a person insists that if a thing is a spade it is nothing but a spade, it is difficult to conceive of other functions for the tool. A construct that sets clear limits to the range of its elements, but also permits them to belong to other realms is a *constellatory construct.* The term "constellatory," however, also implies grouping things that may not belong together. Application of stereotypes is an example of constellatory thinking. To suggest that all college professors are absentminded is not necessarily to exclude them from something else, such as the class of intelligent people, but it is to prevent any college professor from being conceived of as having a good memory. A construct that leaves its elements open to other constructions is a *propositional construct.* The statement "Any roundish mass may be considered, among other things, as a ball" leaves both "roundish masses" and "balls" open to further interpretation. According to Kelly, the individual who uses propositional constructs is much more open to experience and change in his or her construct system.

Fragmentation There are times when people employ constructs that appear to be incompatible with each other. Because of this, we are often surprised by other people's behavior and we cannot always infer what a person is going to do tomorrow from the way he or she behaves today. Such fragmentation is particularly apt to be apparent either when a person's constructs are impermeable and concrete or when they are undergoing change. The fragmentation corollary does not imply, however, that Kelly conceives of individuals as inconsistent. On the contrary, all of a person's constructs operate within a system. Even though certain behaviors may appear to be disorganized, there still is an underlying pattern. Perception of this pattern permits us to recognize the overall unity of an individual's construct system.

Communality When two people share similar constructs, their psychological processes may be said to be similar. This does not mean that their experiences or their constructs concerning those experiences are identical. We have already seen that this cannot be the case. Nevertheless, in certain respects, people can be said to be alike, because they construe experiences in a similar fashion. Kelly's point here is that our obvious ability to share and communicate with other people is based on the fact that we share similar personal constructs with those people. The communality corollary accounts for the fact that we can and do anticipate the behaviors of others and for the fact that certain groups of people behave in similar ways.

Sociality Our potentiality for understanding and communicating with other people depends on our ability to construe another person's constructs or ways of understanding the world. In order to do this, we do not have to share the identical constructs, but we must be able to construe or have some idea of what the other person's constructs are. On a simple level, Kelly points out that the elementary task of driving a car successfully in traffic entails anticipating what other drivers are going to do, even though one might not always choose to imitate them. On a more sophisticated level, our ability to interact socially with other people entails understanding a broad range of their constructs and behaviors. The sociality corollary accounts for our ability to understand and communicate with others.

THE RECONSTRUCTION OF OLD CONCEPTS

Kelly avoids many of the concepts traditionally associated with personality theorizing. Familiar landmarks and terms are given new meanings and subordinated to his theory of personal constructs.

Some of our constructs refer to self-identity or the identity of others. The *self-construct*, according to Kelly, is primarily based on what we perceive as similarities in our own behavior. We believe that we are honest, sincere, friendly, and so forth. The self-construct is developed out of our relationships with other people. When we construe other people, we also construe ourselves. We cannot conceive of another person as "hostile" or "aggressive" without making hostility, aggressiveness, and their opposites, a dimension of our own experience. Our self-interpretation is linked to our role relationships with other people.

Kelly defines the term *role* as a process or behavior that a person plays based on his or her understanding of the behavior and constructs of other people. In order to enter into a relationship or a role with another person, we must have some idea of the way in which he or she behaves and construes our behavior. Interpersonal relationships are predicated on this concept of constructs. Kelly points out that we do not have to be accurate in our constructions to enter into a role. A student may play a certain role with a professor whom he or she believes to be unduly demanding and unfair when in fact the professor is not. Nor does a role have to be reciprocated by the other person. The professor may remain fair in spite of his or her student's misconstruction. What is needed in order to play a role is simply some construct of the other person's behavior.

Kelly's use of "role" should not be confused with its use in social psychology. In social psychology, "role" usually refers to a set of behavioral expectations or roles, such as mother, teacher, physician, ruler, and so on, set forth by a particular society and fulfilled by its members. In Kelly's theory, the role is defined by the individual in his or her efforts to understand the behavior of other people and relate to them. One's self-construct, according to Kelly, may be seen as a core or basic role structure by which one conceives of himself or herself as an integral individual in relation to other people.

For Kelly, the person is a process, an organism in continual activity whose behavior is governed by a system of personal constructs. *Learning* and *motivation* are built into the very structure of the system. Conceiving of the person as a unity, Kelly believes that no special inner forces, such as drives, needs, instincts, or motives, are needed to account for human motivation. Human nature in and of itself implies motivation because it is alive and in process. Nor need behavior be accounted for in terms of external forces, such as stimuli and reinforcements. Learning is synonymous with all of the psychological processes themselves. It is simply inappropriate to conceive of an individual as motivated by internal or external forces other than him- or herself. Kelly reminds us that, "There are pitchfork theories on the one hand and the carrot theories on the other. But our theory is neither of these. Since we prefer to look at the nature of the animal itself, ours is probably best called a jackass theory" (1958). Not all constructs are verbalized, thus, conscious and unconscious processes may be accounted for in terms of our capacity to form constructs that are not put into words.

Emotions are subsumed under the general framework of personal constructs as well. Although some critics (Bruner and Rogers, 1956) suggest that Kelly's theory is too intellectual and mentalistic, Kelly deals with the subject of emotions as one aspect of the unitary character of the person. He refuses to divide the person into cognitive and emotional states. Feelings and emotions refer to inner states that need to be construed. They arise when constructs are in a transitional state. Thus, threat is the awareness of impending inclusive change in one's core structure. Guilt arises when one is dislodged from his or her core role structure. Anxiety is the awareness that one's constructs do not adequately include certain events. In essence, Kelly reconceives emotions and considers them in terms of transition, process, and change.

THE REP TEST

In order to understand how a person interprets his or her world, Kelly developed the Role Construct Repertory Test, known more simply as the "Rep Test." Essentially, the Rep Test permits a person to reveal his or her constructs by comparing and contrasting a number of different persons in his or her life. The following exercise will help you become acquainted with the Rep Test and also tell you about some of your own personal constructs.

EXERCISE:

Rep Test

By completing the Rep Test as it is presented here,* you can learn about your own personal constructs and also gain some familiarity with this important assessment device.

Follow the instructions below indicating how to set up a list of representative persons in your life. Choose from among people you know the individual who most suits each description. Using the form provided (Figure 13.1), write the name of the person in the grid space above the column with the corresponding number to the description.

List of Representative Persons

1. Write your own name in the first blank

2. Write your mother's first name. If you grew up with a stepmother, write her name instead.

3. Write your father's first name. If you grew up with a stepfather, write his name instead.

4. Write the name of your brother who is nearest your own age. If you had no brother, write the name of a boy near your own age who was most like a brother to you during your early teens.

---

* Reprinted from *The Psychology of Personal Constructs* by George A. Kelly, Ph.D. By permission of W. W. Norton & Company, Inc. Copyright 1955 by W. W. Norton & Company, Inc.

FIGURE 13.1 Rep Test Grid

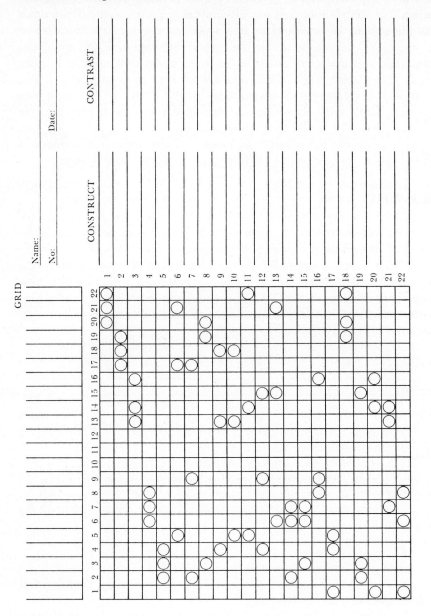

5. Write the name of your sister who is nearest your own age. If you had no sister, write the name of a girl near your own age who was most like a sister to you during your early teens.

From this point on do not repeat any names. If a person has already been listed, simply make a second choice.

6. Your wife (or husband) or, if you are not married, your closest present girl (boy) friend.
7. Your closest girl (boy) friend immediately preceding the person mentioned above.
8. Your closest present friend of the same sex as yourself.
9. A person of the same sex as yourself whom you once thought was a close friend but in whom you were badly disappointed later.
10. The minister, priest, or rabbi with whom you would be most willing to talk over your personal feelings about religion.
11. Your physician.
12. The present neighbor whom you know best.
13. A person with whom you have been associated who, for some unexplained reason, appeared to dislike you.
14. A person whom you would most like to help or for whom you feel sorry.
15. A person with whom you usually feel most uncomfortable.
16. A person whom you have recently met and would like to know better.
17. The teacher who influenced you most when you were in your teens.
18. The teacher whose point of view you found most objectionable.
19. An employer, supervisor, or officer under whom you served during a period of great stress.
20. The most successful person whom you know personally.
21. The happiest person whom you know personally.
22. The person known to you personally who appears to meet the highest ethical standards.

After you have written the names in the space above the columns, look at the first row. There are circles under three persons' names (20, 21, 22). Decide how two of them are alike in an important way and how they differ from the third person. Put an X in each of the two circles under the names of the persons who are alike. Then write on the line under the column headed Construct a word or phrase that identifies the likeness. Write the opposite of this characteristic under the heading Contrast. Now go back and consider all the other people you listed on your grid. If any of them also share the same characteristic, put a checkmark under their name. Repeat this procedure until you have completed every row on the form.

When you have completed the form, take a close look at your results. First consider the nature of the constructs you listed. How many different constructs did you list? What kind of constructs were they? Did you tend to make comparisons on the basis of appearance (skinny versus fat) or personality characteristics (thoughtful versus unthoughtful; honest versus dishonest)? Do any of the constructs overlap? You can discover this by examining the pattern of checks and X's in the various rows. If the pattern for one construct (such as honest versus dishonest) is identical to that of another construct (such as sincere versus insincere), you can suspect that these two constructs may really be one and the same for you. To how many different people did you apply each of the constructs? A construct that is applied to a large number of people may be more permeable than one that is restricted to only one person. Are the constructs divided in terms of their application to persons of the same age or sex? This may give you some idea of the limits on the range of your constructs. Now take a look at your list of contrasting constructs. Are there any constructs that you list only as a difference and never as a similarity? If so, you may be reluctant to use that construct. If you list a contrasting pole for one person only, perhaps that construct is impermeable and limited only to that person. Are any names associated only with contrasting poles? If so, your relationship to those persons may be rigid and unchanging even though you get along with them. Finally, compare your own column to those of the other people on the list. Which of the other people are you most like?

This analysis will not give you definitive answers, rather, it will simply provide a starting point for further questions. It would not be a good idea to consider the results on the grid final, instead, you should use your findings as the basis for additional study of yourself. For example, if you discover identical patterns for two constructs, such as honest versus dishonest and sincere versus insincere, you might ask yourself, "Do I believe that all honest people are sincere?" In other words, use your findings for further questions. Numerous possibilities for self-exploration are initiated by the Rep Test.

PSYCHOTHERAPY

According to Kelly, psychological disorders arise when a person clings to and continues to use personal constructs in spite of the fact that subsequent experience fails to validate them (1955). Such a person has difficulty anticipating and predicting events and is unable to learn from experiences. The neurotic flounders in an effort to develop new ways to interpret the world or rigidly holds onto constructs that are useless; instead of developing more successful constructs and solving problems, the neurotic develops symptoms.

Kelly introduced the *C-P-C cycle* and the *creativity cycle* to show how constructs change and are converted into actions (1955). The C-P-C cycle involves a sequence of circumspection, preemption, and control in a person's constructs that leads to overt behavior. During the phase of circumspection, an individual considers the various ways to look at a problem and its solutions. During the preemptive phase, the person chooses the alternative that seems to be most appropriate. In the final control phase, the choice that the person has made impels him or her to behave in a certain way. Kelly observes that the final "C" might just as well have referred to *choice*, as the person ultimately chooses for him- or herself the alternative that determines behavior. For Kelly, we are at all times free to choose and determine our behavior rather than compelled by outer or inner forces. The creativity cycle entails moving from a loose system of constructs to a tighter, more validated one. Essentially, it involves two phases. During the first phase, the individual deliberately gives his or her imagination and constructs free reign. During the second phase, the constructs are harnessed and channeled into constructive action. The creativity cycle is vital and lies at the heart of the therapeutic process.

George Kelly conceives of his therapeutic methods as "reconstruction" rather than psychotherapy. He seeks to help his patient reconstrue the world in a manner that will foster better predictions and control. The first step in his therapy is usually that of "elaborating the complaint." In this step, the therapist seeks to identify the problem, discover when and under what conditions it first arose, indicate what changes have occurred in the problem, discover any corrective measures that the client may have already taken, and find out under what conditions the problem is most and least noticeable. Elaboration of the complaint usually reveals many aspects of the person's construct system, but Kelly conceives of a second step as that of elaborating the construct system itself. Such elaboration gives a fuller picture of the elements encompassed in the complaint, allows more alternatives to arise, broadens the base of the relationship between therapist and client, and reveals the conceptual framework that created and sustained the symptoms.

In elaborating the construct system, Kelly uses the Rep Test previously described. He also employs the method of self-description. He might ask his client to write out a personal character sketch such as a close friend might write, identifying him- or herself in the third person. He might also ask his client to respond to questions such as, "What kind of child were you?" "What kind of a person do you expect to become?" and "What do you expect from therapy?" All of these methods have proven useful in elaborating the construct system.

Many of the techniques that Kelly employed to effect psychotherapeutic change are similar to those used by other therapists. However, Kelly made a unique contribution to therapeutic methodology by developing and fostering the use of role playing. In the course of therapy, if a client mentioned that he or she was having difficulty with a particular interpersonal relationship, such as an overly demanding boss or unsympathetic professor, Kelly would suggest that they pretend they were in the boss's or the professor's office and re-enact the troublesome scene. Afterwards, alternative methods of handling the scene would be explored and the scene itself re-enacted and changed in the light of various alternative ways in which the client might deal with it in the future. In his use of role playing, Kelly encouraged the use of role reversal, having the client play the role of the significant figures in his or her life while he played the client. Such role reversal allows the client to understand his or her own participation more fully and also to understand the framework of the other person.

EXERCISE:

Role Playing

Kelly's method of role playing can be fruitfully employed as a way of understanding one's own interpersonal relationships. Ask a close friend to help as you play the role of an important figure in your life. You might wish to play the role of your mother, father, professor, boss, or boy or girl friend. Ask your friend to play yourself. Identify a problem situation or a potential problem. First consider how your parent, or whoever, would handle the situation. Then act it out, with your friend playing yourself. It is important that you try to look at the situation and behave as you believe your mother, or the other figure, would. Afterwards, discuss with your friend what happened and consider alternative ways of handling the scene. Seeing yourself through your friend's eyes may help you to a closer understanding of how you come across to other people. Playing the role of other important people in your life can help you construe their interpretation of the way in which you behave.

Kelly also made use of fixed role therapy, in which he had the client enact the role of someone else for a more protracted period of time. Beginning with the client's own character sketch, developed during the phase of elaborating the construct system, the therapist, generally with professional assistance, creates a new fictitious role for his or her client to play that is different from the client's normal role and is designed to help the client explore possible ways of reconstruing his or her own experiences. The client is introduced to the fictitious role and asked to act as if he or she were the fictitious person. The client is to try to think, talk, and behave as if he or she were that other person for a period of a few days or weeks. Obviously, the role must be carefully contrived ahead of time. It must be realistic and not too threatening for the client. Fixed role therapy has proved to be a very creative way to reconstrue the self under professional guidance.

Fixed Role Playing

It is possible for the reader to obtain some of the benefits of fixed role therapy by employing it in a limited scope. Choose one aspect of your personality that you would like to work on. It is important that you choose only one aspect at a time and one with which you feel you can deal relatively comfortably. If you believe that you are generally too passive, you might try to become more assertive. Ask yourself, how does an assertive person think, respond, or behave in certain situations? Then for a period of one day, try to pretend that you are an assertive person. You might even give yourself a new name. Of course, all of your friends will call you by the same old name and assume that you are your same old passive self. However, unknown to them, the passive you is taking a day off and the new you is going to respond to them and other events as an aggressive person would. When the day is over, take time to consider how you performed in your new role. How did other people react to you? You may find yourself quite surprised by the impact that your new role has had on other people.

Kelly believed that his theory had wide implications for social and interpersonal relationships. By actively considering alternative constructions, Kelly suggested that it is possible for us individually and collectively to envision new, more creative ways of dealing with a problematic situation. Take the problem that arises when a teacher observes an inattentive student who does not listen, turns in work late, and appears to put forth very little effort. The teacher might conclude that the pupil is lazy. Kelly would ask us to pose the question: Is this the most fruitful interpretation that the teacher can make, or is it simply a cop out? Perhaps a different construction would give the teacher more latitude in creatively dealing with the problem. At the same time, the student may have his or her own construction of the classroom situation that is hindering rather than facilitating learning. The student may, for instance, perceive that teachers are out to prove the stupidity of their pupils and may only be playing an obliging role.

Kelly also encouraged the use of group therapy to help solve individual and common problems. The technique of role playing is particularly well adapted to groups where several people may assist an individual in acting out a scene. By the end of his life, Kelly was suggesting ways in which his theory could be applied to help solve social and international problems. Much of our difficulty as Americans in international relations has been our problem as a nation in understanding how different events are construed or interpreted variously by people in other countries. You might recall the war in Vietnam and try to look at it from different vantage points.

A RELATED POSITION: LEON FESTINGER'S THEORY OF COGNITIVE DISSONANCE

Somewhat related to George Kelly's cognitive theory is the cognitive dissonance theory of Leon Festinger (1919–   ), which also deals with how people understand their worlds. Festinger has not made any effort to develop a full theory of personality. He simply aims to clarify one aspect of personality and to account for how attitudes change.

Festinger (1957) believes that people seek consistency or consonance within themselves. While there are some exceptions, people generally act in accordance with their beliefs. If a person believes that stealing is wrong, he or she will probably encourage other people not to steal. What is interesting, however, are the exceptions to this rule. Many people believe that smoking is harmful to their health, but they continue to smoke. Many students know the importance of studying in order to earn good grades, but they fail to study. Festinger suggests that in these cases, the person does not really recognize his or her behavior as inconsistent; instead, the person takes steps to perceive the behavior as consistent with the beliefs.

When a person is unable to achieve consistency, a state of *dissonance* or a lack of harmony exists. Festinger describes dissonance as "psychologically uncomfortable." Dissonance leads a person to take steps to reduce the tension that it creates. Dissonance exists among cognitions. Festinger uses the term *cognitions* to refer to any belief about our self, our behavior, or the environment. These cognitive elements reflect reality. They coincide with what we feel or do in our environment. When our beliefs do not correspond with our real actions or environment, pressures arise that lead us to change either the beliefs, the actions, or the environment. In other words, we become uncomfortable if we act or behave in ways that are inconsistent with our ideas about ourselves. If necessary, we will even perceptually distort reality in order to regain some balance. In any event, the state of cognitive dissonance motivates us to undertake some activity that will reduce the inconsistency.

Dissonance may arise for a variety of reasons. A person may encounter new information or events that are at variance with his or her present beliefs. Having purchased a new car, a person may be troubled to learn that the car received a negative review in a reputable consumer magazine. Few decisions or behaviors are completely clear-cut. Most of the time there is some ambiguity in our beliefs, and this ambiguity itself leads to dissonance. Almost any decision that a person makes involves some degree of dissonance. Even trivial decisions, such as how to spend an evening, involve an awareness of different alternatives that one could choose. A person could watch TV or read a good book. However, such decisions usually do not create a great deal of dissonance because the related elements are not very strong. The greater the dissonance, however, the greater the pressure or motivation to reduce it.

Festinger posits three relationships that may exist between elements of cognition. Two elements may be *irrelevant* or have nothing to do with each other. The fact that a letter travels faster by plane than by boat probably has nothing to do with the type of weather that is good for growing crops in Iowa. However, sometimes two seemingly irrelevant elements may later become related. A Frenchman speculating in American corn would not rely on boat travel to get quick information about weather conditions in Iowa. Two elements are *dissonant* if they are contradictory or inconsistent. Elements x and y are dissonant if x implies not-y or the opposite of the original cognition. If a person wants to get out of debt but continues to make extravagant purchases, there is an inconsistency between those two elements of knowledge. People who want to get out of debt are generally conservative in their purchases. If two elements follow from or imply each other, the relationship is one of *consonance*. Knowing that drugs are dangerous and that one is not drug dependent are two elements of cognition that go together.

The degree of dissonance depends on the importance of the cognitive elements for the person. Failure to report all of one's tips as a waiter or waitress usually does not create a great deal of dissonance because this omission is recognized as a customary practice. In fact, the opposite behavior might create greater dissonance for someone in that profession. A student who failed to prepare adequately for a major examination that would change the course of his or her life would probably experience greater dissonance. The degree of dissonance, therefore, depends on the strength of the related elements.

Festinger uses the example of a cigarette smoker to illustrate the ways in which a person can seek to reduce cognitive dissonance. Many smokers were upset some years ago when they learned that the surgeon general had determined that cigarette smoking was dangerous to their health. His warning decorates every pack of American cigarettes. Such information is inconsistent with the knowledge that one is a smoker. Some people handled the dissonance by changing their behavior. Giving up smoking made their behavior consistent with the knowledge that smoking is dangerous. On the other hand, other people handled the situation by changing their beliefs about the effects of smoking. In such cases, the truth of the surgeon general's report was denied or minimized and the positive benefits of smoking were accentuated.

Dissonance may be reduced in three ways. First, one can change one's behavior so that the knowledge of how one behaves is consonant with other cognitive elements. The person who stops smoking when he or she learns of its dangers is reducing the dissonance by altering behavior. Second, one can seek to change the environment or situation in which the cognitive dissonance arises. The efforts to create low tar and nicotine cigarettes, which are less harmful, is an example of this alternative. Changing the environment or situation is feasible and helpful if one is able to do it. This alternative is not always possible. Lastly, one can add new cognitive elements that help to reduce the dissonance. A smoker might seek out research studies that criticize the surgeon general's report and avoid reading those that support it. He or she might observe that crossing the street or driving a car is far more dangerous than smoking and thereby reduce the importance of the cognitive elements that smoking is dangerous. When efforts to reduce dissonance are unsuccessful, however, the pressures to reduce it continue and the person shows signs of psychological discomfort.

Reducing or eliminating dissonance is often difficult because the cognitive elements resist change. Changing our behavior is often painful and entails loss. The withdrawal symptoms of giving up smoking and the satisfaction provided from the activity itself have made many people reluctant to stop. Some changes simply are not possible. Sometimes we may not know of an alternative way to behave. Other behaviors, particularly emotional responses, may not be under voluntary control. Many people wish to stop smoking, but they find it very difficult to do so.

Festinger has explored the implications of his theory in four main areas: the consequences of decisions; the effects of forced compliance; voluntary and involuntary exposure to information; and the role of social support.

Any decision entails a certain amount of dissonance, because it has involved rejecting certain alternatives. Festinger gives the example of having to choose between two attractive jobs. Both jobs have certain positive features, which makes it difficult to choose between them. Once the decision has been made, those cognitive elements that supported the choice of the unchosen alternative create some dissonance. Processes then arise that seek to balance the dissonance. A person begins to alter his or her cognitions so that they fall into line with the decision made.

There are three ways in which dissonance following a decision can be reduced. First, one could change or revoke the decision. Such a solution is rare and often impractical. Moreover, it is usually not effective, because it simply reverses the consonance and dissonance of the elements and restores the very conflict that existed prior to the decision. A more common way to reduce the dissonance is to change the cognitions about the alternatives. By eliminating some of the dissonant elements and adding new consonant elements, the total dissonance will be reduced. A person could actively seek out information emphasizing the benefits of the chosen job and the weak points of the rejected one. Finally, the dissonance can be reduced by creating *cognitive overlap*. If the jobs can be construed as very similar, it makes little difference which offer is accepted and the dissonance is minimized.

A second topic that Festinger has explored is that of forced compliance. At times, a person will comply publicly with certain overt behaviors or statements of belief, while privately maintaining the original stance. A young child may apologize for having committed a certain misbehavior in order to avoid punishment, while inwardly feeling no remorse. A prisoner of war may betray his or her country in order to save colleagues' lives. Public compliance arises because a person is threatened with punishment or is offered a significant reward. Once a person complies there is dissonance, because the overt behavior does not correspond to the inner belief. Festinger believes that the size of the reward or punishment is an important factor in determining the degree of dissonance. If the reward or punishment is very great, there will be little dissonance because one's cognitions of the outcome outweigh other considerations. At the point of a gun, an individual can be coerced into performing many behaviors that he or she would not do otherwise. As the reward or punishment becomes smaller, dissonance increases after compliance. Even if a person does not comply, the fact that he or she was tempted leads to some dissonance. However, in the case of noncompliance, the smaller the reward or punishment, the lesser the dissonance.

Reducing the dissonance after forced compliance can take one of two forms. An individual may change his or her private opinion so that it coincides with the action taken and his or her overt behavior. Such attitudinal change is more likely to occur if the reward or punishment was just sufficient to elicit the response that created considerable later dissonance. A second way to reduce the dissonance is to magnify the value of the reward or punishment so that it coincides with one's behavior.

In a now classic experiment (Festinger and Carlsmith, 1959), subjects were asked to perform a dull tedious task and then were offered rewards of one dollar or twenty dollars to tell prospective subjects that the task was actually interesting. Those who received only one dollar later reported that they found the experiment more interesting than those who were offered twenty dollars. Festinger believes that these subjects experienced greater dissonance because of the small amount of the reward, which led them to change their opinion about the nature of the task. Those who received twenty dollars apparently felt justified in lying about the experiment.

Festinger has also studied the implications of cognitive dissonance for the voluntary or involuntary seeking of information. Apart from active curiosity and seeking knowledge for its own sake, if an area of information is relevant to some behavior that we might engage in, we are more likely to seek out information. We will also seek out information in order to reduce current dissonance. If a person has just bought a new car, he or she might voluntarily attend a lecture that is thought to support the action just taken. On the other hand, if we are experiencing a high degree of dissonance and wish to change our behavior, we may actively seek out dissonance-increasing information that will assist in toppling our resistance to change.

At times, we involuntarily come into contact with information. Knowledge of a new event may be so widespread that we cannot avoid it, other people may not share our opinion, or we can be accidentally exposed to information while in the pursuit of other objectives. When involuntary information is introduced that is dissonant with our present cognitions, the same efforts to reduce dissonance arise. In addition, we may also engage in defensive measures that will prevent the new information from being integrated into our cognitive system. A person might avoid future exposure, misinterpret or misperceive the material, or find some other way to deny its validity. In this regard, Festinger points out that we are likely to distort reality in order to avoid dissonance.

Finally, Festinger has investigated the role of social groups in fostering dissonance. The degree of dissonance that we experience when other people disagree with us depends on the extent to which objective or physical reality substantiates our opinion and the number of other people in the group that agrees with us. It also depends on how important or valuable the group is to us. Voicing the sole dissenting opinion in a group that matters to one a great deal leads to greater dissonance for the individual.

Dissonance that arises from social disagreements is usually reduced by changing one's own opinion, trying to persuade other people to change their views, or finding ways to discount the opinion of the others on the basis that they are not as well informed, intelligent, or knowledgeable as we are.

RESEARCH AND CRITICISM OF COGNITIVE THEORY

Although psychologists are paying increased attention to the role of cognitive factors in personality, surprisingly little research has been generated from George Kelly's theory of constructive alternativism. Most of the empirical studies concern the Rep Test (Bonarius, 1965; Bannister and Mair, 1968) rather than the theory itself. Studies such as Bannister and Fransella (1966) and Bannister and Salmon (1966) suggest the possible usefulness of the Rep Test and Kelly's constructs for understanding the disturbance in thought in schizophrenia. They conclude that the thought constructs of a schizophrenic are less interrelated and more inconsistent than other people's, particularly with reference to interpersonal constructs.

Kelly has been brought to task for his overly intellectual view of the individual and therapy and for his failure to deal adequately with human emotions. Further, Kelly's suggestion that all of our constructs are of a bipolar form is not necessarily true. Some linguistic and cultural systems do not appear to dichotomize. Nevertheless, the biggest criticism of Kelly's work is that in his effort to do justice to the human intellect, he has ignored the full range of the human personality (Bruner and Rogers, 1956).

Festinger's theory of cognitive dissonance has given rise to considerable efforts to test it. Discussion of some of this research is included in Brehmn and Cohen (1962) and Festinger (1964). Two basic criticisms have been made of efforts to test Festinger's theory under controlled laboratory conditions. First, the design of dissonance experiments is such that it is difficult to draw definite conclusions. The variables that require manipulation are so complex that we cannot be sure that the experimenters have succeeded in creating dissonance rather than some other internal states. Second, the statistical analysis of the data has been questioned for its adequacy. Nevertheless, experimental research on dissonance theory has generated some striking, if not controversial, preliminary conclusions. The greatest appeal of Festinger's theory lies in its simplicity. But this very simplicity may be its downfall, as it may mask a great many other variables that remain important and are not adequately accounted for in the theory (Chapanis and Chapanis, 1964).

EVALUATION AND IMPLICATIONS

George Kelly's theory is based on the philosophical stance of constructive alternativism. Kelly and Festinger have made it clear that a person's cognitions are crucial to self-perception and interaction with the external world. Both employ the concept of cognition broadly to include perceptions, ideas, beliefs, and attitudes. They point out that our constructs are subject to modification. When our constructs are dissonant or unconfirmed, we become uncomfortable, experience unpleasant emotions, and are motivated to change our constructs and the behaviors to which they lead.

The primary difference between the theories of Kelly and Festinger is the greater emphasis that Kelly places on the rationality of the human being. Kelly believes that, because we proceed as personal scientists in our increasingly sophisticated scientific world, our constructs are increasingly more successful approximations of the real world. In comparison, Festinger suggests that our efforts to reduce dissonance do not necessarily take reality into account. Indeed, in our efforts to reduce dissonance, we frequently distort or even deny reality.

George Kelly was much more aware of the philosophical basis of his theory than most personality theorists. At times, his discussion of the way in which we validate our personal constructs has overtones of philosophical compellingness rather than sole reliance on empirical evidence, suggesting that we are every bit as much philosophers as we are scientists. Kelly was committed to the philosophical assumptions of rationality and subjectivity, an unusual combination that contributes to the unique character of his work.

George Kelly did not believe that the world or the person is ultimately knowable through a scientific methodology. Science is simply an extremely useful construct system that is helpful for explaining events. It is one system of constructs among many alternatives. Since we cannot posit any objective reality apart from our understanding of it, we cannot assert that science can ever comprehend the real person. It can provide, however, useful constructions that assist us in making predictions. This point of view characterized Kelly's attitude toward his own philosophizing and theorizing as well, since he readily acknowledged and expected that his own theory would ultimately be succeeded by an alternative construction (1970). "At best," he wrote, "it is an ad interim theory" (1955).

In spite of the "ad interim" character of Kelly's theory, it has attracted considerable attention and controversy. Kelly is increasingly included as a major theorist in personality texts, and the influence of cognitive factors in personality, Kelly's primary concern, is an area of intensified interest in psychology.

SUGGESTIONS FOR FURTHER READING

George Kelly was not a prolific writer. Two books and about a dozen articles constitute the sum of his publications. His basic theory was published in a two-volume work called *The Psychology of Personal Constructs* (Norton, 1955). The first three chapters of those volumes were published separately as *A Theory of Personality: a Psychology of Personal Constructs* (Norton, 1963). Kelly's writing is rather academic and difficult reading for the lay person, who might be better advised to begin with a good secondary source such as D. Bannister and F. Fransella, *Inquiring Man: The Theory of Personal Constructs* (Penguin, 1966). Donald Bannister, an Englishman, is Kelly's most fervent disciple, and this book is a concise introduction to Kelly's theory.

Leon Festinger's theory was set forth in *A Theory of Cognitive Dissonance* (Stanford University Press, 1957). Summaries of his experimental efforts to test his theory are included in *Conflict, Decision, and Dissonance* (Stanford University Press, 1964).

PART VII

Personality Theories East and West

During the last few decades there has been a steady growth of interest in the ideas and practices of the East. For the most part, Western psychologists have ignored Asian theories of personality or human behavior because they have lacked scientific validation and substantiation. Recently, however, new teachings about human nature and the cosmos have been entering Western culture from the Orient and the ancient worlds. They are receiving attention from both young and old, lay and professional. Many people have turned to the East with the hope of finding something that could temper or humanize the thrust of modern technology that threatens to destroy the very civilization that developed it. There has been a growing feeling that the dominant concerns of Western science and psychology have ignored the spiritual side of the person. A desire to return to the origins of our own Western tradition where perhaps we may rediscover truths that have since been forgotten is apparent.

By common agreement, the beginning of scientific psychology is generally dated at 1879, the year in which Wilhelm Wundt, a German scholar trained in physiology, physics, and philosophy, established a psychological laboratory in Leipzig in order to explore the experience of consciousness. As a science, psychology is an infant, barely one hundred years old. The scientific study of personality is an even more recent effort. The theory of personality only became a formal and systematic area of specialization in American psychology during the 1930s. Enormous progress has been made during the past half century in gathering together a significant amount of information about human nature and personality. However, while we have learned a great deal about ourselves, we are still far from an adequate understanding of what it means to be a human being. While our modern technology and culture have given rise to practices that may relieve many forms of human illness and suffering, they have yet to provide satisfactory answers to the most fundamental questions of human existence. Those questions about the ultimate meaning, purpose, and goal of our lives continue to haunt us and to demand answers.

Of course, the quest for answers to these questions has hardly been restricted to the past several decades, let alone the past one hundred years. The search of human beings for self-understanding began with the emergence of human self-consciousness, reached great heights in Oriental cultures and ancient Greece, and has found perennial expression in every phase of civilization that has followed. Each one of our various cultural constructs—our philosophy, religion, art, politics, and science—may be seen as expressions of our search for identity. In the broadest sense all these investigations may be seen to be concerned with psychology insofar as they have explored and expressed what it means to be a person.

If psychology is a young science, it also represents the oldest of human concerns. The term *psychology* comes to us from the ancient

Greeks. In their efforts to understand the world, these early people were equally curious about the movements of the heavenly bodies and the nature and attributes of the human soul. Prototypes of all our modern sciences may be found in their writings. In their efforts to understand human nature, the Greeks were greatly impressed by the dramatic differences between the individual in waking life and asleep. A man who is asleep appears to be in repose, however, on awakening, he may report a journey that he undertook or a battle in which he participated. Such phenomena suggested to the Greeks that there was some essence or reality of a person that extends beyond his or her mere physical appearance. Homer labeled this essence the *psyche*, coining that term to refer to the breath or principle of life. Ancient Greeks sought to understand the psyche, which was thought to evidence its reality in the waking state, in dreams, and in the freedom of life after death as well as in life on earth.

Although the Greek *psyche* is commonly translated as "soul," the word as originally introduced by Homer did not represent, as we might suppose, an immaterial, immortal "soul" or "spirit" of a person as opposed to his or her body. Rather, it represented the essence of the human being. Perhaps a better translation of "psyche" would be "self." Later, during the early Christian era, as philosophy and rhetoric came to replace poetry and mythology, the term "psyche" came to be identified with *pneuma* or "spirit." The psyche became progressively disembodied. The path led from *pneuma* to the more rationalistic and intellectual concept of *nous* or "mind." By the time of the enlightenment, "psyche" had become synonymous with consciousness or mental processes. As we have seen, John Watson, the founder of behaviorism, subsequently pointed out that states of consciousness are not objectively verifiable. He deemed them unfit as data for science and encouraged psychologists simply to study behavior. Under Watson's leadership, psychology was transformed from the largely introspective study of consciousness that had concerned earlier investigators into the study of overt or observable behaviors. Thus, in the usual American university, a strange situation prevails. Students of psychology rapidly discover that for the most part, they are not engaged in the study of the psyche but in the study of behavior.

As Westerners, familiar with our own brand of science and psychology, we are frequently unaware of or tend to depreciate many other earlier or current psychologies, such as those that emerge from early Greek philosophy and the Oriental traditions. Socrates, Plato, and Aristotle, philosophers of ancient Greece, each addressed the question of what it means to be a human being, and in so doing developed theories of personality. We have already discussed Hippocrates' theory of the four humors. Hinduism, Buddhism, Confucianism, Taoism, and Sufism, among other Oriental traditions, have raised questions about the ultimate meaning and purpose of human life. All of these movements have developed psychologies insofar as they have explored the psyche or the self, and all have implied personality theories insofar as they have investigated what it means to be a human being. It may come as a surprise to realize that the assumptions that constitute the consensus reality of the twentieth-century Western world are not necessarily universal and shared by other cultures. From the viewpoint of many of these movements, several of our contemporary Western ideas about personality are incredibly foreign. No wonder we have difficulty communicating, as long as we tacitly assume that our comprehension of human behavior is universally shared.

Part VII seeks to explore conceptions of personality as they have appeared in the East and the West. Although there are many varieties of Eastern thought, almost all of them share certain characteristics by which they may be identified and distinguished from Western thought. An examination of these shared characteristics as well as a closer look at an Eastern movement, Zen Buddhism, that is gaining popularity in the West, can give us some familiarity with the Oriental approach to personality. This approach can then be compared with our own Western tradition—past and present—in order to identify points of convergence and divergence.

In directing our attention to patterns of Eastern and early Western thought, the question, as posed by Jacob Needleman, is not simply whether these movements have something that we do not have, but more importantly, do the teachings of the East offer something that the teachings of the West once had, but that we have since lost sight of (1970)? The choice confronting us is not necessarily a choice between East and West. It may be possible for us to integrate the insights of Eastern philosophy with the heritage of the West. In so doing, we might be able to come to a closer realization of the shared humanity of all human beings and the possibility of increased communication and understanding among people of themselves and their places in the cosmos.

CHAPTER 14

Eastern Theories of Personality

There are many varieties of Eastern thought: Hinduism, Buddhism, Confucianism, Taoism, and Sufism, among others. Generally, we think of these movements as Oriental religions or philosophies. However as Alan Watts, a leading exponent of Zen Buddhism, has suggested, in many respects these thought systems do not resemble philosophy or religion as much as they resemble the art of psychology and psychotherapy (1961). Their basic concern is with the human situation: the suffering and frustrations of human beings. They emphasize the importance and development of techniques to accomplish change. Eastern thought aims at transformations in consciousness, feelings, emotions, and one's relation to other people and the world. Thus, each of these movements of Eastern thought may be seen as containing its own psychological categories and be understood as a quest toward self-understanding.

GENERAL CHARACTERISTICS OF EASTERN PSYCHOLOGY

While there are many differences among them, almost all Eastern movements of thought have certain characteristics in common. Jacob Needleman has singled out two features that distinguish Eastern movements from the general pattern of thought in the West (1970).

For the most part, Eastern religions are centered on the self. But the self that is focused on is not the conscious ego or individual mind of Western psychology. Rather, the East conceives of the true self as a deeper, inner consciousness that identifies the individual with the universal or cosmos. Eastern thinkers point out that many of us confuse ourselves with the social role or social identity that others have assigned to us, or what Jung would call the *persona* or mask. This identification is *maya,* or an illusion. Our ego is simply a social convention. When we speak of "I," "you," "him," an "individual," and so forth, we are conforming to the conventions of this world. However, the truth is that there is no "I" or "individual" in ultimate reality, and the "I" should not be confused with reality. Once we can see through the illusion of individual existence, we can recognize ourselves for who we are, both unique and universal. I am universal because my organism is inseparable from the universe at large. I am unique in that I am *I*, not whom others say or expect me to be.

Confusion of oneself with one's social role leads to feelings of isolation, alienation, and loneliness. There is a conflict between who I am and whom others say and expect me to be. Insofar as I attempt to identify myself with my social role or identity, I become further and further estranged from my true identity.

Identification with one's conscious ego or social role leads to a multitude of various contradictory wishes and desires, as well as to vigorous efforts to satisfy them. We seek to satisfy our bodily needs, to be free of pain and fear, to acquire wealth and material possessions, to be loved and love, to receive honor, recognition, and praise from our fellow human beings. At the same time, we seek to be self-sufficient, to control others, and to conquer the fear of death. The problem is that the satisfaction of one of these desires is usually at the expense of another desire, because the desires themselves contradict one another. We become caught in a many-horned dilemma, none of the solutions to which is satisfactory. We seek to satisfy our wants only to discover that in the end none of these worldly interests really satisfies our deepest needs.

In Eastern literature, these desires are frequently symbolized by animals, as if hordes of animals lived within each of us. Each animal seeks its own needs and pleasures. Carnivores feed off of one another to obtain their food. If we identify with the animals, we do not relieve our suffering. As soon as we feed one animal, another appears demanding food. Often it demands for its prey the very animal that we have just cared for. When our concern is to satisfy life's secular and external conditions, we do not find happiness or release from suffering. We merely identify with the animals and increase our internal conflicts. The animals within are concerned only with their own pleasure. They are self-centered in the common meaning of the term. Each seeks to satisfy its own desires. They are not interested in each other or in the truth. Yet it is only by recognizing the truth that their needs may be fully met.

What is required is a higher or deeper form of consciousness that can curb and care for the animals in a manner that fulfills their true needs as part of a whole. The aim of Eastern psychology is transformation of desires rather than their satisfaction. The animals cry out, "I am," "Feed me!" It is this feeling, "I am," "I must be fed," that creates the illusion of self or ego. But that ego has no correspondence with reality. True consciousness involves being whole, rising above the level of individuality, and becoming one with the cosmos and universal, as in a peak experience. This is not easy, however, as the animals within try to con us into *feeling* whole rather than *being* whole (Needleman, 1970).

An Emphasis on the Practical

Eastern psychology is eminently practical. The writings of Eastern thinkers do not concentrate on telling their readers "how" to do it, they present anecdotes concerning a methodology that, if followed, may enable them to do it. Eastern thinkers believe that the truth that we seek is not found in books. It emerges only in the course of living, and to permit it to emerge, we need to undergo a process. The process is not undertaken through following a recipe, rather, through the guidance of a *guru*, or teacher, who is seen as indispensable for such a spiritual journey.

The practice of Eastern psychology entails a systematic training of body and mind that enables one to perceive the truth that lies within his or her inner being. The follower of Eastern thought is introduced to a variety of techniques. He or she is taught to meditate and to engage in physical and psychological exercises. A disciple's life is governed by a great many rules and rituals, whose purpose is to develop a freedom beyond the rules that permits one to be oneself.

Such techniques have not been totally absent in the West. The Socratic dialectic was a particular technique in which the teacher acted as a midwife, permitting the inner life of the person to unfold. Christian monasteries and certain Jewish communities practiced and continue to practice a rich discipline and ritual in order to cultivate the spiritual side of the self. More recently, Sigmund Freud initiated his followers into a precise technique, free association, that is not unlike meditation in that it aims to alter one's normal state of consciousness and to uncover aspects of the self of which one was formerly unaware. However, for most Westerners the rituals and practices that remain or are available today in the West seem empty and meaningless. We may go to church or temple on the Sabbath and enjoy the beautiful service. We may obtain some sort of emotional release from various practices and rituals that temporarily allay our everyday discontents. But these practices do not initiate us into a process that transforms our lives. It is as if we tried to cure an illness by hearing about a new method of treatment but never went to a doctor for treatment itself (Needleman, 1970).

ZEN BUDDHISM

Of the many forms of Eastern thought—Hinduism, Buddhism, Confucianism, Taoism, Sufism, and so forth—one in particular, Zen Buddhism, has caught the interest of the West. In order to introduce the reader to the kinds of personality theorizing characteristic of the East, it seems appropriate to focus on this movement. The study of one conceptual framework, in depth, can be more illuminating than a brief overview of several viewpoints. But we must remember that Zen Buddhism is not the only pattern of personality conception in the East. Other frameworks also illumine the human condition. Nevertheless, Zen Buddhism may be singled out as a system that, while unique, also typifies the East and has had an increasing appeal to the West.

The Japanese Buddhist Daisetz Teitaro Suzuki is the person who is largely responsible for introducing the concepts of Zen Buddhism to the West. Suzuki, undoubtedly the greatest authority on Buddhism and Zen in this century, dedicated his life to the study of Zen and to interpreting its concepts and philosophy for the Western reader. Suzuki was born in 1869; he was educated at Tokyo University and studied Zen Buddhism at Engakuji in Kamakura. He attained his enlightenment in 1896 under the guidance of Soyen Shaku Roshi, a well-known guru. Suzuki was a scholar who wrote and spoke with authority. He studied the original works of Zen in Sanskrit, Pali, Chinese, and Japanese, so he was very familiar with their content. Professor of Buddhist philosophy in the Otani University in Kyoto, Japan, he wrote over twenty books in English on the subject of Buddhism and at least eighteen books in Japanese, which have not yet been translated. The publication of Suzuki's *Essays in Zen Buddhism* in 1927 literally brought Zen Buddhism to the attention of the West and aroused its genuine interest. In large measure the description of Zen that follows is based on the writings of Suzuki, or his followers, and his translations of Zen anecdotes and sayings.*

Suzuki was not simply a scholar, he was also a practicing Buddhist. While he was not a priest of any Buddhist sect, he was well known, respected, and loved in Japan. Those who heard him were greatly impressed by his knowledge of spiritual things. While it is true that Suzuki was sometimes described as a dilettante, popularizing Zen for

---

* The quotations and anecdotes in this chapter are from D. T. Suzuki, *An Introduction to Zen Buddhism*. Reprinted by permission of Grove Press, Inc. and Rider and Company, London. Copyright © 1964. All rights reserved. And also from Alan W. Watts, *The Spirit of Zen*. Reprinted by permission of Grove Press, Inc. Copyright © Hutchinson Publishing Group, Ltd., 1958 by Alan W. Watts and John Murray (Publishers) Ltd.

the West, those who knew him personally attested to his profound spiritual insight. It appeared clear to them that he was searching for words to describe and share his own experience of enlightenment. He spoke of a message that had transformed his life and that would transform others who permitted it to enter into their beings. He referred to a higher level of consciousness in which he dwelt. At the same time, he realized that comprehension of the secrets of Zen lies beyond the power of the intellect alone. Trying to grasp the point of Zen is like trying to hold onto a bar of wet soap. Zen eludes intellectual comprehension; it requires that it be lived. Suzuki's witness to the life of Zen continued until his death in 1966 at the age of ninety-five.

The Origins of Zen

Zen is a school of Buddhism that claims to represent the purest essence of Buddhist teachings. The origins of Zen trace back to the story of Buddha.

Siddhartha Gautama, known after his enlightenment as the Buddha or "enlightened one," was born about 560 B.C. in the city of Kapilavastu in northern India. The exact site of his birthplace is unknown. Unlike some other early religious and philosophical leaders, however, his historical existence has been clearly established. Gautama's father was a wealthy nobleman who tried to protect his son from the harsher, seamier side of life. Gautama was brought up in luxurious surroundings and provided with every conceivable comfort. Nevertheless, he felt uneasy and tormented by the sorrows and evils that he could not avoid seeing around him. He was particularly troubled by the problems of old age, sickness, and death. He asked his father whether there was any solution to the problem of suffering, but his father, distressed by his failure to protect his son, could not answer the question.

At the age of twenty-nine, in spite of his father's judgments and attempts to prevent him, Gautama renounced everything that he had, gave up his rights to his father's throne, and left his wife and newborn son in search of something that would reduce his uneasiness. In his own words, he sought the "incomparable security of a Nirvana," or an exalted state of consciousness and bliss.

Gautama withdrew into the forest and spent the next six years as a mendicant or spiritual beggar. For a time he studied with two Hindu sages who taught him yoga and philosophy, but he continued to feel unsatisfied. Later, he joined a group of five ascetics and practiced severe deprivations. Gautama was merciless in the extremes to which he carried out his asceticism. He fasted, painfully mortified his body, and sought to renounce all human desires. These practices, however, simply brought him to a point near death from starvation. They did little to quell his uneasiness.

According to tradition, on April 8, 508 B.C., during his thirty-sixth year, Gautama, in a state of utter exhaustion, sat down under a peepul tree (an Indian fig tree), later known as the "bodhi tree" or the "tree of enlightenment." He realized that neither intellectual efforts nor ascetic extremes could provide a pathway to the truth. He resolved to wait under that tree until he attained enlightenment. He meditated throughout the night and experienced various levels of consciousness until he reached the stage after which he was known as Buddha, "the enlightened one." His enlightenment awakened him to the ultimate truth, liberating him from the cycles of cause and effect, death and rebirth as expressed in the doctrine of *karma*, or the belief that a person's actions determine his or her destiny in the next life and led to the conviction that the phenomenal world of ordinary appearances is illusory.

After a period of rest, the Buddha decided that he should share his message with others. The remainder of his life was spent teaching. He traveled from place to place and talked to whoever would listen. He led his followers in meditation and discussions. He was described as radiant, compassionate, and charismatic. He continued his work for forty-five years, until his death at the age of over eighty years in about 485 B.C.

After his enlightenment, Buddha developed his doctrine in the form of Four Noble Truths. The first noble truth describes our human situation as one of suffering and frustration that arises from our refusal to accept the basic impermanence and transitory character of life and all things. The second noble truth tells us that the cause of our suffering is ignorance, which arises from clinging or grasping to fixed notions about the world that are actually *maya* or illusions, such as the concept of a separate individual ego. These false concepts lead to the vicious cycle of *karma*, with its unending circle of life and death, cause and effect. The third noble truth states that we can transcend this vicious cycle and reach a state of *nirvana* or unspeakable bliss. The term *nirvana* literally means "waning out." It refers to the extinction of all desire, resentment, and selfishness that is caused by identifying with one's separate ego. Nirvana is not a place, rather, it is a condition of the mind. It entails an exalted state of consciousness in which the self is identified with Brahma, or that which is. To reach nirvana is to attain enlightenment or awakening. The fourth noble truth is Buddha's noble eightfold path that leads to enlightenment and escape from suffering. The eightfold path consists of correct seeing, knowing, speech, conduct, way of living, effort, awareness, and meditation. Essentially, the eightfold path is a method of appropriate ethical action that enjoins moderation or a middle way between extremes of behavior.

Gautama was steeped in the tradition of the *Upanishads*, an early sacred literature of India that goes back as far as 800 B.C. The term "Upanishad" is from Sanskrit and means "to sit by the side of the master and be." The Upanishads are a collection of esoteric or secret discussions between a holy man and a disciple that were designed to initiate the disciple into the inner meaning of life. Over two hundred of these little discourses are believed to have been written. Not one of them, however, is unambiguous and fully clear. They appear to us as a series of notes or aphorisms that give rise to more questions than answers. The Upanishads have also been subject to a number of different interpretations. Nevertheless, they show a general thrust that may be conceptualized as the doctrines of *Brahma,* the ground of existence, and the doctrine of *Atman,* or the illusion of individuality.

According to the Upanishads, the ground of all existence is Brahma. The word "Brahma" means "that which is" and defies any further definition. Brahma is variously described as life, joy, the void, and so forth. In the Upanishads, "Brahma" encompasses all phenomena. Thus, it refers to Being, but also to non-Being. In short, Brahma has no characteristics and cannot be described as having any. Brahma is everything, yet it is nothing.

The Upanishads teach us that Brahma, that which is, expresses itself in a universe where you, Atman, find yourself. Atman denotes the inner self of an individual. In its origin the term "Atman" appears to be related to words in other languages that refer to "breath" or "the breath of life." Such a connotation also applied to Homer's "psyche." The Upanishads maintain that while it is true that Atman appears to be differentiated into individual selves (atmen) or egos, in reality, there is only one Atman. The inner selves of individuals are essentially one and the same. There is only one Atman or Self.

In the final analysis, the doctrines of Brahma and Atman are one and the same. The true essence of the Self or Atman is Brahma or that which is. Therefore, Brahma is Atman and Atman is Brahma. Since there is nothing beyond what has been created, the universe and oneself are composed of Brahma.

Various analogies may be used to describe the relationship of Atman and Brahma. If you place a drop of water into the ocean, it becomes the sea. If a crystal of salt is placed in water, the water and salt mix together. Neither of these analogies, however, can capture the ultimate meaning. Since Brahma defies intellectual conceptualization, its meaning is elusive and cannot be expressed in ordinary language.

The individual "self" or separate "ego" is a misperception of what is really Atman. Thus, the experiences of the individual ego are also misperceptions. This means that the phenomenal world of appearances, as we know it, is illusory and unreal. The ordinary worldly interests and concerns that usually occupy our minds and efforts are fraudulent because they cannot begin to meet our innermost needs. The real problem is not the physical world with its karmic cycles of life and death, cause and effect, but our subjective constructs about the world that lead us to understand it in those terms. The enlightened one finds freedom in meditation on Atman and in conquering his or her individual ego through ascetic practices.

Buddha was silent on the question "What is the Self?" and the doctrines of Atman and Brahma. Most of his followers believe that he accepted the doctrines as facts beyond dispute, and believed that talk about them was unimportant. He felt that it was more important to search than to know. Buddha laid speculation aside in favor of being practical and assisting others in being practical.

It is difficult to describe Buddha's original doctrine, because such a wide variety of Buddhist groups grew out of it. The two main divisions, Hinayana and Mayayana Buddhism, known as the lesser (Hina) and the greater (Maha) vessels of knowledge or wisdom, differ as much as Catholic and Protestant Christianity.

Buddhism divided into two main wings, based on the authority of certain sets of scriptures consisting of sayings and teachings of the Buddha that his followers wrote down after his death. The southern *Theravada* or *Hinayana* school spread throughout Ceylon, Vietnam, Cambodia, Thailand, and Burma. The northern *Mahayana* school spread to Tibet, Mongolia, China, Korea, and Japan. In general, Hinayana Buddhism is more speculative and analytical. Following a formal and rigid school of thought that sticks to the letter of Buddha's teachings as expressed in the Pali version of the scriptures, it teaches that an individual may achieve salvation and release from life's sorrows through rigorous discipline and knowledge. The Hinayana ideal is the *arhat* or monk, who seeks individual deliverance.

Mahayana Buddhism, by contrast, is more fluid. The Mahayana school continually reinterpreted the scriptures, giving rise to a wide variety of changes. Mahayana emphasizes the spiritual needs of common everyday people. Its ideal is the *Bodhisattva*, a Buddhist saint who himself reaches enlightenment and tries to help others find salvation. Mahayana is more relaxed, emphasizing love and action rather than knowledge. Mahayana has given rise to a number of different sects. Strangely enough, in India itself today neither one of these movements is a strong force. For the most part, the Indian people who followed the Buddha incorporated and absorbed his ideas into their own Hindu faith.

Both Mahayana and Hinayana Buddhism agree that the individual self or ego is an illusion. They disagree, however, over what is discovered when the person transcends the barriers of the individual ego and no longer resists the life that extends beyond it. We recall that Buddha was silent on the question, "What is the Self?" The Hinayana believe that his silence meant that there is no self at all. The Mahayana, on the other hand, assume that a true Self emerges when the fallacious ego is abandoned. This true Self is identified with the whole of the universe. According to the Mahayana, to say that there is no Self at all is to be nihilistic, to deny life, and to stress only the temporary character of things. Mahayana believes that any denial must be completed by an affirmation. The individual self is denied, but the true

Self is found in the totality of that which is. At the same time, Mahayana uses the term *sunyata,* or voidness, to refer to the Self, because the Self goes beyond any intellectual conceptualization of it.

Zen Buddhism stems from the Mahayana branch. It arose in China during the sixth century when an obscure and perhaps legendary patriarch called Bodhidharma brought Buddhism to China and founded the Ch'an sect. The term "Ch'an" in Chinese is the same as "Zen" in Japanese. Both words are generally translated as "meditation." This term is rather misleading, however, as Zen does not entail the speculative reflection "meditation" usually implies. On the contrary, Zen avoids all intellectual conceptualization and stresses a higher state of consciousness in which one finds union with ultimate reality. Further, Zen suggests that this higher state of consciousness is to be found in the living of everyday life rather than in solitary meditation and thought.

The Ch'an sect incorporated elements of *Taoism,* a Chinese philosophy, into their system. They identified Brahma and Atman with the *Tao,* an indefinable concept employed by Confucius and Lao-tse, Chinese philosophers who advocated a way of life that was in harmony with the course of nature. The word "Tao" has been variously translated as "the Way," "the Law," "Nature," and "Reality." The Chinese character for "Tao" consists of symbols that indicate movement. The general idea of Tao seems to be one of movement and growth. As the ultimate reality, Tao is the equivalent of the Brahma of the Upanishads. Nevertheless, the concept of Tao, like the concepts of Brahma and Atman, cannot be intellectually defined. Lao-tse told his followers that if Tao could be described in words, it would not be the true Tao. He taught that Tao was elusive and forever in motion. Trying to conceptualize Tao is like trying to catch one's shadow or swim against the current of a river. Our human suffering arises from our efforts to conceptualize and grasp the shadow or the stream that continually eludes us. We can find peace only by going along with the current and permitting it to carry us to our destination.

Tao was thought to manifest itself in two forces: *yin* and *yang.* As the classic diagram shows, however, yin and yang are not static but are dynamically interrelated. One cannot move without the other. Together they compose a circle that continually rotates, and each contains within itself the seed of the other, which is represented by the small circles. Yang is frequently associated with light, creativity, masculinity, and power. Yin is often described as dark, feminine, receptive, and maternal. However, they represent different emphases rather than polar extremes. Since each is dynamically linked to the other, they express, not opposition, but the ultimate unity of all opposites.

In the twelfth century, Zen Buddhism, enriched by its contact with Chinese philosophy, was brought to Japan. In Japan it flourished and became a major form of religion. Japanese painting, sculpture, architecture, and poetry all give witness to the wide variety of cultural

FIGURE 14.1   The Classic Diagram of Yin and Yang

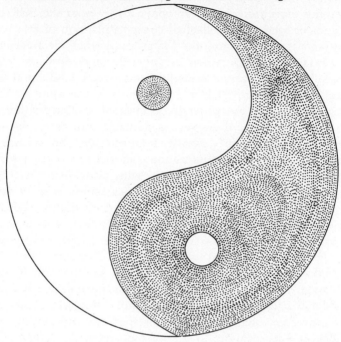

expressions that Zen fostered, although Zen is no longer dominant in Japan. Within the last fifty years, Zen has been introduced to the United States where it already shows signs of giving rise to a potentially significant movement of thought.

The Teachings of Zen

Zen Buddhism is a forthright, vigorous reaction against the strong intellectualism that has characterized the majority of philosophical, religious, and psychological approaches to life. Teachers of Zen suggest that the solution to life's problems cannot be found through intellectual channels, only through the paths of intuition and experience. In its essence, then, it is misleading to describe Zen as a religion or a philosophy. Zen does not set forth a doctrine of religious belief nor does it provide a method of philosophical inquiry. For that matter, it is also inaccurate to refer to Zen as a psychology, as it does not present a theory of the psyche or the self. Zen is totally devoid of all conceptual ideas. To speak of Zen is immediately to distort and misrepresent it. Ideally, one can know Zen only by experiencing its truth and bearing witness to it.

Nevertheless, as Zen spread and penetrated the Western world, it was inevitable that some of its followers would seek to articulate and describe it for the Western mind. Such descriptions are all very well, provided that we realize that to talk about Zen is to conceptualize it and to miss the point at one and the same time. While it is entirely possible to extract a philosophy or psychology of the person from Zen and its teachings, when we do so, we remain outside its secret. The following description, therefore, must immediately be identified as ultimately misleading.

Zen literature consists largely of sayings (the Zen *koan*), anecdotes, and similes. Many of them appear to be straightforward and clear, as they employ common and familiar words. However, Zen teachings are presented in such a fashion that only those disciples who have developed insight and are enlightened can comprehend their real meaning. For example, one Zen master is quoted as having said, "Emptyhanded I go, and behold the spade is in my hands." Such an assertion seems simple enough, but how is it to be understood? To those who have not yet experienced Zen, such teachings appear mysterious and unintelligible, if not downright ludicrous and absurd.

There are some who suggest that teachers of Zen deliberately make their teachings unintelligible so that their profundity may not be questioned. However, followers of Zen point out that their statements are not paradoxical in an effort to hide or obscure the truth. Indeed, they claim they have nothing to hide because nothing is hidden. Their statements are enigmatic or mysterious because human language is inadequate for expressing the truths of Zen. Zen defies logical description and explanation. Its teachings must be personally experienced to be grasped. Zen neither affirms nor denies anything, it merely points the way. Zen seeks a higher affirmation beyond the antitheses of Being and non-Being, Self and not-Self, yes and no, good and evil. This is why it is misleading to identify Zen with a form of meditation. Meditation involves fixing one's thoughts on an object and extracting its vital characteristics; as such, meditation is artificial. Zen masters point out that birds and fish do not meditate, they fly and swim. Meditation is an artificial rather than a natural human activity. Zen asks us to take things as they are, to perceive things, to feel them, without any abstraction or mediation.

Suzuki reminds us that a dog behaves like a dog all of the time, yet it is not aware that it is a dog or that its nature expresses reality itself. A dog eats, sleeps, chases, and romps. It lives Zen, but it does not live by Zen. Human beings, because of the unique character of their consciousness, have the potential to be conscious of living. Thus, they can live Zen and also live by Zen. Most of us are not conscious of life itself; instead, we are conscious of our individual selves, and we conduct our lives according to an artificial set of subjective constructs and moralities that blind us to reality itself. As such, we are circumscribed by our self-consciousness and subjective categories and are out of touch with the innermost Self that coincides with the truth.

Zen seeks to get in touch with the innermost Self and to do it in the most direct possible way. Zen avoids anything that is external or superficial. It renounces all external authorities, stating that whatever truth there is must come from within and be experienced personally. Even human reason itself is rejected as a final authority. Our reason is seen as an intermediary that interferes with the direct perception of what is real. Zen encourages us not to be bound by rules, be they logical, moral, or spiritual; rather, we must create our own rules through the experience of life as we live it.

Truth is in the self. If one cannot find the truth in oneself, no teacher can reveal it to one. When one master was asked, "What is Enlightenment?" he replied, "Your everyday thoughts." Another answered the question "What is the Tao?" with "Usual life is the very Tao."

To search after Tao itself immediately implies a distinction between oneself and the ultimate. This distinction is the basis of egoism and lays the false foundation for an individual ego or self. It suggests that the self is somehow distinct from the rest of life. Tao is not to be sought, it is to be recognized in the commonplace events of everyday living. The individual ego disappears when the self and life move along together.

In Zen all ideas or symbols of Buddha are cast aside as misconceptions. The story is told of Tanka, a monk who burned a wooden statue of Buddha in order to keep his fire going one winter night. The keeper of the temple was outraged at his sacrilege, but Tanka merely began to search in the ashes and said that he was gathering sariras. *Sarira* refers to the holy substance that is found when a Buddha's body is burned. When the keeper inquired how he could possibly get sariras from a wooden Buddha, Tanka pointed out that if there were not sariras in his fire, then the statue was not truly a Buddha. Thereupon, he asked for the two remaining statues of Buddha for his fire. Other Zen masters teach us, "Cleanse the mouth thoroughly when you utter the word Buddha," and "If you encounter the Buddha, kill him." Such false images only serve to separate us from the truth.

Truth is life. It cannot be grasped, held, or conceptualized. All we can possess is our own subjective ideas. Zen masters say that to define is to kill. If the wind were to stop blowing so that we could catch it, it would no longer be wind. Life is elusive in the same way. We try to stop it, to preserve it, to understand it, to define it, so that we can repeat its happy moments and avoid its sad ones. But life moves on and our efforts to halt it are unsuccessful. What brings happiness one moment may bring sorrow the next. Those who try to possess life merely enslave themselves to their own illusions.

When one master was asked, "What is Tao?" he replied, "Walk on." To discuss or talk about bringing the self into harmony with life merely introduces the concept of the self and draws attention away from the process of living itself. Zen is an experience, it is not an explanation.

Therefore, Zen masters do not concentrate on talk. They simply demonstrate life without making any assertions or denials about it. How can one possibly describe the sweetness of sugar? It has to be tasted. Zen masters attach no value to words, because words can only estrange us from what is real. When words are used by teachers of Zen, they are used in a different context. This is why Zen answers are short and to the point. Zen masters do not waste their time on lengthy explanations. Their statements are only to be taken as aids. Zen sayings are no more than a finger pointing to the moon. The finger remains a finger. Many of us, however, take the finger to be the moon.

When asked "Who is the Buddha?" Zen masters have given a variety of answers: "He is no Buddha." "Three pounds of flax." "See the Eastern mountains moving over the waters." In many instances, the answers appear irrelevant. At times they are contradictory. Ordinarily, they pull us away from our philosophical abstractions and draw our attention to the ordinary things of nature and life. Zen teaches that truth does not lie in our intellectual speculations, but in the concrete events of daily living.

Words are words, but facts are facts. When words do not correspond to the facts, it is time to abandon words and return to facts. Most of us hang on to a logical interpretation of things. We have been taught that A is A, and it is unthinkable to suggest that A is not A. But our ordinary processes of logical reasoning do not satisfy our deeper interior and spiritual needs. Words and logic lead us to look at things, to differentiate among them, to develop an attitude toward them, and to judge them. In so doing we stand apart from them and perceive them only through our subjective constructs. Zen teaches us that A is not A. This is an apparent inconsistency. But, by becoming free of the intellect and its logic, we no longer need to be constrained by its constructs. We can stand in the rain and not be wet.

Zen aims at grasping the central fact of life. The fact of experience cannot be captured by any artificial scheme of thought or language. When we conceptualize and talk about our concepts, we make assertions or we make denials. We assert that A is A, and we deny that A is B. Zen aims at a higher synthesis in which there is neither affirmation nor denial. In order to do this, it frequently proposes a series of negations that lead to a higher or more absolute affirmation. Thus we are told, "Coal is black, coal is not black." Such a statement cannot be understood philosophically. It has to be lived.

One problem is that we confuse the order of law with the order of nature. In nature, things simply happen. Our logic imposes on nature the "necessary" laws of affirmation and denial, cause and effect, and so forth. When we believe that things are necessities, life turns into a problem that must be solved. The necessities of affirmation and denial, cause and effect, and other patterns of logic are simply the necessities created by our subjective projection. They are not a problem in the natural order of things. Thus, the "problem" of life is absurd, meaningless, and need not be experienced as a problem.

The point is that we do not need to be prisoners of our thoughts and language. We can call a spade a spade if we want to, and we can consider it an implement for digging. But we do not have to call a spade a spade. Nor must we confine our conception of it to that of a tool. A Zen master may hold up a spade and declare, "I hold a spade, yet I hold it not." In doing so the humble spade becomes the key to the riddle of the entire universe.

Another master may hold up a spade and say, "What do you see?" If a student answers, "I see a spade," the master knows that the student does not have Zen. But if the student replies, "I do not see anything," the master may retort, "How can you deny the fact that I am holding a spade?" To call the spade a spade is to make an assertion. To call it not a spade is to make a denial. The answer lies in perceiving the spade in a way that neither asserts or negates. Such vision sees the spade but does not see it.

Our Western logic tells us that we cannot go beyond the dualistic antitheses of assertion and denial. Life tells us that we can and do. Most of us have been taught to conceive of life and ourselves as logical. Thus, we are encouraged to cultivate and follow our intellect. But the fact of the matter is that life has no such logic; we merely impose a logic on it. Moreover, in our everyday living, we continually behave in illogical ways. We add two and two and get five. We generally act out of our emotions and then use our logic and powers of rationalization to cover up the fact. Because we are not conscious of the illogic of our ways, we imagine that we are governed by logic and correct thought.

What answer should one give when the Zen master holds up a spade and asks his question? The question cannot be answered by logic or ordinary intellectual deduction. Actually, any answer will do, provided it comes from one's innermost being. Such an answer is always an absolute affirmation that goes beyond the logical antithesis of assertion and denial. But such an answer is very difficult to come by.

Zen masters pose riddles such as the following, "If you speak I will give you thirty blows, but if you do not speak, I will give you thirty blows." "How do you interview a wise man if you neither speak or remain silent?" "If a live charcoal is not fire, what is it?" The point of these questions is that they cannot be answered satisfactorily unless one makes the leap to an absolute affirmation that goes beyond the antithesis of the yes and no of ordinary thought. Even if the puzzle could be resolved logically, to resolve it in that way would be to miss the point. The riddles of Zen cannot be answered by our intellect, but only through a consciousness of a higher order. Not to answer the question in this way is to be chained in one's own laws of thought and logic. Zen seeks to jolt us out of our intellectual ruts and conventional morality and demonstrate a different order of things.

A monk, wanting to decide who would be his successor, brought in two of his disciples, showed them a pitcher, and said, "Do not call it a pitcher, but tell me what it is." The first replied, "It cannot be called a piece of wood." The second monk pushed the pitcher over and left the room. The monk who upset the pitcher was chosen as the new abbot.

Upsetting the pitcher appears to have qualified as an absolute affirmation. However, you would not be said to understand Zen if you were to repeat the monk's action under similar circumstances. Zen rejects any form of imitation or repetition. Each one of us must work out our own solution to the puzzle. The statement "If you find the Buddha on the road, kill him" also indicates that you must find your own salvation.

One master's assistant used to imitate his master who lifted his finger in reply to a question. When the master learned of this practice, he cut off the boy's finger. The boy could no longer imitate the master. A harsh lesson, perhaps, but a dramatic illustration that it is the spirit of Zen, not its law, that is to be followed.

The answer of absolute affirmation lies within. Each of us must find it for ourselves. One's innermost self is innately perfect. Thus, each of us has the potential for perfection, waiting to be actualized. The basic nature of our human consciousness is indistinguishable from the pure consciousness of the universe or the void. Our function is to arouse this deeper original consciousness that has been overlaid by intellectualization and the illusions of conventional thought. Most of us behave as someone who dies of starvation while sitting next to a bag of rice or who dies of thirst while standing in the rain. The truth lies within and can be discovered through experiencing the oneness of all things. Zen teaches us that we are ourselves the rice and the water that we need. Yet to discover this truth is more difficult than we think and may take years of work and preparation.

Enlightenment

The goal of Zen Buddhism is *satori* or "enlightenment." Suzuki wrote, "Satori is the *raison d'être* of Zen and without it there is no Zen" (1964). Satori is a concept that again eludes intellectual conceptualization. While most of us understand what the word "enlightenment" means, satori also refers to an art and a way of enlightenment. In order to communicate the message of satori, the writers of Zen again resort to similes and statements that baffle and confuse the Western mind. For example, a monk is said to have gone to a master to inquire where was the entrance to the path of truth. The master asked him, "Do you hear the murmuring of the brook?" When he replied, "Yes, I hear it," the master said, "There is the entrance."

In conceptual language, satori entails being freed of the misconception of self and becoming aware of our innermost truth. This truth enables us to recognize that we are at one with the universal. Satori is best conceived as intuitive perception rather than as intellectual or logical understanding. Moreover, it transforms us so that we are no longer troubled by the ordinary emotions, sorrows, and conflicts of everyday life. Satori, or enlightenment, entails an insight into the nature of the Self in which one's consciousness is freed of the illusory concept of the self as ego. In satori one breaks through the consciousness that is limited to the ego and experiences a non-ego-like-self. When the guru asks, "Do you hear the murmuring of the brook?" the reference is to something other than ordinary hearing, an experience that transcends yet is present in our everyday experience.

Satori must be personally experienced. A guru may point the way, but there are some things that a person can only do for him- or herself. If we are hungry or thirsty, another person's eating and drinking will not fill our stomach or quench our throat. One has to eat and drink for oneself. This is why Zen masters insist that they have nothing to teach or to impart. All they can share is their own experience, but this cannot be said to be identical to any one else's.

Satori does not yield to intellectual analysis. If it is conceptualized, it ceases to be enlightenment. A master can only indicate the way. The story is told of a master and his disciple who passed some wild laurel. "Do you smell it?" the master asked. When his disciple answered, "Yes," he remarked, "There, I have nothing to hide from you."

We are not told how enlightenment comes or what it consists of. The contents of satori cannot be encompassed in an intellectual definition or description. Satori refers to an intuitive perception, not to conceptual ideas. One disciple who acquired satori is reputed to have burned all of his commentaries on the Diamond Sutra, a Buddhist scripture, works that he had formerly cherished and kept by his side at all times. In view of his enlightenment, the wisdom contained in those writings was no more than a drop of water in a vast abyss.

Satori does not arise through concentration or meditation as they are ordinarily practiced. No effort of the will can bring it about even though many Zen Buddhists spend years preparing for it. When satori comes, it is said to come as a sudden jolt or flash. It overturns our minds and crumbles the structure of our normal patterns of thought. False pretensions and illusions disappear as our former framework of logic is torn asunder. This mental upheaval lays the foundation for a new life and a new sense of perception. Satori culminates in a new way of looking at things. It is not possible to describe the contents of satori or this new sense of perception with greater specifications. A person who has been enlightened, however, does not doubt that he or she has been released from the ordinary perception of life. A master who has experienced the enlightenment of satori can also recognize it in his students. Beyond this, however, it belies further description. When Yakusan was asked to give a lecture on Buddhism, he did not utter a word. Another master simply stepped forward and opened out his arms.

The practice of Zen entails a systematic training of the mind. Zen practices are designed to create in the disciples a state of mind that will permit enlightenment to occur. Zen trains the mind to see the ordinary, the everyday as the greatest mystery of living. Zen refuses to deal with abstract concepts; it deals only with living facts of life. It points to truths in the midst of our everyday experience.

Two key elements in the practice of Zen are *zazen,* a form of meditation, and the *koan,* a paradoxical statement or question. Zen masters admit that both of these practices are actually artificial and superfluous. They are devices that are employed to open one's mind to the higher consciousness of Zen. Once the device has served its purpose, it can be discarded. The elements of zazen and the koan are used solely for their instrumental value. Nevertheless, thorough training in these techniques is provided for students of Zen. Their purpose is not the observance of rules and rituals, although the rules permit one to focus on the practice, but to obtain a freedom beyond rules and rituals that expresses the natural order of things.

Zazen (or *dhyana* in Sanskrit) refers to sitting crosslegged in quiet contemplation. The root of the word *dhyana* means to perceive or to reflect. The practice of dhyana or zazen is widespread in the East. In Zen, however, it has taken on a particular role as a means of dealing with the koan and other riddles of life.

The practice of zazen requires an appropriate posture that creates the right state of mind. The student generally sits on a firm, round cushion. In the full lotus position, the right foot is placed on the left thigh, and then the left foot is placed on the right thigh. This position expresses the oneness of duality. Even though we have two legs, in this posture they have become one. The head, neck, and spine are kept in a straight vertical line. The student pushes toward the sky with the back of his head as if trying to support it. The shoulders are relaxed, the chin is tucked in, and the diaphragm is pressed down toward the lower abdomen. The arms are held slightly away from the body and the hands are arranged to form a "cosmic mudra." The left hand is placed on top of the right with the middle joints of the middle fingers together. The thumbs are then held lightly together so that the hands form an oval. This posture provides a firm foundation for prolonged sitting. At first, it may be painful for the initiate since the muscles are unaccustomed to the position, but with practice the posture becomes very natural.

In Japan, students often use a variant posture for meditation. The heels are placed under the buttocks with a cushion between them and the buttocks, in order to take most of the weight off of the lower legs and feet. It is also possible to meditate on a chair, a posture frequently preferred by Zen students in the West, but a cushion is placed under the buttocks so that the angle formed by the body and legs is about 95

FIGURE 14.2 The Posture of Zazen

degrees. Such an angle is mandated to keep the spine straight and erect. The perfectly vertical line of the torso and the erect spine are the hallmarks of all proper zazen postures.

When one sits appropriately, he or she holds his body in perfect balance. Everything exists in the right place and in the right way. In such a position, a person can maintain physical and mental balance. He or she can breathe naturally and deeply. The state of consciousness that exists when one sits in the correct posture is, in itself, enlightenment, according to the teachings of Zen.

Such control over bodily reactions and processes is not unique to Zen, it is shared by many other Eastern disciplines. No doubt the reader has some familiarity with the practice of yoga, a discipline cultivated by certain Hindu sects. Unfortunately, many Westerners have misinterpreted the essence of yoga, perceiving it to be either a form of deception practiced by charlatans or just another set of exercises for physical fitness. In essence, however, yoga is a genuine means whereby one brings the body and mind into harmony. It consists of a posture or series of postures gradually developed through a systematic approach by means of which one gains control over his or her bodily processes. Such discipline permits the trained yogi or yogini to assume for a protracted period of time postures that for most of us would seem unbearable, such as elevating an arm or leg or standing on one's head.

There has been an increased interest in the West in transcendental meditation and biofeedback systems, practices that have grown out of essentially Asian psychologies. Studies suggest that such self-induced altered states of consciousness lead to better health and an increased ability to deal with stress and tension (Benson, Beary, & Carol, 1974). Such practices emphasize internal rather than external control as well as the unity of mind and body, and they are gaining recognition for their efficacy from contemporary Western medicine.

EXERCISE:

The "Corpse Posture"

One of the Hindu postures, known as the "corpse posture," is a method of inducing relaxation. Often used after strenuous exercise, it consists of lying on the back on a mat and progressively relaxing.

An effort to cultivate the Hindu "corpse posture" can be an excellent prelude to an attempt to learn to meditate. Because the posture aims at relaxation, it provides a solid foundation for all other meditational, techniques. Lie down flat on your back on a mat or soft rug, with your arms at your side with the palms up. You should not use a pillow. Allow yourself to relax, beginning with the toes and gradually proceeding to the rest of the body. Simply direct your attention to each part of the body as enumerated: your right big toe, each of the other toes on your right foot, the ball of the foot, arch, heel, the remainder of your foot, and your right ankle. Now direct your attention to your left foot in a similar progressive fashion. Continuing from your left ankle, attend to your leg, beginning with the lower part from the ankle to the knee, including the knee, and doing the same for the right. Attend to the upper parts of your legs and to your hips, one at a time. Then direct your attention to your pelvic area, your stomach, the sides of your body around the stomach area, and the lower part of your back. Move carefully and slowly up your spinal cord to the upper part of your back and shoulder blades. Relax your chest, shoulders, and the upper parts of your arm. Attending to each arm separately, concentrate on the upper arm, elbow, lower arm, wrist, back and palm of the hand, and individual fingers. Pay attention to the back of your neck and its sides, your throat, jaw, and chin. Your lips, tongue, cheeks, nose, right and left ears, eyelids, eyebrows, forehead, and scalp. Gradually take three deep breaths and exhale slowly. Think about something pleasant, such as a tree, a painting, or a person. After you have relaxed for a while, gradually open your eyes, permit yourself to become mentally alert, and arise feeling refreshed.

While meditating one centers his or her mind on a single focus or no focus at all (emptying the mind) and seeks to control other elements. The student sits facing a blank wall in order to avoid abstractions and frequently begins by concentrating on the act of breathing. By becoming aware of this movement, all that exists is the rhythm of breathing. It is no longer necessary to be conscious of one's ego or self. The "I" moves along with the universal nature of breathing. Without air we cannot live, and by concentrating on the experience of breathing, we realize our interrelatedness with all things.

In Zen, zazen is also employed as a means for arriving at the solution to a koan. The term *koan* literally means a "public document." In the practice of Zen, it has come to refer to a paradoxical statement or question, provided by a teacher, that has no intellectual solution. The koan is an instrument for opening one's mind to the higher consciousness of Zen. Being merely a tool, appropriate use can open the mind to the inner truth of Zen. The koan itself is an intellectually unresolvable or meaningless statement or question such as "What is Mu?" "What is the sound of one hand clapping?" "How does one get a goose out of a bottle without breaking the bottle or hurting the goose?"

The koan is given to students to help them realize that what they have accepted as known facts of science or logical inferences are not necessarily so. The koan generally presents two alternatives, neither of which is intellectually possible. Its purpose is to frustrate the intellect in order to reduce its grip and allow a deeper consciousness to emerge. In their efforts to solve the puzzle of the koan, students realize that their former way of looking at things is not always correct nor is it helpful to spiritual growth. The koan cannot be resolved by the discursive intellect that reasons analytically. Our efforts at an intellectual resolution merely lead us to the edge of a mental cliff from which we have no alternative but to leap and leave the field of ordinary consciousness.

While it might be possible to reason about the koan or intellectually try to resolve it, to do so is to miss the point. Our reasoning processes of assertion and denial obscure the truth. They stand in the way of accepting things as they are without judgments or abstractions. This is why the koan is generally designed to shut off the avenue of rationalization. We try to answer the koan, but our efforts are to no avail. Any answer that suggests intellectualization is abruptly dismissed by the master.

But the student's dilemma is the true starting place of Zen. Zen suggests that there are other forms of consciousness besides our ordinary consciousness of reality. Zen Buddhism distinguishes eight levels of consciousness. The first five are the ordinary senses of sight, sound, smell, taste, and touch. The sixth is thought or intellect. The seventh is mind, which entails intuition, and the eighth and highest level is universal consciousness that is at one with all of reality.

The koan arouses doubt and pushes it to its farthest limits. There is no logical way to resolve the koan through the powers of reason. It can be resolved only by a leap of consciousness in which Being is identified with non-Being, thought with non-thought, and Self with non-Self. From an intellectual viewpoint, one could say that the limits of our ordinary dualisms of logic have been transcended. But once we rise above our ordinary consciousness, we discover that in actuality there is nothing more than everyday consciousness. What appeared so mysterious was never hidden at all but was standing in front of us all the time.

We realize that there was, after all, *nothing* to the koan. The koan was an artificial construct or dilemma, just like the other artificial constructs of our thought. When the koan is broken, we return to ordinary consciousness, yet somehow the world is perceived differently.

The koan is a miniature exaggeration of the problem of life. Just as the koan cannot be grasped and comprehended, so life itself cannot be contained and held. The koan, like life itself, cannot be understood, only accepted and lived.

In description, the process sounds deceptively simple. All one has to do is to release the grip of his or her ordinary consciousness and permit a higher consciousness to emerge. But, in fact, the process is extremely hard, frustrating, and time consuming. Zen students work for years, trying to cultivate the proper state of mind that will permit enlightenment to occur. It is ironic that their strenuous efforts do not in themselves create satori. When satori comes, it comes as a flash or jolt that no amount of self-searching can produce because our efforts of will are always confined within the subjective limits of the individual ego.

EXERCISE:

Meditation

For a fuller understanding of the practice of Zen, it would be helpful if you try to meditate yourself. Carefully reread the description of meditation given in the text. Sit in a relaxed position, approximating the classic posture if you wish. Close your eyes and begin to meditate. At the beginning it will probably be most helpful if you concentrate on your breathing. This is most easily done by counting breaths up to ten and then beginning to count again. Try to concentrate solely on the experience of breathing. If anything else comes into your mind, say to yourself, this is a passing thought and go back to counting. In the beginning, you may find it difficult to focus your attention solely on the act of breathing, but with time and practice, you will be able to increase the amount of time spent in alert but relaxed concentration.

As you become more at ease with the process of meditating, it may facilitate your efforts to try to ponder one of the koans cited in this chapter or to contemplate a mantra. A mantra is a spiritual word or formula chanted throughout meditation in order to evoke a deeper level of consciousness. Sometimes the mantra is a syllable or word such as "Om," which appears to have no intellectual meaning but which through use as a meditational tool reveals the essence of the divine. Other mantras are spiritual formulas: Om Sivoham, "I am a part of the cosmos," and Aham Brahmo Smi, "I am a unique creative center of Being." These formulas focus attention on the individual's true identity as part of the unity of the universe. A Zen master frequently assigns personal mantras to each of his students. The mantra then becomes the student's secret meditational device.

Life in a Zen Monastery

The practical and disciplinary character of Zen emerges clearly in the life of a Zen monastery. The center focus of a monastery is the *zendo* or meditation hall, a rectangular building whose size varies according to the number of monks in the monastery. The zendo is the heart of a Zen monastery as it is here that the monks sleep and practice zazen. The monastery complex also includes a kitchen, dining hall, lavatories, master's quarters, guest rooms, and offices. Usually, there are gardens on the property and a farm adjacent or nearby where the monks raise fruit and vegetables for their food.

Hard work and rigid discipline characterize the life of a Zen monk. Po-chang, who founded the first Zen community, is said to have declared, "A day of no working is a day of no food" (Suzuki, 1964). Manual labor occupies a great deal of a monk's time, and no task, even the most menial, is viewed as degrading or beneath a monk's dignity. The monastery is kept immaculately clean, the gardens are beautifully cultivated, and the farm is carefully tended. There is plenty of work to be done: wood to be chopped, food to be prepared, and laundry to be washed. The hard work performed by Zen monks has gained them a reputation for being very industrious. Nevertheless, the monks attend to their chores and labors in a spirit of zest and joy. Laughter and happy facial expressions accompany their efforts at tough manual work.

Economy and simplicity are the hallmarks of the life. In the monastery wants are reduced to a minimum, and the Zen monk leads the simplest of lives. There is little private property. Each monk has his *kesa* and *koromo* (priestly robes), a few books, a razor, and an *oryoki* (set of eating utensils). A monk's possessions are so few that they can be packed into a small wooden box. This box is suspended from the neck by a broad sash and carried in front of the body when the monk is traveling. In the zendo, each monk is provided with a *tatami* (a three by six foot mat) for sitting, meditating, and sleeping. In cold weather, a large quilt provides some protection and warmth.

A monk's day begins long before sunrise, as early as 4:00 A.M. The sound of a gong or bell summons the monks to rise, wash, dress, and prepare for the period of zazen that precedes the early morning meal. The gong also notes the times for the remaining activities of the day. The schedule is demanding and precise. There is no time to waste. A monk has just enough time to do what he has to do, but little if any time to ponder how he feels about it. The purpose of such an exacting schedule is to remove attention from one's personal feelings or tendency to always consider how things ought to be done differently, so that a person may simply do what needs to be done. Zen teachings hold that truth does not reside elsewhere, but in the world of everyday living. By living each moment fully and concentrating simply on what one is doing, one can gain the awareness that he or she is perfect. Usually, we try to change ourselves and to be something or someone other than whom we already are. Likewise, when we are doing something, we tend to be concerned with what we think we should be doing rather than with what we are doing in the present. In the beginning, it is difficult for an initiate to get used to the rigid schedule and to cope with the utter lack of personal time. However, with practice, the schedule becomes second nature, an automatic routine, whose effect is freedom rather than restriction. The purpose of the rules in a Zen monastery is not to restrict the self, but to enable a monk to express himself most freely. Such freedom arises when we no longer have to concentrate on what we should do, but simply on what is being done and how we are doing it.

When it is time for meditation, the monks proceed into the zendo in single file and take their places on low platforms that face the center of the room. The head monk steps forward, prostrates himself before a shrine, and lights a stick of incense to mark the time. Other monks act as monitors and strike the meditators at various times with a *kyosaku* or wooden stick to arouse any of them from drowsiness. This procedure is also believed to stimulate psychic energy. The periods of sitting meditation generally last for about half an hour. A gong summons the monks to *kinhin,* or walking meditation. They proceed slowly around the zendo in single file, still focusing on the koan or some other practice. The combination of sitting and walking meditation provides a perfect balance of needs for both body and mind.

A gong indicates the time for a meal. The monks take their oryoki into the dining hall. The *oryoki* consists of a nest of four or five laquered wooden bowls, chopsticks, spoon, scraping implement, napkin, and cloth for wrapping all the utensils together. Each activity entailed in eating with the oryoki is carefully prescribed. The monks unfold the cloth in a certain manner, remove and place the bowls on the table according to a set pattern, and so forth.

The food is simple, but it provides the essentials for a well-balanced diet. Breakfast, eaten when it is still dark, generally consists of rice gruel and pickled vegetables. The main meal of the day is eaten at about ten in the morning and includes rice, vegetable soup, and pickles. Later in the afternoon, the monks eat what is known as a "medicinal meal." The Zen monk is not supposed to have an evening meal, but the climate of Japan made a compromise mandatory. The final meal of the day, therefore, consists simply of leftovers from the main meal and entails no special preparation.

Each meal begins with a special ceremony during which a short *sutra,* or sacred scripture, and the "Five Meditations on Eating" are recited:

Firstly, let us reflect on our own work, let us see
    whence comes this offering of food;
Second, let us reflect how imperfect our virtue is,
    whether we deserve this offering;
Thirdly, what is most essential is to hold our minds
    in control and be detached from the various faults;
Fourthly, that this is medicinal and is taken to keep
    our bodies in good health;
Fifthly, in order to accomplish the task of
    enlightenment, we accept this food.

                    (Trans. Suzuki, as quoted in Watts, 1958)

Monks act as waiters and serve the food from large bowls. Before they eat, each monk sets aside a few grains of rice and offers them to spirits unseen. Later, these will be taken out to the garden for the birds. The meal is eaten in absolute silence. As they eat, the monks meditate on the principles of Zen Buddhism. The way in which each eating utensil is held and handled is meticulously prescribed. The monks communicate their need for more food with hand gestures. After the meal is finished, the waiters bring in hot water. Each monk fills his largest bowl and carefully washes and wipes all of his utensils according to a predetermined ritual. The bowls are then reassembled and precisely wrapped in their cloth. The monks leave the dining room, as they arrived, in silent procession.

Eating with an oryoki entails much more than simply a Zen version of etiquette. It is essentially a very simple way to eat, in which each movement is accounted for and reduced to the bare minimum. While it takes practice and initial concentration, eventually one's attention is free to focus simply on eating. The practices and rituals of eating with an oryoki, just like the practice of zazen, are designed to remove attention from one's individual self or ego. When one eats in the prescribed manner, just as when one sits in the appropriate posture for zazen, one's movements are symbolic of the truth. Thus, in following these practices, one no longer needs to be concerned with cultivating a proper state of mind, because the practice itself provides the proper framework. The person is not restricted but is allowed to express him- or herself most freely. When we assume the right posture for zazen, the correct stance for eating, and so forth, we are already enlightened.

During periods of *sesshin,* which means "collecting or concentrating the mind," the usual manual labor of monastery life gives way to intensive spiritual training and discipline. Sesshin lasts for a week and is held about four times a year. During sesshin the monks rise even earlier than usual, stay up later, and remain in the zendo for extensive periods of meditation. Sesshin provides extensive opportunities for teisho and sanzen. *Teisho* refers to a lecture or discourse on the inner meaning of Zen that is given by the master. It is generally based on one of the sacred texts. The presentation of a teisho is accompanied by a great deal of ceremony and ritual. The sermon itself is frequently mystifying and obscure to the unenlightened. One master is reported to have said nothing at all. Instead, he called attention to the song of a bird and remarked that the sermon had been given. Such discourses are to be viewed in the same vein as a koan. They baffle the intellect and prepare the mind for a new point of view. *Sanzen* consists of individual consultations between a monk and his master. Many of the written teachings of Zen refer to such interviews. The sanzen is a formal, solemn conference during which the monk presents his view on the koan or some other questions. Before he enters the master's quarters, the monk bows three times. He enters the room with his hands held palm to palm in front of his chest and prostrates himself. Once the conference begins, however, all formalities and conventions are laid aside, and unexpected exchanges may occur. The purpose of sanzen is to make manifest the truth of Zen. Blows and other physical combat may be used to this end. It has been said that a smack on the face expresses the truth of Zen far more than do words. As long as the student gives an intellectual solution to his koan, the master will abruptly reject his answer. The student who attempts to resolve a koan with the intellect is as inept as a mosquito that tries to bite an iron rod. Once the student forgets himself, however, and abandons the pretensions of his individual ego, the flash of satori comes, and he is able to realize that there was nothing in the koan after all. Such enlightenment does not come quickly, however, but only after several years of hard work and innumerable impasses during sessions of sanzen.

This description of life in a Zen community has focused on the life of a monk, or male. Unfortunately, we know little about the role of women in Zen. There are Zen Buddhist nunneries in Japan, but few women have written about their experiences and it appears that the leadership is predominantly male. In America, however, Zen centers are integrated, and women are slowly assuming a more active role.

Zen monks do not remain forever in the monastery. Many return to the everyday life of the world, and some of them marry. Monastic separateness is not an ideal of Zen Buddhist life. Zen Buddhism requires that its disciples be in the world but not of the world. Returning to the world permits a further maturing of one's character. This requires one to act out of his or her full being in the ordinary affairs of everyday life.

Some have suggested that Zen permits and justifies any kind of behavior inasmuch as Zen accepts all things, both good and evil, as evidences of reality. This is not the case. Zen disciples observe a rigorous discipline, both within the monastery and outside in the everyday world. It would be more correct to suggest that Zen commences where conventional morality ceases. Our ordinary morality is a tool that enables us to live in society and get along with other people. As such, it is useful, but it can also become enslaving. Nevertheless, mastery of the moral law is a necessary precedent for awakening to a higher spiritual law. An analogy could be drawn to the cultivation of a garden. A garden must be carefully planned and laid out so that the plants do not choke one another and crowd each other out. But the beauty of a garden does not lie in the planning or position of each individual flower. The beauty resides in the glory of the finished garden as a whole.

In short, Zen is life. Alan Watts, a convert to Zen, describes it as follows: "to chase after Zen is like chasing one's own shadow, and all of the time one is running away from the sun. When at last it is realized that the shadow can never be caught, there is a sudden 'turning about,' a flash of satori, and in the light of the sun the dualism of self and its shadow vanishes; whereas man perceives that what he was chasing was only the unreal image of the one true Self—of That which he ever was, is and shall be. At last he has found Enlightenment" (Watts, 1958).

EASTERN THOUGHT AND PSYCHOTHERAPY

Alan Watts, one of the leading Western authorities on Eastern thought, compared the modes of liberation or psychotherapeutic change developed by the East and the West (1961). Both Western psychotherapy and Eastern ways of life aim at change. However, whereas Western psychotherapy has emphasized change for neurotic or disturbed individuals, Eastern disciplines are concerned with change in the consciousness of normal or healthy people. Eastern psychotherapies recognized long ago that the culture in which one lives not only defines what is normal and abnormal in that particular society, but also provides the context for and fosters a more pervasive form of neurosis that is endured by all of its members.

In the West, Sigmund Freud drew our attention to the offenses that are made against the human being by social repression. In large measure, the task of the psychoanalyst is to liberate his or her patient from stressful social conditioning so that he or she can function more effectively. Eastern psychotherapy, however, goes further than classical Freudian psychoanalysis. It seeks not just to restore the disturbed individual to normal, healthy, social functioning, but to point out that the distress of the normal person, as well as the abnormal, is caused by maya or illusion. The neurosis of all humanity lies in the fact that we take the world picture of our culture too literally and identify ourselves with our social role.

The construct of the self as "individual" is a social process created in the history of our relations with others that gives us our categories of subjective identity. The "I" of the individual ego becomes conscious of itself only in terms of the view of itself given to it by other people. Because the ego is socially constituted, it cannot be identified with anything ultimate or real. The answer does not lie in destroying the illusion, but in recognizing it for what it is.

In his theory of psychoanalysis, Freud emphasized the conflict that arises between the person's sexual desires and impulses and the cultural mores and standards that require him or her to repress them. Eastern thought sees more clearly that social institutions not only repress sexuality, but also the deeper relationship and involvement of the person and the environment. The person does not emerge from the socially created boundaries of self and not-self, inner and outer, subject or object, but from an encounter with what is real. As long as we insist on the reality of these social constructs, we will not encounter ourselves in our full potentiality.

In Eastern ways of liberation, a guru or master points toward enlightenment by persuading disciples to act on their own delusions. Initiating a countergame, the guru provides students with new ways of acting on their premises until they convince themselves that they are false. The students are placed in a dilemma or double bind from which they cannot escape unless they abandon their former conceptions and risk the leap of simply recognizing and accepting things for what they are. To answer a koan, the ego must get rid of the ego. Once we get rid of the ego, we can return to the master and demonstrate that we see through the koan's pretext. There is an obvious parallel here between Eastern liberation and Western psychotherapy, which permits the patient to act on his or her symptoms until he or she realizes their inappropriateness and ceases to use them. Nevertheless, Watts points out that Western psychotherapy falls short of being a way of liberation because it fails to deal with the bigger problem of rectifying the breach between the individual and the world. It is content to limit itself to the individual's adjustment to his or her society. Frequently, its aim is to fortify the ego rather than to dissolve it.

Freud could not begin to resolve the problem of the individual and his or her relationship to reality, partly because he believed that there was an irreparable conflict between the ego and the world. The world, he held, was too poor to meet our needs. Zen points out that we construct our own reality through the development of culture and society. Only by recognizing our construction for the maya that it is can we envision a way to resolve the seemingly irreconcilable opposites brought forth in the Taoist symbol of yin and yang, each of which actually contains the seed of the other.

EVALUATION AND IMPLICATIONS

Eastern thinkers cannot be said to have developed theories of personality comparable to the modern psychological theories of the West. A great deal has been said and written about the relationship of the self and the cosmos. While it is possible to abstract a theory of personality from the writings of the East, to do so is to violate the spirit in which they are presented. Still, it is possible to outline certain broad concepts about personality in Eastern thought that may provide a basis for comparison and impetus for reflection on our own position.

In the East, the emphasis is relational rather than individual. The person is not considered in his or her uniqueness or isolation, but in his or her relation to the self, to others, and the larger cosmos. Identification of oneself with a social role or social identity is maya, an illusion that leads to isolation and alienation.

Eastern philosophies are highly practical. They offer a variety of techniques for cultivating a deeper understanding of self. These practices consist of deliberate movement away from intellectual, rational consciousness and effort to cultivate a deeper level of awareness that transcends our everyday consciousness and logic. Systematically training the body and the mind, Eastern disciplines aim to enable the individual to perceive the truth that lies within his or her inner being.

Eastern theories are generally considered branches of philosophy or religion rather than science. The very need to evaluate and demonstrate a personality theory's usefulness constitutes a bias that is foreign to Eastern psychology. While some efforts have been made in the West to validate through objective techniques claims that certain meditational techniques lead to effective results, the truth of an Eastern psychology could never rest on such grounds. In Zen, truth resides in satori, the compelling vision that accompanies Enlightenment.

SUGGESTIONS FOR FURTHER READING

The writings of D. T. Suzuki and Alan Watts, leading exponents of Zen Buddhism in America, provide an excellent introduction to the thought of Zen. Having introduced Zen to the English-speaking world in his renowned series of *Essays in Zen Buddhism* (Rider and Company, London, beginning in 1927), Suzuki wrote some twenty additional major works in English and at least eighteen in Japanese. Recognizing that the entire set of essays are somewhat lengthy and cumbersome, in 1934, Suzuki re-edited several of the major essays to constitute a shorter work, *An Introduction to Zen Buddhism* (Grove Press, 1964), that is probably the best introduction to Zen for the lay person. The companion volume, *Manual of Zen Buddhism* (Grove, 1960), is recommended for use with it.

Alan Watts wrote numerous books on Eastern thought that have attracted a wide lay audience. His best known is probably *The Spirit of Zen* (Grove Press, 1958), describing the way of life, work, and art in the Far East. Alan Watts's *Psychotherapy East and West* (Pantheon Books, 1961) relates Eastern thought to the needs of Western culture and offers reflection on Western psychotherapy.

A good additional reference for the student who wishes to enter further into the spirit of Zen is R. H. Blyth, *Haiku* (Hokuseido, 1952). Haiku is a short Japanese poem form consisting of only three lines, with usually the first and last lines of five syllables and the second line seven syllables. Other books that are easily available and meaningful to students are Chuang Tsu, *Inner Chapters,* translated by Gia-Fu Feng and Jane English (Vintage Books, 1974); Lao-Tse, *Tao Te Ching,* translated by Gia-Fu Feng and Jane English (Vintage Books, 1972); Jane Hamilton-Merritt, *A Meditator's Diary* (Harper & Row, 1976); and Sheldon Kopp, *If You Meet the Buddha on the Road, Kill Him* (Science and Behavior Books, 1972). A more difficult but useful book is Rune E. A. Johansson's *The Psychology of Nirvana* (Doubleday Anchor, 1970).

CHAPTER 15

Western Personality Theory in Perspective

Toward the end of the nineteenth century, the German philosopher Friedrich Nietzsche (1844–1900) wrote of his fellow Europeans: ". . . art thou not mad? Thy knowledge does not complete Nature, it only kills thine own nature. . . . Thou climbest toward heaven on the sunbeams of thy knowledge—but also down towards chaos. Thy manner of going is fatal to thee; the ground slips from under thy feet into the dark unknown; thy life has no stay but spiders' webs torn asunder by every new stroke of thy knowledge" (1910).

Nietzsche's words are as poignant today as they were then. Nobody has to remind us that we stand in the midst of a cultural crisis. Our spectacular successes in space camouflage a deeper descent toward confusion. The signs of discontent are omnipresent, manifested in the spirited revolts of the 1960s and the perhaps even more disconcerting, apathetic malaise of the 1970s. We sense that our culture and civilization are on the verge of collapse. Modern civilization has been judged and found wanting. Within the last century, doubts have arisen as to the very rationality of our science and technology. Science, which promised us progress, speaks today of our doom. Its greatest triumph may be the power it has given us to bring ourselves and our world to ruin, for technology's by-products may be able to destroy our land and all living organisms (Dasmann, 1972). Science has opened our eyes and increased our knowledge; it has also closed our eyes to the few vital things that really matter.

Erich Fromm suggests that the effects of our "technetronic age" are vividly illustrated in Herman Kahn's book on thermonuclear warfare, a book that raises the question: "How many millions of dead Americans are 'acceptable' if we use as a criterion the ability to rebuild the economic machine after nuclear war in a reasonably short time so that it is as good or better than before?" In Kahn's discussion, figures for gross national production and population increase are primary criteria, whereas human questions of suffering, brutalization, and meaning are ignored (Fromm, 1968). At no other time in human history has the question of the psyche, the human personality, become so problematic. The philosopher Kurt Reinhardt observes that "In this 'progressive' age it is both pitiful and tragic to see the ever increasing discrepancy between the plenitude of scientific knowledge and the helplessness with which governments, peoples, and individuals face the intellectual and moral problems of human life" (1960).

A CRISIS IN WESTERN THEORIZING

Although psychology represents the oldest of human concerns, the science of psychology and the effort to comprehend the human personality within the framework of a scientific methodology is largely a product of the twentieth century. We have seen that Wilhelm Wundt conceived of psychology as an experimental science that ought to emulate the natural science of physics. So committed was Wundt to the experimental method that he limited his study to those psychological processes that could be explored within a laboratory setting. John Watson's dedication to the pursuit of psychology as a natural science went even further. He confined the scope of psychological research to the study of overt behaviors. Since Watson founded the behaviorist movement in the 1920s, behaviorism has come to be the dominant position of psychology in the American university. The mainstream of psychology in America emphasizes extrospective observation and a rigorous scientific methodology. These are the means by which we have sought to understand ourselves in the twentieth century.

Not all of the personality theorists that we have considered agree with the foregoing conceptions. Indeed, some have been very critical of a narrow delimitation of psychology as an experimental science. Their critiques have fostered trends toward a more humanistic approach. Unfortunately, however, as Robert Ornstein, a contemporary American psychologist, points out, humanistic psychology has also become a "divisive force." Its adherents frequently belittle the usefulness of science and generate little research to support their concepts. Thus, "the early promise of this approach, as emphasized by Abraham Maslow and Carl Rogers, was never realized in the mainstream of psychology." Psychologists are divided as to whether they belong to a "humanistic" or a "scientific" camp (Ornstein, 1977). The behaviorist position, with its emphasis on extrospective observation and experimental research, continues to represent the strongest and predominant mode of psychological study in the American academy today, however. Those theorists who choose not to imitate the mainstream run the risk of being considered less respectable, because of a lack of allegiance to a pure scientific approach and methodology. They are tolerated, particularly where they are willing to subject their findings to scientific scrutiny, but they are not fully recognized as sound because they do not emulate those psychologists who conceive of psychology as primarily an experimental science.

We have seen that the keynote of science is observation. Its theories rest on empirical data, that which is based on experience. In Western psychology, however, the term "empirical" has been rendered practically synonymous with "extrospective observation." Empirical data have been largely limited to extrospective or objective findings. Other data of experience or observation, such as subjective introspection, have been discouraged or depreciated, largely because it is so difficult to test these findings experimentally.

Historical, philosophical, and mythological data, because they invariably entail subjective as well as objective elements, are often viewed as incompatible with science. According to this conception, the individual who is a competent scientist does not permit subjective assumptions to interfere with his or her work. The scientist remains detached, objective, and value free. As a result, Western psychology has tended to isolate itself. It has divorced itself from other possible modes of investigation on the ground that their findings, because they are difficult to test experimentally, are not objective, and, therefore, incompatible with science.

Another contemporary American psychologist, David Bakan, has pointed out that the rigorous scientific methodology of the Western experimental psychologist may, at times, actually stand in the way of the empirical and tend to divorce us from experience rather than illuminate it (1969). Any experiment, precisely because it is artificial and contrived, loses its effectiveness in illuminating the everyday world as it becomes more distant and apart from it. In a well-developed experiment the experimenter does not enter into the everyday world; instead, he or she creates a para-world of quantified, logico-mathematical imaginary constructs. In this para-world, events are carefully chosen and precisely controlled in order to avoid the haphazard occurrences of the everyday world that might jeopardize the results. Further, in a well-designed experiment all the possible alternatives and outcomes are anticipated in advance. The experimenter can predict within limits what is going to happen as a result of his or her manipulation of the variables in the experiment. This means that the more carefully designed an experiment is, the more separate and apart it becomes from the world of experience that it seeks to clarify. Rather than talking about the world, the psychologist constructs a para-world. Rather than talking about the person, the psychologist constructs a para-person. The Western psychologists' reliance on a rigid experimental method may, therefore, interfere with the possibility of seeing other ways in which we might learn from experience.

The emphasis on extrospection and rigorous scientific methodology also constrains the scope of psychological findings and personality theorizing. Such a stress limits the findings of psychology to those that can be demonstrated within the experimental laboratory. It circumscribes the study of personality to merely those aspects about the person that can be comprehended in specifically scientific terms. Because of this, many questions about the ultimate meaning, purpose, and goal of human living, questions that traditionally have been and could be included in the study of personality, are ruled out of inquiry.

EARLY WESTERN THEORIZING

We have suggested that personality theorizing entails more than science; it also involves philosophy and art. In the light of present developments, it is often difficult for us to remember that our Western philosophy initially fostered a point of view that was mystical, emphasizing the spiritual side of the person and the world. Not until the modern period, particularly the seventeenth century, did Western thought clearly develop those intellectual patterns that fostered a rigid conception of science. Prior to the seventeenth century there were no clear-cut distinctions between matter and energy, body and soul, or subjective and objective knowledge. Extrospective objectivism and introspective subjectivism were not seen as two different modes of knowing, but as varying emphases. Knowledge was conceived of as the apprehension of the truth, and in authentic knowledge, objectivity and subjectivity were thought to genuinely meet.

Western philosophy begins with the Greeks, arising in the sixth century B.C. in a culture that did not separate science, religion, and philosophy. The philosophers of the early Milesian school did not distinguish between animate and inanimate forms of life. Nor did they make other distinctions that are so familiar to us today: spirit and matter, body and soul, subject and object. Nevertheless, these early philosophers were deeply impressed with the fact of contrast and change. They observed the changes that occur in nature during the course of the seasons. They noted the passage from life to death and from death to life of all things in their world. They perceived that despite all these changes, there had to be something permanent that endures and sustains all of the changes. Thus, they searched for the essential nature or reality of things, which they called *physis* (from which comes our word "physics"), and believed that all forms of life were manifestations of it. Their answers varied as to the essence of physis: Thales (640–550 B.C.) suggested it was water; Anaximander (610–540 B.C.), air; and Heraclitus (530–470 B.C.), fire. But each of them was convinced that beyond the seeming opposites of our everyday world, there was something that persists and unifies them.

In spite of their efforts to identify one or another substance as the ultimate reality, these early philosophers quickly realized that their attempts to identify reality with some element in the natural world were inadequate. Thus, Anaximander suggested that the four basic elements, earth, air, fire, and water, are forms of a more ultimate substance, the Boundless, which assumes different shapes in the course of its many changes. Heraclitus asserted, "Everything flows, but the Logos (or Word) remains." No one element in nature was fixed or final, thus, the concept of a static being was illusory and based on deception. The world presents a myriad of contrasts and opposites, but all seemingly opposite forms were eventually transcended in the Boundless or Logos, which dynamically unifies them.

An early split in this unity was introduced by the Eleatic school of Greek philosophers. Parmenides (520–440 B.C.) countered Heraclitus' emphasis on change with the concept that being or reality was indestructible, unchanging, and indivisible. In order to defend his view, Parmenides developed the art of dialectical argument. He sought to prove an assertion by showing that its denial leads to a logical contradiction and is therefore untenable. Parmenides argued that what is has to be unchanging, because if it changes, it ceases to be what it is and becomes what it is not. It is logically impossible for something to be what it is not. Therefore, what is must be unchanging. Here we have in its earliest form the pattern for a subsequent Western logic based on assertion and denial. The Eleatic school also suggested that a divine principle stands above all human beings and gods, a distinction that ultimately led to the separation of matter and spirit. In the statements attributed to the Eleatic school we can also find, in embryonic form, distinctions between knowledge that comes through the senses and knowledge that comes through the intellect. Nevertheless, subsequent Greek philosophers, such as Plato and Aristotle, did not capitalize on these distinctions, rather, they sought to resolve them.

During the fifth century B.C., the Greek atomists suggested that Being or Reality shows itself in various unchanging substances whose combination and separation leads to changes in the world. This was the view of Democritus (460–360 B.C.), the first to conceive of the atom as the smallest indivisible unit of matter and the basic building block of all material substances. Democritus, however, believed that motion is inherent to the atom. Changes, therefore, arose spontaneously from matter itself. Not until later did the view develop that atoms are moved by forces of energy that are essentially different from matter and that there are sharp divisions between matter and energy.

Mystical concerns and spiritual questions continued to be central in

Western thought up through the historical period of the Renaissance. Socrates, Plato, Aristotle, and later Aquinas stressed the point that questions about the good life and contemplations of ultimate reality were far more important than studies about the material world.

Socrates (469–399 B.C.) conceived of the good life as one of philosophic contemplation, in which the individual person strives to raise him- or herself from the temporal to the eternal and from the particular to the universal. Socrates believed that certain universal concepts or innate ideas about what is good and real are shared by everyone. These universal concepts, which are known subconsciously, need to be brought to our awareness by developing our powers of right thinking. Socrates developed a practical method for assisting his students in their own self-understanding. He asked his students questions, and in the dialogue that followed, led his followers to discover the knowledge that was inherent within themselves. Conceiving of himself as a midwife who assisted in the birth of ideas, Socrates frequently claimed that he was ignorant and had nothing to teach. Nevertheless, he believed that through self-examination, one could recover knowledge that was already latent within one's soul.

Undergoing the Socratic process of self-examination was not a simple process. It was a difficult task, because before Socrates could assist in the birth of new ideas he had to expose false pretenses. Thus, the Socratic dialogue generally had two phases. In the *ironic* phase, by the use of skillful questions, Socrates would expose logically the false assumptions of his followers and lead them into a blind alley so that they were forced to acknowledge their ignorance. Such admissions were painful, but necessary. We cannot begin to understand until we recognize what it is that we do not understand. The second phase was *maieutic* or birth giving. By asking further questions, Socrates would show his disciples that the truth already lay within themselves. There are distinct parallels between the Socratic process of self-examination, Freudian psychoanalysis, and the training of a Zen Buddhist monk.

The Greek philosopher Plato (427–347 B.C.) went beyond Socrates and identified the universals in Socrates' philosophy with essential reality. According to Plato, the absolute forms were not figments of human imagination or construction but referred to a reality that transcends the everyday world of appearances. In the everyday world, Plato argued, there are many objects that assume the shape of a circle. Not one of these, however, in spite of the most sophisticated drawing instruments, is an absolutely perfect circle. Nevertheless, each one of us knows the concept of a perfect circle: a closed plane curve, every point of which is equally distant from the center. This idea of a real circle refers to a reality that transcends the imperfect forms of the everyday world.

In *The Republic*, Plato suggested that we live, as it were, in a cave. Because we are chained to the back of the cave we cannot see the sun or the real world outside. We see only the shadows, but we identify these illusions with what is real. Plato agreed with Socrates: knowledge is reminiscence, the recollection of what was once possessed but now forgotten. Genuine knowledge is present at all times in the person, though latent and unconscious. Discovering the truth entails breaking the chains of bondage, recalling what is latent, and making it conscious.

In his famous painting of Aristotle and Plato, an Italian painter Raphael, significantly portrayed Plato pointing upward to the world of ideal forms and Aristotle pointing outward to the world we live in. By beginning with the everyday world and data of the senses in his theory of knowledge, Aristotle (384–322 B.C.) opened the door to modern science and the scientific method. For Aristotle, nature was dynamic rather than static. He conceived of all being as moving from potentiality to actuality. Each being has an immanent *telos* or goal that its nature strives to achieve. The acorn grows into a mighty oak tree. Humans strive to perfect their reason and acquire wisdom. The dynamic was one of self-actualization. Thus, it was not a contradiction for Aristotle to suggest that something is what it is not, because what is is always in the process of becoming something different as it actualizes its potential. The separate distinctions and categories of Aristotelian thought and logic were ultimately unified under the concept of teleology. The emphasis was on change, seen as the movement from potentiality to actuality. Aristotle's concept of self-actualization finds expression today in the theories of Carl Jung, Carl Rogers, and Abraham Maslow.

Thus, while early contrasts between matter and energy, body and soul, objective and subjective knowledge can be seen in Greek philosophy, these were not sharpened into a clear antithesis until the seventeenth century. In Platonic philosophy, the soul was not conceived as conscious states but rather as the very likeness of reality. For Aristotle, the soul was not a merely intellectual principle but the principle of life itself, a vitality that animates all living beings. According to Aristotle, all substances could be explained in terms of their matter, form, energy, and purpose and any one explanation without the others was incomplete. The person was a body-soul composite. In genuine knowledge, data obtained from sense experience and ideas generated by our intellect were thought to meet authentically.

MOVING TOWARD THE CRISIS

In the seventeenth century, questions arose that began to undercut the earlier assumptions. New problems for philosophical speculation were raised by the sixteenth- and early seventeenth-century renaissance of science. Copernicus (1473–1543), Kepler (1571–1630), and Galileo (1564–1642) investigated the world through careful observations, hypotheses, and tests. A modern scientific method began to emerge. This empirical method of science gradually overthrew the long dominant Aristotelian philosophy of dynamic nature and led to a conception of the universe as physical matters and energies operating within a space-time framework.

The emerging sciences of physics, chemistry, and biology provided answers to the question "What is the world made of?" but left a further question unanswered: "How is the world of human experience related to the physical world?" René Descartes's (1596–1650) assertion "I think, therefore, I am" was an effort to answer that question without resorting to prior authorities. Impressed by the certitude of his own doubt, he became convinced of his existence, and from there he proved the existence of God and the real world.

Descartes's philosophy was to have vast consequences. Not only was it important for physics and the emerging science, it also radically changed the conception of human nature. In Descartes's view, the human being was essentially disembodied thought. This position led people in the West to equate the self with consciousness and posit the locus of a person in the mind, rather than in the entire organism. The view that the self is an isolated ego or mind within a body became common.

Descartes's knowledge of himself was introspective or intuitive. He began by looking into himself, and he discovered one sure thing: "I think, therefore, I am." For Descartes, the self was not just the first existing thing that he could know, it was also the only thing that he could know directly and certainly. All other knowledge was indirect and rested on prior self-apprehension. In short, a person's only direct knowledge was of his or her own thoughts. All other knowledge, of the external world, the body, other minds, and so forth, was indirect.

As a rationalist, Descartes believed that human reason was the final authority in all matters of opinion and conduct. The intellect, through its own power, could form ideas and determine their validity. Once we conceive of innate ideas clearly and distinctly, Descartes suggested that we are on the road to truth, though he could trust his reason only if he protected it against abuse. Descartes said that in order to use our reason properly, we must detach ourselves from sense experience and all non-intellectual inclinations. Descartes's ability to think enabled him to posit the existence of himself. It later enabled him to posit the existence of God and the belief that his mind, if properly used, could discover truths about the external world. While Descartes's strong subjective position led him to certainty, it led later generations to uncertainty and to think of the individual person as essentially isolated and alone.

The Cartesian (from Descartes) position was a radical statement of *subjectivism*. Subjectivism fails to bridge the gap between the knower and the known because the threat of solitude hovers over it. In philosophy this danger was brought to our attention by the subsequent writings of Berkeley (1685–1753), Hume (1711–1776), and Kant (1724–

1804). Because, in the subjectivist view, the constructs of knowledge are creations of the self, one finds oneself in the ego-centric predicament. How do we get outside or beyond our own experiences?

Descartes's subjectivism was too far removed from the emerging science and common sense to permit his view to remain unchallenged. The position of *objectivism* was asserted in reply. In the objectivist view, valid human knowledge arises gradually in the course of experience through observation and experimentation. Experience, in the objectivist position, is primarily sense perception. Obviously, the data of experience must be synthesized by the mind, but the objectivist holds that the ideas and laws thereby formulated rest ultimately on the basis of observation of empirical data. The rigorous scientific methodology of the experimental psychologist expresses the objectivist position today. Valid knowledge is considered to be knowledge grounded in an extrospective consideration of an object in which the subject remains a detached onlooker. There is a tendency to view subjective qualities, observations, feelings, and ideas as inferior, since they are derived from the individual self rather than the external world.

Objectivism, however, is also unable to bridge the gap between the knower and the known. Objectivism, whether in its more radical form in which all knowledge is essentially sensation so that the mind is merely a blank tablet on which is written the perception of our senses, or in more recent versions that concede that the mind is active in the selection and molding of its data of sensation, tends to be left with a para-world. Its notion of sense data, from which knowledge arises, does not establish the reality of the external world and objects, rather, it presupposes them.

Later thinkers have been heir to Descartes's distinctions between mind and body and subjective and objective knowledge, as well as other dichotomies to which his philosophy gave rise. Subsequent Western philosophers and psychologists, even when they have opposed the Cartesian view, have tended to think through their arguments in the terms that Descartes laid down for them. Our thinking reflects the Cartesian dualisms. Most of us assume that knowledge is either subjective or objective. Yet neither objectivism nor subjectivism can bring us into touch with our real selves, because objectivism merely leads to the para-person of the scientist and subjectivism to an isolated individual.

In the aftermath of Descartes's philosophy, Western thought has been left with a host of dualisms that appear unresolvable. A number of these are familiar to us: mind versus body, energy versus matter, subject versus object, cause versus effect, and so forth. Most of our efforts to unify these dualisms have been unsuccessful, because the philosophical assumptions that undergird our efforts assume that they are necessary polarities.

Strangely enough, a major impetus for change in our philosophical assumptions has come from the realm of science itself. Recent developments in physics suggest the need for us to re-examine radically the Cartesian categories that underlie Western philosophy and psychology. In twentieth-century physics, rigorous application of the experimental method has required the physicist to reconceive his or her conceptual framework and to envision a new world that goes beyond the dualisms of nineteenth-century physics and thought. In large measure, these changes have come about through the vast implications of Einstein's theory of relativity and subsequent quantum theory.

Twentieth-century physics has effectively demonstrated that what appears to us to be solid matter is actually a manifestation of energy. For a long time people believed that the mass of a body was constant, but Einstein's theory of relativity showed us that the mass of a body changes with its velocity or speed. Obviously, for most everyday objects in motion, there is no perceivable change in mass because the movement is too slow to make a noticeable difference. Thus, classical physics continues to be a useful theory. However, experiments in which atoms have been smashed by exceedingly high-speed particles have confirmed that mass changes with high speeds. What we think of as matter, therefore, is simply a very high concentration of energy. These findings led Einstein to a formula that expresses the equivalence of matter and energy. The formula, $E = mc^2$, reads as follows: energy (E) is equal to mass (m) times the speed of light (c) squared. The basic building blocks of the universe, the protons, neutrons, and electrons of the atom, have lost their distinct identity as matter.

Quantum theory has further illustrated that the minute units that make up the atom have a dual character. At times, they appear to be particles of matter; at other times, they appear to be waves of energy. According to traditional thought, this represents a case of matter changing into energy, or vice versa. However, the fact that one can change into the other forces us to consider the possibility that matter and energy are actually two aspects of the same thing. The distinction between matter and energy may be artificial and illusory in the light of how readily elementary units appear to switch from one form to the other. Moreover, what is important is not that they change, but that there is a shift in our construct or the way in which we perceive them.

Einstein's theory of relativity has also radically altered the Newtonian concept of the world as material particles that move in absolute, unchanging space and time. Space and time have been shown to be changeable. They flow at different rates relative to the speed of the observer. This means that nature is not composed of isolated, fixed building blocks, it is a complex net of relations between various aspects of a whole. These relations also include the observer. If you were to drop an object while riding a motorcycle, it would appear to you that the object fell almost straight to the road. But a friend standing behind at the side of the road would see the object fall in a distinct arc. From different points of view we perceive things differently. A purely objective description of nature is impossible. We cannot speak of the observed without also speaking of the observer. The implications of these findings are utterly shattering to the Cartesian distinctions. In contemporary physics, the universe is experienced as an indivisible energetic whole that includes the observer. The traditional dichotomies of space and time, subject and object are meaningless.

In addition, traditional notions of cause and effect, concepts central to a scientific method that aims at establishing causal laws in order to make predictions, have become untenable in the light of modern physics. From a different perspective, the event labeled "cause" may appear to be the effect. Tachyons, hypothetical particles that move faster than light, can be received before they are transmitted. At the heart of the experimental method of science is the search for cause and effect. These findings, concerning what appears to be cause and effect, call into question the value of experimentation as a means of gaining insight into the human condition. In a global sense, events are interconnected, but the relationship between them is not necessarily causal. When space and time are limited and events are perceived in a temporal sequence, it is possible to perceive certain events as preceding causes and others as consequent effects. However, in the space-time continuum taken as a whole, there is no before and no after.

Anthropologist Dorothy Lee points out that other cultures, such as the Trobrianders, do not experience sequence in the same causal way that we do. We experience one and the same fruit as changing from ripe to overripe. For the Trobriander, there is no such temporal connection. A *taytu*, or ripe yam, remains a ripe yam. Should an overripe yam appear, it is a totally different being, a *yowana* (1950). Our concept of causation applies only to a limited conception and experience of the world.

Further, the concept of the self as an isolated consciousness within a physical body is called into question. Mind is no more distinct from body than matter is distinct from energy. Gage theory, the only theory to date that has been able to deal with both relativity and quantum theory, suggests that weak and electric forces are ultimately part of the same force. Physicists are impressed by the symmetrical pattern of the forces that they are discovering. At the scale of ordinary life much of nature's symmetry appears broken, giving rise to the rich variety of forms that we know. However, nature's basic symmetry continues to be reflected in many of its patterns, such as the snowflake, the atom, and the bilateral symmetry of our own bodies. The ultimate nature of things may be much simpler than we have suspected heretofore. Affirming the essential nature of all things, the physicist Heisenberg has suggested that what appears to us to be a variety of consciousnesses is more likely only a number of different aspects of one consciousness (1971).

New conceptions of our world have also emerged in the field of philosophy. In 1923, the Israeli existentialist philosopher Martin Buber proposed a new theory of knowledge, one that undercuts the Cartesian distinctions of object and subject and may well represent the most significant philosophical contribution to Western thought since Plato's speculations. His book *I and Thou* was first published in English in 1937; however, Buber's work was not widely recognized in the United States until the 1950s. We have already seen that Buber distinguishes between two primary attitudes to the world: *I-Thou*, which is personal and prereflective, and *I-it*, which involves objectivity and subjectivity. Buber suggests that it is from a primary mode of knowledge, personal and prereflective, that we proceed to knowledge in subjective and objective terms. Out of our confrontation with the whole (in which there is no distinction of self and not-self) we become aware of a self that is *I* and which can organize its world of objects and things. Our belief in the reality of the external world and of ourselves comes from our relations with others. The *I* is not an *I* except through its meeting with an other. Only through such a meeting is one able to be aware of him- or herself as a person and of the external world as separate.

Thus, objective and subjective knowledge are products of a primal knowledge of human relationships. They are derivatives and refinements of aspects of what we shall call *transjective* knowledge, borrowing a term coined by Victor von Weizsacker, one of Buber's followers. The logic of objective and subjective knowledge differs from that of the transjective mode. In the objective mode, the stance is that of a subject turned outward upon an object, viewing it in terms of extrospective apprehension. In the subjective mode, the stance is that of a subject turned back on itself as object, viewing itself in terms of introspective apprehension. In transjective knowledge, the stance is that of person to person and the relationship is one of meeting, confrontation, and encounter. The movement is from transjective knowledge to objective and subjective. Our ability to recognize objects as things, our definitions of the laws of nature, our understanding of cause and effect, are refinements of one aspect of knowing that depends on the transjective knowledge that is primary to us as human beings. Likewise, our identification of feelings as inner and subjective is an elaboration predicated on the prior stance. The transjective mode underlies our subsequent objectivity and subjectivity.

The concept of transjective knowledge cuts across the Cartesian distinctions in two ways. First, it focuses attention on the relationship between persons rather than on an individual object in its causal connections. Second, it identifies feelings with the world of *it* (objective and subjective knowledge), thereby surmounting the opposition between thought and feeling (Farber, 1966). A recognition of the reality of transjective knowledge does not mean that we have to reject the objective and subjective modes. Buber acknowledges that the subject-object relation arises as a condition of our existence. The *I-Thou* relation is self-limited and cannot persist. It fades into the world of *I-it*, of objectivity and subjectivity. Objective and subjective modes of knowing are necessary, inevitable, and desirable forms of knowledge, but they must be recognized for what they are. A subject-object relation is not the sole or primary reality, and the knowledge it yields fulfills its true function only insofar as it retains its symbolic quality of pointing back to the transjective knowledge from which it derives.

In short, a consistent view of the world that is radically different from the predominant concepts of Western psychology is beginning to emerge from contemporary physics and philosophy. We are heir to the Cartesian tradition, whose categories tend to permeate our discussions. Even when we oppose the view of Descartes, we tend to lay down our argument according to the terms he suggested. Nevertheless, contemporary physics and philosophy tell us that the person cannot be divorced from nature. Further, an observed object can be separated from an observing subject only by an artificial disjunction. The conceptual framework of cause and effect may be inappropriate for understanding human behavior. Obviously, there are sequences of behavior, but sequence does not in itself imply causality. A teleological concept of motivation may be more appropriate for comprehending human behavior. Further, a value-free orientation may not answer our questions and fulfill our deeper needs. It may be useful to relate psychological disorders to the problem of existential values and norms. The dualistic framework of Cartesian thinking has lost its utility and ultimacy. We must make an effort to engage in ways of understanding the human condition that transcend the dilemmas of Cartesian philosophy. The framework of early Western philosophy and Eastern thought may prove to be far more amenable to understanding human nature than the bulk of current Western objectivist science and psychology.

A VIEW TOWARD THE FUTURE

Robert Ornstein, who is best known for his research into the relationship of the brain hemispheres to consciousness, has documented that there are two major modes of consciousness: the intellectual and the intuitive. Our tendency to refer to one side of the brain as dominant, and the other as nondominant, reflects our culture rather than our neurology. Contemporary Western culture has emphasized the intellectual mode.

Our methods of science capitalize on the analytic and rational potentialities of the brain. But in doing so, we have neglected the other half with its rich sources of information (Ornstein, 1977).

Mainstream psychology has been insufficiently concerned with understanding the person as a whole. An individual is not simply an object of knowledge or a subject that knows, but a totality. It is vitally important that we attempt to avoid the Cartesian picture of a person as a mind to which a body is attached, operating according to the laws of cause and effect, and restore the unity of the human personality. We need to overcome the Cartesian dualisms, get beneath the traditional polarities, and present a portrait that more accurately reflects the complexity and potentialities of human nature. Contemporary research has documented that an individual's consciousness is limited by his or her assumptions or available categories. The problem is that of freeing the concept of personality from the conceptual structures in which we have tended to enclose it for analysis.

Surprisingly, Sigmund Freud was a forerunner in this movement. While it is true that Freud's concepts operated within a nineteenth-century framework, his ideas underwent a considerable transformation, pointing toward the necessity for a more sophisticated understanding. Originally, Freud's work rendered the Cartesian dualisms more vigorous. His theory emphasized psychic determinism in addition to physical determinism. The dichotomies of mind versus body and cause and effect pervade his work. Nevertheless, the most famous of his dichotomies, that split between a conscious and an unconscious mind, finds a striking parallel in experiments with split-brain individuals. Freud believed that the operations of the conscious mind were accessible to language, rational discourse, and change, whereas the unconscious was less amenable to reason or verbal analysis. When split-brain subjects hold a pencil in their right hand, they are able to describe it verbally even if they cannot see it. If the pencil is held out of sight in the left hand, however, they cannot describe it, but they can later select it from a group of objects presented to the left hand. When the two halves of the brain are severed, they can no longer communicate. The left hand informs the right hemisphere, which is primarily responsible for space and visual orientation but has little language facility. "Normally, when we wish to inquire about the consciousness of another person, we allow the verbal apparatus to determine it—we reduce 'consciousness' to that which a person can report." Research with split-brain individuals shows that this may be "a fundamental error in the study of consciousness. We are aware of more than we can discuss" (Ornstein, 1977).

More important, however, the development of Freud's thought compelled him and those who followed to recognize the inadequacy of the Cartesian picture and to forge forward toward a fresh position. This change emerges most clearly in Freud's practice of psychoanalysis. Using a contemporary version of the Socratic dialogue, Freud revitalized the Platonic view that knowledge is reminiscence of a human condition latent in all of us but overlaid by spurious chains of bondage. Further, in Freud's therapy, the knowledge that arises emerges as a doing, an activity that occurs within an interpersonal relationship (between analyst and analysand) rather than a Cartesian act of thought. Freud's academic discussions remained within the traditional Cartesian conceptualizations; this prevented Freud from recognizing the full implications for understanding personality that were a potential in his therapeutic work. As a result, Freud's writings have raised questions rather than provided sufficient answers. Nevertheless, Freud's effect was to begin to shatter the Cartesian dualisms and conception pf personality. Since Freud, we can no longer conceive of ourselves as primarily rational creatures and ignore the role of emotions and passions in human life. The dichotomy of feeling and thought must somehow be brought together. As subsequent thinkers, we are privileged to be able to grapple with the problem in terms of the legacy he left.

Carl Jung's concept of the collective unconscious, a shared and transpersonal potential consciousness, represents an attempt to compensate for our overdeveloped subjective ego consciousness and permit us to get in touch with archetypal patterns of human life. His notions of individuation and transcendence point toward the eventual unification of existence and essence. The true self emerges, according to Jung, when all of the opposites of human existence coincide. Drawing on the work of both Freud and Jung, Robert Assagioli, an Italian psychiatrist, has developed a system of psychotherapy, *psychosynthesis*, that seeks to integrate the therapeutic and esoteric dimensions of psychology and offers practical techniques for cultivating and integrating our underdeveloped intuition (1971).

Alfred Adler argues against a mechanistic notion of causality as a matrix for understanding human behavior. He points out that if we wish to understand what a person is doing we need to inquire into his or her goals. Gordon Allport radically enriches our understanding of motivation in his postulation of the proprium and its functions. The concept of teleology has re-emerged as a viable framework for comprehending human behavior. A concept of motivation, which implies purpose, understanding, and cognition, may be more viable than a framework of cause and effect for understanding human behavior. Hall and Lindzey point out that most personality theorists today acknowledge that the human being is a purposive creature. Even those who do not emphasize processes of motivation in their theory do not consider the question of purposiveness a matter of grave debate (1978). In the behaviorist movement itself, social learning theorists, such as Albert Bandura, Richard Walters, and Julian Rotter, have found it necessary to reintroduce the organism into the simplistic cause-and-effect link of stimulus-response theory. Cognitive theorists, exploring the dimension of knowledge, recognize that the Cartesian distinction between subject and object is incomplete. Jean Piaget reflects Buber's position in his assertion that children's awareness of external things as objects and themselves as subjects develops slowly out of sensorimotor experience. George Kelly affirms that our concept of reality depends on our interpretation of it. These explorations in cognition point out the need to expand our concept of the variables that influence personality.

Other theorists, whom we have explored, also strike notes that are consonant with contemporary trends in physics and philosophy. Erich Fromm distinguishes between existential dichotomies, which are inevitable, and historical dichotomies, which are self-imposed and unnecessary. Henry Stack Sullivan recognizes the need to translate concepts of personality into interpersonal terms and terms that reflect the modern concept of energy in physics. Carl Rogers picks up directly on Martin Buber's concept of transjective knowledge in his discussion of interpersonal relations and their importance for personality development and therapy. Abraham Maslow explores the characteristics that lead to growth, the development of potential, and self-actualization. In doing so, he, along with other theorists, found it necessary to relate the problem of personality to the problem of existential values and norms. Several theorists express reservations about the direction of Western psychology and science. Some of them explicitly demonstrate an interest in the philosophy of the East, suggesting that it might provide a better framework for understanding the person.

The problem is that several of these theories do not fulfill the criteria for a scientific theory based on the rigorous methodology of the experimental psychologist. Hall and Lindzey have pointed out that few theories of personality resemble the ideal in terms of what a scientific theory should look like. Their assumptions lack explicitness, making it difficult for us to derive empirical statements from the constructs of the theory that would permit us to move from abstract theory to empirical observation. Many of the theories, while provocative, have failed to generate a significant amount of research, thus depriving us of the "most important evaluative comparison" that can be made among theories (Hall & Lindzey, 1978).

In part, the problem results from the fact that theories of personality explore phenomena that by their very nature elude a narrow definition of science and call it into question. At the heart of the experimental method is the search for cause and effect. Theories that emphasize motivation or introduce free will make it difficult to look for underlying causes and limit the possibility of prediction and control. Moreover, they call into question the value of experimentation as a primary means of gaining insight into the human condition.

We need to recall that American psychology struggled valiantly to become a respectable science. This struggle entailed severing its early ties with philosophy and modeling itself along the lines of the natural sciences. Sound training in experimental design and statistical methods characterize the curriculum of academic studies in psychology. Because of the earlier struggle to gain recognition as a science, many psychologists, particularly of a behaviorist orientation, are suspicious of recent efforts by personality theorists to defy strict scientific methodology and reassert the philosophical character of psychology.

To some extent this concern reflects a realistic fear that our present disillusionment with science may foster a tendency to disregard the substantial contributions that it has made to our understanding. We developed the experimental method as a tool, because we discovered through experience, that in certain instances we could increase our understanding and act more efficiently if our activities were guided by information about the determined aspects of our everyday world. While it may be true that the experimental method cannot establish truth, it has provided a very pragmatic means of testing some of our assumptions.

Still, we should recognize that a purely experimental approach is not the only option available to the personality theorist and also consider the effects of a conception of psychology as only science. Moreover, we must not allow the popularity of the behaviorist stance in the American academy to close our eyes to the originality and importance of the ideas of other theorists or to the reality of the phenomena that they draw to our attention. We seek a higher perspective, in which science and philosophy are no longer conceived as in opposition to one another, but as performing complementary functions.

Many contemporary personality theorists urge us to be more, not less, empirical. They point out that our traditional scientific methods may not only fail to do justice to the data, but may also camouflage it. They suggest that we prejudice the results by limiting our analysis to merely those phenomena that can be comprehended in terms of current experimental methodology. By becoming "less scientistic," psychology could become "more scientific" (Bakan, 1969).

It is not wise for a field of investigation that claims to deal with human understanding to refuse to deal with a wide variety of concepts and data simply because they are difficult to cope with in our present scientific terms. The crises in living that we face today mandate that we marshal whatever means are available to assist us in our self-understanding. A true portrait of personality must come to terms with all of the experiences that are central to being a person. It needs to grapple with and express all of the facets of personality, even though they may be difficult to conceptualize, test, or express. To ignore or deny anything that is part of the human condition is not only not to come to grips with it, but to miss or lose an important aspect of what it means to be human. Lopsided theories err not simply because they present us with incomplete portraits that are often biased or stereotyped, but because they fail to develop concepts that adequately represent the human being and his or her potential. In so doing they repress a part of ourselves and deprive us of important aspects of our own consciousness.

This book has suggested that personality theorizing invariably entails more than science; it also involves philosophy and art. Every activity that we engage in rests on certain philosophical assumptions. Our contemporary personality theorizing is tied to and limited by certain assumptions that have come to characterize our view of the world. Frequently, these assumptions are implicit rather than explicit; that is, they are not clearly recognized. Nevertheless, they profoundly influence our concept of the world and its inhabitants. Only by making our assumptions explicit and continually re-examining them can we place ourselves in a better position to understand ourselves and our world. Herein lies the value of the scientific method. It has provided us with a means of testing and consensually validating our theoretical speculations. What we need to do is twofold: to evaluate our philosophical assumptions in the light of contemporary scientific information and to judge our scientific findings in terms of their adequacy as philosophy. In the final analysis, however, neither the intellectual speculations of science nor philosophy can express the ultimate meaning of personality. The ultimate expression of personality does not lie in the constructs of science or philosophy, but in the art of living.

SUGGESTIONS FOR FURTHER READING

For additional information on problems in current psychological research, the reader is referred to David Bakan, *On Method: Towards a Reconstruction of Psychological Investigation* (Jossey Bass, 1969). Bakan points out that our enormous expenditures on psychological research are yielding little information and virtually nothing that is new. He suggests ways in which psychology might become "more scientific" and "less scientistic." Robert Ornstein's *The Psychology of Consciousness*, 2d. ed. (Harcourt Brace Jovanovich, 1977) is an introduction to scientific research and work on the phenomenon of consciousness, as well as a source of information on other questions that the scientific method excludes.

Frederick Copleston's three-volume *A History of Philosophy* (Doubleday, 1962) provides a clear, well-written introduction to Western philosophical thought through the Renaissance. René Descartes's *Discourse on Method* and *Meditations* relate his intellectual biography and philosophical starting point. These are included in *The Philosophical Works of Descartes* (Cambridge University Press, 1931). A good secondary reference for Descartes is A. G. A. Balz, *Descartes and the Modern Mind* (Yale University Press, 1952).

Fritjof Capra, *The Tao of Physics* (Shambhala Publications, 1975) explores parallels between concepts in modern physics and basic ideas of Eastern mysticism. A research physicist, Dr. Capra gives a clear explanation of theories in modern physics that is easy for the lay person to understand. Martin Buber's classic work is *I and Thou* (Scribner's, 1937). The best introduction to Buber's thinking and survey of his philosophy is Maurice Friedman, *Martin Buber: The Life of Dialogue* (Harper & Brothers, 1960).

The following two books were previously recommended in conjunction with Chapter 1; they are again suggested as invaluable for the student who is interested in pursuing personality theory in greater depth: Joseph Rychlak, *A Philosophy of Science for Personality Theory* (Houghton Mifflin, 1968); and Isidor Chein, *The Science of Behavior and the Image of Man* (Basic Books, 1972).

ability traits In Cattell's theory, traits that determine how effectively a person is able to achieve his or her goal.

absence An altered state of consciousness in which there may be considerable personality change and later amnesia or forgetting of the events that occurred.

acceptance A nonjudgmental recognition of oneself, others, and the world.

accommodation In Piaget's theory, the ability to change one's schema in order to introduce new ideas, objects, or experiences.

acquisition In Bandura and Walters's theory, what a person has learned and can do.

active imagination In Jung's psychotherapy, a method for getting in touch with the archetypes.

Adult In Berne's transactional analysis, an ego state that seeks to evaluate and make realistic choices among the alternatives that confront an individual.

alienation In Horney's theory, a state in which the real self and the idealized self are disjunct.

anal stage One of Freud's psychosexual stages in which the major source of pleasure and conflict is the anus.

analytical psychology The school of psychology founded by Carl Jung.

androgyny The presence of both masculine and feminine qualities in an individual and the ability to realize both potentials.

anima In Jung's theory, an archetype representing the feminine side of the male personality.

animism The belief that everything is alive.

animus In Jung's theory, an archetype representing the masculine side of the female personality.

anxiety An emotional state characterized by a vague fear or premonition that something undesirable may happen. a) In Freud's theory, a situation into which we are thrust at birth because of the realistic danger that our needs as helpless infants will not be met. b) In Sullivan's theory, any painful feeling or emotion.

approach-approach conflict A conflict in which two attractive goals are incompatible.

approach-avoidance conflict A conflict in which one and the same goal both attracts and repels.

archetype In Jung's theory, a universal thought form or predisposition to perceive the world in certain ways.

artificialism In Piaget's theory, a schema that all events are accounted for in terms of personal motives.

"as if" a) A philosophical position espoused by Vaihinger and reflected

in Adler's concept of fictional finalisms. b) In Sullivan's theory, a security operation in which an individual acts as if he or she were someone else in interpersonal relations.

assertive training A behavior therapy developed by Wolpe to assist a person to express his or her feelings.

assimilation In Piaget's theory, the ability to incorporate new ideas, objects, and experiences into the existing framework of one's thoughts.

assumption An underlying belief.

asthenic One of Kretschmer's types: thin, long-limbed, narrow-chested individuals who tend to be aloof and shy.

Atman In Buddhist thought, the doctrine of the illusion of individuality.

attitude A positive or negative feeling toward an object. a) In Jung's theory, a basic psychotype. b) In Cattell's theory, a surface dynamic trait.

authoritarian ethic In Fromm's theory, a value system whose source lies outside of the individual.

autism A disorder characterized by absorption into fantasy.

autoeroticism Self-love. In Freud's theory, the child's sexual activity.

autonomy versus doubt Erikson's psychosocial stage, corresponding to Freud's anal stage, in which the child faces the task of developing control over his or her body and bodily activities.

aversion therapy A type of treatment in which an unpleasant stimulus is countered with an undesirable response.

avoidance-avoidance conflict A conflict in which there are two undesirable alternatives.

bad-me self In Sullivan's theory, the content of awareness organized around anxiety-producing experiences concerning the self.

basic anxiety In Horney's theory, feelings of insecurity in which the environment as a whole is dreaded because it is seen as unrealistic, dangerous, unappreciative, and unfair.

basic needs therapy Therapeutic procedures that seek to meet the primary needs of people.

behavior The activity of an organism. a) In learning theory, a response to stimuli. b) In Rogers's theory, the goal-directed attempt of the organism to meet its needs as it perceives them.

behavior modification A form of therapy that applies the principles of learning to achieve changes in behavior.

behavior potential In Rotter's theory, a variable that refers to the likelihood that a particular behavior will occur.

behavior therapy A form of therapy that aims to eliminate symptoms of illness through learning new responses.

behavioral rehearsal A form of role playing used by Wolpe in therapy.

behavioral specificity In Mischel's theory, the concept that an individual's behavior is determined by the specific situation.

behaviorism A movement in psychology founded by John Watson, who suggested that psychologists should focus their attention on the study of overt behavior.

being mode In Fromm's theory, a way of life that depends solely on the fact of existence.

biophilous character In Fromm's theory, a character orientation that is synonymous with the productive orientation.

B-needs A term used by Maslow to refer to being needs that arise from the organism's drive to self-actualize and fulfill its potential.

bodily self In Allport's theory, a propriate function that entails coming to know one's body limits.

Brahma In Buddhist thought, the ground of existence.

brotherly love In Fromm's theory, a sense of responsibility, respect, and knowledge of another human being.

cardinal disposition In Allport's theory, a personal disposition that is so pervasive almost every behavior of an individual appears to be influenced by it.

castration anxiety In Freud's theory, the child's fear of losing the penis.

catharsis An emotional release that occurs when an idea is brought to consciousness and allowed expression.

cathect In Freud's theory, the investment of libidinal energy into an object.

causal laws Established laws of cause and effect.

central disposition In Allport's theory, a highly characteristic tendency of an individual.

centration In Piaget's theory, the tendency to base conclusions on perceptually dominant characteristics.

cerebrotonia In Sheldon's theory, a component of temperament characterized by a predominance of restraint, inhibition, and the desire for concealment.

character a) In Fromm's theory, a system of strivings or objectives that underlies one's behavior. b) In Allport's theory, a certain moral standard or code of behavior against which a person's actions or behaviors may be evaluated or judged.

Child In Berne's transactional analysis, an ego state that records those feelings and experiences one had as a child.

childhood In Sullivan's theory, the period between meaningful speech and development of the need for playmates.

choleric One of Hippocrates' temperaments that refers to an individual who tends to be irascible, hot tempered, and violent.

classical conditioning A form of learning in which a response becomes associated with a previously neutral stimulus.

client-centered psychotherapy A therapeutic technique developed by Rogers that focuses attention on the person seeking help.

closed system A concept of personality that admits little or nothing new from outside of the organism to influence or change it in any significant way.

cognition The process of knowing.

cognitive dissonance theory A theory developed by Festinger which suggests that a person acts to reduce inconsistency between ideas or beliefs.

cognitive processes In Sullivan's theory, developmental modes by which an individual experiences the world and relates to others.

cognitive theories Theories of personality that emphasize cognitive processes such as thinking and judging.

coherence One of the criteria for judging philosophical statements: the quality or state of logical consistency.

collective unconscious In Jung's theory, a shared, transpersonal unconscious consisting of potential ways of being human.

common traits In Allport's theory, hypothetical traits that permit us to compare individuals according to certain dimensions, as contrasted with personal dispositions, which are unique to each individual.

compatibility A criteria for evaluating rival hypotheses. The agreement of the hypothesis with other previously well-established information.

compensation Making up for or overcoming a weakness.

compensatory mechanisms In Adler's theory, safeguarding tendencies that ward off feelings of inferiority.

compellingness One of the criteria for evaluating philosophical statements. The quality of appealing to someone with a driving force.

complex In Jung's theory, an organized group of thoughts, feelings, and memories about a particular concept.

comprehensiveness One of the criteria for evaluating philosophical statements. The quality of having a broad scope or range and depth of coverage.

conceptual The use of symbols and language.

concrete operations In Piaget's theory, a stage of cognitive development in which children begin to think logically but their operations are tied to specific objects.

conditional positive regard In Rogers's theory, positive regard that is given only under certain circumstances.

conditioned response A response that becomes associated with a stimulus through learning.

conditioned stimulus A previously neutral stimulus that becomes associated with a response.

conditions of worth In Rogers's theory, stipulations imposed by other people indicating when an individual will be given positive regard.

conflict a) In Freud's theory, the basic incompatibility that exists among the id, ego, superego, and the external world. b) In Dollard and Miller's theory, frustration that arises from a situation in which incompatible responses occur at the same time.

congruence In Rogers's theory, the state of harmony that exists when a person's symbolized experiences reflect the actual experiences of his or her organism.

conscience In Freud's theory, a subsystem of the superego that refers to the capacity for self-evaluation, criticism, and reproach.

conscious To be aware. In Freud's theory, the thoughts, feelings, and wishes that a person is aware of at any given moment.

consensual validation Agreement among observers about phenomena.

conservation In Piaget's theory, the ability to recognize that the amount, weight, or volume of matter remains the same regardless of changes in its position or shape.

consonance In Festinger's theory, two elements that follow from or imply each other.

constellatory construct In Kelly's theory, a construct that sets clear limits to the range of its elements but also permits them to belong to other realms.

constellatory power In Jung's theory, the power of a complex to admit new ideas into itself.

constitutional traits In Cattell's theory, traits that have their origin in heredity or the physiological condition of the organism.

constructive alternativism In Kelly's theory, the assumption that any one event is open to a variety of interpretations.

constructive reverie In Sullivan's therapy, exploration of the future.

construe To place an interpretation on events.

continuity theory A theory that suggests that the development of personality is essentially an accumulation of skills, habits, and discriminations without anything really new appearing in the make-up of the person.

continuous reinforcement A schedule of reinforcement in which the desired behavior is reinforced every time it occurs.

conventional Referring to one of Kohlberg's stages of moral development, in which behavior is judged in terms of the norms and expectations of society.

coordination of secondary reactions In Piaget's theory, the fourth substage of sensorimotor development, in which children begin to employ responses to achieve specific goals.

correlation A statistical tool for making comparisons by expressing the extent to which two events covary.

covert behavior A behavior that can be observed directly only by the individual actually experiencing it.

C-P-C cycle In Kelly's theory, a sequence of circumspection, preemption, and control in a person's constructs that leads to overt behavior.

CPI California Psychological Inventory; a psychometric device designed to measure a wide range of normal behaviors.

creative self In Adler's theory, that aspect of the person that interprets and makes meaningful the experiences of the organism and establishes the life style.

creativity cycle In Kelly's theory, moving from a loose system of constructs to a tighter, more validated one.

criterion analysis A method of analysis employed by Eysenck that begins with a hypothesis about possible variables and conducts statistical analyses in order to test the hypothesis.

critical periods Periods during which an organism is highly responsive to certain influences that may enhance or disrupt its development.

cue In Dollard and Miller's theory, a specific stimulus that tells the organism when, where, and how to respond.

death instincts In Freud's theory, drives or forces that are the source of aggressiveness.

deductive reasoning Reasoning from the general to the specific.

defense mechanism In Freud's theory, a procedure that wards off anxiety and prevents its conscious perception.

definition A statement that is true because of the way in which we have agreed to use words.

delayed reinforcement Reinforcement that is delayed after a response.

detailed inquiry In Sullivan's theory, the third phase of the interview, in which the therapist tests his or her hypotheses about the patient.

determinism The philosophical view that behavior is controlled by external or internal forces and pressures.

dichotomy An opposite or bipolar construct.

dimensional (or nomothetic) In Allport's theory, an approach to studying personality that considers large groups of individuals in order to infer general variables or universal principles.

directive A term used to describe therapies whose course is primarily structured by the therapist.

discontinuity theory A theory of personality that suggests that in the course of development an organism experiences genuine transformations or changes so that it reaches successively higher levels of organization.

discrimination The learned ability to distinguish among different stimuli.

displacement In Freud's theory, a defense mechanism in which one object of an impulse is substituted for another.

dissonant In Festinger's theory, two elements that are contradictory or inconsistent.

D-needs A term used by Maslow to refer to deficiency needs that arise out of a lack.

double approach-avoidance conflict A conflict in which at one and the same time multiple goals both attract and repel.

dream analysis A technique used by Freud and other analysts to uncover unconscious processes.

dream work In Freud's theory, the process that disguises unconscious wishes and converts them into a manifest dream.

drive The psychological correlate of a need or stimulus that impels an organism into action. a) In Freud's theory, a psychological representation of an inner bodily source of excitement characterized by its source, impetus, aim, and object. b) In Dollard and Miller's theory, the primary motivation for behavior.

drive reduction A concept formulated by Hull that suggests that learning occurs only if an organism's response is followed by the reduction of some need or drive.

dynamic lattice In Cattell's theory, a network by which dynamic traits are related.

dynamic traits In Cattell's theory, traits that motivate an individual toward some goal.

dynamisms In Sullivan's theory, a pattern of energy transformation that characterizes an individual's interpersonal relations.

early adolescence In Sullivan's stages of development, a period marked by physical sexual maturation and the development of a stable heterosexual pattern of expressing sexual feelings.

eclectic Selecting the best from a variety of different theories or concepts.

ectomorphy In Sheldon's theory, a component of physique indicating a predominance of linearity and fragility.

ego The self. a) In Freud's theory, a function of the personality that follows the reality principles and operates according to secondary processes and reality testing. b) In Jung's theory, one's conscious perception of self.

egocentrism Seeing the world from one's own point of view and being unaware that other viewpoints exist.

ego-ideal In Freud's theory, a subsystem of the superego consisting of an ideal self-image.

ego identity versus role confusion Erikson's psychosocial stage of adolescence in which one faces the task of developing a self-image.

ego integrity versus despair Erikson's psychosexual stage of maturity that entails the task of being able to reflect on one's life with satisfaction.

ego-psychoanalytic theory Psychoanalytic theory that emphasizes the role of the ego in personality development.

Electra complex A term that some critics have used to express the feminine counterpart to the male Oedipus complex.

empathy The ability to recognize and understand another's feelings.

empirical Based on experience and observation.

empiricism The philosophical view that human knowledge arises slowly in the course of experience through observation and experiment.

empty organism A phrase used by Skinner's critics to describe his concept of the infant at birth.

endomorphy In Sheldon's theory, a component of physique indicating a predominance of soft roundness throughout the body.

environmental-mold trait In Cattell's theory, traits that originate from the influences of physical and social surroundings.

epiphany A usually sudden manifestation of the essential nature of something.

equilibrium Balance or harmony.

erg In Cattell's theory, a constitutional dynamic trait.

erogenous zones Areas of the body that provide pleasure.

erotic love In Fromm's theory, the craving for union and fusion with one other person.

evaluative response In Rogers's theory, a response that places a value judgment on thoughts, feelings, wishes, or behavior.

existential dichotomy In Fromm's theory, a dilemma or problem that arises simply from the fact of existence.

existentialism A philosophical movement that studies the meaning of existence.

expectancy construct In Rotter's theory, the individual's subjective expectation on the outcome of his or her behavior.

experimental method A scientific method involving a careful study of cause and effect by manipulating variables and observing their effects.

exploitative orientation In Fromm's theory, a character type in which a person exploits others and the world.

expressive behavior In Allport's theory, an individual's manner of performing.

extinction The tendency of a response to disappear when it is not reinforced.

extrinsic A quest that serves other purposes outside the original goal.

extroversion In Jung's theory, an attitude of expansion in which the psyche is oriented toward the external world.

factor analysis Employed by Cattell, a procedure that interrelates many correlations at one time.

fallacy of affirming the consequent An invalid form of reasoning in which affirming the consequence of a premise is thought to affirm the premise itself.

falsify To prove false.

family atmosphere In Adler's theory, the quality of emotional relationships among members of a family.

family constellation In Adler's theory, one's position within the family in terms of birth order among siblings and the presence or absence of parents and other caretakers.

feeling One of Jung's functions involving weighing, valuing, and judging the world.

fictional finalism In Adler's theory, a basic concept or philosophical assumption that cannot be tested against reality.

finalism In Adler's theory, a principle that reflects the concept of goal orientation.

fixation In Freud's theory, a defense mechanism in which there is an arrestment of growth, and excessive needs characteristic of an earlier stage are created due to overindulgence or undue frustration.

fixed schedule of reinforcement A schedule of reinforcement in which the time period or number of responses before reinforcement is identical.

formal operations In Piaget's theory, a stage of cognitive development in which an individual is no longer tied to concrete or specific objects in his or her logical thought.

Four Noble Truths A doctrine developed by Buddha.

frame of orientation and reference In Fromm's thought, the need for a stable thought system by which to organize perceptions and make sense out of the environment.

free association In Freud's psychoanalysis, a technique in which a person verbalizes whatever comes to mind.

frigidity The quality of marked sexual indifference or lack of sexual response.

frustration In Dollard and Miller's theory, an emotion that occurs when one is unable to satisfy a drive because the response that would satisfy it has been blocked.

fully functioning person A term used by Rogers to indicate an individual who is functioning at an optimum level.

functional autonomy In Allport's theory, a concept that implies that present motives are not necessarily tied to the past but may be free of earlier motivations.

functions In Jung's theory, ways of perceiving the environment and orienting experiences.

generalization A statement that may be made, when a number of different instances coincide, that something is true about many or all of the members of a certain class.

generalized conditioned reinforcers In Skinner's theory, learned reinforcers that have the power to reinforce a great number of different behaviors.

generativity versus stagnation Erikson's psychosocial stage of the middle years, in which one faces the dilemma of being productive and creative in life.

genetic epistemology The study of how knowledge is acquired, emphasizing the genetic component.

genital stage Freud's final psychosexual stage, in which an individual reaches sexual maturity.

gestalt Configuration or pattern that forms a whole.

gestalt principle The notion that the whole is more than the sum of its parts.

gestalt psychology A branch of psychology that studies how organisms perceive objects and events.

gestalt therapy A method of psychotherapy developed by Fritz Perls that emphasizes awareness and seeks to discover the how and now of behavior.

goal of superiority In Adler's theory, the ultimate fictional finalism, entailing the desire to be competent and effective in whatever one strives to do and to actualize one's potential.

good-me self In Sullivan's theory, the content of awareness that accompanies being thoroughly satisfied with oneself.

gradient The changing strength of a force, which may be plotted on a graph.

guru Teacher.

habit a) In Dollard and Miller's theory, the basic structure of personality: a learned link or association between a stimulus and response. b) In Allport's theory, a determining tendency that is narrow and limited.

having mode In Fromm's theory, a way of existence that relies on possessions.

heterostasis The desire not to reduce tension, but to seek new stimuli and challenges that will further growth.

heuristic value The ability of a construct to predict future events.

hierarchy of response In Dollard and Miller's theory, a tendency for certain responses to occur before other responses.

historical dichotomy In Fromm's theory, a dilemma or problem that arises out of human history because of various societies and cultures.

hoarding orientation In Fromm's theory, a character type in which the person seeks to save or hoard and protects him- or herself from the world by a wall.

homeostasis Balance or harmony.

homosexuality Primary attraction to the same sex.

hormones Chemicals released into the blood stream by the endrocrine glands.

humanist theories Theories of personality that emphasize human potential.

Humanistic Communitarian Socialism The name of Fromm's ideal society.

humanistic ethic In Fromm's theory, a value system that has its source in the individual acting in accord with the law of his or her human nature and assuming full responsibility for his or her existence.

humors In earlier psychology, bodily fluids thought to enter into the constitution of a body and determine by their proportion a person's constitution and temperament.

hypothesis A preliminary assumption that guides further inquiry.

hysteria An earlier term for an illness in which there are physical symptoms, such as paralysis, but no organic or physiological basis for the problem.

id In Freud's theory, the oldest and original function of the personality, which includes genetic inheritance, reflex capacities, instincts, and drives.

idealized self In Horney's theory, that which a person thinks he or she should be.

identification In Freud's theory, a defense mechanism in which a person reduces anxiety by modeling his or her behavior after that of someone else, and the process whereby the child resolves the Oedipus complex by incorporating the parents into the self.

identity crisis In Erikson's theory, the result of failure to develop a self-image or identity.

immediate reinforcement Reinforcement that immediately follows a response.

imprinting A bond of attraction that develops among members of a species shortly after birth.

inception In Sullivan's theory, the first phase of an interview in which the patient describes the problems that have brought him or her to the session.

incongruence In Rogers's theory, the lack of harmony that results when a person's symbolized experiences do not represent the actual experiences.

Individual Psychology The school of psychology developed by Adler.

individuation In Jung's theory of self-actualization, a process whereby the systems of the individual psyche achieve their fullest degree of differentiation, expression, and development.

inductive reasoning Reasoning from the specific to the general.

industry versus inferiority Erikson's psychosocial stage, corresponding to Freud's latency period, in which children face the task of learning and mastering the technology of their culture.

infancy In Sullivan's stages of development, the period from birth to meaningful speech, in which the significance of oral experiences is emphasized.

inferiority complex In Adler's theory, a neurotic pattern in which an individual feels highly inadequate.

inferiority feelings In Adler's theory, feelings of being inadequate that arise out of childhood experiences.

infrahuman species Species lower than human organisms.

inhibition The prevention of a response from occurring because it is in conflict with other strong unconscious responses.

initiative versus guilt Erikson's psychosexual stage, corresponding to Freud's phallic stage, in which children face the task of directing their curiosity and activity toward specific goals and achievements.

insight A form of therapeutic knowing that combines intellectual and emotional elements and culminates in profound personality change.

insight therapy Therapeutic procedures that seek to increase self-understanding and lead to deep motivational changes.

instinctoid A term used by Maslow to suggest that his hierarchy of human needs is inherent to human nature.

interpretive response In Rogers's theory, a response that seeks to capture the underlying meaning or motive.

interpsychic Between psyches or persons.

interval reinforcement A schedule of reinforcement in which the organism is reinforced after a certain time period has elapsed.

interview Sullivan's term for the interpersonal process that occurs between patient and therapist.

intimacy versus isolation Erikson's psychosocial stage of young adulthood in which one faces the task of establishing a close, deep, and meaningful genital relationship with another person.

intrapsychic Within the psyche or individual self.

intrinsic religion A religious quest that is perceived as an end in itself.

introversion In Jung's theory, an attitude of withdrawal in which personality is oriented inward toward the subjective world.

intuition One of Jung's functions entailing perception via the unconscious.

IQ Intelligence quotient: a number used to express the relative intelligence of a person.

juvenile era In Sullivan's stages of development, a period when the child has a strong need for playmates.

karma In Hindu thought, cycles of cause and effect.

koan In the practice of Zen, a paradoxical statement or question that has no intellectual solution.

late adolescence In Sullivan's stages of development, the last stage before adulthood in which an individual achieves social, vocational, and economic integration and stability.

latency period A period in Freud's psychosexual stages of development in which the sexual drive was thought to go underground.

latent dream In Freud's theory, the real meaning or motive that underlies the dream that we remember.

law of effect A law formulated by Thorndike that states that when a behavior or a performance is attended by satisfaction it tends to increase; if attended by frustration, it tends to decrease.

L-data In Cattell's theory, observations made of a person's behavior in society or everyday life.

learning dilemma In Dollard and Miller's theory, the situation an individual is placed in if present responses are not reinforced.

libido a) In Freud's theory, an emotional and psychic energy derived from the biological drive of sexuality. b) In Jung's theory, an undifferentiated life and psychic energy.

life instincts In Freud's theory, drives or forces that maintain life processes and insure propagation of the species.

love In Fromm's theory, the productive relationship to others and the self, entailing care, responsibility, respect, and knowledge.

love of God In Fromm's theory, love of the highest value and most desired good.

mandala A concentrically arranged figure often found as a symbol in the East that denotes wholeness and unity. In Jung's theory, a symbol for the emerging self.

manifest dream In Freud's theory, the dream as it is remembered the next morning.

mantra In Eastern thought, a spiritual word or formula chanted throughout meditation to evoke a deeper level of consciousness.

marketing orientation In Fromm's theory, a character type in which the person experiences him- or herself as a commodity in the marketplace.

masculine protest In Adler's early theory, the term for the compensation of one's inferiorities.

masochism A sexual disorder in which a person obtains pleasure by receiving pain.

MAVA Multiple abstract variance analysis, a study method employed by Cattell that compares identical twins and siblings with other individuals under various environmental conditions.

maya In Eastern thought, a term that means illusion.

mediational processes In Bandura and Walters's theory, cognitive processes interposed between a stimulus and a response.

melancholic One of Hippocrates' temperaments that refers to an individual characterized by depression.

mental combinations In Piaget's theory, the sixth substage of sensorimotor development, in which children begin to think before they act and to consider the effects of their actions.

mesomorphy In Sheldon's theory, a component of physique indicating a predominance of muscle, bone, and connective tissue.

metamotivation A term used by Maslow to refer to growth tendencies within the organism.

metapsychological A term used by Freud to indicate the fullest possible description of psychic processes.

method of amplification In Jungian therapy, an analytical method whereby one focuses repeatedly on an element and gives multiple associations to it.

MMPI Minnesota Multiphasic Personality Inventory: a psychometric device designed to measure different tendencies of pathology or abnormal behavior.

moral anxiety In Freud's theory, fear of the retribution of one's own conscience.

moral judgment In Piaget's theory, a person's understanding of why certain behaviors are right or wrong.

moral realism In Piaget's theory, the belief that moral laws are as fixed and unchangeable as physical laws.

morphogenic (or idiographic) In Allport's theory, an approach to studying personality that centers on understanding the uniqueness of the individual.

morphology Body measurement.

motherly love In Fromm's theory, the unconditional affirmation of a child's life and needs.

moving against One of Horney's three primary modes of relating to other people, in which one seeks to protect him- or herself by revenge or controlling others.

moving away One of Horney's three primary ways of relating to other people, in which one isolates him- or herself and keeps apart.

moving toward One of Horney's three primary modes of relating to other people, in which one accepts his or her own helplessness and becomes compliant in order to depend on others.

narcissism A form of self-encapsulation in which an individual experiences as real only that which exists within him- or herself.

necrophilous character In Fromm's theory, a character orientation in which an individual is attracted to that which is dead and decaying and seeks to destroy living things.

negative reinforcement Unpleasant or aversive stimuli that can be changed or avoided by certain behavior.

neo-psychoanalytic theories Psychoanalytic theories that revise or modify Freud's original theories.

neurosis An emotional disturbance, usually not so severe as to prevent an individual from functioning in normal society.

neurotic anxiety In Freud's theory, the fear that one's inner impulses cannot be controlled.

nirvana In Buddhist thought, the extinction of all desire, resentment, and selfishness caused by identification with one's separate ego.

nondirective A term used by Rogers to describe therapies whose course is primarily determined by the patient.

normal curve of distribution A bell-shaped curve representing many events in nature in which most events cluster around the mean.

not-me self In Sullivan's theory, an aspect of the self-system, a gradually evolving image of the self that is regarded as dreadful and cannot be permitted conscious awareness and acknowledgment.

objective test In Cattell's theory, a test that is constructed in such a way that the subject taking it cannot know its purpose.

objective data Data acquired through extrospection, the act of looking outward on the world as object.

objectivism The philosophical view that valid knowledge arises gradually in the course of experience through observation and experimentation.

objectivity The quality of recognizing or expressing reality without distortion by personal feeling. In test construction, construction of a test in such a way that it can be given and scored in a way that avoids the scorer's subjective bias.

observational learning In Bandura and Walters's theory, learning that occurs through observation without any direct reinforcement.

Oedipus complex In Freud's theory, an unconscious psychological conflict in which the child loves the parent of the opposite sex.

open system A concept of personality that conceives of it as having a dynamic potential for growth, reconstitution, and change through extensive transactions within itself and the environment.

operant conditioning In Skinner's theory, the process by which an operant response becomes associated with a reinforcement through learning.

operant response In Skinner's theory, a response that acts on the environment and is emitted without a stimulus necessarily being present.

operational definition A definition that specifies those behaviors that are included in the concept.

oral stage One of Freud's psychosexual stages, in which the major source of pleasure and potential conflict is the mouth.

oryoki Utensils used for eating in a Zen monastery.

overcompensation In Adler's theory, an exaggerated effort to cover up a weakness that entails a denial rather than an acceptance of the real situation.

overdetermination In Freud's theory, the view that all events have more than one meaning or explanation.

overt behavior Behavior that can be observed by an external observer.

paradigm A pattern or model.

parataxic distortion In Sullivan's theory, reacting to someone as if he or she were someone else.

parataxic experience In Sullivan's theory, a cognitive process in which one perceives causal relations but not on the basis of reality or logic.

para-world A world of quantified, logical, and mathematical imaginary constructs used by the scientist to draw conclusions about the everyday world.

Parent In Berne's transactional analysis, an ego state that incorporates the values of others.

participant observation In Sullivan's theory, a concept that refers to the fact that an observer of an interpersonal relationship is also a participant in it.

peak experience In Maslow's theory, an intensified experience in which there is a loss of self or transcendence of self.

penis envy In Freud's theory, the concept that women view themselves as castrated males and envy the penis.

performance In Bandura and Walters's theory, what a person actually does.

performance phase In Dollard and Miller's therapy, a phase in which the patient acquires new, more adaptive responses and habits.

perseverative functional autonomy In Allport's theory, acts or behaviors that are repeated even though they may have lost their original function.

persona In Jung's theory, an archetype referring to one's social role and understanding of it.

Personal Data Sheet An inventory developed by Woodworth during World War I as a means of screening out those men who were psychologically unfit for service.

personal dispositions In Allport's theory, traits that are unique to an individual.

personal unconscious In Jung's theory, experiences of an individual's life that have been repressed or temporarily forgotten.

personality a) In social speech, one's public image. b) In Allport's theory, the dynamic organization within the individual of those psychophysical systems that determine his or her characteristic behavior and thought. c) In Fromm's theory, the totality of an individual's psychic qualities. d) In Sullivan's theory, an imaginary construct used to explain and predict certain behaviors. e) In Cattell's theory, that which permits prediction of what a person will do in a given situation.

personification In Sullivan's theory, a group of feelings, attitudes, and thoughts that have arisen out of one's interpersonal experiences.

phallic stage One of Freud's psychosexual stages, in which pleasurable and conflicting feelings are associated with the genital organs.

phenomenal field In Rogers's theory, the total sum of experiences an organism has.

phenomenology The study of phenomena or appearances.

philosophy The systematic love and pursuit of wisdom.

phlegmatic One of Hippocrates' temperaments that refers to an individual who is slow, solid, and apathetic.

physis In ancient Greek philosophy, the essential nature or reality of things.

pleasure principle In Freud's theory, the seeking of tension reduction followed by the id.

POI Personal Orientation Inventory: a test developed by Shostrom to measure self-actualization.

polymorphous perverse A phrase used by Freud to emphasize the point that children deviate in many ways from what is thought to be normal reproductive sexual activity.

positive regard In Rogers's theory, being loved and accepted for who one is.

positive reinforcement Anything that serves to increase the frequency of a response.

postconventional One of Kohlberg's stages of moral development, in which behavior is judged in terms of abstract moral values and one's own conscience.

preadolescence In Sullivan's theory, a stage of development marked by the need for intimacy with a same-sexed peer.

preconscious In Freud's theory, memories of which we are unaware but which are easily accessible to consciousness.

preconventional Referring to one of Kohlberg's stages of moral development, in which behavior is judged in terms of its consequences.

predictive power A criterion for evaluating rival hypotheses: the range or scope of the hypothesis.

preemptive construct In Kelly's theory, a construct that limits its elements to one range only.

preoperational thought In Piaget's theory, a second major stage of cognitive development, which initiates conscious, deliberate, thought-out problem-solving activity.

primary circular reactions In Piaget's theory, the second substage of sensorimotor development, in which behaviors become more deliberate and infants begin to re-enact certain activities for the pleasure that they bring.

primary drive A drive associated with a physiological process that is necessary for the organism's survival.

primary process In Freud's theory, a psychological activity of the id characterized by immediate wish fulfillment and disregard of realistic concerns.

primary reinforcers Reinforcement that is inherently rewarding as it satisfies a primary drive.

proactive Referring to theories of personality that view the human being as acting on his or her own initiative rather than simply reacting.

probing response In Rogers's theory, a response that seeks further information.

productive orientation In Fromm's theory, the character type that represents the ideal of humanistic development.

profile A graph that presents an individual's score on the component parts of a test.

projection In Freud's theory, a defense mechanism that refers to the unconscious attribution of an impulse, attitude, or behavior to someone else or some element in the environment.

projective techniques Personality tests in which an ambiguous stimulus is presented to the subject who is expected to project aspects of his or her personality into the response.

propositional construct In Kelly's theory, a construct that leaves its elements open to other constructions.

propriate functional autonomy In Allport's theory, acquired interests, values, attitudes, intentions, and lifestyle that are directed from the proprium and are genuinely free of earlier motivations.

propriate functions In Allport's theory, the functions of the proprium.

propriate strivings In Allport's theory, a propriate function that entails projection of long-term purposes and goals and development of a plan to attain them.

proprium In Allport's theory, a term that refers to the central experiences of self-awareness that a person has as he or she grows and moves forward.

prototaxic experiences In Sullivan's theory, a cognitive process in which the infant does not distinguish between the self and the external world.

psyche From the Greek term meaning "breath" or "principle of life," often translated as "soul" or "self." a) In Freud's theory, the id, ego, and superego. b) In Jung's theory, the total personality encompassing all psychological processes: thoughts, feelings, sensations, wishes, and so on.

psychoanalysis A method of therapy developed by Freud that concentrates on cultivating a transference relationship and analyzing resistances to the therapeutic process.

psychometrics The quantitative measurement of psychological characteristics through statistical techniques.

psychophysical Entailing components of both the mind and the body.

psychosexual stages In Freud's theory, a series of developmental stages through which all people pass as they move from infancy to adulthood.

psychosexuality In Freud's theory, a term used to express the totality of elements included in the sexual drive.

psychosis An abnormal personality disturbance characterized by loss or distortion of reality testing and the inability to distinguish between reality and fantasy.

psychosocial stages A series of developmental stages proposed by Erikson to emphasize the social dimension of personality.

psychotherapy Treatment of emotional disorders by psychological means.

punishment An undesirable consequence that follows a behavior and is designed to stop or change it.

pyknic One of Kretschmer's types, referring to an individual who is short, fat, barrel-chested, and inclined to fluctuations in mood.

Q-data In Cattell's theory, questionnaires and self-reports.

Q-sort technique A card-sorting technique employed by Rogers for studying the self-concept.

radical behaviorism A label that has been given to B. F. Skinner's point of view.

rationalism The philosophical view that the mind can, in and of its own accord, formulate ideas and determine their truth.

rationalization In Freud's theory, a defense mechanism that entails dealing with an emotion or impulse analytically and intellectually, thereby not involving and avoiding the emotions.

ratio reinforcement A schedule of reinforcement in which the organism is reinforced after a number of appropriate responses.

reaction formation In Freud's theory, a defense mechanism in which an impulse, usually hostile, is expressed by its opposite.

reactive Referring to theories of personality that view the human being as primarily responding to external stimuli.

readiness A concept that implies that if an organism is not prepared or disposed to learn a particular concept, it will be unable to do so because the necessary prerequisites are not present.

reality anxiety In Freud's theory, the fear of a real danger in the external world.

reality principle In Freud's theory, the way in which the ego satisfies the impulses of the id in an appropriate manner in the external world.

real self In Horney's theory, that which a person actually is.

reassuring response In Rogers's theory, a response that attempts to pacify or soothe feelings.

receptive orientation In Fromm's theory, a character type in which the individual reacts to the world passively.

reciprocal inhibition In Wolpe's therapy, the introduction of a response that will compete with a maladaptive response.

reconnaissance In Sullivan's theory, the second phase of the interview, during which the therapist develops a case history and tentative hypotheses.

reconstructive (or intensive) psychotherapy Therapeutic methods that seek to remove defenses and reorganize the basic personality structure.

reflective response In Rogers's theory, a response that seeks to capture the underlying feeling expressed.

reflexes Inborn automatic responses.

regression In Freud's theory, a defense mechanism that entails reverting to earlier forms of behavior.

reinforcement Any event that increases or decreases the likelihood of a particular response.

reinforcement value In Rotter's theory, a variable that indicates the importance or preference of a particular reinforcement for an individual.

relatedness In Fromm's theory, the basic need to relate to and love other people.

relevance One of the criteria for evaluating philosophical statements, the quality of having some bearing or being pertinent to one's view of reality.

reliability The quality of consistently yielding the same results over time.

REP Role Construct Repertory Test: a device developed by Kelly to reveal personal constructs.

repression a) In Freud's theory, the key defense mechanism, which entails blocking a wish or desire from expression so that it cannot be experienced consciously or directly expressed in behavior. b) In Dollard and Miller's theory, a learned process of avoiding certain thoughts and thereby losing verbal control.

resignation One of Horney's three basic orientations, representing the desire to be free of others.

resistance In Freud's theory, a force that prevents an individual from becoming aware of unconscious memories or any obstacle that interferes with the analytic process.

respondent behavior In Skinner's theory, reflexes or automatic responses elicited by a stimulus.

response A behavior that results from a stimulus. In Dollard and Miller's theory, one's reaction to a cue or stimulus.

reversibility In Piaget's theory, the ability to go back to the beginning of a chain of thought and start over again.

role a) In social psychology, a set of behavioral expectations set forth by a particular society and fulfilled by its members. b) In Kelly's theory, a process or behavior that a person plays based on his or her understanding of the behavior and constructs of other people.

role playing A therapeutic technique introduced by Kelly.

rootedness In Fromm's theory, the basic need to feel that one belongs in the world.

Rorschach Test A projective test consisting of a series of inkblots to which a subject is asked to respond.

sadism A sexual disorder in which a person obtains pleasure by inflicting pain.

safeguarding tendencies In Adler's theory, compensatory mechanisms that ward off feelings of insecurity.

sanguine One of Hippocrates' temperaments, referring to a personality marked by sturdiness, high color, and cheerfulness.

sanzen Individual consultations between a Zen Buddhist monk and his master.

satiation Engaging in a behavior until one tires of it.

satori In Zen Buddhism, enlightenment.

schema In Piaget's theory, an individual's cognitive structure or framework of thought.

schema of action In Piaget's theory, a general sensorimotor response that is employed to resolve a number of different problems.

schema of operation In Piaget's theory, a complex function whereby an individual operates on the world with concepts and symbols.

science A system or method of acquiring knowledge based on specific principles of observation and reasoning.

scientific construct An imaginary or hypothetical construct used to explain what is observed in science.

scientific (or empirical) generalization An inductive conclusion based on a number of different instances of observation.

scientific method A method of inquiry that consists of five steps: recognizing a problem, developing a hypothesis, making a prediction, testing the hypothesis, and drawing a conclusion.

scientism Exclusive reliance on a narrow conception of science.

secondary circular reactions In Piaget's theory, the third substage of sensorimotor development, in which behaviors are directed toward objects and events outside of an infant's own body.

secondary dispositions In Allport's theory, more specific focused tendencies of an individual that tend to be situational in character.

secondary drive A drive that is learned or acquired on the basis of a primary drive.

secondary process In Freud's theory, higher intellectual functions that enable the ego to establish suitable courses of action and test them for their effectiveness.

secondary reinforcer A reinforcer that is originally neutral but that acquires reward value on the basis of association with a primary reinforcer.

security In Sullivan's theory, a state of emotional well-being, self-confidence, and optimism in which there are no painful feelings or emotions.

security operation In Sullivan's theory, an interpersonal device that a person uses to minimize anxiety and enhance security.

selective inattention In Sullivan's theory, a security operation in which one fails to notice some factor in an interpersonal relationship that might cause anxiety.

self a) In Jung's theory, a central archetype representing the striving for unity of all parts of the personality. b) In Rogers's theory, the psychological processes that govern a person's behavior.

self-actualization In the theories of Aristotle, Jung, Rogers, and Maslow, a dynamic within the organism leading it to actualize, fulfill, and enhance its inherent potentialities.

self-as-rational coper In Allport's theory, a propriate function that entails the perception of oneself as an active problem-solving agent.

self-concept In Rogers's theory, a portion of the phenomenal field that has become differentiated and is composed of perceptions and values of "I" or "me."

self-construct In Kelly's theory, perception of similarities in one's behavior based on role relationships with other people.

self-effacing solution One of Horney's three basic orientations toward life, which represents an appeal to be loved by others.

self-esteem a) In Sullivan's theory, all the feelings of competence and personal worth that hold a person together. b) In Allport's theory, a propriate function that entails feelings of pride as one develops the ability to do things.

self-expansive solution One of Horney's three basic orientations toward life, which represents a striving for mastery.

self-extension In Allport's theory, a propriate function that entails a sense of possession.

self-identity In Allport's theory, a propriate function that entails an awareness of inner sameness and continuity.

self-image In Allport's theory, a propriate function that entails a sense of the expectations of others and its comparison with one's own behavior.

self-love In Fromm's theory, love of self that is a prerequisite for love of others.

self-sentiment In Cattell's theory, an environmental-mold dynamic source trait composing a person's self-image.

self-system In Sullivan's theory, a dynamism of self-understanding that emerges as a result of interpersonal experiences.

sensation One of Jung's functions referring to sense perception of the world.

sense of identity In Fromm's theory, the need to be aware of oneself as an individual.

sensorimotor A term used by Piaget to describe children's intellectual activity during the first eighteen months of life.

sentiment In Cattell's theory, an environmental-mold dynamic source trait.

seriation In Piaget's theory, the ability to arrange objects in a sequential order according to increasing or decreasing size.

shadow In Jung's theory, an archetype that encompasses one's animalistic and unsocial side.

shaping In Skinner's theory, a process by which an organism's behavior is gradually molded until it approximates the desired behavior.

simplicity A criterion for evaluating rival hypotheses; the quality of being simple and avoiding complicated explanations.

situation The psychological context within which an organism responds.

slips In Freud's theory, bungled acts, such as a slip of the tongue, a slip of the pen, or a memory lapse.

social interest In Adler's theory, an urge in human nature to adapt oneself to the conditions of one's environment and society.

social learning theories Theories that attempt to explain personality in terms of learned behavior within a social context.

social psychoanalytic theories Psychoanalytic theories that emphasize the role of social forces in shaping personality.

sociocentric In Piaget's theory, an awareness that other points of view exist that are different from one's own.

Socratic dialogue A technique developed by Socrates in which the teacher acts as a midwife helping the inner knowledge of a person to unfold.

somatotonia In Sheldon's theory, a component of temperament characterized by a predominance of muscular activity and vigorous bodily assertiveness.

somatotype Sheldon's term for the expression of body type through three numbers that indicate the degree of each physical component.

source traits In Cattell's theory, underlying variables that determine surface manifestations.

species specific behavior Complex automatic behaviors that occur in all members of a species.

specification equation An equation by which Cattell suggests that we may eventually be able to predict human behavior.

spontaneous recovery Following extinction, the return of a learned behavior.

standardization Pre-testing of a large and representative sample in order to determine test norms.

statement An utterance that makes an assertion or a denial.

statistics The application of mathematical principles to the description and analysis of measurements.

stereotype Prejudgment that we make about people on the basis of their membership in certain groups.

stimulus An agent that rouses or excites a response.

stroke In Berne's transactional analysis, an activity that fulfills a physiological or psychological need.

structuralism Early school of psychology that suggested that psychology study conscious experience.

stupidity-misery syndrome Dollard and Miller's term for a neurosis.

style of life In Adler's theory, the specific ways in which an individual seeks to attain the goal of superiority.

subception In Rogers's theory, a discriminative evaluative response of the organism that precedes conscious perception.

subjective data Data acquired through introspection or the act of looking inward on the self as subject.

subjectivism A philosophical view that constructs of knowledge are creations of the self.

sublimation a) One of Freud's defense mechanisms, translating a wish, the direct expression of which is socially unacceptable, into socially acceptable behavior. b) In Sullivan's theory, a security operation in which one expresses and discharges uncomfortable feelings in ways that are interpersonally acceptable.

subsidiation In Cattell's theory, the principle that certain traits are secondary to other traits.

successive approximations In Dollard and Miller's therapy, the interpretations of the therapist that provide increasingly more accurate labels for the patient's responses.

superego In Freud's theory, a function of the personality that represents introjected and internalized values, ideals, and moral standards.

superiority complex In Adler's theory, a neurotic pattern in which an individual exaggerates his or her importance.

supportive psychotherapy Therapeutic measures that seek to strengthen adaptive instincts and defenses.

suppression The conscious, deliberate stopping of a thought or an action.

surface traits In Cattell's theory, clusters of overt behavior responses that appear to go together.

symbiotic relatedness In Fromm's theory, a relationship in which one or the other of two persons loses or never attains his or her own independence.

syntality In Cattell's theory, the behavior of a group as a whole or its "group personality."

syntaxic experience In Sullivan's theory, the highest level of cognitive activity, entailing the use of symbols and relying on consensual validation.

systematic desensitization A behavior therapy developed by Wolpe to condition a patient to substitute a new response for an undesired one.

tabula rasa A blank slate, a phrase associated with John Locke suggesting that the mind is a blank tablet on which experience writes.

talking phase In Dollard and Miller's therapy, a phase in which neurotic habits are studied, examined, and identified so that the patient may unlearn them.

Taoism A Chinese philosophy that advocates a way of life in harmony with the course of nature.

TAT Thematic Apperception Test: a projective test consisting of ambiguous pictures to which a subject is asked to respond.

T-data In Cattell's theory, objective tests.

teisho A lecture or discourse on the inner meaning of Zen.

telos A purpose or goal.

temperament a) In Fromm's theory, one's mode of reaction. b) In Allport's theory, a class of raw materials from which personality is fashioned.

temperament traits In Cattell's theory, traits that determine how a person behaves in order to obtain his or her goal.

termination In Sullivan's theory, the final phase of the interview, which represents a structured conclusion and suggestion for action.

tertiary circular reactions In Piaget's theory, the fifth substage of sensorimotor development, in which children begin to vary their activities in order to explore the environment.

theory A set of abstract concepts made about a group of facts or events to explain them.

therapy The practical application of psychology in ways that will assist individuals.

thinking One of Jung's functions, referring to giving meaning and understanding to the world.

token economy A community based on Skinnerian principles in which individuals are rewarded for appropriate behavior with tokens that can be exchanged for various privileges.

tracing the life line In Adlerian psychotherapy, a method of analyzing early memories and dreams to determine an individual's lifestyle.

trait Continuous dimension that an individual can be seen to possess to a certain degree. a) In Cattell's theory, an imaginary construct or inference from overt behavior that helps to explain it. b) In Allport's theory, a determining tendency to respond that represents the ultimate reality of psychological organization.

trait theories Theories that conceive of personality as being composed primarily of traits.

transactional analysis A system of therapy developed by Eric Berne that conceptualizes human relationships in terms of the roles of Parent, Child, and Adult.

transcendence a) In Jung's theory of self-actualization, a process of integrating the diverse systems of the self toward the goal of wholeness and identification with all humanity. b) In Fromm's theory, the basic human need to rise above the accidental and passive creatureliness of animal existence and become an active creator.

transductive reasoning In Piaget's theory, reasoning from the specific to the specific.

transference In Freudian psychoanalysis, a process in which the patient projects onto the analyst emotional attitudes felt as a child toward important persons.

transjective knowledge In Buber's philosophy, the knowledge that arises out of an encounter between persons.

trust versus mistrust Erikson's psychosocial stage, corresponding to Freud's oral stage, in which infants face the task of trusting the world.

typology Division of human beings into distinct separate categories.

unconditional positive regard In Rogers's theory, positive regard that is not contingent on any specific behaviors.

unconditioned response A reflex or automatic response to a stimuli.

unconditioned stimulus A stimulus that normally elicits a particular reflex or automatic response.

unconscious processes a) In Freud's theory, processes of which a person is unaware because they have been repressed or never permitted to become conscious. b) In Dollard and Miller's theory, drives or cues of which we are unaware because they are unlabeled or repressed.

usefulness a) In scientific theorizing, the ability of a hypothesis to generate predictions about experiences that we might observe. b)

In Adler's theory, the ability of a goal to foster productive living and enhance one's life.

validating evidence Observable consequences that follow an experiment designed to test an hypothesis and are used to support a construct or theory.

validity The quality of measuring what a construct is supposed to measure.

variable A characteristic that can be measured or controlled.

variable schedule of reinforcement A schedule of reinforcement in which the time period or number of responses prior to reinforcement varies.

viscerotonia In Sheldon's theory, a component of temperament characterized by a general love of comfort, relaxation, sociability, people, food, and affection.

voyeurism A sexual disorder in which a person obtains pleasure from seeing sexual organs or acts.

Walden II Skinner's name for his utopian community.

wish fulfillment In Freud's theory, a primary-process activity that seeks to reduce tension by forming an image of the object that would satisfy needs.

withdrawal-destructiveness In Fromm's theory, a relationship characterized by distance, apathy, or aggression.

womb envy In Horney's theory, the concept that men and boys experience jealousy over woman's ability to bear and nurse children.

yin and yang In Taoism, two forces by which Tao manifests itself.

zazen A practice of meditation widespread in the East.

Zen Buddhism A branch of Mahayana Buddhism that teaches meditation and the attainment of enlightenment.

zendo The meditation hall of a Zen monastery.

Adler, A. *Study of organ inferiority and its psychical compensation.* New York: Nervous and Mental Diseases Publishing Co., 1917.

Adler, A. *Practice and theory of individual psychology.* New York: Harcourt, Brace, and World, 1927.

Adler, A. *The science of living.* New York: Greenberg, 1929a.

Adler, A. *Problems of neurosis.* London: Kegan Paul, 1929b.

Adler, A. Individual psychology. In C. Murchison (Ed.), *Psychologies of 1930.* Worcester, Mass.: Clark University Press, 1930.

Adler, A. *What life should mean to you.* Boston: Little, Brown, 1931.

Adler, A. *Social interest.* New York: Putnam, 1939.

Adler, A. *Understanding human nature.* New York: Fawcett, 1954.

Adler, A. *Superiority and social interest: A collection of later writings.* H. L. & R. R. Ansbacher (Eds.). Evanston, Ill.: Northwestern University Press, 1964.

Allport, G. W. *Personality: A psychological interpretation.* New York: Holt, 1937.

Allport, G. W. *The nature of personality: Selected papers.* Cambridge, Mass.: Addison Wesley, 1950.

Allport, G. W. The open system in personality theory. *Journal of Abnormal and Social Psychology*, 1960, *60*, 301–310.

Allport, G. W. *Pattern and growth in personality.* New York: Holt, Rinehart, and Winston, 1961.

Allport, G. W. Traits revisited. *American Psychologist*, 1966, *21*, 1–10.

Allport, G. W. *The person in psychology: Selected essays.* Boston: Beacon, 1968.

Ansbacher, H. L. & R. R. *The individual psychology of Alfred Adler.* New York: Basic Books, 1956.

Arndt, W. B. *Theories of Personality.* New York: Macmillan, 1974.

Assagioli, R. *Psychosynthesis: A manual of principles and techniques.* New York: Hobbs, Dorman and Co., 1971.

Bakan, D. *On method: Toward a reconstruction of psychological investigation.* San Francisco: Jossey-Bass, 1969.

Balz, A. G. A. *Descartes and the modern mind.* New Haven: Yale University Press, 1952.

Bandura, A. Influences of models' reinforcement contingencies with the acquisition of imitative responses. *Journal of Personality and Social Psychology*, 1965, *1*, 589–595.

Bandura, A. *Principles of behavior modification.* New York: Holt, Rinehart & Winston, 1969.

Bandura, A. & Walters, R. *Social learning and personality development*. New York: Holt, Rinehart, & Winston, 1963.

Bannister, D., & Fransella, F. A grid test of schizophrenic thought disorder. *British Journal of Social and Clinical Psychology*, 1966, *5*, 95–102.

Bannister, D., & Mair, J. M. M. *The evaluation of personal constructs*. New York: Academic Press, 1968.

Bannister, D., & Salmon, P. Schizophrenic thought disorder: Specific or diffuse? *British Journal of Medical Psychology*, 1966, *39*, 215–219.

Barrett, W. *Irrational man: A study in existential philosophy*. New York: Doubleday Anchor, 1958.

Barton, A. *Three worlds of therapy: An existential-phenomenological study of the therapies of Freud, Jung, and Rogers*. Palo Alto, Calif.: National Press Books, 1974.

Berne, E. *Games people play*. New York: Grove Press, 1964.

Berson, H., Beary, J., & Carol, M. The relaxation response. *Psychiatry*, 1974, *37*, 37-46.

Bischof, L. J. *Interpreting personality theories* (2nd. ed.). New York: Harper & Row, 1970.

Blitsten, D. *The social theories of Harry Stack Sullivan*. New York: William Frederick Press, 1953.

Borgatta, E. F., & Lambert, W. W. (Eds.). *Handbook of personality and research*. Chicago: Rand McNally, 1968.

Boring, E. G. *A history of experimental psychology*. New York: Appleton Century Crofts, 1929.

Boring, E. G. Mind and mechanism. *American Journal of Psychology*, 1946, *59*, 179–192.

Boring, E. G., & Lindzey, G. (Eds.) *A history of psychology in autobiography* (5 vols.). Worcester, Mass.: Clark University Press, 1930–1967.

Bottome, P. *Alfred Adler*. New York: Vanguard, 1957.

Bouquet, A. C. *Comparative religion*. Baltimore: Penguin, 1954.

Breger, L. *From instinct to identity: The development of personality*. Englewood Cliffs, N.J.: Prentice-Hall, 1974.

Brehm, J., & Cohen, A., *Explanations in cognitive dissonance*. New York: Wiley, 1962.

Brenner, C. *An elementary textbook on psychoanalysis*. New York: Doubleday, 1955.

Brown, B. B. *New mind, new body: Biofeedback: New directions for the mind*. New York: Harper & Row, 1974.

Brown, J. A. C. *Freud and the post-Freudians*. Baltimore, Md.: Penguin, 1961.

Brown, J. S. Gradients of approach and avoidance responses and their relation to motivation. *Journal of Comparative and Physiological Psychology*, 1948, *41*, 450–465.

Bruner, J. S. You are your constructs. *Contemporary Psychology*, 1956, *1*, 355–357.

Bruner, J. S. A cognitive theory of personality. And C. R. Rogers. Intellectualizing psychotherapy. Reviews of G. A. Kelly. *Psychology of personal constructs. Contemporary Psychology*, 1965, *1*, 355–358.

Bruner, J. S. *On knowing: essays for the left hand.* Cambridge: Belknap Press, 1962.

Bruner, J. S. Organization of early skilled action. *Child Development*, 1973, *44*, 1–11.

Buber, M. *I and Thou.* New York: Scribner, 1937.

Candell, W., & Lin, T. (Eds.). *Mental health research in Asia and the Pacific.* Honolulu: East-West Center Press, 1969.

Capri, F. *The Tao of physics.* Boulder, Colo.: Shambhala, 1975.

Caruso, I. A. *Bios, psyche, person.* Freiburg-München: Karl Alber, 1957.

Cattell, R. B. *Personality: a systematic, theoretical and factual study.* New York: McGraw-Hill, 1950.

Cattell, R. B. The multiple abstract variance analysis equations and solutions: for nature-nurture research on continuous variables. *Psychological Review*, 1960, *67*, 353–372.

Cattell, R. B. *The scientific analysis of personality.* Chicago: Aldine, 1965.

Cattell, R. B. (Ed.) *Handbook of multivariate experimental psychology.* Chicago: Rand McNally, 1966.

Cattell, R. B. *A new morality from science: Beyondism.* New York: Pergamon, 1972.

Cattell, R. B. Personality pinned down. *Psychology Today*, July 1973, 40–46.

Cattell, R. B., & Adelson, M. The conformation of ergic and engram structures in attitudes objectively measured. *Australian Journal of Psychology*, 1958, *10*, 287-318.

Cattell, R. B., & Dreger, R. M. (Eds.). *Handbook of modern personality theory.* Washington, D.C.: Hemisphere Publishing Corp., 1977.

Cattell, R. B., & Wispe, L. G. The dimension of syntality in small groups. *Journal of Social Psychology*, 1948, *28*, 57–58.

Chapanis, N., & Chapanis, A. Cognitive dissonance: Five years later. *Psychological Bulletin*, 1964, *61*, 1-22.

Chapman, A. N. *Harry Stack Sullivan: His life and work.* New York: Putnam, 1976.

Chein, I. *The science of behavior and the image of man.* New York: Basic Books, 1972.

Chesler, P. *Women and madness.* New York: Doubleday, 1972.

Chomsky, N. Review of Skinner's *verbal behavior. Language*, 1959, *35*, 26–58; *234*, 246–249.

Conant, J. B. *On understanding science.* New Haven: Yale University Press, 1947.

Copleston, F. *A history of philosophy* (3 vols.). New York: Doubleday, 1962.

Corsini, R. J. *Current personality theories.* Itasca, Ill.: F. E. Peacock Publ. Co., 1977.

Dahlstrom, W., Welsch, G., & Dahlstrom, L. *An MMPI handbook.* Minneapolis: University of Minnesota Press, 1975.

Dasmann, R. F. *Planet in peril: Man and the biosphere today.* New York: World Publishing Meridan Books, 1972.

DiCaprio, N. S. *Personality theories: Guides to living.* Philadelphia: Saunders, 1974.

Dollard, J., & Miller, N. *Social learning and imitation.* New Haven: Yale University Press, 1941.

Dollard, J., & Miller, N. *Personality and psychotherapy: An analysis in terms of learning, thinking, and culture.* New York: McGraw-Hill, 1950.

Dreifurs, R. Adler's contribution to medicine, psychology, education. *American Journal of Individual Psychology*, 1952–1953, *10*, 83–86.

Durant, W. *The story of philosophy.* New York: Pocket Books, 1954.

Elkind, D. *Children and adolescents: Interpretive essays on Jean Piaget* (2nd. ed.). Oxford: Oxford University Press, 1974.

Ellenberger, H. F. *The discovery of the unconscious.* New York: Basic Books, 1970.

Engler, B. Sexuality and knowledge in Sigmund Freud. *Philosophy Today*, Winter 1969, 214–224.

Engler, B. Freud's sexual politics: Heresy or heroism. *Anima*, 1976, *2*, 62–71.

Erikson, E. H. *Childhood and society* (2nd. ed.). New York: Norton, 1963.

Evans, R. I. *Conversations with Carl Jung and reactions from Ernest Jones.* Princeton, N.J.: Van Nostrand, 1964.

Evans, R. I. *Dialogue with Erich Fromm.* New York: Harper & Row, 1966.

Evans, R. I. *Dialogue with Erik Erikson.* New York: Harper & Row, 1967.

Evans, R. I. *B. F. Skinner: The man and his ideas.* New York: Dutton, 1969.

Evans, R. I. *Gordon Allport: The man and his ideas.* New York: Dutton, 1970.

Evans, R. I. *Jean Piaget: The man and his ideas.* New York: Dutton, 1973.

Evans, R. I. *Carl Rogers: The man and his ideas.* New York: Dutton, 1975.

Eysenck, H. J. The effects of psychotherapy: An evaluation. *Journal of Consulting Psychology*, 1952, *16*, 319–324.

Eysenck, H. J. (Ed.). *Handbook of abnormal psychology: An experimental approach*. New York: Basic Books, 1961.

Eysenck, H. J. *The biological basis of personality*. Springfield, Ill.: Thomas, 1967.

Farber, L. H. *The ways of the will: Essays towards a psychology of will*. New York: Basic Books, 1966.

Feeney, E. Vice President, System Performance, Emery Air Freight. Statement made in *Business, behaviorism, and the bottom line*. CRM Films, Del Mar, Calif.: 1972.

Festinger, L. *A theory of cognitive dissonance*. Stanford, Calif.: Stanford University Press, 1957.

Festinger, L. *Conflict, decision & dissonance*. Stanford, Calif.: Stanford University Press, 1964.

Festinger, L., & Carlsmith, J. M. Cognitive consequences of forced compliance. *Journal of Abnormal and Social Psychology*, 1959, *58*, 203–210.

Fisher, S., & Greenberg, R. P. *Scientific Credibility of Freud's Theory and Therapy*. New York: Basic Books, 1977.

Flavell, J. *The developmental psychology of Jean Piaget*. Princeton, N.J.: Van Nostrand, 1963.

Flavell, J. An analysis of cognitive developmental sequences. *Genetic Psychology Monograph*, 1972, *86*, 279–350.

Fordham, F. *An introduction to Jung's psychology*. Baltimore, Md.: Pelican Books, 1953.

Freud, S. *The standard edition of the complete psychological works* (24 vols.). J. Strachey (Ed.). London: Hogarth Press, 1953–   . (Hereafter referred to as *SE* with year of original publication)

Freud, S. Studies in hysteria. *SE* (Vol 2), 1895.

Freud, S. The interpretation of dreams. *SE* (Vols. 4 & 5), 1900.

Freud, S. Psychopathology of everyday life. *SE* (Vol. 6), 1901.

Freud, S. Three essays on sexuality. *SE* (Vol. 7), 1905.

Freud, S. Five lectures on psychoanalysis. *SE* (Vol. 11), 1910.

Freud, S. Instincts and their vicissitudes. *SE* (Vol. 14), 1915.

Freud, S. Introductory lectures on psychoanalysis. *SE* (Vols. 15 & 16), 1917.

Freud, S. Beyond the pleasure principle. *SE* (Vol. 18), 1920.

Freud, S. The ego and the id. *SE* (Vol. 19), 1923.

Freud, S. Inhibitions, symptoms and anxiety. *SE* (Vol. 20), 1926.

Freud, S. The question of lay analysis. *SE* (Vol. 20), 1926.

Freud, S. New introductory lectures on psychoanalysis. *SE* (Vol. 22), 1933.

Freud, S. Analysis terminable and interminable. *SE* (Vol. 23), 1937.

Freud, S. An outline of psychoanalysis. *SE* (Vol. 23), 1940.

Friedan, B. *The feminine mystique*. New York: Norton, 1967.

Friedman, M. *Martin Buber: The life of dialogue.* New York: Harper, 1960.

Fromm, E. *Escape from freedom.* New York: Rinehart, 1941.

Fromm, E. *Man for himself.* New York: Rinehart, 1947.

Fromm, E. *The sane society.* New York: Rinehart, 1955.

Fromm, E. *The art of loving.* New York: Harper & Row, 1956.

Fromm, E. *The heart of man.* New York: Harper & Row, 1964.

Fromm, E. *The revolution of hope.* New York: Harper & Row, 1968.

Fromm, E. *The anatomy of human destructiveness.* New York: Rinehart, 1973.

Fromm, E. *To have and to be.* New York: Harper & Row, 1976.

Fromm, E., & Maccoby, M. *Social character in a Mexican village.* Englewood Cliffs, N.J.: Prentice-Hall, 1970.

Gill, M. Ego psychology and psychotherapy. *Psychoanalytic Quarterly,* 1965, *20,* 62–71.

Giovacchini, P. L. *Psychoanalysis of character disorders.* New York: Jason Aronson, 1975.

Giovacchini, P. L. *Psychoanalysis of primitive mental states.* New York: Jason Aronson, 1977.

Goble, F. *The third force: The psychology of Abraham Maslow.* New York: Grossman, 1970.

Guilford, J. P. *The nature of human intelligence.* New York: McGraw-Hill, 1967.

Hall, C. S. *A primer of Freudian psychology.* New York: World, 1954.

Hall, C. S., & Lindzey, G. *Theories of personality* (3rd. ed.). New York: Wiley, 1978.

Hall, M. H. A conversation with Abraham H. Maslow. *Psychology Today,* July 1968, pp. 34–37; 54–57.

Harlow, H. F. Love in infant monkeys. *Scientific American,* June 1959, *6,* 68–74.

Harris, T. *I'm O.K.—You're O.K.* New York: Harper & Row, 1969.

Hartmann, H. *Ego psychology and the problem of adaption.* New York: International Universities Press, 1958.

Hartmann, H. *Essays in ego psychology: Selected problems on psychoanalytic theory.* New York: International Universities Press, 1964.

Heisenberg, W. *Physics and beyond.* New York: Harper & Row, 1971.

Hilgard, E. R., & Bower, G. H. *Theories of learning.* Englewood Cliffs, N.J.: Prentice-Hall, 1975.

Hoffman, M. L. Moral development. In P. H. Mussen (Ed.). *Carmichael's manual of child psychology* (Vol. 2, 3rd. ed.). New York: Wiley, 1970.

Honig, E. K. (Ed.). *Operant behavior: Areas of research and application.* New York: Appleton-Century-Crofts, 1960.

Horney, K. *Neurotic personality of our times.* New York: Norton, 1937.

Horney, K. *New ways in psychoanalysis.* New York: Norton, 1939.

Horney, K. *Self-analysis.* New York: Norton, 1942.

Horney, K. *Our inner conflicts.* New York: Norton, 1945.

Horney, K. *Neurosis and human growth.* New York: Norton, 1950.

Horney, K. *Feminine psychology.* New York: Norton, 1967.

Hull, R. F. C. *From the life work of C. G. Jung.* New York: Harper & Row, 1971.

Johnson, D. W. *Reaching Out: Interpersonal effectiveness and self-actualization.* Englewood Cliffs, N.J.: Prentice-Hall, 1972.

Jones, E. *The life and work of Sigmund Freud* (3 vols.). New York: Basic Books, 1953–1957.

Jung, C. G. *Collected works.* H. Read, M. Fordham, & G. Adler (Eds.). Princeton: Princeton University Press, 1953– . (Hereafter referred to as *CW* with year of original publication.)

Jung, C. G. The transcendent function. *CW* (Vol. 8), 1916.

Jung, C. G. *Psychological types.* New York: Harcourt, Brace, 1933.

Jung, C. G. *Modern man in search of a soul.* New York: Harcourt, Brace, 1933.

Jung, C. G. A review of complex theory. *CW* (Vol. 8), 1934.

Jung, C. G. The archetypes and the collective unconscious. *CW* (Vol. 9), 1936.

Jung, C. G. Psychology and religion. *CW* (Vol. 11), 1938.

Jung, C. G. Conscious, unconscious, and individuation. *CW* (Vol. 9), 1939.

Jung, C. G. The relations between the ego and the unconscious. *CW* (Vol. 7), 1945.

Jung, C. G. The shadow. *CW* (Vol. 9), 1948.

Jung, C. G. On psychic energy. *CW* (Vol. 8), 1948.

Jung, C. G. Aion. *CW* (Vol. 9), 1951.

Jung, C. G. Psychological aspects of the mother archetype. *CW* (Vol. 9), 1954.

Jung, C. G. Mandalas. *CW* (Vol. 9), 1955.

Jung, C. G. *Memories, dreams, and reflections.* New York: Random House, 1961.

Jung, C. G. *Man and his symbols.* New York: Doubleday, 1964.

Kagan, J. Do infants think? *Scientific American,* 1972, 226: 74–82.

Kagan, J., & Klein, R. E. Cross-cultural perspectives on early development. *American Psychologist,* 1973, *28,* 947–961.

Kaplan, A. G., & Bean, J. P. (Eds.). *Beyond sex-role stereotypes: Readings towards a psychology of androgyny.* Boston: Little, Brown, 1976.

Kelly, G. A. *The psychology of personal constructs* (2 vols.). New York: Norton, 1955.

Kelly, G. A. Man's construction of his alternatives. In G. Lindzey (Ed.), *Assessment of human motives.* New York: Rinehart & Winston, 1958.

Kelly, G. A brief introduction to personal construct theory. In D. Bannister (Ed.), *Perspectives in personality construct theory.* New York: Academic Press, 1970.

Klime, P. *Fact and fantasy in Freudian Theory.* London: Metheien, 1972.

Klopfer, B., & Davidson, H. *The Rorschach technique.* New York: Harcourt, Brace, Jovanovich, 1962.

Koestler, A. Cosmic consciousness. *Psychology Today,* April 1977, pp. 52–54; 104.

Kohlberg, L. The development of moral character and ideology. In M. Hoffman (Ed.), *Review of Child Psychology.* New York: Russell Sage Foundation, 1964.

Kohlberg, L. Continuities in childhood and adult moral development revisited. In P. B. Balles & K. W. Schail (Eds.), *Life-span developmental psychology: Personality and socialization* New York: Academic, 1973.

Lee, D. Codification of reality: Lineal and non-lineal. *Psychosomatic Medicine,* March-April 1950, 2 (12).

Lewin, K. The conflict between Aristotelian and Galileian modes of thought in contemporary psychology. *Journal of General Psychology,* 1931, 5, 141–177.

Lindzey, G. Behavior and morphological variation. In J. N. Spuhler (Ed.), *Genetic diversity and human behavior.* Chicago: Aldine, 1967.

Loevinger, J. Theories of ego development. In L. Breger (Ed.), *Clinical cognitive psychology.* Englewood Cliffs, N.J.: Prentice-Hall, 1969.

Lorenz, K. *King Solomon's ring.* New York: Crowell, 1952.

Lundin, R. W. *Personality: A behavioral analysis* (2nd. ed.). New York: Macmillan, 1974.

MacIntyre, A. *The unconscious: A conceptual analysis.* London: Routledge & Keegan Paul, 1958.

Maddi, S. R. *Personality theories: A comparative analysis* (Rev. ed.). Homewood, Ill.: Dorsey Press, 1972.

Maddi, S., & Costa, P. *Humanism in perspective: Allport, Maslow, and Murray.* Chicago: Aldine Altherton, 1972.

Mahler, M. *On human symbiosis and the vicissitudes of individuation.* New York: Library of Human Behavior, 1976.

Maslow, A. *The psychology of science: A reconnaissance.* Chicago: Henry Regnery, 1966.

Maslow, A. *Toward a psychology of being* (2nd. ed.). New York: Van Nostrand, 1968.

Maslow, A. *Maslow and self-actualization*. Orange, Calif.: Psychological Films, 1969.

▬ Maslow, A. *Motivation and personality* (2nd. ed.). New York: Harper & Row, 1970.

Masters, W. H. & Johnson, V. E. *Human Sexual Response*. Boston: Little, Brown, 1966.

May, R. *Existence: A new dimension in psychiatry and psychology*. New York: Basic Books, 1958.

McGuire, W. (Ed.). *The Freud Jung letters*. Princeton: Princeton University Press, 1974.

Miller, N. E. Experimental studies of conflict. In J. McV. Hunt (Ed.). *Personality and the behavior disorders* (Vol. 1). New York: Ronald Press, 1944.

Miller, N. E. Theory and experiment relating psychoanalytic displacements to stimulus response generalization. *Journal of Abnormal and Social Psychology*, 1948, *43*, 155–178.

Miller, N. E. Learning drives and rewards. In S. S. Stevens (Ed.), *Handbook of experimental psychology*. New York: Wiley, 1951.

Miller, N. E. Comments on theoretical models: Illustrated by the development of a theory of conflict behavior. *Journal of Personality*, 1951, *20*, 82–100.

Miller, N. E. Liberalization of basic S-R concepts: Extensions to conflict behavior, motivation, and social learning. In S. Koch (Ed.), *Psychology: A study of a science* (Vol. 2). New York: McGraw-Hill, 1959.

Miller, N. E., & Dollard, J. *Social learning and imitation*. New Haven: Yale University Press, 1941.

Millett, K. *Sexual politics*. New York: Doubleday, 1970.

Mischel, W. *Personality and assessment*. New York: Wiley, 1968.

Mischel, W. *Introduction to personality*. New York: Holt, Rinehart, & Winston, 1971.

Mitchell, J. *Psychoanalysis and feminism*. New York: Vintage, 1975.

Monroe, R. L. *Schools of psychoanalytic thought*. New York: Holt, Rinehart & Winston, 1955.

Mullahy, P. *The contribution of Harry Stack Sullivan*. New York: Hermitage House, 1952.

Murchison, C. (Ed.) *A history of psychology in autobiography* (Vol. 3). Worcester, Mass: Clark University Press, 1936.

Murphy, G., & Murphy, L. (Eds.). *Asian psychology*. New York: Basic Books, 1968.

Murray, H. A. *Thematic apperception test*. Cambridge, Mass.: Harvard University Press, 1943.

Murray, J. R. Television and violence: Implications of the surgeon general's research program. *American Psychologist*, 1973, *28*, 472–478.

Musak, H. (Ed.). *Alfred Adler: His influence on psychology today.* New York: Noyes, 1973.

Nakamura, H. In P. Wiener (Ed.), *Ways of thinking of eastern peoples: India, China, Tibet, Japan.* Honolulu: University Press of Hawaii, 1964.

Needleman, J. *The new religions.* New York: Doubleday, 1970.

Needleman, J., Bierman, A. K., & Gould, J. A. (Eds.). *Religion for a new generation.* New York: Macmillan, 1973.

Nietzsche, F. *Thoughts out of season, II: The use and abuse of history.* (A. Collins, trans.) Edinburgh & London: T. N. Foulis, 1910.

O'Connell, V., & O'Connell, A. *Choice and change: An introduction to the psychology of growth.* Englewood Cliffs, N.J.: Prentice-Hall, 1974.

Orgler, H. *Alfred Adler: The man and his work.* New York: Liveright, 1963.

Ornstein, R. E. *The psychology of consciousness* (2nd. ed.). New York: Harcourt, Brace, Jovanovich, 1977.

Perls, F., Hefferline, R. F., & Goodman, P. *Gestalt therapy.* New York: Julian Press, 1958.

Piaget, J. *The language and thought of the child.* New York: Harcourt, Brace, & World, 1926.

Piaget, J. *Judgment and reasoning of the child.* New York: Harcourt, Brace, & World, 1928.

Piaget, J. *The moral judgment of the child.* New York: Harcourt, Brace, & World, 1932.

Piaget, J. *The origins of intelligence in children.* New York: International Universities Press, 1952.

Piaget, J. *The child's conception of number.* London: Humanities Press, 1952.

Piaget, J. *The construction of reality in the child* (M. Cook, trans.). New York: Basic Books, 1954.

Piaget, J. The genetic approach to the psychology of thought. *Journal of Educational Psychology,* 1961, *52,* 275–281.

Piaget, J. *Play, dreams, and imitation in childhood.* New York: Norton, 1962.

Piaget, J. *The psychology of intelligence.* Paterson, N.J.: Littlefield Adama, 1963.

Piaget, J. *Six psychological studies.* New York: Vintage, 1967.

Piaget, J., & Inhelder, B. *The psychology of the child.* (H. Weaver, trans.). New York: Basic Books, 1969.

Porter, E. H., Jr. *Therapeutic counseling.* Boston: Houghton Mifflin, 1950.

Progoff, I. *The death and rebirth of psychology.* New York: Julian Press, 1956.

Rapaport, D. A critique of Dollard and Miller's *Personality and psychotherapy.* *American Journal of Orthopsychiatry,* 1953, *23*, 204–208.

Rapaport, D. The structure of psychoanalytic theory: A systematizing attempt. In S. Koch (Ed.), *Psychology: A study of a science* (Vol. 3). New York: McGraw-Hill, 1959.

Rapaport, D. The structure of psychoanalytic theory: A systematizing attempt. *Psychological Issues,* 1960, *6*.

Rees, L. Constitutional factors and abnormal behavior. In H. J. Eysenck (Ed.), *Handbook of abnormal psychology.* New York: Basic Books, 1961.

Reik, T. *The search within.* New York: Farrar, Straus, & Cudahy, 1956.

Reinhardt, K. *The existentialist revolt.* New York: Frederick Ungar Publishing Co., 1960.

Rest, J. *Developmental hierarchy in preference and comprehension of moral judgment.* Unpublished dissertation. University of Chicago, 1968.

Rimm, D., & Masters, J. *Behavior therapy techniques and empirical findings.* New York: Academic Press, 1974.

Roazen, P. *Freud and his followers.* New York: Knopf, 1975.

Rogers, C. R. *Counseling and psychotherapy: Newer concepts in practice.* Boston: Houghton Mifflin, 1942.

Rogers, C. R. *Client-centered therapy: Its current practice, implications, and theory.* Boston: Houghton Mifflin, 1951.

Rogers, C. R. The necessary and sufficient conditions of therapeutic personality change. *Journal of Consulting Psychology,* 1957, *21*, 95–103.

Rogers, C. R. A theory of therapy, personality and interpersonal relationships as developed in the client-centered framework. In S. Koch (Ed.). *Psychology: A study of a science* (Vol. 3). New York: McGraw-Hill, 1959.

Rogers, C. R. *On becoming a person.* Boston: Houghton Mifflin, 1961.

Rogers, C. R. Dealing with psychological tensions. *Journal of Applied Behavior Science,* 1965, *1*, 6–25.

Rogers, C. R. (Ed.). *The therapeutic relationship and its impact: A study of psychotherapy with schizophrenics.* Madison, Wis.: University of Wisconsin Press, 1967.

Rogers, C. R. *Freedom to learn.* Columbus, Ohio: Charles E. Merrill, 1969.

Rogers, C. R., & Dymond, R. F. (Eds.). *Psychotherapy and personality change: Coordinated studies in the client-centered approach.* Chicago: University of Chicago Press, 1954.

Rogers, C. R., & Roethlisberger, F. J. Barriers and gateways to communication. *Harvard Business Review,* July-Aug. 1952, 28–35.

Rotter, J. B. *Social learning and clinical psychology.* Englewood Cliffs, N.J.: Prentice-Hall, 1954.

Rotter, J. B. Generalized expectancies for internal versus external control of reinforcement. *Psychological Monographs,* 1966, *80,* (Whole No. 609).

Rotter, J. B., & Hochreich, D. J. *Personality.* Glenview, Ill.: Scott Foresman, 1975.

Rychlak, J. *A philosophy of science for personality theory.* Boston: Houghton Mifflin, 1968.

Rychlak, J. F. *Introduction to personality and psychotherapy.* Boston: Houghton Mifflin, 1973.

Ryle, G. *The concept of mind.* New York: Barnes & Noble, 1949.

Schafer, R., Berg, I., & McCandless, B. Report on survey of current psychological testing practices. *Supplement to Newsletter, Division of Clinical Abnormal Psychology, American Psychological Association,* 1951, *4*(5).

Schultz, D. *Theories of personality.* Monterey, Calif.: Brooks/Cole, 1976.

Sears, R. R. Survey of objective studies of psychoanalytic concepts. *Social Science Research Council Bulletin,* 1943, *51.*

Seligman, M., and Hagar, J., *Biological boundaries of learning.* Englewood Cliffs, N.J.: Prentice-Hall, 1972.

Sells, S. B. Structured measurement of personality and motivation: A review of contributions of Raymond B. Cattell. *Journal of Clinical Psychology,* 1959, *15,* 3–21.

Sheldon, W. H. (with the collaboration of S. S. Stevens & W. B. Tucker). *The varieties of human physique: An introduction to constitutional psychology.* New York: Harper, 1940.

Sheldon, W. H. (with the collaboration of S. S. Stevens). *The varieties of temperament: A psychology of constitutional differences.* New York: Harper, 1942.

Sheldon, W. H. Constitutional factors in personality. In J. McV. Hunt (Ed.). *Personality and the behavioral disorders.* New York: Ronald Press, 1944.

Sheldon, W. H. (with the collaboration of C. W. Dupertuis & E. McDermott). *Atlas of men: A guide for somatotyping the adult male of all ages.* New York: Harper, 1954.

Sherfey, M. J. *The nature and evolution of female sexuality.* New York: Random House, 1972.

Shostrom, E. An inventory for the measurement of self-actualization. *Educational and Psychological Measurement,* 1965, *24,* 207–218.

Sigel, I. E., Roeper, A., & Hooper, F. H. A training procedure for acquisition of Piaget's conservation of quantity. *British Journal of Educational Psychology,* 1966, *36,* 301–311.

Singer, J. L. *The child's world of make-believe.* New York: Academic Press, 1973.

Skinner, B. F. *The behavior of organisms*. New York: Appleton Century Crofts, 1938.

Skinner, B. F. *Walden II*. New York: Macmillan, 1948.

Skinner, B. F. *Science and human behavior*. New York: Macmillan, 1953.

Skinner, B. F. *Cumulative record*. New York: Appleton Century Croft, 1961.

Skinner, B. F. *Contingencies of reinforcement: A theoretical analysis*. New York: Appleton Century Croft, 1969.

Skinner, B. F. *Beyond Freedom and dignity*. New York: Knopf, 1971.

Skinner, B. F. Will success spoil B. F. Skinner? (Interview). *Psychology Today*, Nov. 1972, *6*, pp. 66–72, 130.

Sperber, M. *Masks of loneliness: Alfred Adler in perspective*. New York: Macmillan, 1974.

Spitz, R. A. The psychogenic diseases in infancy: An attempt at the etiologic classification. *Psychoanalytic Study of the Child*, 1951, *6*, 255–275.

Smith, H. C. *Personality development*. New York: McGraw-Hill, 1968.

Smith, M., & Glass, J. Metaanalysis of psychotherapy outcome studies. *American Psychologist*, Sept. 1977, 752–760.

Spotnitz, H. *Psychotherapy of preoedipal conditions*. New York: Jason Aronson, 1976.

Spranger, E. *Types of men*. New York: Stechert, 1928.

Stoller, R. J. The sense of femaleness. In J. B. Miller (Ed.), *Psychoanalysis and women: Contributions to new theory and therapy*. New York: Brunner/Mazel, 1973.

Stoller, R. J. Overview: The impact of new advances in sex research on psychoanalytic theory. *American Journal of Psychiatry*, 1974, *130*, 241–51.

Stone, I. *Passions of the mind*. New York: Doubleday, 1971.

Stone, L. J., & Church, J. *Childhood and adolescence: A psychology of the growing person*. New York: Random House, 1973.

Sullivan, H. S. *The interpersonal theory of psychiatry*. New York: Norton, 1953.

Sullivan, H. S. *The psychiatric interview*. New York: Norton, 1954.

Sullivan, H. S. *The fusion of psychiatry and social science*. New York: Norton, 1964.

Sullivan, H. S. *Personal psychopathology*. New York: Norton, 1972.

Suzuki, D. T. *An introduction to Zen Buddhism*. New York: Grove, 1964.

Suzuki, D. T. *Zen mind, beginner's mind*. New York: Weatherhill, 1975.

Tart, C. T. (Ed.). *Transpersonal psychologies.* New York: Harper & Row, 1975.

Thurstone, L. L., & Thurstone, T. G. Factorial studies of intelligence. *Psychometric Monographs.* No. 2. Chicago: University of Chicago Press, 1941.

Turner, M. *Philosophy and the science of behavior.* New York: Appleton Century Croft, 1967.

Vockell, E. L., Felker, D. W., & Miley, C. H. Birth order literature 1967–1971: Bibliography and index. *Journal of Individual Psychology,* 1973, *29,* 39–53.

Wadsworth, B. J. *Piaget's theory of cognitive development: An introduction for students of psychology and education.* New York: David McKay, 1971.

Watts, A. W. *The spirit of Zen.* New York: Grove, 1958.

Watts, A. W. *Psychotherapy east and west.* New York: Ballantine, 1961.

Watts, A. W. *In my own way.* New York: Random House, 1972.

Watts, A. W. *Tao: The watercourse way.* New York: Random House, 1975.

Whyte, L. L. *The unconscious before Freud.* New York: Doubleday, 1960.

Wilson, C. *New pathways in psychology: Maslow and the post-Freudian revolution.* New York: Taplinger, 1972.

Wolman, B. Psychoanalysis without libido: An analysis of Karen Horney's contribution to psychoanalytic theory. *American Journal of Psychotherapy,* 1954, *8,* 21–31.

Wolpe, J. *Psychotherapy by reciprocal inhibition.* Stanford, Calif.: Stanford University Press, 1958.

Wolpe, J., & Lazarus, A. *Behavior therapy techniques.* New York: Pergamon Press, 1966.

Word, E. E. *Practical yoga.* North Hollywood, Calif.: Wilshire Book Co., 1972.

Wrightsman, L. *Assumptions about human nature: A social psychological approach.* Monterey, Calif.: Brooks/Cole, 1974.

INDEX

Individual psychology, 113–126
Individuation, 106
Inferiority complex, 122
Inferiority feelings, 118–119
Inhibition, 190–191
Insight, 73, 180, 213
Instinctoid tendencies, 340–341
Instincts, 48, 340–341
Intelligence testing, 263–266
Internal-External Scale, 226
Interpersonal psychiatry, 166–181
Intrapsychic phenomenon, 115, 165
Interview, 177, 179–180, 181
Intrapsychic phenomenon, 115, 165
Introspection, 13, 162, 179, 229, 332, 447, 451. See also Subjective knowledge
Introversion, 104, 260

James, W., 125, 176
Johansson, R., 443
Johnson, V., 86
Jones, E., 35, 59
Jung, C., 35, 41, 92–94, 95–113, 118, 126–127, 240, 260, 292, 294, 303, 416, 450, 458
    and Freud, 35, 95, 97, 105
    biographical background, 95–98
    evaluation and implications, 111–113
    methods of research, 111–112. See also Active imagination, Method of amplification
    personality theory, 98–106
    psychotherapy, 107–111

Kagan, J., 382
Kahn, H., 445
Kant, I., 451
Kaplan, A., 113
Karma, 420
Kelly, G., 18, 361, 386–410, 459
    biographical background, 387–389
    evaluation and implications, 409–410
    methods of research, 397–400, 408–409
    personality theory, 389–400
    psychotherapy, 400–403
Kepler, J., 21, 28, 450
Kierkegaard, S., 304
Klime, P., 77, 89
Koan, 425, 431, 434–435, 441
Koffka, K., 303
Kohlberg, L., 379–381, 382
Kohler, W., 303
Kopp, S., 443

Kraft-Ebing, R., 97
Kretschmer, E., 235–236, 240, 260

Lambert, W., 333
Language, 176, 209, 220, 370–371
Lao-tse, 423
Latency period, 53–54
Law of effect, 162, 206
Learning, 160, 162–163, 183, 184–187, 190–192, 206–213, 256, 386, 396. See also Behavior and learning theories
Learning theories, See Behavior and learning theories
Lee, D., 454
Letters from Jenny, 285, 295–296
Lewin, K., 303
Libido, 48, 50–56, 105, 135
Life instincts, 48–49, 153
Lindzey, G., 141, 155, 248, 259, 274, 292, 295, 458, 459
Linnaeus, C., 234
Locke, J., 160
Loevinger, J., 382
Logic, 6, 18
Logical operations, 376
Loneliness, 144–145
Lorenz, K., 351
Lovass, O., 214
Love, 148, 150–152, 158
Lundin, R., 231

MacIntyre, A., 60
Maddi, S., 55, 341
Mahler, M., 81, 351
Mair, J., 408
Mandala, 101, 109–110
Marx, K., 143, 155
Masculine protest, 119
Maslow, A., 112, 305, 334–355, 445, 450, 459
    biographical background, 334–336
    evaluation and implications, 353–354
    methods of research, 342–343
    personality theory, 337–351
    psychotherapy, 351–353
Masochism, 51, 56
Masters, J., 231
Masters, W., 86
Maturity, 54, 292–294
Maya, 416, 420, 440, 442
Meditation, 417, 425, 435–436, 437. See also Zazen
Mesomorphy, 241–244
Metaphysics, 6
Method of amplification, 108–109